#1 SELLING TELECOMMUNICATIONS DICTIONARY

Third Edition
35% More Definitions
Full ISDN Glossary
New: Mini Tutorials

Newton's TELECOM dictionary

THE OFFICIAL GLOSSARY OF TELECOMMUNICATIONS ACRONYMS, TERMS AND JARGON

by Harry Newton

NEWTON'S TELECOM DICTIONARY

Published by Telecom Library Inc.
Telecom Library publishes books and magazine and runs seminars on telephones, telecommunications, local area networks, PC data processing, desktop office automation, data communications and sales automation software and hardware. It also distributes the books of other publishers, making it the "central source" for all the above materials. Call or write for your **FREE** catalog.

Other Books by Telecom Library
Newton's Telecom Dictionary
The TELECOM LIBRARY Guide to
- T-1 Networking
- Negotiating Telecommunications Contracts
- Buying Short Haul Microwave
- The Perfect RFP
- The Inbound Telephone Call Center
- Using Satellite Communications

The TELECONNECT Guide to
- Automatic Call Distributors
- The Business of Interconnect
- How to Sell Call Accounting Systems
- Professional Selling

and...
- 101 Money-Saving Secrets Your Phone Company Won't Tell You
- 0S2 LANs
- Profit and Control Through Call Accounting
- Telecommunications Management for Business and Government
- The Perfect Proposal
- Which Phone System Should I Buy?

FREE Catalog of Books
Telecom Library publishes books itself, and also distributes the books of every other telecommunications publisher.
You may receive your **FREE** copy of our latest catalog by calling 212-691-8215, or by dropping a line to the Christine Fullam, Telecom Library Manager, at the address below.
You may order your Telecom Library books by calling 1-800-LIBRARY; or fax your order to 212-691-1191.

Quantity Purchases
If you wish to purchase this book, or any others, in quantity, please contact:

Christine Fullam, Manager
Telecom Library Inc.
12 West 21 Street
New York, NY 10010
1-800-LIBRARY or 212-691-8215
Facsimile orders: 212-691-1191

 This book was designed and produced by Randi Ripley, Telecom Library. Printed in USA at BookCrafters, Chelsea, MI
ISBN 0-936648-27-9

Telecom Library Inc., 12 West 21 Street, New York, NY 10010
212-691-8215 1-800-LIBRARY

THE LOGIC OF MY DICTIONARY

by Harry Newton

Most technical dictionaries define terms tersely. As a result, they leave you more confused. This dictionary is different. My definitions tell you what the term is, how it works, how you use it, what its benefits are and how it fits into the greater scheme of things.

This is a working dictionary. The idea is to use it every day. You can give it to your users, to your customers, to your boss. You can even give it to your kids to let them understand what you do.

HOW TO USE MY DICTIONARY

My definitions are in ASCII code order, NOT alphabetical order. ASCII is almost alphabetical order. But with some variations. Here is the order of the more common characters you'll find in this dictionary:

Blank Space	= ASCII 32	5	= ASCII 53
& (Ampersand)	= ASCII 38	6	= ASCII 54
Dash –	=ASCII 45	7	= ASCII 55
Period	= ASCII 46	8	= ASCII 56
/ (Forward slash)	= ASCII 47	9	= ASCII 57
0 (zero)	= ASCII 48	: (colon)	= ASCII 58
1	= ASCII 49	; (semi colon)	= ASCII 59
2	= ASCII 50	A (capital A)	= ASCII 65
3	= ASCII 51	a (lower case a)	= ASCII 97
4	= ASCII 52		

I choose ASCII order over alphabetical order because it's established and logical. When you do "alphabetical," it's hard to figure which comes first: BACK SLASH or BACKSLASH.

NEWTON'S TELECOM DICTIONARY

ON STYLE

Like all high-tech industries, this one makes up new words by joining words together, sometimes with a hyphen and sometimes without one. There are no rules, except with age and familiarity the hyphen tends to disappear.

The plural of PBX is PBXs, not PBX's. The possessive of PBX is PBX's. In some places T1 is T1. Here it's T-1. I follow the style Andy Moore established in TELECONNECT Magazine, and the one he has so rigorously held us to for almost a decade. Yes, it's that long.

THANK YOUs

A big thank you to the dozens of people and dozens of companies who helped. I'd love to name them all. If I do, I'll leave someone out. So thank you all. I do, however, want to especially thank the consultant liaison people from our industry's major long distance carriers, MCI and AT&T. MCI's dial-up consultant liaison bulletin board is just fabulous.

Among the manufacturers, special thanks to Amdahl, Aspect Telecommunications, Bellcore, General Cable, Micom, NEC, Newbridge Networks, New York Telephone, Northern Telecom, Racal Data Communications, Ricoh and Teknekron. They'll recognize some of their words in this dictionary. Special thank yous also to Ken Guy of Micom, Simi Valley (near LA); bugging expert Jim Ross of Ross Engineering, Adamstown, MD; John Perri and Karen Miller of the call-accounting company SoftCom, NYC; to Jane Laino of Corporate Communications Consultants, NYC, to Sharon O'Brien of Hayes Microcomputer Products in Norcross, GA (Atlanta) and B.J. Strode, a Ericsson Network Systems technical editor. In my office, I'm very grateful to Muriel Fullam, Rose Bodin, Andy Moore, Kim Mund, Randi Ripley and Jennifer Cooper-Farrow.

If I've left any definitions out, or if some of my definitions are unclear, drop me a line. This is the third edition of my dictionary. It's one-third bigger than the second edition which was 18 months ago. There'll be many editions. Our industry is exploding.

I wrote this dictionary on a Toshiba T1200XE laptop using ZEdit. We typeset it on a Macintosh IIcx using QuarkXPress and Adobe Illustrator.

Harry Newton

12 West 21 Street

New York, NY 10010

212-691-8215

Fax 212-691-1191

Bulletin Board 212-989-4675

MCI Mail HarryNewton

1.544 MBPS The speed of a T-1 circuit.

193RD BIT The frame bit for a T-1 frame.

10-NET The LAN from Fox Research, Dayton, OH, now a subsidiary of DCA of Atlanta. 10-Net is a baseband, Ethernet CSMA/CD peer-to-peer LAN running on one twisted pair. It is easy to install and has many advantages. See ETHERNET.

23B +D A circuit with a wide range of frequencies that is divided in 23 64 Kbps paths for carrying voice, data, video or other information simultaneously. In ISDN, it is also known as the Primary Rate Interface. It bears a remarkable similarity to today's T-1 link, except that T-1 can carry 24 voice channels. In ISDN, 23B +D gives 23 channels and one D channel for out of band signaling. However, in T-1, signaling is handling in band. So there is considerable difference between today's T-1 and tomorrow's ISDN 23B +D. See ISDN.

2500 SET The "normal" single-line touchtone desk telephone. It has replaced the rotary dial 500 set in most — but definitely not all — areas of the United States and Canada.

2B +D The Basic Rate Interface (BRI) in ISDN. A single ISDN circuit divided into two 64 Kbps digital channels for voice or data and one 16Kbps channel for low speed data (up to 9,600 baud) and signaling. Either or both of the 64 Kbps channels may be used for voice or data. In ISDN 2B+D is known as the Basic Rate Interface. In ISDN, 2B +D is carried on one or two pairs of wires (depending on the interface) — the same wire pairs that today bring a single voice circuit into your home or office. See ISDN.

2B1Q TWO BINARY, ONE QUARTERNARY An ISDN line encoding technique which uses two bits to represent four varia- tions in amplitude and polarity.

2W Two-Wire

486 A shortened name for Intel's new 80486 chip, the successor to and continuation of the line of chips that started with the 8088 and grew into the 8086, 80286 and 80386. The 80486 is a major step forward in speed, complexity and capability. In simple terms, the 486 is a combination microprocessor, floating point math coprocessor, memory cache controller and 8K of RAM cache, all in one chip.

500 SET The older rotary dial telephone deskset.

5ESS A digital central office switching system made by AT&T. It is typically used as an "end-office," serving local subscribers.

64 KBPS The standard speed for V.35 interface, DDS service, and also the effective top speed of a robbed-bit 64 Kbps channel.

800 SERVICE 800-Service. A generic and common (and not trademarked) term for AT&T's, MCI's, US Sprint's and the Bell operating companies' IN-WATS service. All these IN-WATS services have "800" as their "area code." Dialing an 800-number is free to the person making the call. The call is billed to the person or company being called. The telephone company suppliers of 800 services use various ways to configure and bill their 800-services. One way: you can buy an 800 line which will ring on your normal phone line. You'll only pay per call, but you won't receive any incoming call if you're making an outgoing one. (You can even terminate an 800 number on your cellular phone.) For other 800 services you might pay a flat monthly rate plus "so-much" (i.e. timed usage) per call. That timed usage may include some calculation for the distance the incoming call traveled. 800-Service is now available for calls from Canada and some countries in Europe. More and more long distance companies are introducing 800-service.

800 Service works like this: You're somewhere in North America. You dial 1-800 and seven digits. Your local central office sees the "1" and recognizes the call as long distance. It ships that call to a bigger central office (or perhaps processes the call itself). At that central office it's processed, a machine will recognize the 800 "area code" and examine the next three digits. Those three digits will tell which long distance carrier to ship the call to. Each long distance company has been assigned specific 800 three digit "exchanges." For example, MCI has the exchange 999. AT&T has the exchange 542. If you want a phone number beginning with 800-999, then you must subscribe to MCI 800 service. If you want a phone number beginning with 800-542, you must subscribe to AT&T 800 service. Once the 800-call is "passed off" to whichever carrier it belongs to, that carrier sends the call to a switch attached to a huge "translation" database. The call arrives at the switch. The database says the call 800-NNN-XXXX is really 212-555-1234, and sends the 800 line to that number.

As a real-life example, Telecom Library, publishers of this book, has an 800 number, namely 800-LIBRARY (or 800-542-7279). When you call that number, the following number — 212-206-6870 — in New York City rings. Dialing 800-542-7279 is effectively the same as dialing 212-206-6870, except that if you dial 212-206-6870 you'll pay. If you dial 800-542-7279, I'll pay. Because 800 long distance service is essentially a database lookup and translation telephone service, there are endless "800 services" you can create. See EIGHTHUNDRED SERVICE for more, especially all the features you can now get on 800 service.

800 VALUFLEX SERVICE A New York Telephone service which lets you make and receive regular phone calls and 800-number calls from local areas on your normal business phone lines. There are big advantages here. You don't have to rent additional phone lines. You don't have to expand your existing phone system — or buy a new one (if getting extra lines means you'd grow out). And you can combine your incoming 800 lines with features you can get on business lines — like call forwarding, conferencing, etc. Have your 800 calls come into your office during the day. Have them call forwarded at night to your home. 800 Valuflex is aimed at smaller business.

802 IEEE committee on Local Area Networks.

802.1 IEEE standard for overall architecture of LANs and internetworking.

802.1B IEEE standard for network management.

802.1D IEEE standard for inter-LAN bridges (specifically between 802.3, 802.4, and 802.5 networks). Works at the MAC level.

802.2 A data link layer standard used with the IEEE 802.3, 802.4 and 802.5 standards.

802.3 IEEE standard for carrier-sense multiple access with collision detection (CSMA/CD). A physical layer standard specifying a LAN with a CSMA/CD access method on a bus topology. Ethernet and Starlan both follow the 802.3 standard. Typically they transmit at 10 megabits per second.

802.3 1Base5 IEEE standard for baseband Ethernet at 1 Mbps over twisted pair wire to a maximum distance of 500 meters. Also caled "starlan.

802.3 10Base2 IEEE standard for baseband Ethernet at 10 Mbps over coaxial cable to a maximum distance of 185 meters. Also called "Cheapnet" or "Thin Ethernet".

802.3 10Base5 IEEE standard for baseband Ethernet at 10 Mbps over coaxial cable to a maximum distance of 500 meters.

802.3 10Broad36 IEEE standard for broadband Ethernet at 10 Mbps over broadband cable to a maximum distance of 3600 meters.

802.4 A physical layer standard specifying a LAN with a token-passing access method on a bus topology. Used with Manufacturing Automation Protocol (MAP) LANs. Arcnet can work this way. Typical transmission speed is 10 megabits per second.

802.5 A physical layer standard specifying a LAN with a token-passing access method on a ring topology. Used by IBM's Token Ring hardware. Typical transmission speed is 4 or 16 megabits per second.

802.6 IEEE standard for MANs (Metropolitan Area Networks). Formerly known as QPSX (Queued Packet and Synchronous Exchange), now known as DQDB (Distributed Queue DOUBLE Bus).

802.7 IEEE technical advisory group on broadband LANs.

802.8 IEEE technical advisory group of fiber-optic LANs.

8088 This is the name of the chip which drove the original IBM PC and the subsequent IBM XT. It is a hybrid 8-bit processor which addresses 16-bit memory. It has a clock speed of 4.77 mhz. It is made by Intel. See also V20, which is a Japanese NEC version of the 8088. It's about 10% to 20% faster than the 8088. You can pull an 8088 out of your old PC (e.g. the AT&T 6300) and replace it with this chip. You'll get about a 20% (and noticeable) increase in speed. We have. It works fine. Some key systems use this chip.

8088-2 A speeded-up version of the 8088 microprocessor. It has a clock speed of 8 mhz. See also the V20-2 which is the Japanese version of the 8088-2. It's 10% to 20% faster than the 8088-2.

80286 The Intel microprocessor (computer on a chip) which drives the IBM AT. It is a true 16-bit processor (see 8088 above). This chip will run at 6 mhz to 16 mhz.

80386 The Intel microprocessor (computer on a chip) which drives the IBM Model 80 and others. It is a 32-bit processor. It is typically clocked at 16 mhz, but there are now versions of it that will run at 33 mhz.

80486 The Intel microprocessor (computer on a chip) which sports one million transistors. It has a clock speed of 50 mhz. It is very powerful and the newest of Intel's chips as we write.

A & A1 Control leads that come from 1A2 key telephone sets to operate features including flashing of lights to indicate on hold, line ringing, etc.

A & B LEADS Additional leads used typically with a channel bank two-wire E&M interface to certain types of PBXs (also used to return talk battery to the PBX).

A & B SIGNALING Procedure used in most T-1 transmission links where one bit, robbed from each of the 24 subchannels in every sixth frame, is used for carrying dialing and controlling information. A type of in-band signaling used in T-1 transmission. A and B signaling reduces the available user bandwidth from 1.544 to 1.536 Mbps.

A LAW ENCODING The method of encoding sampled audio waveforms used in the 2048K bit(s) 30 channel PCM primary system, widely used outside North America.

A-B TEST Direct comparison of the sound/picture quality of two pieces of audio/TV equipment by playing one, then the other.

A-LAW The PCM coding and companding standard used in Europe.

A/D Analog to digital conversion.

AABS A new software feature being introduced in the telecommunications industry. It allows collect and third-number billed calls to be placed by the caller without using an operator in much the same way as calling card services have been automated. (See 0+ Calls).

AAP Administrative and Accounting Package. The name of a feature on an InteCom PBX which provides call accounting reports relating to usage and cost.

AAR Automatic Alternate Routing.

ABAM A designation for 22 gauge, 110 ohm, plastic insulated, twisted pair Western Electric cable normally used in central offices.

ABANDONED CALL The nontechnical explanation is: A call that is answered but disconnected before any conversation happens. The technical explanation is: A call which has been offered into a communications network or telephone system, but which is terminated by the person originating the call before it is answered by the person being called. Follow this sequence for an explanation: You call an airline. You hear ringing. Their phone rings. A machine, called an automatic call distributor, answers the call, gives some dumb message, "Please don't hang up. A real human will answer eventually." You, the caller, are put on Eternity Hold. You get bored waiting and hang up before a live operator answers. This is an Abandoned Call. Information about abandoned calls is useful for planning how many people (also called operators, agents or telephone attendants) an airline should employ on what days and during what times of the day. Thus you can organize to get the right percentage of incoming calls answered within the "right" amount of time and thus give your callers (i.e. your customers) the service they deserve (or the service you think they deserve, or, the service they think they deserve).

ABBREVIATED DIALING A feature of phone systems which allows users to place calls by dialing typically one or two digits. The system translates the abbreviated number into the destination number. See also SPEED DIALING.

ABC Automatic Bill Calling — a method of billing for payphone calls. Changed in 1982 to Calling Card service.

ABM Asynchronous Balanced Mode.

ABORT To stop doing something. Often to get out of a software program. Also, to discontinue sending or receiving a message.

ABOVE 890 DECISION The 1959 FCC decision which allowed companies to build their own private microwave communications systems. The decision resulted from AT&T Long Lines' reluctance to provide companies with long distance service to remote places, such as oil wells, gas pipelines, power stations and paper plants. The decision got its name because the FCC allowed privately-owned microwave systems using radio frequencies "above 890" megahertz. See also MICROWAVE.

ABR Autobaud rate detect. A process by which a receiving data device determines the speed, code level, and stop bits of incoming data by examining the first character — usually a preselected sign-on character (often a carriage return). ABR allows the receiving device to accept data from a variety of transmitting devices operating at different speeds without needing to establish data rates in advance. TELECONNECT and INBOUND/OUTBOUND Magazine's electronic mail system (212-989-4675) has ABR. It will detect automatically if you are coming in at 300, 1200 or 2400 baud. Try it.

ABRASION RESISTANCE Ability of material or cable to resist surface wear.

ABSENT-SUBSCRIBER SERVICE A service offered by local telephone companies to subscribers who will be away. A live operator or a machine intercepts the calls and delivers a message. When you come back, you get your old number. But in the meantime, while you're away, you pay less money per month than you would for normal phone service.

AC Alternating current. Typically refers to the 120 volt electricity delivered by your local power utility to the three-pin power outlet in your wall. Called "alternating current" because the polarity of the current alternates between plus and minus, 60 times a second. The other form of electricity is DC, or direct current, in which the polarity of the current stays constant. Direct current, for example, is what comes from batteries. Overseas, electricity typically alternates at 50 times a second — which is neither better nor worse than the U.S., just different. See AC POWER and BATTERY.

AC POWER The phone system runs on Alternating Current. Except for very small ones, phone systems need their own dedicated AC power line. This line should be "cleaned" with a power conditioner and voltage regulator. If possible, the phone system should also be backed by a battery-based power pack, called UPS for Uninterruptible Power Supply. The most reliable battery backup is lead acid, the same technology as used in your car. Phone systems consume more power as they process more phone calls. For example, a Fujitsu PBX brochure says that at minimum capacity, it needs less power than eight 100-watt light bulbs. But that at maximum duplex capacity, it needs the same power as 26 100-watt light bulbs — or 2600 watts. See AC and ALTERNATING CURRENT.

ACA Automatic Circuit Assurance.

ACB A Northern Telecom term for Architecture Control Board.

ACC Automatic Callback Calling.

ACCELERATED AGING A test performed on material or cable meant to duplicate long term environmental conditions in a short period of time.

ACCELERATED DEPRECIATION A method which allows greater depreciation charges in the early years of an asset's life and progressively smaller ones later on. The total amount of depreciation charged is still equal to 100% of the asset's value. By taking the charges early on in the asset's life, you get the time value of money, i.e. depreciation charged today (and tax saved today) is worth more than the same amount of depreciation charged (or tax saved) tomorrow.

ACCELERATOR A chemical additive which hastens a chemical reaction under specific conditions. A term used in the telecommunications cable industry.

ACCEPTANCE TEST The final test of a new telephone system. If the system passes the test — i.e. it meets all specifications laid down in the sales contract — and is working well, then, and only then, will the customer finish paying for it.

ACCESS As a verb, to dial into a feature, a circuit or a piece of equipment. As a noun, the point at which you enter a circuit or other communications facility. In data processing, access means to retrieve information from, or store data in memory or mass storage.

ACCESS CHARGES Under deregulation, all users having access to United States public switched long distance networks will pay an Access Charge. The charge will differ for residential and business users and may also differ between Centrex and PBX users. It varies from $1 to $6 per month. The charge is theoretically, to make up for the "subsidies" once paid by AT&T Long Lines (now called AT&T) to the local operating telephone companies — Bell and independent.

ACCESS CODE A series of digits or characters which must be dialed, typed or entered in some way to get use of something. That "something" might be a long distance company, an electronic mail service, a private corporate network, a mainframe computer, a local area network. Once the user dials the main number for the service he must then enter his assigned Access Code to get permission use the system. An Access Code becomes an Account Code when it is used for identifying the caller and doing the billing. Access Code may also mean the digit, or digits, a user must dial to be connected to an outgoing trunk. For example, the user picks up his phone and dials "9" for a local line, dials "8" for long distance, dials "76" for a WATS, etc.

ACCESS CUSTOMER NAME ABBREVIATION A three-character abbreviation assigned to each IntereXchange Carrier (IXC) and listed in the Local Exchange Routing Guide (LERG).

ACCESS EVENT Information with a logical content that the functional user and the Network Access FE (Functional Entity) exchange. Definition from Bellcore.

ACCESS GROUP All terminals or phones have identical rights to make use of the computer, the network or the data PBX.

ACCESS LEVEL Used interchangeably with ACCESS CODE. "Level" in dialing tends to mean a number.

ACCESS LINE A telephone line reaching from the telephone company central office to a point usually on your premises. Beyond this point the wire is considered inside wiring.

ACCESS METHODS Techniques and rules for figuring which of several communications devices — e.g. computers — will be the next to use a shared transmission medium. This term relates especially to Local Area Networks (LANs). Access method is one of the main methods used to distinguish between LAN hardware. How a LAN governs users' physical (electrical) access to the cable significantly affects its features and performance. Examples of access methods are token passing (Arcnet and Token Ring) and Carrier Sense Multiple Access with Collision Detection (CSMA/CD) (Ethernet).

ACCESS TANDEM A type of local phone company central office specifically designed to provide equal access for all long distance carriers in that area.

ACCESS TIME The time between giving an instruction to get data from a computer and when that data becomes available.

ACCOUNT CODE (VOLUNTARY OR ENFORCED) A code assigned to a customer, a project, a department, a division — whatever. Typically, a person dialing a long distance phone call must enter that code so the computer can bill the cost of that call at the end of the month or designated time period. Many service companies, such as law offices, engineering firms, advertising agencies, etc. use account codes to bill their clients. Some account codes are very complicated. They include the client's number and the number of the particular project. The Account Code then includes Client and Matter number. These long codes can tax many call accounting systems, even some very sophisticated ones.

ACCS Automatic Calling Card Service.

ACCUNET A family of digital long distance transmission services from AT&T. Services are leased, switched or high speed. One, called Accunet Packet Service, is a packet switching digital network. Another one is called Accunet Reserved 1.5 Service, which AT&T describes as a general purpose, common user, modal-based digital service using dual 1.544 Mbps terrestrial and satellite facilities. Accunet Spectrum of Digital Services (ASDS) is AT&T's leased line (also called private line) digital service at 56 Kbps. MCI and Sprint have similar services. It is available in N x 56/64 Kbps, for N = 1, 2, 4, 6, 8, 12. The 56/64 Kbps POP-POP service (between long distance carrier central offices) now costs the same as an analog leased line.

ACCURACY Absence of error. The extent to which a transmission or mathematical computation is error-free. There are obvious ways of measuring accuracy, such as the percentage of accurate information received compared to the total transmitted.

AC/DC RINGING A common way of signaling a telephone. An alternating current (AC) rings the phone bell and a direct current (DC) is used to work a relay to stop ringing when the called person answers.

ACD See the next seven definitions, AUTOMATIC CALL DISTRIBUTOR, and ACIS.

ACD APPLICATION BRIDGE Refers to the link between an ACD and a database of information resident on a user's data system. It allows the ACD to communicate with a data system and gain access to a database of call processing information such as Data Directed Call Routing.

ACD APPLICATION-BASED CALL ROUTING In addition to the traditional methods of routing and tracking calls by trunk and agent group, the latest ACDs route and track calls by application. An application is a type of call, e.g. sales vs. service. Tracking calls in this manner allows accurately reported calls especially when they are overflowed to different agent groups.

ACD CALL BACK MESSAGING This ACD capability allows callers to leave messages for agents rather than wait for a live agent. It helps to balance agent workloads between peak and off-peak hours. In specific applications, it offers callers the option of waiting on hold. A good example is someone who only wishes to receive a catalog. Rather than wait while people place extensive orders, they leave their name and address as a message for later followup by an agent. This makes things simpler for them and speeds up service to those wanting to place orders.

ACD CALLER DIRECTED CALL ROUTING Sometimes referred to as an autoattendant capability within the industry, this ACD capability allows callers to direct themselves to the appropriate agent group without the an operator. The caller responds to prompts (Press 1 for sales, Press 2 for service) and is automatically routed to the designated agent group.

ACD CONDITIONAL ROUTING The ability of an ACD to monitor various parameters within the system and call center and to intelligently route calls based on that information. Parameters include volume levels of calls in queue, the number of agents available in designated overflow agent groups, or the length of the longest call. Calls are routed on a conditional basis. "If the number of calls in queue for agent group #1 exceeds 25 and there are at least 4 agents available in agent group #2, then route the call to agent group #2."

ACD DATA DIRECTED CALL ROUTING A capability whereby an ACD can automatically process calls based on data provided by a database of information resident in a separate data system. For example, a caller inputs an account number via touch tone phone. The number is sent to a data system holding a database of information on customers. The number is identified, validated and the call is distributed automatically based on the specific account type (VIP vs. regular business subscri

ber, as an example).

ACD INTELLIGENT CALL PROCESSING (IPC) The ability of the latest ACDs to intelligently route calls based on information provided by the caller, a database on callers and system parameters within the ACD such as call volumes within agent groups and number of agents available.

ACF Advanced Communications Function. A family of software products used by IBM allowing its computers to communicate.

ACIS Automatic Customer/Caller Identification. This is a subset of many sophisticated ACD systems. ACIS allows the capture of incoming network identification digits such as DID or DNIS and interprets them to identify the call type or caller. With greater information, such as ANI, this data can identify a calling subscriber number. This is also possible by employing a voice response device to request an inbound caller to identify themselves with a unique code. This could be a phone number, a subscriber number or some other identifying factor. This data can be used to route the call, inform the agent of the call type and even pre-stage the first data screen associated with this call type automatically.

ACK In data communications, ACK is a character transmitted by the receiver of data to ACKnowledge a signal, information or packet received from the sender. See also ACKNOWLEDGMENT.

ACKNOWLEDGMENT In data communications, the transmission of acknowledgment (ACK) characters from the receiving device to the sending device indicates the data sent has been received correctly.

ACM 1. Address Complete Message. One of the ISUP call set-up messages. A message sent in the backward direction indicating that all the address signals required for routing the call to the called party have been received. See ISUP. 2. Association for Computing Machinery. 3. Automatic Call Manager. The integration of both inbound call distribution and automated outbound call placement from a list of phone contacts to be made from a database. Telemarketing and collections applications are targets for this type of system.

ACOUSTIC COUPLER An acoustic modem. A device used to link data terminals and computers with the telephone network. An acoustic coupler looks like the reverse of a telephone handset and is typically made of rubber. The data communications link is achieved through acoustic (sound) signals rather than through direct electrical connection. It is attached to the computer or data terminal through an RS-232-C connector. To work the acoustic coupler, start the computer's communications program, dial the distant computer on a single line telephone with a normal (e.g. old-fashioned) handset. When the distant computer answers with a higher pitched "carrier tone," you place the telephone handset in the acoustic coupler and transmit data. Since the data is transmitted by sound between the handset and the acoustic coupler (and vice versa), the quality isn't always reliable. You can usually transmit up to 300 baud. People use acoustic couplers when they're short of time or cannot physically connect their modem electrically, e.g. they're using a coin phone.

ACOUSTIC (OR AIR) SUSPENSION A loudspeaker system that uses an air-tight sealed enclosure.

ACOUSTICS That branch of science pertaining to the transmission of sound. The qualities of an enclosed space describing how sound is transmitted, e.g. its clarity.

ACP Activity Concentration Point.

ACRONYM A word formed from the first (or first few) letters of each word or group of words. For example, BASIC, the Beginner's All-Purpose Symbolic Instruction Code, or COBOL, the computer language, which comes from COmmon Business Oriented Language.

ACS 1. Automatic Call Sequencer. A rudimentary automatic call distributor. See AUTOMATIC CALL SEQUENCER. 2. Advanced Communication System. An old name for AT&T's data communications/data processing service, later called Net 1000. In late 1986, after 10 years in birth, AT&T finally buried ACS because it offered too little in the face of what — by then — had become cheap, powerful desktop microcomputers and under $200 1200 baud modems.

ACTGA Attendant Control of Trunk Group Access. A complicated term for a simple concept, namely that your operator completes long distance calls. A primitive form of toll control.

ACTIVE LINE A voice or data communications channel currently in use.

ACTIVITY CONCENTRATION POINT ACP. A location on a telecommunications network where there is high communications traffic, including voice, data, document distribution and teleconferencing. Generally, there will be some switching equipment present at the ACP.

ACTIVITY FACTOR A decimal fraction which represents the percentage of speech on a voice channel versus those periods of (non-talking) silence on that channel. Most voice channels carry actual speech 30% to 40% of the total available time. This represents an activity factor of 0.3 to 0.4.

AC TO DC CONVERTER An electronic device which converts alternating current (AC) to direct current (DC). Most phone systems, computers and consumer electronic devices (from answering machines to TVs) run on DC. Most phone systems have an AC to DC converter in them. Hint: it's probably buried in the power supply.

ACTS Automatic Coin Telephone Service includes a telephone company central office that can complete all types of payphone calls automatically without an operator. Recorded announcements are used to convey instructions to the customer.

ACU Automatic Calling Unit. Also an 801 ACU. A telephone company-provided device instructed by a computer to place a call on behalf of the computer. The call is then connected to a telephone company-provided Data Set. Anyone other than an IBM shop would simply buy a Hayes or Hayes-compatible modem, and not bother with the trouble and expense of an ACU.

ADA 1. Average Delay to Abandon. Average time a caller is held in queue before deciding to abandon. 2. A high level computer language which the Department of Defense has been trying to foist on its suppliers and thus, make a standard. ADA is named for British mathematician Ada Lovelace, known at the time as Lady Lovelace. She was the girlfriend of Charles Babbage, the inventor of the computer.

ADAPTER A device used to connect a terminal to some circuit or channel so it will be compatible with the system to which it is attached.

ADAPTIVE EQUALIZATION An electronic technique that allows a modem to continuously analyze and compensate for variations in the quality of a telephone line.

ADAPTIVE INTERFRAME TRANSFORM CODING A class of compression algorithms commonly used in video codecs to reduce the data transmission rate.

ADAPTIVE PULSE CODE MODULATION A way of encoding analog voice signals into digital signals by adaptively predicting future encodings by looking at the immediate past. The adaptive part reduces the number of bits per second that another rival and more common method called PCM (Pulse Code Modulation) requires to encode voice. Adaptive PCM is not common because, even though it reduces the number of bits required to encode voice, the electronics to do it are expensive. See PULSE CODE MODULATION.

ADAPTIVE ROUTING A method of routing packets of data or data messages in which the system's intelligence selects the best path. This path might change with altered traffic patterns or link failures.

ADC Analog-to-Digital Converter.

ADCCP Advanced Data Communications Control Procedure. ANSI's version of SDLC/HDLC.

ADCU Association of Data Communications Users.

ADD-ON 1. A telephone system feature which allows connecting a third telephone to an existing conversation. This "add-on" feature is initiated by the originator of the call. The feature is also known as "Three-Way Calling." 2. Hardware, often referred to as peripheral equipment, that is added to a system to improve its performance, add memory or increase its capabilities. Voice mail, Automated Attendant and Call Detail Recording Equipment are examples of PBX add-on devices. AT&T and some other manufacturers call them APPLICATIONS PROCESSORS.

ADD-ON CONFERENCE — INTERCOM ONLY Allows a telephone user to add someone else to an existing intercom (within-the-same office) conversation.

ADD-ON DATA MODULE Plug-in circuit cards which allow a PBX to send and receive analog (voice) and digital (data) signals.

ADDITIONAL PERIOD Billing periods charged after initial, first or minimum period on a call. Usually, long distance toll/DDD has a one-minute initial period at premium rate; subsequent "additional" minutes (period) are billed at a lower rate. Additional period billing increments vary by long distance company.

ADDRESS The destination of a message sent through a communications system. A telephone number is considered the Address of the called party on a voice telephone network. In computer terms, it is a set of numbers that uniquely identifies something — a workstation on a LAN, a location in computer memory, a packet of data traveling through a network. Its meaning is similar to that used in reference to postal service.

ADDRESSEE The intended recipient of a message.

ADH Average Delay to Handle. Average time a caller to an automatic call distributor waits before being connected to an agent.

ADJACENT CHANNEL INTERFERENCE When two or more carrier channels are placed too close together, they interfere with each other and mess up each other's conversations.

ADJUNCT Network system in the Advanced Intelligent Network Release 1 architecture that contains SLEE (Service Logic Execution Environment) functionality, and that communicates with an Advanced Intelligent Network Release 1 Switching System in processing AIN Release 1 calls. Definition from Bellcore. See also ADJUNCT PROCESSOR.

ADJUNCT KEY SYSTEM A system installed behind a PBX or a Centrex. Such key system provides the users with several more features than the PBX or Centrex. Not a common term today.

ADJUNCT PROCESSOR A computer outside a telephone switching system that "talks" to the switch and gives it switching commands. An adjunct processor might include a database of customers and their recent buying activities. If the database shows that a customer lives in Indiana, the call from the customer might be switched to the group of agents handling Indiana customers. Adjunct processors might be concerned with energy management, building security etc.

ADMINISTRATION BY TELEPHONE The capability for the system administrator to perform most routine system administrative functions remotely from any Touch Tone pad. Such functions include mailbox maintenance (e.g. create, delete, set password, set class of service, etc.) and disk maintenance.

ADMINISTRATIVE SERVICE LOGIC PROGRAM ASLP. The SLP responsible for managing the feature interactions between Advanced Intelligent Network AIN Release 1 features resident on a single SLEE (Service Logic Execution Environment).

ADN Advanced Digital Network. ADN is Pacific Bell of California's low-cost leased 56-Kbps digital service. ADN is available for intraLATA calls.

ADP Automatic Data Processing. The same as DP, data processing.

ADPCM Adaptive Differential Pulse Code Modulation. A speech coding method which calculates the difference between two consecutive speech samples in standard PCM coded telecom voice signals. This calculation is encoded using as adaptive filter and therefore, is transmitted at a lower rate than the standard 64 Kbps technique. Typically, ADPCM allows an analog voice conversation to be carried within a 32k-kbit/s digital channel; 3 or 4 bits are used to describe each sample, wh

ich represents the difference between two adjacent samples. Sampling is done 8,000 times a second.

ADRMP (pron. add-rump) Autodialing Recorded Message Player. A device that calls a bunch of telephone numbers and upon connection will play a message to the answering person. ADRMPs are used for lead solicitation and message delivery. They are often unpopular due to their indiscriminate dialing pattern and random message playing.

ADVANCED COMMUNICATION SYSTEM ACS. The old name for a proposed packet switched network from AT&T. The service was called Net 1000. AT&T finally killed the service in late 1986. For a bigger explanation, see ACS.

ADVANCED DIGITAL NETWORK ADN is Pacific Bell of California's low-cost leased 56-Kbps digital service. ADN is available for intraLATA calls.

ADVANCED INTELLIGENT NETWORK AIN. The Bell telephone companies' service-independent architecture for the 1990's and beyond.

ADVANCED 800 SERVICES AT&T's name for a family of 800 In-WATS services that include time of day and area code routing, single number 800 service (for both interstate and intrastate), automatic number identification, etc. See also 800 SERVICE.

ADVANCED PRIVATE LINE TERMINATION An AT&T term which means the PBX user gets access to all the services of an Enhanced Private Switched Communications Services (EPCS) network. It also works when it is associated with AT&T's Common Control Switching Arrangement (CCSA) network.

ADVANCENET An Ethernet-based local area network from Hewlett Packard, Palo Alto, CA.

ADVISORY TONES Signals such as dial tone, busy, ringing, fast-busy, call-waiting, camp-on and all the other tones your telephone system uses to tell you that something is happening or about to happen.

AEMIS Automatic Electronic Management Information system. This was the first computerized UCD/ACD reporting system introduced by AT&T for CO UCD (Uniform Call Distribution). This package was updated to become the PRO 150/500 system for UCD management on the Dimension PBX/UCD. AEMIS was the successor to the FADS or Force Administration Data System. It was an electro-mechanical system of peg counters and different colored busy lamp fields used to note trunk and position status.

AERIAL CABLE Cables strung outside and overhead. They're called aerial even though they only hang from poles or buildings. Some aerial cable hangs by its own strength. Some is supported by additional steel wire above it. Stringing aerial cable is cheaper than burying it, though buried cable lasts longer.

AERONAUTICAL RADIO INC. ARINC. The organization that coordinates the design and management of telecommunications systems for the airline industry. It's one of the largest buyers of telecommunications services and equipment in the world.

AFACTS Automatic Facilities Test System. AFACTS is a Rolm CBX feature. An automatic testing system for identifying faulty tie and central office trunks. AFACTS can pinpoint faulty trunks and generate exception and summary reports.

AFCEA Armed Forces Communications and Electronics Association. An organization of military communications personnel and suppliers who fulfill the specialized needs of government and military communications. They run an big convention each year in Washington in May-June. 703-631-4693.

AFE Analog Front End. See ANALOG FRONT END.

AFIPS American Federation of Information Processing Societies. A national, highly-respected organization formed by data processing societies to keep abreast of advances in the field. AFIPS organizes one of the biggest trade shows in the data processing industry — the NCC (National Computer Conference).

AFT Automatic Fine Tuning; SEE AFC.

AGC Automatic Gain Control. There are two electronic ways you can control the recording of something — Manual or Automatic Gain Control (AGC). AGC is an electronic circuit in tape recorders, speakerphones, and other voice devices which is used to maintain volume. AGC is not always a brilliant idea since it will attempt to produce a constant volume level, that is, it will try to equalize all sounds — the volume of your voice, and, when you stop talking, the circuit static

and/or general room noise which you do not want amplified. Never record a seminar or speech using AGC. The recording will be decidedly amateurish. Manual Gain Control means there is record volume control and is thus, preferred in professional applications.

AGENT 1. This term comes from the huge telephone call-in reservation centers which the airlines, hotels and car rental services run. An agent is the person who answers your call, takes your order or answers your question. Agents are also called Telephone Sales Representatives or Communicators. The term "agent" was first used in the airline business. It came from gate or counter ticket agent. 2. An "Agent" is the person or persons who have legal authority to order telephone service and equipment from telephone companies.

AGENT SIGN ON/SIGN OFF A feature which allows any ACD agent to occupy any position in the ACD without losing his or her personal identity. Statistics are collected and consolidated about this agent and calls are routed to this agent no matter where he sits or how many positions he may occupy at one time.

AGGREGATE RATE The sum of the channel data rates for a given application.

AGGREGATOR A new breed of long distance reseller. An aggregator is essentially a sales agent for a long distance company. Here's how it works: The aggregator goes to a long distance company and says "May I sell your long distance service at a discount?" The long distance company says Yes! The aggregator hits the street and sells cut-rate long distance service to any and everyone. The long distance provider installs the service and bills it. The aggregator makes his profit by charging a fixed monthly service fee, a percentage of savings or some other arrangement. The key to it: The end user saves some money because his calls are "aggregated" with those of ALL the customers of the aggregator and the long distance company extends a bulk savings to the aggregator.

Here's what June, 1990 TELECONNECT Magazine wrote about aggregators under the headline, "Aggregator Warning."

"Aggregators are companies which buy long distance wholesale and sell it retail. Aggregators exist because AT&T decided it wanted to win back long distance business it had lost. AT&T sliced its rates, liberalized its bulk billing rules and encouraged those consultants who had recommended their clients switch to MCI and US Sprint to become aggregators. These consultant-turned aggregators simply solicit anyone's long distance business and add it to their collection. AT&T sends their end-user a bill and the consultant-turned-aggregator a commission check.

"Should you — as an end-user — consider buying your long distance from an aggregator? The simple answer is YES. AT&T's discounts are so deep it's not uncommon for a company using AT&T today directly to switch to billing through an aggregator and save 20% to 25% — with nothing of substance happening. They still get their bills from AT&T and they still place and receive calls on AT&T as they had been doing. No wires are touched. No routing is changed.

"What about the pitfalls? There are some: First, don't buy long distance that isn't billed directly by the long distance carrier providing the service. If the aggregator does the billing, there's too much opportunity for "mischief," says Dick Kuehn, Cleveland consultant. "There's opportunity for doing things like increasing each of your calls by 30 seconds. And because a user has no answer supervision on his call detail records, it's very hard for the user to figure his exact timing." The problem, says Dick, is there's no way for a user to verify his own bill. Dick says "Carriers are honest. Resellers (aggregators that bill) are open to question."

"TELECONNECT also believes you probably shouldn't deal with an aggregator who bills you a percentage of "savings." This is also open to abuse. There are so many rates, so many changes monthly, so many options that it's virtually impossible for the user to figure out what he would have paid had he not gone with the aggregator. The calculation is too open to abuse. TELECONNECT's feeling: pay a flat service fee.

"P.S. Imagine buying an automobile tire. The local garage carries two options: a Bridgestone for $30 and a Pirelli for $100. You opt for the Bridgestone at $30. You've thus saved $70. The garage proprietor splits your "savings" with you and charges you $35.

AGGREGATION An AMA (Automatic Message Accounting) function that accumulates AMA data, resulting in a less than detailed AMA record. Definition from Bellcore.

AGING The change in properties of a material with time under specific conditions.

AHD Audio High Density. System of digital audio recording on grooveless discs, employing an electronically-guided capacitance pickup.

AI Artificial Intelligence. Perhaps the next phase of computing. The present forms of AI in computer software are called Expert or Knowledge Based systems.

AIN Advanced Intelligent Network. Bellcore's very detailed vision of what the future holds for the telephone networks of the Bell operating companies in the 1990s.

AIN Release 0 Advanced Intelligent Network Release defined by individual Bell Operating Companies for initial deployment in 1991, or so.

AIN Release 1 Advanced Intelligent Network Release for initial deployment by Bell Operating Companies in 1993 that has a single functional architecture.

AIN Release 1 Logical Resources For Bell Operating Companies, the logical network resources configured and updated to provide Advanced Intelligent Network Release 1 subscriber services (e.g., SLP and trigger data). Definition from Bellcore.

AIN Release 1 Switching System An access tandem, local tandem or end office that contains an ASC (Advanced Intelligent Network Release 1 Switch Capabilities) functional group. Definition from Bellcore.

AIN Release 2 An Advanced Intelligent Network Release for initial deployment in 1995, evolving from AIN Release 1 and supporting an expanded range of information networking services from the Bell operating telephone companies. Definition from Bellcore.

AIN Switch Capabilities ASC. A functional group residing in an Advanced Intelligent Network Release 1 Switching System that contains the Network Access, Service Switching, Information Management, Service Assistance and Operations FEs (Functional Entities). Definition from Bellcore.

AIOD Automatic Identification of Outward Dialing is the ability of the telephone system to know the specific extension placing a call. It's used as part of the process of recording the detail of each telephone call for billback and cost control purposes. See also CALL ACCOUNTING SYSTEM.

AIRLINE MILEAGE The monthly charge for many leased circuits is billed on the basis of "airline mileage" between the two points. Though it sounds as if it's the distance a crow would fly directly between the two points, when in reality, it is the distance in mileage between two Rate Centers whose position is laid down according to industry standards, originally created by AT&T. The entire U.S. is divided by a vertical and horizontal grid. The coordinates — vertical and horizontal — of each rate center are defined and applied to a square root formula which yields the distance between the two points. Think back to school. There's a right-angled triangle. At the top is one Rate Center. At the side is the other Rate Center. The horizontal is the horizontal coordinate. The vertical is the vertical coordinate. The formula is simple: Square the vertical distance. Square the horizontal distance. Add the two together. Then take their square root. That will give you the distance across the hypotenuse — the side opposite the right angle in the triangle. Voila, your "airline" mileage. For sample V and H city coordinates and the formula on how to calculate airline mileage, see V & H under the letter V.

ALARM DISPLAY Attendant console indicators show the status (i.e. what's happening) in the telephone system. There are usually two types of displays — minor and major. Minor displays may be something as "minor" as a "hung" trunk, i.e. one that didn't hang up when the person speaking on it hung up. They can often be remedied by turning the PBX off, counting to ten, and then turning it on. (Before you do, check it will load itself.) Major problems — such as a blown line card in the PBX, one console out or half the trunks out — often require a service call and are often covered under the Emergency Conditions section of telephone service contracts.

ALC 1. Automatic Level Control. 2. Automatic Light Control.

ALERTING A signal sent to a customer, PBX or switching system to indicate an incoming call. A common form is the signal that rings a bell in the telephone set. Others signals can trigger such devices as whistles, gongs and chimes.

ALERTING SIGNAL A ringing signal put on subscriber access lines to indicate an incoming call.

ALGORITHM A prescribed finite set of well defined rules or processes for the solution of a problem in a finite number of steps. In normal English, it is the mathematical formula for an operation, such as computing the check digits on packets of data that travel via packet switched networks.

ALIT Automatic Line Insulation Testing.

ALL CHANNEL TUNING Ability of a television set to receive all assigned channels. VHF and UHF, channels 2 through 83.

ALL NUMBER CALLING Once upon a time, the first two digits of telephone exchanges sort of corresponded to their location. For example, MU-8 meant Murray Hill 8 in Murray Hill, Manhattan, New York City. Then the phone company started running out of letters, so it went to All Number Calling. The All Number Calling provides a theoretical maximum of 792 central office exchange (NNX) codes per area code (NPA). This is derived on the basis of 800 NXX code combinations (8x10x10) leaving out eight special service combinations, including 411, 611, 911.

ALL TRUNKS BUSY When a user tries to make an outside call through a telephone system and receives a "fast" busy signal (twice as many signals as a normal busy in the same amount of time), he is usually experiencing the joy of All Trunks Busy. No trunks are available to handle that call. The trunks are all being used at that time for other calls or are out of service. These days, many long distance companies are replacing a "fast" busy signal with a recording that might say something like, "I'm sorry. All circuits are busy. Please try your call later."

ALL-CALL PAGING With this feature, a user can broadcast an announcement — a page — to someone through the speakers of all the telephones on the system and, possibly, any external loudspeakers. If you want instant fame, ask your secretary to call all the airports in the country and page you. Mike Todd, the movie mogul, used to have this secretary perform this wonderful task. Mr. Todd gave gigantic egos a whole new meaning.

ALLIANCE TELECONFERENCING SERVICE A direct-dial AT&T service which allows you to teleconference as few as three and as many as 58 telephones around the world. You can dial the numbers to call or you can schedule a meeting, called "Meet-Me Service." If you want to set the conference up, you dial 0-700-456-1000, then punch in the number of locations, then put in the numbers, ending each with a #. End your dialing with another # — to add yourself to the teleconference.

ALLOY A combination of two or more metals that forms a new or different metal with specific or desirable qualities.

ALOHA A method of data transmission in which the device transmits whenever it wants to. If it gets an acknowledgement from the device it's trying to reach, it continues to transmit. If not (as in the case of a collision with someone else trying to transmit simultaneously), it starts all over again. The ALOHA method get its name from a dying satellite that was donated to university researchers in the Pacific. It was used to transmit data by satellites among South Sea islands, especially Hawaii. The ALOHA "method" — called "transmit at will" — was invented because the users were short of funds to develop more sophisticated data transmission protocols, and they had a free satellite, which typically had more bandwidth than they had stuff to send.

ALPHA Only alphabetic characters.

ALPHAMERIC Only alphabetic characters. See also ALPHANUMERIC.

ALPHANUMERIC A set of characters that contains both letters and numbers — either individually or in combination. Numeric is 12345. Alphabetic is ABCDEF: Alphanumeric is 1A4F6HH8. American and Australian zip codes are numeric. Canadian and English postal codes are alphanumeric. No one knows why.

ALPHANUMERIC DISPLAY A display on a phone or console showing calling phone number, called number, trunk number, type of call, class of service and perhaps, some other characteristics of the call. It may also contain instructions as to how to move the call around, set up a conference call, etc. The display may be liquid crystal or light emitting diode. Typically, it's liquid crystal.

ALTEL Association of Long Distance Telephone Companies. A trade association composed of alternative (to AT&T) long distance carriers and resellers of long distance services.

ALTERNATE ANSWERING POSITION Usually refers to a second receptionist's desk which has a telephone switchboard or console identical to the main one. Also refers to when the main receptionist is away from his/her desk, or is very busy taking calls, the telephone system automatically sends the calls to another console or to a phone that will be answered.

ALTERNATE BUFFER In a data communications device, the section of memory set aside for the transmission or receipt of data after the primary buffer is full. This helps the device control the flow of data so transmission is not interrupted due to lack of space for the incoming or outgoing data.

ALTERNATE ROUTING A feature used with long distance calls that permits the telephone system (typically a PBX) to throw calls over different (alternate) phone lines, depending on the congestion of the primary phone lines the calls are to be sent over. Alternate routing is often confused with LEAST COST ROUTING, in which the telephone system chooses the least expensive way (available at that time) to route that call. Least Cost Routing typically works with so-called "look-up" tables in the memory of the PBX. These tables are put into the PBX by the user. The PBX does not automatically know how to route each call. It must be told by the user. That "telling" might be as simple as saying "all 312 area codes will go via the AT&T FX line." Or it might be as complex as actually listing which exchanges in the 312 area code go by which method. LEAST COST ROUTING tells the calls to go over the lines which are perceived by the user to be the least cost way of getting the call from point A to point B. Alternate routing happens when the least cost routes get congested and alternate routes (typically more expensive) are found from the look-up tables in the PBX's memory.

ALTERNATING CURRENT See AC.

ALTERNATIVE NON-TRAFFIC SENSITIVE COST-RECOVERY PLANS New charges proposed by the regional Bell holding companies to supplement subscriber line charges. In short, another charge on the subscriber with an interesting, though dubious, justification. They have not been fully implemented.

ALTERNATOR A machine which generates electricity which is alternating current. See AC.

ALU Arithmetic Logic Unit. The part of the CPU (Central Processing Unit) that performs the arithmetic and logical operations.

AM See Amplitude Modulation.

AMA Automatic Message Accounting. AMA is the phone company's name for Call Detail Recording or Station Message Detail Recording (SMDR). See AMA TAPE.

AMA TAPE A telephone company machine-readable magnetic tape which contains the customer's long distance calling and billing data for a given month.

AMA TELEPROCESSING SYSTEM AMATPS. The primary method for delivery of AMA data from the network to billing systems. The current AMATPS architecture consists of an AMA Transmitter (AMAT) and a collector. Definition from Bellcore.

AMATPS AMA Teleprocessing System.

AMBIENT NOISE The level of noise present all the time. There is always noise, unless you're in an anechoic chamber.

AMERICAN BELL, INC. The old name for the unregulated telephone equipment supply subsidiary of American Telephone & Telegraph. American Bell Inc. had its name changed to AT&T Information Systems. At that point it was no longer separately incorporated. It became a division of AT&T. It has been reorganized many times. When it was American Bell, it was only selling telecommunications products and services to end users. When it become AT&T Information Systems, it sold AT&T phone systems and AT&T computer systems. It then merged with AT&T Long Lines, which was then called AT&T Communications and is now simply AT&T. By the time you read this, it will probably be called something else. Sadly, old gadgetry, knick-knacks and momentos bearing the name American Bell, Inc. have no marketable value as antiques or examples of American folk art.

AMERICAN STANDARD CODE FOR INFORMATION INTERCHANGE ASCII. The standard 7-bit code for transferring information asynchronously on local and long distance telecommunications lines. The ASCII code enables you to represent 128 separate numbers, letters, and control characters. By using an eighth bit — as in extended ASCII or IBM's EBCDIC — you can represent 256 different characters. ASCII often uses an eighth bit as a parity check or a way of encoding word processing symbols, not as a way of broadening the number of characters and symbols which it can represent. See also ASCII.

AMERICAN WIRE GAUGE Measurement scale for non-ferrous (copper, bronze, etc.) wire. See AWG for a bigger explanation.

AMERITECH CORP. One of the Regional Bell operating companies formed as a result of the AT&T Divestiture. Ameritech includes the operating telephone companies: Illinois Bell, Indiana Bell, Michigan Bell, Ohio Bell, and Wisconsin Bell. It also includes some other subsidiaries, which fit into two classifications — administrative (centralized buying, real estate, etc.) or entrepreneurial (cellular mobile radio, interconnect equipment, voice mail service bureau, venture capital, etc.).

AMIS See AUDIO MESSAGING INTERCHANGE SPECIFICATION.

AMPERAGE RATING The amperage which may be safely applied to a circuit, service or equipment. See also AMPERE.

AMPERE A measure of electrical current. It is mathematically equal to watts divided by volts. Note that in the electrical context, watts is spelled with two "Ts." In telecommunications, WATS, meaning Wide Area Telecommunications Service, is spelled with only one "T."

AMPHENOL CONNECTOR A brand of cable connector. You see an amphenol connector typically on the end of a 1A2 multi-button key telephone set.

AMPLIFIED HANDSET An amplified handset is the best phone gadget you can buy. You use it to crank up the volume of incoming calls and save yourself enormous amounts of money on callbacks. "We have a bad line. I'll call you back." There are three types of amplified handsets: 1. The handset with a built-in amplifier. These devices suck their power from the phone line and since the phone line doesn't have much power, you won't have much amplification. I'm not overly impressed with amplified handsets. 2. The handset with amplifying circuits built into the phone. Ditto for our comments about power. 3. The handset with the little external box amplifier which is powered by either AC or by several nicad batteries. Such an external amplifier will produce much greater amplification. This is the type we prefer at TELECONNECT Magazine.

AMPLIFIER When telephone conversations travel through a medium, such as a copper wire, they encounter resistance and thus become weaker and more difficult to hear. An amplifier is an electrical device which strengthens the signal. Unfortunately, amplifiers in analog circuits also strengthen noise and other extraneous garbage on the line. Amplifiers are used in all telephone systems, analog and digital. But in digital systems, signals are regenerated and then amplified. As a result, noise is much less prevalent and less likely to be amplified in digital systems.

AMPLITUDE The distance between high or low points of a waveform or signal. Also referred to as the wave "height." See AMPLITUDE MODULATION.

AMPLITUDE DISTORTION The difference between the output wave shape and the input wave shape.

AMPLITUDE MODULATION Also called AM, it's a method of adding information to an electronic signal in which the signal is varied by its height to impose information on it. "Modulation" is the term given to imposing information on an electrical signal. The information being carried causes the amplitude (height of the sine wave) to vary. In the case of LANs, the change in the signal is registered by the receiving device as a 1 or a 0. A combination of these conveys different information, such as words, numbers or punctuation marks.

AMPS Advanced Mobile Phone Service. It's not so "advanced" today — cellular is much better.

AMS Account Management System.

ANA Assigned Night Answer.

ANALOG Comes from the word "analogous," which means "similar to." In telephone transmission, the signal being transmitted is "analogous" to the original signal. In correct English usage, "analog" is meaningless as a word by itself. But in telecommunications, analog means telephone transmission and/or switching which is not digital. See ANALOG TRANSMISSION.

ANALOG BRIDGE A circuit which allows a normal two-person voice conversation to be extended to include a third person without degrading the quality of the call.

ANALOG CHANNEL A channel which transmits in analog waveforms. See ANALOG.

ANALOG COMPUTER A computer that performs its tasks by measuring continuous physical variables — pressure, voltage, flow — and manipulating these variables to produce a solution, which is then converted into a numerical equivalent. Analog computers are largely used as special purpose machines in scientific or technical applications.

ANALOG/DIGITAL CONVERTER An A/D Converter. Pronounced: "A to D Converter." A device which converts an analog signal to a digital signal.

ANALOG FACSIMILE Facsimile which can transmit and receive grey shadings — not just black and white. It is called analog because of its ability to transmit what appear to be continuous shades of grey. "Analog" facsimile is usually transmitted digitally.

ANALOG FRONT END The part of the fax machine that converts between the digitally modulated signal and the analog signal used on the telephone line.

ANALOG LOOP-BACK A method of testing modems and data terminals by disconnecting the device from the telephone line and looping a signal out through the device's transmit side and in through its receive side. The test tells if the trouble is with the telephone line or with the modem.

ANALOG RECORDING System of recording in which music is converted into electrical impulses that form "patterns" in the grooves of phonograph record masters or in the oxide particles of master tapes representing (or analogous to) musical waveforms.

ANALOG SWITCH Telephone switching equipment that switches signals without changing the analog form. The major form of analog switching is circuit switching.

ANALOG TRANSMISSION A way of sending signals — voice, video, data — in which the transmitted signal is analogous to the original signal. In other words, if you spoke into a microphone and saw your voice on an oscilloscope and you took the same voice as it was transmitted on the phone line and threw that signal onto the oscilloscope, the two signals would look essentially the same. The only difference would be that the electrically transmitted signal would be at a higher frequency.

ANC All Number Calling.

AND Automatic Network Dialing.

ANECHOIC CHAMBER A perfectly quiet room. A room in which sound or radio waves do not reflect off the walls. An anechoic chamber is the only place in which a speakerphone will work perfectly. The more a room resembles an anechoic chamber — i.e. lots of drapes, plush carpet, etc. — the better a speakerphone will work.

ANI Automatic Number Identification. A phone call arrives at your home or office. At the front of the phone call is a series of digits which tell you, the receiver, the source of the call. These digits may arrive in analog or digital form, as touchtone digits inside the phone call or in a digital form on a separate circuit. You will need some equipment to decipher the digits AND do "something" with them. That "something" might be throwing them in a database and throwing up your customer's record on a screen in front of your telephone agent as he answers the call. "Good morning, Mr. Smith." Some large users say they could save as much as 20 seconds on the average IN-WATS call if they knew the phone number of the person calling them from the start. They would avoid asking regular customers for routine identification information as it would all be there in the database. ANI is touted as one of ISDN's most compelling advantages — but it is really an advantage of Signaling System 7 (and therefore distinct from ISDN). ANI is also called CLI, which stands for Calling Line ID, or Identification. See ISDN, ISUP and COMMON CHANNEL SIGNALING.

ANM Answer Message. The fourth of the ISUP call set-up messages. A message sent in the backward direction indicating that the call has been answered. See ISUP and COMMON CHANNEL SIGNALING.

ANNEAL The act of using heat to soften a metal such as copper, making it less brittle.

ANNOUNCEMENT SERVICE Allows a phone user to hear a recording when he dials a certain extension. These days, announcement services are provided increasingly by totally solid-state digital announcers. These gadgets are more reliable, deliver a clearer message and last much longer than analog tape-based machines (like answering machines), which use recording tape.

ANNOUNCEMENT SYSTEM A arrangement for providing information by means of recorded announcements.

ANNUNCIATOR A light or bell that tells you something, e.g. the ringing of a phone.

ANS Answer. (What else?)

ANSI American National Standards Institute. A standards-setting, non-government organization, which develops and publishes standards for "voluntary" use in the United States. The British have their own equivalent of ANSI. It's called the BSI, British Standards Institute. Standards set by national organizations are accepted by vendors in that country. See CCITT, ECMA, IEEE, and ISO.

ANSI.SYS A device driver used by MS-DOS to control output to the screen. Some programs require you to have the statement

DEVICE=ANSI.SYS in your CONFIG.SYS file. It provides the "buttons" that these programs then push to make certain things happen on the screen. The "buttons" are pushed by ANSI.SYS commands. The commands begin with Escape (character 27 in ASCII) followed by a left bracket. You can simply type these commands to make the screen change color, blink, etc., if you have the DEVICE=ANSI.SYS statement in your CONFIG.SYS file when you boot your PC. If you put the following line in your AUTOEXEC.BAT you will enjoy an attractive C: prompt. I use this line when I'm working on a color screen: Prompt $e[37;44;1m $_ DATE $d TIME $t $_$P$g

ANSI TIX9.4 ANSI's Sonet standard.

ANSI T1.110-1987 Signaling system number 7 (SS7) - General Information.

ANSI T1.111-1988 Signaling system number 7 (SS7) - Message Transfer Part (MTP)

ANSI T1.112-1988 Signaling System number 7 (SS7) - Signaling Connection Control Part (SCCP)

ANSI T1.113-1988 Signaling System 7 (SS7) - Integrated Services Digital Network (ISDN) user part.

ANSI T1.114-1988 Signaling System 7 (SS7) - Transaction Capability Application Part (TCAP)

ANSI T1.206 Digital Exchanges and PBXs - Digital circuit loopback test lines.

ANSI T1.301 ANSI ADPCM standard.

ANSI T1.401-1988 Interface between carriers and customer installations - Analog voice grade switched access lines using loop-start and ground-start signaling.

ANSI T1.501-1988 Network performance - Tandem encoding limits for 32 Kbit/s Adaptive Differential Pulse-Code Modulation (ADPCM).

ANSI T1.601-1988 Integrated Services Digital Nctwork (ISDN) - Basic access interface for use on metallic loops for application on the network side of the NT (Layer 1 specification).

ANSI T1.605-1989 Integrated Services Digital Network (ISDN) - Basic access interface for S and T reference points (Layer 1 specification).

ANSI T1.Q1 ANSI's standard for telecommunications network performance standards, switched exchange access network transmission performance standard exchange carrier-to-interexchange carrier standards.

ANSWER BACK SUPERVISION Another word for ANSWER SUPERVISION.

ANSWER DETECT The use of a digital signal processing technique to determine the presence of voice energy on a telephone line. It is used with call (answer) supervision, to identify an answered line. It's beginning to be used with computerized dialing equipment as it eliminates the need for a telephone representative to constantly monitor call set-up progress on each telephone line in the event a call is answered. See ANSWER SUPERVISION.

ANSWER MODE When a modem is set by the user to receive data, it is in Answer Mode. In any conversation involving two computers, two terminals or one computer and one terminal, one side of the conversation must always be in Answer Mode. Putting a modem/computer in answer mode is sometimes done through software and sometimes through hardware, i.e. a switch on the side of the machine. You cannot run a data communications "conversation" if both sending and receiving equipment are in "Answer Mode." Computers — mainframe and mini — which receive a lot of phone calls are typically put in "Answer Mode." The terminals or computers calling them are typically in transmit mode.

ANSWER SUPERVISION Follow this scenario: I call you long distance. My central office must know when you answer your phone, so my central office can start billing me for the call. It works like this: when you, the called party, answer your phone, your central office sends a signal back to my central office (the originating CO). This tells my central office to start billing me for the call. This signal is called Answer Supervision. Before the Divestiture of the Bell System in early 1984, most of the nation's long distance companies — with the exception of AT&T Communications — did not receive Answer Supervision. They did not know precisely when the called party answered. So they started their billing cycle after some time — 20 or 30 seconds after the caller completed dialing. These long distance companies presumed that after this time, some one will have answered and the call will be in progress and can then be timed and billed. Without Answer Supervision, their billing of calls is inaccurate. They may bill for calls which didn't occur. And you may pay more for calls which did occur.

With the Divestiture of the Bell System, and the introduction of Equal Access, most long distance companies will eventually be able to recognize Answer Supervision. If you choose to be equal accessed to a long distance carrier other than AT&T, most likely your long distance company will receive answer supervision from the local phone company. And therefore the pricing of your calls will be accurate. But check. If you are "accessing" your preferred long distance carrier by dialing a seven digit local number, then dialing your number and your account code, your carrier is probably not receiving Answer Supervision and the timing and billing of your long distance calls may be inaccurate. Check this out. Remember: just because your town has equal access doesn't mean your preferred long distance phone company has opted for it because it is expensive or for some other reason.

Virtually no hotels have answer supervision. So they start billing you arbitrarily. Some start billing you after three rings. Some after four. When you check out, carefully check your phone bill. You will, in most instances, find you have been billed for many uncompleted calls. Tell you family to pick up the phone quickly when you're out of town and may be calling them. Don't let the phone ring too many times as you're likely to be billed for the dubious pleasure of listening to ringing signals.

ANSWERBACK In data communications, answerback is a response programmed into a data terminal to identify itself when polled by a remote computer or terminal. This response is usually in reply to a Control-E (ASCII Character 5, Inquiry), which is known on the Telex and TWX networks as a "Who Are You?" character, or "WRU." The Answerback allows a remote computer to verify it has dialed correctly (usually on the Telex or TWX networks) by matching the Answerback received with the Answerback expected.

ANSWERING TONE The tone an asynchronous modem will transmit when it answers the phone. The tone indicates that it is willing to accept data.

ANTENNA A device for transmitting, receiving or transmitting and receiving signals. Antennas come in all shapes and sizes. Their shape depends on the frequency signal they're receiving. Electrical signals with frequencies higher on the spectrum, for example, are shorter and more directional. As they get higher on the spectrum, they look more like light. These must be focused and thus, require antennas which are shaped like the mirror reflector of a focusing flashlight. This parabolic shape focuses the broad beam (of the bulb or the electrical signal) into a narrow, focused beam. The weaker the received signal, the bigger the antenna must be. Antennas come in many varieties and have cute names, like parabola, caresgrain, helix, lens and horn.

ANTI-STUFFING A mechanical flap in a coin phone which prevents the blocking by paper or other material of coin chutes. An anti-stuffing flap is meant to assure that you, the user, get your money back after you've tried to make a call but didn't get through.

AOS Alternate Operator Services. Today there are many Operator Services Providers not owned by the Bell Telephone Companies or AT&T. The AOS industry is dropping the descriptive term "alternate" and communicating that they be known as OSPs. AOS was coined by AT&T. See AOSP and OPERATOR SERVICE PROVIDERS.

AOSP Alternate Operator Service Provider. A new breed of long distance phone company. It handles operator-assisted calls, in particular Credit Card, Collect, Third Party Billed and Person to Person. Phone calls provided by OSP companies are more expensive than phone calls provided by "normal" long distance companies, i.e. those which have their own long distance networks and which you see advertised on TV. You normally encounter an OSP only when you're making a phone call from a hotel or hospital phone, or a privately-owned payphone. It's a good idea to ask the operator the cost of your call before you make it.

AOSSVR Auxiliary Operator Services System Voice Response.

AP See ADD-ON or APPLICATIONS PROCESSOR. AP is an AT&T word for a piece of equipment which hangs off the side of their PBX and makes it do more things, like voice mail.

APAD Asynchronous Packet Assembler/Disassembler.

APD Avalanche PhotoDiode. A diode that, when hit by light, increases its electrical conductivity by a multiplication effect. APDs are used in lightwave receivers because the APDs have great sensitivity to weakened light signals (i.e. those which have travelled long distances over fiber).

API Application Programming Interface. A networking interface that serves as a predefined set of procedures that user and vendor software-based programs must follow to gain transparent access to systems services, such as those for network devices, files or interprocess communications. Standardization of APIs at various layers of a communications protocol stack provides a uniform way to write applications.

APL Automatic Program Load in telecom. In data processing, it's a popular programming language.

APLT See Advanced Private Line Termination.

APM Average Positions Manned, the average number of ACD positions manned during the reporting period for a particular group.

APOLOGIZE To lay the foundation for a future offense.

APPC Advanced Peer-to-Peer Communications, also called Logical Unit 6.2, an IBM-specified network node definition featuring high-level program interaction capabilities on a peer-to-peer basis.

APPEARANCE Usually refers to a private branch exchange line or extension which is on (i.e. "appears") on a multi-button key telephone. For example, extension 445 appears on three key systems.

APPEARANCE — TEST POINT The point at which a circuit may be measured by test equipment.

APPLETALK Apple Computer's proprietary local area network for linking Macintosh computers and peripherals, especially LaserWriter printers. Appletalk is a CSMA/CD network that runs at 230.4 kilo bits per second and is therefore, incompatible with any other local area network. Outside manufacturers, however, make gateways which will connect an Appletalk LAN to other local area and telecommunications networks — LANs, WANs and MANs.

APPLICATION A software program that carries out some useful task. Database managers, spreadsheets, communications packages, graphics programs and word processors are all applications.

APPLICATION FOR SERVICE A standard telephone company order form that includes pertinent billing, technical and other descriptive information which enables the company to provide communications network service to the customer and its authorized users.

APPLICATION PROGRAM A computer software program designed for a specific job, such as word processing, accounting, spreadsheet, etc.

APPLICATION PROGRAM INTERFACE API. A set of formalized software calls and routines that can be referenced by an application program to access underlying network services.

APPLICATIONS GENERATOR Basically, software that writes software. Applications generators are software tools that, in response to your input, write software code which a computer can understand. Applications generators have two major benefits: 1. They save time. An applications generator is perfect for demonstrating a quick, though not complete, programming application. 2. They can often be used by non-programmers. Applications generators have two disadvantages. 1. They are often limited in what they can do. 2. The code they produce is not as efficient as the code produced by a good programmer. They may be general purpose tools or they may provide support for specific application segments, such as connecting voice response units to mainframe databases, voice messaging system development, audiotex system development, etc. Applications generators are often used in programming voice processors.

One of applications generators' bigger advantages is their ability to translate user specified screens and menus into programming code. In essence, you produce the screen or menu using an interface as simple as a word processor. Then the applications generator translates that screen into programming code in a language, such as "C." Once translated into "C", a proficient programmer could go through the code and "improve" on it.

APPLICATIONS LAYER The seventh and highest layer of the Open Systems Interconnection data communications model of the International Standards Organization. It supplies functions to applications or nodes allowing them to communicate with other applications or nodes. File transfer and electronic mail work at this layer. See OSI model.

APPLICATIONS PROCESSOR A special purpose computer which attaches to a telephone system and allows it (and the people using it) to perform different "applications," such as voice mail, electronic mail or packet switching. We think AT&T invented the term. See also ADD-ON.

ARCHITECT One who drafts a plan of your office and then plans a draft of your money.

ARCHITECTURE The architecture of a system refers to how the system is designed and how the components of the system are connected to, and operate with, each other. Architecture has become a very "Big" selling feature because of the PBX's increasing importance as a central switcher of all types of office communication systems — voice, video, data, text — each of which have different communications characteristics. Architecture, thus, includes the ability of the system to carry narrow, medium and broadband signals. It also includes the ability of the system to grow "seamlessly" (i.e. without too many large jumps in price).

ARCHIVE A data file not immediately accessible. An archived file may contain backup copies of programs and files in use or data and materials no longer in use, but perhaps needed for historical or tax purposes. Archive files are kept on paper, on microfilm, on disk, on floppies, etc.

ARCNET Attached Resource Computer Network. One of the earliest and most popular local area networks ever invented. A 2.5M-bits-per-second LAN that uses a modified token-passing protocol. Developed by Datapoint, San Antonio, TX, Arcnet interface cards are now manufactured by many vendors, including Standard Microsystems and Pure Data, Ltd.

AREA CODE A three-digit code designating a "toll" center in the United States, Canada and Mexico. The first digit is any number from 2 through 9. The second digit is always a "1" or "0." An Area Code is also called an NPA, Numbering Plan Area. See AREA CODE RESTRICTION.

AREA CODE RESTRICTION The ability of the telephone equipment (or its ancillary devices) to selectively deny calls to specific (but not all) area codes. Area code restriction is often confused with "0/1" (zero/one) restriction which denies calls to all area codes by sampling the first and second dialed digits (is it a 0 or 1?) and thus, identifying and blocking an attempt at making a toll call.

ARINC Aeronautical Radio Inc. The collective organization that coordinates the design and management of telecommunications systems for the airline industry. It's one of the largest buyers of telecommunications services and equipment in the world.

ARITHMETIC UNIT The part of a computing system which contains the circuits that perform the arithmetic operations. See also ALU.

ARL Attendant Release Loop. A feature of the PBX console. See RELEASE.

ARMAGEDDON The fabled battlefield where God's heavenly forces are to defeat the demon-led forces of evil. The final battle.

ARMOR Mechanical protection usually accomplished by a metallic layer of tape, braid or served wires. Normally found only over the outer sheath. See ARMORED CABLE.

ARMORED CABLE A stainless steel handset cord which is meant to resist vandalism. Typically used on a coin phone, most stainless steel handset cords are too short. This is said to be because they were first ordered for use in prisons, where guards wanted to be certain they would not be used by the prisoners as hanging devices. Thus, they requested Western Electric to make them too short for such a use. Whether there is any validity to this story is dubious, however, it is part of telephone industry folk history and therefore, worth preserving.

ARP Address Resolution Protocol. A Transmission Control Protocol/Internet Protocol (TCP/IP) process that maps IP addresses to Ethernet addresses. Required by TCP/IP for use with Ethernet.

ARPA Advanced Research Projects Agency of the U.S. Department of Defense. (The whole DOD annual telecommunications bill exceeds $1 billion.) Much of the country's early work on packet switching was done at ARPA.

ARPANET A Department of Defense data network which ties together many users and computers in universities, government and businesses. ARPANET has been the forerunner of many developments in commercial data communications, including packet switching, which was first tested on a large scale on this network. ARPANET was developed by the Advanced Research Projects Agency.

ARQ Automatic Retransmission Request. The standard method of checking transmitted data, used on virtually all high-speed data communications systems. The sender encodes an error-detection field based on the contents of the message. The receiver recalculates the check field and compares it with that received. If they match, an "ACK" (acknowledgment) is transmitted to the sender. If they don't match, a "NAK" (negative acknowledgment) is returned, and the sender retransmits the message. Note: this method of error correction assumes the sender temporarily or permanently stores the data it has sent. Otherwise, it couldn't possibly retransmit the data. No error detection scheme in data transmission is foolproof. This one is no exception.

ARRAY ANTENNA Take a bunch of directional antennas. Aim them at the same transmitting source. Join them together. Presto, you now have a very powerful giant antenna. Array antennas are used for picking up weak signals. They are often used in astronomical and defense communications systems.

ARRESTOR A device used to protect telephone equipment from lightning, electrical storms, etc. An arrestor is typically gas filled so when lightning strikes, the gas ionizes and, bingo, a low resistance to the ground that drains the damaging high voltage elements of the lightning away.

ARS Automatic Route Selection. An AT&T term for Least Cost Routing. See LEAST COST ROUTING and ALTERNATE ROUTING.

ARTIFICIAL LINE INTERFACE In T-1 transmission, refers to the ability of a piece of transmission equipment to attenuate its output level to meet the required loop loss of 15-22.5 dB normally switch selectable between 0,7.5, and dB.

ARU Automatic Response Unit.

ASA Average Speed of Answer. The average delay an call encounters in an inbound call center where call queuing is used. It is measured and expressed over an hour, a shift or a day.

ASCII Pronounced: as'-kee. American Standard Code for Information Interchange. It's the most popular coding method used by small computers for converting letters, numbers, punctuation and control codes into digital form. Once defined, ASCII characters can be recognized and understood by other computers and by communications devices. ASCII represents characters, numbers, punctuation marks or signals in seven on-off bits. A capital "C", for example, is 1000011, while a "3" is 0110011. As a seven-bit code, and since each bit can only be a "one" or a "zero," ASCII can represent 128 "things," i.e. 2 x 2 x 2 x 2 x 2 x 2 x 2 which equals 128. ASCII is the code virtually every personal computer in the world encodes "things," including IBM, Apple and Radio Shack/Tandy. This compatible encoding (it was developed by ANSI — the American National Standards Institute) allows virtually all personal computers to talk to each other, if they use a compatible modem, or null modem cable and transmit and receive at the same speed. There are variations of ASCII. (Nothing is totally standard anymore.) The most important variation — one originally from IBM — is called Extended ASCII. It codes characters into eight bits (or one byte) and uses those ASCII characters above 127 to represent foreign language letters, and other useful symbols, such as those to draw boxes. But at 127 and below, extended 8-bit ASCII is identical to standard 7-bit ASCII. The CCITT calls ASCII International Telegraph Alphabet 5.

The other major method of encoding is IBM's EBCDIC (pronounced ebb'-si-dick). It's largely used on IBM and IBM-compatible mainframe computers (but not their PCs, which use ASCII and extended ASCII.) EBCDIC is an eight-bit encoding scheme, thus allowing up to 256 "things" to be encoded, i.e. 2 x 2 x 2 x 2 x 2 x 2 x 2 x 2 = 256. EBCDIC codes letters, characters and punctuation marks in a totally different way than ASCII. For ASCII files to be read by an IBM mainframe (one that reads EBCDIC), those ASCII files must be translated into EBCDIC by one of the many translation programs available.

ASDS Accunet Spectrum of Digital Services. AT&T's leased line (also called private line) digital service at 56 Kbps. MCI and Sprint have similar services. It is available in N x 56/64 Kbps, for N = 1, 2, 4, 6, 8, 12. The 56/64 Kbps POP-POP service (between long distance carrier central offices) costs the same as an analog line.

ASIC Application Specific Integrated Circuit.

ASN.1 Abstract Syntax Notation One. LAN "grammar," with rules and symbols, that is used to describe and define protocols and programming languages. ASN.1 is the OSI standard language to describe data types.

ASP A Northern Telecom term for Attached Support Processor.

ASPECT RATIO The ratio of the width of a rectangular image to its height. The aspect ratio of TV is four units of width to every three units of height. This is expressed as 4 x 3 aspect ratio. A 35mm frame measures 24 x 36 mm, which means it has three units of width to two units of height. It is different in size from a TV screen. This is why the side parts of movies are chopped off on TV.

ASR Automatic Send-Receive teletype or telex machine. Such a machine, if left on and loaded with paper, will receive incoming messages and print them, even when nobody is present. See also AUTOMATIC SEND RECEIVE for another definition.

ASSEMBLER A program which translates an assembly programming language into the code of ones and zeros used by computers.

ASSEMBLY LANGUAGE A computer language for writing software. It is a language which is converted by a computer into machine language programs which a computer can understand.

ASSIGNED NIGHT ANSWER ANA. After business hours or when you place your phone system on "Night Answer," this feature sends calls from specified trunks to designated extensions or departments.

ASSIGNED PLANT CONCEPT A pair is dedicated from the central office to the subscriber home and maintained at that address, even when idle. See REASSIGNMENT.

ASSOCIATED VOICE PORT AVP. A Northern Telecom term. A voice port is used to pass signaling and supervision information to establish a connection for the data port. The term is also used in reference to the configuration of modems and voice grade switched circuits connected to the voice-port-data-port pair.

ASSOCIATION A relationship between two connection segments that share a common Leg O (i.e., a common subscriber is in control of connection segments). Definition from Bellcore.

ASTM American Society for Testing and Materials, a non-profit industry-wide organization which publishes standards, methods of test, recommended practices, definitions and other related material.

ASYNCHRONOUS BALANCED MODE ABM. Used in the IBM Token Ring's Logical Link Control (LLC), ABM operates at the SNA data link control and allows devices on a Token Ring to send data link commands at any time and to initiate responses independently.

ASYNCHRONOUS TRANSMISSION Literally, not synchronous. A method of data transmission which allows characters to be sent at irregular intervals by preceding each character with a start bit, and following it with a stop bit. It is the method most small computers (especially PCs) use to communicate with each other and with mainframes today. In every form of data transmission, every letter, number or punctuation mark is transmitted digitally as "ons" or "offs." These characters are also represented as "zeros" and "ones" (See ASCII). The problem in data transmission is to define when the letter, the number or the punctuation mark begins. Without knowing when it begins, the receiving computer or terminal won't be able to figure out what the transmission means. One way to do this is by using some form of clocking signals. At a precise time, the transmission starts, etc. This is called SYNCHRONOUS TRANSMISSION. In ASYNCHRONOUS transmission there's no clocking signal. The receiving terminal or computer knows what's what because each letter, number or punctuation mark begins with a start bit and ends with a stop bit. Transmission of data is called SYNCHRONOUS if the exact sending or receiving of each bit is determined before it is transmitted or received. It is called ASYNCHRONOUS if the timing of the transmission is not determined by the timing of a previous character. ASYNCHRONOUS is used in lower speed transmission and by less expensive computer transmission systems. Large systems and computer networks typically use more sophisticated methods of transmission, such as SYNCHRONOUS or BISYNCHRONOUS, because of the large overhead penalty of 20% in ASYNCHRONOUS transmission. This is caused by adding one start bit and one stop bit to an eight bit word — thus 2 bits out of ten.

The second problem with large transfers is error checking. The user sitting in front of his own screen checks his ASYNCHRONOUS transmission by looking at the screen and re-typing his mistakes. This is impractical for transferring long files at high speed if there is not a person in attendance.

In SYNCHRONOUS transmission start and stop bits are not used.

According to the book Understanding Data Communications, characters are sent in groups called blocks with special synchronization characters placed at the beginning of the block and within it to ensure that enough 0 to 1 or 1 to 0 transitions occur for the receiver clock to remain accurate. Error checking is done automatically on the entire block. If any errors occur, then the entire block is retransmitted. This technique also carries an overhead penalty (nothing is free), but the overhead is far less than 20% for blocks or more than a few dozen characters.

AT Access Tandem

AT COMMAND SET Also known as the Hayes command set. A language that enables communications software to get an asynchronous modem to do what you want it to do. So called "AT" because all the commands begin with "AT," which is short for ATtention. The word "Hayes" comes from the manufacturer of modems called Hayes Microcomputer, the creator of the command set.

ATA American Telemarketing Association.

ATM Asynchronous Transfer Mode

AT&T American Telephone and Telegraph Company. Not much telegraph any more and proportionately less telephone too as it moves increasingly into the computer industry. AT&T, once the largest company in the world, is now 75% smaller as a result of the Divestiture of its operating telephone companies on December 31, 1983. At one stage, it had two main divisions, AT&T Communications (the long distance phone company) and AT&T Technologies (equipment) These were merged to form one AT&T with several divisions. Then we re-wrote this definition. Then they re-organized. Then we re-wrote. We re-wrote this definition so many times during the course of producing this dictionary that we finally gave up. Suffice, AT&T is American Telephone and Telegraph Company. At one stage it provided really good long distance service, made and sold computers, made and sold telephone switches — from small key systems to big central offices. It may still do all this by the time you get this dictionary. It may not. Life is fluid.

AT&T BELL LABS The research and development arm of AT&T. It used to be known simply as Bell Laboratories. It is probably the foremost research laboratory in the United States. Bell Labs is credited with inventing many electronics things including the transistor and is an incredible place, despite its recent trouble focusing its activities on marketable products.

AT&T COMMUNICATIONS AT&T-Comm or AT&T-C. The part of AT&T responsible for long distance services. It used to be called AT&T Long Lines, which we liked better. AT&T Communications is the largest part of AT&T and probably doesn't really exist any longer since it was merged with AT&T Information Systems. Sort of.

AT&T CREDIT CORPORATION AT&T's financing arm, which provides customized leases for telephone equipment including the MERLIN II, MERLIN Plus and SPIRIT Communications Systems, as well as for other equipment, such as AT&T FAX Machines and computers.

AT&T INFORMATION SYSTEMS AT&T-IS is one of AT&T's sales arms (or used to be). It's responsible for sales of certain equipment, including telephone systems and computers, to both end-users and some selected distributors. AT&T-IS used to be responsible for selling a service called Net 1000, which is an end-to-end data communications/data processing service, whose exact service is hard to define and has now been killed. AT&T-IS's precise function and organization within AT&T are also hard to define, since they change regularly. One concept was to use AT&T-IS as the retail on-the-street sales arm for AT&T Technologies. But that is changing and AT&T-IS is also becoming a wholesaler of AT&T products to retail distributors, such as stores and VARs. AT&T-IS used to be called American Bell, Inc., when it was incorporated. It no longer is. AT&T-IS is the second largest part (in employees) after AT&T Communications.

AT&T INTEREXCHANGE COMPANY ATTIX, a suggested name for the long distance part of AT&T, which, at the time was called AT&T Long Lines. It is now called AT&T Communications. Or used to be called AT&T Communications. The reason the name ATTIX was rejected is that it reminded someone at AT&T of the word "drug addicts." No one has explained logically why AT&T ever needed to change the name "Long Lines," which most people in the industry related to very warmly. Including us.

AT&T NETWORK SERVICES This is an AT&T Technologies division which sells equipment primarily to Bell Operating companies, independent phone companies, overseas phone companies and large, Fortune 500-type users. It's doing very well.

AT&T TECHNOLOGIES Formerly called Western Electric, it is the equipment manufacturing arm of AT&T. No one knows why this company changed its name, since Western Electric also (see ATTIX) had a wonderful reputation and is also remembered with great fondness. It has an excellent reputation for high quality products and is still used as a brand name on some AT&T Technologies' products.

ATB See ALL TRUNKS BUSY. One measure which your phone company might give you of telephone traffic in and out of your office.

ATD ATtention Dial the phone. The first three letters in the most frequently-used command in the Hayes command set for asynchronous modems — typically those used with microcomputers.

ATM Automated Teller Machine. The street corner banking machine which is usually hooked up to a central computer through leased local lines and a multiplexed data network.

ATT Automatic Toll Ticketing. A system which telephone companies use to automatically keep call detail records including calling number, number called, time of day and length of call. The phone company uses this information, together with the cost of phone calls, to generate an invoice to its customers.

ATTEMPT Trying to make a telephone call. Also defined as a call offered to a telecommunications system, regardless of whether it is completed.

ATTENDANT The "operator" of a phone system console. Typically, the first person to answer an incoming call. That person usually directs incoming calls to the proper person or department. That person may also assign outgoing lines or trunks to people requesting them. Few companies spend any time training their attendants. They should. There are two types of things attendants should be trained for: 1. Manners, including the correct way to keep people waiting and to screen incoming calls, and 2. The structure of the company. If a caller asks for some help, the attendant should know which department or person might be responsible for providing that help.

ATTENDANT BUSY LAMP FIELD Lamps, lights or LEDs that show whether a PBX or key system extension is busy or not. These days, many attendant busy lamp fields are being incorporated into CRT displays. We hope more will do this as many lamp-based attendant busy lamp fields are difficult to read.

ATTENDANT CALL WAITING INDICATION An unusual feature on a PBX console. The call waiting button on the attendant console lights to indicate a predetermined number of calls in queue. The light flashes when a second (programmable) threshold is reached.

ATTENDANT CAMP-ON If the extension is busy, the attendant or operator can place the call in a queue behind the call already in progress. When the call is over, the "camped-on" call will automatically ring the extension.

ATTENDANT CONFERENCE A conference phone call set up by your telephone operator. Sometimes the quality is good and other times it's not, depending on the quality of the phone lines.

ATTENDANT CONSOLE An attendant console is the larger, specialized telephone set used by the operator or attendant to answer incoming calls and send those calls to the proper extension. Consoles are becoming more sophisticated these days in several ways. Operators need to punch fewer buttons to move calls around, while the information they present to the attendant is more useful for keeping tabs on calls and letting people know what's happening. Many consoles are acquiring TV screens that report the status of each extension, who's speaking, where the call is going, and whether there are problems, such as broken lines or trunks, etc. anywhere on the system. Some of the more modern screens will allow the operator to send messages around the company that can alert someone as to who's calling before he/she picks up the phone. You can also easily program switches through consoles with CRT (also called TV) screens. In the old days you needed to punch in complex codes. Now you can respond to "Yes/No" decisions on a screen with lots of explanatory words and help menus.

ATTENDANT CONTROL OF TRUNK GROUP ACCESS The telephone operator or attendant controls the users' access to trunks for making local and/or long distance calls. This may reduce long distance call abuse.

ATTENDANT DIRECT STATION SELECT This feature gives an operator the ability to reach an extension by simply pushing one button. In direct station select, every extension has its own button. Direct Station Select usually comes with some form of Attendant Busy Lamp Field which shows whether the extensions are busy. Some attendants like direct station select. Others don't, preferring to simply punch in 345, instead of hunting for the button which corresponds to extension 345. The best consoles these days are using some form of easy-to-read screen prompts.

ATTENDANT EXCLUSION A PBX feature which stops the attendant from listening in on a phone call once she or he has passed the call to the correct extension.

ATTENDANT KEY PAD Allows the attendant to perform all functions using a standard touch tone key pad on the console or adjacent to it.

ATTENDANT LOCKOUT This feature denies an attendant the ability to re-enter a phone call unless specifically recalled by that PBX extension.

ATTENDANT OVERRIDE This feature allows a PBX attendant to enter a phone call in progress. Usually, the persons on the call will hear a warning tone.

ATTENDANT POSITION Where a telephone operator sits to answer calls and send them on to the people in the company. This is usually in front of a telephone system with buttons, toggle switches, etc. that facilitate this process.

ATTENDANT RECALL When a phone call has been transferred to a telephone extension and not answered, this telephone system feature sends the call back to the attendant. Sometimes the call will return to a special part of the attendant console which will indicate to the attendant that it is a "returned" call. It's a good idea to pay attention to the speed of recall back to the operator. People hate to be extended into endless ringing. Think of calling a hotel and how aggravating it is to wait until the call comes back to an operator after she/he extended it to the room...and it rings and rings.

ATTENDANT RECALL ON TRUNK HOLD The system will recall the attendant if a trunk placed on hold is not re-entered within a predetermined time.

ATTENDANT TRANSFER OF INCOMING CALLS A PBX and Centrex feature. A telephone extension is talking on a line but that person wants to transfer the call to someone else. The person hits their hookswitch a couple of times. (The hookswitch is the toggle switch the handset depresses when you replace it.) This flashing of the hookswitch signals the attendant to join the call. The person asks the attendant "to please transfer this call." The attendant then transfers the call to the new extension. This feature is totally inefficient as it's hard to reach the attendant, who's always busy, etc. etc. All newer phones can transfer both incoming and outgoing calls automatically by just flashing the hookswitch, dialing the extension number and hanging up.

ATTENDED A telephone system having an attendant or receptionist whose primary job is to answer all incoming calls. Many smaller systems, such as key systems, are not centrally "attended." The phone is simply answered by whoever is near. A non-attended phone system should be set up so anyone can answer an incoming call. Some systems, such as most key systems, come this way from the factory. Others, such as PBXs, have to be specially set up. Some systems can be set up so an attendant will get first shot at answering the incoming call, but then, after a couple of rings, anyone else can answer the call (perhaps a loud "night" bell will ring). This is the system we use at TELECONNECT Magazine.

ATTENTION KEY A key or combination of keys on a computer or terminal which signals the main computer to stop its present task and wait for a new command. The ESCape key is often the Attention Key. In Crosstalk, it's Control A.

ATTENUATE To reduce the amplitude of a signal. To reduce its volume. See ATTENUATION.

ATTENUATION The loss of volume during transmission. The received signal is lower in volume than the transmitted signal due to losses in the transmission medium (such as that caused by resistance in the cable). Attenuation is measured in decibels. It is the opposite of GAIN. Some electrical components are listed as "with attenuation" which means they will compensate for irregular electrical supply (e.g. surges).

ATTENUATOR A device which reduces the volume in a circuit without introducing any distortion.

ATTIX See AT&T INTEREXCHANGE COMPANY.

ATTND Attendant. (What else?)

ATTO Atto means one quintillion, which is 10 to the minus 18. See also FEMTO, which is 10 to the minus 15.

AUDIBLE INDICATION CONTROL Three fancy words for the ability to turn up or down the bell or beeper on your PBX attendant console.

AUDIBLE RING A sound sent from the called party's switch to inform the calling party that the called line is being rung. A long explanation for a bell or buzzer that tells you it's for you.

AUDIO Sound you hear which may be converted to electrical signals for transmission. A human being who hasn't had his ears blown by listening to a Sony Walkman or a ghetto blaster can hear sounds from about 15 to 20,000 hertz.

AUDIO FREQUENCIES Those frequencies which the human ear can detect (usually in the range of 15 to 20,000 hertz). Only those from 300 to 3,000 hertz are transmitted through the phone, which is why the phone doesn't sound "Hi-Fi."

AUDIO MENU Options spoken by a voice processing system. The user can choose what he wants done by simply choosing a menu option by hitting a touchtone on his phone or speaking a word or two. Computer or voice processing software can be organized in two basic ways — menu-driven and non-menu driven. Menu-driven programs are easier for users to use, but they can only present as many options as can be reasonably spoken in a few seconds. Audio menus are typically played to call

ers in automated attendant/voice messaging, voice response and transaction processing applications. See also MENU and PROMPTS.

AUDIO MESSAGING INTERCHANGE SPECIFICATION AMIS. Issued in February, 1990, AMIS is a series of standards aimed at addressing the problem of how voice messaging systems produced by different vendors can network or inter-network. Before AMIS, systems from different vendors could not exchange voice messages. AMIS deals only with the interaction between two systems for the purpose of exchange voice messages. It does not describe the user interface to a voice messaging system, specify how to implement AMIS in a particular systems or limit the features a vendor may implement. AMIS is really two specifications. One, called AMIS-Digital, is based on completely digital interaction between two voice messaging systems. All the control information and the voice message itself, is conveyed between systems in digital form. By contrast, the AMIS-Analog specification calls for the use of DTMF tones to convey control information and transmission of the message itself is in analog form.

AMIS was discussed in detail in the October 1990 issue of Business Communications Review. AMIS specifications are available from Hartfield Associates, Boulder CO. 303-442-5395.

AUDIO RESPONSE UNIT A device which translates computer output into spoken voice. Let's say you dialed up a computer and it said "If you want the weather in Chicago, push button "123," then it would give you the weather. But that weather would be "spoken" by an audio response unit.

AUDIOGRAPHICS The technology which allows sound and visual images to be transmitted simultaneously. According to AT&T, audiographics generally refers to single frame or slow frame visual images as opposed to continuous frame image transmission (e.g. television). Audiographic transmission is often used to teach or train people in remote locations from an educational institution or business training center, saving travel and housing expense.

AUDIOTEX A generic term for interactive voice response equipment and services. Audiotex is to voice what on line data processing is to data terminals. The idea is you call a phone number. A machine answers, presenting you with several options, "Push 1 for information on Plays, Push 2 for information on movies, Push 3 for information on Museums." If you push 2, the machine may come back, "Push 1 for movies on the south side of town, Push 2 for movies on the north side of town, etc." See also INFORMATION CENTER MAILBOX.

AUI Autonomous Unit Interface or Attachment Unit Interface. Most commonly used in reference to the 15 pin D type connector and cables used to connect single and multiple channel equipment in an Ethernet transceiver.

AURAL Relating to the sense of hearing.

AUTHORIZED AGENT Also called Authorized Sales Agent. A term chosen by some of the Bell operating companies to refer to companies which sell their network services on commission. Some of these companies have specific industry knowledge and have written specialized software. The idea is to work with businesses to arm them with the absolute best package of telecommunications hardware, software and services.

AUTHORIZATION Think of charging things on your MasterCard, Visa, or American Express card. If the store cannot authorize the amount of your purchase, your Visa card will not allow you to make the purchase. Authorization is needed for many long distance calls, especially those made using credit cards, telephone company calling card, etc. Authorization is done by the operator's computer checking with the remote validation database service. See BVA, BVS and VALIDATION.

AUTHORIZATION CODE A code in numbers and/or letters employed by a user to gain access to a system or service.

AUTHORIZATION CODES AC. Used to override the facilities restriction level (FRL) of a PBX. If you are making a call out on a line you are not authorized to use, the PBX will ask you for an authorization code. If you have one, your call will go through. If not, your call will be denied (i.e. not go through).

AUTHORIZED USER A person, firm, corporation or any other legal entity authorized by the provider of the service to use the service being provided.

AUTO ANSWER The capability of a terminal, a modem or a computer to answer an incoming call and to set up a data connection without anyone being there.

AUTOBAUD Automatic speed recognition. The ability of a device to adapt to the data rate of a companion device at the other end of the link.

AUTO DIAL A feature of phone systems and modems which allows them to dial a long phone number (usually long distance) by punching fewer buttons than there are numbers to dial. One button auto dial on electronic phones is very common these days. Most communications software programs will allow you to auto dial a string of 35 to 40 digits, which you may need if you're dialing into a long distance company.

AUTO DIAL AUTO ANSWER A modem feature. Auto Dial lets you dial a phone number through your modem, using your personal computer or data terminal keyboard. Auto Answer permits the modem to automatically answer the incoming call without anybody having to be there.

AUTO DIALER See AUTOMATIC DIALER.

AUTODIN The worldwide data communications network of the U.S. Department of Defense. Acronym for "AUTOmatic DIgital Network."

AUTOMATED ATTENDANT A device which is connected to a PBX. When a call comes in, this device answers it and says something like, "Thanks for calling the ABC Company. If you know the extension number you'd like, pushbutton that extension now and you'll be transferred. If you don't know it, pushbutton "0" (zero) and the live operator will come on. Or, wait a few seconds and the operator will come on anyway." Sometimes the automated attendant might give you other options, such as, "dial 3" for a directory. Automated attendants are very new. They are connected also to voice mail systems ("I'm not here. Leave a message for me."). Some people react well to automated attendants. Others don't. A good rule to remember is before you spring an automated attendant on your people/customers/subscribers, etc., let them know. Train them a little. Ease them into it. They'll probably react more favorably than if it comes as a complete surprise. The first impression is rarely forgotten, so try to make it a good experience for the caller.

AUTOMATED COIN TOLL SERVICE ACTS. In the old days, operators handled routine toll calls by counting the sound of coins hitting the box, checking prices, putting calls through, figuring and collecting overtime charges, etc. ACTS does all this automatically. It figures charges, tells those charges by digitized computerized voice to the customer, counts the coins as they are deposited and then sets up the call.

AUTOMATIC BUTTON RESTORATION When the telephone handset of a multi-line instrument (typically a 1A2 multi-line key set) is placed back in its cradle, the line button being used automatically "pops" back up. Conversely, when a user picks up the handset, he must always push down a line button to make a call. Most phones with this feature can be disabled, so the buttons stay down when the handset sits on the cradle. A twist of a single screw inside the instrument will usually solve the aggravation of the automatic button restoration. Some people like automatic button restoration because it saves a user from accidentally barging into someone else's call. This was a much greater problem with 1A2 key systems. It no longer is a problem with most electronic key systems since they usually extend the user automatic privacy once they get on a call so no one else can barge in, even if they wanted to.

AUTOMATIC CALLBACK When a caller dials another internal extension and finds it busy, the caller dials some digits on his phone or presses a special "automatic callback" button. When the person he's calling hangs up, the phone system rings his number and the number of the original caller and the phone system automatically connects the two together. This feature saves a lot of time by automatically retrying the call until the extension is free. See also CAMP ON. Wouldn't it be nice if they had this feature on long distance calls?

AUTOMATIC CALL DISTRIBUTOR ACD. A specialized phone system used for handling many incoming calls. Once used only by airlines, rent-a-car companies, mail order companies, hotels, etc., it is now used for any company that has many incoming calls (e.g. order taking, dispatching of service technicians, taxis, answering technical questions, etc.). There are very few large companies today that don't have at least one ACD. One of the largest systems belongs to General Electric and is used specifically for answering calls regarding the home appliances and equipment they sell.

An ACD performs four functions. 1. It will recognize and answer an incoming call. 2. It will look in its database for instructions on what to do with that call. 3. Based on these instructions, it will send the call to a recording that "somebody will be with you soon, please don't hang up!" 4. It will send the call to an operator within a group of operators as soon as that operator has completed their previous call, and/or the caller has heard the canned message. The term Automatic Call Distributor comes from distributing the incoming calls in some logical pattern to a group of operators. That pattern might be Uniform (to distribute the work uniformly) or it may be Top-down (the same agents in the same order get the calls and are kept busy. The ones on the top are kept busier than the ones on the bottom). Distributing calls logically is the function most people associate with an ACD, though it's not the most important. The management information which the ACD produces is much more valuable. This information is of two sorts: 1. The arrival of incoming calls (when, how many, which lines, from where, etc.) and 2. How many callers were put on hold, asked to wait and didn't. This is called information on ABANDONED CALLS. This information is very important for staffing, buying lines from the phone company, figuring what level of service to provide to the customer and what different levels of service (how long for people to answer the phone) might cost. See ACD. The seven definitions that follow ACD show some of the features which newer ACDs have. See also AUTOMATIC CALL SEQUENCER.

AUTOMATIC CALLING UNIT ACU. A device that places a telephone call on behalf of a computer.

AUTOMATIC CALL INTERCEPT A feature of a Rolm ACD. This feature automatically forwards calls to an attendant if the dialed number is not installed or out of order. It can also intercept an attempted trunk call that is in violation of a Class of Service restriction. Automatic Call Intercept will also recall the attendant after a predetermined period of offhook inactivity (e.g. flash or hold).

AUTOMATIC CALL SEQUENCER A device for handling incoming calls. Typically it performs three functions. 1. It answers an incoming call, gives the caller a message, and puts them on "Hold." 2. It signals the agent (the person who will answer the call) which call on which line to answer. Typically, the call which it signals to be answered is the call which has been on "hold" the longest. 3. It provides management information, such as how many abandoned calls there were, how long the longest person was kept on hold, how long the average "on hold" was, etc. There are three types of devices which handle incoming calls. The least expensive is the Automatic Call Sequencer which is traditionally used with key systems. It differs from Uniform Call Distributors (UCDs) and Automatic Call Distributors (ACDs) in that it has no internal switching mechanism and does not affect the call in any way. It simply recommends which call should be picked up and keeps statistical information on the progress of calls. A more expensive type of device is the UCD. The most full-featured and expensive is the ACD. Distinctions between ACDs and UCDs and/or PBXs with features called

UCDs and ACDs are blurring as UCDs get more sophisticated. The main difference, as we understand it, is that a UCD offers fewer options for routing an incoming call and answering calls in any particular order. ACDs typically produce the most detailed management information reports. One company also makes something called an ELECTRONIC CALL DISTRIBUTOR. It is essentially an automatic call distributor.

AUTOMATIC CIRCUIT ASSURANCE ACA is a PBX feature that helps you find bad trunks. The PBX keeps records of calls of very short and very long duration. If these calls exceed a certain parameter, the attendant is notified. The logic is that a lot of very short calls or one very long call may suggest that a trunk is hung, broken or out of order. The attendant can then physically dial into that trunk and check it.

AUTOMATIC DIALER or AUTODIALER A device which allows the user to dial pre-programmed telephone numbers by pushing one or two buttons. Sometimes referred to as a "repertory" dialer. Dialers can be bought as a separate device and added to a phone, however, today most telephone sets are outfitted with autodialers.

There are four basic measures of an automatic dialer's efficiency. 1. What's the longest number it will dial automatically? This is important because using some of AT&T's long distance competitors requires dialing lots of numbers, with lots of pauses. 2. How many numbers will it dial? Some people like to have a dialer which dials hundreds of numbers. Others like a small one, just for their most frequently called numbers. 3. Will the dialer recognize dial tone? This is important because using a long distance company or dialing through a PBX requires one to recognize consecutive dial tones. 4. Can you "chain" dial? In other words, can you hit one speed dial button after another and have the machine dial through a complex network and throw in authorization codes, etc.?

AUTOMATIC DIALING See SPEED DIALING.

AUTOMATIC EQUALIZATION The process of compensating for distortion of data communications signals over an analog circuit.

AUTOMATIC EXCHANGE A term for a central office which automatically and electronically switches calls between subscribers without using an operator. Not a common term.

AUTOMATIC FACILITIES TEST SYSTEM AFACTS is a Rolm CBX feature. It is an automatic testing system for identifying faulty tie and central office trunks. AFACTS can pinpoint faulty trunks and generate exception and summary reports.

AUTOMATIC FALLBACK A modem's ability to negotiate an appropriate data rate with the modem on the other end of the link, depending on line quality. For example, if two 2400 baud modems can not pass data at 2400 baud, they would "fall back" to 1200 baud automatically in order to transmit data without excessive errors.

AUTOMATIC GAIN This is an electronic circuit which automatically increases the volume when someone is speaking quietly and drops it when someone is speaking loudly. The idea is to keep the transmitted signal even. Most tape recorders, for example, have automatic gain circuits. This allows them to pick up voices of people in a room, even though the volume of each person's conversation arriving at the tape recorder is different. The problem with automatic gain circuits is they're always looking for something to amplify. Such that when it's quiet (and meant to be) the automatic gain circuit will also try and amplify the ambient noise in the room — to keep the sound level constant. All professionally recorded tapes are done on tape reorders with manual volume controls.

AUTOMATIC HOLD — STATION or INTERCOM When a user is having a conversation and receives another call, he may press the button to answer that new call. The call he was on originally is automatically put on hold. There's nothing very sophisticated about this feature, despite the big words describing it.

AUTOMATIC IDENTIFIED OUTWARD DIALING AIOD. The toll calls placed by all extensions on the telephone systems are automatically recorded. This information allows bills to be sent, long distance lines to be chosen, etc. See CALL ACCOUNTING, CALL DETAIL RECORDING, SMDR and AIOD.

AUTOMATIC LEVEL CONTROL ALC. A control system that adjusts the incoming signal to a predetermined level. Somewhat similar to automatic gain control. See AUTOMATIC GAIN CONTROL.

AUTOMATIC LIGHT CONTROL ALC. Vidicon camera control which automatically adjusts the target voltage to compensate for variations in light levels. See also AUTOMATIC GAIN.

AUTOMATIC MESSAGE ACCOUNTING AMA. 1. Service mark of AT&T. A system which records and documents billing information for long distance calls made by a corporate subscriber. The calls must be made to billable destinations to be documented. The information recorded is generally either 20% of all information (CCSA networks) or 100% of the information (all others). 2. The network functionality that measures, collects, formats, and outputs subscriber network-usage data to upstream billing OSs and other OSs (Operations Systems). Definition from Bellcore.

AUTOMATIC MESSAGE SWITCHING A technique of sending messages to their appropriate destination through information contained in the message itself — typically in its "address."

AUTOMATIC NETWORK DIALING A Rolm feature which is said to simplify on-network calling among multiple business locations by providing single-step dialing for private networks and a single numbering/dialing plan.

AUTOMATIC NUMBER IDENTIFICATION ANI. Equipment at your central office which recognizes the telephone number of the person making the call so that information about the call can be sent to the call accounting (i.e. billing) system. There has been some discussion about using ANI capability and sending calling information all over the country along with the call itself. This way the recipient will know who's calling before he/she picks up the phone and answers the call. So far, this service apparently awaits more universal introduction of ISDN, more corporate demand, more standardization, more seminars or whatever. ANI is also called Calling Number Identification. See also ISDN and System Signaling 7.

AUTOMATIC OVERFLOW TO DDD Toll calls jump to expensive direct distance dialed calls, when all lower cost FX, WATS lines, etc. are busy.

AUTOMATIC PRIVACY When someone is speaking on a phone line or on an intercom, this feature ensures no one else can accidentally or deliberately butt into that conversation. If you did, however, want somebody else to come into the conversation (for example, someone to provide some additional information), there's usually another feature called Privacy Release. By pushing this button on the phone, other people who have the same extension button or intercom button on their phones can then push their buttons and join the conversation. Or you can bring them into your conversation by dialing them in. Most modern key systems come with Automatic Privacy. Many people don't like it, especially those who live in small offices. Some newer phone systems are coming standard without it. And you have to program it in, if you want it.

AUTOMATIC PROGRAM LOAD APL is a PBX feature that allows it to load its own software into RAM from a local device such as a hard disk or a floppy disk. All this takes place automatically without human intervention. APL is an important feature since it often determines how fast a PBX can get back into service after some sort of failure — usually a failure in commercial power.

AUTOMATIC QUEUING Queuing is exactly as it sounds. Something you want is being used. So you get placed in line for that device. There are two types of queuing — automatic and manual. Manual is when you're put in queue by a person, for example an operator. Automatic is when you're put in queue by a machine, for example a PBX aided by its software.

AUTOMATIC RECALL A PBX feature which returns a call to the PBX attendant (or alerts the attendant) if a call extended to a telephone is not answered within a pre-set period of time. The most logical time is three rings, or 18 seconds. This feature allows the attendant to give the caller some information, take a message or connect the caller to someone else. Most hotel switches have this feature. And when the call doesn't get answered, the switch sends it back to the operator. The sad thing is that the hotel operator is usually so busy, he/she keeps you waiting another 20 or 30 seconds, irritating you.

AUTOMATIC RECOVERY Your telephone system dies — typically because its power is cut off. Once the power comes on, instructions in the machine direct it to reload its software so that within minutes the system can be back and running normally. Those "instructions" are normally not affected by power drops.

AUTOMATIC RINGDOWN TIE TRUNK A direct path signaling facility to a distant phone. Signaling happens automatically when you lift the receiver on either phone. See also MANUAL RINGDOWN TIE TRUNK.

AUTOMATIC ROUTE SELECTION Your phone system automatically chooses the least cost way of sending a long distance call. See LEAST COST ROUTING and ALTERNATE ROUTING.

AUTOMATIC SEND/RECEIVE ASR. A data device in which the transmitting thing is different from the receiving part, thus enabling the device to receive calls and transmit them simultaneously. See ASR for a different definition. We're not sure precisely which one is right. Both could be.

AUTOMATIC SPEED MATCHING The ability of an asynchronous modem to automatically determine whether it is expected to communicate at 300, 1200 or 2400 bps.

AUTOMATIC TOLL TICKETING A system which makes a record of the calling phone number, the called number, the time of day, the length of the call, etc. and then generates an instant phone bill for that call. Often used in hotel/motels.

AUTOMATIC TRAFFIC OVERLOAD PROTECTION ATOP. A Rolm feature defined as a dynamic form of line-load control, which automatically denies a dial tone during those periods when the Rolm CBX may become overloaded. One wonders why someone would create this feature.

AUTOMATIC WAKEUP The capability for the user to schedule a wake-up call to a predetermined telephone number, either one time or or daily.

AUTOMATIC WAKEUP SERVICE The guest or the operator dials into a machine which records a request for a guest wakeup call the following morning. The auto wakeup machine is a glorified, programmable auto-dial answering machine. The machine is said to save hotels money and make wakeup calls more reliable, and certainly more anonymous.

AUTOSEARCH See RECORDER.

AUTOSEVOCOM The AUTOmatic SEcure Voice COMmunications system of the U.S. Department of Defense.

AUTO-START A standby electrical power system that starts up when the normal supply of commercial power fails.

AUTOTIMED RECALL When a user places a call on hold and forgets about it, AUTOTIMED RECALL will ring that user or the receptionist after a predetermined time. That time is usually programmable. It shouldn't be longer than 30 seconds, otherwise your customers, sitting endlessly on your eternity hold, will go nuts and go elsewhere.

AUTOTIMED TRANSFER This telephone system feature switches unanswered incoming calls to a backup answering position after a predetermined (usually adjustable) interval of time.

AUXILIARY EQUIPMENT See also PERIPHERAL DEVICE or APPLICATIONS PROCESSOR.

AUXILIARY EQUIPMENT ACCESS The ability of a telephone system to interface with (i.e. talk to) auxiliary equipment such as a paging system or dial dictation system.

AUXILIARY LINE A telephone trunk in addition to the main number you rent from the phone company. Phone systems are often equipped for calls to hunt from a busy main number to one or more auxiliary lines (Incoming Service Group, or ISG). For example, The Telecom Library's main number is 212-691-8215. But The Telecom Library also has 8216, 8217, 8218 and several unmarked or coded trunks. These are auxiliary lines and they don't receive their own billing or listing from the phone company. Sometimes, people have single line private lines which "appear" on their phone and no one else's. Sometimes they call these auxiliary lines. Sometimes these are called private lines.

AUXILIARY NETWORK ADDRESS In IBM parlance, in ACF/VTM, any network address except the main network address, assigned to a logical unit which is capable of having parallel sessions. (I think this definition makes sense. I think I will clean it up for the next edition.)

AUXILIARY STORAGE A mass storage device capable of holding a larger amount of information than the main memory (i.e. RAM) of the computer or telephone system, but with slower access time. For example — magnetic tape, floppy disks, etc.

AUTOVON The AUTOmatic VOice Network used worldwide by the US Department of Defense. The system includes conferencing and secure voice communications (scrambling), among other features.

AVAILABLE In automatic call distribution language, an agent state, between calls, when an agent, having finished the previous transaction, returns to accept the next inbound caller. See also AVAILABILITY.

AVAILABILITY The amount of time a computer or a telephone system is available for processing transactions or telephone calls. Contrast this with the term RELIABILITY, which is different.

AVALANCHE PHOTO DIODE APD. A fiber optic transmission device. A light detector that generates an output current many times the light energy striking its face. A photodiode that shows gain in its output power compared to the optical power that it receives through avalanche multiplication (signal gain) of the current that flows through a photosensitive device. This type of diode is used in receivers requiring high light sensitivity. See APD.

AVERAGE PULSE DENSITY In T-1 bipolar transmissions, refers to the number of "1" pulses per "0" conditions and is usually tied to a maximum number of "0"s in a row (i.e., FCC Part 68 requires 12.5% pulse density and no more than 80 consecutive "0"s where as AT&T Pub 62411 uses a formula and no more than 15 consecutive "0"s).

AVC Automatic Volume Control. In radio it maintains constant sound level despite undesired differences in strength of incoming signal.

AVD Alternative Voice Data. See AVD circuits.

AVD CIRCUITS Alternate Voice Data Circuits. Telephone lines which have been electrically treated to handle both voice and data signals. Typically used on leased overseas circuits to save money.

AVERAGE CALL DURATION Divide the total number of minutes of conversation by the number of conversations. Bingo, that's your average call duration.

AVERAGE HOLDING TIME The sum of the lengths (in minutes or seconds) of all phone calls during the busiest hour of the day divided by the number of calls. There are two definitions. The one above refers to average speaking time (it's the more common one). There's a second definition for "average holding time." This refers to how long each call was on hold, and thus not speaking. This second definition is typically found in the automatic call distribution business (ACD). Check before you do your calculations.

AVOIDABLE COSTS A wonderful concept used by the regulated telephone industry. It refers to those costs which would be avoided (i.e. not incurred) if the service were not offered. Examples of costs to avoid are maintenance, taxes, labor, and other direct costs. The concept of Avoidable Costs is to allow the phone industry the justification to price a competitive service very low.

AVP A Northern Telecom word for Associated Voice Port.

AVP-L A Northern Telecom word for Associated Voice Port and Line.

AWC Area-Wide Centrex

AWG American Wire Gauge. Also known as the Brown and Sharpe (B&S) Wire Gauge. A method of measuring the thickness of cable. The AWG numbering system is backwards: The higher the AWG number the thinner the wire. For example, heavy industrial wiring may be No. 2. Homes are typically wired with No. 12 or No. 14. Telephone systems typically use No. 22, No. 24 or No. 26. The thicker the wire, the more current it can carry further. The thicker the wire, the less resistance the current will encounter and therefore the longer it will travel. You need thicker phone cabling when your phones are further away. Some vendors save money by installing systems with thin wire. Make sure you specify.

AZIMUTH The horizontal angle which the radiating lobe of an antenna makes in angular degrees, in a clockwise direction, from a north-south line in the northern hemisphere. In the southern hemisphere, the reference is the south-north line.

B CHANNEL A "bearer" channel that is a fundamental component of ISDN interfaces. It carries 64,000 bits per seconds in either direction, is circuit switched and can carry either voice or data. See BASIC RATE INTERFACE (BRI) and ISDN.

B-ISDN Broadband ISDN.

B8ZS Binary 8 zero substitution. A technique used to accommodate the ones density requirement for digital T-carrier facilities in the public network, while allowing 64 Kbps clear data per channel. Rather than inserting a one for every seven consecutive zeroes, B8ZS inserts two violations of the bipolar line encoding technique for digital transmission links.

BABBLE Just what it sounds like — crosstalk from several interfering communications circuits or channels.

BABBLING TRIBUTARY "A station that continuously transmits meaningless messages," defined by John McNamara, of DEC and author of "Local Area Networks, an introduction to the technology." Some people might argue this was another word for Harry Newton, the author who didn't know when to stop and wanted to make this dictionary the most comprehensive telecom dictionary ever.

BACK BOARD A piece of plywood mounted on a wall. Phone equipment is mounted on the plywood. It is more efficient to first mount phone equipment on plywood in the service bay, test it out while it's convenient and diagnostic tools are handy. Then take the phone equipment and the back board (which typically consists of the KSU, power supply, and 66- blocks) and install them on the customer's premises. This "pre-installation" makes enormous sense — economically and reliably. Sadly, few installation companies do it.

BACK HAUL When a communications channel takes traffic beyond its destination and hauls it back — all because it is cheaper to go that route instead of going directly.

BACK TO BACK CHANNEL BANK The connection of voice frequency and signaling leads between channels banks to allow dropping (i.e. removing) and inserting (i.e. adding) of channels.

BACK-UP SERVER A program or device that copies files so at least two up-to-date copies always exist.

BACKBONE The backbone is the part of the communications network which carries the heaviest traffic. It is one basis for design of the overall network service. The backbone may be the more permanent part of the network.

BACKBONE CLOSET The closet in a building where the backbone cable is terminated and cross connected to either horizontal distribution cable or other backbone cable.

BACKBONE NETWORK A transmission facility designed to interconnect lower-speed distribution channels or clusters of dispersed user devices.

BACKGROUND See BACKGROUND PROCESSING.

BACKGROUND MUSIC Music can be played through speakers in the ceiling and/or through speakers in each telephone, throughout the office, or office-by-office, or selectively. Background music is typically played through paging speakers. In fact, the two — paging and background music — often go hand-in-hand. When you want to page someone, the music turns off automatically and comes back on when the paging is over. The same thing happens on airplanes. Background music is said to motivate workers, often into shutting it off.

BACKGROUND NOISE The noise you hear when nothing else is being transmitted.

BACKGROUND PROCESSING The automatic execution of lower priority computer programs when higher priority programs are not using the computer's resources. A higher priority task would be completing calls. A lower priority task would be running diagnostics. Some PBXs have this feature. Some insist on running their diagnostics even though they are choked with calls. The smarter ones tone down their diagnostics when they get busier, which makes sense.

BACKGROUND TASK A secondary job performed while the user is performing a primary task. For example, many network servers will carry out the duties of the network (like controlling who is talking to whom) in the background, while at the same time the user is running his own foreground application (like word processing). See also BACKGROUND PROCESSING.

BACKOFF When a device attempts to transmit data and it finds trouble, the sending device has to try again. It may not try again immediately. It may "back off" for a little time so the trouble on the line can be cleared. This happens with LANs. For example, an earlier attempt to transmit may have resulted in a collision in a CSMA/CD (Carrier Sense Multiple Access/Collision Detection) Local Area Network (LAN). So the device "backs off," waits a little and then tries again. How long it waits is determined by preset protocols.

BACKOFF ALGORITHM The formula built into a contention local area network used after collision by the media access controller to determine when to try again to get back onto the LAN. See also BACKOFF.

BACKPLANE The high-speed communications line to which individual components of a modern electronic system are connected. For example, all the extensions of a PBX are connected to line cards (circuit boards) which slide into the PBX's cage. At the rear of the PBX cage, there is a connector. Each of these connectors is plugged into the PBX's Backplane. Also called a Backplane Bus. This backplane bus is typically very high speed, since it carries many conversations, address information and considerable signaling. These days, the backplane bus is typically a time division multiplexed line — somewhat like a train with many cars, each representing a time slice of another conversation. The backplane's capacity determines the overall capacity of the switch.

BACKUP A copy of computer data on an external storage medium, such as a floppy disk or tape. Computers and telephone systems (which are computers) are notoriously unreliable. They glitch and lose data for all sorts of unusual and impossible-to-predict reasons. Thus the necessity for backups. The theory is when (not "if") a glitch will occur and the PBX's data base will disappear off the face of the earth. If this happens, you have a backup and you simply retrieve the back-up file, load it up and, presto, you're back live.

Only information changed in the original (since the backup was made) is thus lost. Backups save time in restoring the system after a loss. Most modern PBXs work with a data base and other extensive customized instructions the user loads in. Most PBX users forget to make and keep backups of their PBX data. They expect their vendor to make backups, but he rarely does. This carelessness costs weeks of aggravation, as the PBX's data base and instruction set is manually (and painfully) put back together.

The method by which backups are maintained is also important. The medium should clearly be reliable, i.e. the best quality magnetic medium. The method of backing up is also important. For example, a streaming tape backup is less reliable than a file-by-file backup. In a streaming backup, the backup medium simply captures the original data one bit after another in one long stream. In a file-by-file backup, the data moves over in logical segments — command files, data files, etc. Streaming backups will work if their data is placed back on the same precise device from which they were originally taken. But, if they are placed on a different device (even though the same model number, etc.), they may barf because the tape assumes bad sectors are in the same place. This will probably not be true. Streaming tape backup devices are less expensive to buy and much faster to use. Avoid them.

BAD LINE KEY When the PX attendant encounters a bad trunk, he/she pushes this button on the console, automatically flagging the trunk for later checking and repair.

BAD LINE REPORTING Automatically reports a poor connection without interrupting the current call.

BALANCE To equalize load or current between parts or elements of a telephone line or circuit. Balancing helps get the best out of a phone line.

BALANCED ELECTRICAL INTERFACE An electrical interface on which each circuit consists of a separate pair of wires. A balanced electrical interface generally allows data to be transmitted over longer distances than an unbalanced electrical interface.

BALANCED LINE A transmission line which has two conductors and a ground. When the voltages of the two conductors are equal in strength but opposite in direction, then you have a balanced line.

BALANCED MODULATOR An amplitude modulating circuit that suppresses the carrier signal, producing an output consisting only of upper and lower sidebands.

BALANCED-TO-GROUND In a two-conductor circuit, a balanced ground exists where the impedance-to-ground on one wire equals the impedance-to-ground on the other. This is a preferable condition for decent data communications.

BALANCING NETWORK A network used in a set ending a four-wire circuit to match the impedance of the two-wire circuit.

BALCONY A little platform up a telephone pole where people can work or sleep safely.

BALUN BALanced/UNbalanced. An impedance matching transformer. Baluns are small, passive devices that convert the impedance of coaxial cable so that its signal can run on twisted-pair wiring. They are used often so that IBM 3270-type terminals, which traditionally require coaxial cable connection to their host computer, can run off twisted-pair. Works for some types of protocols and not for others. There is often some performance degradation with baluns. And the signal cannot run as far on twisted wire as it can on coaxial cable.

BAND Usually refers to AT&T's WATS Bands. AT&T WATS service is organized into circles of increasing distance from the caller. Each circle or BAND (also called SERVICE AREA), costs more per minute. But within each service area, each call costs the same per minute, even though the distances the calls it travel might be different. There are typically six interstate bands covering the US and several intrastate bands (depending on how large the state is) which a customer can buy. The word "band" was invented by AT&T Communications (originally known as AT&T Long Lines) when it introduced WATS service. Recently it changed the word band to "Service Area." Nobody knows why. See WATS. BAND can also refer to the range of frequencies between two defined limits. For example, the band of frequencies able to be heard by the human ear ranges between 30 to 25,000 hertz. The ear can hear a band (or more typically bandwidth) of about 25,000 hertz.

BAND, CITIZENS One of two bands used for low power radio transmissions in the United States — either 26.965 to 27.225 megahertz or 462.55 to 469.95 megahertz. Citizens band radio is not allowed in many countries, even some civilized countries. In some countries they use different frequencies. CB radios, in the United States, are limited by FCC rule to four WATTS of power, which gives each CB radio a range of several miles. Some naughty people boost their CBs with external power. The author of this dictionary has actually spoken to Australia while driving on the Santa Monica Freeway in Los Angeles. See also CB.

BAND, FREQUENCY The frequencies between the upper and lower bands. See also BAND. Here is the accepted explanation of "bands:"

Below 300 Hertz	ELF	Extremely low frequency
300-3,000 Hertz	ILF	Infra Low Frequency
3-30 kHz	VLF	Very Low Frequency
30-300 kHz	LF	Low Frequency
300-3,000 kHz	MF	Medium Frequency
3-30 MHz	HF	High Frequency
30-300 MHz	VHF	Very High Frequency
300-3,000 MHz	UHF	Ultra High Frequency
3-30GHz	SHF	Super High Frequency
30-300GHz	EHF	Extremely High Frequency
300-3,000 GHz	THF	Tremendously High Frequency

BANDMARKING A continuous circumferential band applied to an insulated conductor at regular intervals for identification.

BANDPASS The range of frequencies that a channel will pass without excessive attenuation.

BANDPASS FILTER A device which transmits a band of frequencies and blocks or absorbs all other frequencies not in the specified band. Used often in frequency division multiplexing to separate one conversation from many.

BAND SPLITTER Time-division multiplexer (TDM) or frequency division multiplexer (FDM) that divides the composite bandwidth into independent and narrower channels.

BANDWIDTH The range of electrical frequencies a device can handle. The amount of bandwidth a channel is capable of carrying tells you what kinds of communications can be carried on it. A wide band circuit, for example, can carry a TV channel. A wide band circuit that's capable of providing one video channel can also provide 1,200 voice telephone channels.

BANDWIDTH COMPRESSION A technique to reduce the bandwidth needed to transmit a given amount of information. Bandwidth compression is used typically in "picture type" transmissions — such as facsimile or video-conferencing. For example, early facsimile machines scanned each bit of the document to be sent and sent a YES or NO (if there was material in that spot or not). More modern machines simply skip over all the blank spaces and simply transmit a message to the receiving facsimile machine when to start printing dots again. (A facsimile "picture" is made up of tiny dots, similar to printing photos in a magazine.) Today, bandwidth compression is used to transmit voice, video and data. There are many techniques, few of which are standard. The key, of course, is that if you're going to compress a "conversation" at one end, you must "de-compress" it at the other end. Thus, in every bandwidth compressed conversation there must be two sets of equipment, one at each end.

BAR CODE A bunch of blank lines of varying width printed on the label of a product. The bar code is designed to be read optically by some data capturing device. Bar codes are on most things you buy now in supermarkets. By scanning those bar codes at the checkout counter, the supermarket knows what's being sold and not being sold. And presumably the supermarket, or its computer, can order supplies to keep the supermarket stocked with goods that are selling and not re-order those which aren't.

BARBIE, JANE The electronic "Voice With A Smile" on most telephone company intercept recordings. Ms. Barbie does her work for the Audichron Company of Atlanta, GA.

BARE WIRE An electrical conductor having no covering or insulation.

BARGE-IN Interrupting a call in progress.

BARGE-OUT Leaving a call in progress without notice.

BARREL CONTACT A term in cabling. A barrel contact is an insulation displacement type contact consisting of a slotted tube that cuts the insulation when the wire is inserted. **BASEBAND** A form of modulation in which signals are pulsed directly on the transmission medium without frequency division. Local area networks as a whole, fall into two categories — broadband and baseband. The simpler, cheaper and less sophisticated of the two is baseband.

In baseband LANs, the entire bandwidth (capacity) of the LAN cable is used to transmit a single digital signal. In broadband networks, the capacity of the cable is divided into many channels, which can transmit many simultaneous signals. While a baseband channel can only transmit one signal and that signal is usually digital, a broadband LAN can transmit video, voice and data simultaneously by splitting the signals on that cable using frequency division multiplexing. The electronics of a baseband LAN are simpler than a broadband LAN. The digital signals from the sending devices are put directly onto the cable without modulation of any kind. Only one signal is transmitted at a time. Multiple "simultaneous" transmissions can be achieved by a technique called time division multiplexing (see multiplexing). In contrast, broadband networks (which typically run on coaxial cable) need more complex electronics to decipher and pick off the various signals they transmit. Attached devices on a broadband network require modems to transmit. Attached devices to baseband networks do not. Baseband LANs typically work with one high speed channel, which all the attached devices — printers, computers, databases — share. They share it by using it in turns — for example, passing a "token" to the next device. That token entitles the device with the token to transmit. IBM's LAN is a token ring passing local area network. Another way of sharing the baseband LAN is that each device, when it is ready to transmit, simply transmits into the channel and waits for a reply. If it doesn't receive a reply, it retransmits. Thus there are two main network or baseband access control schemes — Token Ring Passing and CSMA/CD. See also CSMA/CD, BROADBAND and LOCAL AREA NETWORKS.

BASEBAND MODEM A modem which does not apply a complex modulation scheme to the data before transmission, but which applies the digital input (or a simple transformation of it) to the transmission channel.

This technique can only be used when a very wide bandwidth is available and only operates over short distances where signal amplification is not necessary. Sometimes called a limited distance or short-haul modem.

BASEBAND SIGNALING Transmission of a digital or analog signal at its original frequencies, i.e., a signal in its original form, not changed by modulation.

BASE LOAD In trunk forecasting, an amount of telephone traffic measuring during a certain defined time. See BASE PERIOD.

BASE PERIOD In trunk forecasting, a time span of consecutive study during which a base load is determined.

BASIC A programming language which stands for Beginners All Symbolic Code. It's an easy language to learn. It's worth learning. Not all "Basics" are the same. A sort of de facto standard is Microsoft Basic. If you're wish to learn some programming, we recommend you begin with Microsoft's QuickBasic.

BASIC CALL A call between two users that does not require Advanced Intelligent Network Release 1 features (e.g. a POTS call). Definition from Bellcore.

BASIC CALL STATE MODEL BCSM. An abstraction of the ASC call processing activities for a basic two-party call. The BCSM is split into Originating and Terminating BCSMs.

BASIC RATE INTERFACE BRI. There are two "interfaces" in ISDN. BRI and PRI. In BRI, you get two bearer B-channels at 64 kilobits per second and a data D-channel at 16 kilobits per second. The bearer B-channels are designed for PCM voice, videoconferencing, group 4 facsimile machines, or whatever you can squeeze into 64,000 bits per second full duplex. The data D-channel is for bringing in information about incoming calls and taking out information about outgoing calls. It is also for access to slow-speed data networks, like videotex, packet switched networks, etc. One BRI standard is the "U" interface, which uses two wires. Another BRI standard is the "T" interface which uses four wires.

BASIC SERVICE A telephone company service limited to providing local switching and transmission. Basic Service does not include equipment. The term Basic Service is unclear and varies between telephone companies and data communications service providers. Check.

BATCH FILE A text file for personal computers with the extension .BAT that contains MS-DOS commands. When you type the name of the file, DOS carries out the commands in the file. Many computer programs are installed on you hard disk or loaded using batch files, as are many LAN operating systems. Batch files simplify life. If used wisely, you can save yourself typing things over and over again. It also means you don't have to remember all the commands to do something, just the first one. Batch files can be used to load other programs or to change the parameters of your computer. Anything that can be done from DOS (and some things that can't) can be done from a batch file. Norton Utilities has an enhanced version of DOS's Batch file.

BATCH PROCESSING There are two basic types of data processing. One is batch processing. Also called deferred time processing and off-line processing. Batch processing occurs where everything relating to one complete job — such as preparing this week's payroll — is bunched together and transmitted for processing (locally, in the same building or long distance, across the country), usually by the same computer and under the same application program. Batch processing does not permit interaction between the program and the user once the program has been read (i.e. fed into) the computer. In batch processing with telecommunications (i.e. sending the task to be done over the phone line), network response time is not critical, since no one is sitting in front of a screen waiting for a response. On the other hand, accuracy of communications is very critical, since no one is sitting in front of a screen checking entries and responses.

The second type of processing is called INTERACTIVE or REAL TIME. Under this method of processing, a user sends in transactions and awaits a response from the distant computer before continuing. In this case, response time on the data communications facility is critical. Seconds count, especially if a customer is sitting at the other end of a voice call awaiting information on whether there's space on that airline flight, for example.

BATTERY All telephone systems work on DC (direct current power). DC power is what you use to talk on. Often the DC power is called "talking battery." Most key systems and many PBXs plug directly into an AC on the wall, but that AC power is converted by a built-in power supply to the DC power the phone system needs. All central offices (public exchanges) used rechargeable lead acid batteries to drive them. These batteries perform several functions: 1. They provide the necessary power. 2. They serve as a filter to smooth out fluctuations in the commercial power and remove the "noise" that power often carries. 3. They provide necessary backup power should commercial power stop, as in a "blackout" or should it get very weak, as in a "brownout."

In short, "battery" is the term used to reference the DC power source of a telephone system. Often called "Talking Battery." 2. Storage battery used with central office switching systems and PBXs serving locations which cannot tolerate outages. Batteries serve the following purposes: Act as a filter across the generator or power rectifier output to smooth out the current and reduce noise; provide a cushion against periodic overloads exceeding the generator/rectifier capacity; supply emergency power for a limited time in event of commercial power failure. See also AC POWER and CENTRAL OFFICE BATTERY.

BATTERY BACKUP A battery which provides power to your phone system when the main AC power fails especially during blackouts and brownouts. Hospitals, brokerage companies, airlines, hotel reservation services must have battery backup because of the integral importance of their phone systems to their business.

BATTERY ELIMINATOR A device which has a rectifier and (hopefully) a filter. This device will convert AC power into the correct DC voltages necessary to drive a telephone system. Such a battery eliminator, or power supply, should deliver "clean" power, i.e. with little "noise" and of low impedance.

BATTERY RESERVE The capability of the fully charged battery cells to carry the central office power load imposed when commercial power fails and the primary power source (generators/rectifiers) is out of service. Properly described in terms of the number of hours the batteries can furnish operating power for dependent CO apparatus for a demand equal to that on the CO during its busy hour. A busy-hour reserve of eight hours is typical for a telephone office battery plant.

BAUD A unit of transmission speed. The speed in baud represents the number of discrete signaling elements transmitted in one second. It is often confused with bits per second, which is a transfer rate measuring exactly how many bits per second can be sent on a channel. At very slow data transmission — typically 300 baud and lower — baud is the same as bits per second. But at higher speeds, advanced coding techniques, such as phase-shift keying, are used. These advanced coding techniques mean that more than one bit can be placed on a baud, so to speak. The newer 1200 bits per second widely used in data transmission by personal computers is actually 600 baud, because each baud actually carries two bits. Thus, the speed of information transmitted is a direct relationship to the baud of transmission plus the encoding scheme used.

BAUDOT CODE The code set used in Telex Transmission, named for French telegrapher Emile Baudot (1845-1903) who invented it. Also known by the CCITT approved name, International Telegraph Alphabet 2. The Baudot code has only five bits, meaning that only 32 separate and distinct characters are possible from this code, i.e. 2 x 2 x 2 x 2 x 2 equals 32. By having one character called Letters (usually marked LTRS on the keyboard) which means "all the characters that follow are alphabetic characters," and having one other key called Figures (marked FIGS), meaning "all characters that follow are numerals or punctuation characters," the Baudot character set can represent 52 (26 x 2) printing characters. The characters "space," "carriage return," "line feed" and "blank" mean the same in either FIGS or LTRS. See also MORSE CODE and ASCII.

BAUD RATE A measure of signaling speed in data communications that specifies the number of signal elements that can be transmitted each second. Over dial up telephone lines, 300 and 1200 Baud are most common. For most purposes, at slow speeds, a baud rate is the same as the speed in bits per second. See also BAUD.

BAY A telephone industry term for a rack. A place you put equipment. Thus the term "rack-mountable equipment."

BBS Bulletin Board Service. Typically a PC, modem/s and communications bulletin board software attached to the end of one or more phone lines. Callers can call the BBS, read messages and download public domain software. TELECONNECT Magazine has a BBS. We call it our InfoBoard. It's open to our readers and friends. Its number is 212-989-4675. Settings to call this number are 8 bit, no parity, one stop bit, 2400 baud. The person who operates a BBS is called a SYSOP (pronounced "sis-op").

BCC Block Check Character. A control character appended to blocks in character-oriented protocols and used for figuring if the block was received in error. BCC is especially used in longitudinal and cyclic redundancy checking. As a packet (or in IBM jargon, a frame) is assembled for transmission, the bits are passed through an algorithm to come up with a BCC. When the packet is received at the other end, the receiving computer also runs the same algorithm. Both machines should come up with the same BCC. If they do, the transmission is correct and the receiving computer sends an ACK — a positive acknowledgement. If they don't, an error has occurred during transmission, and they don't have the same bits in the packet. The receiver transmits a signal (a NAK, for negative acknowledgement) that an error has occurred, and the sender retransmits the packet. This process goes on until the BCC checks.

BCD Binary Coded Decimal. A system of binary numbers where each digit of a number is represented by four bits. See BINARY.

BDOS ERROR (Pronounced "BEE-doss.") It stands for Bad Disk Operating System. When a microcomputer running under CP/M or MS-DOS has trouble reading or writing to a disk, it can produce a "BDOS ERROR" on the screen. BDOS errors are often not very informative as to the source of the trouble or the way to fix it. Sometimes they signal a fatal error and the loss of all information on the disk. Other times, they may mean a sentence or two in a file has been scrambled up. Other times, they may mean you are trying to write information to a disk that is "Write Protected," i.e. deliberately sealed against being recorded onto — the same effect as if you had punched out the little tab at the back of an audio cassette.

An eight inch disk is write-protected when the notch is left exposed. A five and a quarter inch disk is write-protected when its notch is closed. A three and a half inch disk is write protected when the notch is left open.

BDOS errors are a pain in the neck. First, check the disk for write-protect. Second, try and copy all your valuable files on the disk to another disk — FAST. Disks with BDOS errors often get progressively worse the more you play with them. If you get a BDOS error, assume the disk is bad. Check it. If it's scored and obviously ageing, junk it. If not, reformat the disk and start all over again. Don't reformat it UNTIL you've copied everything off it — onto at least two other disks. Remember the cost of new disks is tiny compared to the value of the information on them.

BEAM SPLITTER A device that splits an optical beam into two or more separate beams. Sometimes a partially reflecting mirror.

BELL A bell in a telephone instrument rings when a 20 Hz signal of about 90 volts AC is applied to the subscriber loop. In contrast, the normal voltage applied to a subscriber loop and used for speaking and listening is 48 volts AC.

BELL 103 AT&T specification for a modem providing asynchronous originate/answer transmission at speeds up to 300 bits per second (300 baud). This is the most common standard for modems running with personal computers. Every dial service in the U.S. adheres to this standard. The second most common standard is Bell 212. See below.

BELL 201 AT&T specification for a modem providing synchronous data transmission at 2,400 bits per second.

BELL 202 AT&T specification for a modem providing asynchronous data transmission at speeds up to 1,800 bits per second. Requires four-wire line for full duplex transmission.

BELL 208 AT&T specification for a modem providing synchronous data transmission at speeds up to 4,800 bits per second.

BELL 209 AT&T specification for a modem providing synchronous data transmission at speeds up to 9,600 bits per second.

BELL 212 AT&T specification for a modem providing full duplex asynchronous or synchronous data transmission at speeds up to 1,200 bits per second on the voice dial-up phone network. This is the second common standard for modems running with personal computers. The first is Bell 103.

BELL 43401 Bell Publication defining requirements for transmission over telco-supplied circuits that have dc continuity (that are metallic).

BELL ATLANTIC Formed as a holding company after the AT&T Divestiture. Includes Bell of Pennsylvania, C&P Telephone Companies of D.C., Maryland, Virginia, and West Virginia, Diamond State Telephone (Md.), New Jersey Bell and several Bell Atlantic business activities. Check out Bell Atlantic's logo. It has a wonderful, small wave in the "A" in Atlantic. Very charming. Very subtle.

BELLBOY A public paging system run by local Bell phone companies. The name survived for many years and only drew criticism in the middle to late seventies with the rise of the Women's Liberation movement. It's now not used. Shucks.

BELL COMMUNICATIONS RESEARCH BELLCORE. Formed at Divestiture to provide certain centralized services to the seven Regional Bell Holding Companies (RHCs) and their operating company subsidiaries. Also serves as a coordinating point for national security and emergency preparedness communications matters of the federal government. Bellcore does not work on customer premise equipment or other areas of potential competition between its owners — the seven Regional Bell Operating companies.

Bellcore also works on standardizing methods by which customers of long distance companies will reach their favorite long distance companies. At time of writing, around 8,000 people worked at Bellcore, mostly in northern New Jersey. Bellcore has the unenviable task of trying to service the needs of the seven competitors, which own it. Its annual budget is around $1 billion, paid for by the Bell regional operating companies. It has been doing work on ISDN and common channel signaling standards.

BELL COMPATIBLE A term sometimes applied to modems. A modem is said to be "Bell compatible" if it conforms to the technical specifications set forth by AT&T for the various devices, such as Bell 212.

BELLCORE Bell Communications Research. Formed at Divestiture to provide certain centralized services to the seven Regional Bell Holding Companies (RBOCs) and their operating company subsidiaries. Also serves as a coordinating point for national security and emergency preparedness, and communications matters of the federal government. Bellcore does not work on customer premise equipment (e.g. the telephone set) or other areas of potential competition between its owners — the seven Regional Bell Operating Companies. It is a key player in the design of AIN — the Advanced Intelligent Network. You'll find many AIN definitions in this dictionary.

BELLCORE AMA FORMAT BAF. The standard data format for AMA (Automatic Message Accounting) data to be delivered to the Revenue Accounting Office (RAO) in Advanced Intelligent Network Release 1.

BELLCORE MULTI-VENDOR INTERACTIONS MVI. The process for coordinating the efforts of Bellcore, the Bell Operating telephone companies and vendors to address technical issues associated with Advanced Intelligent Network.

BELL OPERATING COMPANY BOC. The 22 regulated telephone companies of the former Bell System, which was broken apart (the Divestiture of the Bell System) at midnight on December 31, 1983. At Divestiture, the Bell operating companies were grouped into seven Regional Holding Companies (RHCs). According to the terms of the Divestiture Agreement between the Federal Courts, the Federal Government and AT&T, the divested companies must limit their activities to local telephone services, directory service, customer premise equipment, cellular radio and any other ventures as the Federal Court may approve from time to time. See also REGIONAL BELL OPERATING COMPANY.

BELLSOUTH CORP. A regional Bell holding company formed at the Divestiture of AT&T. Includes Southern Bell and South Central Bell and several other BellSouth businesses.

BELL SYSTEM The entire AT&T organization prior to when it was broken up — at the end of 1984. The Bell System included Bell Labs, Long Lines, Western Electric and the 23 Bell operating companies.

BENCHMARK A standardized task to test the capabilities of various devices against each other for such measures as speed.

BENDING RADIUS The minimum allowable curvature of a cable before it breaks. Very critical in all aspects of cable laying, especially with under-carpet cabling and fiber optic cable.

BEP Back End Processor.

BER Bit Error Rate. The ratio of error bits to the total number of bits transmitted. If the BER gets too high, it might be worth while to go to a slower baud rate. Otherwise, you would spend more time retransmitting bad packets than getting good ones through. The theory is that the faster the speed of data transmission the more likelihood of error. This is not always so. But if you are getting lots of errors, the first — and easiest — step is to drop the transmission speed. See also BIT ERROR RATE.

BERT Bit Error Rate Test, or Tester. A known pattern of bits is transmitted, and errors received are counted to figure the BER. The idea is to measure the quality of data transmission. The bit error rate is the ratio of received bits that are in error, relative to the number of bits received. Usually expressed in a power of 10. Sometimes called Block Error Rate Tester.

BETA TEST Typically the last step in the testing of a product before it is officially released. A beta test is often conducted with customers in their offices. Some customers pay for the equipment or software they get under a beta test; some don't. Some beta tests stay in (if they work). Some don't. Most products don't work when they're first introduced. So beta tests are a good idea. Unfortunately, most manufacturers don't do sufficient beta testing. They want to get their product to market before the competition does. This often means we now have two or three new products on the market, none of which work reliably or do exactly what they're meant to do. Our rule: always wait several months after a product is introduced before buying it. By then the major bugs will have been fixed. The test before the beta test is obviously called the Alpha. It isn't that common.

BIAS The deviation of a value from a reference point.

BIAS GENERATOR A CBX printed circuit card that generates a signal that reduces idle channel noise for all coders installed in the CBX.

BIDIRECTIONAL PRINTING A typewriter always prints from left to right. So did the early computer printers. The newer computer printers will print from left to right, drop down a line, then print from right to left. This increases the printer's speed.

BILDSCHIRMTEXT German word for interactive videotex. The German Bundespost likes this service. But the German version isn't as successful as the French because the French gave away the videotex terminals. And the Germans didn't. Also, the French really encourage videotex entrepreneurs by giving a real piece of the action — 60% of the collected revenues.

BILLED NUMBER SCREENING You (at home or your business) establish who can and cannot charge a call to your phone by making an agreement with your local telephone company to screen your calls. (e.g. Refusal of all collect call requests.)

BILLED TELEPHONE NUMBER BTN. The primary telephone number used for billing regardless of the number of telephone lines associated with that number.

BILLIBIT Someone's absolutely awful term for one billion bits. Also (and better) called a gigabit.

BILLING INCREMENT The increments of time in which the phone company (long distance or local) bills. Some services are measured and billed in one minute increments. Others are measured and billed in six or ten second increments. The billing increment is a major competitive weapon between long distance companies. Short billing increments become important to you, as a user, when your average calls are very short — for example, if you're making a lot of very short data calls (say for credit card authorizations).

BILLING MEDIA CONVERTER A Billing Media Converter, as made by the Cook division of Northern Telecom, provides a means of transporting Automatic Message Accounting (AMA) data from DMS-10 central offices to regional accounting offices with the physical transfer of magnetic tapes. The BMC is polled.

BILLING VALIDATION SERVICE See BVA and BVS

BINARY Where only two values or states are possible for a particular condition, such as "ON" or "OFF" or "One" or "Zero." Binary is the way digital computers function because they can only represent things as "ON" or "OFF." This binary system contrasts with the "normal" way we write numbers — i.e. decimal. In decimal, every time you push the number one position to the left, it means you increase it by ten. For example, 100 is ten times the number 10. Computers don't work this way. They work with binary notation. Every time you push the number one position to the right it means you double it. In binary, only two digits are used — the "0" (zero) and the "1" (the one).

If you write the number 10101 in binary, and you want to figure it in decimal as we know it, here's how you do it. 1 is one thing; Zero x 2 = zero; 1 times 2 x 2 = 4; 0 x 2 x 2 x 2 = 0; 1 x 2 x 2 x 2 x 2 = 16. Therefore the total 10101 in binary = 1 + 0 + 4 + 0 + 16 = 21 in decimal.

Binary notation differs slightly from notation used in ASCII or EBCDIC. In ASCII and EBCDIC, the binary values are used for coding of individual characters or keys or symbols on keyboards or in computers. So each string of seven (as in ASCII) or eight (as in EBCDIC) ones and zeros is a unique value — but not a mathematical one.

ASCII uses a seven bit coding scheme. Thus, the maximum number of different things you can code using seven bits is 128, i.e. 2 x 2 x 2 x 2 x 2 x 2 x 2 = 128. The maximum number represented by a byte (8 bits) or the IBM EBCDIC coding system is 256. i.e. 2 x 2 x 2 x 2 x 2 x 2 x 2 x 2 = 256.

BINARY CODED DECIMAL (BCD) A system of binary numbering that uses a 4-bit code to represent each decimal digit from 0 to 9 and multiple 4-bit patterns for higher numbers.

BINARY SYNCHRONOUS COMMUNICATIONS BISYNC or BSC. 1. In data transmission the synchronization of the transmitted characters by timing signals. The timing elements at the sending and receiving terminal define where one character ends and another begins. There are no start or stop elements in this form of transmission. 2. Also a uniform discipline or protocol for synchronized transmission of binary coded data using a set of control characters and control character sequences.

BINARY TO DECIMAL CONVERSION Conversion from base 2 to base 10. See BINARY.

BINARY TRANSFER A data transfer between two computers from files that may not be text based information, and therefore, if sent as ASCII characters, would not be received properly. A Binary Transfer keeps the integrity of the data by sending it in some manner of Error Correcting Protocol such as SNA, or XMODEM.

BIND To set up a condition in a receiving device where it is unreceptive to receiving data it doesn't want.

BINDER Usually a spirally served tape or thread used for holding assembled cable components in place.

BINDING POST A screw with a small nut. You take your wires and join them together on a binding post by wrapping them together around the screw and then tightening the nut on them. These days, 66-blocks have effectively replaced binding posts. 66-blocks are easier and faster to use.

BIOS Basic Input/Output System of desktop computers. The BIOS contains the buffers for sending information from a program to the actual hardware device the information should go to.

BIPOLAR The predominant signaling method used for digital transmission services, such as DDS and T-1. In this method, the signal carrying the binary value successively alternates between positive and negative. Zero and one values are represented by the signal amplitude at either polarity, while no-value "spaces" are at zero amplitude.

BIPOLAR CODING The T carrier line coding systems that inverts the polarity of alternate "one" bits.

BIPOLAR VIOLATION The presence of two consecutive "one" bits of the same polarity on the T carrier line. See also BIPOLAR CODING.

BIRD A satellite. Also an Australian word for woman.

BIS The French term for "second" or "encore." It is used by the CCITT to designate the second in a family of related standards. "ter" designates the third in a family. See V SERIES.

BISYNC BISYNChronous Transmission. A method of transmitting data — a half-duplex, character-oriented, synchronous data communications transmission method originated by IBM in 1964. See SYNCHRONOUS.

BISYNCHRONOUS TRANSMISSION Also called BISYNC. A data character-oriented communications protocol developed by IBM for synchronous transmission of binary-coded data between two devices. BISYNC uses a specific set of control characters to synchronize the transmission of that binary coded data. See also BINARY SYNCHRONOUS COMMUNICATION.

BIT Abbreviation for binary digit. The smallest unit of information (data) and the basic unit in data communications. A bit can have a value of zero (a mark) or one (a space).

BIT BUCKET Slang for throwing out bits — into a wastepaper bucket.

BIT BUFFER A section of memory capable of temporarily storing a single BInary uniT (bit) of information. Used to make data transmission accurate or consistent.

BIT CHECK A bit added to a digital signal and used for error checking, i.e. a parity bit. See also PARITY.

BIT DURATION The time it takes one bit to pass a point on the transmission medium. Used to measure delay times, especially in high speed communications.

BIT ERROR The value of an encoded bit can be changed in transmission and then interpreted incorrectly by the receiver.

BIT ERROR RATE BER. The percentage of received bits in error compared to the total amount of bits received. Usually expressed as a number to the power of 10. For example, 10 to the fifth power means that one in every 100,000 bits transmitted will be wrong. In data transmission just because it's transmitted incorrectly the first time or there's a high error rate on the transmission medium (i.e. some noise), doesn't mean there'll be lots of problems with the final transmission. It just means there'll have to be lots of re-transmissions — "until one gets it right." These re-transmissions cut down the average speed of transmission.

BIT INTERLEAVING/MULTIPLEXING In multiplexing, individual bits from different lower speed channel sources are combined one bit at a time/one channel at a time into one continuous higher speed bit stream compare with byte interleaving/ multiplexing.

BIT ORIENTED Used to describe communications protocols in which control information may be coded in fields as small as a single bit.

BIT ORIENTED PROTOCOL BOP. See BIT ORIENTED TRANSMISSION.

BIT ORIENTED TRANSMISSION An efficient transmission protocol that encodes communications control information in fields of bits rather than characters or bytes.

BIT PATTERN A group of bits arranged in specified ways to represent numbers, letters or symbols, forming a unique binary number for each character. For example, the 7-bit ASCII code produces 128 different characters, i.e. 2 x 2 x 2 x 2 x 2 x 2 x 2 = 128.

BIT RATE The number of bits per second of data transmitted over a phone line. You can usually figure how many characters per second you will be transmitting — in asynchronous communications — if you divide the bit rate by ten. For example, if you are transmitting at 1200 bits per second, you will be transmitting 120 characters per second. In real life, it's never this simple, however. The total bits transmitted will depend on re-transmissions, which depends on the noise of the line, etc.

BIT ROBBING The use of the least significant bit per channel in every sixth frame for signaling. See BIT STUFFING.

BIT STUFFING Process in some data communications protocols where a string of "one" bits is broken by an inserted "zero." This inserted zero is added by the sender and stripped by the receiver. The idea of inserting the zero is to avoid confusing the receiver into thinking the series of one bits mean something else, like a flag control character. See ZERO STUFFING.

BIT STREAM A continuous stream of data bits transmitted over a communications line with no break or separators between the characters.

BIT TRANSFER RATE The number of bits transferred per unit time. Usually expressed in Bits Per Second (BPS).

BIT, PARITY A binary bit appended to an array of bits to make the sum of all the bits always odd or always even. See PARITY.

BITS PER SECOND The number of bits passing a specific point per second.

A KILObit is one thousand bits per second. A MEGAbit is one million bits per second (thousands of kilos). A GIGAbit is one billion bits per second (thousands of millions). A TERAbit is one trillion bits per second (thousands of billions).

BLACK BOX An electronic device that you don't want to take the time to understand. As in, "We'll put the data through a black box that will put it into X.25 format." The term has recently come also to mean PBX switches. While "Black Box" is a generic term, The Black Box Corporation of Pittsburgh, PA, has had the audacity (and brilliance) to register the term as a trademark.

The Phone Phreak community has used the term for decades to describe a device that's put on phone lines in electromechanical central office areas (they don't work under ESS offices). To the phone phreak community, a black box made up of a resistor, a capacitor and a toggle switch that would "fool" the central office into thinking the phone had not been picked up when receiving a long distance call. Since the call was not "answered," the call could not be billed. Clever, eh? (Illegal, too.) See BLUE BOX and RED BOX.

BLACK MATRIX Picture tube in which the color phosphors are surrounded by black for increased contrast.

BLANK A character on teletype terminals that does not punch holes in paper tape (except for feed holes to push the paper through). Also the character between words, usually called a "Space" is referred to in IBM jargon as a Blank.

BLAST BLocked ASynchronous Transmission.

BLERT BLock Error Rate Test.

BLF The Busy Lamp Field is a visual display of the status of all phones in the system or in a section of the system.

BLIND TRANSFER Someone transfers a call to someone else without telling the person who's calling.

BLOCK In data communications, a group of bits transmitted as a unit and treated as a unit of information. Usually consists of its own starting and ending control deliminators, a header, the text to be transmitted and check characters at the end used for error correction. Sometimes called a Packet.

BLOCK CHARACTER CHECK BCC. The result of transmission verification algorithm accumulated over a transmission block, and normally appended at the end, e.g. CRC, LRC.

BLOCK DIAGRAM A graphic way to show different elements of a program or process by the use of squares, rectangles, diamonds and various shapes connected by lines to show what must be done, when it must be done and what happens if it's done this way or that. In short, it shows how all the small decision points add up to the whole process.

BLOCKED CALLS DELAYED A variable in queuing theory to describe what happens when the user is held in queue because his call is blocked and he can't complete it instantly.

BLOCKED CALLS HELD A variable in queuing theory to describe what happens when the user redials the moment he encounters blockage.

BLOCKED CALLS RELEASED A variable in queuing theory to describe what happens when the user, after being blocked, waits a little while before redialing.

BLOCKING When a telephone call cannot be completed it is said that the call is "blocked." Blocking is a fancy way to say that the caller is "receiving a busy." There are many places a call can be blocked: at the user's own telephone switch — PBX or key system, at the user's local central office or in the long distance network. Blocking happens because switching or transmission capacity is not available at that precise time.

The number of calls you try compared to the number of times you get blocked measures "the grade of service" on that network. Blocked calls are different to calls that are not completed because the called number is busy. This is because numbers that are busy are not the fault of the telephone switching and transmission network. One might think the fewer blocked calls, the better. From the user's point of view, the answer is obviously YES, it is better. Less blockage, fewer busies and less frustration.

But as one designs a switching and transmission network for less and less blocking, the network becomes more and more expensive. Logarithmically so. We keep adding extra circuits and extra equipment. Thus, in any telecommunications network design there is always a trade-off: What are you prepared to pay, compared to what can you tolerate?

Everyone designs their network with different tradeoffs depending on what they and their users or customers, can tolerate and/or are willing to pay. Most companies are willing to pay more for better service if someone explains the logic of telephone design to them. Many network salesmen, however, don't believe this. They practice the sales "theory" of selling better service for less money. This doesn't work in business, and especially not in telephony.

The "Grade of Service" is a measurement of blocking. It varies from almost zero (best, but most expensive case, no calls blocked) to one (worst case, all calls blocked). Grade of Service is written as P.05 (five percent blocking). "Blocking" used to be a technical term but has now become a sales tool especially among PBX manufacturers, who increasingly claim their switch to be "non-blocking." This means it will not, they claim, block a call in the switch.

There are several flaws in this logic: First, it's not logical or useful to buy a non-blocking PBX if the chances of being blocked elsewhere — the local lines, the local exchange or the long distance network — are very high. Second, a true non-blocking PBX can be very expensive, perhaps too much power and too much money for most peoples' needs. Third, most manufacturers define "non-blocking" differently. One defines it strictly in terms of switching capability and ignores the fact that his PBX might not have sufficient other "things," like devices which ring bells on phones (to indicate an incoming call) or devices which deliver dial tone to a phone (to indicate the PBX is ready to receive instructions).

BLOCK MULTIPLEXER CHANNEL An IBM mainframe input/output channel that allows interleaving of data blocks.

BLOCK TRANSFER RATE The number of successful block transfers made during a period of time.

BLOWER A microphone.

BLU Northern Telecom word for Basic Link Unit.

BLUE BOX A device used to steal long distance phone calls. The classic blue box was slightly larger than a cigarette container. It had a touchtone pad on the front and a single button on top. Typically, you went to a coin phone and dialed an 800 number. While the distant number was ringing, you punched the single button on the top of the blue box. That button caused the blue box's speaker to emit a 2600 Hz tone. This disconnected the ringing at the other end but left the user inside the long distance network. The user then punched in a series of digits on the touchtone pad. The phone network heard those tones and sent the call according to the instructions in the tones. The tones duplicated the tones which the touchtone pads of long distance operators emitted. They are different from those emitted by normal telephones. The first blue box was "discovered" at MIT in a small utility box that was painted blue, thus the term blue box. When they were young, Steve Jobs and Steve Wozniak, founders of Apple Computer, sold blue boxes, which Wozniak built. People who used blue boxes in their salad days included characters with adopted pseudonyms like Dr. No, The Snark and Captain Crunch, who got his name from the free 2600 Hz whistle included as a promotion in boxes of Captain Crunch breakfast cereal. With the advent of CCIS, Common Channel Interoffice Signaling (i.e. out-of-band signaling), blue boxes no longer work.

BLUE GROMMET The rubber collar over the joint between the handset and the armored cable on a pay phone. Blue identifies a "hearing aid compatible" handset.

BM Burst Modem.

BNA Burroughs Network Architecture. Communications architecture of Burroughs, now Unisys.

BNC A bayonet-locking connector for slim coaxial cables, like those used with Ethernet. BNC is an acronym for Bayonet-Neill-Concelma. Don't ask who Neill and Concelman are.

BNR Bell Northern Research. Northern Telecom's research arm.

BOC Bell Operating Company. The local Bell operating telephone company. These days there are 22 Bell Operating Companies. They are organized into (i.e. owned by) seven Regional Bell holding companies, also called RBOCs, pronounced "R-bocks," or RHCs. See BELL OPERATING COMPANY.

BOOT Abbreviation for the verb to bootstrap. See BOOTSTRAP.

BOOTSTRAP The process of starting up a computer. Think about the following explanation in regard to your desktop MS-DOS machine. Usually, when the computer is turned on, it goes to a location of permanent Read Only Memory (See ROM) for instructions. These instructions, in turn, load the first instructions from the disk telling the computer what tasks to start performing. The name of this process comes from the expression "pulling oneself up by one's own bootstraps." The typical personal computer BOOT (startup) throws a message on the screen instructing the user to "insert a disk."

To confuse matters, there are WARM boots and COLD boots. Cold boots occur when the ac power switch on the computer is turned on. Warm boots occur when you hit the reset button (or CTL/ALT/DELETE) while the ac power switch stays on. A warm boot — reset — is done when you're changing disks or programs, or have done something dumb, like tried to access a drive that didn't access, or tried to print without connecting up to a printer.

You do a cold boot when the machine locks up rock hard and a warm boot doesn't work. To do a cold boot with your computer, turn the ac power off, count to ten and then turn it on. Remember: never leave disks in your computer when you're turning it on and off. The surge of electricity might destroy the disks. When modems give trouble, do a cold boot on them. In fact, when phone systems give trouble, do a cold boot on them also. See also MS-DOS and DEVICE DRIVER.

BOP Bit Oriented Protocol. See BIT ORIENTED TRANSMISSION.

BORSCHT A group of functions provided in Line Circuits (LC). B: Battery supply to subscriber line. O: Overvoltage protection. R: Ringing current supply. S: Supervision of subscriber terminal. C: Coder and decoder. H: Hybrid (2 wire to 4 wire conversion). T: Test.

BOUNDRY NODE In IBM's SNA, a subarea node that can provide certain protocol support for adjacent subarea nodes, including transforming network addresses to local addresses, and vice versa, and performing session level sequencing and flow control and less intelligent peripheral nodes.

BPAD Bisynchronous Packet Assembler/Disassembler.

BPI Bytes Per Inch. How many bytes are recorded per inch of recording surface. Typically used in conjunction with magnetic tape.

BPS Bits Per Second. A measure of the speed of data communications. There are many ways to measure bits per second. So don't assume that just because one LAN or other data communications system has a faster bits per seconds, it will transmit your information faster. You have to factor in speed of writing and reading from the disk and the accuracy of transmission. All datacom schemes have error-checking systems, some better than others. Typically such systems force a re-transmission of data if a mistake is detected. You might have a fast, but "dirty" (i.e. lots of errors) transmission media, which may need lots of re-transmissions. Thus, the "effective" bps of data communications network may actually be quite low. See also BAUD.

BPSK Binary Phase-Shift Key.

BRAID A fibrous or metallic group of filaments interwoven cylindrically to form a covering over one or more insulated conductors.

BRANCH A path in the program which is selected from two or more paths by a program instruction. "To branch" means to choose one of the available paths.

BRANCH FEEDER A cable used between the distribution cable and the main feeder cable to connect phone users to the central office. An outside plant term.

BRANCHING FILTER A device placed in a waveguide to separate or combine different microwave frequency bands.

BREADBOARD A circuit board made by hand, usually in building a prototype. No one knows where the word breadboard came from. Maybe because it looks a little like a breadboard?

BREAK An interruption. As in "Make and Break." Make means contacts which are usually open, but which close during an operation. "Make and Break" accurately describes rotary dialing.

BREAK IN The attendant can interrupt conversations and announce an emergency or an important call.

BREAK KEY A Break Key is found on some PCs. It is usually used to interrupt the current task running on a remote host. Break is not an ASCII character, it is simply a period of start (space) polarity.

BREAKDOWN VOLTAGE The voltage at which the insulation between two conductors breaks down.

BREAKOUT A wire or group of wires in a multi-conductor configuration which terminates somewhere other than at the end of the configuration.

BREAKOUT BOX A device that is plugged in between a computer terminal and its connecting cable in order to re-configure the way the cable is wired. When hooking up a terminal that is wired as if it were a computer itself (such as a VT-100), a break out box is used to break out, or fan out the 25 connections in the RS-232 cable. Each wire in the break out box goes through a switch that can be turned off, and a wire jumper is provided to connect each pin on one side to one or other pin on the other side. This allows you, for example, to switch pins 2 & 3, thus fooling two Computer devices into thinking one is talking to a terminal. (Now you have the essence of a null modem cable.) Break out boxes are necessary because there is no such thing as "standard" pinning on a RS-232 cable. And to connect one computer to a printer one minute and to another computer the next minute, usually requires totally different wiring in the RS-232 cable, i.e. two sets of cables. This lack of standardization is why you'll always see dozens of RS-232 cables lying around where computers are used.

BRI There are two subscriber "interfaces" in ISDN. This one and PRI (Primary Rate Interface). In BRI, you get two bearer B-channels at 64 kilobits per second and a data D-channel at 16 kilobits per second. The bearer B-channels are designed for PCM voice, slow-scan videoconferencing, group 4 facsimile machines, or whatever you can squeeze into 64,000 bits per second full duplex. The data (or D) channel is for bringing in information about incoming calls and taking out information about outgoing calls. It is also for access to slow-speed data networks, like videotex, packet switched networks, etc. See BASIC RATE INTERFACE and ISDN.

BRIDGE 1. To connect one circuit or component to another in parallel. When two single line phones share the same number — line or trunk — they are bridged. Sometimes a bridge has associated components — e.g. amplifiers — to compensate for losses.

2. An interface between two similar local area networks. In more complex language, "A device to expand a LAN by forwarding frames between data link layers associated with two different kinds of physical link. Also called a data link relay or level 2 relay." This second definition is from John McNamara, author of Local Area Networks, an introduction to the technology. See also INTERNETWORKING and ROUTERS.

BRIDGE AMPLIFIER An amplifier installed on a CATV trunk cable to feed branching cables.

BRIDGE EQUIPMENT Equipment which connects different LANs, allowing communication between devices. As in "to bridge" several LANs. Bridges are protocol independent but hardware specific. They will connect LANs with different hardware and different protocols. An example would be a device that connects an Ethernet network to a Starlan network. With this bridge it is possible to send signals between the two networks, and only these two networks. These signals will be understood only if the protocols used on each LAN are the same, e.g. XNS or TCP/IP, but they don't have to be the same for the bridge to do its job for the signals to move on either LAN. They just won't be understood. This differs from gateways and routers. Routers connect LANs with the same protocols but different hardware. The best example are the file servers that accommodate different hardware LANs. Gateways connect two LANs with different protocols by translating between them, enabling them to talk to each other. The bridge does no translation. Bridges are best used to keep networks small by connecting many of them rather than making a large one. This reduces the traffic faced by individual computers and improves network performance.

BRIDGE TAP An undetermined length of wire attached between the normal endpoints of a circuit that introduces unwanted impedance imbalances for data transmission. Also called bridging trap or bridged tap. See BRIDGED TAP.

BRIDGED TAP Any section of a cable pair not on the direct electrical path between the central office and the user's premises.

BRIDGING ADAPTER A box containing several male and female electrical connectors that allows various phones and accessories to be connected to one cable. Bridging adapters work well with 1A2 key systems and single line phones behind PBXs, not so well with electronic key systems and electronic telephones behind PBXs.

BROADBAND A transmission facility that has a bandwidth (capacity) greater than a voice grade line of 4 kHz. (Some say that to be "broadband" it should be 20 kHz.) Such a broadband facility — typically coaxial cable — may carry numerous voice, video and data channels simultaneously. Each "channel" will take up a different frequency on the cable. There'll be "guardbands" (empty spaces) between the channels to make sure each channel doesn't interfere with its neighbor.

A coaxial CATV cable is the "classic" broadband channel. Simultaneously it carries many TV channels. Broadband cables are used in some office LANs. But more common are the BASEBAND variety which have the capacity for one channel only. Everything on that cable to be transmitted or received must use that one channel. That one channel is very fast, so each device needs only to use that high speed channel for only a little of the time. The problem is getting onto the channel. See BASEBAND.

BROADCAST To send information to two or more receiving devices simultaneously — over a data communications network, a voice mail, electronic mail system, a local TV or radio station or a satellite system.

BROADCAST LIST A list of two or more system users to whom messages are sent simultaneously. Master Broadcast Lists are shared by all system users and are set up by the System Administrator. Personal Lists are set up by individual subscribers.

BROADCAST MESSAGE A message from one user sent to all users. Just like a TV station signal. On LANs, all workstations and devices receive the message. On voice mail systems, broadcast messages are important announcement messages from the system administrator that provide information and instructions regarding the voice processing system. Broadcast messages play before standard Voice Mail or Automated Attendant messages.

BROADCAST NET A British Telecom turret feature that enables each trader single key access to a group of outgoing lines. This is designed primarily for sending short messages to multiple destinations. The "net" function allows the user to set up and amend his broadcast group.

BROADCAST TRANSMISSION A fax machine feature that allows automatic transmission of a document to several locations.

BROKERNET A virtual private dedicated network offering from New York Telephone and provided within Manhattan aimed at brokerage, banking and message industries. It uses digital switching to provide virtual private lines, specifically "hot line" service.

BRONZE A mixture of copper and tin and small amounts of other metals.

BROUTER In local area networking, a brouter is a device that combines the dynamic routing capability of an internetwork router with the ability of a bridge to interconnect dissimilar local area networks (LANs).

BSC Binary Synchronous Communication. A set of IBM operating procedures for synchronous transmission used in teleprocessing networks.

BSP Bell System Practice. A very defined way of writing and presenting instruction and installation manuals. Divestiture has changed the rules. There are better ways of writing manuals.

BTAM Basic Telecommunications Access Method. One of IBM's early host-based software programs for controlling remote data communications interface to host applications, supporting pre-SNA protocols. See IBM.

BTN Billed Telephone Number. The primary telephone number used for billing, regardless of the number of phone lines associated with that number.

BTU Basic Transmission Unit.

BUFFER 1. In data transmission, a buffer is a temporary storage location for information being sent or received. Usually located between two different devices that have different abilities or speeds for handling the data. The buffer acts like a dam, capturing the data and then trickling it out at speeds the lower river can handle without, hopefully, flooding or overflowing the banks. 2. A coating material used to cover and protect the fiber. The buffer can be constructed using either a tight jacket or loose tube technique.

BUFFER STORAGE Electronic circuitry where data is kept during buffering.

BUG Sometimes called "An undocumented feature". A problem in software or hardware. The original computer bug, a moth, is enshrined in a log book at the Washington Navy Yard. It was the cause of a hardware failure in an early computer in the 1950's. These days, "bugs" in telecom or computer systems are not insects. They're indescribable glitches that adversely affect smooth operations. Bugs usually originate in poorly-written software. Some programmers call bugs "undocumented features." And they are, indeed.

BUILDING ENTRANCE AREA The area inside a building where cables enter the building and are connected to the cables within the building. Typically this area is the end of the local telephone company's responsibility. From here on it's your responsibility. You should protect your equipment inside the building from spikes and surges and other electrical nonsenses which the phone company's cables might bring in. For the best diaster protection, it's wise to have two building entrances by which your telecommunications cables can enter. And they should enter from separate telephone central offices. Some telephone companies, e.g. New York Telephone, are now tariffing such services.

BULK BILLING A method of billing for long distance telephone services where no detail of calls made is provided. WATS is a bulk billed service. Therein lies the problem for the cost conscious user. There's no verification of calls made. See CALL DETAIL RECORDING.

BULK STORAGE Lots of storage. Usually reels of magnetic tape or hard disks.

BULLETIN BOARD A fancy name for an electronic message system running on a microcomputer. Call up, leave messages, read messages. The system is like a physical bulletin board. That's where the name comes from. Some people call bulletin board systems electronic mail systems. TELECONNECT and Inbound/Outbound Magazines and Telecom Library Inc. have them, too. We call our our InfoBoard. Call us on 212-989-4675. You can use any computer, any communications software and virtually any 300, 1,200 or 2,400 baud modem. You have 15 minutes before our system cuts you off. You can pick up free software and leave us messages and order books and subscriptions. See also BBS.

BUMPER BEEPER Radio beacon transmitter, hidden in or on a vehicle for use with radio tailing equipment.

BUNDLE In T-1, specifically M44 Multiplexing, a bundle is comprised of 12 nibbles (4 bits) and may represent 11 channels of 32 Kbps compressed information plus a delta channel. A bundle is typically a subset of a DSI and treated as an entity with its own signaling delta channel.

BUNDLED Combining several services under one telephone tariff item at a single charge.

BURDEN TEST A semi-legitimate test used in regulation to determine if the offering of a new or continued service will cause consumers of other services to pay prices no higher than if the service were not offered. In other words, the question is "Who carries the Burden?" It's sometimes called the "avoidable cost test."

BURN-IN To run new devices and printed circuits cards, often at high temperatures, in order to pinpoint early failures. The theory is all semiconductor devices show their defects — if any — in the first few weeks of operation. If they pass this "burn-in" period, they will work for a long time, so the theory goes. "Burn-in" should probably be 30-days under full power and working load. Burn-in should also take place in a room with lots of heat and at least 50% humidity, since this will simulate the poorly-ventilated places most people install telephone systems.

BURST MODE A way of doing data transmission in which a continuous block of data is transferred between main memory and an input/output device without interruption until the transfer has been completed.

BUS An electrical connection which allows two or more wires or lines to be connected together. Typically, all circuit cards receive the same information that is put on the BUS. Only the card the information is "addressed" to will use that data. This is convenient so that a circuit card may be plugged in "anywhere on the Bus." See also BACKPLANE and BUS NETWORK.

BUS HOG A device which gets control of and hogs a backplane bus.

BUS NETWORK All communications devices share a common path. Typically in a bus network, a "conversation" from each device is sampled quickly and interleaved using time division multiplexing. Bus networks are very high-speed — millions of bits per second — forms of transmission (e.g. on a local area network) and switching. They often form the major switching and transmission backbone of a modern PBX. The printed circuit cards which connect to each trunk and each line are plugged into the PBX's high-speed "backbone" — i.e. the bus network. See also BUS.

BUSY In use. "Off-hook". There are slow busies and fast busies. Slow busies are when the phone at the other end is busy or off-hook. They happen 60 times a minute. Fast busies (120 times a minute) occur when the network is congested with too many calls. Your distant party may or may not be busy, but you'll never know because you never got that far.

BUSY BACK A busy signal.

BUSY CALL FORWARDING When you call a busy phone extension, your call is automatically sent to another predetermined telephone extension.

BUSY HOUR The hour of the day (or the week, or the month, or the year, — check) during which a telephone system carries the most traffic. For many offices, it is 10:30 A.M. to 11:30 A.M. The "busy hour" is perhaps the most important concept in traffic engineering — the science of figuring what telephone switching and transmission capacities one needs. Since the "busy hour" represents the most traffic carried in a hour, the idea is if you create enough capacity to carry that "busy hour" traffic, you will be able to carry all other traffic. In actuality, one never designs capacity sufficient to carry 100% of the busy hour traffic. That would be too expensive. So, the argument then comes down to, "What percentage of my peak busy or busy hour traffic am I prepared to block?" This percentage might be as low as half of one percent or as high as 10%. Typically, it's between 2% and 5%, depending on what business you're in and the cost to you — in lost sales, etc. — of blocking calls.

BUSY LAMP A light on a telephone showing a certain line or phone is busy. See BUSY LAMP FIELD.

BUSY LAMP FIELD A device with rows of tiny lights that shows which phones in a telephone system are speaking and which aren't. Each light corresponds to a telephone extension on the system. The busy lamp field usually sits attached to the attendant's console, telling the attendant if an extension is busy, free, on hold, etc. The benefit of having a busy lamp field is that the operator doesn't have to dial the number to find out what's happening with the extension. This saves the attendant time in handling incoming calls and gives the caller better service. A busy lamp field is often combined with DSS (DIRECT STATION SELECT). Next to each light on the busy lamp field there is a button which the operator can push which will dial the corresponding extension (i.e. directly select it) and will typically transfer the call automatically. This button is like an autodial button. This saves the time of dialing the two, three or more numbers of the extension. These days, busy lamp fields are often built into phones on a key system, and everyone, not just the operator, can have one. This gives everyone information on what's happening in the system. It makes transferring calls, etc. easier.

BUSY OUT To cause a line to return a busy signal to a caller. Busying out lines going into a computer is useful when the computer is not available, i.e. during maintenance periods. This way callers do not get connected to modems with no computers to talk to. This is also known as "taking the phone off the hook." In a voice phone system with trunks that rotary (or hunt) on, sometimes busying one or more broken trunks out helps calls rotary on to trunks that are still working. This way, someone doesn't end up on your third trunk with endless ringing, while your 4th, 5th, 6th etc. trunks are free, leaving them wondering where you are and you wondering why you're not getting any calls.

BUSY OVERRIDE A feature of some PBXs which allows the attendant or other high priority user to barge in on a telephone conversation. A warning tone is usually thrown into the conversation to alert the parties of an override. The feature is also called "BARGE-IN." Sometimes when conversations are overridden, only the person within the organization can hear the barge-in.

BUSY SEASON An annual recurring and reasonably predictable period of maximum busy hour requirements — normally three months of the year, and typically the three months preceding Christmas.

BUSY SIGNAL A signal indicating the line called is busy. The busy signal is generated by the central office. There are two types of busy signals. See BUSY.

BUSY TEST A method of figuring whether something which can carry traffic is actually doing so or whether it's broken or free and available for use.

BUSY VERIFICATION OF STATION LINES An attendant can confirm that a line is actually in use by establishing a connection (dialing in and listening) to that apparently busy line.

BUTTINSKY Or Butt Set. The one-piece telephone carried on the hips of telephone technicians. It's called buttinsky or butt set because it allows technicians to "butt in" on phone calls, not because the device is worn on their butts. Butt sets used to be essentially telephones without ringers. But now they are much more sophisticated. They will pulse out in rotary or touchtone and allow you to talk or to monitor a call. They will run computerized tests on the line. Some even have the equivalent of an asychronous computer terminal built in, which can be used to talk to a distant computer over a phone line. This distant computer could assign them their next jobs, allow them to check and assign features (touchtone, rotary, hunt), report the time spent on this job, etc. In short, the terminal and the computer could replace a raft of clerks and a deluge of paperwork.

BUTT SET See BUTTINSKY.

BUZZ 1. To check the continuity of a cable pair by putting an audible buzzer on one end and then checking with a "buttinsky" to see if you can hear the buzz and thus identify the correct cable pair. 2. A feature of a Rolm CBX which lets the user signal one Rolm desktop product without picking up the handset. Only one buzz per extension is permitted.

BUZZER LEADS Separate leads that allow a KTU facility to operate a buzzer within a key telephone set (usually in conjunction with a local intercom system).

BVA AT&T's exclusively owned Billing Validation Application database. Today, BVA contains all the Regional Bell Operating Companies (RBOCs) calling cards, and other billing information such as billed number screening and payphone numbers. The RBOCs and AT&T access that database today. Prior to Divestiture three market players, the RBOCs, AT&T and most Independent Companies, dominated the "O" Operator Services business which provided alternate billing arrangements such as collect calls, bill to third number and charging calls to calling cards. The three market players still exclusively employ BVA which allows them to validate or authorize alternate billing arrangements. No other long distance carrier or a company needing access to the data for billing validation can use the system. The database is owned by AT&T and is updated daily by the RBOCs and Independent Companies with local exchange information, billing number screening and calling card information. The scenario is further complicated by the 1984 AT&T Plan of Reorganization's exclusive BVA access restrictions. In other words, the three original market players (AT&T, the RBOCs and Independent Companies) have exclusive access to BVA for a predetermined contract length. In most cases these arrangements run into the 1990s. See BVS.

BVS US West Service Link was the first in the nation to develop and make available a nationwide Billing Validation Service open to any company that needs to verify the legitimacy of their callers' requests to place charge calls to their local telephone calling cards. US West Service Link developed BVS in 1987 and turned up the system for "on-line" customers in early 1988. Today, the US West BVS system is a national validation source containing calling card data of customers served by the RBOCs GTE, Southern New England Telephone, United Telecommunications, Cincinnati Bell, Rochester Telephone and Telecomm Canada, a consortium representing all of Canada's local telephone operating companies. In all, more than 60 million records are stored. US Sprint, MCI and ITI are among the carriers using BVS. BVS uses X.25 and SS7 protocol. See BVA.

BX.25 AT&T's rules for establishing the sequences of events and the specific types and forms of signals required to transfer data between computers. BX.25 includes the international rules known as X.25 and more.

BYPASS A relatively new term coming from the idea of using a method of local communications other than the local telephone company. The theory is you are BYPASSing the local phone company for, typically, two reasons. 1. Because the phone company is too expensive. 2. Because the phone company can't get you the bandwidth, the quality, the fast delivery or the service you want.

Bypass means you might be transmitting between two of your offices in the same city, perhaps between your office and your factory, etc. You might also be transmitting directly to your friendly long distance telephone company, which then carries your calls to distant cities. Bypass means you might be using one, several or many technologies, including your own private microwave, your own cable (metal or fiber), using the local CATV company, etc.

Bypass is a word created by the local telephone industry to sound very threatening. The theory is major users will bypass their local phone company, depriving their phone company of needed revenues. This will drive the phone company close to imminent bankruptcy, or at the very least, to the state regulators for huge rate increases, hurting everyone. The reality of this threat has not been proven. Nevertheless, the rhetoric frightens sufficient regulators to look at the evils of bypass and to outlaw it, or at least severely restrict it — as several states have done. This will strengthen the phone company's local monopoly, the objective of the exercise in the beginning.

BYPASS CABLING Bypass cabling or relays are wired connections in a local area ring network that permit traffic between two nodes that are not normally wired next to each other. Such bypass cabling might be used in an emergency or while other parts of the system are being serviced. Usually such bypass relays are arranged so that any node can be removed from the ring and the two nodes on either side of the removed node can then talk.

BYPASS TRUNK GROUP A trunk group circumvents one or more tandems in its routing ladder.

BYTE A popular microcomputer magazine, which derives its name from the true meaning of BYTE, which is eight bits of information composed of zeros or ones, one of which may include a parity bit. Most character sets, e.g. ASCII or EBCDIC, use one byte per character of information such as a letter, a number or digit, a punctuation mark or a symbol, such as $. A byte is to a bit what a word is to a character. In some circles a byte is called an octet.

BYTE COUNT The number of 8-bit bytes in a message. Since ASCII characters typically have 8-bits, the byte count is also called the character count.

BYTE COUNT PROTOCOL A class of data link protocols in which each frame has a header containing a count of the total number of data characters in the body of the frame.

BYTE MULTIPLEXER CHANNEL An IBM mainframe input/output channel that allows for the interleaving, or multiplexing, of data in bytes. Compare with block multiplexer channel.

BYTE MULTIPLEXING A byte (or character) from one channel is sent as a unit and bytes from different channels follow in successive time slots.

C AT&T programming language used for several of its central office switches. It is also used as the programming language of choice for interactive voice response units. C operates under UNIX, MS-DOS and other systems. It is very powerful and is becoming somewhat of a standard for programming telecom switches.

C LEAD The third of three wires which make up trunk lines between central office switches. There are three wires — positive, negative, and the "c lead." The purpose of the "c lead" is to control the grounding, holding and releasing of trunks.

C MESSAGE WEIGHTING This definition from James Harry Green, author of the excellent Dow Jones Handbook of Telecommunications. C Message Weighting is a factor in noise measurements to approximate the lesser annoying effect on the human ear of high and low-frequency noise compared to mid-range noise.

C-DTE Character mode Data Terminal Equipment. A term to describe most PCs (personal computers) and printer-terminals that use asynchronous signals for data communications.

C-LINK A signaling link used to connect mated pairs of Signal Transfer Points (STPs). An Ericsson term.

CABLE May refer to a number of different types of wires or groups of wires capable of carrying voice or data transmissions. The most common interior telephone cable has been two pair, consisting of four separate wires each covered with plastic insulation and with all four wires wrapped in an outer plastic covering. Typically called quad wiring. The wire and cable business is immense. The assortment of stuff it produces each year is mind-boggling. In telecommunications, there is one rule: The quality of a circuit is only as good as its weakest link. Often that "weak link" is the quality of the wiring or cabling (we used the words interchangeably) that the user himself puts in. Please put in decent quality wiring. Don't skimp.

CABLE BAYS Lots of cable arranged like bays in a harbor.

CABLE LOSS The amount of radio frequency (RF) signal attenuated (lost) while it travels on a cable. There are many reasons for cable loss, including the cable's shape, size, length and what it's made of. See ATTENUATION.

CABLE RACKING Framework fastened to bays to support cabling between them.

CABLE RISER Cable running vertically in a multi-story building to serve the upper floors.

CABLE RUN Conduit used to run cables through a building. Also, path taken by a cable or group of cables.

CABLE SHIELD A metallic component of the cable sheath which prevents outside electrical interference and drain off current induced by lightning.

CABLE VAULT Room under the main distribution frame in a central office building. Cables from the subscribers lines come into the building through the cable vault. From here they snake their way up to the main distribution frame. The cable vault looks like a bad B-movie portrayal of Hell, replete with thousands of dangerous black snakes. Cable vaults are prime targets for the spontaneous starting of fires. They should be protected with Halon gas, but usually aren't because some parts of the phone industry think Halon is too expensive.

CAC Customer Administration Center. A type of terminal used by a PBX user to maintain and troubleshoot his PBX.

CACHE A small part of the computer's high-speed memory set aside to hold recently accessed data. The idea is the user will use that data more than once and therefore, it's worth the software and hardware to load them into this temporary RAM. This location and instant availability gives the computer user the impression that the computer and its programs are actually running a lot faster than they are theoretically capable of. The value of a cache is directly related to how much you will use the last few items of information you have just accessed from your hard or soft disk or from a distant file server. Cache is especially important in a LAN file server. It can be used to "speed up" access to a database stored on the file server, thereby saving workstation users time and aggravation. Caches work because of a phenomenon known as the locality principle which states that a von Neumann CPU (i.e. one that performs instructions one after another) tends to access the same memory locations over and over again. A cache works like this: when the CPU needs data from memory, the cache hardware and software checks to see if the information is already in the cache. If it is, it grabs that information. This is called a cache hit. If it isn't, it's called a cache miss and the computer has to access the disk, which is slower. Data retrieved during a cache miss is often written into the cache.

CAD Computer Aided Design. A computer and its related software and terminals used to design things. A CAD system might be as simple as computerized drafting tools or as complex as detailed layouts of integrated circuits. CAD systems often have terminals on peoples' desks and a central maxi-computer in the company's main computer room.

CAD terminals are often run over LANs (local area networks) or through telephone systems. The terminals are often moved, thus having universal wiring and a universal switching system — a LAN or a phone system — is extremely useful.

CAD/CAM Computer Aided Design/Computer Aided Manufacturing. See CAD.

CAE Computer Aided Engineering.

CAGR Compounded Annual Growth Rate

CAI Computer Assisted Instruction. See also CAD for a discussion on telecom needs.

CALIBRATE To test and reset a measuring or timing device against a standard to make sure it is functioning correctly.

CALL My definition: Two people on the phone. One calls the other. People who speak on phones are called "parties." No one knows why. Bellcore's definition: An arrangement providing for a relation between two or more simultaneously present users for the purpose of exchanging information.

CALL ACCOUNTING SYSTEM A computer, a magnetic storage device (floppy or hard disk), software and some mechanical method of attaching itself to a telephone system. A call accounting system is used to record information about telephone calls, organize that information and upon being asked, prepare reports — printed or to disk. The information which it records (or "captures") about telephone calls typically includes from which extension the call is coming, which number it is calling (local or long distance), which circuit is used for the call (WATS, MCI, etc.), when the call started, how long it lasted, for what purpose the call was made (which client? which project?). A call accounting system might also include information on incoming calls — which trunk was used, where the call came from (if ANI or interactive voice response was used), which extension took the call, if it was transferred and to where and how long it took.

There are 10 basic uses for call accounting systems. 1. Controlling telephone abuse. 2. Controlling telephone misuse — making the wrong call on the wrong line. 3. Allocating telephone calling costs among departments and divisions. 4. Billing clients and projects back for telephone charges incurred on their behalf. 5. Sharing and resale of long distance and local phone calls, as in a hotel/motel, hospital, shared condominium, etc. 6. Management and motivation of sales and customer service departments. For example, correlating the number of phone calls with the amount and quality of sales brought in by telemarketing. 7. Personnel evaluation. Which employees are doing better at being productive on the phone (whatever "productive" is defined as). 8. Network optimization. Two fancy words for figuring which is the best combination of AT&T, MCI, WATS, etc. lines. 9. Phone System diagnostics. Is the phone system working as well as it should? Are all the lines working? Are all the circuit packs (circuit cards) working? 10. Long distance bill verification. Was the bill accurate we received from our chosen long distance phone company/s? Telecom Library has published several books on the subject of Call Accounting Systems and TELECONNECT Magazine publishes regular articles on the subject. For more, call 1-800-999-0345.

CALL ADDRESS The last four digits of a telephone number. The three digits in front of that are the Exchange. In the number 950-1234, the exchange is 950 and the call address is 1234.

CALL ANNOUNCEMENT A PBX operator can announce a call to the called party before putting the call through. All modern PBXs have this feature.

CALL ATTEMPT A try at making a telephone call to someone. Tally up call attempts and compare them to completions and you'll have some idea of corporate frustration and thus, the need for more lines or more phone equipment.

CALL BARRING The ability to prevent all or certain calls from reaching to or from a phone.

CALL BLOCKING Check into a hotel. Dial a 0+ call. You're connected to an Alternate Operator Service company. But you know their rates may be high. You ask to be connected to AT&T or MCI, or whoever is the carrier of your choice. Sadly, the AOS cannot connect and neither can (nor will) your hotel's operator. This is called "Call Blocking." The FCC has disbarred the practice. But it continues. See also CALL SPLASHING.

CALL CONTROL Used generally by the telephone industry to describe the management by network switches of call billing, call completion, call maintenance and call termination.

CALL DELAY The delay encountered when a call reaches busy central office switching equipment. The delay is considered OK if no more than one and a half percent of the calls are delayed by three seconds during the busy hour.

CALL DETAIL RECORDING A feature of a telephone system which allows the system to collect and record information on outgoing phone calls — who made them, where they went, what time of day they were placed, how long they took, etc. It is usually needed if you are to install a Call Accounting System. See also CALL ACCOUNTING SYSTEM.

CALL DIVERTER 1. A device which when connected to a called telephone number intercepts calls to that number and connects them to a telephone operator or prerecorded message. 2. An ancillary device which is connected to a telephone line. The device will, when the called telephone rings, initiate a telephone call on another line to a different telephone number. The calling party may or may not be aware that his call has been diverted to another telephone.

CALL DURATION The time from when the call is actually begun (i.e. answered) to the instant either party hangs up. Call Duration is an important concept for traffic engineering.

CALL FORWARDING A service available in many central offices, and a feature of many PBXs and some hybrid PBX/key systems, which allows an incoming call to be sent elsewhere. There are many variations on call forwarding. Call forwarding busy. Call forwarding don't answer. Call forwarding all calls, etc.

A useful feature. For example, you're going to a meeting but you're expecting an important call. Pick up your phone, punch in some digits and all your calls will go to the new number — perhaps the phone outside the meeting room.

The big disadvantage is that many people return to their offices but forget they forwarded their calls elsewhere. As a result, they usually miss a whole bunch of important calls. Some electronic phones now have a reminder light or message on them saying "all calls are being forwarded." Some people program their PBXs to cancel all call forwards at noon and at midnight every day. This makes sense.

CALL HOLD A phone or PBX feature which allows a call to be placed on hold temporarily by operation of the switch hook or other button, thereby eliminating the need for key telephone sets.

CALL ME CARD A special AT&T Card number which permits others to call you, and only you, and have the call charged to your telephone. Give an AT&T CALL ME Card to your very best customers to encourage them to call you. A Call Me Card is like having a private unlisted 800 toll-free number.

CALL ME MESSAGE A Rolm/IBM feature on their CBX that allows internal users to leave other users a message showing the time, date and the caller's extension number.

CALL MODEL An abstraction of the call processing functionality of the architecture and the relationship that exists between the functionality of the Service Switching FE in an ASC and the Service Logic and Control FE in a SLEE (Service Logic Execution Environment). The call model consists of two components: Connection View and Basic Call State Model. Definition from Bellcore in reference to Advanced Intelligent Network.

CALL PARK The phone call is not for you. Or maybe it is, but you don't want to answer it on your phone. Put it into CALL PARK, then you or anyone else can answer it from another phone. Call Park is similar to placing a call on hold. The attendant may have a call for you, but you're not there. So he places the call in Call Park, pages you and tells you the call in is Call Park. You pick up the nearest phone, dial one or two digits (the code for grabbing the call out of Call Park) and you have the call. It's faster than looking for you, then telling you to hang up while she transfers the call.

CALL PICKUP A phone is ringing but not yours. With call pickup, you can punch in a button or two on your phone and answer that person's ringing phone. Saves time.

CALL PICKUP GROUP All the phones in an area that can be answered by each other by simply punching in a couple of digits. See CALL PICKUP.

CALL PROCESSING The system and process that sets up the intended connection in a switching system. The system scans the trunk and/or station ports for any "requests" for service. Upon detecting a request, the system checks the stored instructions and look-up tables and sets the connection up accordingly.

CALL PROGRESS TONE A tone sent from the switch to tell the caller of the progress of the call. Examples are audible ring, re-order, busy, timing, etc.

CALL QUEUING Incoming or outgoing calls may be queued pending an answer. The idea of call queuing is to save money. See also CALLBACK QUEUING.

CALL RECORD The data record of a call transaction. The record is made up of event details that typically include date, time, trunk(s) used, station(s) used and duration. In an ACD, these events may also include time in queue, call route used, system disposition flag, inbound or outdialled digits and wrap-up data entered.

CALL RELEASE TIME The time it takes from sending equipment a signal to close down the call to the time a "free condition" appears and the system is ready for another call.

CALL RESTRICTOR Equipment inserted in a telephone line or trunk which restricts outgoing calls in some way. Usually from making a toll call.

CALL REQUEST PACKET In packet data networking technology, a call request packet sent by the originating data terminal equipment (DTE) showing requested network terminal number (NTN), network facilities and either X.29 control information or call user data.

CALL SCREENING There are several definitions. Here are two. 1. A PBX feature that looks at the digits dialed by the caller to figure whether the call should be completed. 2. A receptionist or secretary answers the "executive's" phone and checks out that the person calling is important enough be put through to the almighty executive whose calls are being screened.

CALL SECOND A unit for measuring communications traffic. Defined as one user making one second of a phone call. One hundred call seconds are called "ccs," as in Centum call seconds. "ccs" is the U.S. standard of telephone traffic. See also ERLANG and TRAFFIC ENGINEERING.

CALL SEQUENCER A call sequencer, also called an Automatic Call Sequencer, is a piece of equipment which attaches to a key system or a PBX. The Call Sequencer's main function is to direct incoming calls to the next available person to answer that phone. It typically does this by causing lights on telephones to flash at different rates. The light with the fastest flashing is the one whose call has been waiting longest. This call is answered first. Call Sequencers also might answer the phone, deliver a message and put the person on hold. They might keep statistical tabs of incoming calls, how fast they were answered, how long the people waited, how many people abandoned (hung up while they were on hold waiting for their call to be answered by a human being), etc. Call Sequencers are usually simple and inexpensive. Better, but much more expensive devices for answering incoming phone calls are Automatic Call Distributors. These are the devices which typically answer when you call an airline. See AUTOMATIC CALL DISTRIBUTOR.

CALL SETUP The first six PICs (Point In Call) of the Originating BCSM (Basic Call State Model), or the first four PICs of the Terminating BCSM. Definition from Bellcore in reference to Advanced Intelligent Network.

CALL SET-UP TIME The amount of time it takes for a call to be established between two people. Call set-up includes dialing, wait time and time to move through central offices and long distance services. You don't pay for call set-up, but you will need extra lines to take care of it. See also ANSWER SUPERVISION and TRAFFIC ENGINEERING.

CALL SPLASHING A "splash" happens when an Alternate Operator Service (AOS) company, located in a city different to the one you're calling from, connects your call to the long distance carrier of your choice in the city the AOS operator is in. Let's say you're calling from a Hotel in Chicago. You ask AT&T handle your call. The AOS, located in Atlanta, "splashes" your call over to AT&T in Atlanta. But you're calling Los Angeles. Bingo. Your AT&T

call to LA is now more expensive than it would be — if you had been connected to AT&T in Chicago.

CALL SPLITTING A feature allowing a phone user to speak privately with either party of a conference call by alternating between the two parties. Call splitting by an attendant allows the attendant to speak to the called person privately while effectively putting the calling person on hold.

CALL STORE The temporary memory used in a stored program control switch (SPC) to hold records of calls in progress. These records are then transferred to permanent memory.

CALL TRANSFER Allows you to transfer a call from your phone to someone else's. On some phones you do this by punching in a bunch of numbers. Some you do it by hitting the "transfer" button and then the number you want to send the call to. The fewer buttons and numbers you have to punch, the easier it will be for your people.

If you're choosing a telephone system, check how easy it is to transfer a call. It is the most commonly used (and misused) feature on a phone system. How many times have you been told, "I'll transfer you to Mr. Smith, but if we get disconnected, please call back on extension 234." If your people are saying this to your customers or prospects, you are giving the outside world the wrong impression of your business. And since 97% of your prospects' contact with your company is first through your phone system, you could be losing precious business.

CALL USER DATA In packet data networking technology, user information transmitted in a call request packet to the destination data terminal equipment (DTE).

CALL WAITING There are three types of call waiting. 1. From an attendant. 2. From an originating user. 3. To a terminating user. The general concept is as follows: You're speaking on the phone. A call comes in for you. You might hear a beep in your ear or see a light on your phone turn on. Or you might hear a beep and see a message come across the screen of your phone. When you hear the beep, you can, if you wish, put the present call on hold and answer the new one. Or you can ignore the new one, hoping it will go away, and perhaps return to your attendant/operator. The above scenario relates to call waiting put on you by an attendant, another internal user or which you buy as a monthly service from the phone company.

Call Waiting is provided by most modern telephone systems — private ones and central offices. They have slightly different ways of working. These days, even some hotel phones have call waiting. So listen for beep tones. It may be the call you're expecting. Better yet, ask your hotel to put you in a room with two lines.

A major problem with call waiting is if you're on a data call from your PC, the call waiting "beep" will often cause your modem to hang up, thus destroying your data call. There are two solutions to this, the obvious one being turn off call waiting. Some phone systems will allow you to turn it off. The less obvious one is modify your modem. Here's how. In all Hayes and Hayes-compatible modems, there's a S10 register. It tells the modem how long before it hangs up after losing carrier. In Hayes modems, the S10 register is set for 1.4 seconds. The typical call waiting tone is 1.5 seconds. Solution, increase the S10 register to six seconds (to be sure). Use your communications software. Go into terminal mode, then type: ATS10=60. You must put this command in every time you power up, because the Hayes 1200 modem (and others) have volatile memory. But the Hayes 2400 and the 9600 (and other 2400 baud and higher asynchronous modems) have non-volatile memory. They remember the six seconds after they've been switched off. The command to write this to memory is ATS10=60&W. The "&W" means write it to memory.

CALLBACK A feature of some voice and data telephone systems. You dial someone somewhere. Their phone or computer is busy. You hit a button or code for "call-back." When their phone becomes free, the phone system will call you back and call them simultaneously. You can only use this call-back feature on things internally in your phone system — calling other people, calling long distance lines (which might be busy), calling the dictation pool, etc. See CALLBACK QUEUING and CALL WAITING.

CALLBACK MODEM A modem that calls you back. Here's how it works. You dial into a network. A modem answers. You put your password in. It accepts the password. It says "Please hang up. I will now call you back." You hang up. It calls you back. There are two reasons for doing this instead of allowing you to just go straight into the network. 1. It's better security. You have to be at a pre-determined place — an authorized phone number. 2. It may save on phone calls. The modem uses the company's communications network, which is probably cheaper than what the person calling in can use.

CALLBACK QUEUING An option on a PBX which allows outgoing calls to be put in line for one or several trunks. When a trunk becomes available, the PBX calls the user, his phone rings and then the PBX dials the distant party on the trunk it grabbed before calling the user. PBXs typically have two types of queuing. The first is called Hold-On Queuing. With this, the user dials his long distance number, the PBX searches for the correct trunk, finds it's not available and tells the user with a beep or message. The user then elects to stay on the line and wait. The instant the trunk becomes free, the PBX connects the user to it. The second type of queuing is called Callback Queuing. The user hangs up and the phone system calls you back, as we explained above.

There are tradeoffs between the two types of queuing. Callback queuing obviously can tolerate longer queues. The longer you wait, the more chance you have of reaching a very low-cost trunk. But users don't like waiting so long for a trunk. And when the call does come, it may likely reach a phone, newly- deserted by a user who's gone to the bathroom.

In contrast, hold-on queuing is more efficient of the user's time, but less efficient of the user's trunks. The less time you wait, the less chance you have of reaching a low-cost trunk. Life is a trade-off. Queuing is no exception. See also QUEUING.

CALLED DTE A DTE which receives a call from another DTE.

CALLING CARD A sort of credit card issued by Bell operating companies, AT&T, MCI and others used for charging long distance calls. Typically, the number on your calling card is the phone number at which you receive bills (home or business phone) plus a four digit Personal Identification Number (PIN number). Some phone companies — local and long distance — charge more for a call made with a Calling Card. Some don't.

CALLING DTE A DTE which places a call to another DTE.

CALLING LINE ID You are called. As the call comes in, you receive the phone number of the person calling you. Calling Line ID is another term for AUTOMATIC NUMBER IDENTIFICATION. Calling Line ID is used increasingly for the phone numbers of local calls, while ANI tends to be used for the phone numbers of distant phone numbers. Essentially they're the same. See also ANI, CALLING NUMBER DISPLAY, ISDN and SIGNALING SYSTEM 7.

CALLING NUMBER DISPLAY Your phone has a LCD (Liquid Crystal Display) or LED (Light Emitting Diode) display. When your phone rings, it will show which extension in the company or which outside line is calling you. Some phone systems allow you to add the person's name to the calling number display.

CALLING PARTY The person who makes (originates) the phone call.

CALLING PARTY IDENTIFICATION A new service being tested in some areas which tells the person being called the number calling them. They can then decide to answer or not answer it. See ANI, which stands for Automatic Number Identification.

CAM Computer-Aided Manufacture. The actual production of goods implemented and controlled by computers and robots. Often used in conjunction with CAD. Only a few factories are completely automated. Usually, there is some human intervention in the actual construction of the product, often to make sure a part is placed in the robot correctly. This dictionary was written with the aid of CAM. We used a computer and a typesetter, also known as CAP, Computer Aided Publishing.

CAMA Centralized Automatic Message Accounting. See CAMA/LAMA.

CAMA/LAMA Centralized Automatic Message Accounting/Local Automatic Message Accounting. Specific versions of AMA in which the ticketing of toll calls is done automatically at a central location for several COs (CAMA) or only at the local office for that office's subscribers.

CAMP-ON You want to transfer a call to a phone but it's busy. This telephone system feature will allow you to lock the call you're trying to transfer onto the line that's busy. When it becomes free, the phone will ring and the "camped-on" call will be connected automatically.

CAMPUS ENVIRONMENT An environment in which telecom users — voice, video and data — are spread out over a broad geographic area, as in a University, hospital, medical center, prison, etc. There may be several switching nodes on a campus. They will be connected with cable, fiber optic, microwave, etc.

CANCEL By touching the "cancel" button on a phone system you're telling the phone system to ignore the last command you gave it. That command might have been transfer, hold, park, etc. The "cancel" button is often mistakenly confused with the "release" button. The "release" button acts the same as hitting "Enter" on a computer system, i.e. it tells the system to go ahead and do what you just told it to do, no matter how stupid your command. In short, "Cancel" means kill the last command. You use when you make a mistake. "Release" means "Enter" — Do it and do it now, irrespective of whether it's the wrong thing.

CANNIBALIZE To devour a phone system by stripping parts from it to repair another system. A common technique for maintaining equipment whose original manufacturer no longer supplies parts. Before you cannibalize, check out the monthly publication Telecom Gear. That publication lists sources of secondary telecom equipment. Good stuff, too.

CAP Customer Administration Panel. A simplified alternative to CAC, which is a Customer Administration Center. These are AT&T words.

CAPACITANCE The capacity of a media (wire, cable, resistor, bus) to store an electrical charge. Capacitance is measured in farads.

CAPACITY The information carrying ability of a telecommunications facility. What the "facility" is determines the measurement. You might measure a date line's capacity in bits per second. You might measure a switch's capacity in the maximum number of calls it can switch in one hour, or the maximum number of calls it can keep in conversation simultaneously. You might measure a coaxial cable's capacity in bandwidth.

CAPACITY TRANSFER CONTROL A Northern Telecom term for a feature which permits single allocation of capacity to be shared among members in a digital switched broadcast connection. For teleconferencing, for instance, a conference leader can transfer transmission capacity among the digital ports in the circuits. 95% of such transfers will take place within 10 seconds.

CAPSTAN A flangeless pulley used to control speed and motion of magnetic tape through a recorder or playback unit.

CAPTAIN Character And Pattern Telephone Access Information Network System. A form of videotext developed in Japan and operated through the public switched telephone network. Displays are on a TV set. It's interactive.

CAPTURE RATIO The ability of a tuner or receiver to select the stronger of two signals at or near the same frequency. Expressed in decibels, the lower the figure, the better.

CARBON BLOCK A device for protecting cable from being hit by lightning strikes in electrical storms. The carbon block consists of two electrodes spaced so that any voltage above the design level is arced from line to ground. Carbon block protectors are used commonly in both local customer offices and central offices. They are effective, but can be destroyed if high voltage is directly applied — as in a direct strike by lightning. A more expensive, but more effective method of protection is the gas tube. These are glass capsules that are connected between the circuit and the ground. When a voltage higher than the design voltage strikes the line, the gas ionizes and conducts the excess voltage to ground. When the voltage is gone, the protector restores itself to normal. Gas tubes, however, take a tiny time to ionize. This may not be fast enough for very sensitive things, like PBX circuit cards. So gas tube protectors are often equipped with diodes, which clamp the interfering voltage to a safe level until the gas tube ionizes.

CARBON FIBER A strong synthetic material that is low in mass with excellent damping characteristics, used in the manufacture of tonearms.

CARBON TRANSMITTER The microphone of a telephone set which uses carbon granules and a diaphragm. The diaphragm responds to our voice and varies the pressure on the granules and hence, their resistance. If your carbon mike isn't working well, tap it lightly on your desk. The carbon granules will line up and it will work much better. Carbon microphones are very reliable but are being increasingly replaced with more sensitive electronic mikes. Some say electronic mikes are too sensitive, so recently, some manufacturers have gone back to carbon mikes.

CARD DIALER A device attached to a telephone which accepts a special plastic card and then automatically dials the number on the card as indicated by the holes punched in it. A card dialer is now obsolete except for unusual applications, like systems whereby you carry your card with you and use it as a security device.

CAROT Centralized Automatic Reporting On Trunks. A test and maintenance facility associated primarily with electronic toll switching systems like the AT&T Communication's #4-ESS. Enables rapid routine testing of all trunks to ensure quick identification of faults and potential failures.

CARRIAGE RETURN By hitting this key, the printing head or the cursor on your screen will return to the left hand margin. Usually hitting a Carriage Return or the "Enter" key includes a line feed, i.e. the paper will move up one line or the cursor will drop down one line. "Usually" does not mean always. So Check. You can usually correct the problem of not having a line feed with a carriage return by moving a dip switch on the printer, changing one of the parameters of the telecommunications software program (the part where it says something about auto linefeed) or changing the computer's operating system (by doing a "Config" or the like). In most microcomputers, a Carriage Return is equivalent to a "Control M." A line feed is a "Control J".

CARRIED LOAD The load that occupies a group of servers.

CARRIED TRAFFIC The part of the traffic offered to a group of servers that successfully seizes a server.

CARRIER 1. A company which provides communications circuits. Carriers are split into "private" and "common." A private carrier can refuse you service. A "common" carrier can't. Most of the carriers in our industry — your local phone company, AT&T, MCI, US Sprint, etc. — are common carriers. Common carriers are regulated. Private carriers are not. 2. An electrical signal at a continuous frequency capable of being modified to carry information. It is the modifications or the changes from the carrier's basic frequency that become the information carried. Modifications are made via amplitude, frequency or phase. The process of modifying a carrier signal is called modulation. A carrier is modulated and demodulated (the signal extracted at the other end) according to fixed protocols. Some of the wideband (i.e. multi-frequency) circuits are also called "carriers." T-1, which typically has 24-channel PCM voice circuits, is known as a carrier system.

CARRIER BAND A band of continuous frequencies that can be modulated with a signal.

CARRIER BYPASS A long distance phone company provides a direct link between its own switching office and a customer's office, thus bypassing the local phone company. Bypass is done to save the customer or the long distance company money. Bypass is also done to get service faster. Sometimes the local phone company simply can't deliver fast enough.

CARRIER COMMON LINE CHARGE Also called ACCESS CHARGE. The charge which long distance phone companies pay to local phone companies to complete their long distance calls. These charges typically are much more than the local phone company gets from its normal business and residential users for completing local phone calls of the same distance. High access charges are designed to help the local phone company financially. That they do. They also encourage bypass and may, in the long term, be self-defeating.

CARRIER DETECT When you phone a modem and it answers, you hear a constant high-pitched sound. That's called "carrier." Modems can detect (i.e. hear) the carrier of modems they call. When they "detect" the other modem, they know they have a good connection and they are now ready to talk to each other. Most external modems that work with microcomputers have a lamp labelled "CD," meaning Carrier Detect. Typically, when the lamp lights, the modem at the other end has answered, you have a valid connection and you can begin the data conversation.

Communications software programs treat "carrier detect" differently. Some use it to figure if they should begin and end the data conversation. And some ignore it and rely on the person using the program to decide when the data conversation is about to begin and when it should be closed down. (There are advantages to either way. There is no "right" way. Our own preference, however, is to use "carrier detect.") All asynchronous modems have the ability to adjust to either way of handling "carrier detect." In a Hayes or Hayes compatible modem with dip switches, Switch 6 determines whether the carrier detect is "forced true," i.e. the program and the modem will ignore the presence or absence of carrier, or whether it responds to carrier detect. In a Hayes or Hayes compatible modem without dip switches but with "switches" in memory, the command is AT&C1. If your modem has non-volatile memory, the command is AT&C1&W

CARRIER DETECT CIRCUITRY Electronic components which detect the presence of a carrier signal and thus determine if a transmission is about to happen. Used in modems. See CARRIER DETECT.

CARRIER FREQUENCY The frequency of the unmodulated sinusoidal waveform.

CARRIER IDENTIFICATION CODES CIC. Three digit numbers used by end-user customers to reach the services of interexchange carriers through equal access arrangements. The primary carrier of choice is reached by dialing "1" plus the area code and called party number. Secondary IX carriers can still be reached by dialing 10 plus the CIC assigned to the carrier desired.

CARRIER SELECT KEYS Buttons at the bottom of a payphone used to choose a long distance carrier.

CARRIER SELECTION As a result of Judge Greene's Modified Final Judgment which lead to the breakup of the Bell System, most local phone companies must offer their customers (business and home) the opportunity to select which long distance company they would like to be use on a "primary" basis. That means when you dial 1+ (one plus) you get that carrier. To use any other long distance company you have dial more digits, e.g. 1-0288 (for AT&T).

CARRIER SENSE MULTIPLE ACCESS/COLLISION DETECTION A network control scheme. It is a contention access control. It "listens" for conflicting traffic to avoid data collisions. The Ethernet LAN uses CSMA/CD, then waits a small amount of time and then tries again. See ETHERNET.

CARRIER SIGNAL A continuous waveform (usually electrical) whose properties are capable of being modulated or impressed with a second information-carrying signal. The carrier itself conveys no information until altered in some fashion, such as having its amplitude changed (amplitude modulation), its frequency changed (frequency modulation) or its phase changed (phase modulation). These changes convey the information.

CARRIER SYSTEM A system where several different signals can be combined onto one carrier by changing some feature of the signals transmitting them (modulation) and then converting the signals back to their original form (demodulation).

CARRIER TERMINAL The modulation, demodulation and multiplex equipment used to combine and separate individual channels at the ends of a transmission system.

CARRIER TO NOISE RATIO The ratio of the received carrier to the noise level.

CARTERFONE A device for connecting a two-way mobile radio system to the telephone network invented by Thomas Carter. The device was made out of bakelite. It was electrically connected to the base station of the mobile radio system. When someone on the radio wanted to speak on a "landline" (the phone system), the base station operator would dial the number on a separate phone then place the telephone handset in the Carterfone device.

The handset was acoustically, not electrically, connected to the phone system. No more than 4,000 Carterfones were ever installed, yet the Bell System thought they were the most dangerous device ever invented. See CARTERFONE DECISION.

CARTERFONE DECISION In the summer of 1968 the FCC said that the Carterfone and other customer phone devices could be connected to the nation's phone network — if they were "privately beneficial, but not publicly harmful." The Carterfone decision was a landmark. It allowed the connection of non-telephone company equipment to the public telephone network. This decision marked the beginning of the telephone interconnect business as we know it today. The Carterfone decision made a lot of lawyers rich before all the rules on connection to the network got cleared up, and finally codified in something called Part 68 of the FCC's Rules. See CARTERFONE and NETWORK HARM. (Helen and Tom Carter live in Gun Barrel, Texas.)

CARTRIDGE Device to translate (transduce) stylus motion to electrical energy in a phonograph in three basic types - moving magnet, moving coil, induced magnet, also tape container for automatic tape systems. A phono cartridge is also call a pickup.

CAS Centralized Attendant Service. One group of switchboard operators answers all the incoming calls for several telephone systems which are located all over the place, typically in one city. CAS is used by customers with several locations in the same geographic area, i.e. retail stores, banks.

CASCADE To connect the output of a device into the input of another device, often the same type as the first.

CASSETTE TAPE A slow, inefficient method of storing and retrieving data which uses the same technology as audio cassettes — like the Sony Walkman. Some PBXs use cassette tape to backup their user programming and database.

CATHODE RAY TUBE CRT. A TV screen. A CRT is a vacuum tube containing an electron gun which directs an electron beam on the front inside of the tube which has been coated with fluorescent material which reacts to and lights up once the electron beams hit. CRTs are very reliable if they are vented (the electron gun gets hot) and their brightness is turned down when the screen is not in use. CRTs have a "memory." They will memorize what's on their screen and you'll see it even though the screen is turned off. So turn your screen off when it's not in use.

CATLAS AT&T software standing for Centralized Automatic Trouble Locating and Analysis System. CATLAS is used as a maintenance tool for locating and diagnosing problems in AT&T electronic central offices.

CATV May mean either Community Antenna TeleVision or CAble TeleVision. CATV is a broadband transmission facility. It generally uses a 75-ohm coaxial cable which carries many frequency-divided TV channels simultaneously. They are separated by guard channels. See BROADBAND.

CAU Northern Telecom term for Connection Arrangement Unit.

CB Why 10-4, good buddy, that stands for Citizens Band. Also known as

Children's Band, not because of Radio Shack's toy walkie talkies, but for the inane chatter that goes on in these channels. In short, CB is low-frequency (up to four watts permitted) public radio. You do not need permission from the FCC to transmit or receive at these frequencies. Thus CB's great popularity.

CB went through a boom then it ran out of radio frequencies. Its original frequencies were 26.965 to 27.225 Mhz. Now the FCC's given it new frequencies — 462.55 to 469.95 MHz. These new frequencies are much better, clearer and less congested. If you buy a CB set, make sure you get one that operates in these higher frequencies. In some countries they use different frequencies. CB radio is not allowed in many countries, even some civilized countries.

C BAND Portion of the electromagnetic spectrum used heavily for satellite transmission. The uplink frequency is at 6 GHz and the downlink is at 4 GHz. Contrast with Ku band.

CBEMA Computer Business Equipment Manufacturers Association. A lobbying group created to protect the interests of its members.

CBK Change BacK.

CBX COMPUTERIZED BRANCH EXCHANGE. CBX is a registered trademark of the Rolm Corporation, Santa Clara, CA. Rolm is now owned by Siemens and IBM. What CBX is to Rolm, PBX or PABX is to other companies. The term CBX has not received wide acceptance, except at Rolm.

CBX II A Rolm communications controller for larger systems. Two versions exist: the CBX II 8000 (16-bit CPU) and the CBX II 9000 (32-bit CPU).

CCC Clear Coded Channel. A 64 kbps channel in which all 64 kbps is available for data.

CCD Charge-Coupled Devices. A type of scanner technology in which the image is focused on a line of charged devices.

CCDN Corporate Consolidated Data Network. An IBM word.

CCIA Computer and Communications Industry Association. A trade organization of computer, data communications and specialized common carrier services companies headquartered in Arlington VA. It runs seminars, does lobbying and generally tries to take care of the common interests of its members. See CBEMA.

CCIR International Radio Consultative Committee. Also used to describe 625-line television system used primarily in Western Europe. The US system of TV is 525. The high definition TV is scheduled to be 1,125.

CCIS Common Channel Interoffice Signaling. A way of carrying telephone signaling information along a path different from the path used to carry voice. CCIS occurs over a separate packet switched digital network. CCIS is separate from the talk path. A special version of CCIS is called Signaling System #7. SS#7 is integral to ISDN. CCIS offers basically two benefits: first, it dramatically speeds up the setting up and tearing down of phone calls. Second, it allows much more information to be carried about the phone call than what is carried on in-band (old-fashioned) signaling. That information can include the calling number, a message, etc.

Signaling for a group of voice telephone circuits is done on CCIS by encoding the information digitally on one of the voice circuits. In the previous method of signaling — the one replaced by CCIS — multi-frequency tones were sent down the same talkpath and the conversation would eventually travel along. By taking the signaling information out of the talkpath, the "phone phreak" community could no longer get free calls by using so-called "blue boxes" which duplicated the multi-frequency tones used by switching machines. CCIS is a much more efficient method of signaling, since it doesn't require a full voice grade channel just to check if the called party in LA is free and whether the call coming in from New York should be put through. See also COMMON CHANNEL SIGNALING, SYSTEM SIGNALING 7 and COMMON CHANNEL INTEROFFICE SIGNALING.

CCITT Comite Consultatif Internationale de Telegraphique et Telephonique, which, in English, means the International Telephone and Telegraph Consultative Committee. It issues recommendations adopted as standards by most people and most firms. These standards apply to modems, packet switched interfaces, RS-232 connectors. You name it. It's got an exceptionally good track record in terms of adoption. CCITT is one of four permanent parts of the International Telecommunications Union, the ITU. It is based in Geneva, Switzerland. It has no power of enforcement, except moral persuasion. Sometimes, manufacturers adopt the CCITT specs. Sometimes they don't. Mostly they do. CCITT is working on worldwide international ISDN standards.

CCITT V.24 In data communications, a set of standards specifying the characteristics for interfaces. Those standards include descriptions of the various functions provided by each of the pins. This standard is similar to (but not identical to) the RS-232-C as established by the American EIA — Electronics Industries Association.

CCIU Northern Telecom word for Conference Control Interface Unit.

CCR Customer Controlled Reconfiguration. An AT&T service that lets users make changes in their digital access and cross connect (DACS) network configurations at a DSO Level in either real time or according to a preplanned schedule.

CCS One hundred call seconds or one hundred seconds of telephone conversation. One hour of telephone traffic is equal to 36 CCS (60 x 60 = 3600 divided by 100 = 36). CCS are used in network optimization. See also TRAFFIC ENGINEERING.

CCSA Common Control Switching Arrangement. A private network set up by AT&T for very large users and using parts of the public switched network. One important feature of a CCSA is that any user anywhere in a CCSA network can reach any other user by dialing only seven digits. Only very large customers subscribe to this service. It's expensive. AT&T has fewer than 100 customers.

CCSA ACCESS A PBX feature which allows a PBX user to get into a CCSA network. See CCSA.

CCS7 COMMON CHANNEL SIGNALING 7.

CCTV Closed Circuit TV.

CCU Communication Control Unit - Processor, often a minicomputer, associated with a host mainframe computer that performs a number of communications-related functions. Compare with cluster control unit.

CD Compact Disc. A 4.5 inch disk containing digital audio or digital computer information, which can be played back on a laser-equipped player. A compact disc comes in one flavor — read only. You can only "read" it or listen to it. You can't record to it. But it has major uses and it's cheap. Each month, a division of Ford Motor Co. publishes a CD ROM inventory of 300,000 parts for its 2,400 dealers. A CD can typically hold 660 megabytes of information. That is the equivalent of 1,500 floppies or 250,000 pages of print. Most computer CD-ROM drives can play audio CD disks — if they have the software and the speakers. Audio CD players, though, cannot play computer CD-ROM disks. See CD-ROM, CD-I, CD-V and WORM.

CD ROM Compact Disc Read Only Memory. Also called CD. The familiar Compact Disc which you see in the audio stores, but now made for computers. These disks hold huge amounts of data — as much as 660 megabytes. Put into a computer drive, the retrieval time is about 10 times slower than on a hard disk. CD ROMs will be the basis of the new "multimedia" computers, which will combine voice, data and video into one system and put it on the desktop. See CD, CD-ROM XA, CD-V and CD-WO.

CD-I Compact Disc Interactive. Geared toward home entertainment, the drive connects to a television.

CD-ROM XA Microsoft's extensions to CD-ROM that let you interleave audio with data. Though it is not a video specification, limited video can be included on disc. Demand for multimedia applications is increasing use of CD-ROM XA. To use it, you must have a drive that reads the audio portions of the disc and audio card in your computer that translates the digital into sound. Not all drives can recognize the extensions. See CD-WO.

CD-V Compact Disc Video. A format for putting five minutes of video on a 3-inch disc. This format has come and gone. Video is shifting towards CD-ROM XA.

CD-WO Compact Disc Write Once. A CD-ROM version of the WORM (Write Once Read Many) technology. For companies performing all CD-ROM publishing in-house, this format is useful for creating test discs before sending the master for duplication. CD-WO discs conform to ISO 9669 standards and can be played in CD-ROM drives.

CDAR Customer Dialed Account Recording.

CDH INTERFACE An interface once required by the Bell System to protect their phone lines from "foreign" (i.e. non-AT&T) phone equipment. CDH devices were eventually ruled a total waste of money and the phone companies refunded the money — at least to the subscribers who asked. If you still have the stuff installed, you may be due a huge refund. Watch out for the statute of limitations.

CDMA 1. Call Division Multiple Access. 2. Code Division Multiple Access, also called Spread Spectrum, is a name for a new form of digital cellular phone service. The idea is that each phone call is combined with a code which only one cellular phone plucks from the air. Business Week said CDMA works "by spreading all signals across the same broad frequency spectrum and assigning a unique code to each. The dispersed signals are pulled out of the background noise by a receiver which knows the code. This method, developed by a San Diego company called Qualcomm Inc. is very new. Much of the equipment to support it, like the cellular switches, have not yet been developed. See CODE DIVISION MULTIPLE ACCESS.

CDO Community Dial Office. A small automatic central office switching system that is completely unattended. Routine maintenance is provided by a traveling technician once or twice each year, or as troubles develop. Such an office usually serves a small community with a few hundred lines in a rural area.

CDR Call Detail Recording. See CALL ACCOUNTING.

CDR EXCLUDE TABLE A table listing local central office codes which are not monitored (i.e. ignored) by a call accounting system.

CED Capacitance Electronic Disc. System of video recording a grooved disc, employing a groove-guided capacitance pickup.

CEDAR A Rolm desktop computer phone that is part IBM PC, part Rolm phone.

CEI Comparable Efficient Interface. The idea is that the telephone industry will let all its information providers have this interface — defined by technical specs and pricing — and, if it does, then the phone companies can themselves use this information to become information providers themselves. The concept has merit. Implementation has been agonizingly slow.

CELL A hexagonal subdivision of a mobile telephone service area which contains a cell-site controller and radio receivers and transmitters. See CELLULAR RADIO.

CELL SITE CONTROLLER The cellular radio unit which manages the radio channels within a cell.

CELLULAR RADIO A mobile radio system. In the old days, there was one central antenna and everything homed in on that and emanated from it. With cellular radio, a city is broken up into "cells," each maybe no more than several city blocks. Every cell is handled by one transceiver (receiver/transmitter). As a cellular mobile radio moves from one cell to another, it is "handed" off to the next cell by a master computer, which determines from which cell the strength is strongest. Cellular mobile radio has several advantages:

1. You can handle many simultaneous conversations on the same frequencies. One frequency is used in one cell and then re-used in another cell. You can't do this on a normal mobile radio system.

2. Because one cellular system can accommodate many more subscribers than a normal mobile radio system, and therefore because it can achieve certain economies of scale, it has the potential of achieving much lower transmission costs.

3. Because the transceiver is always closer to the user than in a normal mobile system, and the user's radio device thus needs less power, the device can be cheaper and smaller. Cellular radios started at over $5,000 and are now well under $1,500. Some have been spied for under $1,000. From the first portable units, weight has already dropped by more than half. There's at least one unit that will fit in your breast pocket and not overly stretch your suit. But it's pricey at $3,000.

CELLULAR RADIO SWITCHING OFFICE The electronic switching office which switches calls between cellular (mobile) phones and wireline (i.e. normal wired) phones. The switch controls the "handoff" between cells and monitors usage. Different manufacturers call their equipment different things, as usual.

CENLEC European Electrical Standards Institute (Comite European de Normalization Electrique).

CENTEL CORPORATION An independent telephone company serving over one million customer lines. It's based near the Chicago O'Hare Airport.

CENTRALIZED ATTENDANT SERVICE Calls to remote (typically branch) locations are automatically directed to attendants at a central location. Imagine four retail stores in a town. There are three branch stores and one main, downtown store, each having their own phone numbers, which customers call. It's clearly inefficient to put operators at each of the stores — when one group is busy, the other will be free, etc. What this feature does is to direct all the calls coming into each of the stores into one bank of operators, who then send those calls back to the outlying stores. Despite the extra schlepping of calls around town, having one large group of operators is cheaper than maintaining many small groups.

CENTRALIZED AUTOMATIC MESSAGE ACCOUNTING CAMA. The recording of toll calls at a centralized point.

CENTRAL OFFICE Telephone company facility where subscribers' lines are joined to switching equipment for connecting other subscribers to each other, locally and long distance. Also called CO, as in See-Oh.

CENTRAL OFFICE BATTERY A group of wet cells joined in series to provide 48 volts DC. Central office batteries are typically charged off the main 120 volts AC. The batteries have two basic functions. 1. To provide a constant source of DC power for 8 hours or so after AC powers drops, and 2. To isolate the central office from glitches on the AC line.

CENTRAL OFFICE OVERRIDE A third party may interrupt or join in your conversation.

CENTRAL PROCESSING UNIT CPU. The part of a computer which has the logic, computational and decision-making. It interprets and executes instructions as it receives them. Personal computers have one CPU, typically a single chip. It is the so-called "computer on a chip." That chip identifies them as an 8-bit, 16-bit or 32-bit machine.

Telephone systems, especially smaller ones, are not that different. Typically they have one main CPU — a chip — which controls the various functions in the telephone. Today's telephone systems are in reality nothing more than special purpose computers. As phone systems get bigger, the question of CPUs - - central processing units — becomes harder to figure. The design of phone systems has, of late, tended away from single processor-controlled telephone systems (as in single processor controlled PCs). There are several reasons for this move. First, it's more economical for growth. Make modules of "little" switches and join little ones together to make big ones. Second, it's more reliable. It's obviously better not to rely on one big CPU, but to have several. In short, the issue of Central Processing Units — CPUs — is blurring. But the concept is still important because by understanding how your telephone switch works (its architecture), you will understand its strengths and weaknesses.

CENTREX Centrex is a business telephone service offered by a local telephone company from a local central office. Centrex is basically single line telephone service delivered to individual desks (the same as you get at your house) with important features, i.e. "bells and whistles," added. Those "bells and whistles" include features like intercom, call forwarding, call transfer, toll restrict, least cost routing and call hold (on single line phones).

Think about your home phone. You can often get "Custom Calling" features. These features are typically fourfold: Call forwarding, Call Waiting, Call Conferencing and Speed Calling. Centrex is basically Custom Calling, but instead of four features, it has 19 features, and more. Like Custom Calling, Centrex features are provided by the local phone company's central office. Centrex is leased to businesses by the local phone company as a substitute for that business buying its telephone system — its own PBX or a key system.

Before Divestiture, Centrex was presumed dead. AT&T was intent on becoming a major PBX and key system supplier. Then Divestiture came, and the operating phone companies recognized they were no longer part of AT&T, no longer had factories to support, but did have a huge number of Centrex installations providing large monthly revenues. As a result, the local operating companies have injected new life into Centrex, making the service more attractive in features, price, service and attitude. Here are the main reasons businesses go with Centrex as opposed to going with a stand-alone telephone system:

1. Money. Centrex is typically cheaper to get into (the central office already exists). Installation charges can be low. Commitment can also be low, since most Centrex service is leased on a month-to-month basis. So it's perfect for companies planning an early move. There may be some economies of

scale, also. Some phone companies are now offering low cost, large size packages.

2. Multiple locations. Companies with multiple locations in the same city are often cheaper with Centrex than with multiple private phone systems and tie lines, or with one private phone system and OPX lines.

3. Growth. It's theoretically easier to grow Centrex than a standalone PBX or key system, which usually has a finite limit. With Centrex, it's hard to run out of paths, memory, intercom lines, phones, tie lines, CO lines, etc. The limit on the growth of a Centrex is your central office, which may be many thousands of lines.

4. Footprint Space Savings. You don't have to put any switching equipment in your office. All Centrex switching equipment is at the central office. All you need at your office are phones.

5. Fewer Operators because of Centrex's DID features. Fewer operator positions saves money on people and space.

6. Give better service to your customers. Many people prefer to dial whomever they want directly (Centrex DID) rather than going through a central operator. Saves time.

7. Better Reliability. When was the last time a central office crashed? Here are some of the features built into modern central offices: redundancy, load-sharing circuitry, power back-up, on-line diagnostics, 24-hour on-site personnel, mirror image architecture, 100% power failure phones, complete DC battery backup and battery power. Engineered to suffer less than three hours down time in every 40 years.

8. Non-blocking. Trunking constraints are largely eliminated with Centrex, since a central office is so large.

9. Minimal Service Costs. Repair is cheap. Service time is immediate. People are right next to the machine 24-hours a day. Phones are the only off-central office premise repair. But you can plug them in, plug them out yourself. All other equipment is in the central office. You need not hold inventory or test equipment.

10. No technological obsolescence. Renting Centrex means a user has the ultimate flexibility — ability to jump quickly into new technology. Central offices are moving quickly into new technologies, such as ISDN.

The above are pro-Centrex. There are also anti-Centrex arguments. See PBX. Centrex is known by many names among operating phone companies, including Centron and Cenpac. You can now get two important features previously available only on privately-owned self-contained phone systems (like PBXs): 1. The ability for the user to make changes to the programming of his own Centrex installation without having to personally call some representative of the phone company. 2. The ability to get call detail accounting by extension and then have reports printed by a computer on his premises. This CDR function is done by the phone company providing a Centrex customer with a separate "data line" which carries Centrex call records back to the customer as those calls are made.

Centrex comes in two variations — CO and CU. CO means the Centrex service is provided by the Central Office. CU means the central office is on the customer's premises.

CENTREX CCRS Centrex Customer Rearrangement System. Computer software from New York Telephone that allows their Centrex customers to make certain changes in their own line and features arrangements. Other phone companies have similar services under different names.

CENTREX LAN SERVICE Put a modem on a dedicated central office line. Connect that line to a switch. Bingo you have a switched, relatively high-speed service that can connect synchronous and asynchronous terminals and other equipment at speeds up to 19.2 Kbps. Centrex LAN service works with existing wiring Centrex central office to customer premise wiring. Centrex LAN is a name given this service by New York Telephone. Other phone companies have similar services under different names.

CENTRONICS PRINTER STANDARD The Centronics standard was developed by the Centronics company which makes computer printers. The Centronics standard is a 36-pin single plug/connector with eight of the 36-pins carrying their respective bits in parallel (8 bits to one character). There are several types of Centronics male and female plugs and receptacles. So know which you want before you buy. The pinning — the location of and function of each of the 36-individual wires, is standard from one Centronics cable to another.

The Centronics printer standard has been adopted by many printer and PC companies, including IBM. It is a narrower standard than the RS-232-C standard. The Centronics works only between a computer and a printer. It won't work over phone lines, unless conversion is done at either end. However, it is standard and has none of the dumb interface problems the RS-232-C standard does.

CENTUM CALL SECOND 1/36th of an erlang. The formula for a centum call second is the number of calls per hour multiplied by their average duration in seconds, all divided by 100.

CEPT Conference of European Postal and Telecommunications administrations. Standards-setting body whose membership includes European Post, Telephone, and Telegraphy Authorities (PTTs).

CEPT FORMAT Defines how the bits of a PCM carrier system of the 32 channel European type will be used and in what sequence. To correctly receive the transmitted intelligence, the receiving end equipment must know exactly what each bit is used for. Cept format uses 30 VF channels plus 1 channel for supervision/control (signaling) and 1 channel for framing (synchronizing). All 8 bits per channel are used to code the waveshape sample.

CFA Carrier Failure Alarm. The alarm which results from an out-of-frame or loss of carrier condition and which is combined with trunk conditioning to create a CGA.

CFAC Call Forward All Calls.

CFB Call Forward Busy.

CFD Call Forward Don't Answer.

CFGDA Call Forward Group Don't Answer.

CFP Channel Frame Processor

CFW Call Forward.

CGA Carrier Group Alarm. A service alarm generated by a channel bank when an out-of-frame (OOF) condition exists for some predetermined length of time (generally 300 milliseconds to 2.5 seconds). The alarm causes the calls using a trunk to be dropped and trunk conditioning to be applied.

CGA Color Graphics Adapter. An IBM standard for displaying material on personal computer screens. The simplest (and conventional) CGA displays 320 horizontal picture elements, known as pels or pixels, by 200 pels vertically. There is also an Enhanced CGA, which is 640 x 400. See MONITOR.

CHAD The little solid round dots made when paper tape is punched with information.

CHAINING A programming technique linking one activity to another, as in a chain. Each link in the chain may contain a pointer to the next link, or there may be a master control or program instructing the programs to link together.

CHAIN MAILBOXES Mailboxes that are connected together to provide a service or a number of messages (e.g. Directory, Product Information, etc.).

CHANNEL Typically what you rent from the telephone company. A voice-grade transmission facility with defined frequency response, gain and bandwidth. Also, a path of communication, either electrical or electromagnetic, between two or more points. Also called a circuit, facility, line, link or path.

CHANNEL ATTACHED Describing the attachment of devices directly to the input/output channels of a (mainframe) computer. Devices attached to a controlling unit by cables rather than by telecommunications circuits. Same as locally attached (IBM).

CHANNEL BANK A multiplexer. A device which puts many slow speed voice or data conversations onto one high-speed link and controls the flow of those "conversations." Typically the device that sits between a digital circuit — say a T-1 — and a couple of dozen voice grade lines coming out of a PBX. One side of the channel bank will be connections for terminating two pairs of wires or a coaxial cable — those bringing the T-1 carrier in. On the other side are connections for terminating multiple tip and ring single line analog phone lines or several digital data streams. Sometimes you need channel banks. Sometimes, you don't. For example, if you're shipping a bundle of voice conversations from one digital PBX to another across town in a T-1 format — and both PBXs recognize the signal — then you will probably not need a channel bank. You'll need a Channel Service Unit (CSU). If one, or both, of the PBXs is analog, then you will need a channel bank at the end of the transmission path whose PBX won't take a digital signal. See CHANNEL SERVICE UNIT.

CHANNEL LOOPBACK In network management systems, diagnostic test that forms a loop at the multiplexer's channel interface that returns transmitted signals to their source. See also LOOPBACK.

CHANNEL SERVICE UNIT CSU. A device used to connect a digital phone line (T-1 or less) coming in from the phone company to either a multiplexer, channel bank or directly to another device producing a digital signal, e.g. a digital PBX, or data communications device. A CSU performs certain line-conditioning, and equalization functions, and responds to loopback commands sent from the central office. A CSU regenerates digital signals. It monitors them for problems. And it provides a way of testing your digital circuit. You can buy your own CSU or rent one from your local or long distance phone company. See also CSU and DSU.

CHANNELIZATION Subdividing a wideband channel into many smaller channels so it may carry many different streams of information.

CHARACTER A letter, a number or a symbol. A character is sometimes described by the digit represented by the bit pattern that makes up the Character. i.e., the letter A is ASCII code 65, a carriage return is ASCII code 13.

CHARACTER CODE One of several standard sets of binary representations for the alphabet, numerals and common symbols, such as ASCII, EBCDIC, BCD.

CHARACTER IMPEDANCE The impedance termination of an electrically uniform (approximately) transmission line that minimizes reflections from the end of the line.

CHARACTER PRINTER A device which prints a single character at a time. Contrast with a line printer, which prints blocks of characters and is much faster.

CHARACTER SET All the letters, numbers and characters which a computer can use. The symbols used to represent data. The ASCII standard has 256 characters, each represented by a binary number from 1 to 256. This set includes all the letters in the alphabet, numbers, most punctuation marks, some mathematical symbols and some other characters typically used by computers.

CHARACTER-ORIENTED PROTOCOL A communications protocol in which the beginning of the message and the end of a block of data are flagged with special characters.

CHARACTER-ORIENTED WINDOWS (COW) INTERFACE An SAA-compatible user interface for OS/2 applications.

CHARACTERS PER SECOND The number of characters that can be printed on paper or displayed on a CRT screen per horizontal (linear) inch. You can usually figure the number of characters per second by dividing by eight the number of bits transmitted each second. The end result won't be that accurate unless you allow for re-transmissions because of errors on the line.

CHAT A common name for a type of messaging done over a network, involving short, usually one or two line messages sent from one node to another. Usually, a chatting facility is RAM-resident, meaning it can be "popped up" inside an application program. Users are usually notified of an incoming chat by a beep and a message at the bottom of their screens.

CHEAPERNET A slang name for the IEEE 802.3 10 Base2 10 Mbps, baseband, thin wire coaxial cable Ethernet system which has a maximum distance of 185 meters.

CHECK BIT A bit added to a unit of data, say a byte or a word, and used for performing an accuracy check. See also PARITY.

CHECK CHARACTERS Characters added to the end of a block of data which is determined by an algorithm using the data bits which are sent. The receiving device computes its own check characters. It compares them with those sent by the transmitter. If they do not match, the receiver requests the sender to send the block again. If the check characters match, then all the bits used to compute the check characters have been received properly.

CHECK-IN MAILBOX The Centigram VoiceMemo II mailbox used to assign names and passcodes for guests checking into a hotel.

CHECK-OUT MAILBOX The Centigram VoiceMemo II mailbox used to clear out guest mailboxes when the guest checks out of the hotel.

CHECKSUM The sum of a group of data items used for error checking. Checksum is computed by the sending computer based upon an algorithm that counts the bits going out in a packet. The check digit is then sent to the other end as the tail, or trailer of the packet. As the packet is being received, the receiving computer goes through the same algorithm, and if the check digit it comes up with is the same as the one received, all is well. Otherwise, it requests the packet be sent again.

CHILL Ccitt HIgh Level Language. A computer language developed by the CCITT for the standardization of software in telecommunications switches. Not widely adopted. C is more widely adopted.

CHIP The physical structure upon which integrated circuits are fabricated as components of telephone systems, computers, memory systems, etc.

CHROMA Name sometimes applied to color intensity control in a receiver.

CHROMINANCE Portion of color TV signal representing colors.

CHROMIUM DIOXIDE Tape whose coating is of chromium dioxide particles. Noted for its superior frequency output.

CICS Customer Information Control System. An IBM program environment designed to allow transactions entered at remote computers to be processed concurrently by a mainframe host.

CIM Computer-Integrated Manufacturing.

CIRCUIT The physical connection of channels, conductors and equipment between two given points. Includes both sending and receiving capabilities.

CIRCUIT BOARD Same as a Printed Circuit Board, namely a board with microprocessors, transistors and other small electronics components. Such a board slides into a the slot in a telephone system or personal computer.

CIRCUIT PROVISIONING The telephone operating company process that somehow organizes to get you a trunk or other special service circuit.

CIRCUIT SWITCHING The process of setting up and keeping a circuit open between two or more users, such that the users have exclusive and full use of the circuit until the connection is released. There are basically three types of switching — CIRCUIT, PACKET and MESSAGE.

PACKET SWITCHING is like circuit switching in that you can also switch information between people or devices, but in packet switching (as in circuit switching), no circuit is left open on a dedicated basis. Circuit switching is like having your own railroad track for your conversation to travel on that's yours as long as you keep the connection open. Once you hang up, the next caller gets to use that track.

PACKET SWITCHING is a data switching technique only. In packet switching, the addresses on your packets are read by the switches as they approach, and are switched down the tracks. The next packet is read to throw the switches to send THAT packet where it needs to go. The data conversation is sent in packets. Each packet can be sent along different tracks as they are open. The packets are assembled at the other end — typically in the last switching office before the packets reach the distant computer or distant user.

MESSAGE SWITCHING sends a message from one end to the other. But it's not interactive, as in packet or circuit switching. In message switching, the message is typically received in one block, stored in one central place, then retrieved or sent in one clump to the other end.

CIRCUIT, FOUR WIRE A path in which four wires are presented to the terminal equipment (phone or data), thus allowing for simultaneous transmission and reception.

CIRCULAR HUNTING When calling a station, the switching system makes a complete search of all numbers within the hunting group, regardless of the location within that group of the called number. For example, the hunt group is 231, 232, 233 and 234, the call is directed to 233. If it is busy, the equipment will search 234, 231, and 232 to find a non-busy station.

CIRCUMNAURAL A type of headphone that almost totally isolates the listener from room sounds.

CIS Contact Image Sensor. A type of scanner technology in which the photodetectors come in contact with the original document.

CITIZEN'S BAND One of two bands used for low power radio transmissions in the United States — either 26.965 to 27.225 megahertz or 462.55 to 469.95 megahertz. Citizens band radio is not allowed in many countries, even some civilized countries. In some countries they use different frequencies. CB radios, in the United States, are limited by FCC rule to four watts of power, which gives each CB radio a range of several miles. Some naughty people boost their CBs with external power. The author of this dictionary has actually spoken to Australia while driving on the Santa Monica Freeway in Los Angeles. See also CB.

CLADDING Welding of one substance over another. Cladding is used in fiber optics where one form of fiber surrounds the center core. That surrounding is called cladding.

CLAIRE Harry Newton's favorite daughter. Why "favorite?" Simple. She's his only daughter. When he wrote this, she was 10 1/2.

CLAMPER An electronic circuit which sets the level of a signal before the scanning of each line begins to insure that no spurious electronic noise is introduced into the picture signal from the electronics of the video equipment.

CLAS Centrex Line Assignment Service. A service from New York Telephone and other Bell operating companies, which allows Centrex subscribers to change their class of service by dialing in on a personal computer, reaching the phone company's computer and then changing things themselves — without phone company personnel assisting or hindering.

Load your PC with communications software. Dial your local central office. Change your Centrex phone numbers. Turn on, turn off features. Change pickup groups. Add numbers to speed dialing, etc. Your on-line changes are checked by the phone company's computers. If they make sense (i.e. one change doesn't conflict with another), they take effect by early the following day — at which time you can call up and get a report on which took, which didn't and who's got what. Saves calling in person. Is more accurate. And, best of all, saves money. Typically just one flat monthly charge. No charge for any of your changes.

CLASS Custom Local Area Signaling Services. It is based on the availability of channel interoffice signaling. Class consists of number-translation services, such as call-forwarding and caller identification, available within a local exchange of Local Access and Transport Area (LATA). CLASS is a service mark of Bellcore. Some of the phone services which Bellcore promotes for CLASS are Automatic Callback, Automatic Recall, Calling Number Delivery, Customer Originated Trace, Distinctive Ringing/Call Waiting, Selective Call Forwarding and Selective Call Rejection. See also CALLING LINE IDENTIFICATION.

CLASS 1 OFFICE A regional toll center. The highest level toll office in AT&T's long distance switching hierarchy. There are essentially five levels in the hierarchy, with the lowest level — Class 5 — being those central offices owned by the local telephone companies. Each of the classes can complete calls between themselves. But, if the routes are busy, then calls automatically climb the hierarchy. A Class 1 office is the office of "last resort."

CLASS 2 OFFICE The second level in AT&T's long distance toll switching hierarchy.

CLASS 3 OFFICE The third level in AT&T's long distance toll switching hierarchy.

CLASS 4 OFFICE The fourth level in AT&T's long distance toll switching hierarchy — the major switching center to which toll calls from Class 5 offices are sent.

CLASS 5 OFFICE An end office. Your local central office. The lowest level in the hierarchy of local and long distance switching which AT&T set up when it was "The Bell System." A class 5 office is a local Central Office that serves as a network entry point for station loops and certain special-service lines. Also called an End Office. Classes 1, 2, 3 and 4 are toll offices in the telephone network.

CLASS OF OFFICE A ranking assigned to switching points in the telephone network, determined by function, interfaces and transmission needs.

CLASS OF SERVICE Each phone in a system may have a different collection of privileges and features assigned to it, such as access to WATS lines. Class of Service assignments if properly organized, can become an important tool in controlling telephone abuse.

CLASSMARK Indicators of the service privileges and restriction of various lines in a telephone system. See CLASS OF SERVICE.

CLEAR CHANNEL Characteristic of a transmission path where the full bandwidth is available to the user. Primarily of digital circuits that do not require some part of the channel to be reserved for carrier framing or control bits.

CLEAR TO SEND CTS. One of the standard attributes of a modem in which the receiving modem indicates to the calling modem that it is now ready to accept data. One of the standard pins used by the RS-232-C standard. In CCITT V.24, the corresponding pin is called Ready For Sending.

CLIPPING There are two basic meanings of Clipping. The first refers to the effect caused by a simplex (one way at a time) speakerphone. Here the conversation goes one way. When the other person wants to talk, the voice path has to reverse (to "flip"). While the flipping takes place, a few sounds are "clipped" from that person's conversation.

This phenomenon happens on some long distance and many overseas channels. These channels are so expensive, they are simultaneously shared by many conversations. Gaps in your conversation are filled by other people's conversation. But when you start talking, the equipment has to recognize you're now talking, find some capacity for your conversation, and send it. In the process of doing this, your first word or part of your first word might be "clipped" and the conversation will sound "broken."

The second way your voice is clipped is what happens every day on the telephone. You're squeezing your own voice which typically spans 10,000 Hertz into a voice channel which is only 3,000 Hertz. This clips the extremes of your conversation — the higher sounds. As a result, your voice sounds flatter over the phone. As you become more economical and try to squeeze your voice into smaller capacity channels, so it becomes increasingly clipped.

CLOCK Exactly as it sounds. An oscillator-generated signal that provides a timing reference for a transmission link. Used in computers to synchronize certain procedures, such as communication with other devices. It simply keeps track of time, which allows computers to do the same things at the same time so they don't "bump into each other." In short, a clock has two functions. 1. To generate periodic signals for synchronization on a transmission facility. 2. To provide a time base for the sampling of signal elements.

CLOCK SPEED Each CPU contains a special clock circuitry which is connected to a quartz crystal (same as the one in your watch). The quartz crystal's vibrations, which are very fast, coordinate the CPU's operation, keeping everything in step. CPU clock speeds are measured in megahertz, or MHz, which stands for "million cycles per second." The clock speeds of today's computer range from a slow of 4.77 MHz (the original IBM PC) to 25 MHz with some Intel 80386 based machines. Clock speed is a misleading term. It is only one way of measuring the speed of a computer. One other critical way is how fast you can read and write information to the hard disk. How important that is depends on whether you're running a program with lots of access to your hard disk (like a database program) or running a program which uses a lot of calculations in RAM, i.e. a spreadsheet.

CLOSED ARCHITECTURE Proprietary design that is compatible only with hardware and software from a single vendor of single product family. Contrast with OPEN ARCHITECTURE.

CLOSED END The end of a Foreign Exchange — FX — line which ends on a PBX, a key system or a telephone. The closed end is the end of the circuit beyond which a call cannot progress further. The other end of the FX circuit is called the "open end," because calls can progress further.

CLOSED LOOP SYSTEM A closed electrical circuit into which a standard signal is feed and received instantly. A measure of the difference between the input signal and the output signal is a measure of the error, and potentially what's causing it.

CLOSED USER GROUP CUG. A facility for partitioning a data network to enable incoming and outgoing access to be individually tailored for each subscribing DTE.

CLUSTER Collection of terminals or other devices in a single location. A cluster control unit and a cluster controller in IBM 3270 systems are devices that control the input/output operations of a group (cluster) of display stations.

CLUSTER CONTROLLER An interface between several bisynchronous devices and a PAD, NC or communication facility. The cluster controller handles remote communications processing for its attached devices. Most common types are IBM 327X.

CMIP Common Management Information Protocol. A protocol formally adopted by the International Organization for Standardization, used for exchanging network management information. Typically, this information is exchanged between two management stations. CMIP can, however, be used to exchange information between an application and a management station. CMIP has been designed for OSI networks, but it is transport independent. Theoretically, it could run across a variety of transports, including, for example, IBM's Systems Network Architecture.

CMOL Short for "CMIP Over Logical Link Control". An implementation of the CMIP protocol over the second layer of the OSI protocol stack, to be proposed as a standard by 3 Com Corp. and IBM. The goal of CMOL is to create agents that require significantly less memory than CMIP implemented over OSI, or SNMP implemented over UDP.

CMOS Complementary Metal Oxide Semiconductor. A technology for making integrated circuits known for requiring less electricity.

CMOT CMIP Over TCP/IP. The use of CMIP over a TCP/IP-based transport.

CMP Communications Plenum Cable.

CMS Call Management System. This is the AT&T label for their inbound call distribution management reporting package. CMS is found on the Horizon, the Merlin, S/75 and S/85 PBX/ACDs. CMS is the successor product to AEMIS/PRO 150/500.

CMS 8800 Cellular Mobile Telephone Service (North American version).

CNR Telephone company term for re-scheduling a telephone installation appointment because the "Customer is Not Ready."

CO Central Office. In North America, a CO is that location which houses a switch to serve local telephone subscribers. Sometimes the words "central office" are confused with the switch itself. In Europe and abroad, the words "central office" are not known. The more common words are "public exchange." But those words tend to refer more to the switch itself, rather than the site, as in North America. See also CENTRAL OFFICE or PUBLIC EXCHANGE.

CO LINES These are the lines connecting your office to your local telephone company"s Central Office which in turn connects you to the nationwide telephone system.

COAM Customer Owned And Maintained equipment.

COAXIAL CABLE A cable composed of an insulated central conducting wire wrapped in another cylindrical conducting wire. The whole thing is usually wrapped in another insulating layer and an outer protective layer. A coaxial cable has great capacity to carry great quantities of information. It is typically used to carry high-speed data (as in connections of 327X terminals to computer hosts) and in CATV (multiplexed TV stations).

COBOL Common Business Oriented Language. A very popular computer programming language for business applications.

COC Central Office Connection. Separately tariffed part of T-1 circuit.

COCOT Customer Owned Coin Operated Telephone.

CODE A system of numbers and letters, numerical or symbolic signals used for communication, most frequently with a computer.

CODE BLOCKING A switch's ability to block calls to a specified area code, central office code or phone number.

CODE CONVERSION A process which converts the codes coming in from one network into codes that can be recognized on another network, such as converting from the Baudot code in a telex network to the ASCII code on the TWX network. Usually, the hardware will convert differences in transmission speed as well.

CODE DIVISION MULTIPLE ACCESS CDMA, also called Spread Spectrum, is a name for a new form of digital cellular phone service. The idea is that each phone call is combined with a code which only one cellular phone plucks from the air. Business Week said CDMA works "by spreading all signals across the same broad frequency spectrum and assigning a unique code — the company says one of 42 billion — to each. The dispersed signals are pulled out of the background noise by a receiver which knows the code. This method, developed by a San Diego company called Qualcomm Inc. is very new. Much of the equipment to support it — like the cellular switches have not yet been developed.

CODE LEVEL Number of bits used to represent a character.

CODEC CODer-DECoder. This equipment converts voice signals from their analog form to digital signals acceptable to more modern digital PBXs and digital transmission systems. It then converts those digital signals back to analog so that you may hear and understand what the other party is saying. In some phone systems, the CODEC is in the PBX and shared by many analog phone extensions. In some phone systems, the CODEC is actually in the phone. Thus the phone itself sends out a digital signal and can, as a result, be more easily designed to accept a digital RS-232-C signal.

CODED TRUNKS You buy several trunks. They hunt on. The main number is 555-3000. If the main number is busy, the call goes to the next line. There are two types of "next lines." One type can have an actual number, like 555-3001, which you can call directly. The other can be a coded trunk with no actual number and which you can't call directly. It's better to have no coded trunks because it's hard to test coded trunks. You can't dial them directly.

CODER An analog-to-digital converter that changes analog voice signals to their digital equivalents. See CODEC.

CODIAL OFFICE CDO. A small central office designed for unattended operation in a distant community. Usually a community dial office is fairly small, rarely more than 10,000 lines.

COHERENT LIGHT Light emitted from laser and some light-emitting-diodes. It is made up of light of a single frequency in which all the light waves are in phase (i.e., their wave peaks and troughs are all in alignment so the waves reinforce or amplify each other.)

COIN ACCEPTOR/REJECTOR A mechanical or electro-mechanical device that checks and validates the coins deposited in a coin pay phone. They measure the coin's size and weight and steel content. These coin acceptor/rejector units transmit the value of the coin deposits to the processing part of a smart payphone or they signal the information to the telephone company central office via coded tones.

COIN SUPERVISORY TRUNK GROUP A trunk group that lets a switchboard operator collect overtime monies due on coin phones and check for stuck coins.

COIN TELEPHONE A pay telephone that takes coins. See PAY TELEPHONE or PAY STATION.

COLD START Everything starts from scratch. The power to the computer or telephone system is turned off. Everything in the system's volatile memory is erased. A cold start may be needed on a microcomputer when something has happened to "lock up" the keyboard and the Reset button (if there is one) doesn't clear the problem completely. A Cold Start is also needed when you want to load a new operating system. When your phone system gives troubles you find hard to diagnose, turn it off, count to ten and turn it on. This cold boot to your phone system will often fix the problem, as it will typically do on a computer system.

COLLECT CALL A telephone call generally requiring operator-assistance. The called party is verbally asked by an operator if they will pay for the call. The called party is ultimately billed for the call.

COLLIMATE The condition of parallel light rays.

COLLISION The result of two workstations trying to use a shared transmission medium (cable) simultaneously. The electrical signals, which carry the information they are sending bump into each other. This ruins both signals and both will have to re-transmit their information. In most systems, a built in delay will make sure the collision does not occur again. The whole process takes fractions of a second. Collisions in LANs make no sound. Collisions do, however, slow a LAN down. See ALOHA, COLLISION DETECTION and CONTENTION.

COLLISION DETECTION The process of detecting that simultaneous (and therefore damaging) transmission has taken place. Typically, each transmitting workstation that detects the collision will wait some period of time and try again. Collision detection is an essential part of the CSMA/CD access method. Workstations can tell that a collision has taken place if they do not receive an acknowledgement from the receiving station within a certain amount of time (fractions of a second). See ALOHA, CONTENTION AND ETHERNET.

COLLISION WINDOW The time it takes for a data pulse to travel the length of the network. During this interval, the network is vulnerable to collision.

COLOR CODE A color system for circuit identification by use of solid colors, tracers, braids, surface marking, etc.

COMBINATION TRUNK A trunk which will work for both incoming and outgoing phone calls.

COMMAND BUFFER A segment of memory used to temporarily store commands. The command buffer only holds a copy of the last command issued.

COMMAND CONFERENCE SYSTEM A conference calling arrangement in a Northern Telecom PBX which allows a designated phone to originate a conference to and between a group of PBX extensions. Any phone that is busy when the conference begins is automatically connected to the conference as soon as that phone becomes free.

COMMAND LINE INTERPRETER CLI. A Rolm user interface to the CBX software and used for things like testing.

COMMAND PATH The list of path names that tells MS-DOS where to look for files that aren't in the current directory.

COMMAND PORT In network management systems an interface used to monitor and control the system.

COMMON AUDIBLE The same as Common Bell. Ringer wiring is such that ringing occurs on more than one CO or PBX line.

COMMON BATTERY A battery (or several batteries) that acts as a central source of energy for many similar devices. In many telecommunications applications, a common battery provides 48 volts of power to a central office switch and to all its phones.

COMMON BATTERY SIGNALING The signaling power of a telephone is supplied by the battery which drives the central equipment. The most common method of signaling.

COMMON BELL A bell or ringer which rings when any of the lines terminating on that phone rings. A term harking back to 1A2 key system days.

COMMON CARRIER A company that furnishes communications services to the general public. It is typically licensed by a state or federal government agency. A company that is a common carrier cannot refuse to carry you, your information or your freight as long as you conform to the rules and regulations as filed with the state or federal authorities. See OTHER COMMON CARRIER.

COMMON CARRIER BUREAU A department of the Federal Communications Commission responsible for recommending and implementing regulatory policies on interstate and international common carrier (voice, video, data) activities.

COMMON CHANNEL INTEROFFICE SIGNALING CCIS. A way of transmitting all signaling information for a group of trunks by encoding that information and transmitting it over a separate channel using time-division digital methods. By transmitting that signaling information over a separate channel, CCIS saves huge long distance bandwidth, which in the past was used to switch calls across the country only to find a busy signal and then come all the way back again to signal the calling party a busy. For the biggest explanation of common channel signaling, see SIGNALING SYSTEM 7. See also MTP, SCCP, ISUP, and TCAP.

COMMON CHANNEL SIGNALING This is a Bellcore definition: A network architecture which uses Signaling System 7 (SS7) protocol for the exchange of information between telecommunications nodes and networks on an out-of-band basis. It performs three major functions: 1. It allows the exchange of signaling information for interoffice circuit connections. 2. It allows the exchange of additional information services and features, e.g. CLASS, database query/response, etc. 3. It provides improved operations procedures for network management and administration of the telecommunications network. For the biggest explanation of common channel signaling, see SIGNALING SYSTEM 7. See also MTP, SCCP, ISUP, and TCAP.

COMMON CHANNEL TRANSIT EXCHANGE An intermediate exchange where networking of common channel signaling systems occurs.

COMMON CONTROL A switching arrangement where the control of all activities is located centrally. This is in contrast to the control being distributed around the system with multiple control devices.

COMMON CONTROL SWITCHING ARRANGEMENT CCSA. An AT&T offering for very big companies. Those big companies can create their own private networks and dial anywhere on them by dialing a standard seven digit number, similar to a local phone number. The corporate subscriber rents private, dedicated lines and then shares central office switches. CCSA uses special CCSA software at the central office.

COMMON COSTS Costs of the provision of some group of services that cannot be directly attributed to any one of those services.

COMMON EQUIPMENT In telephone systems Common Equipment are items that are used by several or all phones for processing calls. On a key system, the device that permits a light on any instrument to flash on and off may be Common Equipment when used to control all lights on all instruments.

COMMUNICATING WORD PROCESSOR A dedicated word processor that includes software for sending word processed files over phone lines. Communicating word processors have now largely been replaced by PCs (Personal Computers) running word processing programs and asynchronous communications software programs.

COMMUNICATION CHANNEL A two-way path for transmitting voice and/or data signals. See also CIRCUIT.

COMMUNICATIONS ACT OF 1934 Federal legislation which established national telecommunications goals and created the Federal

Communications Commission to regulate all interstate and international communications.

COMMUNICATIONS ACT RE-WRITE A plan to re-write the Communications Act of 1934 to bring telecommunications regulation into the twentieth century. The Act will undoubtedly never been re-written, since Congress typically has more important things to do. However, it is not the function of a dictionary to make predictions. Suffice, a lot of people have spent and are continuing to spend a lot of money to get the Act re-written. They are making a lot of lawyers and a lot of lobbyists rich, but not dictionary writers.

COMMUNICATIONS ADAPTER Device attached to an IBM System 3X computer or an IBM PC that allows communications over RS-232 lines.

COMMUNICATIONS CONTROL CHARACTER A character intended to control or help transmission over data networks. There are ten control characters specified in ASCII which form the basis for character-oriented communications control procedures.

COMMUNICATIONS PROTOCOL Specifications which define hardware and software requirements for that type of communications.

COMMUNICATIONS SATELLITE A satellite circling the earth, usually at a distance of about 22,000 miles, with electronic equipment for relaying signals received from the earth back to other points on the earth. See GEOSTATIONARY SATELLITE.

COMMUNICATIONS SERVER Also called an asynchronous server or asynchronous gateway. A communications server is a type of gateway, that translates the packetized signals of a LAN to asynchronous signals, usually used on telephone lines or on direct connections to DEC and other type minicomputers and mainframes. It handles different asynchronous protocols and allows nodes on a LAN to share modems or host connections. Usually one machine on a LAN will act as a gateway, sharing its serial ports or an RS-232 connection to a minicomputer. All devices on the LAN can use this machine to get to the modems and the minicomputer.

COMMUNICATION WORKERS OF AMERICA CWA. A national union of telephone industry employees, currently very worried about its future membership growth given the phone industry's new propensity to fire workers.

COMMUNITY ANTENNA TELEVISION CATV. Signals from distant TV stations are picked up by a large antenna, typically located on a hill, then amplified and piped all over the community below on coaxial cable.

COMMUNITY CHECK A check to determine whether electrical current flows continously throughout the length of a single wire on individual wires in a cable.

COMMUNITY OF INTEREST A grouping of telephone users that call each other with a high degree of frequency. Often several Communities of Interest exist within an organization. This phenomenon can influence design for service when new switches are planned.

COMPACT DISC See CD-ROM

COMPANDER See COMPANDING.

COMPANDING The word is a contraction of the words "compressing" and "expanding." Companding is the process of compressing signals for economical transmission and then expanding them back to their original form at the receiving end.

COMPATIBLE A widely misused word. In the computer world, two computers are said to be compatible when they will produce the identical result if they run identical programs. Another meaning is whether equipment — peripherals and components — can be used interchangeably with each other, from one computer to another. Compatibility used to be regarded as a useful trait in 1A2 key telephones. But then the electronics revolution came along and now there are almost no compatible electronic key telephones from different manufacturers — although TIE and Vodavi are making an effort with their 612/616 and 1A3 electronic key systems, respectively. And TIE and Toshiba have some compatibility among their own different phone systems.

COMPILATION The translation of programs written in a language understandable to programmers into instructions understandable to the computer. Think of programmers writing in every language but Greek and computers understanding only Greek. In this case, Greek is called machine language. The other languages (the programmer languages) are called things like COBOL, FORTRAN, Pascal, dBASE. A compiler is a special program that translates from all these other languages into machine language.

COMPILER A computer program used to convert symbols meaningful to a human into codes meaningful to a computer. For example, taking instructions written in a "higher" level language such as BASIC, COBOL or ALGOL and converting them into machine code which can be read and acted upon by a computer.

COMPLETED CALL Careful with this one. In telephone dialect, a Completed Call is one that has been switched to its destination and conversation has begun but has not yet ended.

COMPLETION RATIO The proportion of the number of attempted calls to the number of completed calls.

COMPOSITE Output of a multiplexer that includes all data from the multiplexed channels. Contrast with AGGREGATE.

COMPOSITE LINK The datastream composed of all the input channels and control and signaling information in a multiplexed circuit. The Composite Link Speed is the transmission speed of the circuit.

COMPOSITE SIGNALING A direct current signaling system that separates the signals from the voice band by filters. Also called CX signaling.

COMPOUND A term used to designate an insulating or jacketing material made by mixing two or more ingredients.

COMPRESSION Reducing the representation of the information, but not the information itself. Reducing the bandwidth or bits necessary to encode information. Compression saves transmission time or capacity. It also saves storage space on storage devices such as hard disks, tape drives and floppy disks.

COMPRESSION ALGORITHM The arithmetic formulae which convert a signal into smaller bandwidth or few bits.

COMPRESSOR See COMPANDING.

COMPROMISE EQUALIZER Equalizer set for best overall operation for a given range of line conditions. This is often fixed but may be manually adjustable.

COMPUNICATIONS A recent creation meaning the combination of telephones, computers, television and data systems.

COMPUTER This is a definition straight from AT&T Bell Laboratories. "An electronic device that accepts and processes information mathematically according to previous instructions. It provides the result of this processing via visual displays, printed summaries or in an audible form."

COMPUTER AND BUSINESS EQUIPMENT MANUFACTURERS ASSOCIATION CBEMA. Association active before Congress and the FCC promoting the interests of the competitive terminal, computer and peripheral equipment industries.

COMPUTER AND COMMUNICATIONS INDUSTRY ASSOCIATION CCIA. Organization of data processing and communications companies which promotes their interests before Congress and the FCC.

COMPUTER INQUIRY A series of ongoing FCC proceedings examining the distinctions between communications and information processing to determine which services are subject to common carrier regulation. The FCC decision in 1980 resulting from the second inquiry was to limit common carrier regulation to basic services. Enhanced services and customer premises equipment are not to be regulated. This meant the Bell operating companies had to set up separate subsidiaries if they were to offer non-regulated services. Computer Inquiry III, adopted by the FCC in May, 1986, removed the structural separation requirement between basic and enhanced services for the BOCs and for AT&T. CI III replaced that requirement with "nonstructural safeguards." This action resulted in the imposition of such concepts as "comparably efficient interconnection" (CEI) and Open Network Architecture (ONA). The FCC's jurisdiction regarding Computer Inquiry I, II and III has now been usurped by Judge Greene, who insists on fairly tight control over the non-basic telephone company activities of the Bell operating companies. Sometimes he gives dispensations (waivers). Sometimes he doesn't. His word these days is final law on what the Bell operating companies can and can't do.

COMSAT The Communications Satellite Corporation was created by Congress as the exclusive provider to the U.S. of satellite channels for international communications. COMSAT is also the U.S. representative to

Intelsat and Inmarsat, two international groups responsible for satellite and maritime communications. Comsat is now being merged with Continental Telephone, also known as Contel.

COMSPEC Command Specification. A configuration command that tells DOS where to find the program that interprets what is typed at the prompt. Except in unusual circumstances, the program is COMMAND.COM. COMSPEC can be used if you want to load different versions of COMMAND.COM for different applications.

COMSTAR A domestic communications satellite system.

CONCENTRATION A fundamental concept to telephony. Communications from a number of phones are sent out on a smaller number of outgoing lines. The theory is that, since not all the phones are being used at any one time, fewer trunks than phones are needed. Some phone system designs assume that only 5% of the phones will be in use at any one time. Some phone systems design assume 10%. In some phone-intensive industries, you can't make any assumptions about concentration. You have to assume one line per phone. No concentration. TELECONNECT Magazine is around one phone per line. We are very phone intensive. See CONCENTRATION RATIO.

CONCENTRATION RATIO The ratio between lines and trunks in a concentrated carrier system or line concentrator.

CONCENTRATOR This device allows a number of circuits (typically slow speed ones) to be connected to a smaller number of lines for transmission under the assumption that not all of the larger group of lines will be used at the same time. The concentrator allows a shared transmission medium to accommodate more data sources than there are channels currently available within the transmission medium. A concentrator's job is to save money on transmission.

CONCENTRICITY In a wire or cable, the measurement of the location of the center of the conductor with respect to the geometric center of the circular insulation.

CONDITIONING Electrical treatment of transmission lines to improve their performance for specific uses such as data transmission. The "tuning" or addition of equipment to improve the transmission characteristics of a leased voice-grade line so that it meets the specifications for higher-speed data transmission. Voice-grade lines often have too much "noise" on them. By altering the equipment at both ends of the line, this noise on the line can be overcome. This allows transmission of data, which is much more sensitive to noise than voice.

Here is another definition of conditioning: A procedure used to make circuit transmission impairments lie within certain acceptable limits which are specified in a tariff (typically used on telephone lines leased for data transmission to improve transmission speed and quality). Usually done with special equipment or routing.

CONDUCTANCE A measure of the ability of a conductor to carry an electrical charge. Conductance is a ratio of the current flow to the potential difference causing the current flow.

CONDUCTIVITY A term used in describing the capability of a material to carry an electrical charge. Usually expressed as a percentage of copper conductivity - copper being one hundred percent. Conductivity is expressed for a standard configuration of conductor.

CONDUCTOR Any wire or cable that can carry an electrical current.

CONDUIT Any pipe or tubing used to pass telephone cables through. A conduit protects the cable and prevents burning cable from spreading flames or smoke. Many fire codes in large cities thus require that cable be placed in metal conduit.

CONDUIT RUN The path taken by a conduit or group of conduits.

CONFERENCE BRIDGE A telecommunications facility or service which permits callers from several diverse locations to be connected together for a conference call. The conference bridge contains electronics for amplifying and balancing the conference call so everyone can hear each other and speak to each other. The conference call's progress is monitored through the bridge in order to produce a high quality voice conference and to maintain decent quality as people enter or leave the conference.

CONFERENCE CALL Connecting three or more people into one phone conversation. You used to have to place conference calls through an AT&T operator (you still can). But now you can also organize conference calls with most modern phone systems or a conference bridge. See CONFERENCE BRIDGE.

If conferencing is important to you, make sure you ask your supplier if the phone system has amplification and balancing in its conferencing. If not, it will simply electrically join the various conversations together and people at either end won't be able to hear each other. There are different types of conference devices you can buy, including special teleconferencing devices that sit on conference tables and perform the function of a speakerphone, albeit a lot better.

CONFERENCE, MEET-ME A conference call in which each of the people wishing to join the conference simply dials a special "Meet-Me" Conference phone number, which automatically connects them into the conference. It is a feature of some PBXs and also some special Conferencing Equipment. See CONFERENCE BRIDGE.

CONFERENCING Several parties can be added to a phone conversation through Conferencing.

CONFIDENCER A noise-canceling microphone for use on a telephone in noisy places. A confidencer is not an easy device to use.

CONFIG.SYS A file of MS-DOS commands used to set up the computer. DOS reads it each time it starts. This is where you put commands for device drivers for things like a mouse or a RAM drive. Other configuration parameters like how many open files are allowed, how many buffers, how many drives, how often to check for Ctrl-C, etc. are also put in this file.

CONFIGURATION The hardware and software arrangements that define a computer or telecommunications system and thus determine what the system will do and how well it will do it.

CONFIGURATION DATABASES Rolm/IBM words for those databases which represent unique user specifications relating to system and phone features. These databases can be entered on-site and are not part of the generic software which runs the phone system.

CONFORMING END OFFICE Central office with the ability to provide originating and terminating feature group D local access and transport area access service.

CONNECT TIME 1. Measure of computer and telecommunications system usage. The interval during which the user was on-line for a session. 2. Interval during which a request for a connection is being completed.

CONNECTING ARRANGEMENT The manner in which the facilities of a common carrier (phone company) and the customer are interconnected.

CONNECTING BLOCK A device used to connect one group of wires to another. Usually each wire can be connected to several other wires in a bus or common arrangement. A 66-type block is the most common type of connecting block. It was invented by Western Electric. Northern Telecom has one called a Bix block. There are others. These two are probably the most common.

CONNECTION A path between telephones that allows the transmission of speech and other signals.

CONNECTION-ORIENTED OPERATION A communications protocol in which a logical connection is established between communicating devices. Connection-oriented service is also referred to as virtual-circuit service.

CONNECTIONLESS SERVICE A networking mode in which individual data packets in a local area network traveling from one point to another are directed from one intermediate node to the next until they reach their ultimate destination. Because packets may take different routes, they must be reassembled at their destination. The receipt of a transmission is typically acknowledged from the ultimate destination to the point of origin. Connectionless networks may be better than connection-oriented ones for obtaining management information over a failing network because a device doesn't have the additional burden of maintaining a network connection.

CONNECTIVITY Property of a network that allows dissimilar devices to communicate with each other.

CONNECTOR A device at the end of a telephone cable or wire which is used to join that cable to another cable with a matching Connector or to some other telecommunications device. Residential telephones use the RJ-11C connector. Computer terminals with an RS-232-C interface, use the DB-25 connector. The RS-232-C standard is actually the electrical method of using the pins on a DB-25. See RS-232-C.

CONSENT DECREE 1982 The agreement which divested the Bell Operating Companies from AT&T. It took effect at midnight on December 31, 1983.

CONSOLE 1. A large telephone which a PBX attendant uses to answer incoming calls and transfer them around the organization. 2. The device which allows communications between a computer operator and the computer.

Before you buy a PBX for your company, make sure your operator has checked out its console. Some are very difficult to use. Some are easy. Some operators hate some consoles. Some consoles hate some operators. You can measure the efficiency of consoles by comparing keystrokes to do simple jobs and comparing them — e.g. answer an incoming line, dial an extension and transfer the call. How many keystrokes does your PBX take?

CONSOLELESS OPERATION Some PBXs can work without a console. Some must have a console. It's good to check. Consoles are expensive. If you don't want one — because your company is small — you don't want to be forced to buy one, only to have it sit idly by.

CONSTANT CARRIER Physical line specification selection indicating full duplex line in bisync network.

CONSULT To seek another's endorsement of a decision you've already made.

CONSULTANT See CONSULT and CONSULTANT LIAISON PROGRAMS.

CONSULTANT LIAISON PROGRAMS Large users often use communications consultants to help them choose systems and long distance phone lines. In recognition of the important role consultants play, many suppliers have consultant liaison programs. Such programs typically consist of a toll-free number and somebody on the other end to answer technical and pricing questions, a three-ring containing information on all the company's products and services, occasional seminars and, for those extra-privileged consultants, trips to all expense paid trips to exotic places and "something" else. With MCI that "something else" is a dial-up, toll-free, bulletin board. Dial it up with your PC, you can download MCI's latest prices and services. It's truly splendid as most of the paperwork others issue is obsolete the moment it's issued.

CONSULTATION See CONSULTATION HOLD.

CONSULTATION HOLD PBX feature which allows an extension to place a call on hold while speaking with another call. The idea is "consulting with" someone while you have someone else on the phone.

CONTACT A strip or piece of metal which makes an electrical contact when some electromechanical device like a relay or a magnet operates. Contacts are often plated with precious metal to prevent them from oxidizing (i.e. rusting) and thus messing up the switch.

CONTACT REGION The section of the jack wire inside the plug opening as shown in Subpart F of FCC rule 6B, figures 6B.500 (a) (3) and 6B.500 (b) (3).

CONTENDED ACCESS In local area networking technology it's the shared access method that allows stations to use the medium on a first-come, first-served basis.

CONTENDING PORT A programmable port type which can initiate a connection only to a preprogrammed port or group of ports.

CONTENTION Contention occurs when several phones are vying for access to a line and only one of them can get it at one time. Some method is usually established for selecting the winner (first in, first out, camp on, etc.) and accommodating the loser(s) (e.g. giving them a busy tone). When you cannot get an outside line from your extension you have been in contention and lost.

CONTEXT-SENSITIVE A term from the computer industry which means that "Help" is only a keystroke away. Hit F1 and Help information will flash on the screen. That information will be relevant to what you're doing now, i.e. that help is within the context of what's going on right this moment.

CONTIGUOUS PORT Ports occurring in unbroken numeric sequence.

CONTIGUOUS UNITED STATES The area within the boundaries of the District of Columbia and the 48 contiguous states as well as the offshore areas outside the boundaries of the coastal states of the 40 contiguous states, (including artificial islands, anchored vessels and fixed structures erected in such offshore areas for the purpose of exploring for, developing, removing and transporting resources therefrom) to the extent that such areas appertain to and are subject to the jurisdiction and control of the United States within the meaning of the Outer Continental Shelf Land Act, 43 U.S.C. Section 1331, et seq.

CONTINENTAL TELECOM INC. CONTEL. A telephone company made up of more than 600 small phone companies. In 1990 it merged with GTE in a tax-free swap of shares. Contel was formed and grown by Charles Wohlstetter, an ex-stockbroker, who became comfortable in the process of growing Contel.

CONTINUITY An uninterrupted electrical path.

CONTINUOUSLY VARIABLE Capable of having one of an infinite number of values, differing from each other by an arbitrarily small amount. Usually used to describe analog signals or analog transmission.

CONTROL CABLE A multiconductor cable made for operation in control or signal circuits.

CONTROL CHARACTER A non-printing ASCII character which controls the flow of communications. Control Codes are entered from computer terminal keyboards by holding down the Control key (marked CTRL on most terminals, and held down the same way an ordinary Shift key is held down) while the letter is pressed. To ring a bell at the remote terminal, a terminal operator could hold down the CTRL key, and tap the "G" key, since Control-G is the BELL character. Most computers display the "^" character in front of the designated letter. For example, Control-M is the Carriage Return character.

CONTROL EQUIPMENT 1. The central "brains" of a telephone system. That part which controls the signaling and switching to the attached telephones. Known as the KSU (or key service unit) in a key system. 2. Equipment used to transmit orders from an alarm center to remote site to enable you to do things by remote control.

CONTROL SIGNAL Modem interface signal used to announce, start, stop or modify a function. Here's a table showing common RS-232 & CCITT V.24 control signals

Pin	Control Signal	From	To
4	Request-To-Send (RTS)	DTE	DCE
5	Clear-To-Send (CTS)	DCE	DTE
6	Data Set Ready (DSR)	DCE	DTE
8	Carrier Detect (CD)	DCE	DTE
20	Data Terminal Ready (DTR)	DTE	DCE
22	Ring Indicator (RI)	DCE	DTE

CONTROL UNIT An architectural component of a processor chip which orchestrates processor activity and handles timing to make sure the processor doesn't overlap functions.

CONTROL PACKAGE NETWORK A Rolm/IBM term for a multinode network used by the processors in one CBX node to communicate with the processors in other nodes. CPN-1 is used with RolmBus 74. CPN-2 is used with Rolmbus 295. Formerly called HUB.

CONTROLLED ENVIRONMENT VAULT CEV. It is a low maintenance, water-tight concrete or fiberglass container typically buried in the ground which provides permanent housing for remote switches, remote line concentrators, pair gain and fiber transmission systems. Because it is buried, it can often be installed in utility easements or other places where local building laws may be a problem.

CONTROLLER In the true sense, a device which controls the operation of another piece of equipment. In its more common sense, a device between a host and terminals that relays information between them. It administers their communication. Controllers may be housed in the host or on a file server. Typically one controller will be connected to several terminals. The most common controller is the IBM Cluster Controller for their 370 family of mainframes.

CONUS A military term for Contiguous United States (lower 48 states). See CONTIGUOUS UNITED STATES.

CONVECTION COOLING Design techniques used in switching system construction to permit safe heat dissipation from the equipment without the need for cooling fans.

CONVECTOR The device which covers the steam heating radiator in buildings and typically sits underneath a window. Also called a weathermaster.

CONVERSATION PATH The route from originating port to terminating port for a two-way call. A conversation thus typically requires two ports on most PBXs.

CONVERSATION TIME The time spent on a conversation from the time the person at the other end picks up to the time you or him hang up. Conversation time plus dialing, searching and ringing time equal the time your circuit will be used during a call.

COPOLYMER Compound resulting from the polymerization of two different monomers.

COPROCESSOR An additional processor which takes care of specific tasks to reduce the load of the main CPU. Many IBM PCs and their clones will have the capacity to install a coprocessor chip which does only arithmetic functions. This significantly speeds up your computer if you do a lot of calculations.

COPW Customer Owned Premises Wire. You own the telephone wiring in your office.

CORD A small, flexible insulated cable.

CORD BOARD The earliest manual PBX. Usually an elegant wooden device consisting of lots of cords with plugs on them. These cords sat horizontally sticking up, like missiles in a silo. Each cord corresponded to an extension. Whenever the phone rang, the cord board attendant would answer it. Each incoming line was a vertical hole. When the operator had figured for whom the call was, he/she would simply plug the cord corresponding to the desired extension into the hole corresponding to the incoming trunk.

The operator would reverse the process if the internal user wanted to make an external call. Either the operator would dial the call first, or simply plug in the user's extension and thus allow the user to dial the call directly. The tip of the plug and the circular ring of the plug gave the term "tip and ring" to telephony. In electronics, it's known as positive and negative.

CORE The central glass element of a fiber optic cable through which the light is transmitted (typically 8-12 microns in diameter for single mode fiber and 50- 100 microns in diameter for multimode fiber).

CORRELATION The AMA (Automatic Message Accounting) function that permits the association of AMA data generated at the same network system or at physically seperate network systems. There are three levels of correlation that affect Advanced Intelligent Network Release 1: record level, service level, and customer level. Definition from Bellcore in reference to Advanced Intelligent Network.

CORRIDOR OPTIONAL CALLING PLAN New York Telephone offers a discounted way for subscribers in the 212 and 718 area codes to call five northern New Jersey counties — Bergen, Essex, Hudson, Passaic and Union.

CORROSION The destruction of the surface of a metal by chemical reaction.

COS See CLASS OF SERVICE.

COST OF SERVICE PRICING A procedure, rationale or methodology for pricing services strictly on the basis of the cost to provide those services.

COT Continuity Check Message. The second of the ISUP call set-up messages. Indicates success or failure of continuity check if one is needed. See ISUP and COMMON CHANNEL SIGNALING.

COT Central Office Terminal

COUNTRY CODE The one, two or three digit number that, in the world numbering plan, identifies each country or integrated numbering plan in the world.

COVERAGE The percent of completeness with which a metal braid covers the underlying surface.

CP Connection Point in Northern Telecom parlance.

CP/M Control Program for Microcomputers. An erstwhile popular operating system for primarily 8-bit microcomputer systems based on the family of Zilog Z-80 microprocessor chips. The system was designed by Digital Research, who never satisfactorily upgraded it to 16-bit machines. Thus it left the way open for Microsoft to create MS-DOS, which is essentially CP/M with frills for 16-bit microprocessor computers — first the IBM and then all its clones.

CPE Customer Provided Equipment, or Customer Premise Equipment. Originally it referred to equipment on the customer's premises which had been bought from a vendor who was not the local phone company. Now it simply refers to telephone equipment — key systems, PBXs, answering machines, etc. — which reside on the customer's premises. "Premises" might be anything from an office to a factory to a home.

CPI Computer PBX Interface. Computern Private Branch Exchange (PABX) Interface. A voice/data PBX standard for using T-1 transmission that involves T-1-to-64 Kbps conversion prior to connection to the computer bus. CPI represents a move toward an open architecture. Compare with DMI.

CPM Critical Path Method.

CPN Computer PBX Network.

CPODA Compression Priority Demand Assignment. Another protocol for converting voice into data bits. See also PCM.

CPS Characters per second, or cycles per second.

CPU The Central Processing Unit. The computing part of a computer. The "brain" of the computer. It manipulates data and processes instructions coming from software or a human operator. See CENTRAL PROCESSING UNIT.

CR Carriage Return. The key on a computer called Carriage Return or sometimes labelled "ENTER." Touching this key usually signals the computer that the entry has been completed and is now ready for processing by the computer. See CARRIAGE RETURN.

CRACKER A person who "cracks" computer systems by gaining access to passwords, or by "cracking" the copy protection of computer software. Access to passwords may be as simple as guessing what a password is. A Cracker is a "Hacker" who's hacks are beyond the bounds of propriety, and usually beyond the law. See HACKER.

CRASH The complete failure of a hardware device or a software operation. Usually used to mean a "fatal" crash in which the device or software must be started from a "power up" condition. See BOOT.

CRC Cyclic Redundancy Check. A basic error-checking mechanism for link-level data transmissions. A characteristic link-level feature of (typically) bit oriented data communications protocols. The check character is generated by taking the remainder after dividing all the serialized bits in a block of data by a predetermined binary number. CRC is a common method of establishing that data was correctly received in data communications. See CRC CHARACTER and CYCLIC REDUNDANCY CHECK.

CRC CHARACTER A character used to check the integrity of a block of data. The character is generated at the transmission end. Its value depends on the hexadecimal value of the number of ones in the data block. And it is added to the data block. The receiving end makes a similar calculation and compares its results with the added character. If there's a difference, there's been a mistake in transmission. So, please, re-send the data.

CREAM SKIMMING Selecting only the most profitable markets or services to sell into. Choosing the cream of the market. An erstwhile popular economic theory to deny new entrants into the telephone industry.

CREDIT CARD PHONE A pay telephone that accepts credit cards with magnetic strips on them instead of coins.

CROSS WYE A cable used at the host system, or network interface equipment that changes pin/signal assignment in order to conform to a given wiring standard (USOC, AT&T PDS, DEC MMJ,etc).

CROSS-CONNECTION Cross-connection is the connection of one wire to another usually by anchoring each wire to a connecting block and then placing a third wire between them so that an electrical connection is made.

CROSS-LINKED Inter-molecular bonds between long chain thermoplastic polymers created by chemical action or electron bombardment.

CROSS-PLAN TERMINATION The conversion of ten-digit telephone numbers to seven digits, or vice versa.

CROSS-POLARIZATION The relationship between two radio waves where one is polarized vertically and the other horizontally.

CROSS-SUBSIDIZATION Supporting one area of a business from revenues generated by another area.

CROSSBAR A switching system that uses a centrally-controlled matrix switching network of electro-mechanical switches which worked with magnets and which connected horizontal and vertical paths to establish a path through the network. Crossbar is known for its reliability but is now largely obsolete because it takes up a lot of space and isn't programmable.

CROSSLINK An X.25 link connecting two XTX NCs on the same level.

CROSSOVER CABLE Another word for NULL MODEM CABLE. A cable used to joined two computers together.

CROSSTALK Crosstalk occurs when you can hear someone you did not call talking on your telephone line to another party you did not call. There are several technical causes for this phenomenon. They relate to wire placement, shielding and transmission techniques. CROSSTALK is also the name of a very popular telecommunications software program for 8- and 16-bit microcomputers. The program is produced by Microstuf, which is now called Crosstalk Communications, Norcross, GA and is now a subsidiary of DCA, makers of the Irma board. We use this program and can recommend it.

CROSSTALK ATTENUATION The extent to which a communications system resists crosstalk.

CRT Cathode Ray Tube. The glass display device found in television sets and video computer terminals. See CATHODE RAY TUBE.

CRYPTO A term used to describe encrypted information. The use of encryption on data communications circuits lessens the chance that the information will be successfully copied by eavesdroppers.

CSA Abbreviation for Canadian Standards Association, a non-profit, independent organization which operates a listing service for electrical and electronic materials and equipment. The Canadian counterpart of the Underwriters Laboratories.

CSDC An AT&T word for Circuit Switched Digital Capability. They define it as a technique for making end-to-end digital connections. Customers can place telephone calls normally, then use the same private connection to transmit high-speed data.

CSI Called Subscriber Identification. This is an identifier whose coding format contains a number, usually a phone number from the remote terminal used in fax.

CSMA Carrier Sense Multiple Access. In local area networking technology, contended access method in which stations listen before transmission, send a packet and then free the line for other stations. With CSMA, though stations do not transmit unitl the medium is clear, collisions still occur. Two alternative versions (CSMA/CA and CSMA/CD) attempt to reduce both the number of collisions and the severity of their impact.

CSMA/CA Carrier Sense Multiple Access (CSMA) with Collision Avoidance. In local area networking technology, CSMA technique that combines slotted time-division multiplexing (TDM) with carrier sense multiple access/collision detection (CSMA/C) to avoid having collisions occur a second time. CSMA/CA works best if the time allocated is short compared to packet length and if the number of stations is small.

CSMA/CD Carrier Sense Multiple Access with Collision Detection. In local area networking technology, CSMA technique that also listens while transmitting to detect collisions. CSMA/CD is a leading control technique for getting onto and off a local area network. All devices attached to the network listen for transmissions in progress (i.e. carrier sense) before starting to transmit (multiple access). If two or more begin transmitting at the same time and their transmissions crash into each other, each backs off (collision detection) for a different amount of time (determined by an algorithm) before again attempting to transmit.

If you didn't understand the above definition, try this one: CSMA/CD: Abbreviation for Carrier Sense Multiple Access with Collision Detection, a method of having multiple workstations access a transmission medium (multiple access) by listening until no signals are detected (carrier sense), then transmitting and checking to see if more than one signal is present (collision detection). Each workstation attempts to transmit when they "believe" the network to be free. If there is a collision, each workstation attempts to retransmit after a preset delay, which is different for each workstation. It is one of the most popular access methods for PC-based LANs. Think of it as entering a highway from an access road, except that you can crash and still try again. Or think of it as two polite people who start to talk at the same time. Each politely backs off and waits a random amount of time before starting to speak again. Ethernet-based LANs use CSMA/CD. See Ethernet and IEEE 802.3.

CSMDR Centralized Station Message Detail Recording.

CSR Customer Station Rearrangement (as in Centrex).

CSU Channel Service Unit. Also called a Data Service Unit. A device to terminate a digital channel on a customer's premises. It performs certain line-conditioning and equalization functions, and responds to loopback commands sent from the central office. A CSU sits between the digital line coming in from the central office and devices such as channel banks or data communications devices. See CHANNEL SERVICE UNIT.

CTS Clear To Send. Lead on an interface.

CTX Centrex.

CUG Closed User Group. Selected collection of terminal users that do not accept calls from sources not in their group and also often restricted from sending messages outside the group.

CURRENT A measure of how much electricity passes a point on a wire in a given time frame. Current is measured in amperes, or amps. See OHM'S LAW.

CURRENT CARRYING CAPACITY The maximum current an insulated conductor can safely carry without exceeding its insulation and jacket temperature limitations.

CURRENT LOOP A serial transmission system in which a pair of wires connecting the receiving and sending devices transmit binary 0 (zero) when no current flows and a binary 1 (one) when current is flowing.

CURSOR A symbol on a screen indicating where the next character may be typed. Cursors may be solid, blinking, underlines, etc. Many programs, computers and phone systems allow you to reprogram the cursor to what you like. One author of this dictionary, Harry Newton, likes a non-blinking solid block, which came standard with his original CP/M version of WordStar, but doesn't any longer.

CUSTOM CALLING A group of special services available from the central office switching system which the telco can offer its subscribers without the need for any special terminal equipment on their premises. Basic custom calling features now available include call waiting, 3-way calling, abbreviated dialing (speed calling), call forwarding, series completing (busy or no answer) and wake up or reminder service.

CUSTOM INTERCOM Allows phone users to dial 2-digit codes (up to 10 member intercom group) or 3-digit codes to reach frequently-called intercom phones.

CUSTOMER PREMISES EQUIPMENT CPE. Terminal equipment supplied by either the telephone common carrier or by a competitive supplier, which is connected to the nationwide telephone network and resides on the customer's premises.

CUSTOMER PROVIDED TERMINAL EQUIPMENT Or just Customer Provided Equipment (CPE). Terminal equipment connected to the telephone network which is owned by the user or leased from a supplier other than the local telephone operating company.

CUT-THROUGH The act of connecting one circuit to another, or a phone to a circuit.

CUT-THROUGH RESISTANCE A measure of an insulation's ability to withstand penetration by sharp edges.

CUTOVER The physical changing of lines from one phone system to another, or the installation of a new system. It's usually done over the weekend, accompanied by heavy praying that everything will go right.

There are two types of cutovers — flash cuts and parallel cuts. Parallel cuts occur when the old phone system is left functioning and the new one, central switching equipment and phones, is installed around it. This means that for some weeks there are two sets of phones, two sets of wires, two switches, two sets of phone lines, etc. The parallel cut is a far more reliable method of cutting over a new switch. But it's also more expensive.

A "flash cut" occurs in a flash. On Friday, everyone is using the old switch. When everyone comes to work on Monday, the old switch and its phones have disappeared. In its place, there's a brand new system. Sometimes it works. More often than not, there are remaining nagging problems. With any Cutover, it's a good idea to set up a Complaint or Cutover Number. Thus, if anyone's having trouble with their phone, they can call this number and get their problems taken care of. How well these problems are taken care of will determine how well the cutover went and how well the employees perceive the new switch is working. Perception, not reality, is what's at stake here.

CVSD Continuously Variable Slope Delta modulation. A method for coding analog voice signals into digital signals that uses 16,000 to 64,000 bps bandwidth, depending on the sampling rate.

CW Calls Waiting (as in Custom Calling Service).

CXR Carrier.

CX SIGNALING A direct current (DC) signaling system that separates the signal from the voice band by filters. Also called COMPOSITE SIGNALING.

CYCLE One complete sequence of an event or activity. Often refers to electrical phenomena. One electrical cycle is a complete sine wave.

CYCLE TIME The time to complete a cycle. In microcomputers, it's the time between successive RAM read or write operations.

CYCLIC REDUNDANCY CHECK CRC. A check performed on data to see if an error has occurred in the transmitting, reading or writing of the data. A CRC is performed by reading the data, calculating the CRC character and comparing its value to the CRC character already present in the data. If they are equal, the new data is presumed to be the same as the old data. Otherwise, it's wrong. Re-send the data.

A CRC character is figured by treating a block of data as a string of bits that are equal to a binary number. Then we divide that number by another predetermined binary number and append the remainder from the division to the data. We call that appended number the CRC character.

CYPRESS A Rolm/IBM desktop device which combines a data terminal, a digital phone and several time management software features.

D CHANNEL In an ISDN interface, the "D" channel is used to carry control signals and customer call data in a packet switched mode. In the BRI (Basic Rate Interface, i.e. the lowest ISDN service) the "D" channel operates at 16,000 bits per second, part of which will carry setup, teardown, ANI and other characteristics of the call. 9,600 bps will be free for a separate conversation by the user. In the PRI (Primary Rate Interface, i.e. ISDN equivalent of T-1), the "D" channel runs at 64,000 bits per second. See also ISDN and DS-0.

D CONDITIONING A type of conditioning which controls harmonic distortion and signal-to-noise ratio so that they lie within specified limits.

D TYPE The standard connector used for RS-232-C, RS-423 and RS-422 communications. D-type connectors are typically seen in nine, 15 and 25 pin configurations.

D-BANK Another name for channel bank. A device that multiplexes groups of 24 channels of digitized voice input at 64 Kbps into T-1 aggregate outputs of 1,544 Mbps.

D-BIT Also called DBIT. The delivery confirmation bit in an X.25 packet used to indicate whether or not the DTE wishes to receive an end-to-end acknowledgment of delivery. In short, a bit in the X.25 packet header that assures data integrity between the TPAD and the HPAD.

D/A Digital to Analog conversion.

D/I Drop and Insert. See BIT STUFFING and BIT ROBBING.

D1, D1D, D2, D3, D4 and D5 T-1 framing formats developled for channel banks. All formats contain a framing bit in every 193rd bit position. The Superframe (introduced in D2 channel banks) is made up of 12 193-bit frames, with the 193rd bit sequence being repeated every 12 frames. D2 framing also introduced robbed bit signaling, where the eighth bit in frames 6 and 12 were "robbed" for signaling informa- tion (like dial pulses). D1D was introduced after D2 to allow backwards compatibility of Superframe concepts to D1 banks.

D3 FORMAT 24 data channels on one standard (North American standard) T-1/D3 span line. Each data channel is 8-bits wide and has a bandwidth of 8KHz. See also DS-1.

D3/D4 Refers to compliance with AT&T TR (Technical Reference) 62411 definitions for coding, supervision and alarm support. D3/D4 compatibility ensures support of digital PBXs, M24 services, Megacom services and Mode 3 D3/D4 channel banks at a DS-1 level.

D4 CHANNELIZATION Refers to compliance with AT&T TR (Technical Reference) 62411 in regards to the DSI frame layout (the sequential assignment of channels and time slot numbers within the DSI).

D4 FRAMING First read T-1 FRAMING. The most popular framing format in the T-1 environment is D-4 framing. The name stems from the way framing is performed in the D-series of channel banks from AT&T. There are 12 separate 193-bit frames in a super-frame. The D-4 framing bit is used to identify both the channel and the signaling frame. In voice communications, signaling is an important function that is simulated and carried by all the equipment in the transmission path. In D-4 framing, signaling for voice channels is carried "in-band" by every channel, along with the encoded voice. "Robbed-bit-signaling" is a technique used in D-4 channel banks to convey signaling information. With this technique, the eighth bit (least significant bit) of each of the 24 8-bit time slots is "robbed" every sixth frame to convey voice-related signaling information (on-hook, off-hook, etc.) for each voice channel. See also EXTENDED SUPER-FRAME FORMAT.

DA Directory Assistance or Demand Assignment.

DAA Data Access Arrangement. A device required before the FCC registration program if a customer was going to hook up CPE (Customer Provided Equipment), usually modems and other data equipment, to the telephone network. Today, equipment is FCC registered (under Part 68) meaning that the device itself is approved for connection to the phone network. DAAs can still be found in old DP (data processing) installations.

DAB Dynamically Allocable Bandwidth.

DAC Digital to Analog Converter.

DACD Digital Automatic Call Distributor. New York Telephone's name for its central office provided ACD.

DACS Digital Access and Cross-connect System. A digital switching device for routing and switching T-1 lines, and DS-0 portions of lines, among multiple T-1 ports. It performs all the functions of a normal "switch," except connections are typically set up in advance of the call, not together with the call, as in most, normal low-bandwidth communications systems (e.g. voice-band voice and data). A DACS is in essence a manual T-1 switch.

DAF Destination Address Field.

DAISY WHEEL PRINTER A printer that prints its characters on paper using a rotating wheel with "fingers." Mounted on the fingers are the various characters. The wheel rotates, bringing the character in line with the paper, then a hammer strikes the character against the ribbon, forming an image on the paper. Daisy wheel printers are typically used for "letter quality" correspondence and are popular for word processing. Their letters are crisp and attractive. But the speed of printing is slow because of the time it takes to rotate the wheel into place. These days, more and more of what used to be printed by daisy wheel printers is now printed by laser printers which are much faster and very quiet in comparison.

DAL Dedicated Access Line. A private tie line from you to your long distance or local phone company. The line may be analog or digital, e.g. a T-1 circuit.

DAMA Demand Assigned Multiple Access. A way of sharing a channel's capacity by assigning capacity on demand to an idle channel or an unused time slot.

DAMPING Decreasing some dimension of a phenomenon, such as its power.

DARK FIBER Installed fiber not carrying a signal. Sometimes dark fiber is sold by a carrier without the (usually) accompanying transmission service. It's "dark" because it's sold without light communications transmission. The customer is expected to put his own electronics and signals on the fiber and make it light.

DASD Direct Access Storage Device (pronounced "dazz-dee").

DAT Digital Audio Tape used to identify tape recorders and players as well as the tape cassettes.

DATA This is AT&T Bell Labs' definition: "A representation of facts, concepts or instructions in a formalized manner, suitable for communication, interpretation or processing." Typically anything other than voice.

DATA ACCESS ARRANGEMENT DAA. Equipment that allows you to attach your data equipment to the nation's phone system. At one stage, DAAs were required by FCC "law." Now, their limited functions are built into directly attached devices, such as terminals, computers, etc.

DATA BANK A large collection of data collected in one place. The data is not necessarily logically related, nor is it necessarily consistently maintained. See DATA BASE.

DATA BASE A collection of data structured and organized in a disciplined fashion so that access is possible to information of interest. There are many ways of organizing data bases. Most corporate data bases are not one single, huge file. They are multiple data bases related to each other by some common thread — for example an employee identification number. Data bases are made up of two elements, a record and a field. A record is one complete entry in a data base, e.g. Gerry Friesen, 12 West 21 Street, New York, NY 10010, 212-691-8215. A field would be the street address field, namely 12 West 21 Street. Data bases are stored on computers in different ways. Some are comma delineated. They differentiate between their fields with commas — like Gerry's record above. A more common way of storing data bases is with fixed records. Here, all the fields and all the records are of the same length. The computer finds fields by counting. For example, Gerry's first name might occupy the first 15 characters. Gerry's last name might be the next 20 characters, etc. Where Gerry's names are too short to fill the full 15 or 20 characters, their fields are "padded" with specially-chosen characters which the computer recognizes as padded characters to be ignored. The most important thing to remember about databases is that all the common database programs, like dBASE, Paradox, Rbase, etc. don't automatically make backups of their files like word processing programs do. Therefore, before you muck with a database file — sort it, index it, restructure it, etc. Please make sure you make a backup of the main database file.

DATA BASE is sometimes spelled DATABASE, especially by this dictionary's author, who keeps changing his mind as he consulted more and more textbooks, who also couldn't make up his mind on how to spell database. See also DATA FILE and DATABASE MANAGEMENT SYSTEM.

DATA BUS A bus transmits and receives data signals throughout the computer or telephone system. See BUS.

DATA CIRCUIT TERMINATING EQUIPMENT See DATA COMMUNICATIONS EQUIPMENT and DCE.

DATA COMMUNICATIONS The transfer of data between points. This includes all manual and machine operations necessary for this transfer. In short, the movement of encoded information by means of electrical transmission systems. See DATA COMMUNICATIONS EQUIPMENT.

DATA COMMUNICATIONS EQUIPMENT DCE. A definition of an interface standard between computers and printers. A device typically comes configured as a DCE or DTE. See DCE and DTE. Which way it comes determines how you connect it to another device.

DATA COMPRESSION Reducing the size of a file of data by eliminating unnecessary information, such as blanks and redundant data. The idea of reducing the size is to save money on transmission or to save money on storing the data. The file or program which has been compressed is useless in its compressed form and must be "decompressed," i.e. brought back to normal before use. One method of data compression replaces a string of repeated characters by a character count. Another method uses fewer bits to represent the characters that occur more frequently. See also COMPRESSION.

DATA CONTROL BLOCK A data block usually at the beginning of a file containing descriptive information about the file.

DATA CONVERSION Converting data from one format to another. The format can be either to a form usable by the equipment you have, e.g. you convert some data from tape to disk (because you don't have a tape drive), or you convert from EBCDIC to ASCII, because you don't have software which can understand IBM's EBCDIC method of coding. There are many service bureaus whose job is to convert computer data from one form to another.

DATA ENCRYPTION STANDARD See DES.

DATA ENTRY Using an I/O device (input/output device), such as a keyboard on a terminal, to enter data into a computer.

DATA FILE A database typically contains multiple files of information. Each file contains multiple records. Each record is made up of one or more fields. Each field contains one or more bytes of data. The terms file, record and field find their roots in manual office filing systems.

DATA GRADE CIRCUIT A circuit which is suitable for transmitting data. High speed data needs better quality phone lines than normal dial-up phone circuits. You can acquire such circuits from many telephone companies. To upgrade voice phone lines to high-speed data circuits, you must sometimes "condition" the phone line. See CONDITIONING.

DATA GROUP A number of data lines providing access to the same resource.

DATA INTEGRITY A performance measure based on the rate of undetected errors. A measure of how consistent and accurate computer data is. Data integrity can be threatened by hardware problems, power failures and disk crashes, but most often by application software. In a database system, data integrity can be threatened if two users are allowed to update the same item or record of data at the same time. Record locking, where only a single user at a time is allowed access to a given data record, is a method of insuring data integrity.

DATA LINE INTERFACE The point where a data line is connected to a telephone system.

DATA LINE MONITOR A measuring device that bridges a data line and looks at how clean the data is, whether the addressing is accurate, the protocol, etc. Being only a monitor, it does not in any way affect the information traveling on the line. See DATA MONITOR.

DATA LINE PRIVACY Prohibits activities which would insert tones on a data station line used by a facsimile machine, a computer terminal or some other device sensitive to extraneous noise.

DATA LINK A term used to describe the communications link used for data transmission from a source to a destination. In short, a phone line for data transmission.

DATA LINK CONTROL DLC. Characters used in data communications that control transmission by performing various error checking and housekeeping functions — connect, initiate, terminate.

DATA LINK LAYER The second layer of the Open Systems Interconnection data communications model of the International Standards Organization. It puts messages together and coordinates their flow. Also used to refer to a connection between two computers over a phone line. See OSI model.

DATA MONITOR A device used to look at a bit stream as it travels on a circuit. It will show the user what is going down both sides of a data channel. It will show what the user at his terminal is typing, and what the computer is responding with. Extremely useful for troubleshooting data communications problems. Also called a Data Scope.

DATA NETWORK IDENTIFICATION CODE A 14-digit number used for worldwide numbering of data networks. See DNIC and the Appendix.

DATA OBJECT An individually addressable unit of information, specified by a data template and its content, that can persist independently of the invocation of a service.

DATA OVER VOICE A device that takes a voice grade line and multiplexes it so it can carry a voice and a data signal. Typically the data is carried in analog form. Thus, to put data on this type of circuit, you need a modem. It is called Data Over Voice, because the data streams (transmission and reception) travel at a higher frequency than the voice conversations using a a technique called frequency division multiplexing (FDM).

DATA PBX A PBX for only low-speed asynchronous data. A switch that allows a user on an attached circuit to select from among other circuits, usually one at a time and on a contention basis, for the purpose of establishing a through connection. Distinguished from a PBX in that only digital transmissions, and not analog voice, is supported. Like a telecommunications PBX that makes and breaks phone connections, a data PBX makes and breaks connections between computers and peripherals. In response to dynamic demand, it establishes communications paths between devices attached to its input/output ports by receiving, transmitting and processing electrical signals. Usually, data PBXs work off PCs' serial ports rather than through cable attached to a network interface card. For that reason, they are restricted to serial speeds, topping out at about 19.2K bits per second.

DATA PORT Point of access to a computer that uses trunks or lines for transmitting or receiving data.

DATA RATE, DATA SIGNALING RATE The measurement of how quickly data is transmitted. Expressed in bps (bits-per-second).

DATA RECORD See DATA FILE and DATABASE MANAGEMENT SYSTEM.

DATA SCOPE See DATA MONITOR.

DATA SECURE LINE A single tip and ring line off the PBX which is protected against any tones (like call waiting) or break-ins that would otherwise mess up any ongoing data transmission call.

DATA SERVICE UNIT DSU. Device designed to transmit digital data on transmission facilities. Typically a device that interfaces DTE (Data Terminal Equipment) to a line connecting a dataport channel unit to allow digital communications without a modem. It is used with a CSU when the DTE lacks complete digital line interface capability or alone (i.e. without a CSU) when the DTE includes digital line interface capability. See T-1.

DATA SET In AT&T jargon, a data set is a modem, i.e. a device which performs the modulation/demodulation and control functions necessary to provide compatibility between business machines which work in digital (on-off) signals and voice telephone lines. In IBM jargon however, a data set is a collection of data, usually in a file on a disk. See also MODEM.

DATA SET READY One of the control signals on a standard RS-232-C connector. It indicates whether the data communications equipment is connected and ready to start handshaking control signals so that transmission can start. See RS-232-C and see the Appendix.

DATA SHEETS What Business Communications Review calls its statistical and descriptive material comparing PBXs. BCR includes these data sheets in its excellent BCR Manual of PBXs. This manual is the most extensive write-up of larger (more than 200 line) PBXs in the world. It is available from Telecom Library on 1-800-LIBRARY.

DATA SOURCE The originating device in a data communications link.

DATA STREAM Collection of characters and data bits transmitted through a channel.

DATA TERMINAL EQUIPMENT DTE. A definition of hardware specifications that provides for data communications. There are two basic specs your hardware can conform to, DTE (Data Terminal Equipment) or DCE (Data Communications Equipment). See DCE.

DATA TERMINAL READY One of the control signals on a standard RS-232-C connector. It indicates if the data terminal equipment is present, connected and ready and has had handshaking signals verified. See RS-232-C and the Appendix.

DATA TRANSFER RATE The quantity of bits or words per unit of time that can move between two data devices during transmission.

DATABASE See DATA BASE.

DATABASE MANAGEMENT SYSTEM DBMS. Computer software used to create, store, retrieve, change, manipulate, sort, format and print the information in a database. Database management systems are probably the fastest growing part of the computer industry. Increasingly, databases are being organized so they can be accessible from places remote to the computer they're kept on. The "classic" database management system is probably an airline reservation system.

DATABASE SERVER A specialized computer that doles out database data to PCs on a LAN the way a file server doles out files. Where a traditional DBMS runs both a database application and the DBMS program on each PC on the LAN, a database server splits up the two processes. The application you wrote with your DBMS runs on your local PC, while the DBMS program runs on the database server computer. With a regular file server setup, all the database data has to be downloaded over the LAN to your PC, so that the DBMS can pick out what information your application wants. With a database server, the server itself does the picking, sending only the data you need over the network to your PC. So a database server means vastly less network traffic in a multi-user database system. It also provides for better data integrity since one computer handles all the record and file locking.

DATAGRAM A transmission method in which sections of a message are transmitted in scattered order and the correct order is re-established by the receiving workstation. Used on packet-switching networks. The Dow Jones Handbook of Telecommunications defines it as, "A single unacknowledged packet of information that is sent over a network as an individual packet without regard to previous or subsequent packets." Here's another definition I found. A finite-length packet with sufficient information to be independently routed from source to destination. Datagram transmission typically does not involve end-to-end session establishment and may or may not entail delivery confirmation acknowledgment.

DATAPHONE A service mark of AT&T for various data hardware products such as modems and printers and services. See also DDS.

DATASPAN DataSPAN is generally characterized as a "fast packet" service and is based on frame relay standards recommended by the International Consultative Committee for Telephone & Telegraph (CCITT) and the American National Standards Institute (ANSI). Northern Telecom has introduced DataSPAN as a new DMS SuperNode value-added, data-communications service that is targeted toward connecting high-speed Local Area Networks. Northern Telecom asserts that DataSPAN's rapid and efficient data transport assures reliable delivery and substantial performance improvement over current LAN interconnect solutions. DataSpan switching and transmission delay is less than 3 ms per node; X.25 switching and transmission delay can be up to 50 ms per node. Using Frame Relay, wide-area packet switching can be accomplished with the same level of performance that is traditionally limited to complex, dedicated private-line networks. DataSPAN is accessed through standard DS-0 or DS-1 links.

DB Should really be written as dB. Decibel. A unit of measure of signal strength, usually the relation between a transmitted signal and a standard signal source. Therefore, 6 dB of loss would mean that there is 6 dB difference between what arrives down a communications circuit and what was transmitted by a standard signal generator. See DECIBEL for a better explanation.

DB 15/25 Refers to the standard 15/25 pin connectors used in T-1/RS-232C communications.

DB LOSS BUDGET Should be written as dB. dB Loss Budget is the amount of light available to overcome the attenuation in the optical link and still maintain specifications.

DB-9 PLUG This is the standard nine-pin RS-232-C serial port on the IBM AT and most laptop computers. The term DB-9 is used to describe both the male and female plug. So be careful when you order. See also the Appendix in this Dictionary for more information on the pinning of RS-232-C plugs.

DB-25 PLUG The standard 25-pin connector used for RS-232-C serial data communications. The term DB-25 is used to describe both the male and female plug. So be careful when you order. See also the Appendix in this Dictionary for more information on the pinning of RS-232-C plugs.

DBIT Also called D-BIT. The delivery confirmation bit in an X.25 packet that is used to indicate whether or not the DTE wishes to receive an end-to-end acknowledgment of delivery. In short, a bit in the X.25 packet header that assures data integrity between the TPAD and the HPAD.

DBM Should be written as dBm. Output power of a signal referenced to an input signal of 1mW (Milliwatt). Similarly, dBm0 refers to output power, expressed in dBm, with no input signal. (O dBM = 1 milliwatt and -30 dBm = 0.001 milliwatt). See DECIBEL.

DBMS DataBase Management System.

DBRN A ratio expressed in decibels above reference noise.

DC Direct Current. The flow of free electrons in one direction within an electrical conductor, such as a wire. DC also stands for Delayed Call.

DC SIGNALING A collection of ways of transmitting communications signals using direct current — the type of current produced by a dry cell household "D" cell battery. DC signaling is only used on cable. It's an out-of-band signal.

DCE Data Communications Equipment. In the RS-232-C "standard" developed by the Electronic Industries Association, there are DCE devices (typically modems or printers) and DTE (Data Terminal Equipment) devices, which are typically personal computers or data terminals. The main difference between a DCE and DTE is the wiring of pins two and three. But there is, of course, no standardization. When wiring one RS-232-C device to another, it's good to know which device is wired as a DCE and DTE. But it's actually best to go straight to the wiring diagram in the appendix of the device's instruction manual. Then you compare the wiring diagram of the device you want to connect and build yourself a cable that takes into account the peculiar (i.e. strange) vagaries of the engineers who designed each product. In short, with an RS-232-C connection, the modem is usually regarded as DCE, while the user device (terminal or computer) is DTE. In a X.25 connection, the network access and packet switching node is viewed as the DCE. DCE devices typically transmit on pin 3 and receive on pin 2. DTE (Data Terminal Equipment) devices typically transmit on pin 2 and receive on pin 3. See also the Appendix.

DCH D-Channel Handler.

DCM Digital Circuit Multiplication. A means of increasing the effective capacity of primary rate and higher level PCM hierarchies, based upon speech coding at 64 kbit/s. Also a Digital Carrier Module.

DCP TELEPHONE A digital voice telephone of the AT&T model 7400 series, operated with the Digital Communications Protocol (DCP) used in System 75/85 digital PBXs.

DCS 1. Distributed Communications system. See DISTRIBUTED SWITCHING. 2. Digital Crossconnect System. A device for switching and rearranging private line voice, private line analog data and T-1 lines. A DCS performs all the functions of a normal "switch," except that connections are typically set up in advance of when the circuits are to be switched — not together with the call. You make those "connections" by calling an attendant who makes them manually, or dialing in on a computer terminal — one similar to an airline agent's. See also NETWORK RECONFIGURATION SERVICE.

DCT Digital Carrier Termination

DDC Direct Department Calling.

DDCMP Digital Data Communications Message Protocol. A uniform discipline for the transmission of data between stations in a point to point or multipoint data communications system. DDCMP is used by DEC computers.

DDD Direct Distance Dialing. The "brand name" the Bell System used to call its Message Toll Telephone Network. It used the words "Direct Distance

Dialing" to convince the public to dial their own long distance calls directly without the help of an operator.

DDN Defense Data Network (DOD).

DDP Distributed Data Processing. See DISTRIBUTED SWITCHING.

DDS Dataphone Digital Service. DDS is private line digital service, typically with data rates at 2,400; 4,800; 9,600 and 56,000 bits per second. DDS is offered on an inter-LATA basis by AT&T and on an intra-LATA basis by the Bell operating companies. AT&T has now incorporated it into their Accunet family of offerings. But, by the time your read this, they may have a new name for the service.

DDSD Delay Dial Start Dial. A start-stop protocol for dialing into a switch.

DE FACTO Used to describe standards. Reflecting current or actual practice, but not having approval or sanction by any official standards-setting organization. usually created by an individual manufacturer or developer - hence, often used as a synonym for proprietary. The Hayes At auto-dial modem command language is an example of a de facto standard. Very often, de facto standards form the basis for de jure standards (Ethernet was the basis of Institute of Electrical and Electronic Engineers or IEEE standard 802.3). Contrast with de jure.

DE FOREST, Lee Lee de Forest invented the vacuum tube in 1907. Until the invention of the transistor after World War II, all radio, long distance telephony and complicated electronics, including electronic computers, were derived from de Forest's invention.

DE JURE Used to describe standards. Approved or sanctioned by an official standards setting organization. CCITT Recommendation X.25 for packet data networks is an example of a de jure standard. Contrast with de facto.

DEALER BOARD British term meaning "trading turret."

DEALING ROOM British term meaning "trading room."

DEBIT CARD A new form of bank card that handles transactions in the same way as your personal checking account. In a debit card, you get no credit. The instant you make a purchase with your debit card, the money is extracted from your bank account and placed in the bank account of your supplier. Such a card hasn't caught on in a big way, but it may if everyone starts to trust banks not to make mistakes.

DEBUG A MS-DOS program to examine or alter memory, load and look at sectors of data from disk and create assembly-language programs. It is not easy to use.

DEC Digital Equipment Corporation. A leading manufacturer of minicomputers. The Unix operating system, developed at Bell Labs, runs on DEC computers. DEC, with its headquarters in Massachusetts and having sold so many computers to Western Electric for inclusion in central office switches and toll switches, is sometimes referred to as "Eastern Electric". DEC is giving IBM a run for its money. Yippee!

DECIBEL dB. A unit for measuring the power of a sound or the strength of a signal. It is expressed as the ratio of two values. Here is an explanation from James Harry Green's excellent book The Dow Jones-Irwin Handbook of Telecommunications. (Get a copy from Telecom Library 1-800-LIBRARY.) Mr. Green writes, "The power in telecommunications circuits is so low that it is normally measured in milliwatts. However, the milliwatt is not a convenient way to express differences in power level between circuits.

"Voice frequency circuits are designed around the human ear, which has a logarithmic response to changes in power. (Likewise, the human eye has a logarithmic response to changes in light.) Therefore in telephony, the decibel, which is a logarithmic rather than a linear measurement, is used as a measure of relative power between circuits or transmission level points. A change in level of 1 dB is barely perceptible under ideal conditions...Increases or reductions of 3 dB result in doubling or halving the power in a circuit. This ratio is handy to remember when evaluating power differences. The corresponding figure for doubling or halving voltage is 6 dB." See DB.

DECIMAL Our normal numbering system. It is to the base 10.

DECISION SUPPORT SYSTEM An on-line computer system designed to support, enhance and simplify decision-making in business. There are several aspects of the best decision support systems: First, they are connected to mainframe databases. Second, they are accessible by executives from their desktops. Third, there are usually lots of programs for producing graphs, charts and writing simple reports, i.e. for the executives to extract and portray information in forms that are most useful to them.

DECNET DEC's proprietary Ethernet LAN that works across all of the company's machines, endowed with a peer-to-peer methodology. See DEC.

DECODER A device that converts information from one form to another — typically from analog to digital and vice versa. See DECODING.

DECODING Changing a digital signal into analog form or into another type of digital signal. The opposite of Encoding. See also MODEM. Decoding and coding should not be confused with deciphering and ciphering. See DES.

DEDICATED ACCESS A connection between a phone or phone system (like a PBX) and an IntereXchange Carrier (IXC) through a dedicated line. All calls over the line are automatically routed to a particular IXC.

DEDICATED ATTENDANT LINK Assures that there will always be an intercom link available for your attendant or receptionist or operator to announce incoming calls.

DEDICATED CHANNEL OR CIRCUIT A channel leased from a common carrier by an end user used exclusively by that end user. The channel is available for use 24 hours a day, seven days a week, 52 weeks of the year, assuming it works that efficiently.

DEDICATED LINE Another name for a private leased line or dedicated channel. A dedicated line provides the ability to have constant transmission path from point A to point B. A dedicated line may be leased or owned. It may be assigned a single purpose, such as monitoring a distant building. It may be part of a network, with the ability for many to dial into it. It may be a tie-line between your offices or it may be a line to a long distance carrier. In this case, you do not have to dial a local connection number or put in an authorization code. A WATS line is in effect a Dedicated Line to AT&T or whomever you purchased WATS from.

DEDICATED MACHINE A computer used to run only one program or do one thing. This machine cannot easily be re-programmed to do another task, as, for example, a general-purpose machine can. A general-purpose machine, however, can be dedicated to running only one task if programmed to do so.

DEDICATED TRUNK A trunk which bypasses the Attendant Console and rings through to a particular phone, hunt group or distribution group.

DEFAULT This is the preset value from the factory or the software writer that the program or equipment comes with. It will work with default values in the absence of any other command from the user. For example, communications software programs, such as Crosstalk, Blast, etc., have as their default settings 300 baud, 8 bit, one stop bit, no parity. If you want to run at 1,200 baud, you have to change that "default" setting.

DEFAULT CARRIER Generic name given to the long distance carrier which will carry the traffic of customers who haven't presubscribed to a long distance carrier.

DEGAUSSER Device to demagnitize color picture tube for color purity.

DELAY The wait time between two events, such as the time from when a signal is sent to the time it is received. There are all sorts of reasons for delays, such as propagation delays, satellite delays, etc.

DELAY ANNOUNCEMENTS These are pre-recorded announcements to incoming callers that they are being delayed and being placed in an ACD queue. Sample: "Please wait. All our agents are permanently busy. You are being placed on Eternity Hold. Don't go away or you'll never be allowed back."

DELAY DISTORTION The difference, expressed in time, for signals of different frequencies to pass through a phone line.

DELAYED RING TRANSFER An optional KTU facility that provides for automatic transfer to the ringing signal from a principal telephone set to the attendant telephone station after an adjustable number of rings.

DELAYED TRANSMISSION A fax machine feature that allows a document to be transmitted automatically at a specific time.

DELAY EQUALIZER A corrective piece of electronic circuitry designed to make communications circuit delays constant over a desired frequency range.

DELAY MODULATION A modulation scheme that uses different forms of delay in a signal element. Frequently used in radio, microwave and fiberoptic systems.

DELAYED SENDING A feature of fax machines which allows the machine to be programmed to send its transmissions at a later time — to take advantage of lower phone rates, for example.

DELIMITER A special word or character that allows a computer to recognize the beginning or end of a portion of a program or segment of data.

DELPHI FORECASTING One of the silliest methods of forecasting the future. Namely, to ask a bunch of alleged experts (often academic eggheads) what they think might happen and then averaging out their opinions, sort of.

DELTA CHANNEL In T-carrier/ISDN communications, a delta channel/"D channel" contains signaling and status information.

DELTA MODULATION A method for converting analog voice to digital form for transmission. It is the second most common method of digitizing voice after Pulse Code Modulation, PCM. Sampling is done in all conversion of analog voice to digital signals. The method of sampling is what distinguishes the various methods of digitization (Delta vs. PCM, etc.). In delta modulation, the voice signal is scanned 32,000 times a second, and a reading is taken to see if the latest value is greater or less than it was at the previous scan. If it's greater, a "1" is sent. If it's smaller, a "0" is sent.

Delta modulation's sampling rate of 32,000 times a second is four times faster than PCM. But Delta records its samples as a zero (0) or a one (1), while PCM takes an 8-bit sample. Thus PCM encodes voice into 64,000 bits per second, while Delta codes it into 32,000. Because delta has fewer bits, it could theoretically produce a poorer representation of the voice. In actual fact, the human voice can't hear the difference between a PCM and a Delta encoded voice conversation.

Delta modulation has much to recommend it, especially its use of fewer bits. Unfortunately no two delta modulation schemes are compatible with each other. So to get one delta-mod digital PBX to speak to another, you have to convert the voice signals back to analog. With AT&T making T-1 a de facto digital encoding scheme, PCM has become the de facto standard for digitally encoding voice. And although there are three types of PCM in general use, they can be made compatible on direct digital basis (i.e. without having to go back to analog voice). One problem with PCM is that American manufacturers typically put 24 64,000 bit per second voice conversations on a channel and call it T-1. The Europeans put 30 conversations on their equivalent transmission path. Thus, you can't directly interface the American and the European systems. But there are "black boxes" available...(In this business, there are always black boxes available.)

DELUXE QUEUING A feature that allows incoming calls from phone users, tie trunks and attendants to be placed in a queue when all routes for completing a particular call are busy. The queue can be either a Ringback Queue (RBQ)— the user hangs up and is called back when a trunk becomes available — or an Off-Hook Queue (OHQ) — the user waits off-hook and is connected to the next available trunk. Deluxe Queuing is a term used mainly by AT&T. Most modern PBXs have this feature. Most have simpler names, however.

DEMAND ASSIGNED MULTIPLE ACCESS See DAMA.

DEMARC or DE-MARK (Pronounced D-Mark.) The demarcation point between the wiring that comes in from your local telephone company and the wiring you install to hook up your own telephone system — your CPE (Customer Provided Equipment) wiring. A De-Marc might be anything as simple as an RJ-11C jack (one trunk) or an RJ- 14C (two trunks) or an RJ-21X (up to 25 trunks) or a 66-block — a punchdown block on one side of which the telephone company punches down its trunks and on the other, you punch down your connections into your phone system. On a 66 block, there are little metal clips called "bridging clips" between you and the phone company. Lifting these clips off cuts your equipment from the phone company's trunks. This way you can quickly see whose fault it is. Often it's yours. But, if you think it's theirs and they come and find it's yours, they'll bill you megabucks. See DEMARCATION POINT or DEMARCATION STRIP.

DEMARCATION POINT The point or interconnection between telephone company facilities and your terminal equipment. The demarcation point shall be located on the subscriber's side of the telephone company's protector or the equivalent thereof in cases where a protector is not required.

DEMARCATION STRIP The terminal strip or block (typically a 66 block) which is the physical interface between the phone company's lines and the lines going directly to your own phone system. See also DE-MARC.

DEMODULATION The process of retrieving an electrical signal from a carrier signal or wave. The reverse of modulation. See MODEM.

DEMULTIPLEXER A device that pulls several streams of data out of a bigger, fatter or faster stream of data.

DENSITY 1. The number of bits (or bytes) in a defined length on a magnetic medium. Density describes the amount of data that can be stored. 2. The number of circuits that can be packed into an integrated circuit.

DEPOPULATE A technique to reduce the traffic load on a switch by removing devices from the shelf or cabinet. Depopulating reduces the effective device capacity of a switch but can increase switching capacity. This is a ploy used to give older PBX systems traffic capacity nearer true ACD systems.

DEREGULATION The removal of regulatory authority to control certain activities of telephone companies. An attempt by federal authorities to make the telephone industry more competitive. Deregulation is meant to benefit the consumer. Sometimes it does. Sometimes it doesn't. Often, it's a scapegoat for whatever subsequently goes wrong.

DERIVATION EQUIPMENT Produces narrow band facilities from a wider band facility. Such equipment can, for instance, derive telegraph grade lines from the unused portion of a voice circuit.

DES Data Encryption Standard. An algorithm for encrypting (coding) data designed by the National Bureau of Standards so it is impossible for anyone without the decryption key to get the data back in unscrambled form. The DES standard enciphers and deciphers data using a 64-bit key specified in the Federal Information Processing Standard Publication 46, dated January 15, 1977. DES is not the most advanced system in computer security and there are possible problems with its use. Proprietary encryption schemes are also available. Some of these are more modern and more secure. The quality of your data security is typically a function of how much money you spend.

DESCENDERS Those parts (or tails) of the letters p, y, j and g which descend below the base line. This typestyle is much easier to read than one in which the tails rest on the base line. Watch out for true (i.e. real) descenders when you're buying a system. Most have them these days, but many telephone screens don't. Careful.

DESCRAMBLER A device which corrects a signal (often video) that has been intentionally distorted to prevent unauthorized viewing. Used with satellite TV systems. See DES.

DESTINATION ADDRESS That part of a message which indicates for whom the message is intended. Usually a collection of characters or bits. Just like putting a destination address on an envelope.

DESTINATION CODE See DESTINATION FIELD.

DESTINATION FIELD The field in a message header that contains the network address of the individual for whom the message is meant and who will (with luck and good management) receive the message.

DESTINATION NODE Those system nodes which receive messages over the control packet network from the source or transmitting node.

DETENT TUNER "Click" type of TV tuner.

DEVICE DRIVER A piece of software that expands MS-DOS's ability to work with peripherals. The routines that make peripherals (a mouse, a RAM disk, a print spooler) work. They may be part of another program (many applications include device drivers for printers) or separate programs. DOS comes with two device drivers: ANSI.SYS and VDISK.SYS. These are things DOS is not used to. The first is to expand the capabilities of the keyboard. The second is used to carve a RAM disk out of the 640K of RAM that MS-DOS can address. In short, device drivers can be used to expand the abilities of DOS. They are loaded from your CONFIG.SYS file when you boot up the computer. Some network operating systems run as device drivers. They do this to get loaded before anything else so they can get the memory space they want. By being loaded as a device driver they are able to tell DOS how to operate certain "network" things, like virtual drives, shared printers, spoolers, print queues and so on.

DIAGNOSTIC PROGRAMS Programs run by the computer portion of a PBX to detect faults in the system. Such programs may run automatically at regular intervals or continuously. The objective of diagnostic programs is to detect faults before they become serious and to alert someone — typically the attendant — to do fix it. Some diagnostic programs stop running when the switch gets too busy. Some don't. You can dial into some diagnostic programs from afar. And you can't in some. Remote diagnostic programs are probably the greatest boone to improved reliability of telephone systems.

DIA/DCA Document Interchange Architecture/Document Content Architecture. IBM promulgated architectures, part of SNA, for transmission and storage of documents over networks, whether text, data, voice or video. Becoming industry standards by default.

DIAL A PRAYER A sarcastic name for the local 611 number run by the local telephone numbers as their centralized number for repair.

DIAL BACKUP A network scheme using dial-up phone lines as a replacement for failed leased data lines. In one typical case, two dial-up lines can be used. One dial-up link is used to transmit data and the other to receive data, thus giving us full-duplex data transmission.

DIAL CALL PICKUP A phone user on a PBX or hybrid can dial a special code and answer calls ringing on any other phone within his own predefined pickup group.

DIAL PICK-UP A phone behind a PBX can answer another ringing phone by dialing a few digits. Also called an access code.

DIAL PULSING A means of signaling consisting of regular momentary interruptions of a direct or alternating current at the sending end in which the number of interruptions corresponds to the value of the digit or character. In short, the old style of rotary dialing. Dial the number "five" and you'll hear five "clicks." See DIAL SPEED, DIAL TRAIN and DTMF.

DIAL REPEATING TRUNKS PBX tie trunks used with terminating PBX equipment capable of handling telephone signaling without attendant involvement.

DIAL SPEED The number of pulses a rotary dial can send in a given period of time, typically 10 per second. A Hayes modem with a communications package, like Crosstalk, can send 20 pulses per second.

DIAL TONE The sound you hear when you pick up a telephone. Dial tone is a signal (350 + 440 Hz) from your local telephone company to you that it is alive and ready to receive the number you dial. If you have a PBX, dial tone will typically be provided by the PBX. Dial tone does not come from God or the telephone instrument on your desk. It comes from the switch to which your phone is connected to.

DIAL TONE DELAY A measure of the time needed to provide dial tone to customers — a measure of performance. Many of the local public service commissions in the United States claim that 90% of customers receive dial tone in fewer than three seconds.

DIAL TONE FIRST COIN SERVICE A type of pay phone service in which dial tone is received when the caller goes off-hook and coins must be inserted only after the call is connected.

DIAL TRAIN The series of pulses or tones sent from the phone that's calling and the switching system it's attached to in order to signify the call's destination.

DIAL-IT 900 SERVICE A special one-way mass calling service that allows prospects, customers and others to reach you from anywhere across the country. In contrast to 800-service, the caller pays the 900 charge, generally one charge for the first minute, with a lesser charge for each additional minute. DIAL-IT 900 Service is a great way to involve your customers and prospects in a promotion! Premium Billing lets you select a rate above standard DIAL-IT 900 rates. The long distance carriers (through their deals with local phone companies) handle the billing. You, the information provider, split the revenues with the long distance provider. International DIAL-IT 900 service is currently available from a growing number of countries.

DIAL-UP The use of a dial or pushbutton telephone to create a telephone or data call. Dial-up calls are usually billed by time of day, duration of call and distance traveled.

DIAL-UP LINE A telephone line which is part of the switched nationwide telephone system.

DIALAN DMS Integrated Access Local Area Network

DIALED NUMBER RECORDER Also called a Pen Register. An instrument that records telephone dial pulses as inked dashes on paper tape. A touch-tone decoder performs the same thing for a touch-tone telephone.

DIALOGIC Dialogic Corporation, Parsippany, NJ, is one of the leading manufacturers of interactive voice processing equipment and software. They sell equipment through value added resellers, dealers and distributors. Many of their dealers "add value" to the Dialogic components by doing their own specialized software programming, tailoring Dialogic products to particular specialized (and useful) applications.

DIAPHRAGM The thin flexible sheet which vibrates in response to sound waves (as in a microphone) or in response to electrical signals (as in a speaker or the receiver of telephone handset).

DIBIT A group of two bits which can be represented by a single change of modulation of the carrier signal. Usually in phase modulation, one of four phases in four-phase modulation is used to represent 00, 01, 10 or 11.

DICTATION ACCESS AND CONTROL A telephone system feature which allows a user to dial a dictation machine and use that machine (giving it instructions by pushbutton) as if it were in his office. Typically, the material on that dictation machine is taken off by one or several typists of a centralized pool and word processed into letters, reports, legal briefs, etc. Telephone suppliers usually don't supply the dictation equipment. Newer telephone dictation machinery is, in reality, a specialized application of voice processing equipment. See VOICE PROCESSING.

DICTATION TANK A recording gadget which receives messages dictated through the telephone system. This tank contains tape which can then be transcribed into letters or documents. See DICTATION ACCESS AND CONTROL.

DID Direct Inward Dialing. You can dial inside a company directly without going through the attendant. This feature used to be an exclusive feature of Centrex but it can now be provided by virtually all modern PBXs and some modern hybrids.

DIELECTRIC Any insulating medium which intervenes between two conductors and permits electostatic attraction and repulsion to take place across it. A material having the property that energy required to establish an electric field is recoverable in whole or in part, as electric energy.

DIELECTRIC CONSTANT The ratio of the capacitance of an insulated wire with that of the same wire uninsulated in air.

DIELECTRIC STRENGTH The voltage which an insulation can withstand before breakdown occurs. Usually expressed as a voltage gradient (such as volts per mil.).

DIELECTRIC TEST A test in which a voltage higher than the rated voltage is applied for a specified time to determine the adequacy of the insulation under normal conditions.

DIFFERENTIAL MODULATION Type of modulation in which the absolute state of the carrier for the current signal element is dependent on the state after the previous signal element.

DIFFERENTIAL PHASE-SHIFT KEYING DPSK. A modulation technique in which the relative changes of the carrier signal's phase are coded according to the data to be transmitted. See PHASE SHIFT KEYING.

DIGIPATH A New York Telephone service, Digipath Digital Service provides two-point and multi-point duplex, or two-way, private data communications at a synchronous data rate of 2.4, 4.8, 9.6 and 56 Kbps.

DIGIPATH OPTION: SECONDARY CHANNEL CAPABILITY An optional feature for New York Telephone's 56 Kbps Digipath service. It allows customers a second channel at 2.6 Kbps, independent of the primary channel. Customers usually use this "extra" channel for diagnosing the line; for running network management over the same line; or to transmit a second, lower speed data stream through the same line.

DIGIT Any whole number from 0 to 9.

DIGIT DELETION It's nice to make it easy for people to dial their desired numbers. Part of making it "nice" is to keep their pattern of dialing consistent. The charm of our ten-digit numbering system in North America — the three digit area code and seven digit local number — is its consistency, making for easy use and easy remembering. Some corporate networks, however, don't use a common numbering scheme. They might use tie trunks to get to Chicago, and insist on the user dialing 69, instead of the more common 312 area code. They might insist on the user dialing 73 when he wants to go to Los Angeles. But if he wants to reach the LA office, he might dial 235. This can be awfully confusing. So some switches — central office and PBXs — have the ability to insert or delete digits. That is, they will recognize the number dialed and change it as it progresses through the network. The user, however, knows nothing of this. He simply dials a normal phone number and listens as his call progresses normally. Digit insertion and digit deletion is a part of a PBX feature called common number dialing.

DIGIT INSERTION See DIGIT DELETION.

DIGITAL In displays, the use of digits for direct readout. In recording or computing, the use of a binary code to represent information.

DIGITAL ACCESS AND CROSS CONNECT SYSTEM See DACS

DIGITAL AUDIO The storage and processing of audio signals digitally. It usually requires at least 16 bits of linear coding to represent each digital sample.

DIGITAL CIRCUIT MULTIPLICATION DCM is a variation of analog TASI — Time Assigned Speech Interpolation. In DCM, speech is encoded digitally and advanced voiceband coding algorithms are applied to TASI's old speech interpolation techniques. DCM delivers a four to fivefold increase in the effective capacity of normal pulse code modulation (PCM) T-1 links operating at 1.544 megabits per second. DCM equipment is used on the TAT-8 transatlantic optical fiber submarine cable. Most DCM equipment has three operating elements: a speech activity detector. An assignment mapping and message unit, and a speech reconstitution unit. See February, 1987 issue of Data Communications for more.

DIGITAL CROSS-CONNECT SYSTEM DACS or DCS. A specialized type of high-speed data channel switch. It differs from a normal voice switch, which switches transmission paths in response to dialing instructions. In a digital cross-connect system, you give it separate and specific instructions to connect this line to that. These instructions are given independently of any calls that might flow over the system. This contrasts with a normal voice switching in which switching instructions and conversations go together. Commands to a digital cross-connect system can be given by an operator at a console or can be programmed to switch at certain times. For example, you might want to change the T-1 24-voice conversation circuit to Chicago at 11 A.M. each day to allow for the president's 30 minute video-conference call.

DIGITAL FACILITIES MANAGEMENT SYSTEM A Northern Telecom software which integrates the maintenance of all types of digital facilities from T-1 to the high-bit fiber. Largely used by telephone companies.

DIGITAL LOOPBACK A diagnostic feature on a modem, a short-haul microwave or some other digital transmission equipment which allows the user to loop a signal back from one part of the system to another to test the circuit or the equipment. Digital loopbacks can be as long or as short as are necessary to isolate the problem. By looping a signal back and measuring it at both ends of the loop (at the beginning and at the end), you can see if the device carried the message cleanly and is thus, operating correctly.

DIGITAL MICROWAVE A microwave system in which the modulation of the radio frequency carrier is digital. The carrier is still a standard microwave radio wave. The digital modulation may be frequency or phase shift, but the control of that modulation is the digital bit stream.

DIGITAL MICROWAVE CORPORATION DMC makes excellent short-haul digital microwave and optical fiber equipment and systems. They're based in San Jose, CA.

DIGITAL NETWORK A network in which the information is encoded as a series of ones and zeros rather than as a continuously varying wave — as in traditional analog networks. Digital networks have several major pluses over analog ones. First, they're "cleaner." They have far less noise, static, etc. Second, they're easier to monitor because you can measure them more easily. Third, you can typically pump more digital information down a communications line than you can analog information.

DIGITAL PORT ADAPTER DPA. A device which provides conversion from the RS449/422 interface to the more common interfaces of RS-232-C, v.35, WE-306 and others.

DIGITAL RECORDING A system of recording by conversion of musical information into a series of pulses that are translated into a binary code intelligible to computer circuits and stored on magnetic tape or magnetic discs. Also called PCM - Pulse Code Modulation.

DIGITAL SIGNAL A discontinuous signal. One whose state consists of discrete elements, representing very specific information. When viewed on an oscilloscope, a digital signal is "squared." This compares with an analog signal which typically looks more like a sine wave, i.e. curvy. Usually amplitude is represented at discrete time intervals with a digital value.

DIGITAL SIGNAL PROCESSOR A specialized digital microprocessor that performs calculations on digitized signals that were originally analog (e.g. voice) and then sends the results on. The big advantage of a DSP lies in the programmability of digitial microprocessors. DSPs can be used for compression of voice signals to as few as 4,800 bps. They are also used for everything from fetal monitors, to anti-skid brakes, super-sensitive hearing aids, multimedia presentations and low-cost desktop fax machines. DSPs will do for the telecom industry what the general purpose microprocessor (e.g. Intel's 80286 or 80386) did for the personal computer industry.

DIGITAL SPEECH INTERPOLATION DSI. A type of multiplexing. A way of sharing bandwidth among a larger number of users than we really have circuits for. DSI allocates the silent periods in human speech to active users. At least 50% of a voice conversation is always quiet. The technique was originally called TASI (Time Assigned Speech Interpolation). TASI and DSI are lousy for data because they "clip" the first little bit of every new snippet of conversation — unless you hog the channel the whole time by talking incessantly or transmitting continuously. If you pause, you'll get clipping as the system drops you and then reconnects you. Clipping can ruin the meaning of the beginning of data conversations, unless the header knows that TASI or DSI is coming up or the data transmission is following some reasonable protocol and can resend the data. Unfortunately, this slows transmission. DSI and TASI are somewhat similar techniques to STATISTICAL MULTIPLEXING.

DIGITAL SUBSCRIBER LINE A fancy name for an ISDN BRI channel. Here's AT&T's definition: "A three-channel digital line that links the ISDN customer's terminal to the telephone company switch with four ordinary copper telephone wires. Operated at the Basic Rate Interface (with two 64-kilobit per second circuit-switched channels and one 16-kilobit packet switched channel), the DSL can carry both voice and data signals at the same time, in both directions, as well as the signaling date used for call information and customer data. With the introduction of the AT&T 5E5 generic, up to eight different users can be served by a single DSL." See also ISDN.

DIGITAL SWITCHING A connection in which binary encoded information is routed between an input and an output port by means of time-division multiplexing rather than by a dedicated circuit.

DIGITAL VIDEO INTERACTIVE DVI. A compression and playback technology originally developed by RCA's Sarnoff Research Institute and eventually acquired by Intel Corp. DVI is not a compression technique per se but a brand name for a set of processor chips that Intel is developing to compress video onto disk and to de-compress it for playback in real time at the U.S. standard motion video rate of 30 frames per second. The chip set includes both a pixel processor, which performs most of the decompression and also handles special video effects, and a display processor, which performs the rest of the decompression and produces the video output. DVI's greatest long-term advantage, according to Nick Arnett writing in PC Magazine, is that its microprocessors are programmable, so DVI can be adapted to a variety of compression and decompression schemes.

DIGITAL-TO-ANALOG CONVERSION A circuit that accepts digital signals and converts them into analog signals. A modem typically has such a circuit. It also has other circuits, such as those doing with signaling. See MODEM.

DIGITIZE Converting an analog or continuous signal into a series of ones and zeros, i.e. into a digital format. See DELTA MODULATION and PULSE CODE MODULATION. See also the Appendix.

DIGITIZED VOICE Analog voice signals represented in digital form. There are many ways of digitizing voice. See Pulse Code Modulation for the most common.

DIGROUP Two groups of 12 digital channels combined to form one single 24-channel T-1 system.

DIMENSION An analog PBX that used PAM techniques, first introduced in the late 1970s by Western Electric (now AT&T Technologies) for AT&T. Now effectively discontinued except for the hotel/motel version. Some claim Archie McGill was responsible for Dimension. Others claim it was Bob Hawk.

DIODE MATRIX RINGING A method of connecting a common audible line to a system so that all stations do not ring on all lines. See also MATRIX RINGING.

DIODEA A semiconductor device which allows electricity to pass through it in only one direction, restricting flow the other way.

DIP See DIP SWTICH.

DIP SWITCH Dual In-Line Package. A teeny tiny switch usually attached to a printed circuit board. It may peek through an opening in a piece of equipment. It may not. It usually requires a ball point pen or small screwdriver to change. There are only two settings — on or off. Or 1 or 0. But printed circuit boards often have many DIP switches. They're used to configure the board in a semipermanent way. The DIP switches are similar to integrated circuit chips which have two rows (dual) of pins in a row (in-line) that fit into holes on a printed circuit board. If something doesn't work when you first install it, check the dip switches first. Then check the cable connecting it to something else.

DIPLEXER A device that couples a transmitter and a receiver to the same antenna for use in mobile communications.

DIPOLE Antenna fed from the center. Name often applied to "rabbit ear" antenna.

DIRECT BROADCAST SATELLITE DBS. A satellite transmitting TV programs which can be received by small and somewhat inexpensive dish antennas often installed in backyards or on the roofs of houses. Direct broadcast satellites have generated more interest in Europe, which suffers from a lack of TV programs (good and bad), than in the U.S. which has plenty. The backyard satellite antennas you see in America are not receiving signals from Direct Broadcast Satellites. They are receiving them from satellites designed to transmit and receive from large, commercial dishes.

DIRECT CONNECT A term describing a customer hooking directly into a long-distance telephone company's switching office, bypassing the local phone company. Such "direct connect" could be via a leased copper pair, a specially-run copper pair, a fiber optic or a private microwave system. See DIRECT ELECTRICAL CONNECTION, which is different.

DIRECT CONNECT MODEM A modem connected to telephone lines using a modular plug or wired directly to the outside phone line. It thus transfers electrical signals directly to the phone network without any intermediary protective device. Direct connect modems must be certified by the FCC. Direct connect modems are more much reliable and more accurate than acoustically coupled modems. Virtually all modems these days are directly connected. One day payphones will even come with RJ-11 jacks into which you can plug the modem of your portable laptop computer.

DIRECT CONTROL SWITCHING The switching path is set up directly through the network by dial pulses without the use of central control. The telex network is an example of direct control switching. A step by step central office also uses direct control switching.

DIRECT DEPARTMENT CALLING DDC. A telephone service that routes incoming calls on a specific trunk or group of trunks to specific phones or groups of phones.

DIRECT DISTANCE DIALING DDD. A telephone service which lets a user dial long distance calls directly to telephones outside the user's local service area without operator assistance.

DIRECT ELECTRICAL CONNECTION A metallic connection between two things. The normal electrical way of connecting two things. This dumb definition is included in this dictionary because there was a time back in the early 1970s and before, when you couldn't (i.e. weren't allowed to) directly electrically connect your own phone or phone system to the nation's phone network. Those were the "good old days" when they (the Bell System) were trying to convince the world that electrically connecting anyone else's phones could harm the network. They never did prove this, and so today we have direct electrical connection of FCC-certified phone equipment. It's certified so it won't cause any harm to the network. See PART 68.

DIRECT IN TERMINATION Incoming calls on a PBX may be programmed to route directly to preselected telephones without the attendant intervening. DIT features may be assigned to trunk circuits on a day, night or full time basis. Direct In Termination is slightly different from DIRECT INWARD DIALING, though how different depends on whose PBX you're using.

DIRECT INTERLATA CONNECTING TRUNK GROUPS Those trunk groups used for switched LATA access that interconnect Interexchange Carriers (IXCs) used to connect that Point of Presence (POPs) directly with the Bell Operating Company (BOC) end office switching system.

DIRECT INWARD DIALING DID. The ability for a caller outside a company to call an internal extension without having to pass through an operator or attendant. In large PBX systems, the dialed digits are passed down the line from the CO (central office). The PBX then completes the call. Direct Inward Dialing is often proposed as Centrex's major feature. See also DIRECT INWARD SYSTEM ACCESS (DISA) for another approach to DID.

DIRECT INWARD SYSTEM ACCESS DISA. This feature of a telephone system allows an outside caller to dial directly into the telephone system and access all the system's features and facilities. DISA is typically used for making long distance calls from home using the company's less expensive long distance lines, like WATS or tie lines. It's also used for leaving dictation for the typing pool. With DISA, you can dial individual extensions without the aid (or hindrance) of an operator. To use DISA, one must punch in a short string of numbers as a password code. The problem with DISA is that "phone phreakers" (i.e. unauthorized people) often acquire that number or figure it out and run up expensive long distance phone calls. It's best to restrict DISA to trusted people and check the numbers called and bills generated. Changing the password code from time to time can help prevent this. DISA is acquiring a whole new life. It's becoming something called AUTOMATED ATTENDANT. An additional piece of equipment, called an automated attendant, is placed next to the phone system. You dial a special phone number (as you do with DISA). You're answered by a recording that says "Dial the extension you want." In DISA, the response is typically just a tone. An automated attendant is designed to save on operators and speed up outside people getting to talk to your inside people. Automated attendant is being suggested as a lower-cost alternative to Centrex.

DIRECT OUTWARD DIALING DOD. The ability to dial directly from an extension without having to go through an operator or attendant. In PBX and hybrid phone systems, you dial 9, listen for a dial tone, and then dial the number you want to reach. In some phone systems, you don't have to listen for the second dial tone. You can dial straight through. All phone systems now have DOD. The older ones didn't, especially cordboard PBXs. Some Club Meds and lots of cheap hotels (especially the ones Harry — the editor — stays in) do not have DOD.

DIRECT STATION SELECT DSS. A piece of key system equipment usually attached to an operator's phone set. When the operator needs to call a particular extension he/she simply touches the corresponding button on the Direct Station Select equipment. Typically DSS equipment/feature is part of a Busy Lamp Field (BLF), which shows with lights what's happening at each extension. Is it busy? Is it on hold, etc.?

DIRECT STATION SELECT INTERCOM DSS. An interoffice caller can punch one button on his or her phone and dial his desired party, instead of dialing the full intercom number. Direct station select is like having an auto dial or speed dial button for everyone in the office. DSS saves time, but adds more buttons to the phone.

DIRECT TRUNK A trunk between two class 5 central offices.

DIRECT TRUNK ACCESS A PBX feature. By dialing some digits, the attendant can directly access any specific trunk. You'd do this if you want to check the trunk for problems, etc.

DIRECT TRUNK SELECT Permits you, the user, or the attendant to access an individual outgoing trunk instead of one chosen by the PBX from a group of trunks. You may want to grab a special trunk to get access to a specially conditioned data line, for example.

DIRECTIONAL COUPLER A device put in a microwave system's waveguide to couple a transmitter and receiver to the same antenna.

DIRECTORY A listing of all the files on a floppy diskette or hard disk. A directory may also contain other information such as the size of the files and the amount of free space remaining. 2. Also a telephone directory.

DIRECTORY ASSISTANCE DA. Formerly known as "Information," but changed because they were getting too many stupid questions. DA is provided by the local telephone company. It allows the subscriber to call for phone numbers. In most states, the local phone company charges for this service, or will begin to very shortly. AT&T and MCI charge for long distance directory assistance. Most local phone companies will give you the person's address as well as his phone number if you ask for it.

DIRECTORY NUMBER The full complement of digits associated with the name of a subscriber in a telephone directory. This is a very long way of saying the obvious, namely your phone number.

DIRECTORY PACKAGE The process of adding, deleting and moving people attached to PBX or Centrex phones is more than simply programming in new extensions. Or should be. First, there are the changes necessary for the call accounting system. Second, there are changes necessary for "The Corporate Phone Directory." In the past, the directory bore little relation to the telephone system and it was often months, and sometimes years behind the actual phone system. Now some phone systems are incorporating various Directory Software Packages into the PBXs. Some features included in these systems are the ability to dial someone by name — both for the attendant and for the individual phone user, i.e. dial HARRY, or HAR, instead of 3245. Some also include the ability to interface to the call accounting system. So that who's in what corporate department corresponds to which department's bill. There's also that important thing called a Telephone Directory. It would be useful if you could hook a laser printer to the telephone system and tell it to print, in neat, photo-ready columns, an alphabetical (by last name), departmental or any other sorted telephone directory. Some of the newer PBXs have "directory package" features which include some or all of the above. Most users find today's necessity of at least three different systems to be a pain in the behind. Rightly so. The three different systems are CDR, phone directory and extension dialing in the PBX. The three are often out of synch.

DISA See DIRECT INWARD SYSTEM ACCESS.

DISABLE You figured this one. It means to prevent a hardware device from working. Unplugging it is the easiest way. It also refers to a tone or other signal which you send over a phone line to disable the equipment at the other end.

DISC An older method of spelling DISK, as in Floppy DISK. Disc is used in CD (Compact Discs). See also MS-DOS.

DISCHARGE BLOCK A protective device through which unwanted voltages discharge to ground.

DISCONNECT The breaking or release of a circuit connecting two telephones or data devices. 2. The annual April Fools issue of TELECONNECT Magazine. Sometimes funny. Sometimes not.

DISCONNECT SIGNAL The signal that's sent from one end to indicate to the other to shut down the connection.

DISCONNECT SUPERVISION The change in electrical state from off-hook to on-hook. This indicates that the transmission connection is no longer needed.

DISCOUNTED PAYBACK PERIOD The number of years in which a stream of cash flows, discounted at an organization's cost of money, repays an initial investment.

DISCOUNTING The process of computing the present worth of a future cash flow by reducing it by a factor equivalent to the organization's cost of money (or some other measure of the value of money as measured by an interest rate) and the time until the cash flow occurs.

DISCRETIONARY PREVIEW DIALLING A single button dialing

technique where the agent initiates a call with a single key stroke. Often used in association with a CRT tied to a database. Upon hitting a single button the system selects the phone number field from the screen and dials the number. Contrast this with Forced Preview Dialing. When the call ends, the computer brings up the next screen and starts dialing the call without the agent helping or hindering.

DISCRIMINATING RINGING See DISTINCTIVE RINGING.

DISCUSSION A method of confirming others in their errors.

DISH Typically a parabolic microwave antenna — used for receiving line-of-sight terrestrial signals or signals from satellites.

DISK A piece of plastic or metal upon which a coating has been applied and which can thus, record computer information magnetically or optically. See also MS-DOS.

DISK DRIVE A device containing motors, electronics and other gadgetry for storing (writing) and retrieving (reading) data on a disk. See also MS-DOS.

DISK OPERATING SYSTEM See DOS.

DISK PACK A series of disks mounted horizontally and arranged as a single unit. A disk pack contains more space for storing and retrieving information than one single disk.

DISK SECTOR Magnetic diskettes are typically divided into tracks, each of which contains a number of sectors. A sector typically contains a predetermined amount of data, such as 256 bytes.

DISK SERVER A device equipped with disks and a program that permits users to create and store files on the disks. Each user has access to their own section of the disk. It gives users disk space which they would not normally have at their own personal computers. Some sort of connection between the disk server and PC is needed, like a LAN. Compare with file server, which allows users to share files.

DISK/FILE SERVER A mass storage device that can be accessed by several computers, usually through a local area network (LAN).

DISKLESS PC Just what it says: a PC without a disk drive. Used on a LAN, a diskless PC runs by booting DOS from the file server. It does this via a read-only memory chip on its network interface card called a remote boot ROM. Diskless PCs are cheaper than PCs with disks, they're more compact and they offer better security since users can't make off with floppy disks of important and sensitive data or add their own virus-ridden programs to file servers. Diskless PCs appeal primarily to users interested in security. One system of diskless PCs allow the system operator to disable and physically lock the machine's various ports and the computer case itself. Should something go wrong with the machine, the ports can be restored to operating condition by letting the system allow a technician to attach a laptop computer and run diagnostic programs.

DISKLESS WORKSTATION See DISKLESS PC.

DISOSS IBM's Distributed Office Support System.

DISPERSION The degree of scattering taking place in the light beam as it travels along the fiber optic. Or the overlapping of a light signal on one wavelength to different wavelengths because of reflected rays and the different refractive index of the core fiber material.

DISPLAY The visual presentation of information, usually on a TV-like screen or an array of illuminated digits.

DISTANT LEARNING A Pacific Bell term for students sitting in front of TVs and phones and participating in classes that are being held and delivered elsewhere. In one of PacBell's trials, they used a T-1 signal, so the distant lecturer could see and hear his distant students using full-color video.

DISTINCTIVE DIAL TONES In some phone systems, dial tones sound different. An internal dial tone sounds different to an external dial tone. The logical reason for this is simply to alert the user as to whether he or she is making an intercom or an outside local or long distance call.

DISTINCTIVE RINGING Enables telephone users to distinguish types of incoming calls such as outside calls and inside (intercom) calls by the tone of the ringing.

DISTORT To change some characteristic of a signal during its transmission. See DISTORTION.

DISTORTION The difference in values between two measurements of a signal — for example, between the transmitted and received signal. "Distortion" typically refers to analog signals.

DISTRIBUTED COMMON CONTROL There are two elements of telephone switching: The switching itself and the control of that switching. The earliest step-by-step telephone switches had their "Control" built into them. The dialing information at the beginning of the call physically moved switches. You could say, as a result, that control was distributed throughout the switching system. Then came the 1940s and crossbar exchanges, and the economics pointed to centralizing control. Then came computerized or stored program control (SPC) switches in which large computers were used centrally to perform virtually all the functions of the erstwhile electromechanical senders, registers, markers, etc. — those things which affect the setting up and tearing down of the call. As computers got smaller and as microprocessors appeared (the so-called computer on a chip), it became economical and efficient to place inexpensive microprocessors in the telephone circuits themselves, in essence getting much of the processing done before it hits the central processing unit. Increasingly, as special microprocessors (so-called "computers on a chip") for telecommunications evolve, we will see more and more of the processing being distributed to further and further away from the central point and closer and closer to the originating telephone instrument. It will be rare in coming years for telephones to come without microprocessors. One day, each phone will have its own switch and the rest of the system will just be one gigantic loop of cable — not unlike today's local area networks.

DISTRIBUTED DATA PROCESSING DDP. A data processing

arrangement in which the computers are decentralized — i.e. scattered in various places. Hence, processing occurs in a number of distributed locations and only semi-processed information is communicated on data communications lines from remote points to the central computers. The object of DDP is to save telecommunications charges and to improve network response time.

DISTRIBUTED MANAGEMENT ENVIRONMENT A compilation of technologies now being selected by the Open Software Foundation to create a unified network and systems management framework, as well as applications. Those technologies will complement OSF's own Unix implementation, OSF/1, as well as other operating systems.

DISTRIBUTED MICROPROCESSOR COMMON CONTROL This means that the system employs many individual microprocessors to control system and telephone phone functions. They may be located in central processing equipment or in the telephones themselves.

DISTRIBUTED NODES PBX and its "slave" switches which are physically in separate buildings, in separate areas of the campus, in separate parts of the town.

DISTRIBUTED PROCESSING A network of computers such that the processing of information is initiated in local computers, and the resultant data is sent to a central computer for further processing with the data from other local systems. The term also covers computing jobs "farmed out" from a central site to remote processors where faster processing or specialized databases are available. Distributed Processing is often a more efficient use of computer processing power since each CPU can be devoted to a certain task. A LAN is the perfect example of distributed processing. See also DISTRIBUTED DATA PROCESSING.

DISTRIBUTED QUEUE DUAL BUS DQDB. A connectionless packet-switched protocol, normally residing in the Medium-Access Control sublayer of the data link layer. Definition from Bellcore in reference to Advanced Intelligent Network.

DISTRIBUTED SWITCHING When electronics and computers were expensive it made sense to centralize them and run individual lines out for miles to subscribers. Then the economies changed. Electronics and computers became cheaper and running phone lines for miles became very expensive. So switching companies started building small switches which they could put closer to subscribers. Thus, individual local loops would be shorter and the long lines going back to the larger central office would be more efficiently used — namely by more people. The remote, or distributed switches, are called everything from remote switches to slave switches (because they slave off the main one which is distant). Usually these remote switches are unattended.

DISTRIBUTION Refers to the arrangement of premises wiring runs and their associated hardware required to implement the planned customer premises wiring system extending from the Network Interface Jack to each

Communications Outlet.

DISTRIBUTION CABLE Part of the outside cable plant connecting feeder or subfeeder cables to drop wires or buried service wires that connect to the customer's premises. In simpler language, it's the cable from the serving area interface — a box on a pole, in the ground, etc. — to the lightning protection at the entrance to the customer's premises. See also FEEDER PLANT and DROP WIRE.

DISTRIBUTION FRAME Cables coming in from thousands of subscribers need to connect to the correct ports on a central office. Similarly, cables coming in from many PBX extensions need to connect to the PBX. The cables could be directly wired to the CO or to the PBX. This would be inflexible. It would make future moves and changes a nightmare. So the solution is something called a Distribution Frame. Basically it's a giant wire connecting devices made of metal. There's no electronics in it whatsoever. On one side we punch down the wires coming in from the outside world. On the other side, we punch down the wires coming in from the CO or PBX. Both sides are connected with wire that's called "jumper" wire. By pulling off one end of the jumper wire and moving it to another location we can quickly change phone numbers, add or substract cabling (one, two or three pairs for normal or electronic phones, etc.) In big central offices, distribution frames can span whole city blocks and the "jumper" wires can be several hundred yards long. Designing distribution frames and their layout in advance is critical, otherwise it becomes a mess and traces where jumper wires go becomes an enormous time-consuming job.

DISTRIBUTION GROUP A group of telephone extensions on an automatic call distributor (ACD). The ACD answers the incoming calls then checks to see if any agents' phones are free. If none are free, it delivers the caller a message and then puts the caller on hold. Which line the call has come in on may determine which group of agents should handle that call. They would be called a Distribution Group. Once the call is released from hold, it may be sent to a member of that Distribution Group following some pre-determined mathematical formula — for example, so that everyone's workload is kept constant, or a group of people are kept busy.

DIVERSITY In microwave communications, the strength of a microwave signal can decrease for many reasons — heat, rain, fog, etc. This is not good if the objective is to get reliable communications. One solution is to simultaneously send and receive two microwave signals at slightly different frequencies. Since different frequencies respond differently to weather problems, the likelihood is that at least one will get through well. This is called diversity.

DIVESTITURE On January 8, 1982, AT&T signed a Consent Decree with the U.S. Department of Justice, stipulating that on midnight December 30, 1983, AT&T would divest itself of its 22 telephone operating companies. According to the terms of the Divestiture, those 22 operating Bell telephone companies would be formed into seven regional holding companies of roughly equal size. Terms of the Divestiture placed business restrictions on

AT&T and the BOCs. The Federal judge overseeing Divestiture, Judge Harold Greene, has slowly lifted many of the restrictions. So discussing them in this dictionary is meaningless. They'll be changed by the time the dictionary is printed. And changed again by the time you read it.

DLC See DATA LINK CONTROL.

DLE Data Link Escape. A control character used exclusively to provide supplementary line control signals, control character sequences or DLE sequences. In packet switching, Data Link Escape is a name applied to the Control P non-print character which is used to swap the PAD from the data mode to the command mode in packet switched networks.

DLSE Dial Line Service Evaluation.

DMA Direct Memory Access. A fast method of moving data from a storage device or LAN interface card directly to RAM which speeds processing. In essence, DMA is direct access to memory by a peripheral device that bypasses the CPU.

DMC See DIGITAL MICROWAVE CORPORATION.

DMI Digital Multiplexed Interface. In private automatic branch exchange or PABX technology, one of two voice/data PABX standards for using T-1 transmission that involves 64 kbps channels, representing a move toward an open architecture via integrated services digital network (ISDN). Compare with CPI.

DMI AT&T'S Digital Multiplexed Interface. A PBX to computer interface that divides the T-1 trunk into 23 user channels and one signaling channel.

DMI-BOS Digital Multiplexed Interface-Bit Oriented Signaling. A form of signaling, which uses the 24th channel of each DSI to carry signaling information, allowing clear channel 64 Kbps functionality.

DMO Digital Modification Order.

DMS Digital Multiplex System. Also the name of a line of digital central office switches from Northern Telecom. There are DMS-10s, DMS-100s, DMS-100Fs and DMS-200s and, by the time you read this, probably more. See also DMS SUPERNODE.

DMS SUPERNODE The SuperNode is a very flexible central office switch from Northern Telecom which can be configured as a high-capacity local or tandem switch with Common Channel Signaling 7 (CCS7) Service Switching Point (SSP) function, a Signaling Transfer Point (STP), a Service Control Point (SCP), a Digital Network CrossConnect (DNX) system or a network service node with custom programming applications. In 1988, the DMS SuperNode offered twice the capacity of the DMS-100 switch (the older Northern Telecom central office) based on the NT40 processor. This capacity, according to Northern, will double by 1990.

DN See DIRECTORY NUMBER.

DNA Digital Network Architecture. The framework within which Digital Equipment Corporation (DEC) designs and develops all of its communications products. DNA includes many standards of the OSI Model.

Some of these standards will be adopted into ISDN. Acronym also by Network Development Corporation for their network offering.

DNAR Directory Number Analysis Reporting.

DNC Dynamic Network Controller.

DNIC Data Network Identification Code. An address to reach a host computer system residing on a different packet switched network than the one you're on. The data equivalent of a telephone number with country code and area code. Typically the DNIC is a four digit number. The first three digits of a DNIC specify a country. The fourth digit specifies a public data network within that country. See also DATA NETWORK IDENTIFICATION CODE.

DNPIC Directory Number Primary InterLATA Carrier.

DNR 1. Dialed Number Recorder. Also called a Pen Register. An instrument that records telephone dial pulses as inked dashes on paper tape. A touch-tone decoder performs the same thing for a touch-tone telephone. 2. Dynamic Network Reconfiguration. Allows IBM networks to change addresses without reloading and bringing the network down.

DO A word in a high-level language program which comes before a collection of things to be done, i.e. statements to be executed.

DO-NOT-DISTURB Makes a telephone appear busy to any incoming calls. May be used on intercom-only, by extension line-only or both.

DO-WHILE A programming statement used to perform instructions in a loop while a certain condition exists — i.e. the variable Y is less than 20.

DOC See DYNAMIC OVERLOAD CONTROL.

DOCUMENTATION Written text describing the system, how it works and how to work it. In most cases of high technology products, documentation is awful. Better documentation helps sell equipment and software. Please write your instruction manuals better. Please.

DOCKET Formal FCC/State regulatory commission proceeding, also referred to as a case.

DOD Department of Defense.

DOLBY A system of noise/hiss reduction invented by Ray Dolby, widely used in consumer, professional and broadcast audio applications.

DOMAIN In IBM's SNA, domain is a host-based systems services control point (SSCP), the physical units (PUs), logical units, (LUs), links, link stations and all the affiliated resources that the host (SSCP) can control.

DOMESTIC ARC The portion of the geostationary orbit allowing a satellite to return a footprint that almost covers the continental United States.

DOMINANT CARRIER The long distance service provider which dominates a particular market and is subject to tougher regulation than its competitors. An FCC term.

DON'T ANSWER RECALL Allows an extension user on a PBX to automatically retry a call by dialing a special digit code.

DOS Disk Operating System, as in MS-DOS, which stands for MicroSoft

Disk Operating System or PC-DOS which stands for Personal Computer Disk Operating System.

DOS is the software that organizes how a computer reads, writes and reacts with its disks — floppy or hard — and talks to its various input/output devices, including keyboards, screens, serial and parallel ports, printers, modems, etc. The most popular operating system for PCs is MS-DOS from Microsoft, Bellevue, WA. PC-DOS is MS-DOS from IBM. DOS 3.1 was the first version of MS- and PC-DOS that offered functions supporting LANs. It has hooks so that programs can lock data records and files, crucial in multi-user LAN applications. DOS 3.1 (and higher) is now a standard, and any network operating system that supports it also supports applications that lock files and records via 3.1 function calls. This standardization allowed applications to be portable across different LAN systems. Later versions of DOS — 3.2, 3.3 and 4.01 — also support the same locking functions, but the functions still go under the name of 3.1. See MS-DOS for information on the FAT.

DOT ADDRESSABLE GRAPHICS Refers to the mode of operation on a dot matrix printer which allows you to control each element in the dot matrix printhead. With this feature, you may produce complex graphics drawings.

DOUBLE CAMP-ON INDICATION Alerts a phone trying to camp-on to another phone that a call is already camping there.

DOUBLE INTERRUPTED RING Two quick rings followed by a period of silence indicating the arrival of an outside call in some systems.

DOUBLE-POLE A double-pole switch is one which opens and closes both sides of the same circuit simultaneously. Most electrical circuits open and close with only one side being broken.

DOV Data Over Voice. A technology used primarily with local Centrex services or special customer premises PBXs for transmitting data and voice simultaneously over twisted-pair copper wiring. Typical data rates for Centrex operation are 9.6 Kbps and 19.2 Kbps.

DOVPATH TRANSPORT SERVICE A New York Telephone service which lets you transmit both voice and data simultaneously on one phone line. The data is carried on a higher frequency, i.e. "Over the Voice." Hence the name Data Over Voice, or DOV. DOVPATH lets you transmit up to 19.2 Kbps asynchronous data, which could be fast enough for talking to a distant mainframe computer.

DOWNLINE LOADING A system in which programs are loaded into the memory of a computer system via the same communication line(s) the system normally uses to communicate with the rest of a network. As opposed to systems in which all programs are loaded into the computer from a disk or tape associated with the computer. A PC connected to a LAN may use this type of loading when it is first turned on in the morning to get the information it needs from a file server. Diskless PCs always work this way.

DOWNLINK 1. The part of a transmission link reaching from a satellite to the ground. Some satellite transmission circuits, especially international ones, are priced and billed separately for the uplink and the downlink. This is because their transmissions are provided by different carriers. 2. In packet data communications, a downlink is a link from an NC or PAD to another NC or PAD on a different level. The defining of downlinks and uplinks depends on the network configuration of PADs, their relationships to each other and the direction of data transmission.

DOWNLOADING The act of receiving data from another computer into your computer. It's also called to RECEIVE. The opposite is UPLOAD or TRANSMIT. You have to be very careful distinguishing between the two. Choosing the "Download" option in some communications programs automatically erases a file of the same name that was meant for transmission.

DOWNSTREAM In data communications network, downstream is a session established in an MSTX network when an LU and its PU are powered on and connected. The NC establishes a SSCP LU with the LU.

DOWNSTREAM CHANNEL The frequency multiplexed band in a CATV channel which distributes signals from the headend to the users. Compare with UPSTREAM CHANNEL, the band of frequencies on a CATV channel reserved for transmission from the user to the CATV company's headend.

DOWNTIME The total time a telephone system is not working due to some software or hardware failure. You know your vendor is about to lie when he begins to answer a question about "downtime."

DP Dial Pulse (as in dialing a phone) or Data Processing. Also called EDP for Electronic Data Processing. Now more commonly called Management Information Systems — or MIS.

DPA Digital Port Adapter. A Northern Telecom word.

DPN Lanscope A Northern Telecom software package for remote management of local area networks over wide area networks based on Northern's DPN-100 digital data packet networking system. DPN Lanscope provides fault and performance monitoring, resource management, software distribution and usage tracking for geographically dispersed LANs. Network configuration, status, alarms and performance information are presented to a centralized LAN administrator through a graphics interface.

DPBX Digital PBX.

DPN Northern Telecom term for Data Packet Network.

DPP Distributed Processing Peripheral.

DPU Dynamic Path Update. Allows IBM networks to add new network nodes or change backup routing paths while the front-end is still operating.

DPX DataPath loop extension.

DQDB Distributed Queue Double Bus. IEEE's standard 802.6 for MANs (Metropolitan Area Networks). Formerly called QPSX (Queued Packet and Synchronous Exchange).

DRAFT PROPOSAL An ISO standards document that has been registered and numbered but not yet approved.

DRAIN WIRE In a cable, an uninsulated wire laid over the component or components and used as a ground connection.

DRAWING In the manufacture of wire, pulling the metal through a die or series of dies in order to reduce the diameter to a specified size.

DRESSING CABLE You "dress" cable by taking multiple cables and joining them together neatly with cable ties. A nicely dressed, clean installation is a sign of telephony professionalism. It still exists.

DRIFT A slow change in a normally constant signal. The term typically applies to movements in the signal's frequency.

DRIVER A software module that "drives" the data out of a specific hardware port. The port in question will usually have another device connected, such as a printer or modem, and the Driver will be organized in software (i.e. configured) to communicate with the device.

DROP An intermediate terminal point between the connecting ends of a multipoint channel.

DROP AND INSERT A term applied to a device that can add data (insert) to a T-1 data stream, or act as a terminating node (drop) to other devices connected to it.

DROP CABLE In local area networks, a cable that connects perpendicularly to the main network cable or bus, and attaches to the DTE equipment.

DROP CABLET The outside wire pair which connects your house or office to the transmission line coming from the central office. See also DROP WIRE, which is different.

DROP OUTS Drop outs are one major cause of errors in data communications circuits. The technical definition is that the signal level drops more than 12 dB (decibels) for more than 4 milliseconds. It means some of your data will not arrive. A four millisecond dropout in a transmission at 2,400 bits per second will lose about 10 bits. A "dropout" is similar to a person's voice fades away in a telephone conversation. To correct the problem of dropout,we will ask the person (or computer) at the other end to repeat what they just said. "Huh?" This is called retransmission of data.

In telephony, dropouts are defined as incidents when signal level unexpectedly drops at least 12 dB for more than 4 milliseconds. (Bell standard allows no more than two dropouts per 15 minute period.)

DROP SET All parts needed to complete connection from the drop (wall plate, coupling, MOD-MOD) to the terminal equipment. This would typically include a modular line cord and interface adapter.

DROP SIDE Defines all cabling and connectors from the terminal equipment to the patch panel or punch down block designated for terminal equipment at the distribution frame.

DROP WIRE Wires going from your phone company to the 66 Block or protector in your building. See also DISTRIBUTION CABLE.

DRUNKEN SWEDE A way of describing the sound of a computer doing text-to-speech conversion. "Why, he sounds like a drunken Swede." This great definition from Stuart Segal of Phone Base Systems, Inc., in Vienna, VA. Says Stuart, "Our people think that a drunken Swede has recorded this message."

DRY CIRCUIT A circuit over which voice signals are transmitted and which carries no direct current.

DRY CONTACT An electrical contact made by a pair of metallic contacts. You might close a metallic contact, thus operating a relay which might turn something of higher power on or off. For example, a low voltage signal in a key system might cause a dry contact to close, thus causing much higher voltage to flow to a bell, a klaxon, a strobe light. Wheelock Signals makes lots of dry contact devices. There is no such animal as a "wet contact," except maybe an acquaintance who's crying or a phone system under water.

DRY LOOP POWERING Refers to local (not span) plowering, and a transmission medium other than copper wire (microwave/fiber optic).

DRY T-1 A T-1 line with an unpowered interface. A T-1 line with a power is called "Wet."

DRY TWISTED PAIR A normal telephone twisted pair without loading coils. It carries only data, not data and voice.

DS- A hierarchy of digital signal speeds used to classify capacities of lines and trunks. The fundamental speed level is DS-0 (64-kilobits per second) and the highest is DS-4 (about 274 million bits per second. Here are the definitions: DS-1, DS-1C, DS-2, DS-3, DS-4. They correspond to 1.544, 3.152, 6.312, 44.736, and 274.176 Mbps. DS-1 is also called T-1.

DS-0 Digital Service, level 0. It is 64,000 bps, the worldwide standard speed for digitizing one voice conversation. There are 24 DS- channels in a DS-1.

DS-1 Digital Service, level 1. It is 1.544 Mbps in North America, 2.048 Mbps elsewhere. Why there's no consistency is one of those wonderful questions. The 1.544 standard is an old Bell System standard. The 2.048 standard is a CCITT standard. Standard for 1.544 Mbps is 24 voice conversations. Standard for 2.048 megabits is 30 conversations.

DS-1C Digital Service, level 1C. It is 3.152 Mbps in North America and is carried on T-1.

DS-2 Digital Service, level 2. It is 6.312 Mbps in North America and is carried on T-2.

DS-3 Digital Service, level 3. Equivalent of 28 T-1 channels, and operating at 44.736 Mbps. Also called T-3.

DS-4 Digital Service, level 4. A 273 Mbps digital signal carried on T-4.

DSO, DS1 Pronounced "D-S Zero" and "D-S One", these are units of transmission bandwidth. DS1 is the T-1 connection, operating at 1.544 Mbps. A single DSO represents 64 Kbps. Twenty-four DSO's (24x64 Kbps) equal one DS1. See DS-0 and DS-1.

DSO-A Refers to a process where a subrate signal (2.4, 4.8, or 9.6 Kbps) is repeated 20, 10 or 5 times, respectively to make a 64 Kbps DS-0 channel.

DSO-B Refers to a process performed by a subrate multiplexer where twenty 2.4 Kbps, ten 4.8 Kbps, or five 9.6 Kbps signals are bundled into one 64 Kbps DS-0 channel.

DS1/DS-1 Digital Signal Level 1. A telephony term describing a 1.544 Mbps digital signal carried on a T-1 facility. See DS-1.

DSA Distributed Systems Architecture, the network architecture developed by Honeywell.

DSI Digital Speed Interpolation. A technique for squeezing more voice conversations onto a line. DSI digitizes speech so it can be cut into slices, such that no bits are transmitted when no one is speaking. As soon as speech begins, bits flow again.

DSL See DIGITAL SUBSCRIBER LINE.

DSN Distributed Systems Network, the network architecture developed by Hewlett-Packard.

DSP Display System Protocol or Digital Signal Processor. A Digital Signal Processor is a specialized computer chip designed to perform speedy and complex operations on digitized waveforms. Useful in processing sound and video.

DSP MODULE An internal module of the National Sensor Conductor NS32FX16 processor that handles vector operations on complex variables, enhancing DSP performance of the device.

DSR Data Set Ready. This signal is on pin 6 of the RS-232-C connector. It means the modem (which some telephone companies call a "data set") is ready to send data from the terminal. Some modems use Data Set Ready. Some don't. Modems that are snooty enough to give you the DSR signal, are obnoxious enough to not work until they receive the DTR (Data Terminal Ready) signal from the terminal on pin 20. By bridging pins 6 and 20 on the connector at the modem, you can usually get it to work. If it doesn't, bridge in pin 8 (carrier detect) as well.

DSU Digital Service Unit, also called Data Service Unit. Converts RS-232-C or other terminal interface to DSX-1 interface. See DATA SERVICE UNIT.

DSX Digital Signal Cross-connect. See also DACS.

DSX-1 Digital Signal Cross-connect Level 1. The set of parameters for cross connecting DS-1 lines.

DSX-3 The designation for the DS3 point of interface (cross-connect).

DTC Digital Trunk Controller.

DTE Data Terminal Equipment. In the RS-232-C standard specification, the RS-232-C is connected between the DCE (Data Communications Equipment) and a DTE. The main differences between a DCE and a DTE are that pins two and three are reversed. See also DCE and the Appendix.

DTMF Dual Tone Multi-Frequency. A fancy term describing push button or Touchtone dialing. (Touchtone is a registered trademark of AT&T.) In DTMF, when you touch a button on a pushbutton pad, it makes a tone, actually a combination of two tones, one high frequency and one low frequency. Thus the name Dual Tone Multi Frequency. In U.S. telephony, there are actually two types of DTMF signaling, one used on normal business or home pushbutton/touchtone phones, and one used for signaling within the telephone network itself. When you go into a central office, look for the testboard. There you'll see what looks like a standard touchtone pad. Next to the pad there'll be a small toggle switch that allows you to choose the sounds the touchtone pad will make — either normal touchtone dialing or the network version.

DTMF CUT-THROUGH The capability of a voice response system to receive DTMF tones while the voice synethesizer is delivering information, i.e. during speech playback. This capability of DTMF cut-through saves the user waiting until the machine has played the whole message (which typically is a menu with options). The user can simply touchtone his response anytime during the message — when he first hears his selection number, when the message first starts, etc. When the voice processor hears the touchtoned selection (i.e. the DTMF cut-through), it stops speaking and jumps to the chosen selection. For example, the machine starts to say, "If you know the person you're calling, touchtone his extension in now." But before you hear the "If you know" you pushbutton in 230, which you know is Joe's extension. Bingo, the message stops and Joe's extension starts ringing.

DTMF REGISTER A printed circuit card in a switch that converts the DTMF signals coming from the phone into signals which can be used by the switch's stored program control, central computer to do its switching, etc.

DTMF TO DIAL PULSE CONVERSION A PBX feature. DTMF (pushbutton) phones are very popular. But sometimes you install a PBX with pushbutton phones in an area which doesn't have a central office which will respond to pushbutton tones. It's old. In this case, anyone dialing on a pushbutton phone will find that the PBX converts that dialing to rotary pulsing when the PBX accesses a trunk which can't handle pushbutton dialing. All this doesn't speed up the time the call takes to get through. It just speeds up the user's dialing and makes him or her feel she is dealing with a more modern phone system.

DTR Data Terminal Ready. A control signal sent from the DTE to the DCE that indicates that the DTE is powered on and ready to communicate. DTR can also be used for hardware flow control.

DTS Digital Termination Systems. Microwave based transmission technology designed for bypass functions for short-hop, line-of-sight applications. It never converts to analog. Is useful in high-volume, pure-data applications in urban settings where line costs are high. It requires FCC license and is referred to formally by FCC as Digital Electronic Message Service, or DEMS.

DTSR Dial Tone Speed Recording.

DTU Digital Test Unit.

DUAL TONE MULTI-FREQUENCY DTMF. A way of signaling consisting of a pushbutton or touchtone dial that sends out a sound which consists of two discrete tones, picked up and interpreted by telephone switches — either PBXs or central offices. See DTMF.

DUCT A pipe, tube or conduit through which cables or wires are passed. Duct space is always at a premium. If you ever install a duct, make sure it's twice the diameter you think you need. If you're lucky, it will last a couple of years. The cost of putting in thicker or extra ducts is peanuts compared to the cost of having to install additional ones later. Digging up places is getting very expensive, despite Ditch Witch, a company that makes the greatest backhoe trenching equipment. And has also the greatest name.

DUCTILE Capable of being drawn out, hammered thin or being flexed or bent without failure.

DUE DATE The date an event is to occur, i.e. an installation, a change or a connection. Some vendors give accurate due dates. Penalty clauses work most effectively in ensuring due dates are met.

DUMB TERMINAL A computer terminal with no processing or no programming capabilities. Hence, it derives all its power from the computer it is attached to — typically over a local hardwire or a phone line. There are many reasons for "dumb" terminals. They're cheap. They're foolproof. Dumb operators don't have to mess with floppy disks, etc. The require minimal training. Dumb terminals are typically used for simple data entry and data retrieval tasks. Their disadvantage is that everything must come from the central computer — not only the information (data record) but also the form in which to put it. This has led to the creation of "intelligent" terminals, which have a modicum of capabilities — such as an inbuilt (with software) form, some smart function keys and perhaps, a modicum of processing power, etc.

DUMP To copy the entire contents of something — memory, a file on a disk, a complete disk — to a printer or another magnetic storage medium.

DUPLEX Simultaneous two-way transmission in both directions.

DUPLEX CIRCUIT A telephone line or circuit used to transmit in both directions at the same time. Also referred to as full duplex as opposed to half duplex which allows transmission in only one direction at one time.

DUPLEX SIGNALING DX. A direct current signaling system that transmits signals directly on the cable pair.

DUPLEX TRANSMISSION Simultaneous two-way transmission in both directions. A data communications term.

DUTY CYCLE The ratio of operating time to total elapsed time for a device that operates intermittently. Usually expressed as a percentage.

DV-1 As in Northern Telecom's PBX/computer product called the Meridian DV-1.

DVI Digital Video Interactive. Intel's scheme for digitizing and compressing video and audio for storage, editing, playback and integration into PC applications.

DX SIGNALING A form of DC (direct current) signaling in which the differences in voltage on two pairs of a four-wire trunk indicates the supervision information, i.e. the call's beginning, its end, etc. See DUPLEX SIGNALING.

DYNAMIC Events are constantly changing.

DYNAMIC ANSWER This a term typically used in Automatic Call Distributors. The ability to dynamically assign the number of ring cycles (interrupt, more or less) to the queue period when agents are unavailable. The implication of being able to assign this number allows return supervision to the calling in person to be delayed and thus not allow billing on 800 INWATS lines to begin. This is a money saving feature. But it can cost you some customers if they get bored waiting for your phones to pick up.

DYNAMIC BANDWIDTH ALLOCATION A feature available on certain high-end T-1 multiplexers that allows the total bit rate of the multiplexer's tail circuits to exceed the bandwidth of the network trunk. This works because the multiplexer only assigns channels on the network trunk to circuits that are transmitting.

DYNAMIC CAPACITY ALLOCATION The process of determining and changing the amount of shared communications capacity assigned to nodes in the network based on current need.

DYNAMIC LOAD BALANCING A technique where a switching system, particularly multiple ACD systems, apportion the incoming call load to balance the workload. This is done dynamically in real time.

DYNAMIC MEMORY An inexpensive but relatively complicated form of semiconductor memory with two states: presence and absence of electrical charge.

DYNAMIC OVERLOAD CONTROL DOC. The feature of a switch which uses its translation tables and intelligence to allow the switch to adapt to changes in traffic loads by re-routing and blocking call attempts.

DYNAMIC RAM RAM memory that requires data to be refreshed periodically to prevent its loss in memory.

DYNAMIC RANGE In music, the range of amplitudes from loudest to softest. Expressed in decibels. The larger the figure, the more realistic or natural the sound.

DYNAMIC STORAGE ALLOCATION The allocation of memory space while a program is running. The memory is released when the program is complete.

E & M LEADS The pair of wires carrying signals between trunk equipment and a separate signaling equipment unit. The M lead transmits a ground or battery conditions to the signaling equipment. The E lead receives open or ground signals from the signaling equipment. These leads are also known as Ear and Mouth Leads. The Ear lead typically means to receive and the Mouth lead typically means to transmit. Changes of voltage on these leads convey such information as seizure of circuit, recognition of seizure, release of circuit, dialed digits, etc.

E & M SIGNALING See E & M LEADS.

EA SEE EQUAL ACCESS.

EADAS Engineering and Administration Data Acquisition System.

EADAS/NWM EADAS NetWork Management.

EAROM An acronym for Electrically Alterable Read-Only Memory. A type of ROM chip which can be erased and reprogrammed without having to be removed from the circuit board. An EAROM is reprogrammed electrically faster and more conveniently than an EPROM. An EAROM chip does not lose its memory when power is turned off.

EARTH STATION The antenna and associated equipment used to receive and/or transmit telecommunications signals via satellite.

EAS Extended Area Service. A novel name for a larger than normal local telephone calling area. The local phone company extends its subscribers the option of paying less per month for a small calling area and paying extra per individual call outside that area (i.e. the extended area), or paying more per month flat rate but having a larger calling area (i.e. having extended area service).

EAX Electronic Automatic Exchange. Term used throughout the non-Bell telephone industry to refer to an electronic central office. Similar to ESS (Electronic Switching System), the term used by AT&T and the Bell operating telephone companies.

EBCDIC (Pronounced Eb-si-dick.) Extended Binary Coded Decimal Interexchange Code. It is the way IBM codes characters, letters and numbers into a digital binary stream for use in its larger computers. EBCDIC codes characters into eight bits. This gives it 256 possible characters. In EBCDIC you get 256 thus — 2 x 2 x 2 x 2 x 2 x 2 x 2 x 2 = 256. See also EXTENDED CHARACTER SET.

EBCDIC is mainly used in IBM mainframes and minicomputers, while ASCII is used in IBM and non-IBM desktop microcomputers. EBCDIC is not compatible with ASCII, meaning that a computer which understands EBCDIC will not understand ASCII. But there are many real-time and non-real time translation programs around that will convert text files back and forth. See ASCII.

EBS Electronic Business Set.

ECCENTRICITY Like concentricity a measure of the center of a conductor's location with respect to the circular cross section of the insulation.

Expressed as a percentage of center displacement of one circle within the other.

ECHO Exactly what you expect it to mean. You hear yourself speak. Echoes happen in both voice and data conversation. Echoes are good and bad. In voice, an echo happens when the equipment meant to amplify the voice of the party at one end, picks up the signals from the party at the other end, and amplifies them back to that party. Some echo is acceptable (in fact, almost a necessity) in voice conversations. It's called SIDETONE. When the speaker can hear himself speak through the receiver, sidetone gives the speaker some feeling his conversation is actually going through. But too much (i.e. too loud) echo is unacceptable. There are devices called echo suppressors, which do exactly that.

In low speed or on-line data conversations, an echo is positively vital. An echo in a data conversation is where I send my words to the distant computer which "echoes" them back to me and my screen displays them. This way I can visually check if the distant computer received my words/data accurately. In some software programs there's a command called ECHO or ECHOPLEX. Switch it one way, the distant computer echoes the words to my screen. Switch it the other, the words I'm typing on my keyboard are put on my screen.

There are two basic transmission modes in data communications — full duplex and half duplex. In full duplex, I have simultaneous two-way data flowing. In full duplex, I therefore have the capacity to "echo" back the data I am sending and have it displayed on my screen. But this "echoing" depends on the capability and/or programming of the computer at the other end. All dial-up services — Tymnet, GTE Telenet, MCI Mail, etc. — will echo my data back to me so I can check it.

Some computers, such as the extremely dumb Compugraphic typesetter which typeset the first edition of this book, won't send an echo. In this case, if I want to see the data I am sending, I can change the parameters on my communications software to "half duplex." This way I will see what I am sending, but I will not see what the computer is receiving. Which may be very different. (And with our Compugraphic often is.) Of course, watching characters being echoed across your screen is a very poor method of data transmission and only useful in on-line transmissions. Some form of error-checking protocol is much better.

ECHO CANCELLATION Technique used in higher-speed modems that allows for the isolation and filtering of unwanted signal energy caused by echoes from the main transmitted signal.

ECHO CHECK A technique for verifying data sent to another location by returning the received data (echoing it back) to the sending end.

ECHO RETURN LOSS ERL. The difference between a frequency signal and the echo on that signal as it reaches its destination.

ECHO SUPPRESSOR Used to reduce the annoying effects of echoes in telephone connections. The worst echoes occur on satellite circuits. An echo suppressor works by turning off transmission in the reverse direction while a person is talking, thus effectively making the circuit one way. An echo suppressor obviously impedes full-duplex data — data flowing both ways simultaneously. Echo suppressors are turned off by the high-pitched tone (typically 2025 Hz) in the answering modem, which it uses to signal it's answered the phone and is ready for a data conversation.

ECHO SUPPRESSOR DISABLER An echo suppressor disabler is a device which causes an echo suppressor to be disabled (i.e. turned off) when it receives a 2025 Hz tone. A disabled echo suppressor stays disabled until the circuit is disconnected and restored to its "ready" connection. Because an echo suppressor hinders full duplex transmission in data communications, it is necessary to disable the echo suppressor.

ECHOPLEX A way of checking the accuracy of data transmitted whereby the data received are returned to the sender for comparison with the original data. Somewhat time consuming. Used typically in slowspeed transmissions. See ECHO.

ECL Emitter Coupled Logic.

ECM Error Correction Mode.

ECMA European Computer Manufacturers Association.

ECONOMY OF SCALE As throughput gets bigger, so the per unit cost comes down. This is the argument used by economists to justify monopolies — namely that the per unit costs of one supplier are far lower than having two suppliers. The economy of scale argument is used to justify having only one water company in town. It makes more sense in that industry than in the telephone industry.

It was once used in the telephone industry to justify one combined local phone company/long distance phone company/one supplier of terminal equipment. This argument does not really apply to telephony as technological breakthroughs have brought down the cost of getting into the telephone industry and have allowed smaller, competitive companies to become cost effective. Some large telecommunications monopolies, in fact, are experiencing diseconomies of scale. In this case, their cost of per unit business starts to rise as they get very large. Diseconomies of scale are caused by bloated bureaucracies and inertia in management decision making.

ECONOPATH CALLING PLANS Discount plans for New York City businesses to make calls in their regional calling area. For example, Econopath offers a Manhattan business a discount for calls to the East Suffolk region.

ECP Enhanced Call Processing. An Octel term for an interactive customized menu in its voice mail system which provides levels of call routing. See ENHANCED CALL PROCESSING.

ECS Energy Communications Services.

ECSA Exchange Carriers Standards Association.

EDI Electronic Data Interchange. A series of standards which provide computer-to-computer exchange of business documents between different companies and computers over phone lines. These standards allow for companies to send each other purchase orders, shipping documents, invoices, invoice payments, etc. EDI software translates fixed field or "flat" files that are extracted from applications into a standard format and hands off the translated data to communications software for transmission. EDI standards are supported (i.e. have been adopted) by virtually every computer company in the country and increasingly, by every packet switched data communications company. For example, you can use IBM VAN — IBM's Value Added Network for Electronic Data Interchange. See also IES.

EDITOR A software program used to modify programs or files while they are being prepared or after they are (allegedly) complete. An editor is really a very rudimentary word processing program. When you buy MS-DOS, one of the programs you get is a rudimentary editing program called EDLIN. Most programmers, however, now prefer more advanced editors, like ZEdit. For more on ZEdit, call 1-800-999-0345. This dictionary was written in ZEdit.

EDP Electronic Data Processing. Also DP, as in Data Processing. Basically, a machine (also called a computer) that receives, stores, operates on, records and outputs data. The word "electronic" was added to Data Processing when the industry went away from tab cards — the 80 column "do not spindle," etc. — and was able to accept data electronically, instead of electromechanically as with the tab cards. People in the industry used to be called EDPers. Now the term MIS — Management Information System — is more common.

EDUTAINMENT Unpopular answer to the question "What do you get when you cross educational material with interactive video?" A term coined by "someone who obviously knows nothing about either education or entertainment," says Laura Buddine, president of multimedia games maker Tiger Media.

EFT Electronic Funds Transfer. The moving of bits of data from one bank to another. Done in place of moving little green pieces of paper, called money.

EGA Enhanced Graphics Adapter. It offers 640 horizontal x 350 vertical pixels on the color screen of an IBM PC or clone. See MONITOR.

EI Refers to Europe's 2.048 Mbps (T-1 type) digital carrier system.

EIA Electronic Industries Association. A trade organization of manufacturers which sets standards for use of its member companies, conducts educational programs and lobbies in Washington for its members' collective prosperity. In April 1988, a new association called the Telecommunications Industry Association was formed by a merger of the US Telecommunications Suppliers Association (USTSA) and the Electronics Industries Association's Information and Telecommunications Technologies Group (EIA/ITG). TIA and EIA exist separately, each with its own President and governing board. TIA does, however, represent the telecommunications sector for EIA and works with EIA industry groups and divisions and develops technical standards and does market data gathering. See EIA INTERFACE.

EIA INTERFACE A set of signal characteristics (time, duration, voltage and current) set up by the Electronic Industries Association to standardize the transfer of information between different electronic devices, like computers, modems, printers, etc. The most famous EIA interface is the RS-232-C (now called the RS-232-D and shortly to be called the RS-232-E). EIA-232 specifies three things: the functions of the interchange circuits, the electrical characteristics, AND the connector (EIA-232-E includes two different connectors).

In contrast, the CCITT's V.24 specifies ONLY the interchange circuit FUNCTIONS. V.28 specifies electrical characteristics compatible with EIA-232. ISO 2110 is the internal standard that defines the 25-pole D-shell connector compatible with EIA-232.

Following the merger of EIA and the ITG part of EIA, all formed EIA telecommunications standards are now EIA/TIA publications and the standard referred to is now known as EIA/TIE-232-D, edition D, being the most recent. See EIA and RS-232-D.

EIGHT HUNDRED SERVICE 800-Service. A generic and common (and not trademarked) term for AT&T's, MCI's, US Sprint's and the Bell operating companies' IN-WATS service. All these IN-WATS services have "800" as their "area code." Dialing an 800-number is free to the person making the call. The call is billed to the person or company being called. The telephone company suppliers of 800 services use various ways to configure and bill their 800-services. One way: you can buy an 800 line which will ring on your normal phone line. You'll only pay per call, but you won't receive any incoming call if you're making an outgoing one. (You can even terminate an 800 number on your cellular phone.) For other 800 services you might pay a flat monthly rate plus "so-much" (i.e. timed usage) per call which may include some calculation for the distance the incoming call traveled. 800-Service is now available for calls from Canada and some countries in Europe. More and more long distance companies are introducing 800-service.

800 Service works like this: You're somewhere in North America. You dial 1-800 and seven digits. Your local central office sees the "1" and recognizes the call as long distance. It ships that call to a bigger central office (or perhaps processes the call itself). At that central office it's processed, a machine will recognize the 800 "area code" and examine the next three digits. Those three digits will tell which long distance carrier to ship the call to. Each long distance company has been assigned specific 800 three digit "exchanges." For example, MCI has the exchange 999. AT&T has the exchange 542. If you want a phone number beginning with 800-999, then you must subscribe to MCI 800 service. If you want a phone number beginning with 800-542, you must subscribe to AT&T 800 service. Once the 800-call is "passed off" to whichever carrier it belongs to, that carrier sends the call to a switch attached to a huge "translation" database. The call

arrives at the switch. The database says the call 800-NNN-XXXX is really 212-555-1234, and sends the 800 line to that number.

As a real-life example, Telecom Library, publisher of this book, has an 800 number, namely 800-LIBRARY (or 800-542-7279). When you call that number, the following number — 212-206-6870 — in New York City rings. Dialing 800-542-7279 is effectively the same as dialing 212-206-6870, except that if you dial 212-206-6870 you'll pay. If you dial 800-542-7279, I'll pay. Because 800 long distance service is essentially a database lookup and translation telephone service, there are endless "800 services" you can create. Here are a few examples:

- TIME OF DAY ROUTING: Allows you to route incoming calls to alternate, predetermined locations at specified days of the week and times of the day.
- PERCENTAGE ALLOCATION ROUTING: Allows you to route pre-selected percentages of calls from each Originating Routing Group (ORG) to two or more answering locations. Allocation percentages can be defined for each ORG (typically an area code), for each day type and for each time slot.
- SINGLE NUMBER: The same 800 number is used for intrastate and interstate calling.
- CALL BLOCKAGE: You can block calling areas by state or area code. The caller from a blocked area hears the message: "Your 800 call cannot be completed as dialed. Please check the number and dial again or call 1-800-XXX-XXXX for assistance." (You may want to block callers from areas which didn't see your special commercial, for example.)
- POINT OF CALL ROUTING: Allows a customer to route calls made to a single 800 number to different terminating locations based on the call's point of origin (state or area code.) You establish Originating Routing Groups (ORGs) and designate a specific answering location for each ORG's call.
- CALL ATTEMPT PROFILE: A special service that allows subscribers to purchase a record of the number of attempts that are made to an 800 number. The attempts are captured at the Network Control Point, and from this data, a report is produced for the subscriber.
- ALTERNATE ROUTING: Allows a customer to create alternate routing plans that can be activated by the 800 carrier upon command in the event of an emergency. Several alternate plans can be set up using any features previously subscribed to in the main 800 routing plan. Each alternate plan must specify termination in a location previously set up during the order entry process.
- DIALED NUMBER IDENTIFICATION SERVICE: DNIS. Allows a customer to terminate two or more 800 numbers to a single service group and to receive pulsed digits to identify the specific 800 number

called. DNIS is only available on dedicated access lines with four-wire E & M type signaling or a digital interface. The customer's equipment must be configured to process the DNIS digits.

- ANI: The carrier will deliver to you the incoming 800 call plus the phone number of the calling party. See also ANI, COMMON CHANNEL INTEROFFICE SIGNALING and ISDN.
- COMMAND ROUTING: Allows the customer to route calls differently on command at any time his business requires it.

There's one problem with 800 lines: they're hard to test. You may have bought an 800 number to cover the country, but you may be unreachable from certain parts of the country for weeks on end and not know it. That's part of the problem of a service which uses multiple databases lookup tables. The only part of your 800 IN-WATS line you can rigorously test is your local loop — from the local central office to your office. Every IN-WATS line has a local Plant Test Number — a standard seven digit number. You can call this number. If it works, you know that part of your lines are working. Our WATS line is 1-800-LIBRARY. Our first IN-WATS line has a local plant test number of 212-206-6870. So we call this and all the subsequent hunt-on numbers every day first thing. Just to check. And when we go traveling, we call our own numbers. Just to check. The most common problem we have with our 800 numbers is at our local central office. Seems that it crashes every so often for very short amounts of time. When it starts up, it's meant to load all the tables to give us the features we're paying for — like hunting. Sadly, it doesn't always do this. We have to report the trouble to our local phone company. It's usually fixed within minutes.

EISA Extended Industry Standard Architecture. EISA is the independent computer industry's alternate to IBM's Micro-Channel data bus architecture which IBM uses in its high end PS/2 line of desktop computers. EISA, like micro channel, is a 32-bit channel. But, unlike IBM's Micro-Channel, plug-in boards inside the XT and AT-series of IBM and IBM clone desktop computers will work within EISA machines. (They won't work in the Micro-Channel machines.) As of writing, over 200 manufacturers had endorsed EISA.

EITHER WAY OPERATION Same as half-duplex.

EKTS Electronic Key Telephone System.

ELASTICITY OF DEMAND The relationship between price and the quantity sold. The theory is the lower the price, the more you'll sell. In telecommunications, this has traditionally been true, though sometimes it has taken time for demand to catch up with dramatic price cuts.

ELECTROMECHANICAL RINGING The traditional bell or buzzer in a telephone which announces incoming calls.

ELECTRON GUN Device in a television picture tube from which electrons are emitted toward screen.

ELECTRONIC BLACKBOARD This is a teleconferencing tool. At one end there's a large "whiteboard." Write on this board and electronics behind the board pick up your writing and transmit it over phone lines to a remote TV set. The idea is that remote viewers can hear your voice on the phone and see the presentation on the electronic blackboard. The product has not done well because it is expensive — typically several hundred dollars a month just for rent, plus extra hundreds for transmission costs. In Japan, there are similar boards called OABoards — Office Automation Boards. They do one thing differently — they will print a copy on normal letter-size paper of what's written on the board. This takes about 20 seconds. Some of these Japanese OABoards will also transmit their contents over phone lines. So far, neither the OABoards nor the electronic blackboards have found a sizeable market in the United States.

ELECTRONIC CALL DISTRIBUTION Another term for AUTOMATIC CALL DISTRIBUTION.

ELECTRONIC CUSTOM TELEPHONE SERVICE Provides deluxe key telephone features and simplified access to certain AT&T Dimension PBX phones.

ELECTRONIC DATA INTERCHANGE See EDI.

ELECTRONIC DATA PROCESSING See EDP.

ELECTRONIC FUNDS TRANSFER EFT. A system which transfers money electronically between accounts or organizations without moving the actual money.

ELECTRONIC IMAGE MAIL The transmission of slow scan TV or facsimile via "Store and Forward." Not a common term.

ELECTRONIC KEY SYSTEM A key telephone system in which the electromechanical relays and switches have been replaced by electronic devices — often in the phone and in the central cabinet. The innards of the central cabinet of an electronic key system more resemble a computer than a conventional key system. These days, virtually all key systems are electronic. Production of electromechanical key systems (such as 1A2) has been severely curtailed and most manufacturers have ceased making it.

ELECTRONIC MAIL A term which usually means Electronic Text Mail, as opposed to Electronic Voice Mail or Electronic Image Mail. See ELECTRONIC TEXT MAIL, ELECTRONIC VOICE MAIL and ELECTRONIC IMAGE MAIL.

ELECTRONIC MESSAGE REGISTRATION A system to detect and count a phone user's completed local calls and then tell the central office the number of message units used. Also used in hotels.

ELECTRONIC ORDER EXCHANGE EOE. Inter-company transactions between buyers and sellers handled electronically via standard data communications protocols. EOE can be employed to send purchase orders, price and product listings and order-related information.

ELECTRONIC SWITCHING SYSTEM A telephone switch which uses electronics or computers to control the switching of calls, their billing and other functions. The term is now vaguely defined, with each manufacturer defining it as something somewhat different. In fact, every telephone switch sold today is electronic.

The term originally came about because early telephone switches were entirely electro-mechanical. The switch consisted entirely of a moving switch. Devices like relays physically moved in order to send the call through the exchange and on its way. These things moved in direct response to the digits dialed by the telephone subscriber. These switches contained no "intelligence" — i.e. no ability to deviate from a set number of very simple tasks which could be accomplished by electromechanical relays.

Then someone said: it would be more efficient if the "instruction part" of the process were divorced the switching mechanism. This lead to the creation of the "electronic" switch in which the "brains" of the switch are separated from the switching mechanism itself. Thus the "brains" can do simple things like collect the dialed digits as they are slowly dialed and pulse them out quickly to the switch — as fast as it can handle them. Now, the "brains" are typically a digital computer.

ELECTRONIC TANDEM NETWORK Two or more switching systems operating in parallel as part of providing network services (usually voice) to large users.

ELECTRONIC TEXT MAIL A "Store and Forward" service for the transmission of textual messages transmitted in machine readable form from a computer terminal or computer system. A message sent from one computer user to another is stored in the recipient's "mailbox" until that person next logs onto the system. The system then can deliver the message. Telex, in which a machine readable form of message transmission takes place, is also considered an Electronic Text Mail medium, albeit a very slow one. For an example of electronic mail, please dial our electronic mail system on 212-989-4675. It's free. Parameters are 300, 1200 or 2400 baud, 8 data bits, one stop bit, and no parity.

ELECTRONIC VOICE MAIL A system which stores messages usually spoken over a telephone. These messages can be retrieved by the intended recipient when that person next calls into the system. Also called Voice Mail, it operates just like a touch-tone controlled answering machine.

ELECTRONIC WARFARE Known as EW. See EW.

ELECTROSTATIC PRINTING A method of printing very common in photocopying in which charges are beamed onto the surface of paper. The charges attract particles of a very fine (typically, black powder) which sticks to the charges. The black powder is fused permanently on the paper by great heat. "XEROXing" is electrostatic printing. In xeroxing, the black powder is called toner.

ELECTROLYSIS The production of chemical changes by passage of current through an electrolyte.

ELEGANT An elegant program is one that is efficiently written to use the smallest possible amount of main memory and the fewest number of instructions.

ELONGATION The fractional increase in length of a material stressed in tension.

EMBEDDED SYSTEM PROCESSORS National Semiconductor's line of high-performance microprocessors used in dedicated systems, such as fax machines and laser printers.

EMBOSSING A means of marker identification by thermal indentation leaving raised lettering on a cable's sheath material.

EMERGENCY ACCESS An alarm system built into some PBXs. In an emergency it rings all phones.

EMERGENCY DIALING A variation on speed calling to call numbers for police, fire department, ambulance, etc. Typically found as special buttons on an electronic phone.

EMI ElectroMagnetic Interference. Leakage of radiation outside a transmission medium that happens because of high-frequency energy. EMI is reduced by shielding.

EMP A large and fast-moving electromagnetic pulse caused by lightning.

EMULATE To imitate a computer or computer system by a combination of hardware and software that allows programs written for one computer or terminal to run on another. The most common data terminal is a DEC VT-100. Our communications program, Crosstalk, allows us to "emulate" a DEC-VT100 on our IBM PCs and PC clones.

EMULATOR A device or computer program which can act as if it is a different device or program, that is Emulate (i.e. pretend to be) another device. Certain computer terminals are necessary in specific systems and a terminal that is not that type may be able to act as if it was. If it can, it is an Emulator. This is not a common term. See also the verb EMULATE.

ENABLE To make something happen. Or, in more complex language, to set various hardware and software parameters so that the central computer will recognize those parameters and start doing what you want.

ENCODING The reversible process of converting data into code.

ENCRYPTION In security, the ciphering of data by applying an algorithm to plaintext in order to convert it to ciphertext.

END OF FILE EOF. A control character or byte used in data communications that indicates the last character of the last record of a file has been read.

END OF MESSAGE EOM. A control character used in data communications to indicate the end of a message.

END OF TEXT MESSAGE ETX. A control character used in data communications to indicate the end of a text. See ETX.

END OF TRANSMISSION BLOCK CHARACTER A control character used in data communications to indicate the end of a block where data are divided into blocks for transmission purposes.

END OFFICE A central office to which a telephone subscriber is connected. Frequently referred to as a Class 5 office. The last central office before the subscriber's phone equipment. The central office which actually delivers dial tone to the subscriber.

END TO END SIGNALING A signaling system capable of generating and transmitting signals directly from the originating station to the terminating end after the connection is established, without disturbing the connection. Touch-Tone dialing is such a system, allowing the user to send tones to a remote computer for data or other access. See POINT TO POINT.

END USER My definition: The premises occupant who uses and pays the monthly charges for the telephone service received and does not resell it to others. Bellcore's definition: A user who uses a loop-start, ground-start, or ISDN access signaling arrangement. Definition from Bellcore in reference to its concept of the Advanced Intelligent Network.

ENERGY COMMUNICATIONS EC. A PBX feature which communicates with energy consuming and monitoring devices and perform functions like dimming the lights or turning down the heat in a vacant hotel room.

ENFIA Exchange Network Facilities for Interstate Access. A tariff providing a series of options for connecting long distance carriers with local exchange facilities of the local telephone company.

ENHANCED CALL PROCESSING An Octel term for the interactive voice response option in its voice mail system. Here's how Octel defines the term: "Companies and departments that receive a heavy volume of calls can use ECP to create menus that are presented to callers. When the system answers a call, a recorded voice instructs the caller how to use a touch-tone telephone to send call routing instructions to the system. Depending on which option is chosen, ECP's customized call routing feature allows a caller to press a single key to reach a predetermined extension, a voice messaging mailbox where he can leave a message, an Information Center Mailbox where he can listen to a series of recordings giving frequently requested information or additional levels of ECP menus. ECP menus are easily custom-built by the customer to meet its specific needs. Each menu can offer as many as ten options."

ENHANCED PRIVATE SWITCHED COMMUNICATIONS SERVICE EPSCS (pronounced EP-SIS). A private line networking offering from AT&T which provides functions similar to CCSA. Big companies are its customers.

ENHANCED SERIAL INTERFACE ESI. A new, broader serial interface announced by Hayes Microcomputer Products, Norcross, GA, and placed in the public domain. The ESI is an extension of the familiar COM card used in personal computers. ESI includes the definition of I/O, control registers, buffer control, Direct Memory Access (DMA) to the system and interaction with attached modem devices. ESI specification is available from Hayes Customer Service at no charge. Combined with Hayes' announcement of ESI was their announcement of new Enhanced Serial Port hardware products for the IBM microchannel and IBM XT/AT or EISA bus personal computers. According to Hayes, the ESI spec and the supporting ESP hardware provide a "cost-effective' communication co-processor to manager the flow of data between an external high speed modem and PC. This technology prevents loss of data resulting from buffer overflow errors and provides maximum data throughput for high speed modems. Hayes says that the combination of ESP and ESI will allow through-the-phone modem speeds of up to 38.4 kbps.

ENHANCED SERIAL PORT See ENHANCED SERIAL INTERFACE.

ENHANCED SERVICES Services offered over transmission facilities which may be provided without filing a tariff. These services usually involve some computer related feature such as formatting data or restructuring the information. Most Bell operating companies (BOCs) are prohibited from offering enhanced services at present. But the restrictions are disappearing and will probably be gone by the time this dictionary finally sees the light of day.

ENQ/ACK PROTOCOL Hewlett-Packard communications protocol in which the HP3000 computer follows each transmission block with ENQ to determine if the destination terminal is ready to receive more data. The terminal indicates its readiness by responding with ACK.

ENTELEC Energy Telecommunications and Electrical Association, the oldest nationwide user group in telecommunications. It is an association of communications managers and engineers in the oil, gas, pipeline and utility industries. ENTELEC played an important role in the early opening of competition in the telecommunications industry, including the famous Above-980 decision, which allowed private companies to build their own long distance microwave system. ENTELEC was formerly known as the Petroleum Industry Electrical Association.

ENTERPRISE NUMBER A service provided by AT&T and the Bell operating companies (a.k.a. the Bell System) years ago which allowed people to make collect calls and have their calls automatically accepted by the company at the other end. It was very expensive. It has largely been replaced with 800 IN-WATS service, which is much more successful.

ENVELOPE DELAY Circuit characteristics which result in some frequencies arriving ahead of others, even though they were transmitted at the same time.

ENVIRONMENT The place your telephone system's main cabinet and main electronics live. While most PBX vendors will specify the room's characteristics, the ultimate responsibility for the room is yours, the user. Not designing your telephone system's environment correctly is tantamount to jinxing your telephone system from the start.

Here are some things to watch out for (your vendor has a more comprehensive list): 1. Sufficient air conditioning? Telephone systems give off heat. You need some way of getting rid of the heat. If you don't, you will blow some of your phone system's delicate electronic circuitry. 2. Sufficient space? Is there room for technicians to get in and around your telephone system so they can repair it? Will you have room for additional cabinets when you need to grow your phone system? 3. Sufficient and correct power? Will you have sufficient clean commercial AC power? Will you require isolation regulators? Or you will require extensive wet cell batteries? Will you have space? 4. Will you have a solid electrical ground? Can you find somewhere solid to ground your telephone system to — other than the third wire on the AC power, which is not suitable for most telephone systems? Beware of cold water pipes which end in PVC plastic pipes.

EPABX Electronic Private Automatic Branch Exchange. A fancy name for a modern PBX. Other fancy names include CBX, Computerized Branch Exchange.

EO End Office. Typically your own central office.

EO Erasable Optical drive. EO drives act like hard drives yet offer virtually unlimited storage because their cartridges are removable. Each cartridge sports at least 650 MB. Some sport 1 gigabyte.

EOA End Of Address. A header code.

EOB End Of Block. A control character or code that marks the end of a block of data.

EOE See ELECTRONIC ORDER EXCHANGE.

EOM End of Message (indicator).

EOT End of Transmission, End of Tape.

EPAPBX Electronic Private Automatic Branch Exchange.

EPLANS Engineering, Planning and Analysis Systems. Software offered by Western Electric (now called AT&T Technologies) to help operating telephone company people run their business better.

EPROM Erasable Programmable Read Only Memory. A read only memory device which can be erased and reprogrammed. Typically, it is programmed electronically (not electromagnetically) with ultraviolet light. EPROMS are typically returned to the vendor or factory for reprogramming.

EPSCS (Pron. Ep-Sis.) Enhanced Private Switched Communications Service. An AT&T offering for large businesses with offices scattered all over the country. This service allows such businesses to rent space on AT&T electronic switches and join that switching capacity to leased lines. EPSCS customers get a network control center in their offices which gives them information on the continuing operation of their network and allows them some limited options for changing their services.

EPSN Enhanced Private Switched Network.

EQUAL ACCESS All long distance carriers must be accessible by dialing 1 — and not a string of long dialing codes. This is laid down in Judge Green's Modified Final Judgment (MFJ), which spelled out the terms of the Divestiture of the Bell Operating phone Companies (BOCs) from their parent, AT&T. Under the terms of this Divestiture, all long distance common carriers must have Equal Access for their long distance caller customers. City by City telephone subscribers are being asked to choose their primary carrier who they will reach by dialing 1 before their long distance number. All other carriers (including AT&T, if not chosen as primary) can be reached by dialing a five digit code (10XXX), thus providing Equal Access for all carriers. Not all long distance companies will opt for full equal access since this involves considerable expense to the local phone companies. See also FEATURE GROUP A, B, C and D.

EQUAL ACCESS END OFFICE A central office capable of providing equal access. See also EQUAL ACCESS.

EQUALIZATION The process of reducing distortion over transmission paths by putting in compensating devices. The telephone network is equalized by the spacing and operation of amplifiers along the way. In recording, equalization is frequency manipulation to meet the requirements of recording; also the inverse manipulation in playback to achieve uniform or "flat" response. Also called Compensation.

EQUIPMENT CABINET The metal box which houses relays, circuit boards or other phone apparatus. Usually also contains the power supply, which converts the 120 volt AC current into the low voltage direct current necessary to run the telephone system.

EQUIPMENT COMPATIBILITY One computer system will successfully do the same thing that another computer will do with the same data. There are many levels of "equipment compatibility." The only true compatibility, however, is identical machinery. And identical means "identical" down to the very last chip and very last integrated circuit. We have found that some computers — even those consecutively numbered — do not always perform the same. We have empirically proven this for both IBM and AT&T computers.

EQUIPPED-FOR-CAPACITY The maximum number of lines and trunks that can be supported by the available hardware. It is not a totally effective measure of the size of a PBX. See WIRED-FOR-CAPACITY.

EQUIVALENT FOUR-WIRE SYSTEM Transmission using frequency division to get full duplex transmission over only one pair of wires. Normally two pairs are needed for full duplex.

ERASABLE PROGRAMMABLE READ ONLY MEMORY See EPROM.

ERASABLE STORAGE A storage device whose contents can be changed, i.e. random access memory, or RAM. Compare with read-only storage.

ERASE HEAD On a magnetic tape recorder — voice or video — this is the "head" which erases the tape by demagnetizing it immediately before a new recording is placed on the tape by the adjacent record head.

ERLANG A measurement of telephone conversation traffic. One Erlang is equal to one full hour of phone conversation, or 60 x 60 = 3,600 seconds of phone conversation. You convert CCS (hundred call seconds) into Erlangs by multiplying by 100 and then dividing by 3,600. Erlang gets its name from the father of queuing theory, A. K. Erlang, a Danish telephone engineer, who, in 1908, began to study congestion in the telephone service of the Copenhagen Telephone Company. A few years later he arrived at a mathematical approach to assist in designing the size of telephone switches. Central to queuing theory are central facts of queuing life. First, traffic varies widely. Second, anyone who designs a telephone switch to completely handle all peak traffic will find the switch idle for most of the time. This is expensive and uneconomical. Third, it is possible, with varying degrees of certainty to predict upcoming "busy" periods. See also ERLANG, A.K., ERLANG B, ERLANG C and POISSON.

ERLANG B Also known as "Lost Calls Cleared." A formula for designing telephone traffic handling for PBXs and networks. It is used when traffic is random and there is no queuing. Calls which cannot get through, go away and do not return. Using Erlang B will produce a phone network with fewer trunks than one using Poisson formulae. See also ERLANG.

ERLANG C A formula for designing telephone traffic handling for PBXs and networks. Used when traffic is random and there is queuing. It assumes that all callers will wait indefinitely to get through. It is not a perfect traffic engineering formula. But then none are. The best method of "predicting" traffic is to use simulation, but typically, it's based on last month's or the last few months' traffic and there's often little to say about what next month's will be like. See also ERLANG.

ERLANG, A. K. In 1918, A. K. Erlang, a Danish telephone engineer, published his work on blocking in "The Post Office Electrical Engineers' Journal," a British publication. Like E.C. Molina, an AT&T engineer, Erlang assumed a Poisson distribution of calls arriving in a given time. Molina had assumed a constant holding time for all calls, whereas Erlang assumed an exponential distribution for holding times. That means that longer calls occur less frequently than shorter calls. Erlang assumed that blocked calls are immediately cleared and lost and do not return. A formula that Erlang worked out based on these assumptions (Erlang B) is still in use in telephone engineering. See ERLANG B and POISSON.

ERP Effective Radiated Power.

ERROR BURST A sequence of transmitted signals containing one or more errors but regarded as a unit in error in accordance with a predefined measure. Enough consecutive transmitted bits in error to cause a loss of synchronization between sending and receiving stations and to necessitate resynchronization.

ERROR CORRECTING PROTOCOL A method of transmitting bit streams in a mathematical way that the receiving computer verifies to the sending computer that all bits have been received properly. SNA and XMODEM protocols, in the mainframe and microcomputer environments respectively, are Error Correcting Protocols.

ERROR CORRECTION CODE In computers, rules of code construction that facilitate reconstruction of part or all of a message received with errors.

ERROR CORRECTION MODE A method of transmitting and receiving data that eliminates errors.

ERROR LEVEL A numeric value set by some programs that you can test with the errorlevel option of the "If" batch command. It works as follows. Some programs set the DOS errorlevel to a certain number depending on a certain input or response to an event. Let's say when you type the letter "Y" in response to a question the errorlevel is set to 32. Once this is done, you may condition other events based upon this number using an If command in a batch file. You can say "IF ERRORLEVEL = 32 THEN GOTO END." That way, when you type "Y" you will get whatever is at END. This can be very helpful in batch files and other programs for providing "branching" from one event to another based on certain inputs.

ERROR RATE In data transmission, the ratio of the number of incorrect elements transmitted to the total number of elements transmitted.

ESA Emergency Stand Alone.

ESC The ESC key on the keyboard. Often used to leave (escape) a program. Appears on the upper left of some keyboards on the IBM or compatibles but moves around with IBM's latest keyboard redesign whim. See also ESCAPE.

ESCALATION A formal word for taking your trouble up through the levels of management at the vendor — until you get your problem resolved. Some users have formal Escalation Charts, which detail action to be taken depending on how many hours the problem persists, etc. Escalation sometimes works and sometimes doesn't, depending on the vendor. Usually it does. The rule in telecommunications (and we guess most other industries) is that "the squeaky wheel gets the most attention." Escalation works well with honey and flowers and chocolates.

ESCAPE The button on many computer keyboards which allows you to "escape" the present program. EScape is the ASCII control character — code 27. It is often used to mark the beginning of a series of characters that represent a command rather than data. So called "ESCAPE" because it escapes from the usual meaning of the ASCII code and allows commands to be interspersed in a file of data, especially for data transmission. See ESCAPE SEQUENCE.

ESCAPE SEQUENCE A series of characters, usually beginning with the escape character, that is to be interpreted as a command, not as data. Escape sequences are used with ANSI.SYS to change the color of a screen. They are mostly used to send print commands to printers. The name Escape is due to the fact that it "escapes" from the usual meaning of the ASCII code, letting characters be commands instead of data, yet interspersed with data in a transmission.

ESCROW BUCKET A hopper at the outlet of a coin phone's acceptor/rejector that is tipped electrically to return money through the Coin Return or to send the money to the Cash Box as a collection for a completed call.

ESDI Northern Telecom term for Enhanced Serial Data Interface.

ESF Extended Superframe Format. A T-1 format that uses the 193rd bit as a framing bit. ESF provides frame synchronization, cyclic redundancy checking and data link bits. Frames consist of 24 bits instead of the previous standard 12 bits as in the D4 format. The standard allows error information to be stored and retrieved easily, facilitating network performance monitoring and maintenance.

ESI See ENHANCED SERIAL INTERFACE.

ESP Enhanced Serial Port (See ENHANCED SERIAL INTERFACE) or Enhanced Service Provider — a vendor who adds value to telephone lines using his own provided software and hardware. Also called an IP, or Information Provider. An example of an ESP is a public voice mail box provider or a database provider, say one giving the latest airline fares. An ESP is an American term, unknown in Europe, where they're most called VANs, or Value Added Networks. See also ONA and INFORMATION PROVIDER.

ESP Enhanced Service Provider

ESPRIT European Strategic Program for Research and development in Information Technology. A $1.7 billion research and development program funded by the European Community.

ESS Electronic Switching System. ESS was originally a designation for the switching equipment in Bell System central offices but has slightly more general use now. In the independent telephone company industry, the abbreviation for the same thing is EAX.

ESS NO 4 AT&T's large toll telephone switch. It will handle over 100,000 trunks and over 500,000 attempts at making a call each hour. It's large and sophisticated and can probably be configured to be the largest telephone switch in the world.

ESS NO 5 AT&T's Class 5 digital central office. See also END OFFICE.

ETB Abbreviation for End of Transmission Block.

ETERNITY HOLD Our own creation for what happens when someone puts you on long-term hold. Governmental agencies, airlines and police departments (especially when you need them) tend to be firm believers in placing their callers on Eternity Hold. A new service adjunct to Eternity Hold is Conference Hold. Here everyone on Eternity Hold can speak to each other. We made this up. It doesn't exist, but we think it would be great if it did.

ETHERNET A local area network used for connecting computers and terminals, etc., within the same building. Ethernet operates over twisted wire and over coaxial cable at speeds up to 10 Mbps. Ethernet LANs are being promoted by DEC, Intel and Xerox. For LAN interconnection, Ethernet is a physical link and data link protocol reflecting the two lowest layers of the DNA/OSI model. Ethernet is the basis for the IEEE Standard 802.3, which is accepted by the ISO as part of the OSI. IEEE 802.3 LAN can share the same cable and communicate with Ethernet networks.

ETI Electronic Telephone Interface.

ETN Electronic Tandem Network.

ETS See ELECTRONIC TANDEM SWITCHING.

ETX End of Text. Indicates the end of a message. If multiple transmission blocks are contained in a message in Bisynch systems, ETX terminates the last block of the message. ETB is used to terminate preceding blocks. The block check character is sent immediately following ETX. ETX requires a reply indicating the receiving station's status.

EVEN PARITY In data communications there's something called a PARITY BIT that's used for error checking. The transmitting device adds that parity bit to a data word to make the sum of all the "1" ("one" bits) either odd or even. If the sum is odd, the result is called ODD parity. If it's even, it's called EVEN PARITY. See also PARITY.

EVENT An occurrence significant to a task. The completion of an Input/Output (I/O) transfer, for instance, or George Foreman knocking-out Muhammad Ali in Zaire.

EVENT MASK The set of events that the SLEE (Service Logic Execution Environment) designates the ASC (AIN Switch Capabilities) to report for a particular connection segment, and an indication for each event if the ASC should suspend processing events for that connection segment until the SLEE sends a message back. Definition from Bellcore in reference to its concept of the Advanced Intelligent Network.

EW Electronic Warfare. The military uses of radar, electronic counter measures and electronic counter-counter measures to keep an enemy from finding invading forces. It also covers such techniques as jamming radio frequencies, anti-jamming and other military topics of a like nature. It is not the state of Judge Greene's courtroom or the boardroom at the FCC, but it could be.

EXCEPTION When something happens that's "unusual," it's an exception. The key is to define what's "unusual." For example, you might define that every phone call of longer than 15 minutes is an "exception." Now you have defined an "exception," the question is how to use that information. You might ask the phone system to print out each "exception" call on a printer next to your desk immediately after the call is over. Or you might ask the machine to print "Exceptions" reports at the end of the month listing all the calls over 15 minutes. These reports might be by perpetrator. Or in chronological order, or order of phone number called, etc. In short, any event you define by certain strict parameters can be an "exception." Management reports printed in full are almost useless because they contain so much information, so much paper. Management reports which list only previously-defined "exceptions" are more useful. They show you where to focus your attention so as to improve you or your company's performance.

EXCEPTION REPORTS Reports generated by "exceptions," often detailing extra long calls or indications of bad circuits. See EXCEPTION.

EXCESSIVE ZEROS More consecutive zeroes received than are permitted for the selected coding scheme. For AMI-encoded T-1 signals, 16 or more zeroes are excessive. For B8ZS encoded serial data, 8 or more zeroes are excessive.

EXCHANGE 1. Sometimes used to refer to a telephone switching center — a physical room or building. 2. An area in which there is a uniform set of charges for telephone service. Outside North America, telephone central offices are called "Public Exchanges."

EXCHANGE AREA Geographic area in which telephone services and prices are the same. The concept of exchange is based on geography and regulation, not equipment. An exchange might have one or several central offices. Anyone in that exchange area could get service from any one of those central offices. It's good to ask which central offices could serve your home or office and take service from the most modern. There will be no difference in price between being served by a one-year old central office, or a 50-year old step-by-step central office.

EXCHANGE CARRIER ASSOCIATION An organization of long distance telephone companies with specific administrative duties relative to tariffs, access charges and payments.

EXCHANGE CARRIERS STANDARDS ASSOCIATION ECSA. An accredited standards group under ANSI that existed before the AT&T Divestiture and consisted of RBOCs and independent telephone companies.

EXCHANGE NETWORK FACILITIES FOR INTERSTATE ACCESS See ENFIA.

EXCHANGE, PRIVATE AUTOMATIC BRANCH (PABX) A private telephone exchange which transmits calls internally and to and from the public telephone network.

EXCLUSION A PBX feature that prevents the attendant from silently monitoring a call once he/she has extended it.

EXCLUSIVE HOLD Only the telephone putting the call on hold can take it off. This feature assures that the call on hold will not be picked up by someone at another telephone who can then listen to your call.

EXCLUSIVE HOLD RECALL When a call is placed on "Exclusive Hold" and is not picked up after a predetermined amount of time, you will hear a beeping at that phone, which indicates the call is still on hold.

EXCLUSIVE OR PRIVATE UNIT A circuit card installed in each key telephone set sharing the same line or intercom path that causes the first caller on the line to lock out (exclude) all other stations from using or listening in, until the line is released (or privacy feature is defeated by the active caller).

EXECUNET An intercity switched telephone service introduced by MCI in 1975. Execunet was the first dial-up switched service introduced by a long distance phone company in competition with AT&T. At that time, all of AT&T's competitors, including MCI, were selling full-time private lines and shared private lines. The service was named by Carl Vorder-Bruegge, MCI's VP marketing at that time and introduced and made successful by Jerry Taylor, who was MCI's regional manager in Texas. The service was the forerunner of what is today a $4 billion plus industry — the non-AT&T

provided switched long distance business. Gerry Taylor started the service using a 104-port Action WATSBOX in Dallas, Texas. He deserves a place in the history books, not a crummy dictionary.

EXECUTE To complete a task.

EXECUTION TIME The time needed to complete a task.

EXECUTIVE BARGE-IN See EXECUTIVE OVERRIDE.

EXECUTIVE BUSY OVERRIDE See EXECUTIVE OVERRIDE.

EXECUTIVE OVERRIDE A feature of some telephone systems which permits certain users to intrude on conversations on other extensions. In some systems, executive barging-in will not be heard by the person outside the office, only the one inside the office. In some systems, such as the Mitel SX series with the Mitel Superset 4 phones, this feature activates the hands-free speakerphone of the called party, who is using his other line to speak on a normal phone conversation.

EXIT EVENT An event occurring in an ASC (AIN Switch Capabilities) that causes call processing to leave a PIC (Point in Call). Definition from Bellcore in reference to its concept of the Advanced Intelligent Network.

EXM Exit Message. The seventh ISUP call set-up message. It's a message sent in the backward direction from the access tandem to the end office indicating that call setup information has successfully proceeded to the adjacent network. See ISUP and COMMON CHANNEL SIGNALING.

EXPANDED MEMORY Extra RAM that is swapped in and out of the one megabyte (1MB) memory address of an 8088-class computer through the use of special boards and software. See also EXTENDED MEMORY.

EXPANDOR That device in a transmission facility which expands the amplitude of received compressed signals to their approximate normal range. The receiving side of a compandor.

EXPANSION The switching of a number of input channels, such as telephone lines onto a larger number of output channels.

EXPANSION SLOTS In a computer there are card slots for adding accessories such as internal modems, extra drivers, hard disks, monitor adapters, hard disk drivers, etc. Most modern PBXs are actually cabinets with nothing but expansion slots inside. Into these slots we fit trunk cards, line cards, console cards, etc. Some phone systems have "universal" slots, meaning you can put any card in any slot. Some phone systems have dedicated expansion slots, meaning that they expect only a certain card in that slot. In the PC industry, many manufacturers make cards for IBM and IBM compatible slots. In the phone industry, nobody makes cards for expansion slots in anyone else's phone system.

EXPERT SYSTEM A very sophisticated computer program consisting of three parts. 1. A stock of rules or general statements, e.g. Some long distance phone calls are free. 2. A set of particular facts, e.g. Three companies provide long distance service in the United States. 3. Most importantly, a "logical engine" which can apply facts to rules in order to reach all the conclusions that can be drawn from them — one of which might be "Three companies give away long distance phone calls. (Which would be wrong.) The simplest expert systems, according to the Economist Magazine, assume that their rules and facts tell them everything there is to know. So any statement that cannot be deduced from the system's rules and facts is assumed to be false. This can lead machines to answer "YES" or "NO," when they should say "I don't know." Slowly we are beginning to find ways of dealing with the inflexibility of machines. One such gadget is a "truth maintenance machine" invented by Dr. Jon Doyle of MIT. As each fact is fed into the system, Dr. Doyle's program checks to see if it (or the deductions derived from it) contradict any of the facts or deductions already in the system. If there is a contradiction, the machine works backward along its chain of reasoning to find the source and dispose of that troublesome fact or deduction. So the system maintain's one consistent set of beliefs.

EXT See EXTENSION.

EXTEND When the operator (or attendant) answers a call and forwards it to the called party, that call has been extended. "Putting a call through" is a clearer way of saying "extending" a call. The word "extend" probably comes from the old days when the operator extended her arm to plug you in on her cordboard.

EXTENDED ADDRESSING In many bit-oriented protocols, extended addressing is a facility allowing larger addresses than normal to be used. In IBM's SNA, the addition of two high-order bits to the basic addressing scheme.

EXTENDED AREA SERVICE An option offered by local telephone companies where a subscriber can pay a higher rate and reach more areas as local calls (no long distance charges).

EXTENDED BINARY CODED DECIMAL INTERCHANGE CODE EBCDIC. (Pronounced Eb-Si-Dick.) An IBM standard of coding characters. It's an 8-bit code and can represent up to 256 characters. A ninth bit is used as a parity bit. See PARITY and EBCDIC.

EXTENDED CALL MANAGEMENT A Northern Telecom term for a collection of features being added to its DMS Meridian central office Automatic Call Distribution (ACD) service. Using Switch-to-Computer Applications Interface (SCAI), ECM will work with user-provided computer equipment to integrate call processing, voice processing (recorded announcements, voice mail and voice response) and data processing. For example, ECM will allow an outboard computer device to coordinate the presentation of customer data on the ACD agent's computer screen with an incoming call. The D channel of an ISDN Basic Rate Interface (BRI) serves as the transport mechanism from the DMS-100 central office switch to an outboard computing device. Communication is peer-to-peer, meaning that neither the switch or the computer is in a "slave" relationship to the other. The application layer messaging — i.e. layer 7 messaging as defined by the Open Systems Interconnection (OSI) reference model — is in the Q.

932 format and is designed to conform to the T1S1 SCAI message protocol.

EXTENDED CHARACTER SET The characters assigned to ASCII codes 128 through 255 on IBM and IBM-compatible microcomputers. These characters are not defined by the ASCII standard and are therefore not "standard."

EXTENDED KEY CODE The two number code that represents pressing a key outside the typewriter portion of the keyboard, such as a function key, cursor-control key or combinations of CTRL (control) and ALT keys with another key. The first number is always 0 (zero) and is separated from the second number by a semicolon.

EXTENDED MEMORY Memory greater than 1Mb that can be addressed by 80286 or 80386 computers only. Requires an advanced operating system such as Unix or OS/2. See also EXPANDED MEMORY.

EXTENDED SUPER-FRAME FORMAT With this format 24 frames — instead of 12 — are grouped together. In this grouping, the 8,000 bps frame is redefined as follows:

- 2,000 bps for framing and signaling to provide the functions generally defined in the D-4 format.
- 2,000 bps are CRC-6 (Cyclic Redundancy Check-code 6) to detect logic errors caused by line equipment, noise, lightning and other interference. Performance checking is done by both the carrier and the customer without causing any interference with the T-1 traffic.
- 2,000 bps are used as a data link. This link is to perform functions such as enhanced end-to-end diagnostics, networking reporting and control, channel or equipment switching, and/or optional functions or services. See also T-1 FRAMING and D-4 FRAMING.

EXTENSION An additional telephone connected to a line. Allows two or more locations to be served by the same telephone line or line group. May also refer to an intercom phone number in an office.

EXTENSION CORD A multi-conductor, male/female modular line cord generally used to permit greater separation between the Communications Outlet and the telephone equipment. Available in various lengths up to 25 feet. May be of tinsel or stranded wire construction.

EXTERNAL MEMORY Storage devices, such as magnetic disks, drums or tapes which are outside (externally attached) to the main telephone or computer system.

EXTERNAL MODEM A modem external to the computer, it sits in its own little box connected to a computer through the computer's serial port. Compare with an internal modem, which typically comes on one printed circuit card and is placed into one of the computer's expansion slots and thus connects to the computer through the computer's "backplane." Internal modems cost less because they don't need any external housing and separate power supply. But because they're mounted inside the computer, it's harder to see what they're doing. You can't see the various status lights, like OH (for Off-Hook) and CD (for Carrier Detect). They also take up valuable slots instead of a serial port.

EXTERNAL STORAGE See also EXTERNAL MEMORY.

EXTN Extension.

EXTRUSION Method of continuously forcing plastic, rubber or elastometer material through an orifice to apply insulation or jacketing over a conductor or cable core.

EYE PATTERN An oscilloscope display used to visually determine the quality of an equalized transmission line signal being received. So called because portions of the pattern appearing on the scope resemble the elliptical shape of the human eye.

EYE PHONE Several researchers are studying something they call "virtual reality." One version of it, a system developed by a company called VPL Research, Redwood City, CA, is based around three things: a three-dimensional glove worn on the head (called an Eye Phone), an electronic glove (the Data Glove) and a high-speed computer. The whole system cost $250,000 in the fall of 1990.

FAC See FORCED AUTHORIZATION CODE.

FACEPLATE A cover that fits around the pushbuttons or rotary dial of a telephone. Hotels and motels put instructions on them. More businesses should also.

FACILITIES A stupid imprecisely-defined word that means anything and everything. Basically it means the equipment and services which go to make up a telecommunications capability. Most people use the word "facilities" to refer to phone lines. See also FACILITY WORK ORDER.

FACILITIES ADMINISTRATION AND CONTROL A PBX feature which allows you, the subscriber, to assign to your users features and privileges like authorization codes, restriction levels and calling privileges.

FACILITIES ASSURANCE REPORTS This feature allows a subscriber to get an audit trail of the referrals produced by the automatic circuit assurance feature of some PBXs. The audit trail will identify the trunk circuit, the time of referral, the nature of the problem and if a test was performed, the outcome of the test.

FACILITIES RESTRICTION LEVEL Which types of calls a PBX user is entitled to make.

FACILITY A telephone industry term for a phone or data line. Sometimes (but rarely) used to describe equipment.

FACILITY WORK ORDER An order to a phone company to rearrange things.

FACSIMILE EQUIPMENT FAX. Equipment which allows hardcopy (written, typed or drawn material) to be sent through the switched telephone system and printed out elsewhere. There are three internationally accepted specifications for facsimile equipment. Group 1, 2 and 3. Group 2 is faster than Group 1. Group 3 is faster than Group 3, etc. Virtually all machines sold today are Group 3. They send an 8 1/2 x 11 inch page over a normal phone line in about 20 seconds. How much time it actually takes depends on how much stuff is actually on the paper. Unlike older machines, Group 3 machines are "intelligent." They only transmit the stuff that's on the paper. They do not transmit white space, as earlier machines did. Group 3 fax machines are now available in "slimy" (i.e. chemical coated) paper and plain paper. When a fax machine calls a phone line and the phone line answers, the calling fax machine emits a standard CCITT-defined, "CNG tone" — 1100 Hz tone every three seconds. When the receiving fax machine hears this tone, it knows it's an incoming call and it can automatically connect. With this tone it is possible to insert a "fax switch," which would "listen" for an incoming fax call and switch it to a fax machine if it heard the tones or to something else — like a phone — if it didn't. It is not possible to do this with a modem. A modem works backwards — when the receiving machine answers the phone, it emits a tone.

Typically, a Group 3 machine can speak to a Group 2 and a Group 1 machine. A Group 2 can speak to a Group 1. Speaking down means slowing down. Fax machines are dropping in price. "Personal" fax machines are emerging. A Group 4 standard has been promulgated by the CCITT. But, as of writing, the standard has not been fully defined and accepted. Group 4 facsimile machines look as though they will be 100% digital and directly attach to the B (bearer channel) of a digital ISDN line. They will transmit a sheet of 8 1/2 x 11 paper in about six seconds. The author of this dictionary has seen a Group 4 fax machine in operation. It's mighty impressive.

Some warnings on fax machines:

1. All fax machines pose a security risk. Anyone can attach a normal audio cassette recorder to a phone line, record the incoming or outgoing fax "tones," By playing back to another fax machine at a later time, you'll get a perfect reproduction of the fax. There are now fax encryption devices which make the fax transmission unintelligible to any machine other than the one it's intended for — i.e. the one that has a similar un-encryption device.
2. Some plain paper fax machines present a different security risk. They use a carbon ribbon the width of their paper. As a result, if you want to read what came in, you simply read the carbon ribbon, which you open like a scroll, which the cleaning lady finds in the trash.
3. Slimy paper fades. How long it takes to fade depends on a bunch of factors — from what's sitting on top of the fax, to the temperature in the room, to whether it's exposed to sunlight, etc. Recommendation: If you want to retain a fax, make a xerox of it the moment you get it and throw out the original.
4. Poor quality slimy fax paper can abrade the fax machine's drum and cause a costly repair. Don't buy cheap paper. See FAX/DATA MODEM and FACSIMILE SWITCH.

FARAD The standard unit of capacitance. A one farad capacitor is one in which a one coulomb charge produces a one volt potential difference between the plates.

FAX/DATA MODEM A combination facsimile machine/modem. It typically comes as a card which you slip into a vacant slot in your desktop or laptop PC. But it may also come as a small self-contained package about the size of a cigarette package. There are enormous advantages in such a device — including the ability to send and receive data and facsimile calls from your desktop or laptop. There are two main disadvantages:

1. You may still have to print the incoming faxs. If you don't have a decent quality printer, having to buy one will kill the economic advantages of buying a combination fax/modem.
2. Viewing the incoming fax on your PC's screen is not easy. It poses a problem in translating your incoming fax to your computer screen. Here's why:

FAX ENCODING	
Standard, Group III	203 x 98
Fine, Group III	203 x 196
Superfine, Group III	203 x 391
Standard, Group IV	400 x 400

PC SCREEN ENCODING	
CGA	320 x 200
Enhanced CGA	640 x 400
EGA	640 x 350
Hercules	720 x 348
VGA	640 x 480
Super VGA	800 x 600
8514/A	1,024 x 768

FACSIMILE SWITCH A new breed of "black box." Its purpose is to avoid having to lease a separate phone line for your facsimile machine. You buy this box, connect it to an incoming line, your fax machine and your phone system. When a call comes in, the fax switch will answer the call, listen if the call coming in is from a fax machine, switch it to the fax machine, or switch the call to a phone if it's not a fax call. These are the basics. There are variations on this theme. Some fax switches work automatically. Some work by the incoming caller punching in digits. Some even allow a third possibility — namely a modem. But then you usually do have to punch a digit, since an incoming data call is not accompanied by a recognizable tone, in contrast to a fax call, which is.

FADE A reduction in a received signal which is caused by reflecting, refraction or absorption. See also FADING.

FADE MARGIN The depth of fade, expressed in dB, that a microwave receiver can tolerate while still maintaining acceptable circuit quality.

FADING The reduction in signal intensity of one or all of the components of a radio signal.

FADS Force Administration Data System. A system which takes basic statistics on telephone traffic and gives hints as to how many operators should be employed to answer the incoming calls and when they should be present.

FAIL SAFE A specially designed system that allows it to continue working after a failure. There are precious few, genuinely fail safe systems. To be genuinely fail safe, a system needs to be completed duplicated. It is prohibitively, expensive for most commercial users to duplicate every part of their system. But you can duplicate selectively and bring yourself closer to "fail safe." The extent of the duplications you choose (and thus the cost of your telephone equipment and transmission system) depends on how important it is that your system function as close to 100% as possible. The idea is to identify those things most likely to break and to duplicate them. Power is clearly the first area to focus on. These days, the words "FAIL SAFE" are increasingly being replaced with "FAULT TOLERANT." Given the number of times, your local, friendly airline has told you that its "computer is down," you can understand the reason for the wording change.

FAR-END CROSSTALK Crosstalk which travels along a circuit in the same direction as the signals in the circuit.

FAST BUSY A busy signal which sounds at twice the normal rate (120 interruptions/minute vs. 60/minute). A "fast busy" signals indicates that all trunks are busy.

FAST PACKET MULTIPLEXING Multiplexing is putting more than one "conversation" onto one circuit. You can do this in either of two ways — by splitting the channels sideways into subchannels of narrower frequency. This is called Frequency Division Multiplexing. Or you could split it by time. Like a railroad train. The first car carries "Conversation 1." The second carries "Conversation 2." And split them apart at the other end.

Fast packet multiplexing is a combination of three techniques — time division multiplexing, packetizing of voice and other analog signals and computer intelligence. Here are the main advantages fast packet multiplexing has over today's industry standard time division multiplexing:

1. Fast packet multiplexing doesn't blindly slot in "information" from devices if there's no information to send. Most other multiplexing techniques, including the most common — time division and frequency division — slot in capacity, whether the device is "talking" or not.

2. The fast packet multiplexer can start sending a packet before it has completely received the packet. This speed of movement is critical to voice, for example, which must move ultra-fast. Delays are devastating. (No one can afford to replace the phone instruments broken in anger.)

3. Fast packet multiplexing can interrupt the delivery of one packet in favor of sending another. It's OK to delay a packet of data by several milliseconds. It's not OK to delay a packet of voice or video.

FAST PACKET SWITCHING Packet switching that transports a dynamically varying combination of voice, fax, asynchronous and synchronous data, video and LAN traffic. See FAST PACKET MULTIPLEXING.

FAST SELECT In packet switched networks, a calling method which allows the user to send a limited amount of information along with a "call request packet" rather than after the packet.

FAST STAT MUX MICOM's advanced statistical multiplexer that uses data compression, priority echoplex handling and fast packet technology to improve throughput.

FAT File Allocation Table. The FAT is an integral of the MS-DOS operating system. It is like an index of a hard or floppy disk. It keeps track of where the various pieces of each file on a disk are stored. For a much longer explanation, see MS-DOS.

FAULT TOLERANT A method of making a computer or network system resistant to software errors and hardware problems. A fault tolerant LAN system tries to insure that even in the event of a power failure, a disk crash or a major user error, data isn't lost and the system can keep running. Cabling systems can also be fault tolerant, using redundant wiring so that even if a cable is cut, the system can keep running. True fault tolerance is very difficult to achieve.

FAX An abbreviation for FACSIMILE. See FACSIMILE, and FACSIMILE SWITCHES. The plural is FAXS.

FAX DEMODULATION A technique for taking a Group III fax signal and converting it back to its original 9.6 Kbps. It works like this: When a sheet of paper is inserted into a fax machine, the fax machine scans that paper into digital bits — a stream of 9600 bps. Then, for transmission over phone lines, that 9.6 Kbps is converted into an analog signal. But if you wish to transmit the fax signal over a digital line, then it makes sense to convert it back to its original 9.6 Kbps. That means you can put several fax transmissions on one 56 Kbps line — the capacity you'd normally need if you transmitted one voice conversation, or one erstwhile analog fax transmission.

FAXED The past tense of the new verb "to fax," as in "I faxed the document to him."

FAXES The verb for the act of faxing. "He faxes copies of his book to everybody." The plural is FAXS.

FB Framing bit.

FC AND PC Face Contact and Point Contact. Designations for fiber optic connectors designed by Nippon Telegraph and Telephone which feature a movable antirotation key allowing good repeatable performance despite numerous matings.

FCC Fellowship of Companies of Christ, a non-profit transdenominational organization called to motivate and equip Christian CEOs. (I didn't make that up.) See also FEDERAL COMMUNICATIONS COMMISSION.

FCC REGISTRATION NUMBER A number assigned to specific telephone equipment registered with the FCC, as set forth in FCC docket 19528, part 68. The presence of this number affixed to a device indicates that the FCC has approved it as being a compatible device for direct connection to telephone line facilities.

FCC TARIFF #9 The FCC tariff for private line services including Accunet T-1.5, DDS, Voice Grade circuits, and Accunet T45.

FCC TARIFF #11 The FCC tariff for local private line services.

FCC TARIFF #12 The FCC tariff for custom-designed integrated services. A special tariff that allows AT&T to develop custom network solutions, including allowing cus- tomers to install their networking multiplexers in AT&T central offices and letting AT&T manage the network.

FCC TARIFF #15 The proposed FCC tariff that allows AT&T to lower rates after all bids are placed to be competitive with other carriers.

FCFS A silly abbreviation for First Come First Served. See FIFO (First In, First Out).

FCOS Fully programmable classes of service that control user (Feature Class of Service) access to mailbox features, operations and options. Feature Classes of Service (FCOS) are entirely independent of Limits Classes of Service (LCOS).

FCS Frame Check Sequence. In bit-oriented protocols, a 16-bit field that contains transmission error checking information, usually appended to the end of the frame.

FDDI Fiber Distributed Data Interface. FDDI is an emerging ANSI standard for a 100 Mbps fiber optic LAN. It uses a "counter-rotating" token ring topology. It is compatible with the standards for the physical layer of the OSI model.

FDM Frequency Division Multiplexing. A technique in which the available transmission bandwidth of a circuit is divided by frequency into narrower bands, each used for a separate voice or data transmission channel. This means you can carry many conversations on one circuit. The conversations are separated by "guard channels." FDM is still the most used method of multiplexing long-haul conversations. It is typically used in analog transmission.

FDMA Frequency Division Multiple Access.

FDS Frequency Division Switching. Seldom used for voice switching. Primarily used for radio and TV broadcasting.

FDX See FULL DUPLEX.

FE Extended Framing ("F sub E"). An old name for ESF, also known as Extended SuperFrame, a T-1 carrier framing format that provides a 64 Kbps clear channel, error checking, 16 state signaling and some other nice data transmission features.

FE D4 SUPERFRAME EXTENDED Another designation for AT&T's ESF.

FEATURE BUTTONS Pushing a feature button replaces the need for the user to hit the switch hook and to hit the pushbutton pad to activate a feature of the telephone system. For example, hitting the call forward Feature Button sets the system up to forward calls. Think of a Feature Button as just a collection of numbers stored in a bin. When you hit the button, the bin disgorges all the numbers one after another fast.

FEATURE GROUPS A, B, C, D (FGA, FGB, FGC, FGD) Four separate switching arrangements available from local exchange carrier (LEC) end central offices to interexchange (long distance) carriers for accessing the LEC end-users who wish to make toll calls. Feature groups are described in a tariff filed by the National Exchange Carrier Association with the FCC. The feature group used by each IX carrier together with any special access surcharge determines the service they can provide their customers and the carrier common line access fee they will pay to the local exchange carrier involved. See the next four definitions.

FEATURE GROUP A Offers access to the local exchange carrier's network through a subscriber-type line connection rather than a trunk. It is a continuation of the ENFIA arrangement used in the early days of OCCs, until equal access using an access tandem central office is available. Remember, without equal access the IX carrier had to require its customers to dial a local number to reach their OCC's facilities, then dial an identification number, then dial long distance numbers of the called party desired. This service handicap, compared to AT&T's superior connections, qualifies the OCC for a discount off the FGA rate until access is equal. The IX carrier is billed by the LEC based upon actual monthly use rather than the ENFIA method of projected "minutes of use" rate.

FEATURE GROUP B Is similar to FGA, but provides a higher quality trunk line connection from end CO to the IX carrier's facilities, instead of the subscriber-type line. The IX customer can originate a call from anywhere within the LATA, while FGA requires customers to initiate the call from within the local exchange of the exchange carrier connecting to the IXC. FGB billings to the IX are on a flat usage basis, and a discount is applicable.

FEATURE GROUP C Is the traditional toll service arrangements offered by LECs to AT&T prior to breakup of the Bell System. Quality is superior, and the service includes automatic number identification of the calling party, answerback, and disconnection supervision, and the subscribers can use either a dial or touch-tone pad. This FGC service is offered only to AT&T without a discount.

FEATURE GROUP D Is the class of service associated with equal access arrangements. All IX carriers enjoy identical connections to the local exchange carrier. All customers dial the same number of digits, and can reach the predetermined IX of their choice by dialing 1 plus the telephone number being called. When equal access is implemented, all other feature groups convert to FGD and the IX is billed for actual measured use, without discount. In some cases an IX carrier may desire to maintain FGA or FGB arrangements, but the FGD equal access rates will apply.

FEATURE KEYS See FEATURE BUTTONS. A key is to a telephone man what a switch is to an electrical man.

FEATURE PHONE A generic name for a telephone that incorporates extra features (typically one button speed dial buttons) designed to simplify and speed operation.

FEC Forward Error Correction. A technique used by a receiver for correcting errors incurred in transmission over a communications channel without requiring retransmission of any information by the transmitter. Typically involves a convolution of the transmitter using a common algorithm. See FORWARD ERROR CORRECTION.

FED-STD A system of standards numbered FED-STD-1001 to 1008 which set modulation specifications for data transmission.

FEDERAL COMMUNICATIONS COMMISSION The federal organization in Washington, DC, set up by the Communications Act of 1934. It has the authority to regulate all interstate (but not intrastate) communications originating in the United States. The FCC is run by a seven member board appointed by the President. Stripped of all the extensive regulatory and legal mumbo jumbo, the FCC essentially does three things: 1. It sets the prices for interstate phone, data and video service. 2. It determines who can or cannot get into the business of providing telecommunications service or equipment in the United States. 3. It determines the electrical and physical standards for telecommunications equipment. The FCC's powers, although strong, are tempered (limited) by (a) The Federal Courts. Anyone who disagrees with FCC rulings can appeal them to a Federal Court. (b) The Justice Department. The Justice Department changed the industry with Divestiture. (c) Congress and (d) The 50 state public service commissions.

FEDERAL TELECOMMUNICATIONS SYSTEM The private network used primarily by the civilian agencies of the federal government to call other government locations and to place calls to phones connected to the public network.

FEDERAL-STATE JOINT BOARD An organization with representatives from the FCC and the state public service commissions which tries to resolve Federal and State conflicts on telecommunications regulatory issues. Sometimes successfully and sometimes not successfully.

FEEDBACK The return of part of an output signal back to the input side of the device. Think of the high-pitched squeal you hear when someone brings a microphone too close to the loudspeaker. Not all feedback is as obvious or as irritating. Some feedback is good. See SIDETONE, which is what happens when you hear a little in the receiver of you're saying in the transmitter of a phone.

FEEDER CABLE Cabling connecting an intermediate distribution frame to a main distribution frame.

FEEDHOLES Holes punched in paper or papertape which allow the paper or paper tape to be driven by sprocket wheels.

FEFO First Ended, First Out. A rule for dealing with things in a queue. For example, higher priority messages will be sent out first before lower priority messages.

FEMTOSECOND One-millionth of a billionth of a second. Femtoseconds are used in laser transmission. It's 10 to the minus 15.

FEP Front End Processor. The "traffic cop" of the data communications world. Typically sits in front of a computer and is designed to handle the telecommunications burden, so the computer can concentrate on handling the processing burden. Here's a more technical definition: A dedicated communications system that intercepts and handles activity for the host.

Can perform line control, message handling, code conversion, error control, and such applications functions as control and operation of special-purpose terminals. Designed to offload the host computer of data communications functions.

FERNSPRECHVERMITTLUNGSSTELLE A central office in German. In Europe, they call central offices "public exchanges," or just plain "exchange." They look at you kinda strange when you say the North American word, namely "central office."

FERREED ASSEMBLY A glass enclosed reed relay switch in which the reeds are made of some metal which can be opened or closed by an external magnetic field.

FERRI CHROME A tape combining a layer of ferric oxide particles and a layer of chromium dioxide particles, for the attributes of both.

FERRIC OXIDE A tape whose coating is of red iron oxide, the original material used for magnetic recording tapes.

FDDI Fiber Distributed Data Interface

FF Form Feed. A printer function used to skip to the top of the next page or form.

FGB See FEATURE GROUP B.

FGC-EA See FEATURE GROUP C - Equal Access.

FGD See FEATURE GROUP D.

FGD-EA Feature Group D - Equal Access. See FEATURE GROUP D, also See EQUAL ACCESS.

FIBER LOSS Attenuation of the light signal in optical fiber transmission.

FIBER OPTICS Fiber Optics are thin filaments of glass through which light beams are transmitted over long distances carrying enormous amounts of data. Modulating light on thin strands of glass produces major benefits in high bandwidth, relatively low cost, low power consumption, small space needs, total insensitivity to electromagnetic interference and great insensitivity to being bugged. All these benefits have great attraction to anyone who needs vast, clean transmission capacity, to the military and to anyone who runs a factory with lots of electronic machinery.

The first field trial of an AT&T lightwave system took place in Chicago in 1977. There has been a rapid improvement in cost effectiveness of fiber systems, expressed as cost per bit per kilometer. A one hundredfold decrease in cost in one five-year period — from about 1980 to 1985! See LEDs.

FIBERPHONE A battery-powered device that connects to both ends of a fiber optic cable allowing people (typically craftspeople) to talk over the cable. The complete device (two ends) costs $1,000 to $2,000 and often comes with a headset.

FIBERWORLD In simultaneous media events in Washington and Montreal on October 12, 1989, Northern Telecom and Bell Northern Research (BNR) unveiled "FiberWorld," which they referred to "as a vision and commitment to deliver the world's first completely family of fiber-optic access, transport, and switching products."

FIELD 1. One half (every other line) of a television picture "frame". There are 60 fields per second in American television. 2. That indefinable place your salesman is when you want him most urgently. "He's in the field." 3. The specific location of data within a record. In the jargon of data base management systems, many fields make up one record Many records make up one file. Here's another explanation. A field is one of the basic subdivisions of a data record. The record on you in your company's data base might include your name, your address, your salary, etc. A field is simply one of these — e.g. your salary, your last name, or your street address. All the records of all the employees in your company make up a file, also called a data base.

FIELD PROGRAMMABLE The ability of a system to have changes made in its program while it is installed — without having to be returned to the factory.

FIELD STRENGTH METER Electronic instrument that measures the intensity of the magnetic field.

FIFO First In, First Out. All telephone networks are a tradeoff. It's simply too expensive to build a phone network which will be ready to give everyone dial tone and a circuit — if everyone picked up the phone simultaneously and tried to make a call. There are basically two ways of handling calls which cannot be sent on their way — i.e. for which there's no present available capacity. First, you can "block" the call. This means giving the caller a busy or a "nothing" (also called "high and dry"). Second, you can put the call into a queue. Now you have people waiting in queue, how do you handle them? The most equitable — the way most queues work — is to handle the calls on the basis of First In, First Out. (First in, first handled.) There are other ways of handling calls in a queue — including First In, Last Out, by priority (e.g. which line you came in on and how much it cost, or how high you are in the corporation, etc.)

FIFTH GENERATION Fifth generation computers and telephone systems will be based on artificial intelligence. A fifth generation phone system may make far more sophisticated decisions about routing calls across networks. Those decisions may be made on how many calls have already happened so far that month, the choice of carrier by the likely quality of his connection, etc.

FIGS FIGure Shift. A physical shift in a terminal using Baudot Code that enables the printing of numbers, symbols and upper-case letters.

FILE A set of similarly structured data records (such as personnel records using a standardized form). See FIELD.

FILE LOCKING A method of insuring data integrity. With a file locking system, only one user can update a file at a time. Other users are locked out, unable to access the file. Contrast to *record locking.* File server A thing containing files, which are shared by everyone connected to a LAN. In some LANs the device is a microcomputer. In other LANs, this device is a special computer with a huge disk drive and specialized software. In still other LANs, any PC can be a file server, depending on the software it runs. File servers can offer all types of resources, from simple data storage, to gateways and protocol conversion. A file server usually has software rules for allowing LAN users to get into and out of the files and databases it stores. There are also software rules for the other devices, like serial and gateway ports, that a file server shares.

FILE MAINTENANCE The job of keeping your data base files up to date by adding, changing or deleting data.

FILE MANAGEMENT The system of rules and policies for maintaining a set of files — including how files can be created, accessed, retrieved and deleted.

FILE SERVER A file server is an integral part of a multi-user computer network, e.g. a local area network (LAN). It typically is a combination computer, data management software, and large capacity hard disk drive. A file server directs all movement of files and data on a multi-user communications network and gives each user on the network access to files stored on the file server. It allows the user to store information, leave electronic mail messages for other users on the system and access application software on the file server — e.g. word processing, spreadsheet. A file server also stops more than one user accessing (and potentially changing) a file at the same time. A file server might also contain file locking capabilities. This means that certain files are "locked" to certain users, i.e. those users cannot access those files.

FILTER A device which transmits a select range of energy. An electrical filter transmits a selected range of frequencies, while stopping (attenuating) all others. It is used to suppress unwanted frequencies or noise, or to separate channels in communications circuits. Such a filter might be called a BANDPASS filter. You can also use a filter to remove certain characters you might be receiving over a data communications channel, for example control characters, or higher-order nonstandard ASCII bits.

FIPS Federal Information Processing Standard. See also FIPS PUBS nn.

FIPS PUBS nn Various standards for data communications.

FIRMWARE Programs kept in semipermanent storage, such as various types of read-only memory. These programs can be altered, but with difficulty. Firmware is used in conjunction with hardware and software. It also shares the characteristics of both. Firmware is usually stored on PROMS (Programmable Read Only Memory) or EPROMs (Electrical PROMS). Firmware contains software which is so constantly called upon by a computer or phone system that it is "burned" into a chip, thereby becoming Firmware. The computer program is written into the PROM electrically at higher than usual voltage, causing the bits to "retain" the pattern as it is "burned in." Firmware is non-volatile. It will not be "forgotten" when the power is shut off. Hand-held calculators contain firmware with the instructions for doing their various mathematical operations.

FIRST OFFICE APPLICATION The first Ericsson AXE central office to put a new feature into service.

FISH To push a stiff steel wire or tape through a conduit or interior wall. Pull through wires, cable or a heavier pulling-in is then attached to one end of the steel wire. The other end is then pulled until the wire or cable appears.

FIVE BY FIVE Slang expression meaning satisfactory transmission in both directions.

FIXED FORMAT A way of communicating in which everything to be sent follows a predetermined sequence, i.e. it fits into a specific length and format. The idea is to allow you to predict message length, the location of the message, where the control characters are, etc.

FIXED LENGTH RECORDS A set of data records all having the same number of characters in them. For example, everyone has a five digit zip code. This is called a fixed length record.

FIXED RATE A fixed monthly price. See also FLAT RATE.

FLAG 1. A variable in a program to inform the program later on that a condition has been met. 2. In synchronous transmission, a flag is a pattern of six consecutive 1 bits used to mark the beginning and end of a "Frame" (IBM jargon for a packet). The character representation of the six consecutive "1" bits is 01111110. See ZERO STUFFING.

FLAME-RESISTANT Insulated wire which has been chemically treated so it will not aid the spread of flames.

FLAME-RETARDANT Constructed or treated so as not be able to convey flame.

FLAMMABILITY Measure of a material's ability to support combustion.

FLASH Quickly depressing and releasing the plunger in or the actual handset-cradle to create a signal to a PBX or Centrex that special instructions will follow such as transferring the call to another extension.

FLASH BUTTON A button on a phone which performs the same thing as quickly touching the switch hook on a phone. See FLASH and FLASHPHONE.

FLASH CUT The conversion from an old to a new phone system occurs instantly as one is removed from the circuit and the other is brought in. There are advantages and disadvantages to Hot Cuts. For one, they're likely to be much more dangerous than the opposite view, known as a Parallel Cut, in which the two phone systems run side by side for a month or so. Also known as HOT CUT.

FLASHPHONE A Rolm single line analog phone that has a "flash" button. If you pushed this button, it gave the PBX the same signal as if you had flicked the touch hook up and down. The PBX would then give you a dial tone and you could pushbutton in codes to get access to the PBX's features, like transfer, etc. See FLASH.

FLAT RATE An erstwhile common method of pricing local phone calls in the United States. The concept was that for a flat rate amount of money — say

$10 a month — you received a plain old desk telephone and an unlimited number of local calls. For years, most residential and most business phones were on a flat rate service. The first thing to go was the phone instrument. You had to pay a dollar or so a month to continue renting it, or you could send it back and buy your own. Second to go was the size of the local calling area you could call. It got smaller. Third to go were the phone calls themselves. This happened first with businesses and now increasingly with residential service. Under this new "pay-per-call" you get charged a "message unit" for each local calls. A message unit is typically eight to ten cents. But psychologically, "message units" sound better than dimes. Fourth to go was the definition of local calls. What was now a "local" call got smaller, i.e. you could call less far for the price of a local call. And what was now a "local" long distance call changed. Calls which, years ago, were free (i.e. on flat rate service) have now become long distance calls. You can witness this phenomenon of changing local pricing in California, New York and Jersey. In other states, it's taking a little longer. There are cities where flat rate service still exists. Treasure them. They're disappearing, too.

FLEX LIFE The measurement of the ability of a conductor or cable to withstand repeated bending.

FLEXIBLE DIALING PATTERN A PBX dialing pattern that allows you to set your PBX so it can have one, two, three or four digit numbers for its extensions. See also FLEXIBLE NUMBERING OF STATIONS.

FLEXIBLE DRILL BIT A long drill bit that bends and is used for pulling cable and wire through walls in one operation. This means you drill the hole and then reverse the drill and it pulls the cable through the hole, while the drill bit is still inserted. Diversified Manufacturing of Graham, NC makes such a marvelous product.

FLEXIBLE INTERCEPT Allows you to assign "operator intercept" service to those extensions you wish for whatever reason, unassigned number, temporary disconnect, etc.

FLEXIBLE LINE RINGING A PBX feature which allows different phones to have different ringing for incoming calls from inside the building and from outside. Different ringing for intercom calls, different for inter-net calls, different ringing for outside calls, etc.

FLEXIBLE NUMBERING OF STATIONS A PBX feature which allows you some flexibility in the way you number the extensions off your PBX. How much flexibility depends on the particular PBX and the number of extensions you have. Hotels like giving their hotel phones the same number as the rooms. Makes sense. See FLEXIBLE STATION NUMBERING.

FLEXIBLE PRICING TARIFFS A regulatory procedure which permits rates for certain services to be changed quickly to meet market conditions, i.e. competition.

FLEXIBLE RELEASE The ability of the switching system to release a connection when either party hangs up.

FLEXIBLE STATION NUMBERING A feature that allows telephone extensions to be numbered according to their physical location or departmental location, etc. No rewiring is required for in-place telephones. It's all done in software. See FLEXIBLE NUMBERING OF STATIONS.

FLEXIBILITY The quality of a cable or cable component which allows for bending under the influence of outside force, as opposed to limpness which is bending due to the cable's own weight.

FLEXPATH FLEXPATH service provides a 1.544 Mbps interface between a digital PBX and a New York Telephone central office and supports Direct Inward Dialing (DID) and Direct Outward Dialing (DOD).

FLINK A FLash and a wINK makes a flink signal.

FLIP FLOP A device or circuit which can assume either of two stable states. Flip flop devices are used to store one bit of information.

FLOPPY DISK A thin, flexible plastic disk resembling a phonograph record upon which computer data is stored magnetically. Called a floppy disk because it is flexible and can (and will) flop inside a drive as it is being turned. And it may sound as though it is flopping. Floppy disks were never designed as the permanent storage many people are using them for at present. Floppy disks were designed by IBM as a way of having its sellers and engineers carry programs and program updates to its customers. Floppy disks were lighter and less cumbersome than carrying heavy spools of magnetic tape. IBM designed its floppy disks to be thrown away once their information was loaded into the mainframe computer. The moral of this story is that floppy disks are NOT permanent reliable storage. Anything stored on floppy disks should be backed up at least once and, if possible, twice. Floppy disks come in three diameter sizes — 3 1/2, 5 1/4 and 8 inches. Floppy disks should never be put through X-ray machines at airports.

FLOPPY MINI A floppy disk smaller than the traditional 5 1/4 inch diameter floppy disk. Now most commonly the 3 1/2 inch size invented by Sony, and used by the Apple Macintosh, among others. All MS-DOS laptop computers have 3 1/2 inch disks, also called MICROFLOPPIES.

FLOWCHART A graphic or diagram which shows how a complex operation, such as programming, takes place. The flowchart breaks that operation down into its smallest, and easiest-to-understand events.

FLOW CONTROL 1. The hardware, software and procedure for controlling the transfer of messages or characters between two points in a data network — such as between a protocol converter and a printer — to prevent loss of data when the receiving device's buffer begins to reach its capacity. 2. The process of protecting network service by denying access to additional traffic that would further add to congestion. (Think about flow control and the airlines.)

FLUSH OUTLET A Communication Outlet recessed into the wall. This type of outlet may be positioned approximately 12" above the floor level for the connection of portable communications devices or at shoulder height to accept permanent wall telephone installations.

FLUTTER A rapid change in an electrical signal. The change may be in strength, frequency or phase.

FM See FREQUENCY MODULATION.

FM STEREO SEPARATION A measure of a radio tuner's ability to separate the left and right hand channels of a stereo broadcast. The higher the number, the greater the separation. The unit of measure is the Decibel (dB), a logarithmic unit which expresses the ratio between two voltage, current or power levels, usually relating to a standard reference level, or a background noise level.

FOLLOW-ME CALL FORWARDING Rolm's way of saying Progressive Call Forwarding. Allows a previously forwarded call to be forwarded from that to another extension.

FONT A type face. The words you are now reading are in the Helvetica normal type font, also called Helios by some people.

FOOTPRINT 1. The area on the earth's surface where the signals from a specific satellite can be received. A footprint is shown as a series of concentric contour lines that show the area covered and the decreasing power of the signal as it spreads out from the center. 2. The area on a desk a computer will occupy, i.e. the computer's footprint.

FORCE ADMINISTRATION DATA SYSTEM See FADS.

FORCED ACCOUNT CODE BILLING A telephone feature which prevents call from being completed if the user does not pushbutton in a billing code. That billing code may correspond to the department within the company. Or it may conform to the client and to the client's matter number the call must be billed to.

FORCED AUTHORIZATION CODE FAC. A PBX feature which requires all or certain users to enter a code before dialing an outside number.

FORCED RELEASE/DISCONNECT The switching center's automatic hang-up if the calling party fails to do so at the end of a conversation.

FORCED ROUTE OVERRIDE Allows a PBX user to automatically redirect an outgoing call to a different trunk if the first trunk is busy or the connection is poor.

FOREGROUND PROCESSING Automatic execution of computer programs designed to preempt the use of the computing facilities. Usually a real time, urgent program. Contrast this with Background Processing, which might be something less urgent, for example, diagnostics of the system.

FOREIGN AREA TRANSLATION Translating the office codes of a distant (foreign) area to codes that make sense to a PBX which has more than one way of completing the call to that area.

FOREIGN CENTRAL OFFICE SERVICE Getting telephone service in a multi-office exchange from a central office other than the one you are normally served by. Not a common term any longer. Foreign central office service is the same price as normal local telephone service. It typically just involves asking for service off another central office. For example, our main number in New York City is 212-691-8215. Our 691- central office is in the 18th Street Exchange, a tall building on 18th Street. There is another central office in the same building. It is 206- and it is a more modern central office. When we ordered additional lines, we ordered them from this central office. You can now also call us on 212-206-6660.

FOREIGN EMF Any unwanted voltage on a telecommunications circuit.

FOREIGN EXCHANGE SERVICE FX. Provides local telephone service from a central office which is outside (foreign to) the subscriber's exchange area. In its simplest form, a user picks up the phone in one city and receives a dial tone in the foreign city. He will also receive calls dialed to the phone in the foreign city. This means that people located in the foreign city can place a local call to get the user. The airlines use a lot of foreign exchange service. Many times, the seven digit local phone number for the airline you just called will be answered in another city, hundreds of miles away.

FORTRAN FORmula TRANslating System. A computer programming language.

FORWARD CHANNEL The communications path carrying data or voice from the person who made the call. The Forward Channel is the opposite of the Reverse Channel.

FORWARD ERROR CORRECTION A system of data transmission in which redundant bits generated at the transmitted end are used at the receiving terminal to detect, locate and correct any transmission errors before delivery to the local data communications link. The idea of forward error correction is to avoid having to retransmit information sent incorrectly. This technique is consuming of bandwidth.

FOTS Fiber Optics Transmission Systems. Not the same as POTS. But a neat acronym, nevertheless.

FOURIER'S THEOREM In the early 1800s, the French mathematician Emile Fourier proved that a repeating, time-varying function may be expressed as the sum of a (possibly infinite) series of sine and cosine waves. Digital data is a bit stream, which can be sent as a sequence of square waves. Fourier's Theorem shows that to send a square wave (digital signal), a series of sine waves (analog signals) are actually summed together. If 1,000 square waves are to be sent every second, for example, the frequency components of the sine waves that are summed together are 1 kHz, 3 kHz, 5 kHz, 7 kHz, etc. The point of this analysis is to show that high frequency signals are required to form a stable, recognizable square wave. As the bit rate increases, the square wave frequency increases and the width of the square waves decrease. Thus, narrower square waves require sine waves of even higher frequencies to form the digital signal. Note, then, that there is insufficient bandwidth in the 3 kHz voiceband to send square waves due to the absence of frequency components above 3,300 Hz. Even low frequency square waves cannot be sent because sine waves below 300 Hz are also absent. Thus, the local loop, according to Fourier's Theorem, cannot be used for the transmission of digital signals!

The last paragraph is, in fact, no longer totally correct, as the increasingly successful ISDN trials are proving.

FOUR-WIRE A transmission path that allows physical separation of transmit and receive channels. At one time, 4-wire was the only method for implementing full-duplex transmission.

FOUR-WIRE ADAPTER A device which allows the connection of two-wire telephone equipment to a four-wire line. See FOUR-WIRE CIRCUITS.

FOUR-WIRE CIRCUITS Telephone lines using two wires for transmitting and two wires for receiving, i.e. four altogether. All long distance circuits are four-wire. Almost all local phone lines are two-wire. All analog phones are two-wire. Four-wire circuits offer much higher quality.

FOUR-WIRE REPEATER A repeater with two amplifiers, one used to amplify the signal going. The other used to amplify the signal coming. See FOUR-WIRE CIRCUITS.

FOUR-WIRE TERMINATING SET An electrical device which takes a four-wire circuit — one pair coming and one pair going — and turns it into the "normal" tip and ring circuit you need for a typical telephone, key system or PBX. See FOUR-WIRE CIRCUITS.

FOX MESSAGE A standard sentence for testing teletypewriter circuits because it uses all the letters on the keyboard. That sentence is The quick brown fox jumped over the lazy sleeping dog.

FP File Processor

FP Feature Package. A software release for AT&T's Dimension PBX.

FR-1 A flammability rating established by Underwriters Laboratories for wires and cables that pass a specially designed vertical flame test. This designation has been replaced by VW-1.

FRACTIONAL T-1 Service offering data rates between 64 kbps (DSO rate) and 768 kbps (half the full T-1 rate). See also ASDS.

FRAME 1. A group of bits sent serially (one after another). Generally a frame is a logical transmission unit. A frame usually contains its own control information for addressing and error checking. A frame is the basic data transmission unit employed in bit-oriented protocols. In this way, a frame is similar to a block. In video transmission, a frame is usually 525 electron scan lines that comprise one TV picture. 2. One complete cycle of events in time-division multiplexing. The frame usually includes a sequence of time slots for the various sub-channels as well as extra bits for control, calibration, etc. 3. A distributing frame. A rectangular steel bar framework having "verticals and horizontals" which is used to place semipermanent wire cross connections to permanent equipment. Found in telephone rooms and central offices. See FRAME RELAY and DISTRIBUTION FRAME.

FRAME CHECK SEQUENCE Bits added to the end of a frame for error detection. Similar to a block check character (BCC). In bit-oriented protocols, a frame check sequence is a 16-bit field added to the end of a frame that contains transmission error-checking information.

FRAME ERRORS In the 12-bit, D4 frame word, an error is counted when the 12-bit frame word received does not conform to the standard 12-bit frame word pattern.

FRAME GRABBER A device in a visual display unit which allows you to store and display one frame of information.

FRAME GROUND FGD. Frame Ground is connected to the equipment chassis and thus provides a protective ground. Frame Ground is usually connected to an external ground such as the ground pin of an AC power plug.

FRAME RELAY Frame relay switching is a form of switching that lies between circuit switching and packet switching. Like X.25 packet networks, frame relay networks use bandwidth only when there is traffic to send. However, like circuit switching, frame relay is transparent to most data communications protocols in use today and can switch traffic at relatively high speeds.

Frame relay does not support voice. The reason is that voice traffic is highly sensitive to variations in the transmission delay introduced by the networks, while such small variations are usually not as critical to data traffic. In order for voice to be supported satisfactorily in a packet mode environment, each packet must have a time-stamp which is monitored by the network. Frame relay lacks such a mechanism.

In a late September 1990 press US Sprint, which announced it was making frame relay switches, said that frame relay was:

- A new high-speed, statistically multiplexed interface standard.
- Two layers of the OSI network model, as compared to X.25, which is three layers.
- Relies on intelligent end user devices such as LAN routers and front end processors (FEPs) for error control.
- Works best when used in conjunction with high quality transmission facilities, such as fiber optics.
- A packet mode technology using "virtual circuit" functionality for bandwidth-on-demand connectivity.
- Designed to carry data and (still) image, not voice.

Frame Relay is also a new international standard for efficiently handling high-speed, bursty data over wide area networks. It offers lower costs and higher performance for those applications in contrast to the traditional point-to-point services. With frame relay, a pool of bandwidth is made instantly available to any of the concurrent data sessions sharing the circuit whenever a burst of data occurs. An addressed frame is sent into the network, which in turn interprets the address and sends the information to its destination at up to 2.048 Mbps.

The American National Standards Institute (ANSI) describes frame relay service in the following documents:

ANSI T1.602 — Telecommunications - ISDN — Data Link Layer Signaling Specification for Application at the User Network Interface.

ANSI T1.606 — Frame Relaying Bearer Service — Architectural Framework and Service Description.

ANSI T1S1/90 - 175 - Addendum to T1.606 - Frame Relaying Bearer Service — Architectural Framework and Service Description.

ANSI T1S1/90-214 - DSS1 - Core Aspects of Frame Protocol for Use with Frame Relay Bearer Service.

ANSI T1S1/90-213 - DSS1 — Signaling Specific for Frame Relay Bearer Service.

US Sprint put an edition of its TeleNotes on "the Frame Relay Solution."

FRAMING An error control procedure with multiplexed digital channels, such as T-1, where bits are inserted so that the receiver can identify the time slots that are allocated to each subchannel. Framing bits may also carry alarm signals indicating specific alarms.

FRAMING ERROR An error occurring when a receiver improperly interprets the set of bits within a frame.

FRANCHISE The exclusive right to operate telephone service in a community. This right — also called the franchise — is granted by some government agency. Some phone companies existed before the appropriate regulatory authority, so they're "grandfathered" in their exclusivity. Some phone companies have an exclusive area to serve more because of their presence than because of the legal right conferred on them. The question of who has a franchise to serve what community with what service is becoming increasingly unclear as competition penetrates all aspects of the phone industry.

FRD Fire RetarDant. A rating used for cable within duPont's Teflon or equivalent fluorpolymer material. FRD cable is used when local fire codes call for low flame and low smoke cable. FRD cable is typically run in forced air plenums as an alternative to metal conduits.

FREEPHONE The overseas name for what we know as 800 IN-WATS service, international 800 service. And it means you can now have your overseas customers call you for free on an 800 line, just as your domestic customers do. The service is available from companies including Australia, Brazil, France, Hong Kong, Israel, Italy, Japan, Sweden, Switzerland and the United Kingdom. See EIGHTHUNDRED SERVICE.

FREEZE FRAME The transmission of discrete video picture frames at a data rate which is too slow to provide the psychovisual perception of natural motion, referred to as "full-motion." An uncompressed, digitized full-motion video signal is typically transmitted at a rate of 90 Mbps. Freeze frame can be carried on anything from a simple voice grade phone line operating at 9.6 Kbps (the same speed as a Group 3 facsimile machine) or a DDS channel at 64 Kbps.

FREQUENCY The rate at which an electrical current alternates, usually measured in Hertz. Hertz is a unit of measure which means "cycles per second."

FREQUENCY AGILITY The ability of a cellular mobile telephone system to shift automatically between frequencies.

FREQUENCY BAND The portion of the electromagnetic spectrum within a specified upper- and lower-frequency limit. Also known as Frequency Range.

FREQUENCY DIVERSITY A way of protecting a radio signal by providing a second, continuously operating radio signal on a different frequency which will assume the load when the regular channel fails.

FREQUENCY DIVISION MULTIPLE ACCESS A technique for sharing a single transmission channel (such as a satellite transponder) among two or more users by assigning each to an exclusive frequency band within the channel.

FREQUENCY DIVISION MULTIPLEXING FDM. An older technique in which the available transmission bandwidth of a circuit is divided by frequency into narrower bands, each used for a separate voice or data transmission channel. This means you can carry many conversations on one circuit.

FREQUENCY HOPPING Another name for spread spectrum transmission. A technique developed during the second world war for through-the-air transmissions to prevent the enemy from jamming or eavesdropping on conversations. The idea is to jump from one frequency to another as you transmit information.

FREQUENCY MODULATION A modulation technique in which the carrier frequency is shifted by an amount proportional to the value of the modulating signal. The amplitude of the carrier signals remains constant. The deviation of the carrier frequency determines the signal content of the message. Commercial TV and FM radio use this technique, which is much less sensitive to noise and interference.

FREQUENCY RESPONSE The variation (dB) in relative strength between frequencies in a given frequency band, usually the voice frequency band of an analog telephone line.

FREQUENCY SHIFT KEYING FSK. A modulation technique for data transmission. It shifts the frequency above the carrier for a 1 and below the carrier for a 0 (zero). See also FSK.

FRIESEN, GERRY The world's best telecommunications sales authority. Formerly the world's best telecommunications seller. These two definitions contributed by Mr. Friesen, who is a half-integral part of the operation which published this dictionary and who is not shy. But we love him all the same. Call him if you find any mistakes in this dictionary. He didn't write it. But he should take the blame, anyway. His phone number is 215-355-2886.

FRL Facility Restriction Level. A term created by AT&T for its Dimension PBX. Refers to imposing dialing restrictions on telephone extensions.

FROGGING Frogging is the process of inverting line frequencies of a carrier system so that incoming high-frequency channels leave at low frequencies and vice versa. Frogging equalizes the transmission loss between high and low frequency channels.

FRONT END CONTROLLER See FRONT END PROCESSOR.

FRONT END EQUIPMENT The equipment positioned between a computer and the communications line(s). Its purpose is to organize data being sent and received.

FRONT END PROCESSOR FEP. An FEP is a computer under the control of another, larger computer in a communications network. That FEP does simple, basic "housekeeping" operations on the data streams as they arrive to be processed by the bigger computer. The FEP acts as a sort of intelligent traffic cop. It relieves the bigger, host computer of some of its telecommunications Input/Output burden. Depending on its sophistication, the front end processor might also perform serial to parallel conversion, protocol conversion, block or message assembly, etc.

FSK Frequency Shift Keying. A modulation technique for translating 1's and 0's into something that can be carried over telephone lines, like sounds. A "1" will be assigned a certain frequency of tone, and a "0" to another tone. The transmission of the bits keys the sounds to shift from one frequency to the other. See also FREQUENCY SHIFT KEYING.

FTP File Transfer Protocol. In local area networking technology, file-sharing protocol that operates at layers 5 through 7 of the Open Systems Interconnection (OSI) model.

FTS Federal Telecommunications System is a private telephone network sometimes shared enthusiastically by all federal government agencies.

FULL AVAILABILITY Idealized condition which exists when your phone system can provide connections for every telephone connected to it. Also called NON-BLOCKING.

FULL DUPLEX Transmission in two directions simultaneously, or, more technically, bidirectional, simultaneous two-way communications. The best two-way phone conversations take place on four-wire circuits, two for transmission in one direction and two for transmission in the other. All long distance circuits are four wire. Most local lines are two wire, which means they're a compromise. Most speakerphones are half-duplex, meaning they only transmit in one direction at one time. The speakerphone flips its direction based on who's talking, or, more precisely, who's talking the loudest. Full duplex speakerphones are the best, but they're expensive. See also SPEAKERPHONES. See also FOUR-WIRE CIRCUITS.

FULL ECHO SUPPRESSOR An echo suppressor in which the speech signals on each path are used to control the suppression loss in the other path of a 4-wire circuit. Used for long-distance communications. Compare with split echo compressor.

FULL MOTION VIDEO Television transmission where images are sent and displayed in real-time and motion is continuous. Compare with freeze frame. See FREEZE FRAME VIDEO.

FULL SYSTEM BATTERY BACKUP This means there's sufficient battery power backing the phone system so that during a power outage, the telephone system will continue to work, i.e. you won't even know the commercial power has gone out. All programming will be intact. Calls will get through, etc. Full System Battery Backup is critical to many businesses, especially those in the "life or death" business, such as hospitals, police, fire departments, etc. Other businesses who depend highly on the phone for their revenues — airlines, brokerage companies, hotel/motels, etc. — often also use full system battery backup.

FULLY CONNECTED NETWORK A network topology in which each node is directly connected by branches to all other nodes. This architecture becomes impractical as the number of nodes in the network increases in complexity. Such networks normally go to distributed nodes.

FULLY PERFORATED Paper tape which has information on it as represented by the holes punched through it.

FULLY RESTRICTED STATIONS In a PBX, fully restricted stations (also called phones) can't place any outside calls. They can make intercom calls as well as receive incoming calls.

FUNCTION KEY 1. A key on a computer keyboard that has a defined function, such as the DELETE or BACK SPACE key. 2. An undefined key that can be defined to perform one function, which would normally require the user hitting one or several keys in succession. For example, one function key might move a block of data from one point in a file to another point.

FUNCTIONAL ENTITY FE. A set of functions that provides one or more specified capabilities. Seven FEs have been identified for the Advanced Intelligent Network Release 1 architecture: Network Access, Service Switching, Service Logic and Control, Information Management, Service Assistance, Automatic Message Accounting and Operations. Definition from Bellcore in reference to its concept of the Advanced Intelligent Network.

FUNCTIONAL GROUP A collection of FEs (Functional Entities) that reside together in a system.

FUNCTIONAL RESOURCE An abstraction of physical entities (e.g., voice synthesizers) that the Service Assistance FE (Functional Entities) can manipulate.

FUNCTIONAL SPECIFICATION A description of a system from a working point of view. It differs from a precise technical description which includes each piece of equipment precisely spelled out. A system can often work functionally the same using different hardware and software configurations. By functionally describing a system, a user allows sellers to use their imagination to solve the problem in the most creative, cost-effective way. Most sellers prefer functional descriptions.

FUNCTIONAL SPLIT A division within an automatic call distributor (ACD) which allows incoming calls to be directed from a specific group of trunks to a specific group of agents.

FUNCTIONAL TEST A test carried out under normal working conditions to verify that a circuit or particular part of the equipment works properly.

FUNCTIONAL USER An entity external to the functional architecture that uses the functional architecture capabilities to exchange information with other functional users. Definition from Bellcore in reference to its concept of the Advanced Intelligent Network.

FX See FOREIGN EXCHANGE.

G-STYLE HANDSET A G-style handset is a standard round handset, as compared to the K-style handset, which is the newer square handset with the two screws in the middle.

GAIN The increase in signaling power that occurs as the signal is boosted by an electronic device. It's measured in decibels (dB).

GAIN HIT A cause of errors in data transmission over phone lines. Usually the signal surges more than 3dB and lasts for more than four milliseconds. AT&T's standard calls for eight or fewer gain hits in a 15-minute period.

GALLIUM ARSENIDE A substance from which microprocessor and memory chips are made. Compared with silicon, GaAs:

- is three to 10 times faster or, depending on its speed, uses as little as one-tenth the power,
- can detect, emit and convert light into electrical signals, opening the possibility of providing optoelectronic properties on a single chip.
- can resist up to 10,000 times the radiation.
- can withstand operating temperatures of 200 degrees Centigrade, and
- has a higher electron mobility.

GALVANOMETER A device used to measure small currents.

GARAGE Silicon Valley, according to contemporary lore, started in a garage in Palo Alto in 1939. In that year Bill Hewlett and Dave Packard started Hewlett Packard with $538. Hewlett was the inventor and Packard the manager. Their first product, an audio oscillator, was an immediate success. Walt Disney used it in making Fantasia.

GARBAGE IN, GARBAGE OUT GIGO. If the input data is wrong or inaccurate, the output data will be inaccurate or wrong. GIGO is problem with data entered by hand into computer systems. Ask yourself how many times you've received "junk" mail with the wrong spelling of your name? That's called Garbage In, Garbage Out.

GAS TUBE A method of protecting phone lines and phone equipment from high voltage caused by lightning strikes. See CARBON BLOCK (another protection technology) for a more detailed explanation.

GATE This a term typically used in Automatic Call Distributors, devices used for handling many incoming telephone calls. Gate refers to a telephone trunk or business transaction grouping that may be handled by one group of telephone answerers (called attendants, operators, agents or telemarketers). That one group of telephone answerers is called "the gate." All calls coming into that gate can, theoretically, be handled by any of the telephone answerers. A telephone call is homogeneous throughout the gate. An automatic call distributor may have one gate — all calls coming in can be handled by everyone. Or it may have many gates, each one consisting of the line (or lines) bringing the call in — e.g. Band 5 WATS, New York City foreign exchange line. Or it may have two gates — one for orders and one for service. ACDs with multiple gates will establish rules for moving the calls between the gates, should one gate become overloaded.

GATEWAY A gateway is what it sounds like. It's an entrance and exit into a communications network. Gateways exist at the point where AT&T Communications ends and Comsat begins — for taking my call overseas. Gateways also exist between data networks. In data communications, they're typically referred to as a node on a network that connects two otherwise incompatible networks. Gateways on data networks often perform code and protocol conversion processes as well. Gateways also connect compatible networks owned by different entities, such as X.25 networks linked by X.75 gateways.

GATING Enabling or disabling a signal through applied logic. If it's turned on, the signal gets through. If not, the signal doesn't get through.

GAUGE A term for specifying the thickness (diameter) of cables. Thicker cables have a lower number in the American Wire Gauge (AWG) scale. (It doesn't make sense. But that's the way it is.) Thicker gauge cables can carry phone conversations further and more cleanly than thinner gauge cable. But thicker cables cost more and take up more room, especially when you bundle them together and put them in a duct. When buying a phone system it is good to specify the thickness of the cables that will be installed — especially if some of your extensions will be a great distance from the central telephone switch, if you intend to carry high-speed data on them or you intend to live with your cabling scheme for more than a few months. You should, of course, not only specify the cable's thickness, but also whether it's stranded or solid core, coax, etc. Gauge is but one part of a cable description. See AWG.

GAUSSIAN NOISE Gaussian noise is white noise uniform across the whole range of frequencies. "Gaussian" refers to the measurement of the noise. It is essentially the assumption you make when working on the problem of noise mathematically.

GENERATIONS, COMPUTER As computers have improved, so the industry's pundits have assigned "generations" to those improvements. The concept of generations is not perfect nor finite. Here's our best shot on generations in computers:

First generation: 1951-1958, core memory 8Kbytes to 32 Kbytes.

Second generation: 1958-1964, transistor technology, memory 32Kbytes to 64 Kbytes.

Third generation: 1964-1975, integrated circuitry.

Fourth generation: 1975-date, nonprocedural languages, software driven.

Fifth generation: into the 1990s, natural language programming, parallel processing and supercomputing.

Sixth generation: in the 2000, will process knowledge rather than data.

GENERATIONS, PBX As PBXs have improved, so the industry's pundits have assigned "generations" to those improvements, as they did in computers. The concept of generations is not perfect nor finite. Here's our best shot on generations in PBXs:

First generation: 1920s to the late 1960s. Step-by-step mechanical equipment. The first and the last of the step-by-step Bell PBXs switches was called a 701. Lee Goeller says the 701 "was the best PBX ever built. It was infinitely flexible. It was just too BIG. In fact, it was usually bigger than the office it served. This era of the stepper will be remembered as the era the Bell System was intact and had the gall to rent operator chairs."

Second Generation: Late 1960s: Bell 801 reed relay switch. Stromberg Carlson 800 series reed relay switch. GTE had a series, also. Reed relay switches were not very popular.

Third Generation: 1974 and 1975: Rolm introduces its first CBX, an electronic, solid-state PBX. AT&T introduces Dimension. Digital Telephone Systems introduced the D1200. Northern introduced its first stored-program controlled SL-1. Some of these PBXs switched voice digitally, though they used different techniques, including PCM, PAM and Delta Modulation. The codecs were in the switch, not in the instruments.

Fourth generation: early 1980s. Distributed processing. Northern, Rolm and NEC and others introduced remote modules — slaves to the master switch at headquarters. These switches also added the capability of handling data without using modems. Switches like Lexar and InteCom were designed from the beginning to handle data without modems, thus requiring digital capability out to the set.

Fifth generation: CXC, Anderson Jacobson and Ztel and others called themselves "fourth generation." When they started to fail, some people called them the "fifth generation." It wasn't clear exactly what that generation was. But they all got lots of publicity and the PBXs from CXC, Anderson Jacobson and Ztel ultimately failed.

Sixth generation: Networked PBXs. Sit in New York. Operate your national network as if it were in the same building. Bingo, you can transfer calls across the country. All your messaging is the same wherever you sit on the network. Lee Goeller, however, says you can network stepper PBXs. In fact, in 1971 he says he managed one of the biggest integrated voice and data networks in the US using step-by-step electromechanical PBXs (701s made by AT&T). It was the world's largest dial tandem network. He had 63 different locations and three hubs.

Seventh generation: Open Architecture. You can now program your own PBX. For more, see the NORSTAR COMMAND SET.

In reality, the concept of generations among PBXs is very flimsy. But it's the stuff good dictionaries are made of.

GENERATOR A machine which converts mechanical energy, such as the power from a piston engine into electrical energy.

GENERIC PROGRAM A set of instructions for an ESS or electronic PBX that is the same for all installations of that equipment. Detailed differences for each individual installation are listed in a separate parameter table.

GEOSTATIONARY SATELLITE A satellite in geostationary orbit, also called geosynchronous orbit. A satellite placed in an geosynchronous orbit — 22,300 miles directly over the earth's equator — will appear to be stationary in the sky, turning synchronously with the earth. This means you can plant a satellite receiving/transmitting antenna on the ground, and point it at that one place in the sky to receive signals from and transmit signals to "the bird," as satellites are sometimes called. Most communications satellites are in geostationary or geosynchronous orbit. The Russians have some satellites that orbit the earth and require antennae which move. These satellites are used to transmit to far northern communities which are difficult to reach with normal geosynchronous satellites.

GEOSYNCHRONOUS ORBIT Synchronous with the Earth. An orbit above the earth's equator where satellites circle at the same rate as the earth's rotation, thereby appearing stationary to an earth-bound observer. See also GEOSTATIONARY ORBIT.

GFI Group Format Identifier. In packet switching, refers to the first four bits in a packet header. Contains the Q bit, D bit and modulus value.

GFLOPS One billion FLoating point Operations Per Second. (G stands for GIGA, meaning million). Today's fastest supercomputers are able to maintain a sustained throughput of over one billion floating point operations per second (GFLOPS) while performing real-world applications. By contrast, a 25-MHz 486 personal computer can sustain about one million floating operations per second (one MFLOP), or about one-thousandth the throughput of a supercomputer.

GIGA Prefix meaning one billion, which is one thousand million. 1,000,000,000. See also GFLOPS.

GIGABITS One thousand million bits. One billion bits.

GIGAHERTZ A measurement of the frequency of a signal equivalent to one billion cycles per second, or one thousand million cycles per second.

GLARE Glare occurs when both ends of a telephone line or trunk are seized at the same time for different purposes or by different users. Most embarrassing. See GLARE RESOLUTION.

GLARE RESOLUTION Ability of a system to ensure that if a trunk is seized by both ends simultaneously, one caller is given priority and the other is switched to another trunk.

GLITCH A problem with a system or procedure as in "Who glitched this thing up?"

GLOBAL Universal. An adjective meaning the whole world. See GLOBAL SEARCH.

GLOBAL SEARCH A word processing term meaning to automatically find a character or group of characters wherever they appear in a document.

GLOBAL SEARCH AND REPLACE A word processing term meaning to automatically find a character or group of characters wherever they appear in a document and replace them with something else.

GLOBAL SOFTWARE DEFINED NETWORK AT&T's international virtual private network. It provides business customers with point-to-point, two-way voice and voiceband data communications between the US and various overseas countries. Features include:

- International two-way on-net calling
- Abbreviated user defined 7-digit dialing.
- Usage sensitivity.
- SDN call screening.

GNX DEVELOPMENT TOOLS A set of fax software development tools offered by National Semiconductor.

GO LOCAL A command typically given in a microcomputer asynchronous data communications program to tell the computer that it will connect to something without a modem over a null modem cable. The command "Go Local" also refers to modem connections and can tell one modem to overlook some of the handshaking and assume it's already taken place.

GOLD NUMBER Also called vanity number. A service of New York Telephone. It's a phone number that's easy for your customers to remember, e.g. 555-LIMO. But occasionally hard for them to dial. Tip: If you buy a vanity number, make sure it doesn't have numbers in it. 555-LIMO is harder to remember than CAR-RENT.

GORIZONT The Russian geostationary telecommunications satellite.

GOSIP The U.S. Government OSI Profile. GOSIP addresses communication and interoperation among end systems and intermediate systems. It provides specific peer-level, process-to-process and terminal access functionality between computer system users within and across government agencies.

GRACEFUL CLOSE Method terminating a connection at the transport layer with no loss of data.

GRADE OF SERVICE A term associated with telephone service indicating the probability that a call attempted will receive a busy signal. A P.01 Grade of Service means the user has a 1% chance of reaching a busy signal.

GRADED INDEX FIBER Graded index fiber is a multimode fiber optic cable that is made with progressively lower refractive index fiber toward the outer core. This reduces dispersion, which is fiber's equivalent of fading.

GRANDFATHERED Something that has a right to be a thing or own a thing by reason of it being or owning that thing before laws or rules were introduced to formalize the process. The derivation of term is unclear, but clearly has something to do with age. See also GRANDFATHERED EQUIPMENT.

GRANDFATHERED EQUIPMENT Non-FCC registered telephone equipment that was directly connected to the telecommunications network without a phone company-provided protective connecting arrangement (PCA) prior to the formalized FCC registration program.

GRAPHIC EQUALIZER A device that permits altering the tonal balance of an audio component/system at several frequency levels.

GRAY SCALE Early facsimile machines could only receive black and white images and print them in black or white. Now they can print 16 shades of gray. This way if they receive a photo, it will look like a photo.

GRAY WHALE One of the first non-Bell key systems sold in North America. It was a 1A2 electro-mechanical key system from TIE/communications. TIE was a shortening of the words Telephone Interconnect Equipment. It was a wonderfully reliable phone system. A gray whale is now a prized possession.

GREETING ONLY MAILBOXES Mailboxes that deliver a message to incoming callers but do not allow a message to be left. The Greeting Only mailbox may transfer a caller to a designated telephone number.

GROOM/FILL In telephony, terms associated with more efficient use of T-1 trunks by combining partially filled input T-1 trunks into fully filled outgoing T-1 trunks.

GROUND 1. An problem that exists when a circuit is accidentally crossed with a grounded conductor. 2. Connecting equipment by some conductor (wire) to some route that winds up in the earth (Ground) for electrical purposes. The idea of a "ground" wire is to carry spurious voltage (e.g. lightning strikes) away from the electrical and electronic circuits it can cause harm to. Incorrect grounding is probably the major cause of telephone systems problems. See GROUND RETURN.

GROUND BUTTON A button needed on phones used for power failure transfer behind a PBX. You need the button because many trunks behind a PBX are ground start (as compared to loop start).

GROUND LOOP This occurs when a circuit is grounded at one or more points. It can cause telephone system problems.

GROUND RETURN If a battery is connected to a closed electrical circuit, an electric current will flow in the circuit. In the early days of the telegraph, the circuit consisted of a long wire, the telegraph key, the electromagnet of a telegraph sounder and a return path through the ground, which served as a conductor. Thus the current flowed from one terminal of the battery through the wire, through the electromagnet, to a metal stake driven into the ground (a "ground" electrode), back through hundreds of miles of earth to the distant stake at the distant telegraph office and then to the other terminal of the battery. In later telecommunications, the ground return path was replaced by a second wire.

GROUND START A way of signaling on subscriber trunks in which one side of the two wire trunk (typically the "Ring" conductor of the Tip and Ring) is momentarily grounded to get dialtone. There are two types of switched trunks typically for lease by a local phone company — ground start and loop start. PBXs work best on ground start trunks, though many will work — albeit intermittently — on both types. Normal single line phones and key systems typically work on loop start lines. You must be careful to order the correct type of trunk from your local phone company and correctly install your telephone system at your end — so that they both match. In technical language, a ground start trunk initiates an out-going trunk seizure by applying a maximum local resistance of 550 ohms to the tip conductor. See LOOP START.

GROUND START SUPERVISION Telephone circuitry developed to prevent Glare.

GROUND STATION A cluster of communications equipment, usually including signal generator, transmitter, receiver and antenna that receives and/or transmits to and from a communications satellite. Also called a satellite earth station.

GROUP 1. In automatic call distributors, the same as GATE or SPLIT. 2. A collection of voice channels, typically 12. In AT&T jargon, a group is 12 channels. A supergroup is 60 channels. A mastergroup is 10 supergroups or 600 voice channels.

GROUP 1, 2, 3 & 4 These relate to the facsimile machine business. They are essentially standards of speed and sophistication. They were created by the CCITT in Geneva, Switzerland, to make sure facsimile machines from one maker could speak to facsimile machines of another maker.

> Group 1 transmits an 8 1/2 by 11-inch page in around six minutes. It conforms to CCITT Recommendation T.2.
>
> Group 2 transmits an 8 1/2 by 11-inch page in around three minutes. It conforms to CCITT Recommendation T.3.
>
> Group 3 transmits an 8 1/2 by 11-inch page in as little as 20 seconds. It is a digital machine and includes a 9,600 baud modem. It transmits over dial up phone lines.
>
> Group 4 Fax. The latest and fastest international standard for facsimile machines. It specifies a machine which operates at 64 Kbps, which can only work on a digital channel and which takes six seconds to transmit a 8 1/2 x 11 inch page. The Group 4 standard was promulgated in January, 1987. Group 4 fax machines are designed to use one of the 64,000 bit per second B (Bearer) channels on ISDN.

Most Group 3 machines will transmit and receive from Group 1, Group 2 and Group 3 machines (but at their slower speeds). If you're buying a facsimile machine check its compatibility with other machines. See FACSIMILE.

GROUP ADDRESSING In transmission, the use of an address that is common to two or more stations. On a multipoint line, where all stations recognize addressing characters but only one station responds.

GROUP CALL A special type of station hunting that requires a special access number to permit a call to the special access number and ring the first available phone in that group.

GROUP HUNTING Automatically finds free telephones in a designated group. See HUNT

GROUPING A facsimile term for periodic error in the spacing or recorded lines.

GS General Services Administration.

GSD See GLOBAL SOFTWARE DEFINED NETWORK.

GSTN General Switched Telephone Network. Same as public telephone network.

GTA Government Telecommunications Association. An association of local, state and federal telecommunications professionals, located in the Washington, DC, metropolitan area.

GTE General Telephone and Electronics. A major telecommunications company, whose main business is owning and operating "independent" (i.e. non Bell) telephone companies. In 1990 it bought Continental Telephone. GTE also has part of a long distance company called US Sprint, a packet switched operation called Telenet and various equity interests in various manufacturing operations making most things in telecommunications — from central offices to PBXs. Its partners in these joint ventures include Fujitsu and Siemens.

GTE SPRINT A long distance service once provided by GTE, then a 50-50 joint venture of GTE and United Telecom. Now majority owned (80%) by United Telecom and called US Sprint.

GTE TELENET A public data network which operates by using the CCITT approved X.25 packet switching protocol.

GUARD BAND A narrow bandwidth between adjacent channels in a communications amplifier which serves to reduce interference between adjacent channels. That interference might be crosstalk. Guard bands are typically used in frequency division multiplexing.

GUARDING The process of holding a circuit busy for a certain interval after its release to assure that a necessary minimum disconnect interval will occur between calls.

GUEST MAILBOX A mailbox used by a hotel or motel to set up temporary mailboxes for their guests.

GUI Graphical User Interface.

H.R.nnnn A proposed law introduced into the House of Representatives by a Congressman. Typically, four digits follow the H.R., signifying the proposed bill's number. The reason for including this definition in this dictionary is that every few months since divestiture some Congressman has attempted to introduce a bill into the House of Representatives changing the Communications Act of 1934. Such a bill is generally supported by a bevy of Bell telephone companies trying to use the proposed bill to remove those restrictions placed on them by Divestiture — manufacturing, creating information content and getting into long distance.

HACK The output of a hacker. Usually good programs, but sometimes just something clever of no discernible use. Just a "good hack," or something done for the "hack value."

HACKER A person who "hacks" away at a computer until his program works. The term has been wrongly used by the press to mean people who break into computer systems. See CRACKER.

HALF-DUPLEX A circuit designed for data transmission in both directions, but not at the same time. Telex is an example of a half duplex system, as is speaking on the telephone via most (but, not all) speakerphones. (The best speakerphones are full duplex. They're rare and expensive.)

HAMMING CODE An error correcting code named after R. W. Hamming of Bell Labs. The code has four information bits and three check bits per character.

HANDOFF The process of changing cellular radio channels when a car equipped with the cellular radio moves from one cell to another.

HANDSET The part of a phone held in the hand to speak and listen, it contains a transmitter and receiver. In the old days, the transmitter was a carbon mike. Now it's mostly electronic. Some electronic mikes are awful. Some phone makers are going back to carbon mikes.

HANDS-FREE ANSWERBACK Permits the telephone user to listen and reply to intercom calls without lifting his/her handset.

HANDS-FREE DIALING A telephone feature which allows the user to place outside calls and listen to the progress of those calls without lifting the handset of his telephone. Unbelievably useful when calling airlines which inevitably put you on "eternity hold." (We made that term up.)

HANDS-FREE MONITORING You can dial an outside call and hear the call's progress without having to lift your handset. Similar to hands-free dialing. With hands-free monitoring, you can only listen. To speak, you must pick up the handset. To be able to speak, you need a full speakerphone. Be careful of the distinction. Many people have been caught.

HANDS-FREE TELEPHONE Could be another word for a speakerphone or for a phone that does hands-free dialing. See HANDS-FREE DIALING.

HANDSHAKE IN HIN. A general purpose control signal sent from the DTE to DCE in a Newbridge Networks RS-232-C connection. HIN can be used in place of Request to Send (RTS), Carrier Detect (CD) or Ring

Indicator (RI).

HANDSHAKE OUT HOUT. A general purpose control signal sent from the DCE to the DTE. For example, in the case of a Newbridge Networks Mainstreet Data Controller with ports configured as DCE, HOUT is sent from the Data Controller to an attached device. HOUT can be used in place of Clear to Send (CTS), Carrier Detect (CD) or Ring Indicator (RI).

HANDSHAKING The electrical exchange of predetermined signals when a connection is made between two modems or other devices carrying data. Just as people shake hands, and go through a perfunctory "Hi, how are ya?", computers must go through a procedure of greeting the opposite party, verifying the identity of the other party, and other functions that can be described by this "humanizing term." As with human contacts, once the Handshaking is complete, the business of communications begins.

HARD COPY Anything on paper. It is all well and good to have information flash by on your CRT or video display terminal, but there are times when you want to take a Hard Copy with you. This dictionary was written on a computer screen. Now you have a hard copy in your hands. In this case, that's a lot more useful than having a disk.

HARD DISK ASSEMBLY A sealed mass storage unit used for storing large amounts of data. Now available on personal computers.

HARD DRAWN COPPER WIRE Copper wire that has been drawn to size and not annealed.

HARD SECTORING Physically marking the sector boundaries of a magnetic disk by punching holes in the disk where there's space available to store data. Hard sectored disks are not very common these days. Most disks — like those used on the IBM PC — are soft-sectored.

HARDWARE The actual physical computing machinery, as opposed to Software which is the list of instructions to operate the hardware, or the Firmware which is combination hardware/software that is "burned into" a Programmable Read Only Memory chip or chips. See FIRMWARE and SOFTWARE.

HARDWIRE To permanently connect by wire two or more devices rather than to connect them temporarily through connectors or switches. Hardwire is a term also used to represent a leased line.

HARM See NETWORK HARM.

HARMONIC DISTORTION A problem caused when the nonlinearities in communication channel cause the harmonics of the input frequencies to appear in the output channel.

HARMONIC RINGING A way of stopping users on a party line from hearing other than their own ring. We do this by tuning the ringer in their phone to a given ringing frequency, so it only rings when their frequency comes down the line.

HARMONICA A device that is attached to the end of a connectorized feeder cable that converts the 25 pairs into individual 4-, 6- or 8-wire modular channels.

HASH TOTAL Adding up one or more information fields in order to provide a check number for error control. The addition is not intended to have any meaning other than for checking.

HASP Houston Automatic Spooling Program. A control protocol adopted by IBM for transmitting data processing files and jobs to IBM 360 and 370 computers. An early job control language still in limited use.

HAYES AT COMMAND SET Before 1981, the modem was a dumb device. It had no memory or ability to recognize commands. It simply modulated and demodulated signals between the telephone line and the computer or terminal. In 1981, Hayes Microcomputer Products, Inc. in Norcross, GA produced the first "smart" modem, appropriately named the Smartmodem 300. It was "smart" because it understood commands, such as "ATD" which means "ATention, Dial the phone." The Hayes Command Set — a language for modems — has been accepted as a standard by the modem industry. And now many modems claim to be 100% Hayes compatible, which may mean they are and may mean they aren't. As in all cases of claimed compatibility, one should check.

HAYES MICROCOMPUTER PRODUCTS, Inc. The company that made modems for PCs affordable and intelligent. Continues to make great modems. Still the standard against which most PC modems are measured. Based in Norcross, GA. See also HAYES COMMAND SET.

HAYES ULTRA 96 New Hayes 9600 bps modem with CCITT V.32, V.42 error correction and V.42 bis data compression. 9600 bps communications does not require data compression, although most modem manufacturers do have compression at 9600 bps. What happens is that the two 9600 bps modems will first negotiate modulation, then they'll negotiate error-control, and finally, they'll negotiate data compression. Hayes' ULTRA 96 has "Automatic Feature Negotiation" which means that this whole process occurs automatically without the user's help.

HCI Host Command Interface. Mitel's PBX-Computer link. For more, talk to Digital Equipment Corporation.

HCS Hundred Call Seconds. One hundred seconds of telephone conversation. See CCS.

HDB3 High Density Bipolar 3. A bipolar coding method that does not allow more than 3 consecutive zeroes.

HDLC High-level Data Link Control. A standard bit-oriented protocol developed by the International Standards Organization (ISO). In HDLC, control information is always placed in the same position. And specific bit patterns used for control differ dramatically from those used in representing data, so that errors are less likely to occur. SDLC and ADCCP are similar protocols. See also HIGH LEVEL DATA LINK CONTROL.

HDTV High Definition TeleVision. Today's typical TV set in North America contains 336,000 pixels. A high definition TV set — one giving at least the definition of a movie theater, or 35 mm slide — will require at least two million pixels. Researchers are pursuing at least two dozen technologies to achieve this level of quality. The ideal HDTV would be flat screen, cheap, reliable and require very little electrical power.

HDX Half duplex.

HEAD The device which comes in contact with or comes very close to the magnetic storage device (disk, diskette, drum, tape) and reads and/or writes to the medium. In computer devices, it performs the same function as the head on a home cassette tape recorder.

HEAD-END The originating point of a signal in Cable TV systems. At the head-end, you'll often find large tall TV and dish satellite receiving antennae.

HEADER The information at the beginning of a data message or packet which indicates the intended addressee and other "housekeeping" information to assist in the transmission of the information.

HEADSET A telephone transmitter and receiver assembly worn on the head. Headsets are becoming very light and very comfortable and are no longer worn only by switchboard attendants and airline clerks.

HEADSET JACK A place on a phone or console into which you can plug a headset.

HEARING AID COMPATIBLE A hearing aid compatible phone may be used with inductively coupled hearing aid devices. You can find hearing aid compatible coin phones by looking for the blue grommet between the handset and the cord.

HEHO Head-End Hop Off. You have a private network. You overflow a long distance call to WATS or DDD at the originating end (the end the call is coming from). This HEHO (Head-End Hop Off) is done because it's usually cheaper than carrying the call part way through the network, then jumping off the network at that point (because the network is busy or it won't reach the end point). The opposite of HEHO is TEHO — Tail-End Hop Off. In TEHO, you carry the call as far as possible through the network, then pass it off to WATS or DDD as close to its destination as possible. The decision to go HEHO or TEHO has to do with economics, primarily which is cheaper.

HELD ORDERS A telephone company term for requests for telephone lines which the phone company cannot fill. Thus it is "holding" the orders. The reasons for holding customer orders might range from lack of capacity at the serving central office to a lack of local cable plant.

HELICAL STRIPE A continuous, colored, spiral stripe applied over the outer perimeter of an insulated conductor for circuit identification purposes.

HERCULES A method of encoding a PC's screen. See MONITOR and FACSIMILE.

HERTZ A measurement of frequency (Hz) in cycles per second. A hertz is one cycle per second.

HETERODYNING Here is an explanation from James Harry Green's book, the Dow Jones Handbook of Telecommunications: Analog microwave repeaters use either of two techniques to amplify the received signal for retransmission: HETERODYNING or BASEBAND. In a baseband repeater, the signal is demodulated to the multiplex (or video) signal at every repeater point. In heterodyne repeaters the signal is demodulated to an intermediate frequency, typically 70 MHz, and modulated or heterodyned to the transmitter output frequency. Heterodyne radio is reduced to baseband only at main repeater stations where the baseband signal is required to drop off voice channels. The primary advantage of baseband radio is that some carrier channel groups can be dropped off at repeater stations. Heterodyne radio has the advantage of avoiding the distortions caused by multiple modulation/demodulation and amplification of a baseband signal. Therefore, heterodyne radio is employed for transcontinental use with drop-off points only at major junctions.

HEURISTIC Using much trial and error to arrive at a solution to a problem.

HEXADECIMAL A numbering system of 16 characters, ten digits and six letters. It is used to condense the long strings of zeros and ones in large binary numbers. It makes life simpler for programmers. Uses the base 16. A hexadecimal or "hex" digit can be represented by the letters "A" through "F" and the numerals "0" through "9."

HIERARCHY See HIERARCHICAL NETWORK.

HIERARCHICAL NETWORK A network that includes two or more different classes of switching systems in a defined homing arrangement, meaning to home in on the telephone you wish to be connected to. This is a fancy Bell System (Oops, I mean AT&T — old habits die hard) term meaning that when direct circuits between two switches are busy or too far apart to be directly connected, the machinery will seek a higher level of switches to route the call through.

HIGH AND DRY What happens when you dial into a long distance network and nothing happens. You don't hear anything. Your call doesn't go anywhere. You're simply left High and Dry!

HIGH CAPACITY SERVICE Generally refers to tariffed, digital-data transmission service equal to, or in excess of T-1 data rates (1,544 Mbit/s.)

HIGH DEFINITION TV HDTV. A system for transmitting a TV signal with far greater resolution than the standard NTSC standards. NTSC is the National Television System Committee. See HDTV.

HIGH LEVEL DATA LINK CONTROL HDLC. A communications protocol that is bit oriented in which control codes differ according to their bit positions and patterns.

HIGH LEVEL LANGUAGES Essentially any of the computer languages whose code is not unique to the hardware or architecture of a particular computer. High level languages are more like human language than the machine language which computers talk. High level languages translate human instructions into the machine language computers can understand, but which humans don't have to (in order to tell the computer what to do). Computer languages such as BASIC, FORTRAN, COBOL and Pascal are high level languages. They are a number of levels (at a High Level) away from the actual bit manipulation (machine language, also called "bit twiddling" by the Hackers). Compare with LOW LEVEL.

HIGH PASS FILTER A filter which passes frequencies above a certain frequency and stops (attenuates) those below.

HIGH POWER AMPLIFIER HPA. A device which provides the high power needed to shoot signals 22,000 miles plus from an earth station to a satellite.

HIGH SPEED PRINTER Any printer which can print at over 100 lines a minute. Like many definitions, this one is arbitrary. Some people claim a dot matrix is "high speed" and a letter quality, daisy wheel is a "low speed" printer. Laser printers could be classed as high speed printers, maybe.

HIGH USAGE GROUPS Trunk groups established between two central office switching machines to serve as the first choice path between the machines and thus, handle the bulk of the traffic.

HIGH/LOW TARIFF A tariff in which two prices are given for something — a high price and a low price. The first high/low tariff from AT&T was for leased voice lines where a lower charge was made per mile for connections between routes that have much traffic (High Density) and greater charges per mile are made for all other (Low Density) routes. The High/Low tariff was significant because it was AT&T's response to competition from long distance carriers like MCI and it was one of the first moves away from nationwide rate averaging, which was the way things were done under monopoly.

HIGHWAY Another word for BUS. A common path or set of paths over which many channels of information are transmitted. The channels of the highway are separated by some electrical technique.

HIT Electrical interference that causes the loss or introduction of spurious bits into a data stream.

HOBIC HOtel BIlling Information Center used by hotels for getting immediate charges for long distance calls placed by their guests. A service of AT&T and the local telephone operating company delivered through a distinct and separate trunk and usually terminating on a telex machine, which prints guest long distance charges.

HOBIS HOtel Billing Information System.

HOLD To temporarily leave a phone call without disconnecting it. You can return to the call at any time, sometimes from other extensions. There are several types of "HOLD" on a telephone system. How they work and what lamping they put on instruments varies from phone system to phone system.

Exclusive Hold: Prevents every other telephone from picking up the call. Only the telephone instrument that put the call on hold can retrieve it.

I-Hold: Effectively the same as Exclusive Hold.

Line Hold: The call is on hold. Anyone with a phone with the held line appearing on it can pick up the phone.

HOLDING TANK A queue in which a call is held until it can either use its assigned route or overflow into the next available route.

HOLDING TIME The total time from the instant you pick up the handset, to dialing a call, to waiting for it to answer, to speaking on the phone, to hanging up and replacing the handset in its cradle. You are never billed for holding time. You are always billed for conversation time which is shorter than holding time. But holding time is an important figure to know when you're trying to determine how many circuits you need. For you will need sufficient circuits to take care of dialing, etc. — even though you're not being billed for that time.

HOLD RECALL A telephone system feature which reminds you periodically that you've put someone on hold.

HOLLERITH CARD A punched-hole 80 column card used for storing information for input into a computer. Remember the cards you got telling you "not to fold, bend, punch, spindle, etc."? They were Hollerith Cards. They're now falling into disfavor as other, less tamper-proof methods appear.

HOLLOW PIPELINE Jargon for a broad bandwidth circuit that has no framing. It is so named that it typically needs framing, and timing.

HOME The beginning place of a cursor on a CRT screen. Usually it's the top left hand corner. The function key on an IBM PC or clone marked "Home" will take the cursor to the home position, namely the top left hand corner.

HOME RUN Phone system wiring where the individual cables run from each phone directly back to the central switching equipment. Home run cabling can be thought of as "star" cabling. Every cable radiates out from the central phone equipment. All PBXs and most key systems work on home run cabling. Some local area networks work on home run wiring. Most don't. See LOOP THROUGH.

HOMEOSTASIS The state of a system in which the input and output are exactly balanced, so there is no change.

HOMING When you dial a long distance number, your central office will choose a special set of trunks to send your call onto the next switching center for movement through the nationwide toll system. Those trunks are said to be the homing trunks for your central office. In other words, your central office is said to home on these trunks. If you're consistently encountering lousy long distance lines (and so are others on your central office), then ask your telephone company to check these trunks out.

HOOK FLASH See FLASH

HOOK-UP WIRE A wire used for low current, low voltage (under 1000 volts) applications within enclosed electronic equipment.

HOOKING SIGNAL An on-hook signal of 0.1 to 0.2 seconds duration used to indicate that a subscriber intends to initiate a new process such as "add-on."

HOOKSWITCH Also called SWITCHHOOK. The place on your telephone instrument where you lay your handset. When you lift the handset, you are said to be going "off hook." When you place your handset back, you are said to be "on hook." When you lift the handset (i.e. go off hook) you are, in effect, signaling your central office that you'd like to make a call or that you have answered the incoming ringing call.

HOOKSWITCH DIALING You can make phone calls by depressing the hookswitch carefully. If you push it five times, you dial five. Push it ten times you dial 0. Some coin phones discourage hookswitch dialing. Some don't.

HOST COMPUTER A computer attached to a network providing primarily services such as computation, data base access or specific programs of special programming languages. The central computer in a time-sharing operation.

HOST PROCESSOR Same as HOST COMPUTER.

HOST SWITCH A central office switching system which provides certain functions to a smaller switch located remotely.

HOT Live wire. A conductor carrying a signal is said to be a hot conductor, i.e. the wire carrying the signal as opposed to a ground wire.

HOT CUT The conversion from an old to a new phone system which occurs instantly as one is removed from the circuit and the other is brought in. There are advantages and disadvantages to Hot Cuts. For one, they're likely to be much more dangerous than a Parallel Cut, in which the two phone systems run side by side for a month or so. Also known as FLASH CUT.

HOT LINE A private line dedicated between two phones. When you pick up either phone or do some act of signaling (like push a button), the other phone rings instantly. Hot lines are useful in emergency applications and other areas where time is of the essence — e.g. trading currencies.

HOT LINE SERVICE When you pick up the phone, you're automatically connected with a phone number. Such Hot-Line Service on a PBX typically gets you emergency service, etc. See also HOT-LINE.

HOT STANDBY Backup equipment kept turned on and running in case some equipment fails.

HOTEL/MOTEL CONSOLE A specialized PBX console or a normal console programmed to work specifically in hotels and motels. The console will often show room status information.

HOUSE CABLE The riser cable going up the building. Unless you own the building, the riser cable is usually owned by the phone company.

HOWLER A device which produces a loud tone that may be applied to a subscriber's line or Private Branch Exchange (PBX) extension to indicate that the handset is off-hook.

HOWLER TONE A tone which gets increasingly louder over a short period of time. It is used to notify a user that his phone handset is off its hook.

HPA See HIGH POWER AMPLIFIER.

HPAD Host Packet Assembler/Disassembler. The HPAD can link to a host or FEP with native protocol data, or if the host can accept it, with X.25 input. The 4400 PAD functions as either an HPAD or a TPAD See TPAD.

HPO High Performance Option. A way of improving equipment transmission characteristics. For instance, the upgrading of a voice-grade line to meet standards for data transmission.

HSDA High Speed Data Access.

HSDU High Speed Data Unit.

HUB The point on a network where a bunch of circuits are connected. Also, a switching node.

HUB POLLING A polling system in which a polled station sends its traffic and passes the polling message (after it's sent its message) to the next station.

HUB JUNCTION BOX A box used to connect a Hub Interface when a node is placed at a remote location.

HUNDRED CALL SECONDS Known by the initials CCS where C is the roman numeral for Hundred. See CCS. One CCS is 36 times the traffic expressed in Erlangs.

HUNT Refers to the progress of a call reaching a group of lines. The call will try the first line of the group. If that line is busy, it will try the second line, then it will hunt to the third, etc. See also HUNT GROUP.

HUNT GROUP A series of telephone lines organized in such a way that if the first line is busy the next line is hunted and so on until a free line is found. Often this arrangement is used on a group of incoming lines. Hunt groups may start with one trunk and hunt downwards. They may start randomly and hunt in clockwise circles. They may start randomly and hunt in counter-clockwise circles. Inter-Tel uses the terms "Linear, Distributed and Terminal" to refer to different types of hunt groups. In data communications, a hunt group is a set of links which provides a common resource and which is assigned a single hunt group designation. A user requesting that designation may then be connected to any member of the hunt group. Hunt group members may also receive calls by station address.

HYBRID A device used for converting a conversation coming in on two pairs (one pair for each direction of the conversation) onto one pair and vice versa. This is necessary because all long distance circuits are two pairs, while most local circuits are one pair. Here is a longer explanation from "Signals, The Science of Telecommunications," by John Pierce and Mike Noll:

The telephone instrument in your home is connected to a single pair of wires called the subscriber loop or local loop, which carries both the outgoing voice signal and the incoming one. This pair of wires creates an electrical circuit for each of the two signals. A device in your phone called a hybrid or bybrid coil keeps the two signals separate, more or less, so that what you say into your phone's transmitter doesn't blast into your ear from the receiver.

In contrast, all multiplex systems provide separate talking paths in two directions. Separate paths are necessary because the amplifiers placed along the lines between terminals amplify signals traveling in one direction only. When two people talk between New York and San Francisco the call goes from one phone through a local two-wire voice circuit to a multiplex terminal. There the call is transferred to a four-wire long distance circuit that consists of two separate one-way circuits. At the end of the system, a hybrid reconverts each four-wire circuit into a two-wire circuit.

HYBRID COIL Transformer used in a balancing network to connect a 4-wire line to a 2-wire line.

HYBRID KEY SYSTEM Term used to describe a system which has attributes of both Key Telephone Systems and PBXs. The one distinguishing feature these days is that a hybrid key system can use normal single line phones in addition to the normal electronic key phones. A single line phone behind a hybrid works very much like a single line phone behind a PBX. The second distinguishing feature of a hybrid is that it's "non-squared." This means that not every trunk appears as a button on every phone in the system — as occurs on virtually every electronic key system manufactured today.

HYBRID NETWORK 1. A communications network which has some links capable of sending and receiving only analog signals and other links capable of handling only digital signals. The current public switched telephone network is Hybrid. 2. An amalgam of public and private network transmission facilities.

HYGROSCOPIC Capable of absorbing moisture from the air.

HYPERMEDIA A way of delivering information that provides multiple connected pathways through a body of information. Hypermedia allows the user to jump easily from one topic to related or supplementary material found in various forms, such as text, graphics, audio or video.

Another definition we found is: Non-linear media, of which multimedia can be a form. Just as hypertext is a non-sequential, random-access arrangement of text, hypermedia is a non-sequential, random-access arrangement of multiple media such as video, sound and computer data.

HYPERWARE New hardware that has been announced and perhaps even publicly demonstrated, but is not being shipped to commercial customers. Vaporware is software which has been announced, but is not yet shipping to commercial customers. Years can pass between public announcement and actual commercial shipment. Be wary.

HZ See Hertz.

I&R Installation And Repair. The telephone company department responsible for these jobs.

I-HOLD INDICATION A telephone system feature. If I put someone on hold at my phone, all the other phones which have the same line appearing on them will start flashing — indicating that the call is on hold.

I-USE Shows a user which line the phone is connected to when the receiver is off-hook. It does this by illuminating a small light below that line button. Most key sets and PBX sets have I-Use buttons. Most of the newer two-line phones do also.

I/O Input/Output.

I/O CHANNEL Equipment forming part of the input/output system of a computer.

I/O CONTROLLER Provides communications between the central processor and the I/O devices.

IAB Internet Activities Board. A policy-setting and decision-review board for the TCP/IP-based Internet.

IAM Initial address message in the ISUP Call Set Up Messages. A mandatory message sent in the forward direction to initiate seizure of an outgoing circuit and to transmit address and other information relating to the routing and handling of a call. See also ISUP and COMMON CHANNEL SIGNALING.

IBM International Business Machines. Also known affectionately as I've Been Moved, International Big Mother, Itty Bitty Machines, It's Better Manually, along with others not suitable for printing (but used in the back of better computer rooms all across the North American continent). IBM dominates the computer industry. This is why many of the IBM terms in this book are described as how IBM defines them. It is a remarkable company.

IBM TOKEN RING A local area network using star wiring architecture of two pair cabling to each drop location — one pair from the hub to the workstation and one pair from the workstation back to the hub to continue the ring. The IBM 8228 Multiple Access Unit (MAU) will support communications for eight personal computers (workstations). Up to 33 IBM 8228 MAUs may be connected together into a single ring, supporting up to 260 data devices. MAU to MAU connection is accomplished with data connectors equipped with Type 1 cables from a MAU's RO (Ring Out) connection to the next MAU's RI (Ring In). The final MAU's RO connects back to the initial MAU's RI to complete the ring. See also TOKEN PASSING and TOKEN RING.

IBX Integrated Business Exchange. Another name for a PBX. This is the name InteCom calls their large PBX. InteCom is now owned by Matra, a French company.

IC See INTEGRATED CIRCUIT.

ICA International Communications Association. The biggest trade association of the biggest corporate telecommunications users — the ones who spend the most. It was once called the Industrial Communication Association. The ICA holds one of the largest telecommunications trade shows in the United States. It happens every May. A schedule is published in the back of TELECONNECT Magazine.

ICEA Abbreviation for Insulated Cable Engineers Association.

ICM See Integrated Call Management.

IDC Insulation Displacement Connection. A type of wire connection device in which the wire is "punched down" into a double metal holder and as it is the metal holders strip the insulation away from the wire, thus causing the electrical connection to be made. The alternate method of connecting wires is with a screw-down post. There are advantages and disadvantages to both systems. The IDC system, obviously, is faster and uses less space. But it requires a special tool. The screw system takes more time, but may produce a longer-lasting and stronger, more thorough (more of the wire exposed) electrical connection. The most common IDC wiring scheme is the 66-block, originally invented by Western Electric.

IDCMA Independent Data Communications Manufacturers Association, a lobbying and education group.

IDDD International Direct Distance Dialing. The capability to directly dial telephones in foreign countries from your own home or office telephone.

IDENTIFICATION FAILURE Automatic Number Identification (ANI) equipment in the originating office failed to identify the calling number. See ANI.

IDENTIFIED OUTWARD DIALING Same as AIOD. It's a PBX feature which provides identification of the PBX extension making outward toll calls. This identification may be provided by automatic equipment or by attendant identification of the extension.

IDF See INTERMEDIATE DISTRIBUTION FRAME.

IDLE Not being used but ready.

IDLE CHANNEL NOISE Noise which exists in a communications channel when no signals are present.

IDLE LINE TERMINATION An electronic network which is switch controlled to maintain a desired impedance at a trunk or line terminal when that terminal is in an idle state.

IDLING SIGNAL Any signal that indicates no data is being sent. Because if nothing was sent, you might think it meant nothing, or a pause....you could get confused, or the computer might hang up.

IDN Integrated Digital Network.

IEC Inter Exchange Carrier. Also called an IXC. Any common carrier authorized by the FCC to carry customer transmissions between LATA's. In practice this means anyone and his brother who print up stationery, rent a few lines and proclaim themselves to be in the long distance phone business. Except for AT&T, regulation of long distance carriers by the FCC is perfunctory. It is less perfunctory by the local state authorities, some of whom still think competition is a mild form of insanity.

IEEE Abbreviation for the Institute of Electrical and Electronic Engineers, a publishing and standards-making body responsible for many standards used in LANs, including the 802 series.

IEEE 802.2 A data link layer standard used with the IEEE 802.3, 802.4 and 802.5 standards. For more on the 802 series, see the numbers definitions at the front of this dictionary.

IEEE 802.3 A physical layer standard specifying a LAN with a CSMA/CD access method on a bus topology. Ethernet and Starlan both follow the 802.3 standard. Typically they transmit at 10 megabits per second.

IEEE 802.4 A physical layer standard specifying a LAN with a token-passing access method on a bus topology. Used with Manufacturing Automation Protocol (MAP) LANs. Arcnet can work this way. Typical transmission speed is 10 megabits per second.

IEEE 802.5 A physical layer standard specifying a LAN with a token-passing access method on a ring topology. Used by IBM's Token Ring hardware. Typical transmission speed is 4 or 16 megabits per second.

IES Inter-Enterprise Systems is EDI (Electronic Data Interchange) AND inter-company electronic mail, fax, electronic funds transfer, videotex/online databases and the exchange of CAD/CAM graphics. See also EDI.

IETF Internet Engineering Task Force. One of two technical working bodies of the Internet Activities Board. The IETF is the primary working body developing new TCP/IP (Transmission Control Protocol/Internet Protocol) standards for the Internet.

ILS Input buffer Limiting Scheme. A flow control scheme used in data communications that blocks overload by limiting the number of blocks arriving at a buffer.

IMAS Intelligent Maintenance Administration System. Northern Telecom software which is a menu-driven PC-based program that provides enhanced maintenance and administrative capabilities for DMS-10 central offices.

IMMEDIATE RINGING A PBX feature which makes the called telephone begin ringing the instant the phone has been dialed. Normally there's a small wait between dialing the number and having the phone ring.

IMPACT STRENGTH A test designed to ascertain the abuse a cable configuration can absorb, without physical or electrical breakdown. Done by impacting with a given weight, dropped from a given height, in a controlled environment.

IMPEDANCE The effect of resistance, inductance and capacitance on a transmitted signal. The effect varies at different frequencies. Ohm's law says that voltage equals the product of current and impedance at any single frequency. The unit of impedance is the ohm.

IMPEDANCE MATCHING The connection of additional impedance to existing impedance one in order to improve the performance of an electrical circuit. Impedance Matching is done to minimize distortion, especially to data circuits.

IMPROVED MOBILE TELEPHONE SERVICE In the beginning, there was dispatch mobile service. The base operator broadcast a message to you. Everyone could hear it. You responded. Then they had mobile telephone service. You picked up the phone in your car, the operator responded. You asked for the number you wanted and she/he dialed it and connected you. You had the channel to yourself but others could still tune in. Then came Improved Mobile Telephone Service (IMTS). Now you could dial from your car without using an operator with some assurance of privacy. The latest development is cellular mobile telephone service. See CELLULAR.

IMPULSE HITS Errors in telephone-line data transmission that are caused by voltage surges lasting from 1/3 to 4 milliseconds and at a level within 6 dB of the normal signal level (Bell standard allows no more than 15 impulse hits per 15 minute period).

IMPULSE NOISE High-level, short duration noise that comes on a circuit. You can get impulse noise from electromechanical relays. These noise "spikes" have little effect on voice transmission but can be devastating to data. You can get a piece of test equipment called an impulse noise measuring set. Such a machine establishes a threshold and counts the number of impulses (hits) above that threshold.

IMS/VS Information Management System/Virtual Storage. An IBM host operating environment.

IMTS See IMPROVED MOBILE TELEPHONE SERVICE.

IN Intelligent Network

IN-BAND SIGNALING Signaling made up of tones which pass within the voice frequency band and are carried along the same circuit as the talk path that is being established by the signals. Virtually all signaling — request for service, dialing, disconnect, etc. — in the U.S. today is in-band signaling. Most of that signaling is MF — multi-frequency dialing. The more modern form of signaling is out-of-band. Several local and long distance companies provide ANI (Automatic Number Identification) via in-band signaling. Some long distance companies provide it out-of-band, using the D-channel in a PRI ISDN loop. See ISDN and SS7 (CCITT Signaling System Number 7).

INCOMING CALL IDENTIFICATION Some way of telling the user who's calling him. It might be the caller's extension number on an LCD screen or even the caller's name spelled out, e.g. "KATE BRODIE-DAVID CALLING." Today, most "incoming call identification" is done totally within one PBX. However, the days of ISDN and CCITT Signaling System Number 7 are arriving. They promise to deliver to us the phone number of everyone calling us — from within the PBX or key system and from the outside world.

INCREMENT A small change in the value of a quantity.

INDEPENDENT TELEPHONE COMPANY A telephone company not affiliated with one of the "Bell" telephone companies. There are about 1,400 independent phone companies. They serve more than half the geographic area of the United States, but only around 15% of its telephones. The independent phone companies used to be represented by the United States Independent Telephone Association (USITA). But once Divestiture happened, the association dropped the word "Independent" from its name, accepted membership of the Bell operating companies (but not AT&T) and became USTA.

INDICATION OF Lights, bells and buzzers indicating to you that something has or is about to happen. For example, indication of camp-on to a station: short bursts of tone are periodically transmitted to the busy phone to indicate that another call is camped on and waiting.

INDIVIDUAL LOAD CYCLING FEATURE This is one of the features of AT&T's Dimension Energy Communications Service Adjunct. Individual Load Cycling reduces energy consumption by turning devices on and off (e.g. airconditioning) on an hourly basis.

INDIVIDUAL SPEED CALLING A key system or PBX feature by which a user can dial a longer number by punching one or two buttons on his phone. Sometimes this speed dial ability is programmed into the phone. Sometimes it's programmed into the system. Whichever it is, each user has a bunch of numbers he/she can speed dial. These are his/her own. No one else can speed dial them.

INDUCTANCE Inductance is the property of an electric force field built up around a conductor. When current flows through a wire, lines of force are built up around the wire. The field created by DC current is steady. When AC flows through a wire, the lines of force are constantly building and collapsing. A inductor is formed by winding a conductor into a coil. In long local loops, conversation gets difficult because the long wires encounter capacitive resistance. To counter this, inductors known as load coils are connected in series, increasing the inductance. When load coils, or inductors are connected in parallel, they reduce the inductance. See also INDUCTIVE CONNECTION.

INDUCTIVE CONNECTION A connection between a telephone instrument and another device by means of the electromagnetic field generated by the telephone instrument. No direct electrical connection is established between the two things. See INDUCTANCE.

INDUCTIVE PICKUP A coil used to tap phone lines without direct connection.

INDUCTIVE TAP Wiretap that is not physically connected to the telephone wires. A voltage proportional to the varying line current is induced into a coil.

INDUCTOR See INDUCTANCE and INDUCTIVE CONNECTION.

INFERENCE ENGINE The AI (Artificial Intelligence) heart of a knowledge base system. The inference engine is the technology which directs the reasoning process.

INFINITE LOOP A state in which specific steps of a program are executed repeatedly, not allowing the program execution to advance further.

INFO-LOOK Gateway Service A NYNEX service. Use your PC,

modem and communications software to dial Info-Look and check on news, weather, health, finance, sports. Do some shopping. Info-Look connects you to many computer services and databases, none of which are provided by NYNEX, New York Telephone or New England Telephone. That's why Info-Look is called a "gateway." It's a gateway to a myriad of services.

INFOPATH PACKET SWITCHING SERVICE A New York Telephone service using a switched data network, where users share all network facilities. Offered for only the NY Metropolitan RCA. Its Low Throughput (private dial access) is dedicated to one customer, Medium Throughput uses a Data Over Voice channel and High Throughput uses a Digipath Digital Service facility.

INFORMATION CENTER MAILBOXES An Octel term for a voice bulletin board on a voice mail system. Here's their explanation: Multiple callers can access, directly or indirectly, recorded announcements containing information that would otherwise have been given live by employees. Callers are frequently "outside" users of the system. One type of "listen only" mailbox simply plays the messages to the callers. This technology, sometimes known as audiotex, makes it possible to create a verbal database so callers can select which information they want to hear. Another type of Information Center Mailbox prompts callers to reply to announcements. Callers wanting further information can be given the opportunity to leave their names and phone numbers after listening to a product description. They can also be transferred to a designated employee who can immediately take an order. If desired, a password can be required before confidential or controlled access information can be heard.

INFORMATION ENGINEERING Coined by James Martin, the most prolific writer in data processing, the term refers to systems within data processing and their impact on giving the corporation a greater competitive edge. In short, a fancy term for Management Information Systems (MIS), which itself was a fancy term for DP, namely Data Processing.

INFORMATION PROVIDER A business or person providing information to the public for money. The information is typically selected by the caller through touchtones, delivered using voice processing equipment and transmitted over tariffed phone lines, e.g., 900, 976, 970. Typically, billing for information providers' services is done by a local or long distance phone company. Sometimes the revenues for the service are split by the information provider and the phone company. Sometimes the phone company simply bills a per minute or flat charge. A typical "information provider" is American Express, which provides a service — 1-900-WEATHER. By dialing that number you can touchtone in city names and find out temperatures, weather forecasts, etc. Calling 1-900-WEATHER costs several dollars a minute.

INFORMATION TECHNOLOGY MANAGEMENT An AT&T term used to encompass telecommunications and data management.

INFRARED Portion of the electromagnetic spectrum used for fiber-optical transmission and also for short-haul through-the-air data transmission.

Infrared occupies the wavelengths between 0.75 and 1000 microns.

INITIAL PERIOD The minimum billing period on a call. For interstate or inter-LATA AT&T calls, the initial period is one-minute. Some non-AT&T long distance companies have initial periods under one-minute. This also applies to local calls in Measured areas.

INITIAL PROGRAM LOAD The initial loading of generic and/or configuration software into a PBX or other phone system. The Initial Program Load is a pain in the rear end. But an even bigger pain is what happens when you lose your programming and you've forgotten to back it all up.

INITIATING EVENT An event that causes the ASC (AIN Switch Capabilities) to assign an ID to a connection segment for a certain user ID and to communicate with a SLEE (Service Logic Execution Environment) for the first time with respect to the combination of the specific user ID and connection segment ID.

INL See InterNode Link.

INMARSAT The International Maritime Satellite Service that provides communications to ships. Comsat runs this service. Typically you buy a small earth station and install it on your ship and pay Comsat a per minute charge for the use of the single phone and single telex service most customers subscribe to. As of writing, a ship earth station cost $50,000 and a minute of calling was $10. Not cheap!

INN See InterNode Network.

INP BOARD Intelligent Network Processor board for synchronous transmission on an Hewlett Packard 3000 system.

INPUT A signal fed into a circuit.

INQUIRY A request for specific information.

INSERTION LOSS The difference in the amount of power received before and after something is inserted into the circuit (viz. another telephone instrument) or a call is connected.

INSIDE PLANT Inside plant is everything inside a telephone company central office. See also INSIDE WIRING.

INSIDE WIRING That telephone wiring located inside your premises or building or home. Inside Wiring starts at the telephone company's Demarcation Point and extends to the individual phone extensions. Traditionally, Inside Wiring was installed and owned by the telephone company. But now you can install your own wiring. And most companies installing new phone systems are installing their own new wiring because of potential problems with reusing the old telephone company cable. See also INSIDE PLANT.

INSTABUS1080 and INSTABUS1480 Trademarks for MICOM's direct host attachment products.

INSTALINK and INSTALINK460 Trademarks for MICOM's data-over-voice products.

INSTANET Trademark for MICOM's family of local data distribution and data private automatic branch exchange (PABX) products.

INSTANTANEOUS OVERRIDE ENERGY FUNCTION IOEF. A feature of the AT&T PBX Dimension Energy Communications Service Adjunct (ECSA), which allows the user to turn all the ECSA energy functions ON or OFF. IOEF is most often used for periodic maintenance, or to adjust to sudden changes in weather.

INSTATRUNK and INSTATRUNK480 Trademarks for MICOM's local T-1 multiplexer products.

INSTRUCTION REGISTER The register which contains the instruction to be executed and functions as the source for the subsequent operations of the arithmetic unit.

INSULATION A material which does not conduct electricity but is suitable for surrounding conductors to prevent the loss of current.

INSULATION DISPLACEMENT CONNECTION IDC. A type of wire connection device in which the wire is "punched down" into a double metal holder and as it is, the metal holders strip the insulation away from the wire, thus causing the electrical connection to be made. The alternate method of connecting wires is with a screw-down post. There are advantages and disadvantages to both systems. The IDC system, obviously, is faster and uses less space. But it requires a special tool. The screw system takes more time, but may produce a longer-lasting and stronger, more thorough (more of the wire exposed) electrical connection. The most common IDC wiring scheme is the 66-block, invented by Western Electric.

INSULATION RESISTANCE That property of an insulating material which resists electrical current flow through the insulating material when a potential difference is applied.

INSULATOR A material which does not conduct electricity and is traditionally used to separate or protect wiring used for carrying signals.

INTEGRATED CALL MANAGEMENT ICM. A family of Rolm networking products and services for single-site and multi-site CBX installations.

INTEGRATED CIRCUIT IC. A single electronic device that contains hundreds or thousands of previously separate (discrete) components. The so-called "computer on a chip" is a special purpose integrated circuit.

INTEGRATED PERSONAL COMPUTER INTERFACE IPCI. A Rolm-designed communications printed circuit card designed to provide an IBM PC with asynchronous data transmission over two-strand wiring to and from a Rolm CBX PBX.

INTEGRATED SERVICES DIGITAL NETWORK See ISDN and SIGNALING SYSTEM 7.

INTEGRATED SERVICES DIGITAL NETWORK USER PART ISDN-UP. The part of SS7 (Signaling System Number 7) that encompasses the signaling functions required to provide voice and non-voice services in ISDN and pre-ISDN architectures. The basic service offered by the ISDN-UP is the control of circuit-switched connections between subscriber line exchange terminations. Definition from Bellcore in reference to its concept of the Advanced Intelligent Network.

INTEGRATED VOICE DATA There are many different meanings to this concept. The most common (we'll get arguments on this) is that a workstation or a combination telephone/personal computer on a desk can combine voice and data signals over a single communications channel. That channel might be carried digitally on one pair of wires. That is "the most integrated" voice/data. Less integrated is when you carry voice and data digitally on two pairs — one pair for transmitting and one pair for receiving. Even less integrated are some systems which use three pairs of cabling set up as one voice analog pair, one digital data pair and one power/signaling pair. In short, "integrated voice/data" means different things to different people and depends on the technology. See also ISDN.

INTEGRATED VOICE DATA WORKSTATION See ISDN, IVDT and INTEGRATED VOICE/DATA.

INTELLIGENCE The part of a computer which performs the arithmetic and logic functions. Also, the information impressed or modulated on a transmission carrier — either voice or data.

INTELLIGENT NETWORK See SIGNALING SYSTEM SEVEN.

INTELLIGENT PERIPHERAL IP. A network system in the Advanced Intelligent Network Release 1 architecture containing an Resource containing an Resource Control Execution Environment (RCEE) functional group that enables flexible information interactions between a user and the network.

INTELLIGENT TERMINAL A terminal is an input/output device to a distant computer. The terminal may communicate with the computer over a dedicated collection of wires or over phone lines. In the early days, terminals contained no processing power. They simply reflected what the user typed in and what the distant computer responded. As computers became cheaper and with the advent of the "computer on a chip," so it was economically possible to put computing power into a terminal. This reduced the load on the main computer and cut down on communications costs. There are levels of "intelligence" in terminals. An intelligent terminal might perform simple arithmetic functions or it might check the accuracy of input data (does the zip code match the state?). It may perform far more comprehensive processing — as doing virtually all the local processing, and only transmitting summary results to corporate headquarters once a day. A personal computer can be used and act as an Intelligent Terminal. Many personal computer communications software can emulate terminals, the most common being the DEC VT-100.

INTELLIDIAL Intellidial is basically a New York Telephone Centrex service for small offices of big businesses or small businesses. You can get from two to nine lines. And you get to buy "packages" of features. Features in the packages include touch-tone, three-Way calling, call transfer, call hold, call pick-up, intercom, call forward-variable, call forward busy, call forward-don't answer, speed calling and call waiting.

INTELLIHUB A New York Telephone service which offers its larger customers large, local bandwidth. The service was developed primarily as a response to the threat of bypass. INTELLIHUB integrates and modifies FLEXPATH Digital PBX Service, INTELLIPATH, INTELLIPATH II Digital Centrex Service and INFOPATH Packet Switching Service for large multi-location business customers within an regional calling area.

INTELLIPATH DIGITAL CENTREX SERVICE Intellipath Digital Centrex Service is a New York Telephone digital Centrex service for smaller businesses with fewer than 99 lines. It has the basic features — such as call transfer, hold and three-way calling. One nice feature: each user can have his own 30-number speed calling list.

INTELLIPATH II Digital Centrex Service INTELLIPATH II Digital Centrex Service is a New York Telephone service for businesses needing over 100 lines. It has voice and data features. It has over 100 voice features — from automatic call back, to call pickup, to intercept and three-way calling. Its data features let you plug computers and terminals directly into a digital circuit.

INTERNODE LINK A data line for high-bandwidth connections between PBXs.

INTELSAT International Telecommunications Satellite Organization. A worldwide consortium of national satellite communications organizations. COMSAT acts as manager for Intelsat. Comsat is also the U.S. representative.

INTER- Means between two things, as opposed to INTRA-, which means inside one thing. INTERSTATE means communications between states. INTRASTATE means communications inside one state.

INTERACTIVE The ability to interact with a computer or to be in a conversational mode with a computer. Interactive processing is very time dependent since a user is waiting for the computer to ask him/her questions. The opposite of Interactive processing is batch processing. See BATCH.

INTERACTIVE VOICE RESPONSE IVR. Think of Interactive Voice Response as a voice computer. Where a computer has a keyboard for entering information, an IVR uses remote touchtone telephones. Where a computer has a screen for showing the results, an IVR uses a digitized synthesized voice to "read" the screen to the distant caller.

Whatever a computer can do, an IVR can too, from looking up train timetables to moving calls around an automatic call distributor (ACD). The only limitation on an IVR is that you can't present as many alternatives on a phone as you can on a screen. The caller's brain simply won't remember more than a few. With IVR, you have to present the menus in smaller chunks.

INTERAXIAL SPACING Center to center conductor spacing between any two wires.

INTERBUILDING WIRING Consists of underground or aerial telephone wire/cables used on the premises to connect structures remote from the primary building to the premises telephone system.

INTERCEPT Calls which cannot reach their destination may be intercepted and diverted to a station attendant, a recording or some other place. See INTERCEPT RECORDING and INTERCEPT SERVICE.

INTERCEPT RECORDING You make a phone call. It doesn't go through. The phone company intercepts that call and sends it somewhere. Intercept Recording is a recording telling you your call cannot be completed and has been intercepted on its way to the destination number for some reason that will be explained by the recording. The most common voice you hear on intercept announcements is Jane Barbie's. See BARBIE, JANE and INTERCEPT SERVICE.

INTERCEPT SERVICE A service of the local phone in which a phone call is redirected by an operator or a recording to another phone number or a message.

INTERCOM INTERCOMmunication. An internal communication system which allows you to dial another phone in your building, office complex, factory or home. There are three types of intercom: 1. Dial: It allows you to dial or pushbutton another extension. 2. Automatic: One phone goes off hook and automatically dials another. 3. Manual: The user can manually signal another phone by pushing a button for that phone. An example is a buzzer between a boss and a secretary.

INTERCOM BLOCKING A PBX feature by which phones with a particular Class Of Service (COS) are blocked from calling certain phones. A rare feature.

INTERCONNECT COMPANIES Companies which sell, install and maintain telephone systems for end users, typically businesses. AT&T coined the word "interconnect" as a pejorative word — to indicate that these companies "interconnected" to AT&T's telephone network — but didn't really belong there. These "interconnect" companies contrasted with true-blue companies belonging to AT&T which did a sterling job — such as AT&T itself or its local operating companies. Anyway, the term stuck but the nasty associations went away. Now the irony is that the CPE (Customer Premise Equipment) equipment subsidiaries and divisions of both AT&T and the local Bell operating telephone companies are, in fact, interconnect companies, though they don't call themselves that. The industry is looking for a better word. We at TELECONNECT Magazine started a campaign to make "TELECONNECT" a better replacement for interconnect. But our lawyers and the lawyers for a manufacturing/interconnect company called Teleconnect told us to lay off and stop trying to make the word generic. We rather like the term "Telecommunications Systems Integrator." That seems to be catching on. Anybody with a better name will be immortalized in Edition Four of this dictionary.

INTEREXCHANGE CARRIER IXC. A telephone company that is allowed to provide long-distance telephone service between LATAs but not within any one LATA. See IXC.

INTEREXCHANGE CHANNEL IXC. A communications channel or path between two or more telephone exchanges.

INTERFACE 1. A mechanical or electrical link connecting two or more pieces of equipment together. 2. A shared boundary. A physical point of demarcation between two devices where the electrical signals, connectors, timing and handshaking are defined. The procedures, codes and protocols that enable two entities to interact for a meaningful exchange of information. 3. To bring two things or people together to allow them to talk. 4. A poorly-defined word often used when the speaker is incapable of figuring precisely what he means. 5. An annual data communications trade show organized by Shelly Adelson. See also INTERFACE DEVICE.

INTERFACE DEVICE A device which meets a standard electrical interface on one side and meets some other nonstandard interface on the other. The purpose of the device is to allow a device with a nonstandard interface to connect to a device with a standard interface.

INTERFACE OVERHEAD the interface overhead is the remaining portion of the bit stream after deducting the information payload. The interface overhead may be essential (e.g. framing for an interface shared by users) or ancillary (e.g. performance monitoring).

INTERFACE PAYLOAD The portion of the bit stream which can be used for telecommunications services. Any signaling is included in the interface payload. See also INTERFACE OVERHEAD.

INTERFACE SHELVES Shelves in a Rolm PBX cabinet containing the printed circuit card groups that connect telephones, terminals, lines and trunks to CBX interface channels. These shelves also contain shared electronics cards.

INTERFERENCE Energy you receive with a signal. You don't want the energy. You want the signal. Getting rid of the interference may be a pain. The interference may be manmade (e.g. elevator motors) or it be GOD-made (e.g. lightning, thunderstorms.)

INTERFLOW The ability to establish a connection to a second ACD and overflow a call from one ACD to the other. This provides a greater level of service to the caller.

INTERFRAME ENCODING A way of video compression that transmits only changed information between successive frames. This saves bandwidth.

INTERLATA Telecommunications services that originate in one and terminate in another Local Access and Transport Area (LATA). Under provisions of Divestiture, the Bell operating companies cannot provide Inter-LATA service, but can provide Intra-LATA service. Some LATAs are very large. So some "local" phone companies provide the equivalent of long distance service. And some of these phone companies have different pricing packages. Some of these packages are cheap, but not highly-publicized.

See also LATA.

INTERLEAVE Refers to the way a computer writes to and reads from a hard disk. Interleaving is critical to understand if you want to get your hard disk to work at its maximum speed (without in any way damaging the disk). Let's look at the way MS-DOS reads information from a hard disk. All hard disks are controlled by a special card called a hard disk controller card. Let's say the computer wants a file. It tells the hard disk controller card it wants the file. The controller searches the disk for the first sector of the requested file, reads that sector (usually 512 bytes) to your computer's RAM and then transfers the information to the CPU to be processed. When this is complete, the controller goes back to the hard disk and searches for the file's second sector. The process continues in this way until the file is completely read.

The problem is that while the controller and the CPU are doing their things, the hard disk itself is spinning 3,600 times a minute. By the time the controller reads one sector and it is ready to return to the disk, the next consecutive file sector has spun past the read/write head. If the file is stored in contiguous sectors, the controller must wait for the disk to complete its revolution before it can read the next file sector. To solve this problem, hard drive makers developed a concept called interleave setting, which tells the hard drive controller to skip a certain number of sectors when it writes a file to disk. Thus, when the file is later read back, the appropriate file sectors should fall under the read/write heads at the appropriate time.

Setting the "correct" interleave settings on your hard disk is critical to getting maximum performance out of your hard disk. Here's a test that a writer for PCResource Magazine did. He copied the same files from one part of his hard disk to another part using different interleave settings:

Interleave	Time to copy file
3	1 min 15 seconds
4	1 min 17 seconds
5	1 min 1 second
6	35 seconds
7	41 seconds
8	1 min 10 seconds

Clearly his best interleave setting is 6. There are two ways of choosing the correct interleave setting. You can do it by trial and error as the writer did. His test took three hours. Or buy a program and do it in seconds. The best one is called Disk Technician. It's from a company called Prime Solutions in San Diego. Sadly, the program doesn't work on certain laptops.

INTERMEDIATE DISTRIBUTION FRAME IDF. The IDF provides connections between the Main Distribution Frame (MDF) and individual phone wiring. There's usually a permanent big, fat cable running between the MDF and IDF. The changes in wiring are done at the IDF. This saves confusion in wiring.

INTERNAL MODEM A modem on a printed circuit card which is inserted into one of the slots on a PC (personal computer). The other type of modem for a PC is an external modem — essentially a modem with the same circuitry as an internal modem but with a metal or plastic case. An internal modem costs slightly less than an external one. Internal modems are good if you're short of deskspace and afraid your external modem will be stolen. External modems have lights so it's easier to tell what's going on. Everybody has their theories on which type of modem is best. We prefer the external ones — largely for their lights and ease of moving around.

INTERNATIONAL 800 SERVICE You can now have your customers overseas call you for free on an 800 line, just as your domestic customers do. The service is available from countries including Australia, Brazil, France, Hong Kong, Israel, Italy, Japan, Sweden, Switzerland and the United Kingdom. Overseas 800 service is often known as "Freephone."

INTERNATIONAL CENTER FOR INFORMATION TECHNOLOGIES A Washington "think tank" whose mission is to bring together discussion on new telecommunications and computer technologies. Targeted at senior executives who are looking for ways to apply new technologies to gaining competitive edges for their company.

INTERNATIONAL DIRECT DISTANCE DIALING IDDD. Being able to automatically dial international long distance calls from your own phone.

INTERNATIONAL ORGANIZATION FOR STANDARDIZATION ISO. An organization established to create standards. See ISO.

INTERNATIONAL TELECOMMUNICATIONS UNION ITU. The specialized agency of the United Nations which tries to establish standardized communications procedures and practices. Its most successful work is done in the allocation of radio frequencies worldwide — including satellites, etc. See ITU.

INTERNATIONAL TELEPHONE ADDRESS A four-part code specifying a unique address for any telephone company in the world.

INTERNET MIB SUBTREE A tree-shaped data structure in which network devices on a local area network and their attributes can be identified within the confines of a network management scheme. The name of an object or attribute is derived from its location on this tree.

For example, an object in MIB-I might be named 1.2.1.1.1.0. the first 1 indicates the object is on the Internet. The 2 denotes that it falls within the Management category. The second 1 shows the object is part of the first fully defined MIB, known as MIB-I. The third 1 indicates which of the eight object groups is being referenced. And the fourth 1 is a textual description of the network component. The 0 indicates there is only one object instance. An object instance links a particular object to a specific node on the network. The numbering system is infinitely extendible to accommodate additions to this base identification scheme. This common naming structure permits equipment from a variety of vendors to be managed by a single management station that uses SNMP. The four main categories of the tree are Directory, Management, Experimental and Private/Enterprises.

INTERNET PROTOCOL IP. Used in gateways to connect networks at OSI network Level 3 and above.

INTERNETWORK ROUTER In local area networking technology. Device used for communications between networks. Messages for the connected network are addressed to the internetwork router, which chooses the best path to the selected destination via dynamic routing. Internetwork routers function at the network layer of the Open Systems Interconnection (OSI) model. Also known as a network router or simply as a router.

INTERNETWORKING A term indicating the reach of local area networks (LANs) to other networks, so users can get access to new files, databases and applications. Bridges and routers are the devices which typically accomplish the task of joining LANs. According to a press release from Telebit Corporation,

INTERNODE Communication paths which originate in one node and terminate in another.

INTERNODE LINK A data line for high-bandwidth connections between PBXs.

INTEROFFICE Between two telephone company switching offices.

INTEROFFICE CHANNEL A transmission path between two AT&T serving offices.

INTEROFFICE TRUNK A trunk circuit connecting two local telephone company central offices.

INTERPBX Calls coming into one PBX can be transferred to extensions on another PBX using direct tie lines between the two PBXs.

INTERPOSITION CALLING One operator in a multi-position system calling another.

INTERPOSITION TRANSFER Transfer of a call from one operator to another.

INTERROGATE To determine the state of a device or unit.

INTERRUPT 1. To temporarily suspend the program you're working on and jump into another. 2. An access method used in some bus and ring local area networks where workstations can "interrupt" a server to get service. The server will stop doing what its doing, give the workstation a file or whatever it wants, then return to its previous task. Interrupt is preferred over polling, an older, less efficient easier-to-implement method of getting the attention of the server (central computer). See also INTERRUPT REQUEST and POLLING.

INTERRUPT REQUEST IRQ. This is the communications channel through which devices issue interrupts to the interrupt handler of an IBM PC or IBM compatible PC's microprocessor. It's the channel through which these devices get the microprocessor's attention. Different IRQs are assigned to different devices. This assignment pattern differs from PC to PC. Many LAN interface cards use an IRQ to get to the microprocessor. You must be sure that your LAN interface card is not trying to use the IRQ assigned to another peripheral, like the hard disk controller or EGA card.

INTERRUPTER An automatically operated electromechanical device used to turn lights, bells or other signals on and off in timed sequences. An interrupter makes lights wink on and off on a key system. Or did, when everything was electromechanical. It was used on 1A key telephone systems.

INTERSTATE Between different states (crossing a state line).

INTERSTICES In cable construction, the spaces, valleys or voids between or around the cable's components.

INTERTOLL TRUNKS Trunks connecting Class 4 and higher switching machines in the AT&T long distance network.

INTERVAL Time. Pulse interval, for example, means the time from the start of one pulse to the start of the next.

INTERSWITCH TRUNK A circuit between two switching machines.

INTRACALLING This is an outside plant term. Intracalling refers to the ability of a remote line concentrator to interconnect users served by the same concentrator without providing two trunks directly back to the central office.

INTRAFLOW This is an automatic call distribution term. It refers to the ability to select a second or subsequent group of agents to backup the primary agent group. This is designed to allow the caller to be serviced more efficiently and less expensively.

INTRAFRAME ENCODING A way of video compression that divides the TV picture into blocks and transmits only changed blocks between successive frames.

INTRALATA Telecommunications services that originate in and end in the same Local Access and Transport Area.

INTRANODE Communications path which originates and terminates in the same node.

INTRAOFFICE TRUNK A telephone channel between two pieces of equipment within the same central office.

INTRASTATE Remaining entirely within the boundaries of a single state and, therefore, if related to telephone, falling under the jurisdiction of that state's telephone regulatory procedures.

INVERTER A device which converts DC electricity to AC electricity or which converts pulses from positive to negative and vice versa.

INVITATION TO SEND A character or sequence of characters which calls for a station to begin transmission. Usually this is part of a polling arrangement.

INWARD RESTRICTION A Centrex service feature which stops Centrex lines receiving certain incoming calls.

INWARD TRUNK Used only for incoming calls, these trunks cannot dial out. "800" lines, for example, can only be used to receive calls.

INWATS Inward Wide Area Telephone Service. A service of AT&T, MCI, US Sprint and the Bell operating companies which allows subscribers to receive calls from specified areas (depending on the rate band chosen) with no charge to the person who's calling. See 800 SERVICE for a much bigger explanation.

IOD Identified Outward Dialing. See also AIOD and CALL ACCOUNTING SYSTEM.

IP Internetwork Protocol in ISO or in ARPA.

IPCI See INTEGRATED PERSONAL COMPUTER INTERFACE.

IPL Initial Program Load.

IPM Interruptions Per Minute or Impulses Per Minute.

IRC International Record (i.e. non-voice) Carrier. One of a group of common carriers that, until a few years ago, exclusively carried data and text traffic from gateway cities in the U.S. to other countries. The distinction between international companies providing "record" and data has eroded and now both types of companies provide voice and data services internationally.

IRQ See INTERRUPT REQUEST.

IRRADIATION In insulations, the exposure of the material to high energy emissions for the purpose of favorably altering the molecular structure by crosslinking.

IS Information Separator. A type of control character used to separate and qualify data logically. Its specific meaning has to be defined for each application.

ISB InterShelf Bus.

ISDN Integrated Services Digital Network. A totally new concept of what the world's telephone system should be. According to AT&T, today's public switched phone network has the following limitations: 1. Each voice line is only 4 kHz, which is very narrow. 2. Most signaling is in-band signaling, which is very consuming of bandwidth (i.e. it's expensive and inefficient). 3. The little out-of-band signaling that exists today runs on lines separate to the network. (This includes signaling for PBX attendants, hotel/motel, Centrex and PBX calling information.) 4. Most users have separate voice and data networks (which is inefficient, expensive and limiting). 5. Premises telephone and data equipment must be separately administered from the network it runs on. 6. There is a wide and growing variety of voice, data and digital interface standards, many of which are incompatible. ISDN's "vision" is to overcome these deficiencies in four ways: 1. By providing an internationally accepted standard for voice, data and signaling. 2. By making all transmission circuits end-to-end digital. 3. By adopting a standard out-of-band signaling system. 4. By bringing significantly more bandwidth to the desk top. An ISDN central office will deliver to the user's office or factory four basic ISDN services, also called interfaces.

1. The 2B+D "S" interface (also called the "T" interface). The 2B+D is called

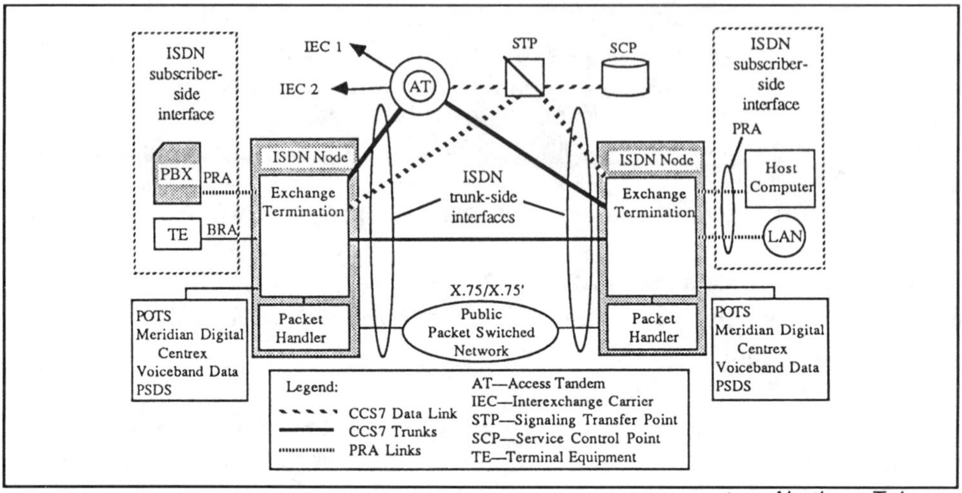

courtesy Northern Telecom

the Basic Rate Interface (BRI). The "S" interface uses four unshielded normal telephone wires (two twisted wire pairs) to deliver two "Bearer" 64,000 bits per second channels and one "data" signaling channel of 16,000 bits per second. An S-interfaced phone can be located up to one kilometer from the central office switch driving it. Each of the two 64 kpbs "bearer" or B channels can be used to carry a voice conversation, or one high speed data or several data channels, which are multiplexed into one 64 kbps high speed data line. The "D" channel of 16 kbps will carry control and signaling information to set up and break down the voice and data calls. The "D" channel can also carry data up to 9600 bits per second in addition to the control and signaling information. Signalling and control on the D channel conforms to a protocol (LAPD) and a messaging structure (Q.931). These two allow intelligent endpoints and switching nodes from different vendors to talk a common language and thus be able to transfer features across a network, from one switch to another, e.g. to transfer a Centrex call across town through several switches and to have it arrive at the end phone with the calling party's name.

2. The 2B+D "T" interface. This "T" interface delivers the same two 64 kbps bearer channels and one 16 kbps data channel, except that it uses 2-wires (one pair) and can work at 5-10 kilometers from the central office switch driving it.

3. The 23B+D or 30B+D. This is called the Primary Rate Interface (PRI). At 23B+D, it is 1.544 megabits per second. At 30B+D, it is 2.048 megabits per second. The first, 23B+D is the standard T-1 line in the U.S. which operates on two pairs. The second 30B+D is the standard T-1 line in Europe, which also operates on two pairs.

4. A standard single line analog phone. A 2500 or a 500 set. (A connection to tradition?)

Integral to ISDN's ability to produce new customer services is CCITT

Signaling System 7. This is a CCITT recommendation which does two basic things: First, it removes all phone signaling from the present network onto a separate packet switched data network, thus providing enormous economies of bandwidth. Second, it broadens the information that is generated by a call, or call attempt. This information — like the phone number of the person who's calling — will significantly broaden the number of useful new services the ISDN telephone network of tomorrow will be able to deliver.

Here are some sample ISDN services which the various vendors have publicized. They are "mind-blowing." Most are possible in some way today. They reflect early ISDN "thinking," not ISDN "doing." They remind us of the applications we thought were possible with PCs when we only had CP/M eight bit machines — before the 16-bit IBM PC machine debuted in 1983:

Simultaneous Data Calls: Two users can talk and exchange information over the D packet and/or the B circuit or packet switched channel.

Citywide Centrex: A myriad of services: Specialized numbering and dialing plans. Central management of all ISDN terminals, including PBXs, key systems, etc.

Call waiting: A line is busy. A call comes in. The user knows who is calling. He can then accept, reject, ignore, transfer the call.

Credit card calling: Automatic billing of certain or all calls into accounts independent of the calling line/s.

Calling line identification presentation: Provides the calling party the ISDN "phone" number, possibly with additional address information, of the called party. Such information may flash across the screen of an ISDN phone or be announced by a synthesized voice. The called party can then accept, reject or transfer the call. If the called party is not there, then his/her phone will automatically record the incoming call's phone number and allow automatic callbacks when he/she returns or calls back in from elsewhere.

Calling line identification restriction: Restricts presentation of the calling party's ISDN "phone" number, possibly with additional address information, to the called party.

Closed user group: Restricts conversations to or among a select group of phone numbers, local, long distance or international.

E-Mail (aka Personal mailbox): ISDN can carry information to and from unattended phones as long as they're equipped with proper hardware and software.

Multi-location ringing: An ISDN subscriber can specify several locations where an incoming call should ring simultaneously.

In the summer of 1990 Southwestern Bell issued a press release announcing their signing up of several ISDN customers. In that release, they also included a small listing of what they felt were ISDN benefits:

Most people who use the telephone or a personal computer probably don't care why ISDN works, but they may be very interested in what it can do for them. A few examples: Selective Call Screening — Within a business, this application displays the phone number of the calling party before the phone is answered. If two people call simultaneously, the person answering can choose which call is the higher priority to answer by seeing both calling numbers.

Shared Screen — Switched data services provided via ISDN lets two people in remote locations, both equipped with a computer terminal, to view the same information on their screens and discuss its contents while making changes — all over one telephone line.

Network Access — Most large companies have many computer networks and databases, but only those workers who regularly use those databases have easy access to them. ISDN allows a person at a personal computer to gain access to virtually any database.

Less Down Time/Cost Savings Moves — When a company moves an employee within an office, there can be hours or days of lost production while a computer terminal and phone set are being installed. In some cases, the terminal is connected to a network via coaxial cable. ISDN virtually eliminates down time, as well as the need for coaxial cable.

For more on ISDN capabilities, see ISDN TELEPHONE, ISUP, NETWORK TERMINATION 1, PERSONAL COMPUTER TERMINAL ADAPTER, Q.931, SIGNALING SYSTEM 7, and TCAP.

ISDN TELEPHONE An ISDN phone can attach to an ISDN basic rate interface. It typically has one voice channel and two data options — one for packet switched services (up to 9600 bps) and another for circuit switched data (up to 64 kbps). It will also have an RS-232-C connector on its back and a two line, 48-character LCD adjustable display. It will also have a bunch of dedicated buttons for standard stuff — last number redial, speed dial, on-hook dialing, listen-on-hold, etc. Some ISDN phones work behind most ISDN central offices — e.g. the Telrad phones. Most don't. They have

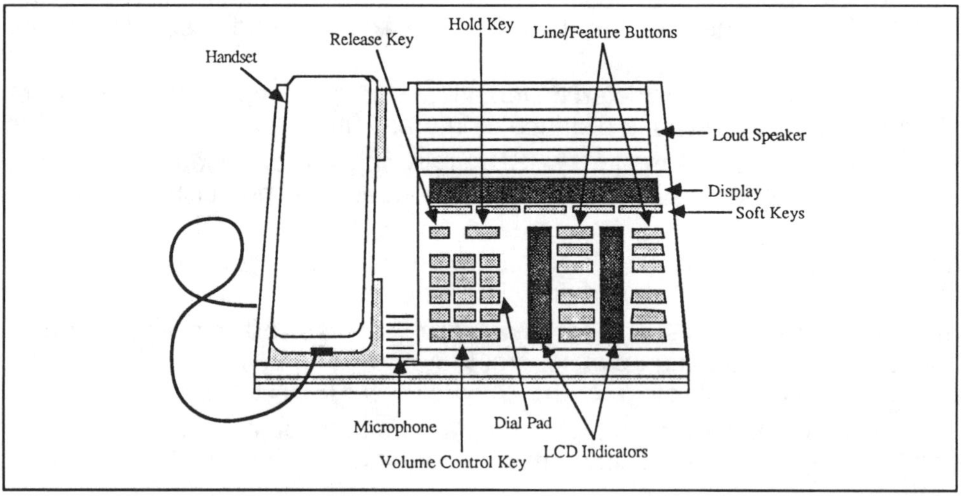

courtesy Northern Telecom

to work behind the central office they're designed for. Most ISDN phones cost over $600. Some cost nearly $1,000. Some cost more than a personal computer. See ISDN. See ISDN.

ISL Northern Telecom term for ISDN Signaling Link.

ISO 1. International Standards Organization in Paris, devoted to figuring standards for international and national data communications. The U.S. representative to the ISO is ANSI. 2. The initials also stand for Independent Service Organizations or Independent Sales Organizations in the computer sales community.

ISOCHRONOUS A term used with digital transmission of data indicating that the timing, or synchronizing, signal is derived from the signal carrying the data.

ISUP Integrated Services Digital Network User Part. The call control part of the SS7 protocol. ISUP determines the procedures for setting up, coordinating, and taking down trunk calls on the SS7 network. ISUP is defined by CCITT recommendations Q.761 and Q.764. ISUP also provides:

- Calling party number information (including privacy indicator).
- Call status checking, to keep trunks in consistent states at both ends.
- Trunk management, and
- Relates of trunks and the application of tones and/or announcements in the originating switch upon encountering error, blockage or busy conditions.

There are seven ISUP Messages: Initial Address Message (IAM), Continuity Check Message (COT), Address Complete Message (ACM), Answer Message(ANM), Release Message (REL), Release Complete Message (RLC) and Exit Message (EXM). For you to benefit from these capabilities, your phone equipment must first be able to access the CCS7 network. One suggested way (but not the only way) is through the ISDN primary rate access (PRA) standard, which supports Q.931 protocol. See IAM, ISDN and COMMON CHANNEL SIGNALING.

IT Information Technology. An European term favored by Siemens and Nixdorf who merged in 1989. IT is one of the broader terms ever created.

ITB Intermediate Block Character. A transmission control character that terminates an intermediate block. A Block Check Character (BCC) usually follows. Using ITBs allows for error checking of smaller blocks in data communications.

ITERATIVE PROCESS The process of repeatedly processing a bunch of instructions. Each repetition, theoretically, comes progressively closer to the desired result, the "correct" answer, etc.

ITI Idle Trunk Indicator.

ITM See Information Technology Management.

ITT International Telephone and Telegraph. A company that once was the largest manufacturer of telecommunications equipment outside the U.S.

ITU International Telecommunications Union. An organization established by the United Nations with membership from virtually every government in the world. ITU's objective is to set telecommunications standards, allocate frequencies to various uses and hold trade shows every four years. As satellites have become more important as a method of long distance communications, so the ITU's allocation of scarce satellite frequencies among countries has become a hot bed of controversy. There are many who believe the ITU to be the most important telecommunications organization in the world.

IVDT Integrated Voice/Data Terminal. A device with a terminal keyboard/display and a voice telephone with or without its own processing power. See INTEGRATED VOICE/DATA TERMINAL.

IVR Interactive Voice Response. Think of IVR as a voice computer. Where a computer has a keyboard for entering information, an IVR uses remote touchtone telephones. Where a computer has a screen for showing the results, an IVR uses a digitized synthesized voice to "read" the screen to the distant caller.

Whatever a computer can do, an IVR can too, from looking up train timetables to moving calls around an automatic call distributor (ACD). The only limitation on an IVR is that you can't present as many alternatives on a phone as you can on a screen. The caller's brain simply won't remember more than a few. With IVR, you have to present the menus in smaller chunks.

IXC InterExchange Channel, or InterExchange Carrier — as contrasted to the LEC — the Local Exchange Carrier, a new word for a local phone company. InterExchange Carriers used to be called "Other Common Carriers," except that didn't include AT&T. Now, AT&T, MCI, Sprint and all the Other Common Carriers are called InterExchange Carriers.

JABBER, JABBERING In local area networking technology, continuously sending random data (garbage). Normally used to describe the action of a station (whose circuitry or logic has failed) that locks up the network with its incessant transmission.

JACK A receptacle used to connect a cord or line to a telephone system. A jack can be female or male.

JACK CONTACTS Metallic elements of telephone jacks that carry the central office currents/voltages to the CPE plus contacts.

JACK PINS See JACK CONTACTS.

JACK POSITIONS A numbering scheme to permit consistent identification of the Jack Contact(s) position. Position identification helps assure compatibility between the wiring system and the associated terminal equipment.

JACKET The protective and insulating housing of a cable.

JAMMING The interference of through-the-air radio transmission, the object being to hinder the receiver's ability to pick up and understand the signal. An example is the Russians' jamming Radio Free Europe.

JANE BARBIE The electronic "Voice With A Smile" on most telephone company intercept recordings. Ms. Barbie does her work for the Audichron Company of Atlanta, GA.

JCL Job Control Language.

JEOPARDY A wonderful AT&T word meaning anything occurring during the course of accomplishing scheduled work which might cause the scheduled completion date to slip.

JES Job Entry Subsystem. Control protocol and procedure for directing host processing of a task in an IBM host environment. Also the specific IBM software release, host-based, that performs job control functions.

JITTER A tendency towards lack of synchronization caused by mechanical or electrical changes. Technically, the phase shift of digital pulses over a transmission medium.

JOB A file, typically sent in batch mode. Specifically a set of data, including programs, files and instructions to a computer, that together amount to a unit of work to be done by a computer.

JOINT USER SERVICE An arrangement whereby a corporation, association, partnership or individual whose telecommunications needs do not warrant the provision of separate leased service, is permitted to use the service of another customer by mutual agreement. The primary objective of joint user service is to save money by buying circuits in bulk.

JOURNAL PRINTERS These are special purpose printers which provide hard-copy output for audit trail and demand printing functions associated with hotel/motel management features.

JPEG Proposed worldwide standard for image compression devised by the Joint Photographic Experts Group, experts sanctioned by the International

Standards Organization (ISO).

JUDGE HAROLD GREENE Judge Greene presided over the 1982 AT&T Antitrust settlement, enforcing its provisions and making decisions about requests from the participants to modify or reinterpret the provisions of the settlement. As long as he doesn't allow AT&T to be completely free of regulation, Judge Greene will probably always be involved in figuring the future of the telecommunications industry.

JUMBO GROUP A 3,600 channel band of frequencies formed from the inputs of six master groups. See MASTERGROUP and SUPERGROUP.

JUMPER 1. A wire used to connect equipment and cable on a distributing frame. 2. A patch cable or wire used to establish a circuit, often temporarily, for testing or diagnostics. 3. When errors are found on printed circuit boards, a Jumper cable is sometimes soldered in to correct the problem.

JUMP HUNTING See NONCONSECUTIVE HUNTING.

JUNCTION BOX Metal box inside which cables are connected together.

JUNCTOR A connection or circuit between inlets and outlets of the same or different switching networks.

JUNIPER A Rolm/IBM product that consists of a digital phone and a printed circuit for dropping into an IBM PC or clone.

K 1. See K-style handset below. 2. In metric terms it means one thousand — 1,000. It is often appended to a measurement such as KHertz or kHz, which means 1,000 Hertz. In data communications, a kilobit means a thousand bits per second. In computer memory terms, it means 1,024, which is the figure for two raised to the tenth power, i.e. 2 x 2 x 2 x 2 x 2 x 2 x 2 x 2 x 2 x 2.

K BAND That portion of the electromagnetic spectrum in the high microwave/millimeter range — from 10.9 GHz to 36 GHz. See also Ka BAND.

K PLANS Also call keysheets. When designing a phone system, you need to assign features and line assignments to each extension. A keysheet or a K Plan is an organized way of figuring and keeping track of those features and assignments. Typically it's one page per extension. These days, keysheets are often done on computer.

K-STYLE HANDSET A K-style handset is the newer, square telephone handset with the two screws in the middle of the handset. The older, round handset is called the G-style handset.

Ka BAND That portion of the electromagnetic spectrum in the high microwave/millimeter range — approximately 33 to 36 GHz.

KBIT/S Kilobits per second. Standard measure of data rate and transmission capacity. SEE K.

KBPS KiloBits Per Second. One thousand bits per second.

KEEP-ALIVE SIGNAL A generic term for a T-1 signal transmitted when a DTE detects a loss of input from the customer's equipment for 150 msec. (sometimes called a blue signal or AIS).

KERMIT An asynchronous file transfer protocol designed for PC communications at Columbia University. The protocol has become popular because of its flexibility. Kermit is found most frequently on DEC VAX computers, IBM mainframes and other minicomputers. One of the clearest advantages of Kermit is its ability to be tailored for virtually any equipment. Protocols break a file into equal parts called blocks or packets. These packets are sent and the receiving computer checks the arriving packet and sends an acknowledgement (ACK) back to the sending computer. Because modems use phone lines to transfer data, noise or interference on the line will often mess up the block. When a block is damaged in transit, an error occurs. The purpose of a protocol is to set up a mathematical way of measuring if the block came through accurately. And if it didn't, ask the distant end to re-transmit the block until it gets it right.

KEY 1. One or more characters or perhaps a field within data record used to identify the data and perhaps control its use. 2. The physical button on a telephone set. (What normal people call a "Switch," telephone people call a "Key.") 3. The device which unlocks your front door or perhaps your terminal or computer.

KEY ILLUMINATION A lamp under a button (called a "key" in telephony) which flashes at different rates to signal an incoming call, a steady busy and "wink" (fast) hold.

KEY PAD The touch-tone dial pad on a pushbutton phone. Touchtone is a registered trademark of AT&T, so most people use the word "pushbutton." But there's really no difference.

KEY PULSE In multifrequency (MF) tone signaling, a signal used to prepare the distant equipment to receive digits.

KEY PULSING A pulsing system in which digits are transmitted using pushbuttons. Each button corresponds to a digit and generates a unique set of tones.

KEY SERVICE PANEL An old 1A2 key telephone term. Wired or unwired connector panel for modular expansion of key system service by allowing the installation of additional Line Cards and/or other KTUs. Typically, Key Service Panels are available in different jack configurations to accommodate 18-, 20-, 36- and 40-pin KTU's. Commonly abbreviated as KSP. Most KSPs are supplied as rack-mount equipment.

KEY SERVICE UNIT KSU. This is a small metal cabinet which contains all the switching electronics of a business key telephone system. The KSU fits between the lines coming in from the central office and the lines going to the individual phones. Be careful where you place the Key Service Unit. That place should be well-ventilated as the KSU gets hot. It should be near a power outlet (it needs one). Unless it's a very small phone system, it should be plugged into a power outlet dedicated to it (other devices, such as typewriters, plugged into the same electrical circuit could affect it). And the power outlet should be above the reach of the mops and brooms of the local cleaning lady. Otherwise the plug will get knocked out and the phone system won't work the next day. See KEY TELEPHONE SYSTEM.

KEY SET Also called Key Telephone Set. A telephone set having several buttons which can be used for call holding, line pick-up, auto-dialing, intercom and other features. Ericsson calls a keyset a touchtone telephone.

KEY STRIP The row(s) of additional buttons on key telephone sets used for call hold, intercom and other KTU function control.

KEY SYSTEM POWER SUPPLY The local source for all DC voltages required for talking and lamp signaling within the Key Telephone System. The power supply may or may not also provide an AC voltage output for ringing. If it does, a separate Ringing Generator will normally not be required.

KEY TELEPHONE SYSTEM A system in which the telephones have multiple buttons permitting the user to select outgoing or incoming central office phone lines directly. With a key system you don't have to dial 9 to get obtain an outside line. With a PBX, you have to dial "9" to make a call outside the building. Dialing 9 is the major difference these days between a key telephone systems and PBXs. PBXs are usually, but not always, larger.

KEY TELEPHONE UNIT A modular 1A2 Key Telephone System building block that plugs into a KSU or KSP. Commonly abbreviated as KTU. Typical KTU examples include 4000 Series Line Cards, 4448 Delayed Ring Transfer

Card, 6606 Interrupter, etc.

KEY TO DISK A method of entering data whereby it's sent directly from the keyboard to a disk, usually a hard disk.

KEYBOARD A series of switches, arranged somewhat like a standard "QWERTY" typewriter that allows you to send information to a computer. There is no such animal as a "standard" computer keyboard. For speed typists, this is a terrible pity. If you are buying multiple computers for your office, check out your peoples' preference for keyboards. Getting the right one can make a big difference. You can often buy PCs without keyboards and buy third party differently-designed keyboards.

KEYBOARD CALL SETUP Allows you to set up a data call using the keys of a telephone, or vice versa. That is, it allows you to set up a voice call using the keyboard of your PC. Which definition you choose — setting up a voice or a data call — depends on which manufacturer you're working with.

KEYING Modulation of a carrier signal, usually by frequency or phase, to encode binary (digital) information, (as in FSK or Frequency Shift Keying).

KHz KiloHertz. See K.

KILO One thousand.

KILOCHARACTER One thousand characters. Used as a measure of billing for data communications by some overseas phone companies. See also KILOSEGMENT.

KILOSEGMENT 64,000 characters. Used as a measure of billing for data communications by some overseas phone companies. See also KILOCHARACTER.

KINGSBURY COMMITMENT December 13, 1913: A letter from Nathan C. Kingsbury, VP AT&T, to the attorney-general of the United States committed AT&T to dispose of its stock in Western Union Telegraph Company. It also promised to provide long distance connection of Bell System lines to independent phone companies (where there was no local competition) and further agreed not to purchase any more independent telephone companies, except as approved by the Interstate Commerce Commission which regulated the phone industry at that time.

KLUDGE A hardware solution that has been improvised from various mismatched parts. A slang word meaning makeshift. A kludge can also be in software. It may not be elegant and is probably only a temporary fix. As in, "That patch to the software is a real kludge." See KLUGE.

KLUGE Another way of spelling KLUDGE. We don't know which is correct.

KNOWLEDGE BASE SYSTEM Software in which application specific information is programmed into something called the "knowledge base" in the form of rules. The system uses artificial intelligence (AI) procedures to mimic human problem-solving. It applies the rules stored in the knowledge base and the facts supplied to the system to solve a particular business problem.

KSR Keyboard Send Receive. A combination teleprinter/transmitter/receiver with transmission capability from the keyboard only, i.e. there is no punch paper tape device and no magnetic memory device, such as a floppy disk.

KSU Key Service Unit. The main cabinet containing all electronics necessary to run a key telephone system. See also KEY SERVICE UNIT.

KTA Key Telephone Adapter. A Rolm multiplexing unit which connects a standard 1A2 key telephone to a three-pair cable coming in from the Rolm CBX.

KTI Key Telephone Interface.

KTU Key Telephone Unit. The circuit cards found in a KSU that control telephone sets and their features in a key system.

KU BAND Portion of the electromagnetic spectrum in the 12 to 14 GHz range. Used for satellites.

KWH KiloWatt Hour. One thousand watts of electricity used for one hour.

L BAND Portion of the electromagnetic spectrum commonly used in satellite and microwave applications, with frequencies in the 1 GHz region.

L CARRIER A long haul frequency division multiplexed coax-cabled long haul carrier system. It was first introduced just before the second World War. Eventually it grew to a capacity of 13,300 voice channels over a pair of coaxial tubes. L Carrier systems are still used today. They are the most widely-used analog long distance transmission system.

L MULTIPLEX A system of analog multiplexers built up through groups, supergroups, master groups and jumbo groups of circuits. See L CARRIER.

L-to-T CONNECTOR A device that mates two FDM (Frequency Division Multiplexed) groups with one TDM (Time Division Multiplexed) digigroup to allow 24 voice conversations in analog form to talk to (tie into) a DS-1 line — a T-1 line.

LABEL A set of symbols used to identify or describe an item, record, message or file. It can also be the same as the address in storage.

LADT Local Area Data Transport. A service of your local phone company which provides you, the user, with synchronous data communications.

LAMA Local Automatic Message Accounting. A process using equipment in the central office which records the information necessary to bill your local phone calls by your local phone company.

LAMP BATTERY A steady (unpulsing) 10 VAC source of power to operate the lamps in key telephone sets; usually one of the outputs of the local Key System Power Supply.

LAMP FLASH A pulsed 10 VAC source of lamp power sent to a key telephone set to indicate a CO or PBX line is ringing in. Pulse repetition rate is normally 60 Hertz with a duty cycle of .5 sec on and .5 sec off. This signal is usually provided by the local Interrupter KTU.

LAMP LEADS Lamp and Lamp Ground (L&LG) wires connected to all lamps in the key telephone set over which steady and pulsed 10 VAC signaling signals from the Line Card KTU are sent.

LAMP STEADY A steady (unpulsed) 10 VAC source of lamp power sent to a key telephone set to indicate that the line is in use. See also Lamp Battery.

LAMP WINK A pulsed 10 VAC source of lamp power sent to a key telephone set to indicate that the line is on Hold status; pulse repetition rate is normally 120 Hertz with a duty cycle of .4 sec on and .1 sec off. This signalling signal is usually provided by the local Interrupter KTU.

LAN Local Area Network. A short distance network (typically within a building or campus) used to link together computers and peripheral devices (such as printers) under some form of standard control. LANs have two main advantages — anyone on the LAN can typically access a centralized database, and anyone on the LAN can send messages to and work jointly with others on the LAN. A LAN does not use common carrier circuits, although it may have gateways and/or bridges to public telecommunications networks. See LAN MANAGER, TOKEN RING and ETHERNET.

LAN MAGAZINE BOOKSTORE The mail order bookstore which carries all books on local area networks. For a copy of the bookstore's free catalog of books for sale, please call 1-800-999-0345 or 1-800-LIBRARY.

LAN MANAGER A person who manages a LAN. Duties can includes adding new users, installing new hardware and software, diagnosing network problems, helping users, performing backup and setting up a security system. Unlike MIS managers, LAN managers are rarely formally trained in LAN management. Sometimes they're called LAN Network Managers.

LANDLINE A telephone circuit that travels over terrestrial circuits, be they wire or microwave. A call may originate from a source not connected to the "terrestrial" network, as from a car telephone or a ship to shore radio connection, and the call be completed via a Landline.

LANDSCAPE Most computer screens are horizontal, i.e. they are wider than they are high. In the new language of computer screens, such screens are called "landscape." When a computer screen is higher than it is wide, it's called "portrait." Some computer screens can actually work both ways. Some even have a small mercury switch in them that determines which way the screen is standing (portrait or landscape) and will adjust their image accordingly.

LANGUAGE Computer software that allows you to write programs.

LANGUAGE INTERPRETER Any processor, assembler or software that accepts statements in one software language and then produces equivalent statements in another language.

LAP Link Access Procedure.

LAPB Link Access Procedure Balanced. The data link level of X.25 in a packet switched network. Same as a subset of the asynchronous balanced mode of HDLC. Link initialization procedure that establishes and maintains communications between the data terminal equipment (DTE) and data communications equipment (DCE). All public packet data networks (PDNs) support LAPB.

LAPD Link Access Procedure-D. Link-level protocol devised for ISDN connections, differing from LAPB (LAP-Balanced) in its framing sequence. Likely to be used as basis for LAPM, the proposed CCITT modem error-control standard.

LAPTOP COMPUTER A portable computer you can use on your lap. Usually weighing less than 15 pounds. Probably the most useful gadget to come along in years. Much of this dictionary was written in planes, trains, airports, etc. on a laptop computer — a Toshiba T1200 HB, sporting one megabyte of RAM, one 21 megabyte drive, one 3 1/2 inch disk drives with a capacity of 730K and a 1200 baud modem.

LATA Local Access and Transport Area. One of 161 local telephone service areas in the United States. As a result of the Bell divestiture, switched calls with both endpoints within the LATA (intraLATA) are generally the sole responsibility of the local telephone company, while calls that cross outside the LATA (interLATA) are passed on to an interexchange carrier.

LARGE SQUARING CAPABILITY A feature on the AT&T Merlin key system which permits all lines to appear on all telephone sets.

LASER An acronym for Light Amplification by Stimulated Emission of Radiation. It is a device which produces a single frequency light. By turning on and off the laser light signal quickly, you can transmit the ones and zeros of a digital communications channel. Lasers carried through glass fiber are ideal for telecommunications transmission for two major reasons. 1. Glass fiber of such purity has now been developed that only a very minute portion of the laser light traveling through it is lost. In telecom terms, this means very little of the laser signal is attenuated. The signal maintains its strength and thus reduces the need for frequent and expensive repeaters (the digital word for "amplifiers.") Laser transmission systems can now carry thousands of voice conversations for hundreds of miles without repeaters on two fibers each no thicker than a human hair. (You need two fibers — one for the conversations coming and one for them going.) 2. Laser fiber optics telecom systems are totally immune to electromagnetic interference of any kind. There's no humming from electrical motors. You can't pick up the local TV station in the background.

In recent years, laser fiber optic transmission has been getting cheaper, more reliable and more powerful at roughly the same rate as computers, and like computers, nobody believes there is an end in sight. As we were writing this dictionary, Russell Dewitt of Contel delivered a paper entitled Evolution of fiber optics in rural telephone networks. In it, he talked about "Fiber Optics Progress" and said:

"In 1860, the Pony Express could deliver a letter from St. Louis to San Francisco in ten days. For three typed pages the data transmission rate was about three bits per minute. In comparison, today in Contel we are transmitting at the rate of 565 Mbps (million bits per second) over single mode fiber. This is a capacity of 8064 voice channels. Gigabit per second systems will be available for use this year (a gigabit is a million million) and a 20 Gbps system has been demonstrated in the laboratory. For the future, the ultimate potential of a single mode fiber has been estimated. It is about 25,000 Gbps (25,000,000,000,000,000 bits per second). At that rate you could transmit all the knowledge recorded since the beginning of time in 20 seconds. See also LCD and FIBER OPTICS.

LASER FAX A conventional laser printer that is also capable of being used as a fax machine when combined with an optional plug-in cartridge and used with a personal computer.

LASER OPTICAL System of recording on grooveless discs using a laser-optical-tracking pickup. Originally, the technology was WORM — Write Once (i.e. not erasable) Read Many. It's now erasable.

LASER PRINTER A high speed nonimpact dot matrix printer which uses a laser beam to electrostatically form characters on paper. The printer then heats the paper which melts a metallic dust attracted to the electrostatic areas which form the inked images on the paper. Laser printers are fast and the quality of their printing beautiful, rivaling that produced by conventional photo-typesetting.

LAST DIGIT DIALED SIGNAL Allows the use of the # sign on touchtone telephones to indicate that the last digit has been dialed on outgoing calls. This signal enables the PBX to process calls more rapidly, since some PBXs count the time after a digit was dialed. If nothing else is dialed within a certain time, it assumes that the dialing is complete and then pulses out the call.

LAST EXTENSION CALLED Same as LAST NUMBER REDIAL.

LAST IN FIRST OUT LIFO. The last phone call (or data) arriving is the first call (or data) to leave — to be processed, to be saved, whatever. The term LIFO comes from accounting. It's one of several ways to value an inventory.

LAST NUMBER REDIAL Most modern electronic phones have a button on them called "Last Number Redial." When you touch this button, your phone will automatically dial the last number you dialed. If you also have speed dial numbers on your phone, any number you dialed with a Speed Dial button will not appear in Last Number Redial. Most Last Number Redial buttons on electronic phones attached to a PBX will only recognize completely dialed numbers. Last Number Redial buttons are useful. Also useful — but less common — is a stored number dial button. Dial a number, punch in "save," then that number will be saved to that button, ready to be dialed later, even though you might dial some other numbers in the meantime.

LATA Local Access and Transport Area. The geographical areas within which a local telephone company may offer telecommunications services — local or long distance. AT&T is expressly prohibited from offering intra-LATA calls by the terms of the Divestiture. Other competitors are not, though rules vary by state, according to state regulation.

LATENCY The time interval between when a network station seeks access to a transmission channel and when access is granted or received. Same as waiting time.

LAY A term used in cable manufacturing to denote the distance of advance of one member of a group of spirally twisted members, in one turn, measured axially.

LAYER In the seven layered OSI model, it refers to a collection of network processing-functions that together comprise a set of rules and standards for successful data communication. See OSI MODEL.

LAYERED NETWORK SALES STRATEGY An AT&T sales strategy which involves segmenting customer network needs into four usage levels or layers, then pursuing sales opportunities at these various entry points. The layers are Premises Networks, Office Networks, "metropolitan" or " campus" networks and Wide Area Networks.

LBRV, LOW BIT RATE VOICE Digitized voice that requires a bandwidth of less than 32 kbps. LBRV digitizing techniques include packetized voice, APV, DSI, and LPC.

LCD Liquid Crystal Display. An alphanumeric display using liquid crystal sealed between two pieces of glass. The display is divided into hundreds or thousands of individual dots, which are charged or not charged, reflecting or not reflecting external light to form characters, letters and numbers. LCD displays have certain advantages. They use little electricity and react quickly. However, they are not very legible. The newer so-called "supertwist" LCDs are much more readable. See also FIBER OPTICS.

LCM Line Control Module.

LCR Least Cost Routing. A telephone system feature that automatically chooses the lowest cost phone line to the destination. What actually is the "lowest cost" is determined by algorithms, equations and decision trees programmed into the PBX. Least Cost Routing typically works with "look-up" tables in the PBX's memory. These tables are put into the PBX by the user. The PBX does not automatically know how to route each call. It must be told so by the user. That "telling" might be as simple as saying "all 312 area codes will go via the AT&T FX line." Or it might be as complex as actually listing which exchanges in the 312 area code go by which method. LEAST COST ROUTING tells the calls to go over the lines which are perceived by the user to be the least cost way of getting the call from point A to point B. There are typically two types of "least cost routing" translation — that which examines the first three digits of the phone number (i.e. just the area code) and the first six digits of the phone number (i.e. the area code and the three digits of the local central office). Six digit translation is preferred because it allows you more flexibility in routing — particularly to big area codes, like 213 in LA, where there are long distance calls within the area code. See also AUTOMATIC ROUTE SELECTION, ALTERNATE ROUTING and SIX DIGIT TRANSLATION.

LD Long Distance.

LDM See LIMITED DISTANCE MODEM.

LDN Listed Directory Number.

LEAD AGENT The first agent in an ACD group. See also AUTOMATIC CALL DISTRIBUTOR.

LEAD-IN Wire or cable from antenna to TV set.

LEADER The section at the beginning of a roll of magnetic tape which holds no data and often is not even magnetic tape. A leader is used to feed the magnetic tape through the tape mechanism and secure it onto the roll.

LEAKY PBX One of those really silly terms the phone industry is famous for. Picture this. You dial a distant PBX. If you can dial on — either locally or make a long distance call, that distant PBX is referred to as "leaky." All PBXs are, of course, "leaky," or at least capable of being made leaky. But there are some tariffs which the FCC insists on you paying more for if your PBX is being used as a "leaky" PBX. So, to avoid the extra surcharge, almost everyone lies on the little form the carrier sends you.

LEAS LATA Equal Access System.

LEASED CIRCUIT Same as LEASED LINE or PRIVATE LINE.

LEASED LINE Same as a LEASED or DEDICATED CIRCUIT, PRIVATE LINE, LEASED CHANNEL. A telephone line rented for exclusive use 24-hour a day, seven days a week from a telephone company — a local phone company (like New York Telephone) or a long distance company like AT&T or MCI.

LEAST COST ROUTING LCR. A telephone system feature which automatically chooses the "least cost" long distance line to send out a long distance call. The user typically dials "9" and then his 10-digit long distance number which is routed over the least costly service. See also LCR.

LEAVE WORD CALLING For AT&T System 75 and 85 users for internal messages. The caller's name, time of call and extension number are taken and can be retrieved on a Digital Display Monitor or BCT. The service is accompanied by an Integrated Directory — a simple electronic listing of employee names and extension numbers, access by a terminal equipped with a DDM or via the attendant console.

LEC Local Exchange Company. The local phone companies, which can be either a Bell Operating Company (BOC) or an independent (e.g. GTE) which provide local transmission services. Prior to divestiture, the LECs were called telephone companies or telcos.

LED Light Emitting Diode. A semiconductor diode which emits light when a current is passed through it. In lightwave transmission systems, light emitting diodes or lasers are used as sources of light. These devices are fabricated from multilayered structures of compound semiconductors epitaxially grown on a single-crystal substrate. LEDs are used as sources for optical data link applications in which the data rates are less than about 500 megabits per second and the transmission distances do not exceed a few kilometers. LEDs are also used in alphanumeric displays on calculators and computer devices. LEDs use less power than normal incandescent light bulbs, but more power than LCDs (Liquid Crystal Displays).

LEG My definition: A segment of a multipoint circuit which lies between any two of the points. Bellcore's definition: An object within a connection view that represents a communication path toward some addressable entity.

LEN Line Equipment Number.

LENGTH The number of bits or bytes in a computer word, a field, a record, etc.

LETTER OF AGENCY A letter sent by an end user to a telephone company — local or long distance — authorizing the end user's equipment vendor to deal on the end user's behalf with the phone company. A letter of agency is actually a specialized Power of Attorney.

LETTERS SHIFT A physical shift in a teletypewriter, specifically Telex, which enables the printing of alphabetic characters.

LEVEL 1. The power of a signal measured at a certain point in the circuit. 2. Your management position (i.e. "level" in the management structure) in a telephone company. In AT&T and members of the operating Bell telephone companies, employees are identified by their "Levels." At the bottom of the totem pole are craftspeople, the installers, the repair people, the trench diggers, etc. They do not have a level. They are often unionized. Management begins one level above the union. They are called first level. They are often also called supervisors. Above them are second level managers. They are called second level managers. Above them are third level managers. They are called district managers. Above them are fourth level managers. They are division managers. Fifth level managers are assistant vice presidents. Sixth level managers are vice presidents. Above vice presidents, levels get fairly vague. Salary is contingent upon level. And there are several levels with different salary levels within each level. It is not uncommon for AT&T or for a Bell phone company to have as many as 16 different management levels. At one stage, there was talk about eliminating the fourth level altogether.

LF Line Feed. ASCII character 10. This character is now identified in the ASCII code set as New Line. See NEW LINE.

LGC Line Group Controller.

LIBRARY As in TELECOM LIBRARY the source of all good books on telecommunications, local area networks and personal computers. Send for your FREE catalog today. Call 212-691-8215 or 1-800-LIBRARY.

LIDB Line Information Data Bases which are being developed by the Regional Companies will include such services as Originating Line number Screening, Calling Card Validation, Billing Number Screening, Calling Card Fraud and Public Telephone Check. The LIDB systems will contain all valid telephone and calling card numbers in their regions, and will have the necessary information to perform billing validation. The LIDB systems are expected to be operational in 1989. A national interconnecting system is planned for 1990.

LIFE CYCLE A test performed on a material or configuration to determine the length of time before failure in a controlled, usually accelerated, environment.

LIFELINE SERVICE A minimal telephone service designed for the poor and elderly to assure they can be reached by phone and have a "Lifeline" to the world in case of emergency. The basic rate for this limited service is less than standard rates and varies by state. Typically, Lifeline Service entitles you to a phone line, a listing in the directory and a minimal number of outgoing local calls, e.g. 10. Some people who are neither poor nor elderly, subscribe to Lifeline Service and use it for incoming calls — for an answering machine or a computer electronic mail or bulletin boards. There's no difference in the quality of service provided by Lifeline Rates and normal phone lines.

LIFO Last In First Out. A method of organizing queues. See LAST IN

FIRST OUT.

LIGHT EMITTING DIODE See LED.

LIGHT PEN A video terminal input device which is a light sensitive stylus connected by a cable to the video terminal. The user brings it to the desired point on the screen surface and presses a button. A light pen is used to select options from a menu on the screen or to draw images by dragging the cursor around the screen on a graphics terminal.

LIGHTWAVE COMMUNICATIONS (Fiber Optic) Communications using light to carry information.

LIGHTWAVE TRANSMISSION This term now means laser communications systems shot through the air (as opposed to glass fiber). Also called "free space lightwave communications." Typically, a signal is radiated directly from a light transmitter to a receiver less than a mile away. Advantages to lightwave transmission: easy to install, no digging of cables, wide bandwidth, reliable, cheap, no FCC frequency clearance approvals required and the receiving and transmitting equipment occupy little space. Disadvantages: only works for a mile or so and is subject to attenuation (fading) from fog and dust. It's perfect for between downtown buildings, where installing cables is too expensive, too cumbersome, too slow, etc. See LASER.

LIMITED DISTANCE MODEM LDM. A special-purpose conversion device designed to connect two DTEs (data communications devices) over a relatively short distance, typically up to several miles. An LDM is not really a modem since it does not perform a digital-to-analog conversion, but transmits a special type of digital signal to the other LDM on the circuit. Also called a line driver, local dataset or short-haul modem.

LIMITER A circuit which shapes a signal sent through it to conform to certain preset tolerances, used in both audio and video to regulate signal flow and prevent overloading, which would lead to distortion and the introduction of spurious noise.

LINE An electrical path (two wires) between a phone company central office and a subscriber, usually with an individual phone number that can be used for incoming and outgoing calls.

LINEAR DISTORTION Amplitude distortion wherein the output signal envelope is not proportional to the input signal envelope. This distortion is often caused by part of the signal being bounced off something, while part arrives free and clear. Thus the receiver hears the same signal but bits of it arrive earlier and later than other bits, causing distortion. Anyone coming across a more understandable definition, please send it to the editors for the next edition.

LINEAR PREDICTIVE CODING A speech coding method that analyzes a speech waveform to produce a time-varying filter as a model of the human vocal tract. See also Digital Signal Processing.

LINEAR PROGRAMMING Techniques in Operations Research (OR) to find an optimum solution to a linear function, given certain restrictions and typically expressed in many equations. A typical linear programming problem might be to find the least expensive, most efficient route between various pick-up and drop-off points in a transportation route.

LINEARITY The straightness of a frequency response curve as an indication of true or accurate sound reproduction. In an A/D (Analog to Digital) or D/A (Digital to Analog), linearity measures the precision with which the digital output/input tracks the analog input/output.

LINE BUILD OUT Because T-1 circuits require the last span to lose 15-22.5 dB, a selectable out put attenuation is generally required of DTE equipment (typical selections include O.O, 7.5, and 15 dB of loss at 772 KHz).

LINE CARD A plug-in electronic Printed Circuit (PC) card that operates lamps, ringing, holding and other features associated with one or several telephone lines or telephones in a telephone system.

LINE CIRCUIT The sensor in the CO which detects and advises the switching system that one of its subscribers has gone off-hook and wishes to make a call. One line circuit is dedicated to each line of each subscriber.

LINE CONDITIONING A service offered by telephone companies to reduce envelope delay, noise and amplitude distortion. By doing this, you allow for transmission of higher speed data than over a traditional dial-up phone line.

LINE CORD The connecting cord between the phone and the jack in the wall.

LINE DISCIPLINE Archaic term for communications protocol.

LINE DRIVER Signal converter that conditions the digital signal transmitted by an RS-232 interface to ensure reliable transmission beyond the 50-foot RS-232 limit and often up to several miles; it is a baseband transmission device. Also called baseband modem, limited distance modem, or short-haul modem. See also LIMITED DISTANCE MODEM.

LINE EQUIPMENT Equipment in a central office which is there to serve one phone line. That line equipment includes a line relay or equivalent which starts to work when the customer's telephone goes off-hook.

LINE FEED The act of moving a cursor or the head or a printer or telex machine down one line. These days, on the keyboards of most equipment — Personal Computers, etc. — there's no single key that says "Line Feed." There's usually a key that's labeled "Enter" or "Return." This key does two functions — a line feed and a carriage return (i.e. sending the print head or cursor to the left hand side of the carriage or the screen). In many (but not all) programs, a line feed is control J or ASCII character 10. The name for this character has been changed to New Line. See NEW LINE.

LINE FINDER The first switching element of a step-by-step phone system which recognizes a calling party is waiting for dial tone to make a call, identifies the party, and connects that party to the switching system so that the processing of the call may begin. Normally line finders serve 100 or 200 subscriber lines.

LINE HIT Electrical interference that causes a hit, that is, a loss or introduction of spurious bits into a data stream.

LINE HOLD Provides a winking, blinking flash on the line lamp at every telephone which has the line appearing on it.

LINE INSULATION TEST LIT. A test performed from the central office, which measures resistance and voltages on local lines to find faults.

LINE LINK FRAME LLF. An arrangement that permits a crossbar office to transmit dial pulse information over a line to a PBX for switching Direct Inward Dial (DID) calls to the indicated phone. See CROSSBAR SWITCHING

LINE LOCKOUT when a phone stays off-hook for longer than a predetermined time, line lockout provides some loud noise and then puts the phone line out of service — until someone puts the phone back on hook again.

LINE NOISE Spurious signals introduced into a line by static, or other imbalances in the circuit. Line Noise is the most common cause of "Hits" or problems in data calls.

LINE OF SIGHT Some through the air transmission media — such as microwave, infrared, and laser — operate at a frequency which transmit in a perfectly straight line. Or in "line of sight." In other words, the area between a transmitter and a receiver must be clear of obstructions.

LINE POWERED Telephone equipment that is powered solely by the CO talk battery supplied in a standard phone line.

LINE PREFERENCE User selects the line to be used simply by pressing the button associated with that line from the central office or from the PBX or key system.

LINE PRINTER The class of printer where an entire line of text is printed at one time. This printer is obviously a high speed printer. It is used, for example, to print TELECONNECT Magazine's monthly mailing list

LINE PROTOCOL Rules for controlling transmission on a synchronous data transmission line. Includes rules for bidding for the line, for positive and negative acknowledgements, requests for retransmission, and transmitter time-outs.

LINE QUEUING Dial an outside line (typically a long distance line). It's busy. Your phone system will put you in queue for that line. The queue might involve your waiting a few seconds on hold; or it might involve your hanging up and having the phone system call you back. There are thus two types of Line Queuing — hold-on and callback queuing.

LINE RINGING Provides the user with an audible indication of a call on a specific line that appears on his/her telephone.

LINE SPEED The maximum number of bits you can transmit over a line in a certain defined time, say one second.

LINE STATUS INDICATION Provides a visual indication on an ECTS (electronic telephone set) telephone of the idle, busy, ringing or held state for each line appearing on the telephone.

LINE SWITCHING Another term for circuit switching. See CIRCUIT SWITCHING and SWITCHING.

LINE TURNAROUND The delay in a circuit as the direction of communications changes, usually in half duplex communications. When one side of the communications stops sending, there is a delay before the other party stars sending in return. This is the Line Turnaround delay.

LINEMAN'S CLIMBERS Telephone pole climbing irons which are strapped to the telephone lineman's legs, allowing him or her to climb a wooden telephone line. You can tell when a pole has been climbed by the holes left in it by the lineman's climbers.

LINES PER MINUTE The way of measuring the speed of a line printer. Like any measure of speed, the speed you will get from your printer may be different from what the manufacturer says. Your speed will depend on how fast you feed the printer from your computer — a function of how fast you're transmitting, what software you're running, how fast that software can get the information to be printed off your disk, etc.

LINK Another name for a communications channel or circuit.

LINK ATTACHED Describing devices that are connected to a network, a communications data link, or telecommunications circuit; compare with channel-attached.

LINK CONVERTER A device for an InteCom S/80 which connects distributed switching modules to the centralized switching equipment through a coaxial cable or a fiber optic cable.

LINK PROTOCOL The set of rules by which a logical data link is set up and by which data transfers across the link. It includes formatting of the data.

LIQUID CRYSTAL DISPLAY LCD. A low power display that aligns material suspended in a liquid under the influence of a low voltage so it reflects ambient light and displays alphanumeric characters. LCD displays are finding great use as methods of displaying information on new electronic telephones, especially those positioned behind PBXs. The advantage of putting such displays on telephones is that the power to drive the display is very small. The display can be line powered -- i.e. powered by the one or two pairs coming from the PBX. This avoids the necessity and cost of a transformer/rectifier — the little black box you plug into the wall to run your answering machine or to power up your rechargeable calculator/laptop computer. Such LCD displays on electronic phones can perform many functions. The most useful is that of "walking" the user through the call. Showing him/her how to transfer a call, to make a conference call, to split a conference, etc. An LCD can also alert you as to who's calling you — but, only at this point, if it's an internal call. (Eventually, when ISDN and CCITT Signaling System 7 arrives, it will at everyone's phone.) See also LCD.

LISTED DIRECTORY NUMBER LDN, incoming exchange network calls to the PBX via assigned listed local telephone directory number are directed to the attendant.

LIT See LINE INSULATION TEST.

LLC Logical Link Control. A protocol developed by the IEEE 802 committee for data-link-level transmission control; the upper sublayer of the IEEE Layer 2 (OSI) protocol that complements the MAC protocol; IEEE standard 802.2; includes end-system addressing and error checking.

LLF Line Link Frame, see CROSSBAR SWITCHING

LNA Low Noise Amplifier.

LOAD The act of taking a program or data from external storage — a cassette, a floppy or hard disk, etc. and storing it in the computer main RAM memory.

LOAD BALANCING FOR STATION/TRUNK LINES A PBX feature. You can change phone and trunk terminations on PBX in order to even out traffic on the network. An example: You have a PBX of three separate cabinets, each of which are joined by tie lines. Instead of having each cabinet serve anyone in the building, you might figure which groups talk to each other the most and concentrate them into specific cabinets. The objective is to maximize the number of calls that can be handled inside each cabinet and reduce the number of calls that need to travel between the cabinets. This makes the calls go faster and reduces the need for inter-cabinet lines.

LOAD COIL An inductor used to increase the inductance of a pair of metal wires in a local loop. The use of the inductor improves the voice transmission characteristics of the loop, but it must be removed if you are running digitally over the line. See LOADING and LOADING COIL.

LOAD NUMBER Load number is the Canadian equivalent of the U.S. concept of Ringer Equivalence. The idea is that each phone or "phone thing" you buy (e.g. answering machine) comes with a number. You add the numbers together and if you get above a certain number, you are drawing too much current and none of the bells on the phones will ring. In Canada, single line phones are typically rated at 10 for the newer ones with electronic "bells" or 20 for the older electro-mechanical ones with real metal bells. In Canada, the rule is not more than 100 points on a line. In the U.S., phones are typically one and the rule is not more than five points on a line.

LOAD SHARING In data processing, load sharing is the technique of using two computers to balance the processing normally assigned to one of them.

LOADED LINE A telephone line equipped with loading coils to add inductance in order to minimize amplitude distortion. See LOADING and LOADING COIL.

LOADING A method of improving the voice quality of a phone line. Telephone companies put load coils on local lines. What this loading does is to insert inductance in a local loop circuit to offset the effect of capacitance in the cable. Loading "tunes" the circuit to the voice frequency band (500 to

2500 Hz) and thus improves the quality at the expense of overall bandwidth. You usually have to ask that the loading coils be removed if you're planning to transmit high-speed data exclusively on that circuit. See LOADING COIL.

LOADING COIL An induction device employed in local loops exceeding 18,000 feet in length, that compensates for wire capacitance and boosts voice grade frequencies. Loading coils are often removed for higher speed data services, as distortion will occur at frequencies higher than those used for voice. See LOADING.

LOCAL ACCESS AND TRANSPORT AREA LATA. The geographical area within which a Local Exchange Company (a local phone company) can provide communications services. See LATA.

LOCAL AREA AND TRANSPORT AREA See LATA.

LOCAL AREA DATA TRANSPORT LADT. A service of your local phone company which provides you, the user, with synchronous data communications.

LOCAL AREA NETWORK LAN. A data communications network spanning a limited geographical area, a few miles at most. It provides communications between computers and peripherals, some switching to direct messages. See LAN.

LOCAL AUTOMATIC MESSAGE ACCOUNTING LAMA. A combination of automatic message accounting equipment and automatic number identification equipment in your telephone company's central office and used by them to bill your local phone calls.

LOCAL BATTERY Having "local battery" means the telecom equipment — the telephone, the PBX, the key system, etc. — has its own source of power and does not draw from the power coming down the phone line. The term came from telegraphy and was used to distinguish the battery which provided power to the telegraphic station as against the power that went to drive the line and the signal down it. See BATTERY.

LOCAL CALL Any call within the local service area of the calling phone. Individual local calls may or may not cost money. In many parts of the US, the phone company bills its local service as a "flat" monthly fee. This means you can make as many local calls per month as you wish and not pay extra. Increasingly this luxury is dying and individual calls are costing money.

LOCAL CALL ACCOUNTING Computes the dollar amount for local calls based on the total message units stored for each phone.

LOCAL CALL BILLING Computes dollar amount for local calls placed by guests based on total message units.

LOCAL CENTRAL OFFICE Switching office in which a subscriber's lines terminate.

LOCAL CHANNEL CONTROLLER An AT&T name for its family of 3270 compatible cluster controllers.

LOCAL COMPOSITE LOOPBACK In network management systems. Composite loopback test that forms the loop at the output of the local multiplexer that returns transmitted signals to their source. See also loopback.

LOCAL DATASET Signal converter that conditions the digital signal transmitted by an RS-232 interface to ensure reliable transmission over a dc continuous metallic circuit without interfering with adjacent pairs in the same telephone cable. Normally conforms with Bell 43401. Also called baseband modem, limited distance modem, local modem, or short-haul modem. See also line driver.

LOCAL DISTRIBUTION FRAME LDF. Another word for an Intermediate Distribution Frame. It's a device for cross connecting cables — from one thing to another. On one side of the LDF are the pairs from individual phones in that part of the building or area. On the other side are trunks coming in from a central office or cables coming in from the central, larger PBX. LDFs typically help with the organization of cables in a building or area. See also INTERMEDIATE DISTRIBUTION FRAME.

LOCAL EXCHANGE The telephone company exchange where subscribers lines are terminated. Also called an "End Office."

LOCAL EXCHANGE CARRIER A local phone company. See also LEC.

LOCAL LOOP The physical wires that run from the subscriber's telephone set, or PBX or key telephone system, to the telephone company central office. Increasingly, the local loop now goes from the main distribution frame in the basement to the phone company. And the subscriber is responsible for getting his/her wires from the box in the basement to his phone, PBX or key system.

LOCAL MEASURED SERVICE LMS. Years ago virtually all phone lines in the United States were FLAT RATE. That meant that for a fixed amount of money each month, you, the customer (a.k.a. subscriber) were allowed to make as many local calls as you wanted. For many reasons, the U.S. phone industry has progressively moved to LOCAL MEASURED SERVICE for local calls. Typically this means that for a fixed amount of money each month, you, the customer, can receive as many calls as you want and can make a finite number of outgoing local calls — typically 50. Each additional call beyond the 50 (or whatever the number is) costs extra. How much that call costs depends on the distant the call travels, the time of day, the day of the week, and the local company's tariffs.

LOCAL NET The broadband architecture used in Sytek's work. Also the product name of their network. Sytek is in Sunnyvale, CA.

LOCAL ORDER WIRE A communications circuit between a technical control center and selected terminal or repeater locations.

LOCAL SERVICE AREA The geographic area that telephones may call without incurring toll charges. A flat rate calling area. Increasingly rare.

LOCAL TANDEM A central office, usually in large metropolitan areas, serving as a transit switch between noncontiguous class 5 exchanges. It connects end office trunks.

LOCAL TEST DESK A testing system that is used to test local loops and central office subscriber line equipment from a central point, typically a central office.

LOCAL TRUNK Trunks between Class 5 offices (local central offices)

LOCATION One definition is the place where a telephone jack is located. This location is given a number. The wire going to that location is given a number. All this in hope of being organized for installation, moves, changes and maintenance.

LOCKING Preventing several people getting to and changing the same data simultaneously. Locks may be permanent and prevent access completely, or they may be "advisory." A user is warned the data is being used by someone else and that the data is not presently available. Locks prevent the destruction of data that can occur if two people access a file at the same time. In any data base or other computer system, there are typically two types of "locks" — record and file locks. A record lock occurs when an airline agent pulls up your travel plans. No other travel agent can access those records at that time. A file lock occurs when the whole file is locked up. This might occur in a centralized word processing program. The whole document will be locked when it is being used by someone.

LOCK ON The process by which an earth station initially acquires the signal from a satellite.

LOCK OUT In a satellite telephone circuit controlled by an echo suppressor, one or both subscribers can't get through because of excessive noise at one end. You get this also with speakerphones. The person with the speakerphone can simply hog the conversation because his speakerphone keeps transmitting his voice. There are weird variations on this. Sometimes you might call someone on your speakerphone and wait for them to pick up. They do. They shout into the phone "I'm here." All they can hear is you at the other end talking or typing. The sound at your end is hogging the channel and thus locking out the person at the other end. The solution? Turn the "mute" button on your speakerphone. This will stop your end transmitting and allow the other end to say "Hello, I'm here."

LOG IN The process of identifying and authenticating oneself to a computer system. Used to control access to computer systems.

LOG OFF To type in the needed keystrokes for ending a session that's on-line with a computer. Often those keystrokes are "Logoff." Usually it's very easy to Log Off. It's more difficult to Log On.

LOG ON To enter the needed keystrokes to start an on-line session with a computer. "Logging On" may be done with a computer that's local or one that's long distance and your work is done over communications lines.

LOGICAL CHANNEL NUMBER Virtual circuit identified at the packet level of X.25.

LOGICAL LINK A virtual circuit concept of DNA, existing at the End communications and Session control layer above.

LOGICAL LINK CONTROL LLC; A protocol developed by the IEEE 802 committee, common to all of its LAN standards, for data link-level transmission control; the upper sublayer of the IEEE Layer 2 (OSI) protocol that complements the MAC protocol; IEEE standard 802.2; includes end-system addressing and error checking.

LOGICAL UNIT INTERFACE See LU 6.2.

LONG DISTANCE Any telephone call to a location outside the local service area. Also called toll call or trunk call.

LONG HAUL COMMUNICATIONS That type of phone call which reaches outside a local exchange or serving area.

LONGITUDINAL BALANCE A measure of the electrical balance between the two conductors (tip and ring) of a telephone circuit; specifically, the difference between the tip-to-ground and ring-to-ground AC signal voltages, expressed in decibels.

LONGITUDINAL REDUNDANCY CHECK LRC. An error checking technique based on an accumulated collection of transmitted characters. An LRC character is accumulated at both the sending and receiving stations during the transmission of a block. This accumulation is called the Block Check Character (BCC) and is transmitted in the last character in the block. The transmitted BCC is compared with the accumulated BCC character at the receiving station for an equal condition. An equal comparison indicates a good transmission of the block.

LONGITUDINAL TRANSMISSION CHECK LTC. An even or odd parity check at fixed intervals during data transmission.

LONGITUDINAL WRAP A tape applied longitudinally with the axis of the core being covered, a opposed to a helical, or spiral, tape wrapped core.

LONG LINES AT&T Long Lines. The department of AT&T which operates long distance toll service. It is no longer called Long Lines. It is called AT&T Communications.

LOOK-UP TABLE A translation table. You dial a certain number. But the number is meaningless. For the phone system to complete the call, it needs routing instructions. It gets that by "looking up" that number in a table, which translates that number to another number that is now meaningful to the switching network. There are lots of applications for Look-up Tables. Least Cost Routing tables are essentially look up tables. IN-WATS dialing works by looking up the 800 number and finding its real 10-digit normal number. Most private networks use look up tables to translate the number dialed by the internal user into a number that the network can recognize.

LOOP 1. Typically a complete electrical circuit. 2. The loop is also the pair of wires that wends its way from the central office to the telephone set or system at the customer's office, home or factory, i.e. "premises" in telephonese. 3. In computer software. A loop repeats a series of instructions many times until some prestated event has happened or until some test has been passed.

LOOPBACK Type of diagnostic test in which the transmitted signal is returned to the sending device after passing through a data communications link or network. This allows a technician (or built-in diagnostic circuit) to compare the returned signal with the transmitted signal and get some sense of what's wrong. Loopbacks are often done by excluding one piece of equipment after another. This allows you to figure out logically what's wrong. (It's called Sherlock Holmes deductive reasoning.) See LOOPBACK TEST.

LOOPBACK TEST A test typically run on a four-wire circuit. You take the two transmit leads and join them to the two receive leads. Then you put a signal around the loop and see what happens. Measuring differences between the sent and the received signal is the essence of a loopback test. See LOOPBACK.

LOOP CHECKING A method of checking the accuracy of transmission of data in which the received data are returned to the sending end for comparison with the original data.

LOOP CIRCUIT Generally refers to the circuit connecting the subscriber's set with the local switching equipment.

LOOP EXTENDER Device in the central office that supplies augmented voltage out to subscribers who are at considerable distances. It provides satisfactory signaling and speech for such subscribers.

LOOP SIGNALING SYSTEMS Any of three types of signaling which transmit signaling information over the metallic loop formed by the trunk conductors and the terminating equipment bridges.

LOOP START You "start" (seize) a phone line or trunk by giving it a supervisory signal. That signal is typically taking your phone off hook. There are two ways you can do that — ground start or loop start. With loop start, you seize a line by bridging through a resistance the tip and ring (both wires) of your telephone line.

LOOP TEST A way of testing a circuit to find a fault in it by completing a loop and sending a signal around that loop. See LOOPBACK.

LOOP THROUGH A type of phone system wiring that allows phones to connect to one cable in parallel going to the common central switching equipment. The most common type of Loop Through wiring is that which you have in your home. You have one cable with two conductors — a red and a green — wending through your home. Whenever you want to connect a phone, you simply attach it to the red and green conductors. The other way of connecting phones is called HOME RUN. In that system, every phone has its own one, two or three pairs of conductors which wind their lonely way back to the central PBX or key system cabinet. In Loop Through wiring, many phones share one set of cables. In Home Run Cabling, only one phone sits on that line.

LOOP TIMING A way of synchronizing a circuit that works by taking a synchronizing clock signal from incoming digital pulses.

LOOPING Problem encountered in distributed datagram routing in which packets return to a previously visited node.

LOOP UP/LOOP DOWN In T-1, there are generally two loopback types, LLB (line loopback) and TLB or DLB (terminal or DTE loopback). Loop Up refers to activating one of these loop backs, where as Loop Down refers to deactivating one of these loopbacks.

LOOSE TUBE BUFFER A cable construction in which the optical fiber is placed in a plastic tube having an inner diameter much larger than the fiber itself. The loose tube isolates the fiber from the exterior mechanical forces acting on the cable. The space between the tube and the fiber is often filled with a gel to cushion the fiber.

LOOSELY COUPLED Describing processors connected by means of channel-to-channel adapters that are used to pass control information between each other (IBM). Compare with TIGHTLY COUPLED.

LORAN A radio-navigation system which times the difference in reception of pulses from one or more fixed transmitters. Often used on boats.

LOSS The drop in signal level between two points on a network. It is important to distinguish between LOSS and LEVEL. Level is measured at a finite point. Loss is the difference between levels. Loss occurs constantly throughout telephony — from long distance circuits to switches. Loss is usually measured in dB — decibels. Loss is cumulative. Add two circuits each with a loss of 10 dB. You will have 20 dB loss in the total circuit. The human ear can detect a 3 dB loss.

LOST CALL ATTEMPT A call attempt that cannot be further advanced to its destination due to an equipment shortage or failure in the network.

LOUDSPEAKER PAGING ACCESS Interface to customer-provided paging equipment.

LOW ENTRY NETWORKING LEN. A peer-oriented extension to SNA, first implemented on IBM's System/36, that allows networks to be more easily built and managed by means of such techniques as topology database exchange and dynamic route selection.

LOW FREQUENCY The band of frequencies between 30 and 300 kilohertz.

LOW LEVEL LANGUAGE A programming language that uses symbols — one step away from the machine language of a computer. Low level computer languages, such as Assembler and C, actually manipulate the bits in computer registers. Higher level languages such as Basic and Fortran will take care of the piddling details of doing specific functions when you give it a broad command like "PRINT". In a lower level language, you must provide all the details of instruction necessary in the code (program) to perform the operation. It is possible to do this by calling standard routines, but still takes up the programmers' time in deciding which routines, and keeping the registers straight as he designs the program.

LOW NOISE AMPLIFIER LNA. Typically a parametric amplifier in a satellite earth station.

LOW PASS A specific frequency below which a filter will allow all frequencies to pass. Opposite of high pass.

LPC Linear Predictive Coding. Low bit rate voice (LBRV) digitizing technique that requires a bandwidth of only 2.4 or 4.8 kbps. This technique may result in poor quality voice signals.

LPI Lines Per Inch. The number of lines both horizontal and vertical, that a facsimile machine will print in a square inch.

LPP Link Peripheral Processor

LRC Longitudinal Redundancy Check.

LSI Large Scale Integration. Refers to microelectronic components which combine many hundreds of transistors on an integrated circuit. See CHIP.

LTB Last Trunk Busy.

LTRS Letters Shift. 1 Physical shift in a terminal using Baudot Code that enables the printing of alphabetic characters. 2 Character that causes the shift.

LU Logical Unit, access port for users in SNA. In a bisync network, a port through which the user gains access to the network services. A LU can support sessions with the host-based System Services Control Point (SSCP) and other LUs.

LU 6.2 Logical Unit Interface. Version 6.2. An IBM SNA protocol that allows for peer-to-peer or program-to-program communications. The LU 6.2 protocol standard frees application programs from network specific details. On an IBM PC, a LU 6.2 program accepts commands and passes them on to an SDLC card to communicate directly with the mainframe or a token ring handler. LU 6.2 enables users to develop applications programs for peer-to-peer communications between PC's and IBM host systems. It increases the processing power of the PC user without the constraints of mainframe-based slave devices, i.e. 3274/3276 controllers. It creates a transparent environment for application-to-application communications, regardless of the types of systems used or their relative locations.

LUG Something which sticks out onto which a wire may be connected by wrapping or soldering.

LUMINA 100 CALL DISPLAY A small Northern Telecom device which sits between the incoming central office line and the telephone and records the incoming number delivered via Calling Line IDentification (CLID) services on Custom Local area Signaling Services (CLASS). The Lumina 100 can store up to 14 of the last unique calling numbers. It will also store the date and time of the call, whether the call is new or a repeated call, whether the calls comes from an area not equipped for calling number delivery, whether the call has previously been displayed during a review of the caller's list. Lumina only displays the last 14 numbers, using the FIFO method — First In, First Out. See also MAESTRO.

LUMINANCE That part of the video signal which carries the information on how bright the TV signal is to be.

LZW The Lempel-Ziv-Welsh compression algorithm is another way of reducing the number of bits to transfer. Northern Telecom uses this compression algorithm for its Distributed Processing Peripheral (DPP) — the Automatic Message Accounting Transmitter (AMAT) for the DMS-100 family of central office switches. Northern Telecom selected this nonproprietary protocol and helped promote it as an industry standard. The nominal compression ration is 2.8:1, without considering field suppression. Transmitting data compressed at a ratio of 2.8:1 at 9600 bps is equivalent to transmitting noncompressed data at 27 kbps. Compatible compression collectors can poll the DPP in compressed or noncompressed mode. DPPs equipped with the Data Compression feature can transmit in either compressed or noncompressed mode, based on the collector's polling request for a specific polling session. To preserve data integrity, AMA data are still stored in noncompressed form on the DPP disks.

M m (small letter) Milli. One-thousandth. M (big letter) Mega. One million, e.g. Mbps or Mbit/s, one million bits per second.

M BIT The More Data mark in an X.25 packet that allows the DTE or DCE to indicate a sequence of more than one packet.

M1 Multiplexer in the U.S. digital signal hierarchy. See M1, which is listed as if it were M-ONE in this dictionary.

M12 A designation for a multiplex which interfaces between four DSIs and one DS2 circuit.

M13 The multiplexer equivalent of T-1. In the U.S. digital hierarchy, multiplexers are called by the digital signal levels they interface with. For example, a multiplexer, which joins DS-1 channels to DS-3 is called a M1-3. A M1-3 takes 28 DS-1 inputs and combines them into a single 45 megabit per second stream. (The bit stream is actually 44.736 megabits.)

M24 A T-1 service that allows a user to multiplex up to 24 voice or data channels into a single T-1 link, compatible with AT&T central office based channel banks (M24 compatability generally refers to compliance with the channelization and coding techniques specified by AT&T TR62411).

M34 A designation for a multiplex which interfaces between six DS3s and one DS4 circuit.

M44 A T-1 service that allows up to 44 voice channels (48 without signaling) to operate over a single T-1 link by using ADPCM, and is compatible with AT&T central office based equipment. MJ44 compatibility generally refers to the ability to accept the 44 channel T-1 aggregate and break out one of the channels individually for routing purposes.

MA BELL A term used to refer affectionately to the old AT&T and the old Bell System. Several Women's Lib organizations objected to it some years ago on the basis that there were no women in the higher corporate structure of AT&T, and that women, as over-supervised operators, were the downtrodden majority within the Bell System. There was a movement afoot to change it Pa Bell. But then came Divestiture and the breakup of the Bell System. The term, MA BELL, now largely belongs in the history books. And there are now many women in senior management in the Bell operating companies.

MAC Media Access Control. A media-specific access control protocol within IEEE 802 specifications. Currently includes variations for the token ring, token bus and CSMA/CD. The lower sublayer of the IEEE's link layer (OSI) which complements the Logical Link Control (LLC).

MACHINE CODE Same as Machine Language.

MACHINE DEPENDENT Software which will only run (i.e. is dependent) on a certain computer.

MACHINE LANGUAGE A binary code. The native language of computer hardware.

MACINTOSH A family of Apple microcomputers that represents the first wide-scale PC (personal computer) deployment of icons, windows, "mice" and a consistent user interface.

MACROS A common name for a microcomputer software program which lets you alter the definitions of what the keys on your computer keyboard are. With a "macro" software program, you could change the letter "M" on your keyboard to type "Michael" every time you hit it. But this would be stupid. Better to hit a combination of letters to get "Michael." Most personal computers have extra non-alphabetic keys, like Control and Alternate. And some macro software programs typically allow you to define a "Supershift" key. This means you can define one of your keys as a second Shift key. When you hit it (or Control or Alt) and then hit another key on the keyboard that key will type something different. For example, when we hit ALT T on the macro we've programmed for this dictionary, we get T103 in square brackets, which means to change the typeface to Helvetica Bold. When we first started writing this dictionary, we were using Radio Shack Model II machines running an operating system called CP/M. On that machine, we had no ALT key. It had only a control key. So we defined our Macro key to be "Control 6." When we hit the Control Key and the "6" key simultaneously, nothing happened on the screen, but the next character, number or letter was different, depending on how we defined it. For example, if we hit Control 6 and then T, we'd get T103 in square brackets. Our biggest use for macros is typesetting commands. We have about 40 macro translations loaded on every MS-DOS machine in our office. Macros are among the most useful and, curiously least expensive, of all PC software programs. Increasingly, macro capability is being built into most major word processors. ZEdit, the word processor we used to write this dictionary, has extensive macros. You can pretty well define any key or combination of keys to type out words or executive commands.

MADN Multiple Appearance Directory Number.

MAGAZINE Hardware unit, mounted in a frame, containing printed board assemblies.

MAESTRO A Northern Telecom telephone designed for CLASS service, in particular the CLID — Calling Line IDentification service available with SS7. Maestro has a 16-character display and logging capability that retains and displays on command the last 15 unanswered incoming directory numbers, and allows return dialing from the unanswered call log. Maestro's ten programmable one-touch memory memory keys can be used either for storing phone numbers or for one-button access to CLASS and other custom calling features that are otherwise accessed by dialing a code. MAESTRO also has a Call Forwarding Lamp which makes it easy to tell when call forwarding has been activated from the Maestro. List price for the Maestro was set originally at $136. See also CLASS and LUMINA.

MAGIC WAND One of the devices used by con men when pretending to do TSCM (Technical Surveillance CounterMeasures). A magic want is typically a field strength meter or box with many fancy lights.

MAGNETIC BUBBLE A device in which information is stored in a magnetic film as a pattern of oppositely directed magnetic fields. Magnetic bubble devices hold their memory even if you lose power.

MAGNETIC INK An ink that contains particles of a magnetic substance whose presence can be detected by magnetic sensors. Typical is the ink on your checks, which carry your name, your account number and the check's number.

MAGNETIC MEDIUM Any data-storage medium and related technology including diskettes and tapes, in which different patterns of magnetization are used to represent the values of stored bits and bytes.

MAGNETIC STRIPE A strip of magnetic material, usually tape, attached to a credit card containing data relating to the card holder. You have a magnetic stripe now on the back of most of your credit cards. That stripe tells a computer who you are, what your account number is, etc.

MAGNETIC TAPE A tape made of magnetic material upon which data may be stored for later retrieval by a computer.

MAGNETO A hand-cranked AC generator which can make electricity to ring telephone bells.

MAGNETO OPTICAL DRIVE A computer data storage device that uses light to read and write data to a disk that resembles a CR-ROM disk. Such a magneto optical drive holds huge amounts of information — as much as 500 megabytes on a single disk.

MAILGRAM An overnight electronic mail service of Western Union. The letter is phoned in or sent by computer to a central Western Union computer, from where it is sent to teleprinter machines located in post offices in major cities. When it's printed at the post office, the Mailgram is placed in an envelope and hand-delivered by your friendly, local mailman in next day's mail.

MAIN PBX or Centrex switch into which other PBXs or remote concentration of switching modules are homed. A PBX or Centrex connected directly to an electronic tandem switch (ETS). Also, a power source.

MAIN DISTRIBUTION FRAME MDF. A wiring arrangement which connects the telephone lines coming from outside on one side and the internal lines on the other. A main distribution frame may also carry protective devices as well as function as a central testing point. See MAIN DISTRIBUTION FRAME FILL, DISTRIBUTION FRAME and FRAME.

MAIN DISTRIBUTION FRAME FILL The central office mainframe is the termination point for outside plant cables. The "fill" is the percentage of pairs used by customers of the total number of pairs on the frame. Optimum fills vary based on the size of the central office and the amount of growth in the area. A low fill means idle lines and wasted investment in outside plant. A high fill, plus unexpected growth, forces budget busting and crisis construction projects.

MAIN FEEDER Feeder cable that transports pairs from the central office to branching or taper points.

MAIN LOBE The main lobe is the area with the maximum intensity in the pattern of radiation produced by an antenna. One presumes it's called "lobe" because the pattern in a microwave signal of the main lobe typically looks like a ear lobe.

MAIN MEMORY The principal random storage area inside the computer. Used for storing data and programs and under the direct control of the CPU — the main processor. Also called RAM memory.

MAIN NETWORK ADDRESS In IBM's SNA, the logical unit (LU) network address within ACF/VTAM used for SSCP-to-LU sessions for certain LU-to-LU sessions. Compare with auxiliary network address.

MAIN SATELLITE SERVICE A PBX feature that allows multi-location customers to concentrate their attendant positions at one location referred to as the Main. Other unattended locations are referred to as Satellites.

MAIN STATION A subscriber's telephone instrument, terminal or workstation used to originate and receive calls. Very often if two instruments have the same extension number (are bridged), one becomes the Main Station and the other is a bridged station for inventory purposes.

MAINFRAME A large computer with hundreds of thousands of bytes of RAM memory and hundreds of megabytes of mass storage. The term — main frame — derives from the racks that typically hold a large computer and its memory.

MAINFRAME GATEWAY A hardware/software system that allows PCs on a LAN (Local Area Network) to communicate with a mainframe. A single, usually dedicated, PC acts as the gateway. PCs on the LAN share its hardware and its communication link, communicating with it over the LAN cable. The most common mainframe gateway is an SNA gateway, which hooks a LAN into an IBM mainframe.

MAINS Some countries call their normal commercial power outlets — "mains." In Europe the frequency of commercial power is 50 Hz. In the United States, its frequency is 60 Hz. It's hard to convert the frequency of commercial power. It's easier to convert voltage. In Europe and Australia, normal voltage is 240 volts. In the U.S., it's 120 volts.

MAINTENANCE 1. All work needed to keep the telephone system operating properly, including periodic testing, repairs, etc. See PREVENTIVE MAINTENANCE. 2. All work needed to keep a software program operating properly, operating on new machinery and operating with new management needs. Often, software maintenance means substantially re-writing the original software program. Most of the work done by data processing departments in large companies involves maintaining old programs. This is not a put-down.

MAINTENANCE CONTROL CENTER MCC. A central place in a stored program control central office from which system configuration and trouble testing are controlled.

MAINTENANCE SERVICES In IBM's SNA, network services performed between a host SSCP and remote physical units (PUs) that test links and collect and record error information. Related facilities include configuration services, management services and session services.

MAINTENANCE TERMINATION UNIT MTU - An MTU is an electronic circuit that is owned and deployed by a telephone company to aid in fault sectionalization and is installed at the network interface. The MTU should meet the requirements of Bellcore Technical Advisory TSY-000324 and be testable with the Mechanized Loop Test System (MLT). The MTU is designed to work on single line residence or business service.

MAKE BUSY To make a communication circuit unavailable for connection. The technical term for taking the phone off the hook and leaving it off hook.

MALICIOUS CALL TRACING An ISDN service which enables to User to Network message to be sent while the call is in progress, ensuring that origination details are captured at the local exchange.

MAN Metropolitan Area Network. Extends to 50-kilometers, operates at speeds from 1 Mbit/s to 200 Mbps and provides an integrated set of services for real-time data, voice and image transmission. Two standards bodies are involved with work on MANs: IEEE 802.3 and ANSI X3T9.5.

MAN MACHINE INTERFACE A term coined by James Martin to designate the ease (or lack of ease) of a person working with a computer.

MANAGEMENT INFORMATION SYSTEM MIS. Management information provided by computer data processing. Once upon a time called data processing.

MANAGEMENT SERVICES In IBM's SNA, network services performed between a host SSCP and remote physical units (PUs) that include the request and retrieval of network statistics.

MANCHESTER ENCODING A digital encoding technique in which each bit period is divided into two complementary halves. A negative-to-positive (voltage) transition in the middle of the bit period designates a binary "1" while a positive-to-negative transition represents a "0". This encoding technique is self-clocking (the receiving device can recover transmitted clock from the data stream).

MANUAL EXCLUSION A PBX extension user, by entering a certain code, can block all other phones on that line from entering the call. Assures privacy on the line.

MANUAL GAIN CONTROL MGC. There are two electronic ways you can control the recording of something — Manual or Automatic Gain Control (AGC). AGC is an electronic circuit in tape recorders, speakerphones and other voice devices which is used to maintain volume. AGC is not always a brilliant idea since it attempts to produce a constant volume level. This means it will try to equalize all sounds — the volume of your voice and, when you stop talking, the circuit static and/or general room noise which you undoubtedly do not want amplified. Sometimes it's better to have quiet, when you want quiet. Manual Gain Control is preferred in professional applications. Manual Gain Control is simply an elegant way of saying there's a record volume control. Never record a seminar or speech using AGC. The end result will be decidedly amateurish.

MANUAL HOLD The method of placing a line circuit on "hold' by activating a non-locking "hold" button on the phone, usually one colored red.

MANUAL INTERCOM A crude, single-path communications link between telephones without the ability to signal the receiving party.

MANUAL MODEM ADAPTER An external device for the Merlin key system from AT&T. It allows connection of single line accessories to any Merlin telephone. The device, in effect, draws a standard tip and ring line out of the Merlin proprietary cabling/signaling scheme. Some other key systems have similar devices. Comdial calls theirs a "data port" and their phones contain extra RJ-11 jacks.

MANUAL ORIGINATING LINE SERVICE The attendant must complete all outgoing calls. All other calls are blocked. This "feature" is used to cut down on long distance phone abuse. There's a wonderful story. When many of the PBXs in Europe went from manual originating line service to automatic dial "9" long distance, the number of long distance calls doubled within two months. Some of these calls were legitimate. Some were not. How much abuse there was varied from company to company. Typically, those companies with employees who were more bored suffered (or enjoyed?) more abuse.

MANUAL PBXs Refers to PBXs which are not automatic and which require that all calls, including intercom calls, be placed through the attendant. Such PBXs are still used today, though in limited applications. You can still find manual PBXs in vacation hotels, nursing homes and in the data communications departments of some firms, who use manual PBXs as manual dataPBXs. These are especially useful in places where long data calls and sold metal-to-metal connections are an advantage.

MANUAL RINGDOWN TIE TRUNK A direct talk path between two distant phones. Signaling must be done manually from either phone. Contrast this with Automatic Ringdown Tie Trunk, in which the signaling occurs the moment one of the phones is lifted off hook.

MANUAL SIGNALING Pushing a button on a telephone sends an audible signal to a predetermined phone. Manual signaling can be used for secretary/boss communications.

MANUAL TELEPHONE A telephone without a dial. Taking the receiver off hook automatically rings a predetermined number. A courtesy phone.

MANUAL TERMINATING LINE SERVICE Provides extension lines that require all calls be completed by the attendant. For a better explanation see MANUAL ORIGINATING LINE SERVICE.

MANUFACTURING AND AUTOMATION PROTOCOL See MAP.

MAP 1. Maintenance and Administration Position 2. Manufacturing and Automation Protocol. A protocol initially developed as an internal specification for its own factory floor equipment and now championed by General Motors as the industry standard to facilitate communications among the diverse automation devices found in production environments. AT&T, IBM and DEC have endorsed this standard and have already or will introduce MAP-compatible products. TOP (Technical and Office Protocol) was initiated by Boeing Computer Services (one of the nine companies that helped form the MAP Users Group in 1984) and is designed for use in the engineering and office environment and to move information from the factory floor to other parts of the company. Implementation of these protocols would lead to GM's factory of the future concept.

MAP/MAAP Maintenance and Administration Panel. A device attached to a PBX to allow you to maintain and administer the system — to change phone features, etc.

MAPPING In network operations, the logical association of one set of values, such as addresses on one network, with quantities or values of another set, such as devices on another network (e.g. name-address mapping, internetwork-route mapping).

MARATHON A family of products that are combination fast packet multiplexer, data compression, voice compression and fax de-modulation devices that fit many, varied voice, data, fax and LAN "conversations" onto one leased circuit — analog or digital. The idea of Marathon is to save money on telecommunications charges. The Marathon family of products is made by Micom Communications Corporation, Simi Valley, CA.

MARCONI, GUGLIELMO Guglielmo Marconi was born in Bologna, Italy in 1874. In 1896, in England, Marconi obtained the first patent on the wireless. By 1897 he had transmitted messages over a distance of nearly 20 kilometers. In 1897 he formed Marconi's Wireless Telegraph Co. Ltd. In 1901 he succeeded in transmitting signals across the Atlantic. In 1909 he received jointly with C. F. Braun the Nobel Prize in Physics. Marconi was made a Marchese and a member of the Italian senate. He died in Rome on July 20, 1937.

MARISAT A satellite for marine use. Conversations on MARISAT are crystal clear. Call Comsat and ask them for a demo call to a ship somewhere in the world. It's very exciting.

MARK A term that originated with the telegraph. It currently indicates the binary digit "1" (one) in most coding schemes.

MARK-HOLD The normal no-traffic line condition where a steady mark is transmitted.

MARKER The logic circuitry in a crossbar central office that controls call processing functions.

MARKER TAPE A tape laid parallel to the conductors under the sheath in a cable imprinted with the manufacturer's name and the specification to which the cable is made. Other information such as date of manufacture may also be included.

MARKER THREAD A colored thread laid parallel and adjacent to the strands of an insulated conductor which identifies the cable manufacturer. It may also denote a temperature rating or the specification to which the cable is made.

MASER Microwave Amplification by Stimulated Emission of Radiation. A device that generates electromagnetic signals in the microwave range, known for relatively low-noise characteristics.

MASTER CLOCK An electronic timing circuit which synchronizes the entire data communications network. The source of timing signals, or the signals themselves, that all network stations use for synchronization.

MASTER CONTROL UNIT MCU. An InteCom word for the device which controls the main operating functions of the system.

MASTER NUMBER HUNTING When a call is directed to the pilot number of a hunt group, it will hunt to the first non-busy station in that group. If a call is directed to a specific station in that hunt group it will go directly to that station and not hunt to another station in the group.

MASTER SLAVE SWITCHING SYSTEM A configuration consisting of a central switch and one or more remote switches. The master switch typically controls all I/O (input/output) information. The slave system performs tasks as directed by the master, including switching calls between phones attached to that remote module — without sending those calls back to the central switch. There are enormous savings in wiring since not every remote phone has to have a pair back to the central switch.

MASTER STATION 1. The main phone or station in a group. The one controlling the transmission of the others. 2. The unit which controls all the workstations on a LAN, usually through some type of polling. The master station on a token-passing ring allows recovery from error conditions, such as lost, busy or duplicate tokens, usually by generating a new token. Sometimes servers are referred to as master stations.

MASTERGROUP A mastergroup consists of 600 voice channels, or 10 supergroups. Six mastergroups is equal to one jumbogroup.

MATEL A Multiplex Automatic Telephone System. Picture one long, up-to-two miles wire (any decent quality works). You roll it out, then you clip phones anywhere into the wire. Then you have, in effect, a seven channel bus PBX. You have two digit extension dialing between the phones (up to 60). You also have conferencing, broadcast, call back, DID and connection to one central office line and one radio channel. The uses? String it around a rioting prison, a siege, an airport hijack, an emergency in New York City subway, etc. Three advantages: instant communications, communications where radio is bad and radio silence — you keep the press and the bad guys in the dark. This definition from John McCann, general manager of Racal Acoustics Limited, Frederick, MD, which makes the MATEL.

MATR Minimum Average Time Requirement.

MATRIX A switch. A device for moving calls from one input to the desired output. There are many types of switching matrices — from simple step-by-step matrices to complex digital pulse code modulated matrices. Most switching matrices are "blocking." They do not have sufficient capacity to switch every call. There are some switches that are "non-blocking." These have the ability to switch every call simultaneously. By definition, non-blocking matrices are more expensive. They are only needed in special situations of high traffic.

MATRIX RINGING Two key system phones picking up the same extensions with different lines ringing on different phones. These days, with electronic phones, matrix ringing is easy. In the old days, with 1A2 phones, you needed to do considerable wiring.

MATV Master Antenna System, such as used in apartment buildings and motels.

MAU Math Acceleration Unit, Multiple Access Unit, which is a node on a token ring network that provides eight terminal ports. The mechanical interface is the IBM data connector.

MAU MULTISTATION ACCESS UNIT A wiring concentrator used in local area networks.

MBE Micom Business Exchange. Trademark for MICOM's series of communications processors.

MBPS Mbps. M/bps. Megabits per second. Million bits per second.

MCA Micro Channel Architecture. The new internal bus inside IBM's new line of PS/2 MCA machines.

MCCS Mechanized Calling Card Service was formerly known as ABC Service. MCCS is a CO switch facility that automatically bills credit card calls made on DDD without the involvement of an operator.

MCI Once upon a time it was called Microwave Communications Inc. Thus the MCI. But now it's just MCI and it stands for nothing. It is the largest long distance phone company in the US after AT&T. In MCI's early days, the initials were said to stand for "Money Coming In." Now MCI is a $5 billion corporation and its stock is selling for more than AT&T's (or was at the time of writing). MCI is a full-service long distance company offering every service from switched single channel voice to leased T-1. See also MCI FAX and MCI MAIL.

MCI FAX A way of sending facsimile messages. You can send them directly from fax machine to fax machine. Or you can send them from your personal computer (equipped with a modem) to any fax machine anywhere in the world. If you send faxes from your PC, you don't need a fax machine and you can send the same fax to a lot of people very easily. MCI Fax is cheaper than sending faxes by dialing directly. A good service.

MCI MAIL A way of sending electronic messages from your PC instantly to other people who have MCI Mail Mailboxes. It's the easiest, fastest, least expensive way to keep in touch in North America and in most industrialized countries around the globe. If you want to send us a message, send a message to TELECONNECT or to HARRY NEWTON. They're both subscribers to MCI Mail. Some of the definitions in this dictionary came to us via MCI Mail. MCI FAX is a subset of MCI Mail, an alternate delivery vehicle. See MCI FAX.

MCVF Multi-Channel Voice Frequency.

MDC Meridian Digital Centrex. A Northern Telecom abbreviation.

MDF See MAIN DISTRIBUTION FRAME.

MDT Mean Down Time.

MEAN BUSY HOUR For a telephone line or group of lines or a switch the Mean Busy hour is the 60 minute period where traffic is the greatest.

MEAN TIME BETWEEN FAILURE MTBF. The average time a manufacturer estimates before a failure occurs in a component, a printed circuit board or a complete telephone system. One must check, since MTBFs are cumulative.

MEAN TIME BETWEEN OUTAGES MTBO. The mean time between equipment failures or significant outages which essentially render transmission useless. See MEAN TIME BETWEEN FAILURE.

MEAN TIME TO REPAIR MTTR. The vendor's estimated average time required to do routine repairs on equipment.

MEASURED RATE A message rate structure in which the monthly phone line rental includes a specified number of calls within a defined area, plus a charge for additional calls. See LOCAL MEASURED SERVICE.

MEASURED SERVICE Also known as USAGE SENSITIVE PRICING (USP). A local phone company method of pricing used to bill local phone calls. Measured service is often charged on the number of calls, the time of day, the distance traveled and the length of the call. See LOCAL MEASURED SERVICE.

MECHANIZED CALLING CARD SERVICE MCCS was formerly known as ABC Service. MCCS is a central office switch feature that automatically bills credit card calls made on DDD (direct distance dial) rates without the involvement of an operator.

MECHANIZED LINE TESTING MLT. The system provides computer control of accurate and extensive loop testing functions in the customer contact, screening, testing, dispatch and closeout phases of trouble report handling. It also provides full diagnostic outputs instead of just pass/fail indications.

MEDIA COMPATIBLE Usually used to refer to floppy disk media. Even though two different computers (e.g. an AT&T PC 6300 and an Apple IIe) both use 5 1/4 inch floppy disks, the information recorded on them is recorded in a different format and thus, they are not media compatible. You can put one disk in another's machine. But it won't work. You'll get a dumb error message.

MEDIA PATH Same as wire run. The means by which telephone signals are conveyed from the Network Interface Jack to the Communications Outlet.

MEDIUM Any material substance that can be used for the telecommunications transmission of signals. "Mediums'" (or media) include optical fiber, cable, wire, dielectric slab, water, air or free space.

MEET-ME INTERCOM CONFERENCE Dial a special number ("access code") and any telephone can join an intercom conference call.

MEET-ME PAGE A feature which allows a person to answer an intercom page from any phone in the system.

MEGA A prefix meaning one million, also represented as an M. MEGABIT = one million bits. MEGABYTE = one million bytes. MEGAHERTZ = one million cycles per second.

MEGACOM Megacom 800 and Megacom. Two AT&T services which are variations on INWATS and OUTWATS. Both are normal WATS services except that the local lines to and from the customer's office to and from AT&T's serving class 4 central office are the responsibility of the customer. Such lines tend to be T-1. And they are usually direct wiring through the local phone company, or short-haul microwave, or leased fiber optic.

MEGAFLOPS Millions of floating point operations per second. A measure of computer performance.

MEMORY The part of a computer or sophisticated phone system which stores information or instructions for use. Memory comes in many variations. There is memory which is lost when the power is switched off. There is memory which is retained when power is turned off.

MEMORY ADMINISTRATION MA. A set of functions that provide network system database updates, network system database integrity, network system database security and network system database backup and restoration. Definition from Bellcore in reference to its concept of the Advanced Intelligent Network.

MEMORY MAP An indication of what type of data is stored where in a computer's RAM memory.

MEMORY RESERVE POWER The operating voltage, generally provided by a battery, which supplies power to the memory modules when your commercial power fails. You should check your memory reserve power before it's too late. You should test it even when you don't need it.

MENU Options displayed on a computer terminal screen or spoken by a voice processing system. The user can choose what he wants done by simply choosing a menu option — either typing it on the computer keyboard, hitting a touchtone on his phone or speaking a word or two. There are basically two ways of organizing computer or voice processing software — menu-driven and non-menu driven. Menu-driven programs are easier to use but they can only present as many options as can be reasonably crammed on a screen or spoken in a few seconds. Non-menu driven screens allow more alternatives but are much more complex and frightening. It's the difference between receiving a bland "A" or "C" prompt on the screen — as in MS-DOS and receiving a menu of "Press A if you want Word Processing," "Press B if you want Spread Sheet," etc. It's very easy to write menus in MS-DOS using BATch files. See also AUDIO MENUS and PROMPTS.

MERLIN COMMUNICATIONS SYSTEMS Five microprocessor based key/hybrid phone systems from AT&T — the 206, 410, 820, 1030 and 3070.

The last two numbers is the size, in phones, the system will handle. The first two or one number is the size, in trunks, the system will handle.

MERS Most Economical Route Selection. A term used by GTE and some other PBX manufacturers to mean Least Cost Routing. See LEAST COST ROUTING.

MESA ARCHITECTURE Centigram's trademarked brand name for its architecture that stands for Modularly Expandable System Architecture: 1. The capability to expand and/or enhance a VoiceMemo II system hardware and software in a modula fashion. 2. The capability to expand a single module VoiceMemo II into a multi-module system with a single database and centralized control.

MESA-FLEX Centigram's service design utility that allows a VoiceMemo II system to be fully customized through individually designed Feature Class of Service, independent Limits Classes of Service, Group Classes of Service and Network Classes of Service.

MESALINK Centigram's registered trademark for its inter-processor high speed bus that carries control information to the distributed processors.

MESSAGE A sequence of characters used to convey information or data. In data communications, messages are usually in an agreed format with a heading which establishes the address to which the message will be sent and the text which is the actual message and maybe some information to signify the end of the message.

MESSAGE CENTER A centralized place within the corporation where messages are taken and (occasionally) delivered. Message centers are good if they are staffed with competent, motivated people and the various phones in the place have message waiting lights (like they do in hotels). If staffed by talented people, message centers work a lot better than the amateur message takers called secretaries and their part-time short-term replacements.

MESSAGE DETAIL RECORDING See CALL DETAIL RECORDING and CALL ACCOUNTING SYSTEMS.

MESSAGE FORMAT The rules for placing information necessary for an electronic message. The format includes where the heading is and how long it will be as well as other control information.

MESSAGE HEADER The header before a string of data containing information regarding the destination of the data, usually in a packet in X.25 format.

MESSAGE REGISTRATION A phone system feature that records the number of message units incurred by each phone. Useful in hotels which bill local calls by message units.

MESSAGE RETRIEVAL The ability of a fax machine to store material already transmitted so it can be retransmitted.

MESSAGE SIGNAL UNIT Signal unit of CCS that carries a message corresponding to the information part or packet of the HDLC frame plus a message transfer part corresponding to the HDLC frame header.

MESSAGE SWITCHING A technique for receiving a message, storing it for a while and then sending it on. Message switching is normally used when the desired recipient is not there. The message switch will keep attempting delivery, freeing the calling party to handle other work. Unlike voice phone calls no direct connection is made in message switching between the incoming and outgoing messages.

MESSAGE SWITCHING NETWORK A public data communications network over which subscribers send primarily text messages to one another.

MESSAGE TELECOMMUNICATIONS SERVICE MTS. The regulatory term for long distance or message toll voice service. Misnamed. Actually there's nothing "message-y" about this service. This is a 100% switched voice service (though it can obviously be used for data).

MESSAGE TELEPHONE SERVICE MTS. Official designation for tariffed long-distance, or toll, telephone service. See MESSAGE TELECOMMUNICATIONS SERVICE.

MESSAGE UNIT The charge for one unit of local telephone service. How many message units you will find on your bill is a function of how many calls you made, how far the calls traveled, what time of the day or night you called and for how long you talked.

MESSAGE UNIT DETAIL MUD. A service offered by local telephone companies in which they give you a report listing the phone number of all local calls made from each of your billing numbers. The billing number may be the main number for a PBX or the individual extensions if Centrex service is used. MUD reports are usually available to a telephone company customer at additional cost. MUD reports generally have to be requested in advance. Some telephone company central offices cannot generate MUD reports. When available, MUD reports may not be in machine processible form.

MESSAGE WAITING A light on the phone or some letters or characters on the phone's display indicating there's a message waiting somewhere for the owner of the phone. That message might be with a special message center (as in a hotel or a larger company), with the operator or with a computer attached to the phone system or with someone else in the company. Message waiting lights are incredibly useful at hotels. It's amazing more companies don't use them also.

MESSAGE-HANDLING SYSTEM MHS. The standard defined by CCITT as X.400 and by ISO as Message-Oriented Text Interchange Standard (MOTIS).

MESSENGER A piece of heavy metal cabling attached to a pole line to support aerial phone cable.

MET Multibutton Electronic Telephone for an old phone system called AT&T Horizon.

METAL TAPE Recording tape coated with iron particles and noted for its wide dynamic range and wide frequency response.

METALLIC CIRCUIT A circuit completely provided by wire, and not containing any carrier, radio or fiber.

METERING PULSES In virtually all foreign countries, periodic pulses are returned from the distant exchange to the exchange (central office) of the calling number. These pulses determine the cost of the call, local or long distance. Typically, all pulses cost the same. However, the farther you call, the quicker the pulses come. This system contrasts to the North American long distance billing scheme which typically charges a certain amount for the first minute — no matter how much of the minute is actually used in conversation. After the first minute in the U.S., conversations are billed in one minute increments. Overseas pulses can be as short as three or four seconds (especially for international calls).

METROPOLITAN AREA NETWORK A broadband network that links non-contiguous premises within the metropolitan or LATA area and moves information between buildings. See MAN.

MF See MULTI-FREQUENCY SIGNALING.

MFJ The Modified Final Judgment is the federal court ruling that set up the rules and regulations concerning deregulation and divestiture of AT&T and the Bell system.

MFM Modified Frequency Modulation. A perfectly fine hard disk interface specification that is the oldest and slowest of the Winchester hard disk interface standards. Other and newer standards include RLL (Run Length Limited encoding), IDE (Integrated Drive Electronics), ESDI (Enhanced Small Device Interface) and SCSI (Small Computer System Interface).

MFLOPS An acronym for Million Floating point Operations Per Second. A measure of computing power usually associated with large computers.

MIB Management Information Base. A repository or virtual database in which managed objects on a network node and their attributes are described. Method of storage is irrelevant. Within the Internet MIB employed for SNMP(Simple Network Management Protocol)-based management, ASN.1 (Abstract Syntax Notation One) is used to describe network management variables. These variables, which include such information as error counts or on/off status of a device, are assigned a place on a tree data structure. See INTERNET MIB TREE.

MIB-I The initial collection of objects and attributes defined by the TCP/IP (Transmission Control Protocol/Internet Protocol) standards community. MIB-I was elevated to Internet standard status in May 1990.

MH Modified Huffman data compression method.

MHS MESSAGE HANDLING SYSTEM An ISO standard Application Layer protocol that defines a framework for distributing data from one network to several others. It transfers relatively small messages in a store-and-forward manner (defined by CCITT as X.400 and by ISO as MOTIS/Message-Oriented Text Interchange Standard).

MHz An abbreviation for Megahertz. One million Hertz. One million cycles per second.

MIC A designation for a multiplex which interfaces between two DSIs and one DSIC circuit.

MICHAEL Harry's favorite son. (His only one, in case you hadn't guessed already.)

MICOM A manufacturer of data and voice equipment located in Simi Valley, CA.

MICR Magnetic Ink Character Recognition. A process of character recognition where printed characters containing particles of magnetic material, are read by a scanner and converted into a computer-readable digital format.

MICRO One-millionth.

MICRO CASSETTE Miniaturized version of the standard audio cassette.

MICRO CHANNEL A proprietary bus developed by IBM for its PS/2 family of computers' internal expansion cards. Also offered by Tandy and other vendors. Compare with EISA bus.

MICRO COMPONENTS Miniaturized audio components that provide the benefits of traditional sized components in far less space.

MICRO FARAD One millionth of a farad. This is the common unit for designation capacitance in electronics and communications.

MICRO-TO-MAINFRAME LINK The telecommunications path over which data between a microcomputer and a mainframe computer travels.

MICRO-TO-MAINFRAME SOFTWARE Software which provides the logic by which data can be transferred back and forth between a microcomputer and a mainframe computer.

MICROCODE Programmed instructions that typically are unalterable. Usually synonymous with firmware and programmable read-only-memory (PROM). MICROCOM NETWORK PROTOCOL. See MNP.

MICROCOMPUTER The combination of CPU (Central Processing Unit) and other peripherals (I/O, memory, etc.) that form a basic computer system.

MICROFLOPPIES The latest generation of floppy disks at 3 1/2 inches diameter, invented by Sony. The microfloppy is used in the Apple Macintosh and most MS-DOS laptop computers. Used in an MS-DOS machine, a 3 1/2 inch microfloppy diskette will currently format to carry 730K of data — equivalent to about 500 pages of double-spaced text. The latest IBM personal computers can format microfloppies to carry exactly twice as much — 1.4 million bits.

MICROGRAPHICS Conversion of information into or from microfilm or microfiche.

MICRON One thousandth of a millimeter. Or one millionth of a meter.

MICROPROCESSOR An electronic circuit, usually on a single chip, which performs arithmetic, logic and control operations, with the assistance of internal memory. The microprocessor is the fabled "computer on a chip," the "brains" behind all desk top personal computers. Typically, the microprocessor contains the following parts: read only memory — ROM — (permanently stored instructions), read and write memory — RAM, and a control decoder for breaking down the instructions stored in ROM into detailed steps for action by the arithmetic logic unit — ALU — which actually carries out the numerical calculations. There's also a clock circuitry which connects the chip to an exterior quartz crystal whose vibrations coordinate the chip's operations, keeping everything in step. And finally, the input/output section directs communications with devices on the outside of the chip, such as the keyboard, the screen and the various disk drives.

MICROSECOND One millionth of a second.

MICROVAX II DEC's minicomputer operating system which runs on Berkeley UNIX (also known as 4.2).

MICROWAVE Electromagnetic waves in the radio frequency spectrum above 890 Megahertz (million cycles per second) and below 20 Gigahertz (billion cycles per second). Microwave is a common form of transmitting telephone, facsimile, video and data conversations used by common carriers as well as by private networks. Microwave signals only travel in straight lines. In terrestrial microwave systems, they're typically good for 30 miles, at which point you need another repeater tower. Microwave is the frequency for communicating to and from satellites.

MIF Minimum Internetworking Functionality. A general principle within the ISO that calls for minimum local area network station complexity when interconnecting with resources outside the local area network.

MIGRATION An AT&T marketing strategy designed to encourage all phone equipment month-to-month renters into long-term contracts for AT&T's "flagship products", i.e., System 75, 85 and Definity PBXs.

MIL 1/1000 of an inch.

MILEAGE See AIRLINE MILEAGE.

MILLI One thousandth. Millisecond equals one thousand of a second.

MILLIWATT One thousandth of a watt. Used as a reference point for signal levels at a given point in a circuit.

MINI-FLOPPY A floppy disk that is 3 1/2 inches in diameter. Also called a microfloppy. See MICROFLOPPY.

MINI-MAP (Mini-Manufacturing Automation Protocol): A version of MAP consisting of only physical, link and application layers intended for lower-cost process-control networks. With mini-MAP, a device with a token can request a response from an addressed device. Unlike a standard MAP protocol, the addressed Mini-MAP device need not wait for the token to respond.

MINICLAS A service from New York Telephone which allows a small (up to 199 lines) Centrex III user to make certain changes to his own Centrex features and lines with an easy-to-use computer program or a touch-tone phone. See also CLAS.

MINIMUM INTERNETWORKING FUNCTIONALITY MIF. A general principle within the ISO that calls for minimum local network station complexity when interconnecting with resources outside the local network.

MINITEL French name for videotex. Very popular. See VIDEOTEX and packet switched networks.

MIPS Millions of Instructions Per Second. A measure of computer speed.

MIS Management Information System. A fancy name for Data Processing. MIS are also the first three letters of the word MISanthrope and MISguided and lots of other MIS words. MIS departments are taking over corporate telecommunications departments which is why there's little love lost between the two.

MISCELLANEOUS COMMON CARRIER A communications common carrier (typically one using microwave) which is not offering switched service to the public or to companies. A miscellaneous common carrier usually provides video and radio leased line transmission services to TV and radio networks.

MISCELLANEOUS TRUNK RESTRICTIONS Denies preselected lines access to preselected trunk groups (e.g., FX or WATS trunks). A call attempt over a restricted group routes to an intercept tone.

MIXED CABLE Cables have characteristic impedances which vary according to the cables' physical parameters. When cables of different characteristic impedance are mixed, an impedance imbalance will occur. It is thus bad practice to mix different wire gauges, and twisted or non-twisted pair cables. However, it is accepted practice to combine long runs of twisted pair cable with short lengths of modular patch cords and line cords. Baluns are an exception to this rule.

MIXED MODE An imprecise term which suggests that one digital bit stream can carry voice, data, facsimile and video signals.

MIXED MODE NIGHT SERVICE After-hours answering of incoming calls in which Assigned Night Answer (ANA) is specified for some trunks, and Universal Night Answer (UNA) specified for others.

MIXED STATION DIALING A telephone system feature which allows you to install both rotary and pushbutton phones on your phone system. Most modern PBXs have this feature.

MLPP See MULTILEVEL PRECEDENCE PREEMPTION.

MMJ A six wire modular jack with the locking tab shifted off to the right hand side. Used in the DEC wiring system.

MMR Modified Modified Read data compression method.

MNEMONIC A shorthand label or term that is easy to remember, usually made up from the initials of the words in a term or process. LASER is a mnemonic. See LASER.

MNEMONIC DIAL PLAN A way of dialing using characters typed on the keyboard of a terminal. An option of the InteCom PBX.

MNEMONIC PROMPTS System commands represented by the appropriate alphabet letter rather than by a number, (for example, "P" to "Play", "A" to Answer").

MNP Microcom Network Protocol. MNP is a modem standard like the Hayes standard. There are five Classes of MNP modem protocols. Classes 1 through 4 are error checking protocols. Class 5 is a data compression protocol in which the sending modem automatically compresses the file and the receiving modem automatically decompresses the file. MNP Class 5 boosts modem throughput by as much as 200%. MNP Class 5 is the most important protocol. More and more modem manufacturers are beginning to adopt MNP Class 5 protocol. It makes sense to buy only high-speed dial-up modems that support MNP Class 5 protocol.

MNP MICROCOM NETWORKING PROTOCOL A proprietary error-correcting data compression protocol for modems (2.4 to 9.6 Kbps).

MOBILE TELEPHONE Radio telephone service provided to vehicles from a broadcast point located within range of the moving vehicle. The broadcast point in turn can be connected to the public network so that calls can be completed to or from any stationary telephone. See also CELLULAR.

MODAL DISPERSION Digital pulse rounding in lightwave communications that takes place because of the slightly different paths followed by the laser light rays as they arrive at the detector slightly out of phase.

MODEM Acronym for MOdulator/DEModulator. Equipment which converts digital signals to analog signals and vice-versa. Modems are used to send data signals (digital) over the telephone network, which usually is analog. The Modem modulates the "1s" and "0s" into tones which can be carried by the phone network. At the other end, the demodulator part of the modem converts the tones back into digital 1s and 0s.

MODEM ELIMINATOR You can connect a PC to a printer, or a PC to another printer using a cable. But you can only go a certain distance — maybe 100 feet. After that, the traditional solution has been to use a modem and go over traditional phone lines. A newer approach is to connect the two devices directly by wire and use a device called a Modem Eliminator. There are two advantages of a Modem Eliminator over a normal modem. The eliminator is cheaper and it can often transmit faster.

MODEM POOL A collection of modems which a user can dial up from his terminal, access one and use that one to make a data call over the switched telephone network. Modem pools are obviously designed to allow many users to share few modems, thus saving on modems. Now that modems have become less expensive, the advantages of modem pooling are no longer as great. There are also some advantages in having a modem right next to your terminal or computer — namely you can see how it is functioning. And modems have lights to indicate what they're doing. One of the most useful lights on most modems indicates whether the line is "off hook" or not. It is possible for your computer to instruct your modem to hang up the line and for your modem to forget to do it, leaving you with a huge phone bill. One problem with giving people their own modems is they (the modems) have a tendency to get pinched. It's hard to screw down modems. Harder, anyway, than computers and disk drives.

MODEM STANDARDS Definitions of electrical and telecommunications characteristics which enable modems from dissimilar manufacturers to speak to each other. Bell 103...US standard for 300 bps; CCITT V.21...International standard for 300 bps; Bell 212A...US standard for 1200 bps; CCITT V.22...International standard for 1200 bps; CCITT V.22 bis...US and international standard for 2400 bps; CCITT V.23...International videotex standard (1200/75 bps or 75/1200 bps). See also HAYES COMMAND SET.

MODEM TURNAROUND TIME The time needed for a half-duplex modem (an old-fashioned one) to reverse its transmission direction.

MODULAR Equipment is said to be modular when it is made of "plug-in units" which can be added together to make the system larger, improve its capabilities or expand its size. There are very few phone systems that are truly modular.

MODULAR PLUG A series of connecting devices adopted by the FCC as the standard interface for telephone and data equipment to the public network. The most common is the RJ-11, used to connect a single line phone.

MODULATION The process of varying some characteristic of the electrical carrier wave as the information to be transmitted on that carrier wave varies. Three types of modulation are commonly used for communications, Amplitude Modulation, Frequency Modulation and Phase Modulation. And there are variations on these themes called Phase Shift Keying (PSK) and Quadrature Amplitude Modulation (QAM).

MODULATOR A device which converts a voice or data signal into a form that can be transmitted.

MODULO Term used to express the maximum number of states for a counter. Used to describe several packet-switched network parameters, such as packet number (usually set to modulo 8 — counted from 0 to 7). When the maximum count is exceeded, the counter is reset to 0.

MODULO N In communications, refers to a quantity, such as the number of frames or packets to be counted before the counter resets to zero. Relates to the number of frames or packets that can be outstanding from a transmitter before an acknowledgement is required from the receiver. Also indicates the maximum number of frames or packets stored, in case a retransmission is required (i.e., Modulo 8 or Modulo 128).

MOH Music On Hold.

MOISTURE RESISTANCE The ability of a material to resist absorbing moisture from the air or when immersed in water.

MONITOR 1. To listen in on a conversation for the purpose of determining the quality of the attendant's or agent's response and politeness to customers. 2. Video monitor. TV screen and surrounding electronics. IBM personal computer monitors come in monochrome and color. The more you pay the better quality the monitor is. The quality of monitors is typically measured by how monitor's screen resolution, which is measured by pixels, or picture elements. In monochrome monitors, the "standard" is Hercules Graphics, which offers a resolution of 720 pixels horizontally by 348 vertically. The worst color monitor is called CGA, which stands for Color Graphics Adapter. It offers 320 x 200. Most low-end laptops have this resolution screen. Next better is EGA, Enhanced Graphics Adapter. It offers 640 x 350 pixels. Next better is VGA, or Video Graphics Array, which offers 640 x 480. Next up is 8514/A, which is IBM's high-resolution extension to its VGA adapter. It provides a resolution of 1,024 x 768. It will only work on IBM machines with the Micro Channel Architecture (MCA). See FACSIMILE EQUIPMENT.

MONITOR ON HOLD A telephone feature. If the person you're speaking with puts you "on hold," you can turn your speaker on your phone and hang up your handset but keep listening until the other person comes back to the phone.

MONTH-TO-MONTH The standard way of paying for telephone service. Some services now come in "rate stability" packages, which means if you commit to keeping the service for a while — typically three or five years — it's cheaper each month.

MORSE CODE The International Morse code, named for Samuel F. B. Morse who invented telegraph, is referred to as International Telegraph Alphabet 1. Mr. Morse first demonstrated the telegraph in 1844. It is still used in radio telegraphy to ships at sea, though many ships now carry satellite antennae and subscribe to MARISAT.

Morse code represents letters by combinations of long and short signals. Morse code can be written in dots and dashes or signaled with flashlights and radio bleeps. In 1912 the easily memorized letters SOS were chosen as the international distress signal. "Save Our Souls" was the catchphrase devised later.

See also MORSE, SAMUEL

MORSE CODE

A .- B -... C -.-. D -.. E . F ..-. G --.
H .... I .. J .--- K -.- L .-.. M -- N -.
O --- P .--. Q --.- R .-. S ... T -
U ..- V ...- W .-- X -..- Y -.-- Z —..

MORSE, SAMUEL Samuel Finley Breese Morse was born in Charlestown (now a part of Boston) on April 27, 1791. He entered Yale University at the age of 14 and graduated in 1810. Although he attended lectures on electricity while at Yale, after graduation he went to England to study art. He returned to the United States in 1815 and became a well-known painter. In 1832, while returning from Europe, he and a fellow passenger discussed the electromagnet and Morse conceived the idea of his telegraph. He made a working model about 1835 and filed for a patent in 1838 and in 1844 inaugurated public service between Washington and Baltimore with his famous message, "What hath God wrought?" He died in 1872. See MORSE CODE.

MOS Metal Oxide Semiconductor. Technology describing a transistor composed of a semiconductor layer including "source" and "drain" regions separated by a channel. Above the channel is a thin layer of oxide and over that a metal electrode called a gate. A voltage applied to this gate controls the current between the source and drain regions, or in another format, stops a flow between the two areas. (Definition courtesy of Bell Labs)

MOST ECONOMICAL ROUTE SELECTION MERS. Used by several phone companies and several manufacturers to mean Least Cost Routing — the feature of a telephone system which automatically chooses the least cost route for a long distance call. See LEAST COST ROUTING.

MOST FAVORED NATION CLAUSE A clause added to a purchase contract with a vendor saying that for a certain period after signing the contract, if the buyer finds out that the product has been bought for less, then the seller will refund the difference. The idea is to give the purchaser the assurance of the least expensive price.

MOTHERBOARD The main circuit board of a computer system. The motherboard contains edge connectors or sockets so other PC (printed circuit) boards can be plugged into it. On IBM's new OS series of personal computers, the motherboard is called the PLANAR BOARD. Motherboards are common in key systems and hybrid key/PBXs. They are not common in PBXs, where all the electronics are typically on printed circuit cards which slide into the PBX's cage and can be replaced (and thus upgraded) easily.

MOV Metal Oxide Varistor. A type of surge suppressor which absorbs voltage and current surges and spikes. Many trunk boards inside PBX are protected by MOVs. This means that the first device a trunk coming in hits on the circuit board is an MOV. If the voltage or current is high, it will blow the MOV, thus protecting the remaining and far more valuable devices on the board.

MPEG An image-compression scheme more sophisticated than the JPEG scheme, proposed by the Motion Picture Experts Group, which is also ISO-sanctioned. While JPEG compresses each still frame in a video sequence as much as possible, MPEG also performs "differencing," noting differences between consecutive frames. If two consecutive frames are identical, the second can be stored with the appropriate information. MPEG condenses moving images about three times more tightly than JPEG, but probably won't be implemented until 1991 or 1992.

MPG Microwave Pulse Generator. A device that generates electrical pulses at microwave frequencies.

MS-DOS MicroSoft Disk Operating System. Being dumb, a computer needs to be told from the very basic steps what to do. MS-DOS is the basic command system for IBM and IBM clone personal computers. It explains to the computer how to talk to its keyboard, to its screen, to its various "ports" — serial and parallel — and how to talk to its internal bus — the broadband communications system that sends messages between PC (printed circuit) cards that are slid into the empty slots most personal computers come with.

One critical MS-DOS function is to "talk" to its disk/s — hard and/or soft. Let me explain: In MS-DOS when you format a disk, you actually put temporary dummy data all throughout the disk. The smallest unit of storage on a disk is 512 bytes. When you create a file (say a letter), MS-DOS stores the file in clusters, which are typically groups of sectors. MS-DOS doesn't store these clusters contiguously (i.e. next to each other). Rather, it stores them all over the disk. Each cluster thus contains only a portion of the file. This is efficient, since MS-DOS then doesn't require long uninterrupted areas of space on the disk for each file.

If your files are stored all over the disk, clearly you need an index or roadmap to where the files are. When you format a disk, in addition to laying down dummy data, MS-DOS makes two other things — first, an area of the disk containing the boot-up logic MS-DOS needs to start the machine. And second, two copies of something called the File Allocation Table. The FAT is like an index to what's on the disk. When you make a new file, MS-DOS automatically checks the FAT to figure where the chunks of your new file should be stored. When you do a DIR, you can't see the FAT. It's hidden away. But it's there. And it's duplicated (just in case).

Sometimes the FAT becomes corrupted. This is a nice term for "messed up." When the FAT and the directory entries fall out of synch with each other, you could be in trouble. The most common problem is a lost cluster. MS-DOS wrote a portion of a file to the disk, but didn't connect it with a file. In other words, MS-DOS has simply misplaced the cluster. To solve the problem you must use the CHKDSK command. You do this by typing a C: prompt CHKDSK /F

That means check the disk and fix it. One more point: How to bring back a file you've erased. MS-DOS doesn't actually "erase" a file. It marks the directory entry of the file as "erased" and frees the sectors (i.e. space) listed in the FAT. When you create a new file or add to an existing one, MS-DOS may then use these freed-up sectors. The key to recovering a file you've erased is not to have written anything to disk after you erased the file. If you erase a file, say "Drat" and then instantly use a program like Norton Utilities' UNERASE program. You'll be able to bring your erased file back to life with absolutely no problem and totally intact. The key is NOT to write anything over it. See also DEVICE DRIVER.

MS-NET An enhancement Microsoft included in the 3.1 version of MS-DOS to support their MS-NET local area network software.

MSNF Multisystem Networking Facility. An optional feature of certain IBM telecommunications access methods that allows more than one host running

ACF/TCAM or VTAM to jointly control an ACF/NCP program.

MTA Message Transfer Agent.

MTBF Mean Time Between Failure. The length of time a user may reasonably expect a device or system to work before an incapacitating fault occurs.

MTP Message Transfer Part of the SS7 Protocol. It provides functions for basic routing of signaling messages between signaling points.

MTS Message Telecommunications Service. AT&T's name for standard switched telephone service. Also called DDD, for Direct Distance Dial.

MTTR Mean Time to Repair. The average time required to return a failed device or system to service.

MU-LAW The PCM coding and companding standard used in Japan and North America. See A- LAW.

MULDEM A contraction for Multiplexer Demultiplexer, referring to a piece of equipment which performs both functions and generally operates between two of the AT&T digital hierarchy rates (i.e., DSI to DS3).

MULTI-ACCESS The ability of several users to communicate with a computer at the same time with each working independently on their own job.

MULTI-CAST The broadcast of messages to a selected group of workstations on a LAN.

MULTI-CAST USER MESSAGE A user message generated at the source node and distributed to two or more destination nodes.

MULTI-CHANNEL The use of a common channel to make two or more channels either by splitting the frequency band of the common channel into several narrower bands (called frequency-division multiplexing) or by allocating time slots in the entire channel (time-division multiplexing).

MULTI-CONDUCTOR More than one conductor within a single cable complex.

MULTI-DROP A communications circuit with multiple terminals and peripherals. Only one may transmit at any time.

MULTI-DROP LINE A communications channel that services many data terminals at different geographical locations and in which a computer (node) controls utilization of the channel by polling one distant terminal after another and asking it, in effect, "Do you have anything for me?"

MULTI-FREQUENCY PULSING An in-band address signaling method in which ten decimal digits (the numbers on the touchtone pad) and five auxiliary signals are each represented by selecting two frequencies and combining them into one tone. The frequencies are selected from five separate frequencies — 700, 900, 1100, 1300 and 1500 Hz.

MULTI-HOP An example of a single hop system is a microwave system between one building (let's say downtown San Francisco) and another across town (let's say uptown San Francisco). Each with one microwave antenna on its roof. Let's say we wanted to extend that system to Oakland. We'd put a second antenna on the uptown San Francisco building and shoot across to an antenna in Oakland. That building would now have a multi-hop transmission system.

MULTI-LEAVING In communications, the transmission (usually via bisync facilities and using bisync protocols) of a variable number of data streams between user devices and a computer.

MULTI-LEVEL PRECEDENCE PREEMPTION MLPP. A system in which selected customers may exercise preemption capabilities to seize facilities being used for calls with lower precedence levels.

MULTI-LINE HUNT The ability of switching equipment to connect calls to another phone in the group when other numbers in the group are busy.

MULTI-LINE TELEPHONE Any telephone set with buttons which can answer or originate calls on one or more central office lines or trunks. Originally all multi-line telephones were 1A2 and they came in sizes of 2, 3, 5, 9, 11, 17, 19, 29, and 60 lines. Now, skinny wire electronic key systems come in all sizes. See KEY TELEPHONE SYSTEM.

MULTI-LINE TERMINATING SYSTEM Premises switching equipment and key telephone type systems which are capable of terminating more than one local exchange service line, WATS access line, FX circuit, etc.

MULTI-MEDIA Multi-media is the combination of multiple forms of media in the communication of information between users and machines. Communication formats vary, but they usually include voice communications (vocoding, speech recognition, speaker verification and text-to-speech), audio processing (music synthesis, CD-ROMs), data communications, image processing and telecommunications using LANs, MANs and WANs in ISDN and POTS networks.

MULTI-MODE In fiber-optics, an optical fiber designed to carry multiple signals distinguished by frequency or phase at the same time (contrasts with single- mode). (Also spelled multimode.)

MULTI-PATH Multiple routes taken by RF energy between the transmitter and the receiver. Signal can cancel or reinforce. Varying multipath (at sunset or sunrise) causes varying signal strength that sounds like a train's steam engine starting up.

MULTI-POINT A configuration or topology, designed to transmit data between a central site and a number of remote terminals on the same circuit. Individual terminals will generally be able to transmit to the central site but not to each other.

MULTI-POINT CIRCUIT A circuit connecting three or more locations. It is often called a multidrop circuit. See also MULTI-POINT and MULTI-DROP LINE.

MULTI-POINT LINE A single communications channel to which more than one data terminal is attached, though only one may transmit at a time, but several devices on the line may receive transmissions.

MULTI-PROCESSING The simultaneous execution of two or more computer programs by a computer or computer network. Similar to parallel processing.

MULTI-PROGRAMMING Computer system operation whereby a number of independent jobs are processed together.

MULTI-STAGE QUEUING This a term typically used in Automatic Call Distributors. It is the ability to array a number of agent groups in a routing table. The notion of multiple agent groups being addressed may mean that the system may be able to "look-back" and "look forward" as it searches for a free agent in the right group to take the call presently holding.

MULTI-STATION Any network of stations capable of communicating with each other on one circuit or through a switching center.

MULTI-TASKING Doing several different tasks at the same time on one computer. This should not be confused with TASK SWITCHING. In task switching, the computer jumps from one task to another, typically in response to a command from you, the user. For example, in task switching, you might temporarily stop your word processing, jump into your communications package, dial up a database, grab some information, then jump back into your word processor and put that new information into the document you're word processing. However, in true multi-tasking, you could have told your computer to dial the database, grab the information and alert you when it had grabbed the material. At that point you could have included it in your document. But in the meantime, you could have been happily word processing. Multi- tasking is touted as a great new feature in the IBM line of PCs — the OS series. If this were the only reason to buy the new PCs, it would be cheaper simply to buy two of the old PCs and put them next to each other on your desk, which is exactly what many of us do.

MULTI-TENANT SHARING The capability of a PBX to serve more than one tenant in a building. This process is a new option for building owners. They now become the Telephone Company for tenants in the building. There is money in this business, but chiefly on the resale of long distance phone calls.

MULTI-THREADING Concurrent processing of more than one message by an application program.

MULTI-TIER TARIFFS A way of paying for something (i.e. equipment) from your local phone company. The idea is that one tier of your monthly payments is to pay off the equipment, and after a finite period, this tier payment drops to zero. The next tier is to pay for your monthly service and it is on-going. Other tiers are for other reasons. As this technique was practiced by the Bell System, it was called "two tier." You will no longer find two tier tariffs in common use.

MULTI-USER PC A microcomputer that has several terminals attached to it, so that multiple users can simultaneously use its resources. Multi-user PCs can either slice up the time of a single microprocessor or can give each terminal-based user his own microprocessor. Multi-user PCs are an alternative to LANs and are typically used in specialized, one-application solutions, such as a doctor's office billing system.

MULTIPLE ACCESS The ability of several personal computers connected to a Local Area Network to access one another through a common addressing scheme and protocol.

MULTIPLE ADDRESS MESSAGE A message to be delivered to more than one destination.

MULTIPLE CONSOLE OPERATION A phone system with this feature can use more than one attendant console. It's good to know the maximum number of consoles your chosen PBX can use.

MULTIPLE CUSTOMER GROUP OPERATION A PBX shared by several different companies, each having separate consoles and trunks.

MULTIPLE LISTED DIRECTORY NUMBER SERVICE Permits more than one listed directory number to be associated with a single PBX.

MULTIPLE ROUTING The process of sending a message to more than one recipient, usually when all destinations are specified in the header of the message.

MULTIPLEX To transmit two or more signals over a single channel.

MULTIPLEX HIERARCHY According to the U.S. multiplex hierarchy, 2 channels = 1 group, 5 groups = 1 supergroup, 10 supergroups = 1 mastergroup, (CCITT standard says 5 supergroups = 1 mastergroup), 6 mastergroups = 1 jumbo group.

MULTIPLEXED CHANNEL A communications channel capable of carrying the telecommunications transmissions of a number of devices or users at one time.

MULTIPLEXER Electronic equipment which allows two or more signals to pass over one communications circuit. That "circuit' may be a phone line, a microwave circuit, a through-the-air TV signal. That circuit may be analog or digital. There are many multiplexing techniques to accommodate both.

MULTIPLEXING EFFICIENCY Figure of merit for multiplexers. The ratio of the aggregate channel input data rate to the composite output data rate. Many statistical multiplexers achieve a multiplexing efficiency of 8 or more.

MURIEL Muriel Fullam worked for me for 10 years before she worked with me on this dictionary. That had to be the longest apprenticeship ever. It shows. She did great work. Thanks. She is married to Jerry who will freak when he sees his name here.

MUSIC-ON-CAMP Audio source input for use with attendant camp-on. See also MUSIC-ON-HOLD.

MUSIC-ON-HOLD Background music heard when someone is put on hold, letting them know they are still connected. Some modern phone systems generate their own electronic synthesized music. Most phone systems have the ability to connect any sound-producing device, e.g. a radio or a cassette player. Most companies, unfortunately, devote little attention to the sound source they select. Sometimes competitors will deliberately advertise on the radio station that callers will hear on hold. Thus, Macys is now selling Gimbels. It's better to use pre-recorded music. Better yet are tapes of "specials" and other happenings around your firm. Use the "Music-on-Hold" feature as another method of selling. "Ask the operator about our special on ladies underwear." "Ask our operator to send you a copy of our latest annual report."

MUTE A feature which disconnects the handset microphone or speakerphone microphone so that side conversations won't be heard.

MUTUAL CAPACITANCE The capacitance between two conductors when all other conductors, including the shield, are short circuited to ground.

MUX See MULTIPLEXER.

MVS Multiple Virtual Storage.

MX3 A designation for a multiplex which interfaces between any of the following circuit combinations: 28 DSIs to one DS3 (M13), 14 DSICs to one DS3 (MC3), or 7 DS2s to one DS3 (M23).

N1 The first short-haul multiplex carrier in the U.S. by the Bell System was Western Electric's N1. The N1 transmitted 12 voice frequency channels over separate transmit and receive pairs in a single cable. N carriers have been progressively improving.

N2 In packet data networking technology, parameter used to specify the allowable number of retransmissions before disconnection.

NA See NIGHT ANSWER.

NAILED CONNECTION A PBX feature. Defined by Fujitsu, their Omni SI provides up to eight dedicated (constant) trunk-to-trunk connections for special applications. See also NAILED DATA CONNECTION.

NAILED DATA CONNECTION A permanently established connection between two InteCom IBM S/80 data interfaces. This connection is defined in the IBM data base and the switch paths are established when the call processing software is first brought on line.

NAK Negative Acknowledgement. NAK is a control character in ASCII that means a packet arrived with the check digits in error. It is sent from the computer receiving the packets to the sender, implying that the packet should be retransmitted so that all bits will arrive intact in the next go-round. See CHECK DIGITS and ACK.

NAME SERVER A directory service located in the SLEE (Service Logic Execution Environment) that provides a mapping between a resource's global name and its physical location in the network.

NANOMETER One-billionth of a meter. Written nm.

NANOSECOND One billionth of a second. Written nsec.

NAP Network Action Point. An AT&T term describing the switching point through which a call is processed. The NAP switches the call based on routing instructions received from the NCP.

NAPI Numbering/Addressing Plan Identifier.

NAPLPS North American Presentation-Level Protocol Syntax. A protocol for videotex text graphics and screen formats, developed by AT&T and since standardized within ANSI, based on Canada's Telidon videographics protocol.

NARROWBAND An imprecise term. Some people think it's sub-voice grade channels capable of only carrying 100 to 200 bits per second. Others think it means lines or circuits able to carry data up to 2400 bits per second. So as lines get broader, narrowband gets broader.

NARTE National Association of Radio and Telecommunications Engineers, based in Salem, OR. 800-933-1470.

NARUC National Association of Regulatory and Utility Commissioners. Members are representatives of state regulatory agencies concerned with telephone regulatory and other utility matters.

NASA National Aeronautics and Space Administration.

NATA North American Telecommunications Association. A trade association of manufacturers and distributors of telephone equipment and now also telephone companies and, more recently, some computer companies.

NATIONAL ELECTRICAL CODE A code giving rules for the installation of electrical and telephone cabling published by the National Fire Protection Association, Boston, MA. This code has been adopted and enforced by many states and municipalities as law.

NAU Network Addressable Unit. SNA term for LU, PU and SSCP. Each unit in SNA has a unique address.

NAUTICAL MILE 6076 feet. 15% longer than a normal mile (5280 feet).

NBS, NATIONAL BUREAU OF STANDARDS US government agency that produces Federal Information Processing Standards (FIPS) for all other agencies except the Department of Defense (DoD).

NBS/ICST National Bureau of Standards/Institute for Computer Sciences and Technology. The NBS directorate, based in Gaithersburg, MD, is concerned with developing computer and data communications.

NCA Number of Calls Abandoned. The number of calls accepted into the ACD on the trunks only but lost before being connected to a person.

NCC 1. Network Control Center. A central location on a network where remote diagnostics and network management are controlled. 2. National Computer Conference, the erstwhile largest annual conference of the computer industry.

NCCF Network Communication Control Facility. An IBM term. See NETVIEW.

NCEO NonCompliant End Office

NCO Network Control Office.

NCP 1. In AT&T language, Network Control Point. 2. In IBM language, Network Control Program, which is a program that controls the operations of the communication controllers, 3704 and 3705 in an IBM SNA network. 3. In Northern Telecom language, it means Network Configuration Process.

NCTA National Cable Television Association. A trade organization representing U.S. cable-television carriers.

NCTE Network Channel Terminating Equipment. Equipment considered necessary for terminating a telephone circuit or facility at the customer premises. Recent FCC decisions have established that most NCTE is customer premises equipment (CPE) and may therefore, by supplied by third-party vendors as well as the telephone company.

NDT No Dial Tone.

NEAR-END CROSSTALK Signal distortion caused by the coupling of an outgoing signal at the originating end of a circuit with the incoming signal being received from the other end of the circuit.

NECA National Exchange Carrier Association. Nonprofit organization established by the FCC in 1983 to implement the access charge objectives being introduced replacing interstate division of revenue procedures. Membership includes all U.S. local exchange carriers. NECA files interstate access charges with the FCC, and after approval, pools such collections from the LECs and distributes these revenues equitably to the members based on each one's contribution in terms of expenses and capital investment for interstate toll.

NEGATIVE ABSORPTION Amplification. The positive difference between stimulated and absorbed radiation.

NEGATIVE ACKNOWLEDGEMENT NAK. A communications control character sent by a receiving station to indicate that the last message or block received was not received correctly.

NEMA National Electrical Manufacturers Association.

NEPER Np. A method of expressing the ratio between two quantities (Q1,Q2). Np=log(n)xQ1/Q2. One Neper equals 8,686 decibels.

NEST To embed a set of instructions or a block data within another.

NET NETwork.

NET 1000 A data communications network and processing service of AT&T that never got off the ground and was closed down at a cost of about $1 billion. At one stage it was called Advanced Communications Service.

NET ADDRESS The location on a network where an addressee's mail is held, usually in storage until the user logs into the system. The system delivers the message at that time. The Net Address in the header of a message gives the information required by an automated message processing or message switch, to deliver a message to an intended addressee. A net address of RA3Y#SAIL would designate that the message was addressed to the user with the "Net Name" of "RA3Y" (pronounced "Ray". The 3 is silent) located at (signified by the symbol "#") the system in the network called "SAIL", in this case, the Stanford (University) Artificial Intelligence Laboratory.

NET LOSS The signal loss encountered in a transmission facility or network, or the sum of all the losses the signal encounters on its way to its final destination.

NET/ONE The family of local area network products, bridges, gateways, network interfaces and software from Ungermann-Bass, Santa Clara, CA.

NETBIOS Network Basic Input/Output System. Originally designed as the network controller for IBM's PC Network LAN, NetBIOS has now been extended to allow programs written using the NetBIOS interface to operate on the IBM Token ring. Application programs adhering to the NetBIOS interface standard will end up sending the same PU 2.1 calls to the token ring card handler as APPC programs do when using the more extensive LU 6.2. NetBIOS has been adopted as something of an industry standard. It offers LAN applications, a variety of "hooks" to carry out inter-application communications and data transfer. To run an application that works with NetBIOS, a non-IBM network operating system or network interface card must offer a NetBIOS emulator. More and more hardware and software vendors offer these emulators. They aren't always perfectly compatible, though.

NETVIEW An IBM network management product that integrates the functions of three formerly separate Communications Network Management (CNM) software programs: 1. NCCF. Network Communication Control Facility. 2. NLDM. Network Logical Data Manager, which uses functions from NCCF and helps pinpoint problems along the logical connection/path of an SNA session. 3. NPDA. Network Problem Determination Application, which displays various alerts using IBM equipment located at strategic points in the network and allows diagnostic information to be displayed. Also, NetView incorporates some of the functions from two other programs: VNCA (Virtual Telecommunications Access Method/Node Control Application) which monitors the status and current activity of all resources in a domain, and NMPF (Network Management Productivity Facility) which helps the network operator to install, learn and use many network management products. See also NETWORK and NETWORK MANAGEMENT.

NETWARE An extremely popular local area network operating system from Novell, Orem, UT.

NETWORK 1. Networks are common in our lives. Think about trains and phones. A networks ties things together. Computer networks connect all types of computers and computer-related things — terminals, printers, modems, door entry sensors, temperature monitors, etc. The networks we're most familiar with are long distance ones, like phones and trains. But there are also Local Area Networks (LANs) which exist within a limited geographic area — like the few hundred feet of a small office, an entire building or even a "campus," such as a university or industrial park. There are also Metropolitan Area Networks (MANs). See also LAN and MAN.

NETWORK ACCESS CONTROL Electronic circuitry that determines which workstation may transmit next or when a particular workstation may transmit.

NETWORK ADDRESS The signaling code containing network identification.

NETWORK ADDRESSABLE UNIT NAU. In IBM's SNA, a logical unit (LU), physical unit (PU) or system services control point (SSCP), which is host-based, that is the origin or destination of information transmitted by the path control portion of an SNA network.

NETWORK ARCHITECTURE The structure and protocols of a computer network. See ARCHITECTURE.

NETWORK BALANCING 1. Lumped circuit elements (inductances, capacitances and resistances) connected so as to simulate the impedance of a uniform cable or open-wire circuit over a band of frequencies. 2. Moving circuits around in a multi-node switching network such the switching loads on each of similar switching modules are roughly equal.

NETWORK CHANNEL TERMINATING EQUIPMENT NCTE. A

device mounted on the user's premises used to amplify, match impedance or match network signaling to the customer's equipment connected to the network. Basically, network channel terminating equipment is a general name for equipment linking the network to a customer's premises.

NETWORK RECONFIGURATION SERVICE NRS is a New York Telephone service that lets you control, rearrange and switch your private line voice, private line analog data and Superpath 1.544 Mbps lines. You might wish to do this because you want to temporarily join one office to another for a high-speed data dump, or for a videoconference. Or in case something happens and you may want to route yourself around the trouble. You can reconfigure you own network in one of two ways — using a computer terminal or PC to dial in your instructions or call an 800 number and have an NYTel attendant do it for you. Rearrangements can be made in near-real time or scheduled for an appointed time.

NETWORK CONTROL POINT In IBM SNA networks, a host-generated program that controls the operation of a communications controller (such as an IBM 3705 or 3725).

NETWORK CONTROL SIGNALING The transmission of signals used in the telecommunications system which perform functions such as supervision, address signaling and audible tone signals to control the operation of switching machines in the telecommunication system.

NETWORK CONTROL SIGNALING UNIT A telephone set that controls the transmission of signals into the telephone system which will perform supervision, number identification and control of the switching machines.

NETWORK CONTROLLER A powerful microprocessor device designed to perform communications protocol translations between various terminals and computers and an X.25 packet switching network.

NETWORK, DISTRIBUTED See DISTRIBUTED NETWORK.

NETWORK ELEMENTS NE. Entities defined by the functionality of the functional groups they contain and by their interfaces. Definition from Bellcore in reference to its concept of the Advanced Intelligent Network.

NETWORK EQUALIZING A device connected to a transmission path in order to alter the characteristics of that path in a specified way. Often used to equalize the frequency response characteristic of a circuit for data transmission.

NETWORK EXTENSION UNIT NEU. An AT&T thing which sits in a telephone satellite closet (their words) which links up to 11 Starlan daisy chained clusters of PCs, etc. in a star configuration through standard telephone wiring, modular cords and plugs.

NETWORK HARM The reasoning behind the Bell System's insistence that the public could not hook its own equipment to the telephone line for fear it would produce "Irreparable Harm To The Network." A Bell System publication quoted the National Academy of Sciences as identifying four areas of potential harm. They were: Excessive signal power, hazardous voltage, improper network control signaling and line imbalance. Since the Carterfone Decision in the summer of 1968, the FCC has seen fit to allow devices, which pass an FCC Registration program, to be connected to the network, and while the quality of the stuff is occasionally poor, the fears of Network Harm have proven groundless. The fears were, of course, raised to preserve the Bell System's erstwhile almost-monopoly on the manufacture of telephone equipment in the U.S.

NETWORK INTERFACE The point of interconnection between Telephone Company communications facilities and terminal equipment, protective apparatus or wiring at a subscriber's premises. The network interface or demarcation point shall be located on the subscriber's side of the Telephone Company's protector, or the equivalent thereof in cases where a protector is not employed, as provided under the local telephone company's reasonable and nondiscriminatory standard operating practices.

NETWORK INTERFACE CARD Electronic circuitry connecting a workstation to a network. Usually a card that fits into one of the expansion slots inside a personal computer. It works with the network software and computer operating system to transmit and receive messages on the network.

NETWORK INTERFACE CONTROLLER Same as a Network Interface Card.

NETWORK INTERFACE DEVICE NID. A device wired between a telephone protector and the inside wiring to isolate the customer's equipment from the network.

NETWORK INWARD DIALING NID. See DIRECT INWARD DIALING.

NETWORK LAYER Third layer of the OSI model of data communications. Involves routing data messages through the network on alternate routes. See OSI STANDARDS.

NETWORK MANAGEMENT A set of procedures, software, equipment and operations designed to keep a network operating near maximum efficiency. Network management generally falls into five areas:

1. CONFIGURATION MANAGEMENT deals with installing, initializing, "boot" loading, modifying and tracking the configuration parameters of network hardware and software.
2. FAULT LOCATION and REPAIR MANAGEMENT tools let you find out what's going wrong with what equipment or lines and give you the ability to fix those resources — by re-routing traffic on different lines or reporting problems to the carrier, or suggesting to whoever that certain equipments should be replaced. Fault location and management tools have strong error and alarm characteristics.
3. SECURITY MANAGEMENT tools allow the network manager to restrict access to various resources in the network. There are devices such as password protection schemes, giving users different levels of access to different network resources.

4. PERFORMANCE MANAGEMENT tools provide real-time and historical statistical information about the network's operation. Such tools show, for example, how many packets are being transmitted at any given moment, the number of users logged into a specific server and use of network lines.
5. ACCOUNTING MANAGEMENT applications help users allocate the costs of the various network resources — from lines to PBXs, from access to a mainframe to time used on printers.

See NETVIEW.

NETWORK MANAGEMENT CONTROL CENTER NMCC. A central place from which the network is maintained and changed and from where statistical information is collected.

NETWORK MANAGEMENT SYSTEM A comprehensive system of equipment used in monitoring, controlling and managing a data communications network. Usually consists of testing devices, CRT displays and printers, patch panels and circuitry for diagnostics and reconfiguration of channels, generally housed together in an operator console unit.

NETWORK OPERATING SYSTEM NOS. The software side of a LAN. The program that controls the operation of a network. It allows users to communicate and share files and peripherals. It provides the user interface to the LAN, and it communicates with the LAN hardware or network interface card. It is important to note that a network operating system is different from a network interface card: IBM's Token Ring, for example, is an interface card, not a NOS. IBM's NOS is called the PC LAN Support Program. A variety of other vendors also offer NOSs, including Novell and 3Com. Most have drivers to support a variety of network interface cards.

NETWORK OPERATIONS Functions that provide, maintain and administer services supported by the network systems. These functions reside in network systems or network operations applications that interface directly to network systems and include memory administration, surveillance, testing, network traffic management and network data collection. Definition from Bellcore in reference to its concept of the Advanced Intelligent Network.

NETWORK OPERATIONS CENTER A name for the central place which monitors the status of a corporate network and sends out instructions to repair bits and pieces of the network when they break. In more formal terms, monitoring of network status, supervision and coordination of network maintenance, accumulation of accounting and usage data and user support.

NETWORK OUTWARD DIALING See DIRECT OUTWARD DIALING.

NETWORK PROBLEM DETERMINATION APPLICATION NPDA. A host-resident IBM program product that aids a network operator in interactively identifying network problems from a central point.

NETWORK PROTECTION DEVICE NPD. A device which provides isolation between PBX circuits and CO trunks or tie lines.

NETWORK SERVICES In IBM's SNA, the services within network addressable units (NAUs) that control network operations via sessions to and from the SSCP.

NETWORK TERMINAL NUMBER NTN. The number assigned to a data terminal under the Data Network Identification Code system.

NETWORK TERMINAL OPTION NTO. An IBM program product that enables an SNA network to accommodate a select group of non-SNA asynchronous and bisynch devices via the NCP-driven communications controller.

NETWORK TERMINATING UNIT NTU. The part of the network equipment which connects directly to the data terminal equipment.

NETWORK TERMINATION 1 The ISDN Network Termination 1 (NT1) provides an interface between the ISDN loop and an S or T interface terminal, such as an ISDN phone, or the PCTA (Personal Computer Terminal Adapter). The PCTA is the device which turns a normal IBM PC or IBM clone into an ISDN terminal/phone. The NTI is the classic ISDN "black box." It sits on the subscribers premises at the end of the subscriber loop coming in from the phone company. It talks to the ISDN central office. And, in turn, all ISDN terminals, phones and other devices on the subscriber premises are plugged into this black box. The basic NT1 functions are:

- Line transmission termination;
- Layer 1 line maintenance functions and performance monitoring;
- Layer 1 multiplexing; and
- Interface termination, including multidrop termination employing layer 1 contention resolution.

See ISDN.

NETWORK TOPOLOGY The geometric arrangement of links and nodes of a network. The geography of a network. Networks are typically of either a

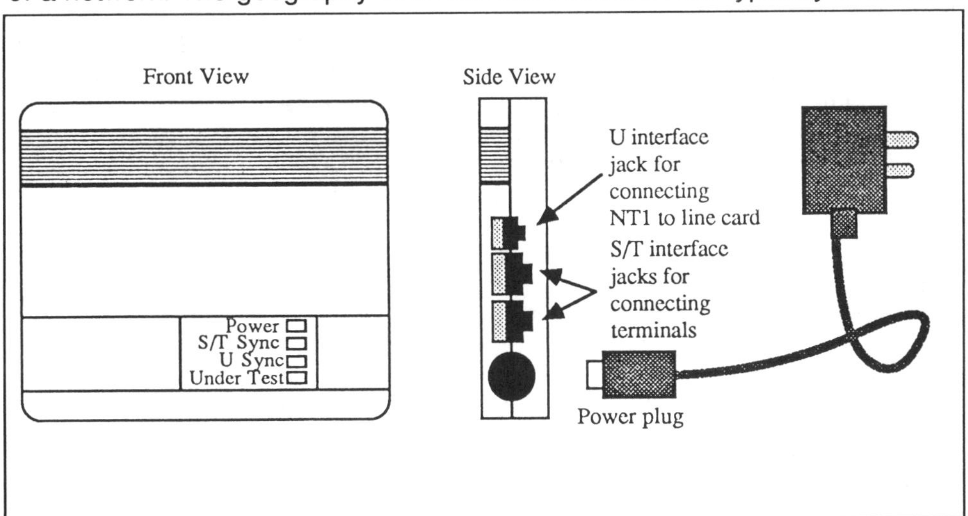

courtesy Northern Telecom

star, ring, tree or bus topology, or some hybrid combination.

NETWORK TRAFFIC MANAGEMENT NTM. Functionality that maximizes the traffic throughput of the network during times of overload or failure and minimizes the impact of one service on the performance of others. This is done through centralized surveillance of maintenance conditions and traffic, and centralized control of traffic volumes being originated in network systems (e.g., call gapping). Definition from Bellcore in reference to its concept of the Advanced Intelligent Network.

NETWORK VIRTUAL TERMINAL A communications concept wherein a variety of DTEs, with different data rates, protocols, codes and formats, are accommodated in the same network. This is done as a result of network processing, where each device's data is converted into a network standard format and then converted into the format of the receiving device at the destination end.

NEURAL NETWORK COMPUTER A very different kind of computer. Neural network computers are built from webs of randomly connected electronic neurons. These machines are designed to be trained, not programmed. In design and in function, they are meant to closely resemble the human brain. As in the brain, the neurons send signals to one another through thousands of adjustable connections, or synapses. As the machine learns, the settings of these controls are automatically turned up or down. And the chaos of connections evolves into a finely tuned machine, one that can read handwritten letters or recognize the spoken words. With a neural network computer, a trainer simply speaks words to the machine, rewarding it if it acts correctly and punishing it when it acts incorrectly. There is hope that neural network computers may perform better than traditional computers in running artificial intelligence software.

NEUTRAL TRANSMISSION Unipolar transmission. A form of signaling which employs two distinct states, one of which represents the existence of a space as well as the absence of current.

NEW LINE ASCII character 10, abbreviated "NL". This character replaced the abbreviation "LF" which meant Line Feed. Newer terminals accept the NL character to mean both CR (Carriage Return) and LF functions for "end of line" sequences. The function of transmitting an "end of line" sequence to a printer or remote computer system is to designate to a computer to print what follows on the next line of a print out. This usually consists of transmitting the characters CR, LF (Carriage Return, followed by Line Feed). On older printing terminals, these two characters would be followed by a number of null characters whose job would be to waste time until the print head got back to the left margin before printing the first letter of the next line on the page. Otherwise, that character would be in the middle of the page, and the second character would start the line. Telex machines usually send the sequence CR, LF, CR as a New Line sequence to give the head enough time to get back.

NEWBRIDGE NETWORKS A manufacturer of good T-1 muxes, channel banks and other digital communications devices founded by Terry Matthews, co-founder of Mitel, and Peter Madsen, who also made his fortune with Mitel. Newbridge is one of our favorite companies. Terry and Peter will be pleased when they see their name in this dictionary.

NI Network Interface. Demarkation point between PSTN and CPE.

NIA Network Interface Adapter. An IBM hardware device that with certain software, will allow an SNA device to communicate over a packet switching network.

NIBBLE Four bits or half a byte.

NIBBLE INTERLEAVING/MULTIPLEXING A technique where 4 bit nibbles (one at a time) from each lower speed input a channel are used to build the higher speed frame output of a multiplexer.

NIC Near Instantaneous Companding. This describes the very fast, essentially real-time, process of quantizing an analog signal into digital symbols.

NIF Network Interface Function.

NIGHT ANSWER Incoming calls to a switchboard during evening and weekend hours are automatically rerouted to ring only at designated night answering phones such as the security desk. See the next few definitions.

NIGHT ANSWER — ASSIGNED Night answer going to specific, assigned telephones.

NIGHT ANSWER — OFFSITE Phones being answered after hours by people and machinery located offsite — someplace else.

NIGHT ANSWER — UNIVERSAL Anybody and everybody can answer the incoming calls from any phone. In TELECONNECT, if the phone rings after hours, we simply touch "6" on any phone and we can answer that incoming call — whether it's a local, normal DDD or incoming WATS.

NIGHT AUDIT This feature provides automatic printout of message registration data for all quest rooms at the front desk console.

NIGHT CHIME An auxiliary ringer, usually wall mounted, used to indicate a ringing trunk during night operations or used as a "phantom" extension for overflow applications.

NIGHT CONSOLE POSITION Provides an alternate attendant position which can be used at night in lieu of the regular console. Usually cheaper than buying a second normal console.

NIGHT PATCH Assigned Night Answer, Fixed Night Service, Programmable Night Connections. Provides arrangements (which are prewired into the system) to route incoming central office calls normally answered at the attendant position, to preselected stations within the PBX system when the attendant is not on duty.

NIGHT SERVICE AUTOMATIC SWITCHING Should the attendant neglect to place the console in the night answering mode, after a certain period of timed ringing from an incoming central office call, the entire system will automatically jump to the night service.

NIGHT SERVICE — EXPANDED SERVICE Routes calls normally directed to the attendant to preselected station lines within the system when it is arranged for night service. Calls to specific exchange trunks can be arranged to route to specific station lines and can be assigned on a flexible basis. Trunk Answer From Any Station capability is provided for calls which are handled by assigned night stations.

NIGHT SERVICE — FIXED SERVICE Provides arrangements to route calls normally directed to the attendant to preselected station lines within the PBX system when regular attendant positions are not in use. In addition, calls to specific trunks can be arranged to ring on specific phones. The receiving phone can then transfer the call.

NIGHT STATION The phone assigned to automatically handle incoming calls after the main switchboard has shut down for the day.

NIH Not Invented Here. The tendency of organizations to reject ideas and inventions which they didn't think of. A major and continuing problem in the telephone industry.

NIOD Network Inward/Outward Dialing.

NL See NEW LINE.

NLDM Network Logical Data Manager. An IBM term. See also NETVIEW.

NMOS N-channel Metal Oxide Semiconductor.

NNX/NXX A three-digit code to identify the local central office in which N represents any digit from 2 to 9 and X is any digit. NNX/NXX means the first three digits of a North American telephone number. Originally, only NNX codes were used to identify and number local central offices. Now all subscribers dial 1+ when making a direct distance dialed long distance call. And central offices are being changed to be NXX — which gives us more numbers. Area codes are also being expanded to include NXX codes.

NO ATTENDANT OPTION CBX systems with Direct Inward Dialing may be designed (configured) without an attendant console.

NO LINE PREFERENCE Requires the user to manually select (i.e. punch down) a line for each call.

NON-BLOCKING A PBX is Non-Blocking if all callers can be switched through the PBX even during the busiest time of day. However, the caller may find no trunks are available and thus may not be able to complete the call. The trunk availability is a different problem than the ability of the switch to handle all the traffic it gets. But if your call does not go through do you care? A more technical explanation from InteCom of non-blocking: "Indicates that the internal network of the switching system is such that the total number of available transmission paths is equal to the number of ports. Therefore, all ports can have simultaneous access through the network."

NONCONSECUTIVE HUNTING Often referred to as "jump hunting." Nonconsecutive lines, trunks or extensions can be accessed upon dialing the initial number in the hunting group. Nonconsecutive hunting can be used on incoming and outgoing lines. For example, you could order four trunks from your local phone company which are to "hunt" on. Should the first be busy, the call will go to the next. If the next is busy, then it will hunt to the next. TELECONNECT Magazine has "consecutive" numbering in its first four phone numbers — 212-691-8215, 8216, 8217 and 8218. But let's say we only started with one number and then, because of growth, we needed three more. It's possible consecutive numbers might be taken. Therefore to get the hunting feature, the phone company might have assigned us NONCONSECUTIVE hunting numbers like 691-8220, 8256, 8678. Sometimes the phone company will also assign us "coded" trunks as part of our trunk group. These are trunks which have no dialable number associated with them. It's best to get real numbers so you can test them by calling them individually. You cannot test coded trunks.

NON-ERASABLE A switch where a through traffic path always exists for each attached phone. Generically, a switch or switching environment designed never to experience a busy condition due to call volume. See NON-BLOCKING, which is a better term.

NON-IMPACT PRINTER Refers to printers that do not strike a hammer to a platen as typewriters do. Usually a heat sensitive paper or laser/xerox type technology is involved.

NON-INTELLIGIBLE CROSSTALK Crosstalk which is not of sufficient level to be understood by a listener but which is more annoying than other crosstalk because you think it's intelligible. Or think it should be intelligible.

NON-LINEAR DISTORTION Amplitude distortion of a signal in which the output signal does not have a linear relationship to the input signal.

NON-LOADED LINES Cable pairs or transmission lines with no added inductive loading coils. In short, straight, raw copper pairs. See LOAD COILS.

NON-PERSISTENT In local area networking technology, describes a carrier sense multiple access (CSMA) local area network (LAN) in which the stations involved in a collision do not try to retransmit immediately — even if the network is quiet. Compare with persistent and p-persistent.

NON-PRINTING CHARACTER A character in a transmission code which performs a control function but is not reproduced when the transmission is printed.

NON-PROPRIETARY LAN A Local Area Network that can connect the equipment of many vendors. See PROPRIETARY LAN.

NON-SENT PAID Utility industry term for calls made as third party billings, reversed charges or with a Calling Card.

NON-SESSION A type of synchronous access mode that can exist between an end user and a host computer in an Amdahl packet network. In non-session access, the calling line (PU) is mapped to a specific offering line (LU). The offering line is reserved for that calling line at all times.

NON-SIMULTANEOUS TRANSMISSION Half duplex transmission. Transmission in one direction at a time. This mode of transmission may be the result of limitations of the transmission channel or of the transmitting/receiving equipment.

NON-SYNCHRONOUS COMMUNICATIONS See ASYNCHRONOUS COMMUNICATIONS.

NON-TRAFFIC SENSITIVE PLANT Telephone company facilities which are unaffected by changes in volume of telephone activity.

NON-TRANSPARENT MODE A transmission environment, mainly of bisynch transmission, in which control characters and control-character sequences are recognized through the examination of all transmitted data. Compare with transparent mode. Also called normal mode.

NON-VOLATILE Memory which is not lost (i.e. that does not "forget") when the power is shut off.

NON-WIRELINE FCC regulations restrict providers of cellular telephone service in any given market to one wireline carrier (the local telephone company) and one nonwireline carrier (any company other than local telephone company).

NOC Networks Operations Center.

NOD Network Outward Dialing. See DIRECT OUTWARD DIALING.

NODE A point of connection into a network. In multipoint networks, it means it's a unit that's polled. In LANs, it's a device on the ring. In packet switched networks, it's one of the many packet switches which form the network's backbone.

NODE TYPE In IBM's SNA, the classification of a network device based on the protocols it supports and the network addressable units (NAUs) it can contain. Type 1 and Type 2 nodes are peripheral nodes. Type 4 and 5 nodes are subarea nodes.

NOISE Unwanted electrical signals introduced into telephone lines by circuit components or natural disturbances which tend to degrade the performance of the line. Also known as Line Noise.

NOISE MEASUREMENT UNITS A series of terms used to express circuit noise. These units include: -dB RN — Decibel rated noise -dBrnC — C message weighting refers to the noise measured at 1000 Hz.

NOISE SUPPRESSOR Filtering or digital signal-processing circuitry in a receiver or transmitter that automatically eliminates or reduces noise.

NOISE WEIGHTING A method of assigning a specific value to the transmission impairment due to the noise encountered by an average user operating a particular telephone. Noise weightings generally in use have been established by regulatory agencies concerned with public telephone service. They are tightened as technology improves.

NORTH AMERICAN NUMBERING PLAN The method of identifying telephone trunks in the public network of North America, called World Numbering Zone 1 by the CCITT. The Plan has three ways of identifying phone numbers in North America — a three digit area code, a three digit exchange or central office code and four digit subscriber code. Other countries have much more complicated numbering schemes. There are some countries, for example, where the length of the area code actually exceeds the subscriber code. There are many countries where there is no consistency in the length of phone numbers. Some are nine-digit. Some are 12-digit, etc. All these varying number lengths may be within 100 miles of each other.

NORTH AMERICAN TELECOMMUNICATIONS ASSOCIATION NATA. The national trade association for companies providing customer premise telephone equipment. NATA represents the interests of the industry before the Congress, the FCC and in court actions. See also NATA.

NORSTAR A family of telephone systems from Northern Telecom.

NORSTAR COMMAND SET A series of standard commands for programming a telephone system. These commands were created by Northern Telecom to program their Norstar telephone system. The Norstar Command Set includes commands such as:

mDisconnectCall

mDialDigits

mJoinCalls

mOnEvent

mOnErrorEvent

mTermWrite (which means to write to the phone's screen).

In creating this command set, Northern Telecom saw two types of applications for its Norstar telephone system:

1. Server applications and, 2. Personal telephony applications. Server applications would include automatic call distribution, dial by name, predictive dialing, dial from a computer and transfer a database record and the call to an agent.

Personal telephony applications include on-screen dialing for telemarketing. placing a call in an electronic rolodex by hitting "ENTER."

Under the Norstar Command set, a programmer can take complete control of a phone system away from its central factory-programming. Using the Norstar command set, one momeent a phone could be an ACD agent terminal, the next moment a data input terminal and the third an operator position.

NPA 1. Numbering Plan Area. A fancy way of saying Area Codes. There are over 200 area codes in the United States, Canada, Bermuda, the Caribbean, Northwestern Mexico, Alaska and Hawaii. Within any of these area codes, no two telephone lines may have the same seven digit phone number. The middle number has been either "1" or "0" creating "N 1/0 x" codes. The number of codes available on this basis were nearing depletion. Bellcore has now modified the plan to obtain more area codes. Future area codes will be NXX like the central office numbering scheme. Switching systems in the national network will differentiate between the central office and area codes by recognizing the subscriber always dials 1+ or 0+ preceding an area code when direct dialing such long distance calls.

2. In IBM language, it means Network Performance Analyzer, a product for network tuning, determining performance, degradation and determining the affect of network growth.

3. AT&T National Pricing Agreement. A multi-year agreement an AT&T customer signs with AT&T which specifies that the customer will buy $xxx of equipment and services from AT&T at a "deep" discount. (This definition from AT&T.)

NPD See NETWORK PROTECTION DEVICE.

NPDA Network Problem Determination Application. An IBM term. See NETVIEW.

NPM Network Process Monitor.

NPSI Network Packet Switching Interface. Software package that allows Systems Network Architecture (SNA) 3270 traffic to be transmitted over an X.25 packet data network (PDN). See also QLLC. Contrast with DSP.

NRM NORMAL RESPONSE of HDLC.

NRZ Non-Return to Zero. A binary encoding scheme in which ones and zeroes are represented by opposite and alternating high and low voltages and where there is no return to a zero (reference) voltage between encoded bits.

NRZI Non-Return to Zero Inverted. A binary encoding scheme that inverts the signal on a "one" and leaves the signal unchanged for a "zero". Where a change in the voltage signals a "one" bit, and the absence of a change denotes a "zero" bit value. Also called transition coding.

NSC Network Service Center. See NETWORK CONTROL POINT and SDN.

NT-1 Network Termination type 1. The NT-1 is a customer premise device in ISDN which converts from two-wire transmission (or "U" Interface). It supports network maintenance functions such as loop testing. Up to 8 terminal devices may be addressed by an NT-1. See NETWORK TERMINATION 1.

NT-2 In ISDN, the Network Termination type 2 is an intelligent customer premise device which can perform switching and concentration, such as a digital PBX. It typically terminates primary rate access lines from the local ISDN CO switch. It may include the Layer 1 functions of a NT-1, and the protocol handling functions of Layers 2 and 3. See NETWORK TERMINATION 1.

NTIA National Telecommunications and Information Administration. An agency of the U.S. Department of Commerce concerned with the development of communications (primarily telephony) standards.

NTCA National Telephone Cooperative Association. A trade association representing primarily rural telephone cooperatives and other small telephone companies.

NTN See NETWORK TERMINAL NUMBER.

NTO Network Terminal Option. An IBM program product that enables an SNA network to accommodate a select group non-SNA asynchronous and bisynchronous devices via the NCP-driven communications controller.

NTS Network Test System.

NTSC North American Television Standards Committee. The initials are used to describe the standard method of television transmission in North America. PAL is the name of the format for color TV signals used in West Germany, England, Holland, Australia and several other countries. It uses an interlaced format with 25 frames per second and 625 lines per frame. In contrast, the US system called NTSC uses interlaced scans and 525 horizontal lines per frame at a rate of 30 frames per second. The two systems are not compatible. You cannot view an Australian videotape on a US TV.

When TV engineers get together to hoist some brews, however, the initials for the various standards for TV broadcast take on other meanings, such as: NTSC, Never Twice the Same Color. PAL, Peace at Last. PAL-M, Peace At Last — Maybe. SECAM (French system) becomes System Essentially Contrary to the American Method. We bother mentioning it because if you try to take computer terminals outside the country and connect the video outputs to monitors, you will be made aware of the many TV and video monitor "standards" in use.

NTSC SIGNAL National Television System Committee specified signal. De-facto standard governing the format of television transmission signals in the United States.

NUI Network User Identifier. A unique alphanumeric number provided to dial-up users to identify them to packet switched networks around the world. The number is used to get onto the network and for billing.

NULL CHARACTERS Characters transmitted to fill space, time or to "pad" something. They add nothing to the meaning of a transmitted message, but the null characters are expected by the system. On older teletype machines, for example, when the type head reaches the end of a line and the New Line sequence is transmitted, it usually includes a number of Null Characters in order to give the mechanical type head enough time to reach the left margin of the page before transmitting the next line to the terminal. In this manner, no characters are lost. MCI Mail uses five null characters at the beginning of every line — unless you tell it otherwise.

NULL MODEM CABLE Special wiring of an RS-232-C cable such that a computer can talk to another computer without a modem (thus "null" modem) or a computer can talk to a printer. Essentially, a null modem cable reverses pins 2 and 3 on an RS-232-C cable. But there are no standard null modem cables. And other pins need changing and jumpering together. Control Cable in Baltimore, MD sells one that works for us.

NUMBER CRUNCHING A repetitive series of mathematical calculations.

NUMBERING PLAN 1. In Wide Area Networks, the method for assigning NNX codes to provide a unique telephone address for each subscriber, special line or trunk destination. 2. In PBX's, the method of assigning extension numbers and trunk designations at the local premises.

NUMBERING PLAN AREA NPA. A fancy term the Bell System came up with years ago to mean Area Codes. See NPA.

NUMBERS SHIFT A character in the Baudot code which establishes that the characters following in the transmission are to be interpreted as numeric characters. See LETTERS SHIFT.

NUMERIC KEY PAD A separate section of a computer keyboard which contains all the numerals 0 through 9. Sometimes, some special keys are included — a plus sign, a minus sign, a multiplication sign and a division sign. The numeric key pad on a computer is the same as that found on calculators and adding machines. The top row is 789. The second top row is 456. The third top row is 123. The lowest row is typically 0, "." and "+". The numeric key pad is exactly opposite that of the touchtone telephone keypad, which was designed deliberately to be unfamiliar to users, so they may not input digits into the nation's telephone system faster than it could take them. Early touchtone central offices were very slow.

NXX In a seven digit local phone number, the first three digits identify the specific telco central office which serves that number. These digits are referred to as the NXX where N can be any number from 2 to 9 and X can be any number from 0 through 9. Until recently the middle digit was a 0 or 1. But the need for more exchange codes has forced this to change. The phone industry solved the confusion by forcing users to dial "1" for a "long distance" number within their own area code. This little trick allowed us to introduce telephone exchanges with the same three digits as area codes. For example, one of our numbers is 212-206-6660. The "206" elsewhere is an area code for Seattle and other parts of Washington state.

NYNEX CORPORATION One of the seven Regional Holding Companies formed at Divestiture. It includes New England Telephone and New York Telephone Company and sundry other service and cellular radio companies.

NYQUIST THEOREM In communications theory, a formula stating that two samples per cycle is sufficient to characterize an analog signal. In other words, the sampling rate must be twice the highest frequency component of the signal (i.e., sample 4 KHz analog voice channels 8,000 times per second.)

O+ CALLS Called "OH PLUS." O+ plus calls are calls made by dialing zero plus the desired telephone number. Calls made this way may be interrupted by a live operator requesting billing information, or a recorded announcement requesting the caller to enter the billing information.

O- CALLS Called "OH MINUS." O- calls are operator-assisted calls. The caller dials zero and waits for the operator to pick up the line and talk to the caller.

O/E Optic to Electric conversion.

OA Office Automation. Nobody knows what it means. But there are many consultants out there who will tell you for the right amount of money.

OAM Operations, Administration and Maintenance. Some switches have computers devoted to OAM. Northern Telecom, for example, uses a Sun Microsystems 3/80 B-4 processor in one of its central office switches.

OAMP Operation, Administration, Maintenance and Provisioning.

OBJECT CODE Instruction code in machine language produced as the output of a compiler or a assembler. The original program, or code, is called the source Code.

OC-1 Optical Carrier level-1. The optical counterpart of STS-1 (the basic rate, 51.840 Mbps, on which Sonet is based). Direct electrical-to-optical mapping of the STS-1 signal with frame synchronous scrambling. All higher levels are direct multiples of OC-1 (i.e., OC-3 = 3 times OC-1,etc).

OCC Other Common Carriers. Carriers providing long distance communications service other than AT&T. Nowadays, these companies (including AT&T) are called IXCs — IntereXchange Carriers.

OCCUPANCY The time a circuit or a switch is in use, i.e. occupied.

OCR See OPTICAL CHARACTER RECOGNITION or OUTGOING CALL RESTRICTION.

OCTAL A numbering system with the base eight.

OCTET An eight-bit byte.

OCTOPUS A device attached to the end of a connectorized feeder cable that converts the single 25-pair cable into individual 2, 4, 6 and 8 wire connectors.

OCUDP Office Channel Unit Data Port. A channel bank unit used to interface between the channel bank and a customer's DDS CSU or DSU.

ODA OFFICE DOCUMENT ARCHITECTURE ISO's standard 8613-1/8 for document architecture and interchange format adopted by MAP/TOP 3.O, GOSIP, and standardized by ECMA as ECMA-101.

ODD PARITY One of many methods for detecting errors in transmitted data. An extra bit is added to each character sent and that bit is given a value of 0 ("zero") or 1 ("one") such that the total number of ones in the character (including the parity bit) will be odd.

OEM Original Equipment Manufacturer. The maker of equipment marketed by another vendor, usually under the name of the reseller. The OEM may only manufacture certain components, or complete computers, which are then often configured with software and/or other hardware, by the reseller.

OFF-HOOK When the handset is lifted from its cradle it's Off-Hook. Lifting the hookswitch alerts the central office that the user wants the phone to do something like dial a call. A dial tone is a sign saying "Give me an order." The term "off-hook" originated when the early handsets were actually suspended from a metal hook on the phone. When the handset is removed from its hook or its cradle (in modern phones), it completes the electrical loop, thus signaling the central office that it wishes dial tone. Some leased line channels work by lifting the handset, signaling the central office at the other end which rings the phone at the other end. Some phones have autodialers in them. Lifting the phone signals the phone to dial that one number. An example is a phone without a dial at an airport, which automatically dials the local taxi company. All this by simply lifting the handset at one end — going "off-hook."

OFF-HOOK QUEUE There are two types of queuing: ON-HOOK and OFF-HOOK. In On-Hook Queuing, the user dials his number, the switch tells him the outgoing trunks are busy. The user then hangs up. The switch calls him back when a trunk becomes available. In Off-Hook dialing, the user waits with his receiver screwed into his ear until a trunk comes free and the PBX connects him to the next available trunk. Off-Hook queues are usually shorter than on-hook queues. If a trunk doesn't come free quickly in off-hook queuing, the call will often flow over onto the more expensive DDD trunks. Off-hook queuing costs more but keeps the user waiting less. On-hook queuing costs less by waiting for a cheaper trunk but can be tiring and frustrating for the workers waiting for their calls to go through.

OFF-HOOK ROUTING See OFFHOOK and RINGDOWN.

OFF-HOOK VOICE ANNOUNCE A telephone system feature. A telephone has a speaker. If the person is speaking on the phone, another person (inside the building, on the same phone system) can "off-hook voice announce" you and can give you a message or speak with you. You will hear their voice coming through the speaker on your phone. (So may the person on the other end.) Depending on your phone, you may be able to put your hand over your telephone handset and whisper something back to the person who's "off-hook voice announcing" you. Otherwise you'll have to hang up or put the person on hold, and speak to the person on another line.

OFF-LINE Any equipment not actively connected to a phone line but which can be activated to work with that system is Off-Line. This concept also applies to computer systems. For example, a modem attached to or built into a microcomputer can be plugged permanently into a phone line. But the microcomputer can be used for word processing most of the time. While it's doing word processing, it is "off-line." When the user loads the communications software and turns on the modem, the microcomputer is now said to be "on line."

OFF-NET CALLING Phone calls which are carried in part on a network but are destined for a phone not on the network, i.e. some part of the conversation's journey will be over the public switched network.

OFF-NETWORK ACCESS LINE ONAL. A circuit in a private network which allows the user to go off the private network and complete calls on the public dial network.

OFF-PREMISE EXTENSION OPX. Now also called OPS for Off-Premise Station. A telephone located in a different office or building from the main phone system. The OPX is connected by a phone line dedicated to it. It acts as if it were in the same place as the main phone system and can use its full capabilities. Here's another explanation a reader sent in. OPX is the appearance of an actual telephone line (such as 212-691-8215) in two physically separate locations. For example, this line (212-691-8215) could appear and ring in my office and at my home without my home phone being a part of the office telephone system. An OPX is commonly used for answering services or for small businesses. Bell operating phone companies are sharply increasing the charge for dedicated OPS lines — often by several hundred percent per year.

OFF-THE-SHELF When something has already been produced and is available for immediate delivery, it is said to be available "off-the shelf." It is presumably sitting on the shelf in a warehouse waiting for your order.

OFFERED LOAD The total telephone traffic load, including load that results from retries, submitted to a group of servers. See also OFFERED TRAFFIC.

OFFERED TRAFFIC The total attempts to seize a group of servers.

OFFICE CLASS Functional ranking of a telephone central office switch depending on transmission requirements and hierarchical relationship to other switching centers. (Awful mouthful!) There used to be five classes of switches in the U.S. telephone network hierarchy, with the one closest to the end-subscriber being a class 5 central office. But technology and marketing is changing things and, by distributing intelligence closer to the end user, it is diffusing our traditional definitions of network hierarchies and the class of switches. See CLASS 5 central office.

OFFICE CODE The first three digits of your seven-digit local telephone number. Also called NNX code.

OFFICE NETWORK A network within an office. An older term for a Local Area Network. User concern is with application sharing, file/database sharing, electronic mail, word processing and circuit switching.

OFFICE TELESYSTEM OTS. An AT&T office automation solution that runs on 3B computers and includes a family of allegedly low-cost, easy-to-use workstations.

OFFICE USER INTERFACE A special shell program which sets up windows with menus of available utilities and applications.

OFFICE WINDOW INTERFACE See OFFICE USER INTERFACE.

OFFSITE NIGHT ANSWER This mode allows incoming after-hours calls to be forwarded automatically to an offsite location.

OGT OutGoing trunk.

OHMS Measures of resistance. A resistance of one Ohm allows one Ampere to flow when a potential difference of one volt is applied to the resistance. See OHM'S LAW.

OHM'S LAW The law which relates current measured as Amps (I), voltage (V) and resistance measured as Ohms (R). Ohm's Law is E = I x R. It can also be expressed as I = V/R, or R = V/I. See OHMS.

OHQ Off-Hook Queue. See OFF-HOOK QUEUING.

OHSA Abbreviation for Occupational Safety and Health Act. Specifically the Williams-Steiger law passed in 1970 covering all factors relating to safety in places of employment.

OMAT Operational Measurement and Analysis Tool.

OMNI-DIRECTIONAL A microphone with a pickup pattern essentially uniform in all directions.

ON-HOOK When the phone handset is resting in its cradle. The phone is not connected to any particular line. Only the bell is active, i.e. it will ring if a call comes in. See OFF-HOOK.

ON-HOOK DIALING Allows a caller to dial a call without lifting his handset. After dialing, the caller can listen to the progress of the call over the phone's built-in speaker. When you hear the called person answer, you can pick up the handset and speak or you can talk hands-free in the direction of your phone, if it's a speakerphone. Critical: Many phones have speakers for hands-free listening. Not all phones with speakers are speakerphones — i.e. have microphones, which allow you to speak, also.

ON-LINE When a device is actively connected to a PBX or a computer, it is On-Line. Terminals, PCs, modems and phones are often On-Line.

ON-NET Telephone calls which stay on a customer's private network, traveling by private line from beginning to end are said to be on-net.

ONA See OPEN NETWORK ARCHITECTURE.

ONAC Operations Network Administration Center.

ONAL Off Network Access Line.

ONE NUMBER PRESENCE This is the consistent use of one telephone number (particularly an 800 number) across all advertising media. The long distance vendors can arrange this for both in-state and national 800 services.

ONE-WAY OPERATION See SIMPLEX.

ONE-WAY SPLITTING When the attendant is connected to an outside trunk and an internal phone, pushing a button on the console allows her to speak privately with the internal extension, thus "splitting" her off from the external trunk.

ONE-WAY TRUNK A trunk between a switch (PBX) and a central office, or between central offices, where traffic originates from only one end. You can, of course, still speak and listen on the trunk. It's just like a normal two-way trunk except that a one-way trunk can only be used for dialing out or only to receive calls.

ONES DENSITY The requirement for digital transmission lines in the public switched telephone network that eight consecutive zeros cannot be in a digital data streams. Ones density exists because repeaters and clocking devices within the network will lose timing after receiving eight zeros in a row. Any number of techniques or algorithms used to insert a one after every seventh-consecutive zero. See BIT STUFFING.

ONI Operator Number Identification.

OOF Out Of Frame. A designation for a condition defined as either the network or the DTE equipment sensing an error in framing bits. It's declared when 2 of 4 or 2 of 5 framing bits are missed (the OOF condition existing for 2.5 seconds generally creates a local Red Alarm).

OPEN Means the circuit is not complete. There is a break in it. A break does not necessarily mean it's malfunctioning, only that it's been turned off.

OPEN AIR TRANSMISSION Referring to a transmission type or associated equipment, that uses no physical communications medium other than air. Most radio communications systems, including microwave, shortwave and FM radio and infrared are open-air (also called "through-the-air") transmission systems.

OPEN CIRCUIT A circuit is not complete. There is no complete path for current flow. Electrical current cannot flow in the circuit.

OPEN ENDED ACCESS Term used to describe the ability to terminate a call to any public network destination. For example, on the open end of a foreign exchange circuit, the customer may call any number in the local calling area without being charged for long distance service.

OPEN LINE DEALING This is a term used by British Telecom in its turrets. The system electronically recreates the original "pit" share trading environment in the stock exchange in which everybody could talk to everybody else. In open line dealing, the trader has the ability to program a number of counterparties onto speakers. Full duplex speech is achieved using the associated microphones and all lines receive a simultaneous broadcast.

OPEN LOOP SYSTEM A control system which does not use feedback to determine its output.

OPEN NETWORK ARCHITECTURE ONA. If the FCC is to allow the Bell operating companies into the value-added business — voice mail, electronic mail, data processing etc. — then it must figure a way that the Bell operating companies don't organize things so they have an unfair advantage and greater chance of survival. The FCC wants other companies to get into these businesses also. Its latest idea is called ONA — Open Network Architecture. Under this concept, the telephone companies are obliged to provide a certain class of service to their own internal value-added divisions and the same class of service to external, nonaffiliated valued added companies. The concept is that the phone company's architecture is to be "open" and that everyone and anyone can gain access to it on equal footing. ONA is only a concept at present and still needs some rigorous defining.

OPEN SYSTEMS INTERCONNECTION See OSI.

OPEN WIRE A transmission facility comprised of pairs of bare (uninsulated) conductors supported on insulators which are mounted on poles to form an aerial (above ground) pole line. Most basic of all practical types of transmission media.

OPERAND That which is being operated on. An operand is usually identified by the address part of an instruction.

OPERATING ENVIRONMENT Referring to the combination of (usually IBM) host software that includes operating system, telecommunications access method, database software and user applications. Some common operating environments include MVS/CICS and MVS/TSO.

OPERATING SYSTEM A software program which manages the basic operations of a computer system. It figures how the computer main memory will be apportioned, how and in what order it will handle tasks assigned to it, how it will manage the flow of information into and out of the main processor, how it will get material to the printer for printing, to the screen for viewing, how it will receive information from the keyboard, etc. In short, the operating system handles the computer's basic housekeeping.

OPERATING TIME The time required for seizing the line, dialing the call and waiting for the connection to be established.

OPERATION CODE The command part of a machine instruction.

OPERATOR ASSISTED A phone call placed with the assistance of the carrier's operator. You pay more when you use an operator.

OPERATOR CONSOLE Same as attendant console. See ATTENDANT CONSOLE.

OPERATOR SERVICES Any of a variety of telephone services which need the assistance of an operator. Such services include collect calls, third-party billed calls and person-to-person calls.

OPS Off-Premises Station. See OFF PREMISES EXTENSIONS.

OPTICAL CHARACTER RECOGNITION OCR. Reading data using a machine that visually scans the characters in a document and converts that data into standard form which can be stored on conventional magnetic medium, e.g. floppy or hard disk. See OPTICAL SCANNER.

OPTICAL COMPUTER A computer that uses photons, not electrons as in today's old-fashioned computers. Scientists think photon computers and photon switches could be a thousand times faster than present computers and switches, and, of course, totally impervious to electromagnetic interference.

OPTICAL DISK Peripheral storage disk for programs and information. Optical disks are emerging as computer storage devices because of their tremendous storage capacities in comparison to magnetic disk. Optical disks are WORM — which stands for Write Once, Read Many Times, meaning you write once to the disk, and read that information many times. But with today's technology, you can't erase the information on the optical disk. It is not uncommon to be able to store 600 megabytes of information on an optical disk the size and shape of one you currently buy recorded music on.

OPTICAL FIBER Glass fiber for carrying lightwave communications. There are two types of optical fiber: Single Mode and Multimode. In single mode fiber, light can only take a single path through a core that measures about 10 microns in diameter. (A micron is one millionth of a meter.) Multimode fibers have thicker cores — typically 50 to 200 microns. Single mode fiber is more efficient. It offers low dispersion, travels great distances without repeaters and has enormous information carrying capacity. But it's more expensive to make. The relatively large core of multimode fiber lightguide allows light pulses to zig-zag along many different paths. It's also ideal for light sources larger than lasers, such as LEDs (Light Emitting Diodes). Multimode fiber is not the preferred method of optical telecommunications.

OPTICAL FIBER FACILITY Transmission system which uses glass fibers as the transmission medium.

OPTICAL SCANNER A hardware device that recognizes images on paper, film and other media and converts them into digital form which can be stored in a conventional computer readable magnetic medium, such as floppy or hard disk. Optical scanners are getting better and better but are still not perfect. See OCR.

OPTICAL TIME DOMAIN REFLECTOMETER OTDR. A device which measures the transparency of lightguide by means of an optical pulse. The ratio of incident and reflected light power is measured. By using this device you can figure precisely where a fiber optic link is broken. This device sends a pulse down the cable and waits for it to return. It measures the time taken and calculates the distance, based on the speed of light through the fiber optic.

OPTO-ELECTRICAL TRANSDUCER A device which converts electrical energy to optical energy and vice versa. Used as transmitters and receivers in fiber optic communications systems.

OPX See OFF PREMISE EXTENSION.

ORB Office Repeater Bay

ORDER WIRE 1. A circuit used by telephone personnel for fixing, installing and removing phone lines. 2. Equipment and the circuit providing a telephone company with the means to establish voice contact between central office and carrier repeater locations.

ORDER WIRE CIRCUIT A voice or data circuit used by telephone company technical control and maintenance personnel for the coordination and control action relating to activation, deactivation, change, rerouting, reporting and maintenance of communication systems and services.

ORIGINATE MODE The "originate mode" sets the modem to begin a data phone call — i.e. dial the phone, listen for a carrier tone from a remote modem and connect to that modem. The modem at the receiving end must be set to "Answer" mode. In any asynchronous data conversation, one side must be set to "Originate" and the other to "Answer." Such settings are usually made in software.

ORIGINATING RESTRICTION A phone line with this restriction cannot place calls at any time. Calls directed to the phone, however, will be completed normally.

ORM Optical Remote Module.

OS Operating System, as in MS-DOS (MicroSoft- Disk Operating System) or OS/2. See OPERATING SYSTEM.

OSCILLATOR 1. A device for generating an analog test signal. 2. Electronic circuit that creates a single frequency signal.

OSI Open Systems Interconnection. The only internationally accepted framework of standards for communication between two systems made by different vendors. ISO's major goal is to create an open systems networking environment where any vendor's computer system, connected to any network, can freely share data with any other computer system on that network or a linked network. OSI was developed by the International Standards Organization. And much of it will have to be included in ISDN if ISDN is to become the transparent data network we all hope. OSI is a seven-layer model:

Layer 1 — The Physical layer deals with the physical means of sending data over lines (i.e. the electrical, mechanical and functional control of data circuits).

Layer 2 — The Data Link layer is concerned with procedures and protocols for operating the communications lines. It also has a way of detecting and correcting message errors.

Layer 3 — The Network layer determines how data is transferred between computers. It also addresses routing within and between individual networks.

Layer 4 — The Transport layer defines the rules for information exchange and manages end-to-end delivery of information within and between networks, including error recovery and flow control.

Layer 5 — The Session layer is concerned with dialog management. It controls the use of the basic communications facility provided by the Transport layer.

Layer 6 — The Presentation layer provides transparent communications services by masking the differences of varying data formats (character codes, for example) between dissimilar systems.

Layer 7 — The Applications layer contains functions for particular applications services, such as file transfer, remote file access and virtual terminals.

See also OSI STANDARDS.

OSI STANDARDS The International Standards Organization (ISO) has established the Open Systems Interconnection (OSI). The idea of OSI is to provide a network design framework to allow equipment from different vendors to be able to communicate. Codex of Mansfield, MA. has published an excellent booklet called "The Basics Booklet of Local Area Networking." Here is a shortened excerpt of what Codex says about standards.

"Standards allow us to buy items such as batteries and bulbs. Many of us have learned "the hard way" that the lack of computer standards can make it impossible for computers from different vendors to talk to each other Because a major goal of a LAN (Local Area Network) is to connect varied systems, standards are being developed to specify the set of rules networks will follow. The OSI Model is a design in which groups of protocols, or rules for communicating, are arranged in layers. Each layer performs a specific data communications function. The concept of layered protocols is analogous to the steps we follow in making a phone call:

Step 1 — Listen for dial tone.

Step 2 — Dial a phone number.

Step 3 — Wait for a ring.

Step 4 — Exchange greetings.

Step 5 — Communicate message.

Step 6 — Say Good-bye.

Step 7 — Hang up.

Each of these steps, or OSI "layers," builds upon the one below it. Although each step must be performed in preset order, within each layer there are several options. Within the OSI model, there are seven layers. The first three are the PHYSICAL, DATA LINK, and NETWORK layers, all of which are concerned with data transmission and routing. The last three — SESSION, PRESENTATION and APPLICATIONS — focus on user applications. The fourth layer TRANSMISSION provides an interface between the first and last three layers. The X.25 PROTOCOL which created a standard for data transmission and routing is equivalent to the last three layers of the OSI Model. The OSI model is quickly becoming the standard for how LAN products should be built." See also OSI and X.25.

OSINET A test network sponsored by the National Bureau of Standards (NBS) designed to provide vendors of products based on the OSI model a forum for doing interoperability testing.

OSP Operator Service Provider. A new breed of long distance phone company. It handles operator-assisted calls, in particular Credit Card, Collect, Third Party Billed and Person-to-Person. Phone calls provided by OSP companies are often more expensive than phone calls provided by "normal" long distance companies, i.e. those which have their own long distance networks and which you see advertised on TV. You normally encounter an OSP only when you're making a phone call from a hotel or hospital phone, or privately-owned payphone. It's a good idea to ask the operator what the cost of your call will be before you make it.

OSPS An AT&T word for Operator Services Position System.

OTHER COMMON CARRIERS Providers of long distance telephone service in competition with AT&T. OCCs often (but not always) have lower rates than AT&T. All long distance carriers — including AT&T — are now called interexchange carriers.

OTS See OFFICE TELESYSTEM.

OUT-OF-BAND SIGNALING Signaling that is separated from the channel carrying the information — the voice, data, video, etc. Typically the separation is accomplished by a filter. The signaling includes dialing and other supervisory signals.

OUT-OF-ORDER TONE A tone which indicates the phone line is broken.

OUTAGE Service interrupted.

OUTGOING ACCESS The capability of a user in one network to communicate with a user in another network (CCITT).

OUTGOING LINE RESTRICTION The ability of the system to selectively restrict any outgoing line to "incoming only."

OUTGOING STATION RESTRICTION The ability of the system to restrict any given phone from making outside calls.

OUTGOING TRUNK A line or trunk used to make calls.

OUTGOING TRUNK QUEUING OTQ. Extensions can dial a busy outgoing trunk group, be automatically placed in a queue and then called back when a trunk in the group is available. This feature allows more efficient use of expensive special lines such as WATS or FX. Instead of having to redial the trunk access code until a line is free, the caller can activate OTQ. See also OFF-HOOK QUEUING.

OUTPULSE DIAL A pushbutton dial which allows rotary dial users the convenience of "Touch-Tone" dialing. Pushing the buttons makes the phone pretend to be a rotary dial phone. This is necessary because touch-tones are not recognized everywhere.

OUTPULSING The process of transmitting address information over a trunk from one switching center to another.

OUTPUT Data that flows out of a computer to any device.

OUTPUT DEVICE A device by which a computer transfers its information to the outside world. For example, a printer.

OUTSIDE PLANT The outside plant includes all cables and wires extending outward from the network protectors on the main distribution frame, supporting structures and other associated apparatus necessary to connect the terminal equipment to the outside plant.

OUTWARD RESTRICTION Phone lines within the PBX can be denied the ability to access the exchange network without the assistance of the attendant. Restricted calls are routed to intercept tone.

OUTWARD TRUNK QUEUING A process of holding outgoing long distance calls in queue until the appropriate long distance facility is available. See OFF-HOOK QUEUING.

OUTWATS See WATS.

OVERFLOW Additional traffic beyond the capacity of a specific trunking group which is then offered to another group or line. For example, overflowing calls from WATS lines to (DDD) direct distance dial lines.

OVERHEAD In communications, all information, such as control, routing and error-checking characters, that is in addition to user-transmitted data. Includes information that carries network status or operational instructions, network routing information, as well as retransmissions of user-data messages that are received in error.

OVERHEAD BIT A bit other than one containing information. It may be an error checking bit or a framing bit.

OVERRIDE When a circuit already in use is seized. For example, when your boss can break into your telephone conversation.

OVERRIDE PROMPTS The ability of callers and users to key over system prompts.

OVERRUN Loss of data because the receiving equipment could not accept the data at the speed at which it was being transmitted.

OVERSAMPLING Time division multiplexing (TDM) technique where each bit from each channel is sampled more than once.

OVERSPEED Condition in which the transmitting device runs slightly faster than the data presented for transmission. Overspeeds of 0.1% for data PABXs are typical.

OVERTIME PERIOD Those minutes of use of a telephone service beyond the initially defined period for which a basic charge is quoted. The initial period on many calls is one or three minutes. After that, the next minute is overtime.

P/AR Peak to Average Ratio. A standard analog transmission-line test signal of varying frequencies and amplitudes, which is then compared with the received signal. Composite results are a weighted number from 1 to 100 being the maximum. The P/AR is used increasingly as a standard quick test of a telecommunications channel comparative quality. Per Bell standard, the minimal acceptable P/AR rating for medium-speed data transmission is 48.

P01, P.01, Pnn or P.nn The Grade of Service for a telephone system. The digits following the P, i.e. nn, indicate the number of calls per hundred that are or can be blocked by the system. It is a goal or a measure of an event. In this example, P01 means one call in a hundred can be blocked, so the system is designed to meet this criterion. Typically, grade of service is designed for the peak busy hour — the busiest hour of the busiest day of the year.

PA Public Address. Loud speaker system, sometimes used for paging.

PABX Private Automatic Branch Exchange. Originally, PBX was the word for a switch inside a private business (as against one serving the public). PBX means a Private Branch Exchange. Such a "PBX" was typically a manual device, requiring operator assistance to complete a call. Then the PBX went "modern" (i.e. automatic) and no operator was needed any longer to complete outgoing calls. You could dial "9." Thus it became a "PABX." Now all PABXs are modern. And a PABX is now commonly referred to as a "PBX." Some manufacturers have tried to make their PBX appear different by calling it something else. Rolm/IBM calls theirs the "CBX" (Computerized Branch Exchange). Some others call theirs the "EPABX" (the electronic Private Automatic Branch Exchange. Then there are special ones, like Wang's WBX, SRX's SRX, NEC's IMS (Information Management System), etc.

PACIFIC TELESIS One of the seven, now-independent Regional Holding Companies formed at the Divestiture of AT&T of 1983. It holds Pacific Bell, Nevada Bell and several non-regulated subsidiaries.

PACING A method of flow control in IBM's SNA. See PACING GROUP.

PACING ALGORITHM The mathematical rules established to control the rate at which calls are placed by an automatic dialing machine.

PACING CONTROL SNA term for flow control. See PACING GROUP.

PACING GROUP In IBM's SNA, the number of data units (Path Information Units, or PIUs) that can be sent before a response is received. An IBM term for window.

PACK To compress data items so they take up less space.

PACKET A bundle of data, usually in binary form, organized in a specific way for transmission. Three principal elements are included in the packet: 1. Control information — destination, origin, length of packet, etc., 2. the data to be transmitted and 3. error detection and correction bits.

PACKET BUFFER Memory set aside for storing a packet awaiting transmission or for storing a received packet. The memory may be located in the network interface controller or in the computer to which the controller is connected. See BUFFER.

PACKET CONTROLLER The hub of the AT&T ISN system. It acts as a fast packet switch providing virtual circuit services to the devices hooked to the system.

PACKET LEVEL In packet data networking technology, level 3 of X.25. Defines how user messages are broken into packets, how calls are established and cleared over the packet data network (PDN) and how data flows across the entire PDN. The packet level also handles missing and duplicate packets.

PACKET SIZE The length of a packet, expressed in bytes.

PACKET SWITCHING Sending data in packets through a network to some remote location. The data to be sent is subdivided into individual packets of data, each having a unique identification and carrying its destination address. This way each packet can go by a different route. It may also arrive in a different order than it was shipped. The packet ID lets the data be reassembled in proper sequence. Packet switching is a very efficient method of moving digital data around. It is not useful for voice, yet, though experiments are underway.

PACKET SWITCHING NETWORK A network designed to carry data in the form of packets. See PACKET SWITCHING.

PACKET TYPE IDENTIFIER In packet data networking technology, the third octet in the packet header that identifies the packet's function and, if applicable, its sequence number.

PACKETIZED VOICE First read the definition of "Packet Switching" just above. The idea is to digitize voice and then slice it up into packets and sent those packets from the sender by various routes and assemble them as they get to the receiver. Packet switching for data makes sense. Packet switching for voice has not made sense because the voice is too sensitive to small delays. Yet the logic and the economics are there. And experiments continue.

PAD 1. A device inserted into a circuit to introduce loss. 2. Packet Assembler/Disassembler. A device that accepts characters from a terminal or host computer and puts the characters into packets that can be handled by a packet switching network. It also accepts packets from the network, and disassembles them into character streams that can be handled by the terminal or host.

PAD CHARACTERS In (primarily) synchronous transmission, characters that are inserted to ensure that the first and last characters of a packet or block are received correctly. Inserted characters that aid in clock synchronization at the receiving end of a synchronous transmission link. Also called fill characters.

PAD SWITCHING A technique of automatically cutting a transmission loss pad into and out of a transmission circuit for different operating conditions.

PAGER A small one-way receiver you carry with you. When someone wants you, they make your pager receiver sound an alarm. They can activate your pager in a number of ways, including dialing your pager digits directly into a computer, or giving your name and pager number to an operator who then punches out your numbers. Pagers have become small, cheap and very reliable. Monthly service costs have dropped and the area which you can be paged in most areas has widened dramatically. With some pagers you can be reached in most major metropolitan areas of the US. Some pagers also display small alphanumeric messages — like phone numbers to call and names of babies born. All this has made the pager far more useful. See also PAGING.

PAGING To give a message to someone who is somewhere, but where we don't know. Paging can be done with a little "beeper" carried in her purse or on his belt. Paging can also be done through speakers in phones or from speakers in the ceiling. Most phone systems offer a paging channel access. You dial that number and page your party. The system comes "live" and your voice is heard everywhere. Similar to the stuff they have at airline terminals. Paging systems as an accessory to phone systems always cost extra. They're one of the most valuable features on a phone system. Don't skimp, however, on the quality of the speakers or the power of the paging system. If you do, your system will sound awful and people will not use it. See PAGER.

PAGING ACCESS, RAPID Your attendant and you or anybody else with an extension off your PBX can make a page (access the paging equipment) by pushbuttoning one or several digits. Sometimes you can dial one several numbers for different paging alternatives. One number gives you the tenth floor. One number gives you the fourth floor, etc. And one number to page everyone — also called an "ALL CALL" page. See also RAPID PAGING ACCESS.

PAGING BY ZONE By dialing the appropriate access code, any phone is able to selectively page "groups" of predesignated phones or speakers.

PAGING CODE CALL ACCESS A feature of the Rolm Attendant Console which offers direct, one-touch access to the paging or code call features.

PAGING SPEAKERS Speakers in the telephone. Also external units located in ceilings, on walls, etc.

PAGING TOTAL SYSTEM Upon dialing the appropriate special code, any station may make a paging announcement through all the loudspeakers.

PAID CALL The usual type of a toll telephone call automatically billed to the calling telephone number.

PAIR The two wires of a circuit. Those which make up the subscriber's loop from his office to the central office.

PAIR GAIN The multiplexing of x phone conversations over a lesser number of physical facilities. Pair gain usually refers to electronic systems used in outside plant — from the central office to the subscriber's premises. In "pair gain" you might do something as simple as take one pair of wires and carry two conversations on it. You might also take two pairs and carry

128 conversations. "Pair gain" is actually the number of conversations you get minus the number of wire pairs used by the system.

AT&T Technologies has various subscriber pair gain devices called "SLC" (pronounced "slick" and standing for Subscriber Loop Carrier Systems). Other companies, like Rockwell, have comparable systems. The more circuits these devices produce, i.e. the more cable pairs they save you, the more they cost. The cost of subscriber pair gain equipment — like all electronics — has been dropping in recent years, reducing the phone company's need to install outside cable and thus making better use of the presently installed cable. T-1 is a type of subscriber pair gain equipment.

PAIRED CABLE A cable in which all conductors are arranged in twisted pairs. This form of cable is the most common for communications.

PAL 1. Programmable Array Logic. 2. PAL is also the format for color TV signals used in West Germany, England, Holland, Australia and several other countries. It uses an interlaced format with 25 frames per second and 625 lines per frame. In contrast, the US system called NTSC uses interlaced scans and 525 horizontonal lines per frames at a rate of 30 frames per second. The two systems are not compatible. You cannot view an Australian videotape on a US TV. 3. Proprietary Algorithm. A designation for a privately designed and owned intelligence-based electronic method for performing a task (such as voice compression).

PAM Pulse Amplitude Modulation. Process of representing a continuous analog signal (a voice conversation) with a series of discrete analog samples. This concept is based on the information theory which suggests that the signal can be accurately recreated from a sufficient sample. Why bother? Sampling allows several signals to then be combined on a channel that otherwise would only carry one telephone conversation. PAM was used as part of a method of switching phones calls in several PBXs. It is not a truly "digital" switching system. PAM is the basis of PCM, Pulse Code Modulation. See PCM.

PANEL, PATCH See PATCH PANEL.

PANNE FATALE An equipment crash in Italian.

PANS Pretty Amazing New Services. PANS is a term coined to describe ISDN Capabilities which should eventually replace POTS. Contrast with POTS.

PAPER TAPE A long thin paper roll on which data is stored in the form of punched holes. Usually used as input to other systems. Many old-fashioned telex machines still use paper tape as their storage medium. Punch up the message on the paper tape, rewind the paper tape, call the distant telex machine, then start the paper tape containing the message. The primary benefit of paper tape is that you save on transmission line cost. The paper tape will run through at the maximum speed of the line, while a human operator typing manually would be slower. The disadvantage of paper tape is that you can't change the message once you've typed it. Magnetic medium — floppy disks, hard disks, bubble memory — are much more flexible. They are rapidly replacing paper tape, even on telex machines, or on personal computers, which are replacing telex machines as telex data entry devices.

PAPER TAPE PUNCH A device to physically punch holes in a roll of paper tape in order to store information.

PAPER TAPE READER A device which translates the holes in coded perforated tape into electrical signals suitable for further handling. The reader may be attached to a keyboard-printer or it may be a free standing device.

PARABOLA A shape which can focus a microwave signal into one narrow beam. All satellite and microwave antennae are parabolic, not spherical.

PARABOLIC REFLECTOR The technical name for a dish antenna shaped like a perfect parabola.

PARALLEL CIRCUIT A circuit in which electricity can take more than one path. Household wiring is the most common type of parallel circuitry. Every outlet is parallel with every other outlet on the same circuit-breaker. So, if a bulb blows in a light fixture on that circuit, all the other devices on that circuit will still function. By contrast, a string of Christmas tree lights is strung in a SERIES circuit. Should one bulb go out, usually the rest will also. See also PARALLEL DATA.

PARALLEL DATA The transmission of bits over multiple wires at one time. This is usually accomplished by having one wire for each bit of an eight-bit byte going from a device, usually a computer, to another device, usually a printer. Thus the word "Parallel." Data transmission in parallel is very fast, but usually happens only over short distances (typically under 500 feet) because of the need for huge amounts of cable. In contrast, the other common method of data transmission, serial transmission, takes place over one pair of wires and is usually slower than parallel transmission, but can happen over much longer distances, especially using phone lines. Parallel data transmission does not happen on phone lines. See SERIAL DATA and see the APPENDIX.

PARALLEL INTERFACING A method of interfacing peripherals to computers, usually printers. Not as common as RS-232-C serial interfacing.

PARALLEL PORT An output receptacle often located on the rear of a computer. Unlike serial, there is no EIA standard for parallel transmission, but most equipment adheres to a quasi-standard called the Centronics Parallel Standard.

PARALLEL PROCESSING A computer performs two or more tasks simultaneously. This contrasts with multi-tasking in which the computer works fast and gives the impression of performing several tasks at once.

PARALLEL SESSIONS In IBM's SNA, two or more concurrently active sessions between the same two logical units (LUs), using different network addresses. Each session can have different transmission parameters.

PARALLEL TRANSMISSION 1. Method of information transfer in which all bits of a character are sent simultaneously as opposed to serial transmission where the bits are sent one after another. 2. Method of achieving higher system reliability through use of completely redundant transmission facilities.

PARAMETERS The record in a stored program control central office's data base that specifies equipment and software and options and addresses of peripheral equipment for use in call processing.

PARASITE A radio tap that takes its power from the phone line.

PARITY A process for detecting whether bits of data (parts of characters) have been altered during transmission of that data. Since data is transmitted as a stream of bits with values of one or zero, each character of data composed of, say seven bits has another bit added to it. The value of that bit is chosen so that either the total number of one bits is always even if Even Parity error correction is to be obeyed or always Odd if odd Parity error correction is chosen. Here's an explanation (better, but longer) from The Black Box Corporation in Pittsburgh:

Many asynchronous systems append a parity bit following the data bits for error detection. Parity bits trap errors in the following way. When the transmitting device frames a character, it counts either the number of 0s or 1s in the data bits and appends a parity bit that corresponds to whether or not the count in the data bits was even or odd. The receiving end also counts the data bit 0s or 1s as it receives them and then compares the computation to the parity bit. If an error is detected, a flag can be set and retransmission may be requested. When even parity is chosen, the parity bit is set at 0 if the number of 1's in the data bits is even and it is set at 1 if the number of 1s is odd. Conversely, odd parity sets the parity bit at 1 if the number of 1s in the data bits is even, and it is set at 0 if the number of 1s is odd. Other parity selections include mark, space or off. Mark parity always sets parity at 1. Space parity always sets parity at 0, and "off" tells the system to ignore the parity bit.

PARITY BIT A binary bit appended to an array of bits to make the sum of all the bits always odd or always even. See PARITY and ASCII. See PARITY.

PARITY CHECK A method of error-detection in binary data transmission whereby an extra bit is added to each group of bits (usually a character of data). If parity is to be odd, then the extra or parity bit is assigned either a one or zero so the total number of ones in the character will be odd. If the parity is even, the parity bit is assigned a value so that the total number of ones in the character is even. This way errors can be detected. See PARITY.

PARK 1. A telephone system feature that (like many features) may mean different things depending on who created it. One definition of "park" is that I dial another extension and park the call at that extension. It doesn't ring. Then I go over to that extension and pick up the phone and I'll be speaking with whoever I parked over there. This feature is useful if I have to go to another phone to find some information the caller wants. There's another definition of the telephone system meaning of "park." You have a single line phone. You put that call on a variation of hold. Then you or anyone else can pick up any phone in that pickup group and you will have your parked call.

2. In the language of hard disks, "parking" means moving the read/write head to a safe area of the hard disk when you're ready to turn the disk off. This is useful also when you need to move the hard disk because it keeps the head from bouncing on data areas of the disk and damaging the disk. Some hard disks have a program called "park" which you run before you turn off the machine. Others do it automatically. Some don't do it all. You ought to check. It's very important.

PART 68 REQUIREMENTS (REGISTRATION) Specifications established by the FCC as the minimum acceptable protection communications equipment must provide the telephone network. Meeting these requirements does not certify that equipment performs any task.

PARTIALLY PERFORATED TAPE Same as CHADLESS TAPE.

PARTITIONED EMULATION PROGRAMMING EXTENSION PEP. An IBM special software package that, with the Network Control Program (NCP), allows the same communications controller to operate in split mode, controlling an SNA network while at the same time managing a number of non-SNA communications lines. It was developed by IBM to facilitate migration of users to SNA.

PARTY A stupid word for the person making or receiving a phone call. Also now used in the airline business, as in "How many people will there be in your Party?"

PARTY IDENTIFICATION Identifying the person who is placing a call on a party line, i.e. phone line with several people sharing it. Often found in rural locations.

PARTY LINE 1. Saying what your company or boss wants you to say or, 2. A telephone line with several subscribers sharing its use.

PARTY LINE SERVICE Telephone service which provides for two or more phones to share the same loop circuit. Party line service, which is becoming less common, is offered in two-party, four-party and eight-party versions. Interestingly, there is a version of ISDN in which several subscribers do share the same ISDN line — but they would rarely be affected by it because of ISDN's specialized signaling and the two phone lines in its 2B+D bandwidth.

PARTY LINE STATIONS Two party phone service can be expanded to support to multi-party service.

PAS A Northern Telecom word for Port Adapter System.

PASCAL A programming language designed for general information processing and noted for its structured design.

PASSBAND The range of frequencies that can pass through a filter without being attenuated (i.e. stopped).

PASSIVE LEG A leg of a call representing the communication path toward another user. Definition from Bellcore in reference to its concept of the Advanced Intelligent Network.

PASSIVE STAR In fiber optics, a passive device that accepts a light signal on its input fiber and retransmits it on multiple output fibers with minimal loss (the fibers are actually fused together). Also called a star coupler or a retransmissive star.

PASSTHROUGH Gaining access to one network through another element.

PASSWORD A word or string of characters recognized by automatic means permitting a user access to a place or to protected storage, files or input or output devices.

PASSWORD CONTROL OF CHANGES A feature that makes it impossible to alter the performance of a piece of equipment without first entering a password.

PATCH 1. Instructions added to a software program, usually at the last moment, to get the program to run. The "patch" is usually not part of the original planning or logic of the program. Too many patches make it difficult to effectively manage the program over a long term. Patches, like the main programming, should be extensively documented. 2. To connect circuits temporarily with a jack and a cable. Patching is typically done on devices called PATCH BAYS, PATCHBOARDS or PATCH PANELS.

PATCH BAY A collection of hardware put together in such a way that circuits appear on jacks and can be connected together for transmission, monitoring and testing. See PATCH PANEL.

PATCH PANEL A device in which temporary connections can be made between incoming lines and outgoing lines. It is used for modifying or reconfiguring a communications system or for connecting devices such as test instruments to specific lines. A patch panel differs from a distribution frame in that the interconnections on a distribution frame are intended to be permanent.

PATCHBOARD Same as a PATCH BAY.

PATCHMASTER A patch panel in which multiple pair lines can be interconnected as a group.

PATH The route a signal follows through a circuit or through the air.

PATH CLEARANCE In through-the-air microwave transmission, you must find a line-of-sight path, free of obstruction of buildings, trees, other microwave towers, etc.

PATH CONTROL LAYER In IBM's SNA, the network processing layer that handles primarily the routing of data units as they travel through the network and manages shared link resources.

PAX Private Automatic Exchange. Typically an intercom system not joined to the public telephone system. PAXes are more common in Europe, where is it common for business people to have two phones on their desk — one for internal intercom calls and one for external calls.

PAYLOAD In Sonet, the STS-1 signal is divided into a transport overhead section and an information payload section (similar to signaling and data).

See SPE (Synchronous Payload Envelope) for a description of what would be found in the payload.

PAYPHONE Used to be just a public phone that accepted only coins. Now pay phones can be coinless and can read credit cards.

PAYPHONE-POSTPAY Calls are paid for after they are completed, typically with a credit card or calling card, etc.

PAYPHONE-PREPAY At a coin phone, calls must be paid for before they can de dialed. Virtually all local calls are prepay.

PAYPHONE-PRIVATE Referred to as Customer Owned Coin Operated Telephones (COCOTs). Installed and maintained by companies other than local exchange carriers who are rapidly entering this industry. COCOTs may have access to more than one IXC.

PAYPHONE-PUBLIC A coin phone installed in a "public" place. The local operating Company is totally responsible for its installation. The phone company will typically pay someone — the city, the bus station owner — a commission on the calls made from this phone. Also see PAYPHONE SEMI-PUBLIC.

PAYPHONE-SEMI-PUBLIC A coin phone installed for public use but installed in a "semi-public" place, such as a restaurant or bar. The proprietor of the establishment is obliged to guarantee that the phone company will receive a minimum amount of money out of the phone. The phone company will typically not pay a commission on this type of phone and takes all the money in the coin box for itself. What is a "public" and what is a "semi-public" phone is a decision made by the local telephone company for whatever reason it chooses. The pay phone business is rapidly deregulating. It is now legal to own your own payphone.

PAYSTATION, POSTPAY Calls are paid for after they are completed, typically with a credit or calling card, etc.

PAYSTATION, PREPAY Calls must be paid for before they can be dialed. Virtually all local calls are prepay.

PAYSTATION, PUBLIC A coin phone installed in a "public" place. The phone company is totally responsible for its installation. The phone company will typically pay someone — the city, the bus station owner — a commission on the calls made from this phone. See PAYSTATION, SEMI-PUBLIC.

PAYSTATION, SEMI-PUBLIC A coin phone installed for public use but installed in a "semi-private" place, such as a restaurant or bar. The proprietor of the establishment is obliged to guarantee that the phone company will receive a minimum amount of money out of the phone. The phone company will typically not pay a commission on this type of phone and takes all the money in the coin box for itself. What is a "Public" and what is a "Semi- Public" phone is a decision made by the local telephone company for whatever reasons it chooses. The pay phone business is rapidly deregulating. So the rules are changing. And it is now legal to own your own payphone.

PBX Private Branch Exchange. A private phone system allowing communication within a business and between the business and the outside world. A PBX differs from a key system in that to make an outgoing call on a PBX, you must first dial "9". PBXs are also larger than key systems. An old name for a PBX was a PABX. Key systems are getting larger and becoming "hybrid key/PBX" systems. This distinction between hybrid key systems and PBXs is vanishing. On most hybrid key system/PBX you now have to dial "9" to access an outside line.

PBX EXTENSION A telephone line connected to a PBX.

PBX LINE ACCESS An AT&T term. Provides for a PBX line to appear in a line access button on 16 ECTS telephones. A single-line telephone may be used for an appearance of a PBX.

PBX STATION LINE A transmission path extending from the station (phone instrument) location to the switching equipment.

PBX TIE LINE A tie line between two PBX's, permitting extensions in one PBX to be connected to extensions in the other without having to dial through the public switched network. See also OPX and OPS, which are different and are lines between PBXs and distant extensions, not tie lines between PBXs.

PBX TRUNK A circuit which connects the PBX to the local telephone company's central office switching center or other switching system center.

PC Personal Computer. Peg Count. Printed Circuit. Product Committee.

PC NETWORK IBM's first LAN (Local Area Network).

PC-DOS What IBM calls a version of the operating system on its older personal computers. If PC-DOS runs on an IBM compatible, it is called MS-DOS, which stands for MicroSoft Disk Operating System. Microsoft of Bellevue, Washington, is the company that wrote the operating system.

PCA Protective Connecting Arrangement. A device that AT&T and members of the Bell System insisted be connected between a telecommunications device (like a phone) that wasn't made and sold by AT&T and a phone line provided by an AT&T Bell operating company. Many years later, the PCAs were found by the FCC to be totally unnecessary and AT&T and members of the Bell System were ordered to refund all payments received for rental of PCAs. The Bell System insisted on the PCAs as a way of protecting AT&T's effective monopoly of telecommunications equipment. See also PROTECTIVE CONNECTIVE ARRANGEMENT.

PCB Printed Circuit Board.

PCL A page description language used for sending data to a laser printer.

PCM Pulse Code Modulation. A method of taking an analog voice signal and encoding it into a digital bit stream. First, the amplitude of the voice conversation is sampled. This is called PAM, Pulse Amplitude Modulation. This PAM sample is then coded into a binary (digital) number. This digital number consists of zeros and ones. It can then be switched and transmitted digitally. There are three basic advantages to PCM voice. They are the three basic advantages of digital switching and transmission. First, it is less expensive to switch and transmit a digital signal. Second, by making an analog voice signal into a digital signal, you can interleave it with other digital signals — such as those from computers or facsimile machines. Third, a voice signal which is switched and transmitted end-to-end in a digital format will usually come through "cleaner," i.e. have less noise, than one transmitted and switched in analog. The reason is simple: An electrical signal loses strength over a distance. It must then be amplified. In analog transmission, everything is amplified, including the noise and static the signal has collected along the way. In digital transmission, the signal is "regenerated," i.e. put back together again, by comparing the incoming signal to a logical question: Is it a one or a zero? Then, the signal is regenerated, amplified and sent along its way.

PCM refers to a technique of digitization. It does not refer to a universally accepted standard of digitizing voice. The most common PCM method is to sample a voice conversation at 8000 times a seconds. The theory is that if the sampling is at least twice the highest frequency on the channel, then the result sounds OK. (See NYQUIST THEOREM.) Thus, the highest frequency on a voice phone line is 4,000 Hertz. So one must sample it at 8,000 times a second. Many PCM digital voice conversations are typically put on one communications channel. In North America, the most typical channel is called the T-1 (also spelled T1). It places 24 voice conversations on two pairs of copper wires (one for receiving and one for transmitting). It contains 8000 frames each of 8 bits of 24 voice channels plus one framing (synchronizing bit) bit which equals 1.544 Mbps, i.e. 8000 x (8 x 24 + 1) equals 1.544 megabits.

Europe uses a different scheme for multiplexing voice conversations. It is based not on 24 voice channels, but on 32. This scheme keeps two of the 32 channels for control, actually transmitting 30 voice conversations at a data rate of 2.048 Mbps. The European system is calculated as 8 bits x 32 channels x 8000 frames per second. European PCM multiplexing is not compatible with North American multiplexing. The two systems cannot be directly connected. Some PBXs in the U.S. conform to the U.S. standard only.

Some (very few) conform to both. Both the European and North American T-1 "standards" have now been accepted as ISDN "standards." In addition to PCM, there are many other ways of digitally encoding voice. PCM remains the most common. See T-1 and VOICE COMPRESSION.

PCM-30 Short name of international 2.048 Mbps T-1 (also known as E1) service derived from the fact that 30 channels are available for 64 Kbps digitized voice each using pulse code modulation (PCM).

PCN Personal Communications Network

PCS Personal Communications Software — available in Rolm Cedar, Cypress and Juniper — makes for easy access to external data bases, rapid transfer of data files and one-touch access to most telephone features. Other PCS features include built-in calculator, small phone list, reminder function and internal clock.

PCTA Personal Computer Terminal Adapter. A printed circuit card that slips into an IBM PC or PC compatible and allows that PC to be connected to the ISDN T-interface. See PERSONAL COMPUTER TERMINAL ADAPTER.

PDM See PERSONAL DATA MODULE.

PDN Public Data Network. A public network for the transmission of data, particularly a network compatible with X.25 protocol. A public data network is to data what the Public Switched Voice Network is to voice. To access a public data network, you typically dial a local number, receive a carrier tone and then follow very specific instructions. Public data networks send their digital data in packets over high speed channels. The major reason to use a PDN is that it may be cheaper than dialing directly on a switched voice line. Also, they get you into some databases and services which are hard to get into by dialing direct. There are many public data networks in the United States. The two best-known public data networks are Tymnet and Telenet. But there are probably 30 more. Every industrialized foreign country has at least one, usually owned by the local government phone company.

PDP See POWER DISTRIBUTION PANEL.

PDS Premises Distribution System.

PDU Protocol Data Unit. The unit of data in the OSI Reference Model containing both protocol-control information and user data from the layer above.

PE Processing Element.

PEAK LOAD A higher than average quantity of traffic. Peak Load is usually expressed for a one-hour period, often the busiest hour of the busiest day of the year. See BUSY HOUR.

PEAK-TO-AVERAGE RATIO P/AR. An analog test that provides a measure of data circuit quality by sending a pulse into one end of a circuit and measuring its envelope at the distant end of the circuit. See P/AR.

PEDESTAL A mounting device used in pay telephone installations where the instrument is not attached to a wall. Pedestals are usually too small and rarely have a shelf big enough to take notes on.

PEER-TO-PEER NETWORK 1. A network in which every node has equal access to the network and can send and receive data at any time without having to wait for permission from a control node. 2. Picture a switch acting as an automatic call distributor and an outboard computer processor. The idea is to coordinate the call and the screen at the agent. Communication must take place between the switch and the computer. If that communication is peer-to-peer, as it is, for example, in the DMS Meridian ACD, then neither the switch nor the computer is in a "slave" relationship to the other. See EXTENDED CALL MANAGEMENT.

PEG COUNT A raw count of some event. Because this was originally maintained by moving pegs on a board with units of 1,10s,100, 1000s it became a peg count. A count of the number of calls placed or received at a certain point or over certain lines during a period such as an hour or day or week. A peg count simply tells you how many calls you made or received. It does not tell you how long they were or where they went or anything else. In the old days before we had accurate and relatively inexpensive call accounting equipment, we relied on Peg Counts to figure out how many circuits we needed. No more. The peg count method is too inaccurate.

PEL Picture Element. Also called a pixel. The smallest unit of a video screen image. The single point on a CRT display. The single point in a facsimile transmission. See also VGA.

PEN REGISTER Also called a Dialed Number Recorder (DNR). An instrument that records telephone dial pulses as inked dashes on paper tape. A touch-tone decoder performs the same thing for a touch-tone telephone.

PERCENTAGE ATB Percentage of All Trunks Busy. Percentage of time during a reporting period that all trunks in a group or split were busy. This may be measured in two ways, actual simultaneous busies and call length per event, or backed into statistically. Neither technique is absolutely accurate as each depends on "snap shots" in a environment of random interleaved call events.

PERCENTAGE CA Percentage of Calls Abandoned. Indicates the percentage of calls abandoned by callers after being accepted by the ACD.

PERCENTAGE HLD Percentage of total calls HeLD in queue within a reporting group.

PERCENTAGE NCO Percentage of total of Number of Calls Offered to a particular reporting group.

PERCENTAGE TUT Percentage of Trunk Utilization Time. The percentage of a time during a reporting period that a trunk is in use and not idle.

PERFORATOR An instrument for the manual preparation of a perforated tape, on which telegraph signals are represented by holes punched in accordance with a predetermined code.

PERFORATOR, PAPER TAPE An electromechanical device which converts electrical signals into coded holes in a paper tape. See PAPER TAPE PUNCH.

PERIPHERAL DEVICE See PERIPHERAL EQUIPMENT or APPLICATIONS PROCESSOR.

PERIPHERAL EQUIPMENT Equipment not integral to but working with a phone system. An example might be a printer or television screen on which calling traffic statistics are displayed. It might also be a voice mail system. AT&T once called PBX peripheral equipment "applications processors," because they process specific applications. Some people now call them Adjunct Processor or Outboard Processors.

PERMANENT SIGNAL A sustained off-hook supervisory signal originating outside a switching system and not related to a call in progress. Permanent signals can occupy a substantial part of the capacity of a switching system.

PERMANENT VIRTUAL CIRCUIT A virtual circuit that provides the equivalent of a dedicated private line service over a packet switching network between two DTEs. The path between users is fixed. A PVC uses a fixed logical channel to maintain a permanent association between the FTEs. Once a PVC is defined, it requires no setup operation before data is sent and no disconnect operation after data is sent. A new connection between the same users may be routed along a different path. See also SDN for another type of virtual network.

PERMUTER TABLE Routing table in TYMNET.

PERSISTENT COMMUNICATION A dialogue between an ASC (AIN Switch Capabilities) and a SLEE (Service Logic Execution Environment) that may involve a sequence of messages. Definition from Bellcore in reference to its concept of the Advanced Intelligent Network.

PERSISTENT INFORMATION Information for which a permanent data object exists. Definition from Bellcore in reference to its concept of the Advanced Intelligent Network.

PERSONAL CENTRAL OFFICE TRUNK LINE Allows a user to access a central office trunk line dedicated to him. A trunk line can appear in a line access button on his PBX phone or his 16 ECTS telephones on a AT&T PBX.

PERSONAL COMPUTER PC. A computer for personal single-user use, as opposed to other types of computers — mainframes and minis — typically shared by many users.

PERSONAL COMPUTER TERMINAL ADAPTER PCTA. A printed circuit card that slips into an IBM PC or PC compatible and connects the PC to the ISDN T-interface. As of writing, such devices cost between $1,250 and $1,750 and are available in almost-commercial form from about six manufacturers. The PCTA basically turns a normal PC into an ISDN phone and ISDN terminal, ready for voice and data communications. According to Northern Telecom, one of the manufacturers of such a device, the PCTA does:

- Functional signaling call setup;
- B channel for circuit switched data;
- X.25 packet data services on the B or D channel;
- Simultaneous operation of the B and D channels;
- M5317T digital telephone to PC messaging for integrated voice and data operation;
- NetBIOS interface to applications software, such as Microsoft Networks. For more, see Northern Telecom's brochure ISDN PC Terminal Adapter NetBIOS Interface Description (D307-1).

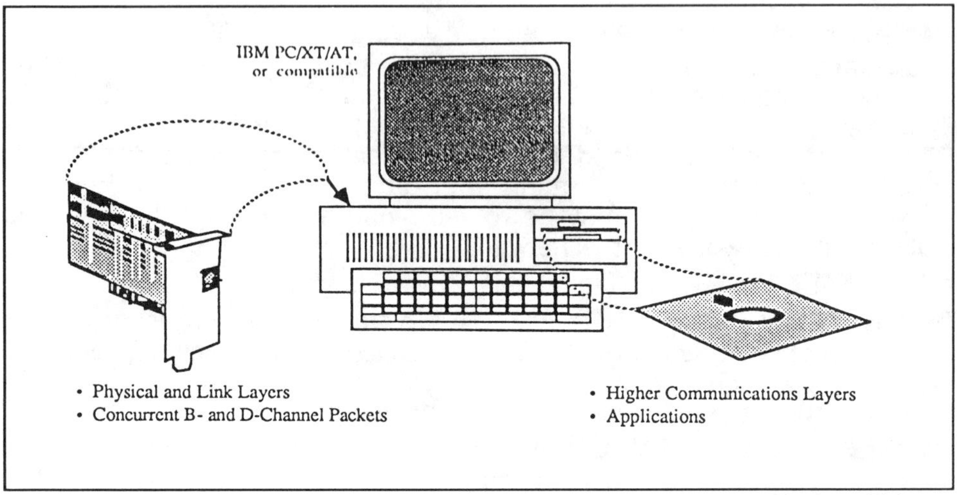

courtesy Northern Telecom

PERSONAL DATA MODULE A removable module, unique to the Rolm Cypress and Cedar, which stores all information entered by the user. Such items as phone numbers, terminal profiles and log-on sequences are stored in the PDM, which also features battery backup to protect the memory in the event of a power failure. The user can take his personal data module with him, plug it into another Cypress or Cedar and get all his speed dial and other personalized programming on his phone he just moved from.

PERSONAL IDENTIFICATION NUMBER PIN number. 1. An AT&T term meaning the last four digits of your AT&T, MCI Bell operating company Credit Card — the card you use for making long distance numbers. 2. Some banks and financial institutions issue credit cards for machine, teller-less banking. These machines, called Automated Teller Machines, ask you for a password consisting of several numbers or characters. These are not on your credit card. These numbers or characters, called PIN numbers, are designed to make sure the right person is using your card. It's not a good idea to use your birthday as you PIN number.

PERSONAL LINE A feature which allows specific key telephones to have their own private Central Office line. Sometimes called an AUXILIARY LINE. You can typically receive and make calls on this line. No one else can answer it, since it does not appear on any other phone instrument in the office. You can give this number to your wife or girlfriend. It is not a good idea to give it to both.

PERSONAL SYSTEM/2 PS/2. IBM's current family of microcomputers that sports one major difference from its predecessors, namely the existence of a 32-bit micro-channel bus. This "bus" serves the same purpose as a PBX's backplane — namely to move information from the printed circuit cards and to other printed circuit cards, which may contain their own individual microprocessors (computers on a chip) and which may communicate with the outside world through their own communications ports. Some PS/2 machines are designed to use IBM/Microsoft's new PC operating system, called OS/2.

PERSONALIZED RINGING A telephone feature which allows you to select different ringing sounds for your telephone. This feature is useful if you work in a big room with lots of other people and it's hard to tell whose phone is ringing.

PERSON-TO-PERSON CALL The most expensive way to make a long distance call. Call the operator. Say "I want to speak to Andy Moore on 212-691-8215." The operator dials Mr. Moore's phone number, gets Mr. Moore on the phone. "Are you Mr. Moore?" Mr. Moore replies: "Yes, I am." The operator bows out of the conversation and sends you, the caller, a hefty bill for that personalized service. Until recently, person-to-person service was only offered by AT&T. Now it's offered by many companies. But prices are not regulated. And some companies charge an arm and a leg. Please be careful.

PERT Project Evaluation and Review Technique. A variation on the Critical Path Method of organizing the completion of projects. Projects are examined for the their worst, best, average completion times. A critical path is determined and overall standards for completion times are created. The PERT technique was created by the military. It is used for organizing complex tasks.

PF XFER Power Failure Transfer.

PGA Programmable Gain Amplifier, a part of the Analog Front End.

PH Packet Handler, or Packet Handling function.

PHANTOM CIRCUIT A third circuit derived from two physical circuits by means of repeating coils installed at the terminals of the physical (side) circuits.

PHASE DELAY, ENVELOPE DELAY See ENVELOPE DELAY.

PHASE DISTORTION An unwanted modification of a transmitted signal caused by the non-uniform transmission of the different frequency components of the signal. Same as Delay Distortion.

PHASE HIT In telephony, the unwanted and significant shifting in phase of an analog signal. As defined by AT&T: any case where the phase of a 1004 HZ test signal shifts more than 20 degrees. Also, error-causing events more severe than phase jitter, especially for data transmission equipment using PSK modulation.

PHASE JITTER In telephony, the measurement, in degrees out of phase, that an analog signal deviates from the referenced phase of the main data-carrying signal. Phase jitter is often caused by alternating current components in a network.

PHASE LOCK LOOP In electronics, a circuit that acts as a phase detector by comparing the frequency of a known oscillator with an incoming signal and then feeds back the output of the detector to keep the oscillator in phase with the incoming frequency.

PHASE MODULATION One of three ways to change a sine wave (or L signal) to let it carry information. In this case, the phase of the sine wave is changed as the information to be carried is changed. See PHASE SHIFT KEYING and MODULATION.

PHASE SHIFT A change in the time or amplitude that a signal is delayed with respect to a reference signal.

PHASE SHIFT KEYING Used for transmitting digital signals over analog phone lines. Some modems use phase shift keying. Picture a sine wave. The sine wave is the carrier. We want to place a digital signal on it. We want the signal to change in some way to reflect the presence of a "1" or the absence of a one, i.e. a zero. In phase shift keying, we simply change the phase of the signal. See the diagrams in the APPENDIX.

PHASING The process of ensuring that both sending and receiving facsimile machines start at the same position on a page.

PHASOR Temporary buffer storage that compensates for slight differences in data rate between TDM I/O ports and devices.

PHI Northern Telecom term for Packet Handler Interface or PBX-to-Host Interface.

PHONE PHREAKS Communication hobbyists. People, usually kids, who like to figure out how the telephone network works and sometimes make free calls on the network by figuring a way to bypass billing mechanisms. Phone Phreaks have become Computer Phreaks with the boom of microcomputers and the advent of out-of-band signaling, making it a lot more difficult to make long distance calls for free.

PHONEMAIL A Rolm term for Voice Mail. Rolm's PhoneMail is a voice messaging system that provides telephone answering (with the user's own greeting), the capability to store and forward voice messages and the capability to turn on a message waiting light or message on the recipient's phone. PhoneMail can be used positively to speed the flow of information. It can also be used negatively to allow the user to "hide behind" the system and avoid the outside world and anyone in the outside world who might actually want to buy something. See also VOICE MAIL.

PHOSPHOR Substance which glows when struck by electrons. The back of a picture tube face is coated with phosphor.

PHOTOCONDUCTOR Any transducer that produces a current which varies in accordance with the incident light energy. A fiber optic communications term.

PHOTODETECTOR In a lightwave system, a device which turns pulses of light into bursts of electricity.

PHOTOELECTRIC EFFECT The emission of electrons by a material when it is exposed to light. Albert Einstein received a Nobel Prize for explaining this phenomenon. Amazingly, he never received one for his brilliant theories of relativity.

PHOTON The fundamental unit of light and other forms of electromagnetic energy. Photons are to optical fibers what electrons are to copper wires. Like electrons they have a wave motion.

PHOTONICS The technology that uses light particles (photons) to carry information over hair-thin fibers of very pure glass.

PHOTOVOLTAIC Adjective to describe material which develops voltage and electrical current when light shines on it.

PHYSICAL ADDRESS A six digit number giving the physical location of an extension within the Rolm CBX. The number is in the form of xxyyzz, where xx = shelf, yy = slot and zz = channel.

PHYSICAL LAYER Within the OSI model, the lowest level of network processing, below the link layer, that is concerned with the electrical, mechanical and handshaking procedures over the interface that connects a device to a transmission medium.

PHYSICAL UNIT PU. In IBM's SNA, the component that manages and monitors the resources of a node, such as attached links and adjacent link stations. PU types follow the same classification as node types.

PHYSICAL UNIT CONTROL POINT PUCP. In SNA, the component that provides a subset of the system-services control point (SSCP) within a node. Types 1, 2 and 4 nodes contain a PUCP, while a Type 5 (host) contains a SSCP.

PIC Plastic Insulated Conductor. Conductors covered with an extruded coating of plastic.

PICK The computer operating system of VMark Computer Inc. Pick is a neat operating system that unfortunately, never really caught on.

PICKUP Means you can answer a call from your phone. There all sorts of "pickups." The most common is GROUP PICKUP. Here you are part of a group and you can answer — from your phone — the call of anybody in that group, usually by punching a digit or a button or two. There's also NIGHT PICKUP, which typically allows anyone to answer an incoming call after hours, again by punching down a digit or a button or two. In TELECONNECT Magazine, we have one GROUP PICKUP. Everybody in the company belongs to that Group and everyone can answer everyone else's phone. We believe this simplifies things. It also allows anyone, anywhere, from any phone, to play telephone attendant, answering any and all incoming calls and transferring them through the system.

PICKUP PATTERN A determination of the directions from which a microphone is sensitive to sound waves. It varies with the mike element and mike design. The two most common pickup patterns are omni- and uni-directional.

PICO Prefix meaning one-trillionth.

PICOFARAD One-trillionth of a farad. A unit of capacitance usually used to designate capacitance unbalance between pairs and capacitance unbalance of the two wires of a pair to ground.

PICOSECOND One-millionth of a millionth of a second. NANO is a billionth of a second, (or, for those in England, Australia or New Zealand, one thousand millionth of a second).

PICTURE ELEMENT See PIXEL.

PICTUREPHONE AT&T's trademark for a video telephone service that permits the user to see as well as talk with the person at the distant end. It was introduced in 1963 but failed in the marketplace when AT&T discovered no one wanted to pay $100 a month and more for it. AT&T has changed the offering to Picturephone Meeting Service to provide full video Teleconferencing for business. We believe, as of writing, AT&T has abandoned Picturephone, the product, and has closed down its Picturephone Meeting Service rooms it had rented to corporations at one stage.

PICTUREPHONE MEETING SERVICE An AT&T service once provided under experimental tariff. It combined TV techniques with voice transmission. PMS is usually only available between telephone company-located picturephone centers. Most have now been closed down. The venture was losing too much money.

PIECE Productivity, Information, Education, Creativity, Entertainment. Microsoft's trick for remembering the big five multimedia computing applications.

PIGTAIL 1. Multiple pieces of short cable with single circuit connectors connected to a multi-conductor cable. 2. A short, permanently attached piece of optical fiber used to link the transmitter and receiver to the transmission fiber.

PILOT NUMBER Identifies a Hunt Group or Distribution Group.

PIN Positive Intrinsic Negative. Type of photodetector used to sense lightwave energy and then to convert it into electrical signals. See PIN DIODE. Also PERSONAL IDENTIFICATION NUMBER.

PIN DIODE A photodiode made with an intrinsic layer of undoped material between doped P and N layers and used as a lightwave detector.

PIN NUMBER Personal Identification Number. A group of characters entered as a secret code to gain access to a computer system, such as the one that completes long distance calls. See PERSONAL IDENTIFICATION NUMBER.

PIN PHOTODIODE An optical detector that converts light into electricity. This type is the typical diode used in a fiber optic receiver.

PING PONG A method of getting full duplex data transmission over a two wire circuit by rapidly alternating the transmission direction.

PINK NOISE Noise in which power distribution is logarithmic through the spectrum, with an equal amount of power in each octave.

PINOSECOND One-trillionth of a second. One-millionth of a microsecond.

PITCH CONTROL Variable control for increasing or decreasing the speed of a tape deck or turntable.

PIU Path Information Unit in SNA.

PIXEL Picture Element. Also called a Pel. The smallest unit of a video screen image. The single point on a CRT display. The single point in a facsimile transmission. See also VGA.

PJ-327 A double RCA dipole plug for connecting a headset into a PBX console. When you buy a headset you need to specify — 4-pin modular jack (for connecting to a telephone) or two prong plug (for connecting to a PBX console).

PL Private Line.

PL/1 Programming Language One (IBM).

PLAN A route to an end or objective usually achieved accidentally and often written in hindsight. Derived from the expression: "Most people spend more time planning their annual vacation than they do planning their careers."

PLANAR BOARD IBM's new name for a motherboard in their new series of System/2 Personal Computers. A motherboard is the main board in a PC on which the main CPU, the main memory, the clock and sundry other things like serial and parallel ports are mounted. Other boards, i.e. graphics boards, are plugged into the motherboard. Thus the expression "motherboard." No one knows why IBM dropped the word. Maybe it was too risque? Maybe they included more on their motherboards in the System/2 series that they would no longer function as motherboards? Maybe a feminist group of mothers objected?

PLANT A general term for all equipment used by a telephone company to provide telecommunications services. Usually divided into outside and inside plant.

PLANT TEST NUMBERS Virtually every 800 IN-WATS number has a plant test number. This is its equivalent seven digit local number. That number looks like a normal local seven digit number, with a standard three-digit central office exchange code and a four-digit extension. The purpose of plant test numbers is to allow the telephone company to test the local part of the incoming 800 number by simply dialing that number. For example, TELECOM LIBRARY and TELECONNECT Magazine, which published this dictionary have an 800 number — 800-LIBRARY (or 800-542-7279). The plant test number of the first line of that 800-LIBRARY group is 212-206-6870. The second line is 212-206-6871 and so on. It is valuable to know the plant test numbers of your incoming WATS lines so you can test the local loop part of those lines. The local loop part is the part which typically gives the most problem. It is, unfortunately, the only part of your 800 lines you can test yourself — unless you ask someone (or several people) to call you regularly on your 800 lines, just to test them. You can get plant test numbers out of your local and/or your long distance carrier. When they tell you those numbers are "not available," beg a little. They are available and you are entitled to them. Calling plant test numbers costs exactly what a normal long distance IN-WATS call on that line costs. So keep your test calls short. You should call your plant test numbers once a day.

PLAR Private Line, Automatic Ringdown. In telecommunications, leased voice circuit that connects two single instruments together. When either handset is lifted, the other instrument automatically rings.

PLASMA An ionized gas with a mixture of positive and negative electrons. See PLASMA DISPLAY.

PLASMA DISPLAY Type of flat visual display device in which selected electrodes, part of a grid of crisscross electrodes in a gas-filled panel, are energized, causing the gas to be ionized and light to be emitted. Some computer use plasma displays. They're fabulous, and quite expensive.

PLASTICIZER A chemical agent added in compounding plastics to make them softer and more flexible.

PLAYBACK HEAD The part which converts the magnetic information on the tape or disk into an electrical signal. Moving the magnetic fields on the medium (tape or disk) past the playback head generates a tiny voltage, which is picked up in a conductor (a coil) in the payback head and sent onto the electronic equipment where it is amplified or transmitted.

PLENUM In some modern buildings, the ducts carrying the air conditioning are not metal ducts but actually are part of the ceiling. This is called a plenum ceiling. Most cities now have rules and regulations which say that if you run cabling through these plenum ceilings, you must not use cabling sheathed in PVC (polyvinyl chloride), the standard jacketing of most electrical cable. The reason is that PVC burns and emits toxic smoke ferociously. Plenum cable is low smoking so that if it catches fire it won't circulate toxic smoke through the vent system and suffocate everyone. Plenum cabling is often made of teflon. It's much more expensive than normal cabling.

PLENUM AREA The space between the drop ceiling and the floor above. Continuous throughout the length and width of each commercial building floor.

PLENUM CABLE Fluoropolymer insulated and jacketed cable with fully color coded insulated copper conductors. Available in various pair sizes. Can be either 22 or 24 AWG.

PLESIOCHRONOUS In T-1, refers to a condition where the Bell System and an OCC (other common carrier) both provide very accurate clock sources. A signal traversing through them will maintain synchronization, although any one node in the network may not be referenced to the same clock as any other node.

PLOTTER A type of computer peripheral printer that displays data in two-dimensional graphics form.

PLS Premises Lightwave System.

PLUG A male element of a plug/jack connector system. In the Premises Wiring System it provides the means for the user to connect his communications devices to the Communications Outlet as well as the means to disconnect his service at the Network Interface Jack when trouble analysis is required.

PLUG-COMPATIBLE Devices made by different manufacturers that are totally interchangeable. The word derives from the fact that the devices are so totally interchangeable that you can simply unplug one device and plug in another device made by different manufacturer and it will work the same, or better.

PLUG-IN STATIONS The telephone need stays constant for all types of phones. For ease in phone "moves" and rearrangements, all phones are provided (and installed) as plug-in instruments.

PLUGBOARD A telephone switchboard on which connections are made by a jack and an attached cord representing a trunk (the male jack and the cord) and a female plug (the telephone extension). Early plugboards needed an operator to place outside calls and connect incoming calls. All calls were completed by the operator. Plugboards were common in the days of "PBXs." Then came PABXs (Private Automated Branch Exchanges) and you could dial out without the help of an operator. Then electronic PABXs came in and you could dial directly in to many internal extensions, using a feature called DID (Direct Inward Dial). Now PABXs are called PBXs because they're all automatic. Plugboards are rapidly disappearing. They do have two great uses, however. First, operators who grew up with them, still like them Operators who now live in nursing homes like them. Second, because the jack and plug make a pure metallic connection, they're great for data transmission and occasional data switching.

PLV Production-Level Video. The DVI video quality recommended for end-user applications, Intel performs PLV's 120-to-1 compression for customers on its own parallel processors. It takes three hours to compress one minute of video.

PMS See PICTUREPHONE MEETING SERVICE or PROPERTY MANAGEMENT SYSTEM, which is a computer software program that controls all guest billing and guest services functions in a hotel. See PMS INTERFACE.

PMS INTERFACE An interface that allows VoiceMemo functions to be administered through a hotel's Property Management System.

POINT IN CALL PIC. A representation of a sequence of activities that the ASC (AIN Switch Capabilities) performs in setting up and maintaining a basic two-party call. PICs occur in Originating and Terminating BCSMs (Basic Call State Model).

POINT OF INTERFACE The physical telecommunications interface between the LATA access and the interLATA functions.

POINT OF PRESENCE POP. Physical place within a LATA where a long distance carrier interfaces with the network of the local exchange carrier (LEC), also called the local telephone company. The point at which the local telephone company terminates subscribers circuits for long-distance dial-up or leased-line communications.

POINT OF SALE TERMINAL A special type of computer terminal which is used to collect and store retail sales data. This terminal may be connected to a bar code reader and it may query a central computer for the current price of that item. It may also contain a device for getting authorizations on credit cards.

POINT OF TERMINATION The physical telecommunications interface that establishes the technical interface, the test points and the points of operational responsibility.

POINT TO MULTIPOINT A circuit by which a single signal goes from one origination point to many destination points. The classic example is a TV signal (say a Home Box Office program) being broadcast from one satellite to many CATV subscribers all around the country. Not to be confused with a multi-drop circuit.

POINT TO POINT A private circuit, conversation or teleconference in which there is one person at each end, usually connected by some dedicated transmission line. See also POINT TO MULTIPOINT.

POINT TO POINT CONNECTION An uninterrupted connection between one piece of equipment and another.

POINT TO POINT SIGNALING A signaling method where signals must be completely received by an intermediate station before that station can set up a call connection. See END TO END SIGNALING.

POISSON See POISSON DISTRIBUTION.

POISSON DISTRIBUTION A mathematical formula named after the French mathematician S. D. Poisson, which indicates the probability of certain events occurring. It is used in traffic engineering to design telephone networks. It is one method of figuring how many trunks you will need in the future based on measurements of past calls. Poisson distribution describes how calls react when they encounter blockage (see QUEUING THEORY for a detailed explanation of blockage). There are two main formulas used today in traffic engineering: Erlang B and Poisson. The Erlang B formula assumes all blocked calls are cleared. This means they disappear, never to reappear. The Poisson formula assumes no blocked calls disappear. The user simply redials and redials. If you use the Poisson method of prediction, you will buy more trunks than if you use Erlang B. Poisson typically overestimates the number of trunks you will need, while Erlang B typically underestimates the number of trunks you will need. There are other more complex but more accurate ways of figuring trunks — Erlang C (blocked calls delayed or queued) and computer simulation. Poisson has been used extensively by AT&T to recommend to its customers the number of trunks they needed. Since AT&T was selling the circuits and preferred its customers to have excellent service, it made sense to use the Poisson formula. As competition in long distance has heated up, as circuits have become more costly and as companies have become more economically-minded (more aware of their rising phone bills), Poisson has become widely ignored.

POISSON PROCESS See POISSON DISTRIBUTION.

POKE-THROUGH A wiring method in which a hole is drilled though the floor and wiring is routed through the hole to a termination in the space above.

POLAR KEYING A transmission technique for digital signals in which the current flows in opposite directions for 1s and 0s or marks and spaces. It is used in telegraph signaling. It is also known as polar transmission.

POLAR RELAY A relay containing a permanent magnet that centers the armature. The direction of movement of the armature is governed by the direction of current flow.

POLARITY Which side of an electrical circuit is the positive? Which is the negative? Polarity is the term describing which is which. Knowing polarity is not critical with rotary phones. They will work irrespective of which way the telephone circuit's polarity is. Touchtone phones, however, need correct polarity for their touchtone pads to work. How to tell? If you can receive an incoming call, can speak on the phone clearly, but can't "break" dial tone by touching a digit on your touchtone pad, then the polarity of your line is reversed. Simply reverse the red and green wires. Some electronic phones behind PBXs and key systems are also sensitive to polarity. If in doubt, simply reverse the wires. In video, reversed polarity results in a negative picture.

POLARIZATION Characteristic of electromagnetic radiation (e.g. lightwave, radio or microwave) where the electric-field vector of the wave energy is perpendicular to the main direction, or vector, of the electromagnetic beam.

POLITENESS The most acceptable hypocrisy. Mostly seen before the sale.

POLITICS A clash of interests masquerading as a clash of principles. Also, the technique by which most telephone systems are bought in large corporations.

POLL In data communications, an individual control message from a central controller to an individual station on a multipoint network inviting that station to send if it has any traffic to send. See POLLING.

POLL CYCLE The complete sequence in which stations are polled on a polled network.

POLLING Refers to some form of data or fax network arrangement whereby a central computer or fax machine asks each remote location in turn (and very quickly) whether they want to send some information. The purpose is to give each user or each remote data terminal an opportunity to transmit and receive information on a circuit or using facilities which are being shared. Polling is typically used on a multipoint or multidrop line. Polling is done to save money on telephone lines.

POLLING DELAY Communications control procedure where a master station systematically invites tributary stations on a multipoint circuit to transmit data. Polling delay is a measure of the time to transmit and receive on a polled network versus a direct point-to-point circuit.

POLYETHYLENE A family of insulating materials derived from polymerization of ethylene gas. They are basically pure hydrocarbon resins with excellent dielectric properties.

POLYMER A material having molecules of high molecular weight formed by polymerization of lower molecular weight molecules.

POLYMERIZATION A chemical reaction in which low molecular weight molecules unite with each other to form molecules with higher molecular weights.

POLYOLEFIN Any of the polymers and copolymers of the ethylene family of hydrocarbons.

POLYPROPYLENE A thermoplastic similar to polyethylene but stiffer and having a higher softening point (temperature) and excellent electric properties.

POLYVINYL CHLORIDE PVC. A thermoplastic material composed of polymers of vinyl chloride. A tough, water and flame resistant insulator used for wire insulation. Unfortunately, it burns and gives out noxious gases which kill. Most towns, therefore, don't allow PVC to be run in their plenum ceilings. See PLENUM.

POOL A collection of things available to all for the asking or the dialing. A modem pool is a collection of modems typically attached to a PBX. Dial a special extension and you can use the modem, which answers that extension (or one of the extensions in the hunt group) to make a data call. Pooling is sharing. The purpose of having a "pool" is to avoid buying everybody one of whatever it is you're pooling. Actually, "pooling" is a fancy word for something we've been doing in the telephone business for the past 100 years — sharing. We started sharing lines, then sharing switches, then sharing voice mail devices, now we're sharing equipment, like modems.

POP Point-Of-Presence. A long distance carrier's office in your local community (defined as your LATA). A POP is the place your long distance carrier, called an IntereXchange Carrier (IXC), terminates your long distance lines just before those lines are connected to your local phone company's lines or to your own direct hookup. Each IXC can have multiple POPs within one LATA. All long distance phone connections go through the POPs.

PORT 1. An entrance to or exit from a network. 2. The physical or electrical interface through which one gains access. 3. The interface between a process or program and a communications or transmission facility. 4. To move a process, program or subroutine from one processor to controller to another ("port it over").

PORT SHARING DEVICE A system which connects multiple lines to a single port by means of a manual or automatic line selection method.

PORTABILITY The ability of software designed for one computer system to be used on other systems. Little software outside MS-DOS software for IBM and IBM clone computers is portable. UNIX software is portable to an extent.

PORTRAIT Most computer screens are horizontal, i.e. they are wider than they are high. In the new language of computer screens, this is called "landscape." When a computer screen is higher than it is wide, it's called "portrait." Some computer screens can actually work both ways. Some even have a small mercury switch in them that determines which way the screen is standing (portrait or landscape) and will adjust their image accordingly.

POS Point Of Service. Also called Point of Presence. See that.

POSITION A telephone console at a switchboard manned, er, staffed by an attendant, or operator, or agent, or whatever the latest fashionable word is.

POSITIVE ACTION DIGIT A digit that must be dialed before a PBX will advance a call to a higher-cost route. The WATS lines are busy. Time on the queue is over. It's time to move the call to the more expensive direct distance dial. Before it can go that route, the caller must punch in a positive action digit. This affirms that the user knows he is now making a more expensive call. It causes him to think twice, allegedly.

POSIX Portable Operating Systems for Computer Environments.

POST PAY A method of coin phone operation characterized by the operation of a lever or button that causes the collection of deposits after the called party answers. This method of "A" and "Buttons" is still used on coin phones overseas, especially in Great Britain.

POSTSCRIPT PostScript is a page description language for personal computers. It allows users to create fancy documents. Most business documents and most business programs — spreadsheets, word processors and databases — do not require its sophistication. It is standard for many graphics and desktop publishing applications. Computer printers capable of using PostScript typically cost twice as much as non-PostScript printers. The Apple Laserwriter printers are the leaders among PostScript machines.

POTENTIAL The difference in voltage between one point and another. One point is usually ground.

POTS Plain Old Telephone Service. The basic service supplying standard single line telephones, telephone lines and access to the public switched network. Nothing fancy. No added features. Just receive and place calls. Nothing like Call Waiting or Call Forwarding. They are not POTS services. Pronounced POTS, like in pots and pans.

PANS (Pretty Amazing New Stuff) is a term coined to describe ISDN Capabilities eventually to replace POTS.

POWER The term which describes the amount of work an electric current can do in a unit of time. We measure power in watts (note it's spelled with two "T"s.) A WATT measures the amount of work done in lifting a quarter-pound weight a distance of one yard in one second. Metric watts are a little more powerful. They go the distance of one meter. Power is the product of the current in amperes times the voltage, i.e. P = IV. See OHM's LAW.

POWER DISTRIBUTION PANEL A part of the Rolm CBX power distribution system that receives voltages from the main power supply and distributes them to the cabinet shelves.

POWER DOWN The sequence of things you to have to do to turn off a computer or telephone system. Not following the correct power down procedures can cause a loss of data.

POWER FAIL BYPASS A feature that allows analog trunks to be answered if your commercial AC power or your telephone system crashes.

POWER FAILURE BACKUP If your AC power fails, your telephone system can still operate by switching to a backup battery power supply, often called a UPS — Uninterruptible Power Supply.

POWER FAILURE TRANSFER When the commercial AC power fails and there is no backup power source — such as a battery or a generator — this feature switches some of the trunks connected to the phone system to several single line phones, which don't need external power and can draw their power from the phone lines.

POWER LEVEL The measure of signal power at some point. The measure can be referenced to some power level in which case the measurement is expressed in dB (decibels). It may also be referenced to 1 milliwatt in which case the measurement is expressed in dBm.

POWER ON See POWER UP.

POWER REGULATOR Equipment that regulates the power delivered to a system. Designed to mitigate transients in the commercial electric power source.

POWER SUPPLY That part of a phone system or a computer which converts the normal 120 or 240 volts AC power to AC and DC at the various voltages and frequencies as needed by the components and circuits of a system. Power supplies are usually the least reliable part of modern electronic gadgetry. This is because they take the hits and the garbage power the local utility sends in and also, many manufacturers skimp on the quality of their power supplies. A cheap power supply is not evident immediately. It may take time to break down. Whenever you're having intermittent problems with your phone system or computer, suspect the power supply. Most often you'll be right.

POWER UP The sequence of things you have to do in order to turn a computer or telephone system on. You can't cut corners starting up electronic equipment. It must be done carefully and in the correct order. Always count to ten after turning something off before turning it back on again. See also POWER DOWN.

PPI Pixels Per Inch. See RESOLUTION.

PPM Northern Telecom term for Periodic Pulse Metering.

PPS Pulses Per Second.

PRA See PRIMARY RATE ACCESS.

PRACTICE The technical and installation manuals often used by Bell Operating Companies. A poor use of the word. A better word would be procedure.

PRBS PSEUDO-RANDOM BIT SEQUENCE/PATTERN A test pattern

having the properties of random data (generally 511 or 2047 bits), but generated in such a manner that another circuit, operating independently, can synchronize on the pattern and detect individual transmission bit errors.

PRE-AMPLIFIER An electronic circuit which maintains or establishes an audio or video signal at a predetermined signal strength, prior to that signal being amplified for reproduction through a monitor or speaker.

PRE-SUBSCRIPTION A local Bell or local independent operating telephone company service that encourages each subscriber to select one long distance carrier he may use without having to dial a multiple digit access code. If you pre-subscribe to MCI, you will simply reach MCI by dialing "1" plus the 10-digit long distance number.

PRE-WIRING The practice of concealing telephone wiring or cable in the wall of a building while the building is being constructed.

PRECEDENCE PROSIGN An introductory character or set of characters which indicate how a message is to be handled by the receiving unit.

PREDICTIVE DIALING A term for the algorithm used by Teknekron Infoswitch to automatically place calls from a dialing machine, then, using answer detection capability, switch only answered calls to telemarketing or collection personnel. The goal is to eliminate non-productive calling.

PREFIX One or several digits dialed or touchtoned in front of a phone number, usually to indicate something to the phone system. For example, dialing a zero in front of a long distance number in the United States would indicate to the phone company you wanted operator assistance on the call.

PREFORM Optical fiber source material. Preform is glass rod formed and used as source material for drawing an optical fiber.

PREMISES Denotes the space occupied by a customer or authorized or joint user in a building or buildings on continuous or contiguous property (except railroad rights of way, etc.) not separated by a public road or highway.

PREMISES DISTRIBUTION SYSTEM PDS. A multi-functional distribution system from AT&T to support voice, data, graphics and video communications on premise. PDS includes cables, adapters, electronics, 8 pin universal wall jacks and protective devices, all arranged in a logically coherent and economic fashion. It uses fiber optic cable and twisted pair copper wire and is suitable for single building, multi-tenant high rise or campus environment.

PREMISES LIGHTWAVE SYSTEM The fiber optic part of the Premises Distribution System (PDS) from AT&T. PDS, which can replace the coaxial cables linking IBM terminals and printers, consists of two fiber optic interface units, one at a controller-end and the optic interface units and one at a terminal-end linked by a fiber optic pair. The fiber optic interface units connect to the terminals through four-pair building wiring and balun adaptors. Balun adaptors also enable direct connections of the terminals to the cluster controller through building wiring.

PREMISES WIRE The twisted-pair, quad or other wire installed at the user's location to provide telephone service. Includes both intra-building and inter-building wiring.

PREMISES WIRING SYSTEM The entire wiring system on the user's premises, especially the supporting wiring that connects the communications outlets to the network interface jack.

PREPAY The industry standard for coin phone operation which requires that the full cost of a call be deposited before a connection is attempted through the Central Office.

PREPROCESSOR A device or information handling system which converts raw data into a form more easily processed with standard equipment.

PRESENTATION LAYER The sixth layer of the OSI model of data communications. It controls the formats of screens and files. Control codes, special graphics and character sets work in this layer. See OSI standards.

PRESET The "programming" of radio station frequencies on a tuner or receiver or musical selections on a tape, for instant recall at the push of a button.

PRESET CALL FORWARDING Incoming calls will be re-routed to a pre-determined secondary number.

PRESS-TO-TALK Telephone circuits are two way. Some circuits, such as mobile dispatch services for taxis, etc., are one-way. They use a microphone or handset with a button you must press-to-talk and release to listen. You can also buy a normal telephone handset with a press-to-talk button. Such a handset is useful in noisy places.

PRESTEL A videotex system used only in Britain.

PRESSURIZATION Pumping inert gas into a heavy casing in which a couple of thick cables will be joined. The pressure is usually maintained at a few pounds above the surrounding atmospheric pressure. The idea is that the higher pressure inside keeps moisture out of the splice and thus improves the quality of phone service.

PREVAIL An office automation UNIX software package which combines functions usually available only in individual programs, such as spreadsheet, a word processor, a database management system, communication capabilities and more.

PREVENTIVE MAINTENANCE The periodic inspection, cleaning, adjusting and repair to eliminate problems before they affect service. Usually ignored.

PRICE CAP The phone industry has always been regulated on the basis of the profits it earns compared to the investment it had. That was called Rate of Return Regulation. How you figure profits — since you also have to figure what are allowable expenses — has been the subject of on-going debate for over 100 years. The latest idea in regulation is to replace the rate of return regulation with something called "Price caps" which allow the price of phone company services to rise by x% at maximum — the so-called price cap.

PRI See PRIMARY RATE INTERFACE and ISDN.

PRIMARY AGENT GROUP An automatic call distributor term: Primary agent group for which the inbound calls are intended. Intraflow goes to secondary and tertiary groups if the primary group does not have an agent available after the time or after overflow parameters are exceeded. Different ACD systems label this process differently.

PRIMARY BUFFER A part of a computer's memory where fast incoming or outgoing data is kept until the computer has a chance to process it.

PRIMARY CENTER A control center connecting toll centers — a Class 3 Central Office. It can also serve as a toll center for its local end offices.

PRIMARY GROUP A group of basic signals which are combined by multiplexing. The lowest level of the multiplexing hierarchy.

PRIMARY INSULATION The first layer of non-conductive material applied over a conductor to act as electrical insulation.

PRIMARY RATE INTERFACE The ISDN equivalent of a T-1 circuit. The Primary Rate Interface (that which is delivered to the customer's premises) provides 23B+D or 30B+D running at 1.544 megabits per second and 2.048 megabits per second, respectively. There is another ISDN interface. It's called the Basic Rate Interface. It delivers 2B+D over either one or two pairs. In ISDN, the "B" stands for Bearer, which is 64,000 bits per second, which can carry PCM-digitized voice or data. See ISDN for a much better explanation.

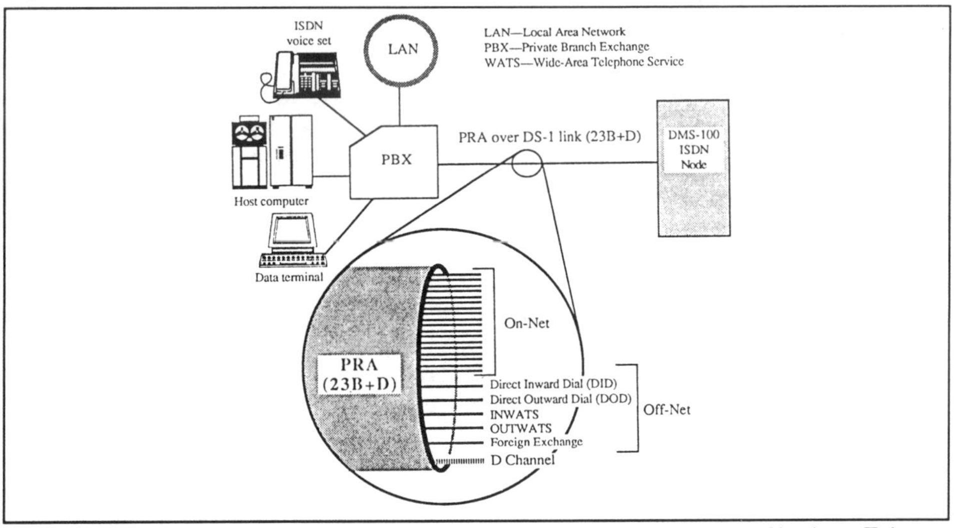

courtesy Northern Telecom

PRIMARY STATION A network node that controls the flow of information on a communications link. Also, the station that, for some period of time, has control of information flow on a communications link (in this case primary status is temporary).

PRIMARY STORAGE The main internal storage.

PRIMARY WIRE CENTER A switching center in the AT&T/Bell system hierarchy of exchange classes. The primary center is a Class 3 exchange. It is used to connect toll offices and less frequently to connect a toll center with a local end office. Primary centers are capable of connecting toll centers through sectional centers and then to local end offices to establish communication connections when simple routing possibilities are busy.

PRIMITIVES Abstract representations of interactions across the service access points indicating information is passed between the service user and service provider. There are four types of primitives in the OSI Reference Model — request, indication, response and confirm.

PRIME LINE PREFERENCE When you pick up the handset on your key system or hybrid key, you are automatically connected to your preferred line (central office or intercom), rather than having to punch down an extra line button. Some phone systems tout this as a feature. Some have it set up where you simply leave one of the line buttons depressed and it doesn't pop up when you put your handset back into its cradle. Most 1A2 phone systems have this feature. Not all electronic phone systems do. Walker breaks the features into Prime Line Outgoing and Prime Line Incoming, and allows you to program the phones separately.

PRINCIPAL First or highest in importance. An owner or part-owner of a business. A person who authorizes another, as an agent, to represent him. Often confused incorrectly with PRINCIPLE.

PRINCIPLE A general or fundamental truth on which others are based. A rule of conduct. Often confused incorrectly with PRINCIPAL.

PRINT SPOOLING A technique used to schedule printing tasks to one printer and to free up computer time from the slow task of feeding a slow printer (Any printer is slow compared to the speed of a computer). A small program or program/machine called the spooler does the scheduling. A user loads the print task to the spooler and when the print task's turn comes, the job is printed. Print spooling is handled several ways: You can allocate part of the computer's main memory to become a print spooler. You can allocate part of the company's disk memory to become a print spooler. You can get an external device called a print spooler. It will have all the storage space and software necessary. There are two primary advantages to Print Spooling: 1. You can use the spooler to save your and your computer's time. Dump the report to a print spooler at thousands of bits per second. Get on with something else on the computer. 2. You can use a print spooler to schedule several users' printing requests. This is particularly good in multi-user environments — for example, where the printer is a laser printer (and therefore expensive) and is attached to a LAN (Local Area Network).

PRINT CONTROL CHARACTER A coded control character used to instruct the receiving unit on how a message is to be formatted in hard copy. Print control characters include carriage returns, back spaces, line feeds, tabs, etc.

PRINTED CIRCUIT BOARD PCB. Flat material (fiberglass/epoxy) o which electronic components are mounted. A PCB also provides electrica pathways called traces, that connect components. Printed circuit boards are what PBXs and computers are made of these days. Be careful when you're replacing PCBs. They're usually very sensitive to static electricity. Handle them only when you're attached to a static electricity strap that is properly grounded. Lay them down only on a surface you're sure is static electricity free. And don't touch the components on PCBs whatever you do.

PRINTER A device which takes computer information and prints it on paper.

PRINTER SERVER A computer and/or program providing LAN (Local Area Network) users with access to a centralized printer. A person using the LAN will send a message to the printer server computer. This computer will then assign it a piece of memory or disk space to store its file while it waits to be printed. With a printer server, users can send to the printer any time. Their print jobs are usually handled in the order they are received. But "big bosses" can be given priority and can be bumped to the top of the queue. Print servers allow fewer printers to satisfy more users. Print servers are also especially useful for expensive, laser or high speed printers because they (the print servers) spread the cost of these expensive machines over many users, making them more affordable. See PRINT SPOOLING.

PRINTER, WIRE A matrix printer which prints using a set of wire hammers which strike the page through a carbon ribbon to generate the matrix characters.

PRIORITIZATION The process of assigning different values to network users, such that a user with higher priority will be offered access or service before a user with lower priority. Increasingly available as an added option with network operation. Any procedure where different levels of precedence exist.

PRIORITY BUMPING The process during a link, trunk or facility failure where lower priority user access to network services is interrupted in order to offer those services or bandwidth to a predesignated higher priority user.

PRIORITY CALL Emergency calls to the attendant bypass the normal queue and alert the attendant with some special signal.

PRIORITY INDICATOR A character or group of characters which determine the position in queue of the message in relation to the urgency of other messages. Priority indicators control the order in which messages are to be delivered.

PRIORITY TRUNK QUEUING Through user-chosen trunk access level, this PBX feature places any caller with this or higher level in the class of service assignment ahead of callers waiting for the same trunk group (or Agent Group in the case of incoming ACD calls).

PRIVACY Privacy usually means that once a caller "seizes" a line, no other user can access that same line even though it appears on his/her key set. Privacy can be automatic or selected for each call.

PRIVACY AND PRIVACY RELEASE All other extensions of a line are unable to enter a conversation in progress unless the initiating telephone releases the feature.

PRIVACY LOCKOUT Privacy automatically splits the connection whenever an attendant would otherwise be included on the call, i.e. the attendant can't listen in to a call she's just extended to someone. A tone warning is generated when the attendant bridges into a conversation in progress.

PRIVACY OVERRIDE Activation of a special pushbutton allows the phone user to access a given busy line, even though the automatic exclusion facility is being used by the station on that line. This privilege of Privacy Override is usually only given to Big Bosses.

PRIVATE AUTOMATIC BRANCH EXCHANGE PABX. A private telephone switch for a business or an organization in which people have to dial "9" to access a local line. In the old days, private branch exchanges were manual, meaning that operators/attendants were needed to manually place calls. Then the systems improved and you were able to dial the outside world from your extension without the help (or hindrance?) of an operator. Thus they became known as private automatic branch exchanges. But then all PBXs became Automatic. So these days, PABXs are all called PBXs, except in some countries outside North America, where they're still called PABXs. See also the next definition.

PRIVATE BRANCH EXCHANGE PBX. Term used now interchangeably with PABX. PBX is a private telephone switching system, usually located on a customer's premises with an attendant console. It is connected to a common group of lines from one or more central offices to provide service to a number of individual phones, such as in a hotel, business or government office. See also PABX.

PRIVATE DIAL-IN PORTS. A packet network term. For customers who have many calls, the packet network operator provides dedicated, unpublished phone numbers. The idea is to give the preferred user better service.

PRIVATE EXCHANGE PX. A telephone switch serving a particular organization and having no means of connection with a public exchange. In other words, a phone system just for intercom calls.

PRIVATE LINE A direct channel specifically dedicated to a customer's use between specified points. A line leased from a carrier, local or long distance. A non-switched circuit. One end of the line is directly connected to the other end. Here's the AT&T definition of a private line. "A dedicated, nonswitchable link from one or more customer-specified locations to one or more customer-specified locations..."

PRIVATE LINE SERVICE An outside telephone number separate from the PABX, can be set up to appear on one of the buttons of a key telephone. Also called an Auxiliary Line.

PRIVATE MESSAGE A message designation which prevents that message from being given to another mailbox.

PRIVATE NETWORK A series of offices connected together by leased and non-leased phone lines with switching facilities and transmission equipment owned and operated by the user or by the carrier and leased to the user. This is a broad definition. But these days with SDN and other virtual private networks, it's hard to see the difference between using a private network and using the public network except that you hope your private network will be cheaper, better quality and perhaps offer a little more flexibility in the types of traffic — voice, video, data and fax — you carry on it. See PRIVATE VOICEBAND NETWORK.

PRIVATE VOICEBAND NETWORK A network that is made up of voice band circuits, and sometimes switching arrangements, for the exclusive use of one customer. These networks can be nationwide in scope and typically serve large corporations or government agencies.

PRIVATE WIRE A private line. Derives its name from the old telegraph days when messages were carried on wires that strung across the nation.

PRO WATS PRO WATS I is AT&T's discount long distance service for companies which spend over $120 a month on long distance. AT&T PRO WATS II and III are designed for companies with higher calling volumes. Charges and discounts increase with plan size.

PRO-ACTIVE Taking the initiative. Doing it before someone (most likely your competition) forces you to do it. The word is currently in vogue among those people who believe the telephone companies should do all the positive, forward-looking actions before the competition does them and gets the public kudos. The word has no real meaning, but serves a purpose as a cry to action. The word actually is grammatically incorrect. The real word is "active." It is the opposite of "reactive." The person who told us this is Norm Brust, a wonderful man and one of the more active (not proactive) people in our industry.

PROCESS A software application. Any activity or systematic sequence of operations that produces a specified result. Typically, a computer function that consists of, or involves, procedure code, data storage and an interface for communicating with other processes.

PROCESSING, BATCH A method of computer operation in which a number of similar input items are accumulated and sorted for processing. Compare with ON-LINE or INTERACTIVE PROCESSING.

PROCESSOR The intelligent central element of a computer or other information handling system. Also called the Central Processing Unit (CPU).

PROCESSOR DATA MODULE AT&T's PDM performs conversion between the EIA signal protocol and the System 85 Digital Communications Protocol (DCP).

PROCESSOR OCCUPANCY The time the telephone system processor is in use. There are two typical demands on the central processor in a telephone system, moving calls around and running self-diagnostics. Be sure you factor in the second when you're trying to figure out how many calls your telephone system processor will handle before it dies.

PROFILE A set of parameters defining the way a device acts. In the LAN world, a profile is often used by one or more workstations to determine the connections they will have with other devices and those devices they will offer for use by other devices. Often called a login file. Profiles and login files usually work like batch files, automatically executing a number of commands when you turn on the machine.

PROFS PRofessional Office System. An IBM software package/s that is/are part of the Virtual Machine (VM) Productivity System. PROFS is said to give a user a productivity edge in three areas: business communications (including electronic mail), time management and document handling.

PROGRAM Instructions given to a computer or automated phone system to perform certain tasks. Most vendors improve (update) their software programs continuously. It's a good idea to ask what the deal is with getting updates.

PROGRAM CIRCUIT A voice circuit used for the transmission of radio program materials. It is a telephone circuit which has been equalized to handle a wider range of frequencies than are required for ordinary speech signals.

PROGRAM COUNTER A device inside a computer which keeps track of which instruction in the program is next, etc.

PROGRAM EVALUATION REVIEW TECHNIQUE PERT. A management tool for graphically displaying projected tasks and milestones, schedules and discrepancies between tasks.

PROGRAM LOGIC The particular sequence of instructions in a program.

PROGRAMMABLE In telephony, the ability to change a feature or a function or the extension assigned to a telephone without rewiring.

PROGRAMMABLE CALL FORWARDING This feature of a telephone system allows a user to instruct his phone to send all his calls to another phone. That phone might be another extension in the same phone system or it might be another phone number altogether in a different part of the country. This feature is great. You're going to a meeting but don't want to miss that one special call. You can send your calls to a person close to the meeting and ask them to interrupt you if that "special" call comes in. The problem with this feature is that often people forget their phone is on "forwarding" and when they return to their office, they sit around all afternoon waiting for that special call, which got call forwarded elsewhere. There are two ways to overcome this. Some phones have lights or messages on their screens which indicate all calls are being forwarded. Also, some telecom managers program their total phone systems so that twice a day, all call forwarding shall cease and all calls shall return to their original phone.

PROGRAMMABLE MEMORY Memory that can be both read from and be written into by the processor. Synonym for RANDOM ACCESS MEMORY — RAM.

PROGRAMMABLE TERMINAL A user terminal that has some limited processing power. Also, intelligent terminal.

PROGRAMMING LANGUAGE A language used by a programmer to develop instructions for the computer. It is translated into machine language by language software called assemblers, compilers and interpreters. Each programming language has its own grammar and syntax.

PROGRAM SHARING The ability of several users or computers to use a program simultaneously.

PROGRAM STORE Permanent memory in a stored program control central office that contains the machine's generic software program, parameters and translations.

PROJECT EVALUATION REVIEW TECHNIQUE PERT. A technique for managing a project — say the installation of a PBX — which produces a guess at the project's critical path (longest task to complete) and of project milestone completion dates. See PERT.

PROM Programmable Read Only Memory. A chip that acts like non-volatile memory. It is difficult to re-program. Least cost routing instructions can be programmed into the PROM by the vendor and then installed by service technicians. When changes in routing are needed, the vendor "burns" in a new PROM, and the old one is then replaced.

PROMPT Request from a system for information or action on the part of the operator of the system. See also PROMPTS.

PROMPTS 1. Recorded instructions delivered by voice processing units. Prompts may include MENUS or other information that is played each time you get into the system. 2. Messages from the computer instructing the user on how to use the system. See MENU and AUDIO MENU.

PRONET A family of token-passing local area networks from Proteon, Natick, MA. The fastest of Proteon's networks is an extremely fast 80 Mbps.

PROPAGATION DELAY The time it takes for a signal to travel from one point on a circuit to another.

PROPAGATION TIME Time required for an electrical wave to travel between two points on a transmission line.

PROPERTY MANAGEMENT INTERFACE PMI. A telephone system's ability to talk to a hotel's computer system.

PROPRIETARY If something is proprietary it means it will only work with one vendor's telephone system. There are many telephones that are proprietary to one telephone system or one manufacturer. These Proprietary phones are usually the electronic and multi-line instruments. For example, Rolm's Cedar, Juniper and Cypress phones will only work connected to a Rolm PBX. Similarly with the CXC Rose TeleTerminal which will only worked connected to a CXC Rose PBX. However, the Mitel SuperSet 4s will work with Solid State PBXs and ACDs.

PROPRIETARY LAN A LAN that runs the equipment of only one vendor. A proprietary LAN, for example, cannot join IBM PC's to DEC minicomputers. DEC and Wang both make proprietary LANs. Some people say such LANs are more "bug-free" because they have only one vendors' wares to deal with. They also tend to be more expensive. They also tend to tie you to one vendor, although some makers are now coming out with bridges which connect proprietary LANs to non-proprietary LANs.

PROSPECTIVE The opposite of Retrospective or Retroactive. Most regulatory commission rate cases are prospective, which means they relate to prices and things in the future. Some rate cases, however, are retroactive or retrospective, which means they apply to prices and things in the past. Most of these decisions involve forcing the company to return money to its subscribers in the form of a refund. Interestingly — try this one — most retroactive commission decisions are prospectively retroactive. In other words, they only take effect some time in the future, when the decision is voted upon by all the commission members.

PROTECTIVE CONNECTING ARRANGEMENT PCA. A device leased from the telephone company and placed between your own (customer-provided) telephone equipment and the lines of the telephone company. The idea was to protect their lines from your junky equipment. No instance/case was ever proven of harm occurring to the network from faulty customer-provided equipment and the PCAs were thrown out and replaced by the FCC's Part 68 Registration Program. Under this program, customer-owned equipment which passes FCC tests can be registered and connected directly to the phone network without these devices. The phone industry eventually refunded most of the fees it charged on the PCAs. NATA and many manufacturers claimed the PCAs were designed to prevent the growth of the interconnect or customer-owned phone industry. They were probably right. The question is now moot, since the charges and the devices no longer exist, except in a museum or attached to very old equipment. See also PROTECTIVE COUPLING ARRANGEMENT and PCA.

PROTECTIVE COUPLING ARRANGEMENT PCA. A device placed between the phone company's trunks and your particular telephone gadget. The objective of the PCA is to isolate the telephone company's lines from your equipment and thus protect their lines from your equipment. The device is not needed if your equipment has passed FCC approval — under Part 68 of the FCC's rules. See also PROTECTIVE CONNECTIVE ARRANGEMENT, which is another term for the same thing.

PROTECTOR BLOCK A device interconnected to an exchange access line to protect the connected equipment from over-voltage and/or over-current of 600 volts or greater. Hazardous voltages and currents are shunted to ground.

PROTOCOL A specific set of rules, procedures or conventions relating to format and timing of data transmission between two devices. A standard procedure that two data devices must accept and use to be able to understand each other. Sort of like us both speaking English so we can communicate. The protocols for data communications cover such things as framing, error handling, transparency and line control. There are three basic types of protocol: character-oriented, byte-oriented and bit-oriented.

Protocols break a file into equal parts called blocks or packets. These packets are sent and the receiving computer checks the arriving packet and sends an acknowledgement (ACK) back to the sending computer. Because modems use phone lines to transfer data, noise or interference on the line will often mess up the block. When a block is damaged in transit, an error occurs. The purpose of a protocol is to set up a mathematical way of measuring if the block came through accurately. And if it didn't, ask the distant end to re-transmit the block until it gets it right.

PROTOCOL ANALYZER A specialized computer and/or program that hooks into a LAN and analyzes its traffic. Good protocol analyzers can record and display data on all levels of traffic on a LAN cable, from the lowest media access control packets to NetBIOS commands and application data. They are excellent for diagnosing network problems, but they require some expertise, as their data output can be obscure.

PROTOCOL CONVERSION A data communications procedure which permits computers operating with different protocols to communicate with each other. See PROTOCOL and PROTOCOL CONVERTER.

PROTOCOL CONVERTER A device which does protocol conversion. It's your classic "black box." Compare with bridge and gateway, which are different animals and may contain protocol converters...and more.

PRX Program.

PSC/PUC Public Service Commission. Also known as Public Utility Commission. It's the state agency charged with regulating the local phone company utility. In reality, there are only two things the PSC can do: 1. Allow the phone company to increase its prices, and 2. Restrict competition to the phone company by creating all sorts of restrictive rules and regulations. As competition in the telecommunications industry grows — chiefly because of Federal rulings — the state PSCs are losing their power. This bothers them.

PSDS Public Switched Digital Service. A BOC service. AT&T Circuit Switched Digital Capability (CSDC), also known commercially as AT&T's Accunet Switched 56 service. It allows a full-duplex, dial up, 56-kbit/s digital circuits on an end-to-end basis.

PSEUDO CODE A code which must be translated before it can be executed or acted upon.

PSEUDO-RANDOM BIT PATTERN Test message consisting of 511 or 2,047 bits ensuring that all possible bit combinations can pass through a network without error.

PSEUDOTERNARY A term used in ISDN Basic rate interface data coding. Refers to three encoded signal levels representing two-level binary data (binary "1"s are represented by no line signal, and binary "O"s by alternating positive and negative pulses).

PSI Packet Switching Interface.

PSK Phase Shift Keying. A method of modulating the phase of a signal to carry information. See PHASE MODULATION.

PSTN Public Switched Telephone Network. An abbreviation used by the CCITT. See PUBLIC SWITCHED TELEPHONE NETWORK and PUBLIC DATA NETWORK.

PTT Post Telephone & Telegraph Administration. The PTTs, usually controlled by their governments, provide telephone and telecommunications services in most foreign countries. In CCITT documents, these are the Administrations referred to as Operating Administrations. The term Operating Administrations also refers to "Private Recognized Operating Agencies" which are the private companies that provide communications services in those very few countries that allow private ownership of telecommunications equipment.

PTY Party.

PU Physical Unit. In IBM's SNA, the component that manages and monitors the resources of a node, such as attached links and adjacent link stations. PU types follow the same classification as node types.

PU 2.0 & 2.1 IBM protocols which allow applications written to APCC and interpreted by LU 6.2 to access the mainframe (2.0) and token ring LAN (2.1).

PUBLIC ACCESS TERMINAL A kiosk (SK series), enclosure (TK series) or a system for special enclosures and custom applications (XE Series) which provides the public access to service. Contains a color monitor and keypad for customer interaction.

PUBLIC ANNOUNCEMENT TRUNK GROUP A trunk group used to provide multiple types of announcements, such as the weather, time and sports results.

PUBLIC ASYNCHRONOUS DIAL-IN PORT A term used in packet switching networks referring to the local phone number of a port into the packet switched network. Some networks provide different numbers for different speeds. Some provide different speeds on the same numbers. See also PRIVATE DIAL-IN PORTS.

PUBLIC DATA NETWORK A network available to the public for the transmission of data, usually using packet switching under the CCITT X.25 packet switching protocol. See PACKET SWITCHED NETWORK.

PUBLIC DIAL-UP PORT A port on a computer system or on a communications network which is accessible to devices operating over the public switched telephone network.

PUBLIC EXCHANGE A British word for Central Office. Outside North America, central offices are all called "public exchanges." In the US, a public exchange is typically a local telephone switch. TELECONNECT's phone number in North America is 212-691-8215. The 212 is our area code. The 691 designates the central office or public exchange which serves us. That public exchange belongs to New York Telephone Company. See also CENTRAL OFFICE and CO.

PUBLIC NETWORK A network operated by common carriers or telecommunications administrations for the provision of circuit-switched, packet-switched and leased-lined circuits to the public. Compare with private network.

PUBLIC SERVICE COMMISSION PSC. The state regulatory authority responsible for communications regulation. Also known as Public Utility Commission, Corporate Commission and in some states, the Railway Commission.

PUBLIC SWITCHED NETWORK Any common carrier network that provides circuit switching between public users. The term is usually applied to the public telephone network but it could be applied more generally to other switched networks such as Telex, MCI's Execunet, etc.

PUBLIC SWITCHED TELEPHONE NETWORK Usually refers to the worldwide voice telephone network accessible to all those with telephones and access privileges (i.e. In the U.S., it was formerly called the Bell System network or the AT&T long distance network).

PUBLIC TELEPHONE STATION Coin phone. Pay phone.

PUBLIC UTILITY COMMISSION PUC. State body charged with regulating phone companies. Also called Public Service Commissions. See PUBLIC SERVICE COMMISSION.

PUC See PUBLIC UTILITY COMMISSION.

PULL BOX A box with a cover inserted in a long conduit run, particularly at a corner. It makes it easier to pull wire or cable into the conduits.

PULP A type of older telephone twisted-pair cable whose wood-pulp "paper" insulation is formed on the cable during manufacture.

PULSE A quick change in the current or voltage produced in a circuit used to operate an electrical switch or relay or which can be detected by a logic circuit.

PULSE AMPLITUDE MODULATION PAM. A technique for placing binary information on a carrier to transmit that information. PAM is a technique for analog multiplexing. The amplitude of the information being modulated controls the amplitude of the modulated pulses. Samples of each input voltage are placed between voltage samples from other channels. The cycle is repeated fast enough so the sampling rate of any one channel is more than twice the highest frequency transmitted. See also PAM and PCM.

PULSE CABLE A type of coaxial cable constructed to transmit repeated high voltage pulses without degradation.

PULSE CODE MODULATION PCM. The most common and most important method a telephone system in North America can use to sample a voice signal and convert that sample into an equivalent digital code. PCM is a digital modulation method that encodes a Pulse Amplitude Modulated (PAM) signal into a PCM signal. See PCM and T-1.

PULSE DENSITY In T-1, since "O"s are represented by no pulse and "1"s by alternating pulses, pulse density refers to the number of no pulse ("O") periods allowed before a pulse ("1") must occur. Typically, no more than 15 no pulse periods ("O"s) are allowed before a pulse ("1") must occur.

PULSE LINK REPEATER A signaling set that interconnects the E and M leads of two circuits.

PULSE OVERSHOOT In T-1, the amount of signal voltage that can remain at the trailing end of a pulse. It can be no more than 10-30% of the pulse amplitude. Also called afterkick.

PULSE STUFFING When timing signals on digital circuits get out of whack, some method of allowing mismatches must be provided. In time division multiplexing, this is called pulse stuffing. One stream of data has bits added to it so its final rate is the same as the master clock.

PULSE TRAIN The resulting electronic impulses that transmit encoded information.

PULSE WIDTH In T-1, refers to the width (at half amplitude) of the bipolar pulse (typically 324 + or -45 nsec).

PULSE WIDTH MODULATION Another but not very common method of modulating a signal, in which an analog input signal's DC level controls the pulse width of the digital output pulses. See PULSE CODE MODULATION and PULSE AMPLITUDE MODULATION.

PULSENET ALERT TRANSPORT SERVICE A service from New York Telephone, PULSENET Alert Transport Service lets monitoring agencies use a business or residence customer's existing POTS telephone line to transport information (burglar, fire, medical, alert, etc.) without interfering with their basic voice telephone service.

PULSING The method used for transmitting the phone number dialed to a telephone company switching office.

PUNCH 1. The process of perforating a paper tape or card in order to code information into machine readable form. 2. The process of connecting jumper interconnection wires on a distribution frame. It is called punching because of the tool which places the wire on the metal post of the frame. It is called a PUNCH and requires a heavy "punch" to make it strip its wires, then connect into the PUNCH-DOWN BLOCK.

PUNCH-DOWN BLOCK See QUICK-CONNECT BLOCK or 66 BLOCK.

PURE ALOHA A random access technique developed by the University of Hawaii in the early 1970s. In this scheme, a user wishing to transmit does so at will. Collisions are resolved by retransmitting after a random period of time.

PUSH Mechanism in TCP for ensuring immediate transmission of data.

PUSH-TO-TALK A method of payphone operation in which a push button switch is touched by the caller when the called party answers. Once pushed, money is collected and handset microphone turned on. This system deprives the phone company of revenues for calls to 976 numbers, answering machines or answering services.

PUSHBUTTON DIALING Instead of rotary dialing, buttons are pushed to generate the tones needed to place a phone call. Also called Touchtone and Touch-call. Some pushbutton phones do not produce tones, but generate the dial pulses of rotary dials. Some phones and phone systems will generate both rotary dial pulses and tone signaling.

PUSHBUTTON DIALING TO STATIONS A special attendant console feature in which the switching system is served by rotary dial central office trunk circuits. A ten-button keyset is provided on the console which allows fast dialing of extension numbers to complete incoming calls.

PUSHBUTTON ORIGINATING REGISTER A register used to store information about originating calls with pushbutton signals.

PUT-UP Refers to the packaging of wire and cable. The term itself refers to the packaged product that is ready to be stored or shipped.

PVC 1. Premises Visit Charge. 2. PolyVinyl Chloride, a type of plastic. Or, Permanent Virtual Circuit, a permanent association between two DTEs established by configuration. A PVC uses a fixed logical channel to maintain a permanent association between the DTEs. Once a PVC is defined, it requires no setup operation before data is sent and no disconnect operation after. A new connection between the same users may be routed along a different path.

PVN Private Virtual Network.

PWB Printed Wire Board.

PWM Pulse Width Modulation. In communications, encoding information based on variations of the duration of carrier pulses. Also called Pulse Duration Modulation or PDM.

PWR Power.

PYRAMID CONFIGURATION A communications network in which the data link(s) of one or more multiplexers are connected to I/O ports of another multiplexer.

Q Queue.

Q BIT The qualifier bit in an X.25 packet that allows the DTE to indicate that it wishes to transmit data on more than one level.

Q.931 Q.931 is the powerful message-oriented signaling protocol in the PRA D-channel. It is also referred as CCITT Recommendation I.451. This protocol describes what goes into a signaling packet and defines the message type and content. Specifically, Q.931 provides:

- call setup and take down;
- called party number, with type of number indication (private or public);
- calling party number information (including privacy and authenticity indicators);
- bearer capability (to distinguish, for example, voice versus data for compatibility check between terminals;
- status checking (for recovery from abnormal events, such as protocol failures or the manual busying of trunks); and
- release of B-channels and the application of tones and/or announcements in the originating switch upon encountering errors.

Q.931 makes it possible to interwork PBX features with features in the public network. In addition to offering users more access to a wider range of services, this interaction, according to Northern Telecom, will improve the revenue potential of service providers. Service provided over PRA, using Q.931, include:

- access to the public network, such as equal access, WATS, DDD, international DDD, dial-800 and other special number services and operator assisted calls.
- access to and from such private networks as Northern Telecom's Meridian Switched Network (previously call Electronic Switched Network — ESN), tandem tie networks, and extension dialing network; and
- integration of voice and circuit-switched data traffic (up to 64 kbps).

The Q.931 protocol also enables corporations to use B-channels — that is voice and data channels — in ways currently not possible. Today, for example, a separate trunk from the PBX to the central office is often required for each different service, such as voice, data, foreign exchange, 800-service. With PRA, one common trunk between the PBX and the central office can carry multiple call types. Moreover each B-channel within the PRA trunk can be assigned dynamically to carry whatever service is needed at the moment.

QAM, QSAM Quadrature Amplitude Modulation, Quadrature Sideband Amplitude Modulation. A sophisticated modulation technique, using variations in signal amplitude, that allows data-encoded symbols to be represented as any of 16 or 32 different states. Some QAM modems allow dial-up data rates of up to 9,600 bits per second.

QBF A test message containing the "Quick Brown Fox" text. Used to test data terminals. The text is "The Quick Brown Fox jumped over the lazy dog." It contains every letter of the alphabet. Check it out.

QLLC Qualified Logical Link Control. Software package that allows Systems Network Architecture (SNA) commands to be transmitted over an X.25 packet data network (PDN). See also NPSI. Contrast with DSP.

QPSK Quaternary Phase Shift Keying. Another way of sending data through a modem over an analog phone line.

QPSX Queued Packed and Synchronous Exchange. Technology used in Institute of Electrical and Electronic Engineers (IEEE) standard 802.6 for metropolitan area networks (MANs).

QUAD Term used to describe the four-wire (2 twisted pair) cable used in homes. Typically, one pair is used for "tip and ring," also called positive and negative. These two wires carry the phone conversation and the ringing. Typically these wires are red and green. The other pair of the quad is usually black and white and is used as a spare, as a second line or to carry power to a lamp in the dial of the phone, etc.

QUADDED CABLE A cable in which at least some of the conductors are arranged in the form of a quad.

QUALITY OF SERVICE A measure of the telephone service quality provided to a subscriber. It's not easy to define "quality" of telephone service. It's very subjective. Is the call easy to hear? Is it "clear?" Is it loud enough, etc.? The state public service commissions have various measures which they insist phone companies conform to. They tend to be more measurable. They include the longest time someone should wait after picking up the handset before they receive dial tone (three seconds in most states).

QUANTIZATION Take an analog voice signal, sample it and put numbers on those samples. That's called quantization. Here's an explanation from Understanding Telephone Electronics: "A circuit called a quantizer takes in the analog signal and produces an equivalent number. Threshold levels are established and numbers are assigned to the analog samples as their amplitudes fall within the bands formed by the threshold numbers. (For example, everything within the range 1000.05 and 1000.06 Hz is given the number 14568.) The assigned number in most costs is an approximation rather than a true value because the true value would require many more bits (i.e. more threshold limits) in the binary code...This approximation causes an error which is the difference between the approximate number and the true sample. This quantization error adds noise to the signal, called quantization noise, which is heard in the telephone as hissing. Quantization noise can be reduced by making the threshold bands narrower...However, providing more intervals requires more bits in the binary code. Therefore, more bandwidth is needed. There is a tradeoff between small quantizing intervals (higher bandwidth, lower noise), and fewer intervals (lower bandwidth, higher noise)."

QUANTIZATION NOISE Signal errors which result from the process of digitizing (and therefore ascribing finite quantities to) a continuously variable signal. See QUANTIZATION.

QUANTIZE The process of encoding a PAM signal (Pulse Amplitude Signal) into a PCM signal (Pulse Code Modulation). See QUANTIZATION.

QUANTIZING The second stage of pulse code modulation (PCM). The waveform samples obtained from each communication channel are measured to obtain a discrete value of amplitude. These quantized values are converted to a binary code and transmitted to a distant location to reconstruct the original waveform. See QUANTIZE and QUANTIZATION.

QUANTIZING NOISE Noise caused by the inability of an analog signal to be exactly replicated in digital form.

QUANTUM In physics, quantum means a very small indivisible piece of energy. This word is widely misused by people who refer to "a quantum leap," meaning a big leap.

QUARTER SPEED An international leased teletype line capable of transmitting one quarter of Telex speed of 16 2/3 words per minute.

QUARTZ CRYSTAL A small piece of quartz which is cut to a precise size. When electricity is applied to the crystal, it vibrates at a specific and precise frequency. Quartz crystals are often used in watches. They vibrate quickly and make the watch far more accurate than a timing device which vibrates far more slowly, like a pendulum, for example, or a tick tock watch.

QUERY In data communications, it's the process by which a master station (or mainframe or boss computer) asks a slave station to identify itself and tell its status, i.e. is it busy, alive, OK, waiting, etc.?

QUEUE A stream of tasks waiting to be executed. A series of calls or messages waiting for connection to a line. See QUEUING.

QUEUED MODE Calls entering an Automatic Call Distributing system wait in a queue are presented, one at a time, to the first idle trunk in the chosen group.

QUEUED TELECOMMUNICATIONS ACCESS METHOD QTAM. A program component in a computer which handles some of the communications processing tasks for an application program. QTAM is employed in data collection, message switching and many other teleprocessing applications.

QUEUING The act of "stacking" or holding calls to be handled by a specific person, trunk or trunk group. There are two reasons to queue telephone calls:

1. Because you simply don't have enough trunks.

2. Because you want to save money.

You can queue calls mechanically using your telephone switch or manually using a human operator or attendant. There are two ways you can queue calls — hold-on or call-back. In "hold-on" queuing, you dial, you get some queuing tone (or the operator tells you you're being queued), then you wait on-line until a line becomes free and you're connected. In "call-back" queuing, you tell the operator or the machine you want to dial a call. And you hang up. When the line becomes free you are called back and connected. There are advantages and disadvantages to both systems. In "hold-on" queuing, you waste your time but save on phone time. In call-back queuing, you waste less of your time, but more phone line time. In call-back queuing, the operator or the phone system has to grab the line you want and simultaneously call you. By then, you may have left your desk. The call may be wasted, etc. The line given to you could have been used by someone else, etc. Queuing calls as a method to save money on long distance calling makes sense ONLY:

1. IF you are out of trunks because of a temporary surge in telephone traffic — perhaps at your peak, peak busy time and it's very expensive to buy sufficient "cheap long distance" trunks to handle every conceivable peak, and
2. IF you never plan on having a queue longer than 20 seconds for a hold-on queue and 60 seconds for a call-back queue and
3. IF you are queuing calls into an expensive fixed-cost line. For example a tie-line between New York and London. If you queue calls into a variable cost line, like an interstate WATS line, you will save money over throwing the call onto DDD, but the pennies you save usually won't be worth it — considering the aggravation you're going to cause your people. Queuing is a very sensitive subject in corporate telecommunications departments. People don't like to wait for telephone lines. They consider that insulting to them personally, damaging to their "productivity" and to heck with the cost. Queues do, however, make enormous sense. Even a queue as short as ten seconds can save big amounts of money. Queues of a maximum length of ten seconds are rarely noticed. These days some of the more modern PBXs will allow you to offer "selective" queuing, or levels of queuing. Upper management doesn't have to queue for the cheap long distance lines before it's bounced to the expensive ones. While lower management has to wait up to 30 seconds. And the worker bees (non-management) have to wait even longer. Queuing is also used on incoming trunks.

See ACD and QUEUING THEORY.

QUEUING THEORY The study of the behavior of a system that uses queuing, such as a telephone system. Much of queuing theory derives from the science of Operations Research (OR). Dr. Leonard Kleinrock has written the authoritative books on the subject. He is probably a genius. His books are very difficult to understand for laymen. Here is an explanation of Queuing Theory from James Henry Green's Dow Jones-Irwin Handbook of Telecommunications (you can get a copy from Telecom Library at 1-800-LIBRARY.):

"The most common (telephone) network design method involves modeling the (phone) network according to principles of queuing theory, which describes how customers or users behave in a queue. Three variables are considered in network design. The first is the arrival or input process that describes the way users array themselves as they arrive to request service...The second variable is the service process, which describes the way users are handled when they are taken from queue and admitted into the service providing mechanism. The third method is the queue discipline, which describes the way users behave when they encounter blockage in the network...Three reactions to blockage are possible:

- Blocked calls held (BCH). When users encounter blockage, they immediately redial and reenter the queue.
- Blocked calls cleared (BCC). When users encounter blockage, they wait for some time before redialing.
- Blocked calls delayed (BCD). When users encounter blockage, they are placed in a holding circuit until capacity to serve them is available. (See QUEUE.)

"Traffic engineers have different formulas or tables to apply, corresponding to the assumption about how users behave when they encounter blockage." See POISSON.

QUICK-CONNECT BLOCK Also called a 66-block or punch-down block. It's a two foot piece of metal and plastic which allows you to connect telephone wiring coming from two remote points. The quick-connect block has multiple metal "jaws" ranging horizontally and vertically. To connect up, you "punch" (or push) a wire between the two metal teeth of the "jaws." This both holds it firm and strips the wire's insulation, thus allowing for a good electrical connection. (There are special "punch-down" tools for punching wires into 66-blocks.) On a 66-block, one horizontal row of "jaws" is always the same conductor. To connect other wires to it, you simply punch those wires down along the row. Some 66-blocks have a gap between one side of the 66-block and the other. To connect one wire on one side to the wire on the other side, you have to use a BRIDGING CLIP. This is a small metal clip about one inch long. The bridging clip has one purpose: you can slip it off easily and thus cut one side of the circuit from the other. For example, if you connected central office trunks on one side of the 66-block and a PBX on the other, by removing the bridging clips, you can tell instantly if the trouble is in the PBX or in the central office. Two conductors on a 66-block makes a circuit — a trunk or a line. Therefore, the trunk 212-691-8215 (our main number) takes up the first two horizontal rows on our 66-block. The second two horizontal rows are taken up with 212-691-8216, and so on.

It is good to learn where your main 66-block is — the one that connects you to the telephone company's central office lines. The 66-block is what the telephone company calls the "demarcation point." And they (the phone company) usually install the 66-block. On one side (the trunk side) of their block, they're responsible. On the other (the PBX, key system or phone side), you're responsible. By knowing how to test your lines at this point, you can know whose fault it is — the phone company's or your equipment's. This can avoid having to wait until the phone company arrives, discovers it's not their problem and then sends you a hefty bill. Or the interconnect company arrives, finds out it's not their problem, and sends you a hefty bill, etc.

Quick Connect Blocks or 66-blocks are found in the Main Distribution Frame — where lines coming out of the PBX are connected to the individual wires going to the phones, or to big cables going to clumps of phones in other parts of the building. They're also found in Satellite Distribution Frames where they take big cable coming in from the main distribution frame and connect it to the individual cable pairs going to the individual phones.

QUIESCENT A fancy word for quiet. No noise. No activity. Quiescent time is the best time to write this dictionary. Sadly, it wasn't always to be.

QUORUM A family of teleconferencing products linked in a system designed to meet a customer's teleconferencing needs.

QWERTY A standard typewriter keyboard. The left side top row of letter keys on the keyboard spell QWERTY. In reality, the last "standard" keyboard was IBM's Selectric keyboard. And even then there were variations to suit different tasks, languages, etc. Computer keyboards typically have 20 to 30 extra keys more than "standard" typewriter keyboards. Many of the keys on computer keyboards are called "function" keys. If you hit one of them, they might perform a complete function on the computer, e.g. save a file, move to the end of the file, etc. There is absolutely no such thing as a standard computer keyboard.

QZ Special billing arrangement provided by your local telephone company. Before there was automatic call accounting and before there was Centrex, the phone company would give you "time and charges" on every outgoing call. This service was called "QZ" billing. It was used by engineers, lawyers, accountants, consultants and other service people who had to bill their calls back to their clients.

RACE An association in the European Economic Community, Research and development for Advanced Communications in Europe.

RACEWAYS A metal or plastic channel used for loosely holding electrical and telephone wires in buildings. A raceway is usually located in the floor and is encased on three or four sides by concrete. A raceway is used for interior wiring and performs the same job as a conduit but is typically larger.

RACK A structure onto which equipment is mounted. What a rack is to equipment, so a frame is to wiring. See also DISTRIBUTION FRAME.

RADAR RAdio Detection And Ranging.

RADIO The science of communicating over a distance by converting sounds or signals to electromagnetic waves and radiating them through the air or through space. Also called Wireless by the British and the Australians.

RADIO COMMUNICATION Any telecommunication by means of radio waves.

RADIO FREQUENCY That group of electromagnetic energy whose wavelengths are between the audio and the light range. Electromagnetic waves transmitted usually are between 500 KHz and 300 GHz.

RADIO FREQUENCY INTERFERENCE The disruption of radio signal reception caused by any source which generates radio waves at the same frequency and along the same path as the desired wave.

RADIO PAGING ACCESS Provides attendant and phone user dial access to customer-owned radio paging equipment to selectively tone-alert, or voice-page individuals carrying pocket radio receivers. The paged party can answer by dialing an answering code from a phone within the PBX.

RADIO PAGING ACCESS WITH ANSWER BACK Allows access to customer-provided paging systems and provides the capability in the PBX to connect the paged party when the former answers the radio page by dialing a special code from any PBX.

RADIO WAVE Electromagnetic waves of frequencies between 10 KHz and 3MHz, propagated without guide in free space (air).

RADOME A plastic cover for a microwave antenna. Protects the antenna from awful weather.

RAIN ATTENUATION Signal losses due to absorption are common when radio signals encounter a heavily moisture laden atmosphere. Generally, the higher the radio frequency, the more attenuation (i.e. the more losses). Since microwave signals for satellite and for land line are essentially line-of-sight, microwave radio is very susceptible to signal attenuation in heavy rain. Modern microwave paths are engineered with weather patterns in mind. In areas where heavy rainfalls occur, microwave links may be closer together or more attention is paid to diverse routing.

RAIN BARREL EFFECT Signal distortion of a voice telephone line caused by the under-attenuated echoes on the return path.

RAM Random Access Memory. The primary memory in a computer. Memory that can be overwritten with new information. The "random access" part of its name comes from the fact that the next "bit" of information in RAM can be located — no matter where it is — in an equal amount of time. This means that access to and from RAM memory is extraordinarily fast. By contrast, other storage media — like magnetic tape — have their information stored serially, one bit after another. Therefore you have to search for them. And your search time will depend on how far from the bit you're searching for you are. Floppy disks are faster than magnetic tape because their information is readily at hand, though the read/write head will have to search for it. Hard disks are even faster because there are multiple heads and because the disks spin faster and everything moves faster. RAM memory is the fastest of all. The problem with RAM memory is that it's volatile. This means when power is turned off (or power glitches occur) RAM memory is erased. RAM memory can be protected with rechargeable batteries — just remember to charge the batteries.

RANDOM ACCESS Usually refers to computer memory or storage. Random Access is the ability to reach any piece of data in the memory directly without having to pass by other pieces of data. In telephony, this means the ability to reach any other subscriber through the telco switching network. See SEQUENTIAL ACCESS.

RANDOM ACCESS MEMORY See RAM.

RANDOM NOISE Interference to telephone communications occurring at irregular intervals.

RANGE EXTENDER A device that increases the length of a local loop by boosting battery voltage being sent out from the telephone company central office.

RASTER A pattern of horizontal scanning lines on a TV screen. Input data causes the beam of the TV tube to illuminate the correct dots to produce the required characters.

RATE The price of a particular service or piece of equipment from a telephone company. Telephone companies don't use the word "price." They use the word "rate." No one knows why, except that if they didn't cultivate their own jargon, there'd be no job for telecommunications dictionary writers. God forbid!

RATE ARRANGEMENTS Telephone customer prices charged by tariffs for specified telephone services.

RATE AVERAGING Telephone companies' method for establishing uniform pricing by distance rather than on the relative cost (to them) of the particular route. The theory is that some routes are more heavily trafficked, have huge transmission equipment and achieve great economies of scale. Some routes, on the other hand, have little traffic, small transmission equipment and achieve no economies of scale. Therefore, it costs more to provide calls on these less-trafficked routes. But the phone industry doesn't charge more to call small towns than big cities. The phone industry simply charges by distance, averaging its costs. This is called rate averaging.

RATE BASE A regulated telephone company's plant and equipment which forms the dollar base upon which a specified rate of return can be earned. The total invested capital on which a regulated company is entitled to earn a reasonable rate of return.

RATE CENTER Telephone company-designated geographic locations assigned vertical and horizontal coordinates between which airline mileages are determined for the charging of private lines. See AIRLINE MILEAGE.

RATE CHIP A standard, nonvolatile memory device used to retain data base information on call pricing by Area Code and Central Office. Typically used in call accounting equipment.

RATE ELEMENTS The pricing structure of various telecommunications service offerings usually described in tariffs.

RATE OF RETURN The percentage of net profit which a telephone company is authorized (by a regulatory commission) to earn on its rate base. See RATE BASE.

RATE PERIOD Dividing a day into various slices of time for the purpose of charging differently for long distance and local calls. There are three rate periods in force today in North America for intra-North America calls. One rate period is from 11:00 P.M. to 8:00 A.M.; one is from 8:00 A.M. to 5:00 P.M. and one is from 5:00 P.M. to 11:00 P.M. If you call outside the United States, there are different rate periods.

RATE STABILITY PLAN Commit yourself to keeping a New York Telephone service for several years and you'll pay less than if you keep it only from month to month. Other phone companies have similar schemes, typically by other names.

RATE TABLE A data base that contains the cost of calls referenced to the Area Code and/or number dialed plus time of day considerations. See RATE PERIOD.

RATE ZONE A defined geographic division of an exchange area used as the primary basis for figuring toll rates.

RATED TEMPERATURE The maximum temperature at which an electric component can operate for extended periods without loss of its basic properties.

RATED VOLTAGE The maximum voltage at which an electric component can operate for extended periods without undue degradation or safety hazard.

RAYLEIGH SCATTERING Scattering due to tiny impurities in the optical fiber which are fractions of the wavelength of the infrared rays.

RB Reverse Battery.

RBOC Regional Bell Operating Company. There are seven RBOCs each of which own two or more BOCs (Bell Operating Companies). The RBOCs were carved out of the old AT&T/Bell System by Judge Harold Greene when he signed off on the divestiture of the Bell operating companies from AT&T at the end of 1984. There is nothing magical about seven — nor the grouping of BOCs into RBOCS — except the Judge wanted to keep them all roughly the same size.

RCA Regional Calling Area. The geographical area covered by a telephone company.

RCC Radio Common Carrier.

RCL ReCaLl.

RDF Radio Direction Finding.

RDT Recall Dial Tone.

RDY Ready.

RE-422 A high-speed electrical interface defined by the CCITT, supporting data rates of up to 768 Kbit/s over up to 300 feet of cable.

RE-INITIATION TIME The time required for a device or system to restart (usually after a power outage).

REA Rural Electrification Administration. A federal agency which makes loans to extend telephone service into rural areas. The REA has been one of the most successful federal government programs ever.

READ To glean information from a storage device, like a floppy disk. The opposite of READ is to WRITE. That's when you put information onto that storage device. Some storage devices can only be READ, but not written to. On a floppy disk that's called being "WRITE PROTECTED." See also WORM, which stands for Write Once, Read Many.

READER 1. A device which converts information into a format recognized by a machine as input. 2. A device which interprets coded data in the process of transferring that data from one coded state of storage to another.

READ ONLY MEMORY ROM. A memory device which is programmed at the factory and whose contents thereafter cannot be altered, even by a power breakdown, or being written to, or anything else. ROM memory is also random-access, which means accessing its information is very fast. See also RAM.

READ-WRITE CYCLE Time of reading and writing data onto a memory device. See READ.

READYLINE 800 A toll-free service designed with the small business user in mind. Receive "800" dialed calls over your existing telephone lines and equipment - no new lines to install, no new equipment needed. And you can still use those same lines to make and receive local and long distance calls as you always have. Choose the geographic areas you want to cover - from a single area code to an entire state or the whole country. Even decide when you want your toll-free number to be available, based on your seasonal needs. You pay an affordable, one-time start-up charge and a low monthly fee. Calling prices are based on the market coverage you choose. There are time-of-day and day-of-week discounts, and a volume usage discount. Calls are priced on a mileage/distance-sensitive basis.

REAL TIME A voice telephone conversation is conducted in Real Time. That is, there is no perceived delay in the transmission of the voice message or in the response to it. This concept often applies to interaction between a computer and a terminal. See also REAL TIME CAPACITY. In data processing or data communications, real time means the data is processed the moment it enters a computer, as opposed to BATCH processing where the information enters the system, is stored and is operated on a later time.

REAL TIME CAPACITY The capacity of the central computer processor of a stored program control telephone system to process the instructions coming at it. Real Time Capacity is probably the most important measure of the size of a telephone system relying on a single main processor.

REARRANGEMENT A fancy word for moving phone extensions around.

REASONABLENESS CHECKS Tests made on information reaching a real-time system or being transmitted from it to ensure that the data lie within a given range.

REASSIGNMENT Here is an explanation by Bill Etling, a senior planner for GTE. "Under the assigned plant concept, a pair is dedicated from the central office to the subscriber home and maintained at that address, even when idle. The likelihood of such a pair being reused, thus eliminating a field visit and extra assignment work, more than makes up for lost revenue while the pair is vacant. In areas of high cable fills, such a pair, when vacant, is often used to fill an order at a different address. Reassignment quickly snowballs, generating many installation field visits and assignment changes, increasing paperwork and the chance of errors."

REBOOTING Repeating a Boot. Turning on or resetting the telephone system or the computer. The word derives from "boot-strapping." Starting from scratch. Pulling oneself up by one's own bootstraps. Booting a telephone system or a computer means starting it from scratch, usually by turning its AC power on. Rebooting a telephone system is done by simply turning it off, counting to ten and turning it back on again. Rebooting is done to clear the volatile part of the telephone system's or computer's memory and its various processing and clock chips. You reboot typically when your PC "locks" inexplicably or when your telephone system does something you can't explain logically — like ring phones randomly or give strange error messages on the console. On a computer, "Lock" means that no matter which key or combination of keys you touch on your keyboard, you can't get your computer to do anything. In addition to "unlocking" your computer, you also reboot to clear RAM or RAM-resident programs. On an IBM or an IBM clone, rebooting is done by pressing the CONTROL, ALT and DELETE keys simultaneously. You can also reboot by pressing the reset button if your computer has one. (Not all do.) You can reboot any computer by turning its power off, then turning it back on. This is usually not a good idea, since the surge of power that accompanies a computer being turned on and off will reduce the life of many of its electronic components. Some experts recommend leaving computers running full-time. They also recommend turning your screen off, or at least running a public domain program such as SCRNSAVE.COM or SCRN.COM which turn off your screen after several minutes of doing nothing (inactivity).

RECALL BUTTON Provides the flash function needed to operate many of the Dimension PBX features. Another word for FLASH BUTTON, as this button is called on other phones of other PBXs.

RECALL DIAL TONE A stutter or interrupted dial tone indicating to the extension user that the hookswitch flash has been properly used to gain access to system features.

RECALL KEY Used to get dial-tone or to transfer calls on a key system installed within a PBX. See also RECALL BUTTON.

RECEIVE INTERRUPTION The interruption of a transmission to a terminal to receive or send a higher priority message from the terminal.

RECEIVE ONLY RO. Describing operation of a device, usually a page printer, that can receive transmissions but cannot transmit.

RECEIVED LINE SIGNAL DETECTOR Modem interface signal defined in RS-232-C EIA interface which indicates to the attached data terminal equipment that it is receiving a signal from the distant modem.

RECEIVED SIGNAL LEVEL RSL. The strength of a radio signal received at the input to a radio receiver.

RECEIVER Any device which receives a transmission signal. 2. Any portion of a telecommunications device which decodes an encoded signal into its desired form. 3. The earpiece portion of a telephone handset, which converts an alternating electric current into sound waves, usually through an electromagnet moving a diaphragm. 4. An electronic component capable of collecting radio frequency broadcasts and reproducing them in their original audio and/or video form, e.g. a TV or radio receiver.

RECEIVER OFF-HOOK TONE The loud tone sent by the central office to tell the telephone user that his/her phone is off the hook.

RECEIVER SENSITIVITY The magnitude of the received signal necessary to produce objective BER or channel noise performance.

RECEIVING PERFORATOR REPERFORATOR. A telegraph instrument in which the received signals cause the code of the corresponding characters or functions to be punched in a tape.

RECENT CHANGE Changes to line and trunk translations in a stored program control switching machine that have not been merged with the permanent data base.

RECONFIGURATION A fancy word for rearranging equipment, features and options.

RECORD In a database, a record is a group of related data items treated as one unit of information — for example, your name, address and phone number. Each Record is made up of several fields. A field is simply your last name.

RECORD COMMUNICATIONS Any form of communication which produces a "written" record of the transmission. Teletypewriter and facsimile are examples or record communications. Companies such as RCA Globecom, ITT Worldcom, TRT and MCI, which provide international telex, are known as international record carriers. Before deregulation, that business was exceptionally profitable.

RECORD HEAD The electromagnetic device which magnetizes the surface of a magnetic recording — tape, disk, etc. — in proportion to an electrical signal.

RECORD LENGTH The number of bytes in a record. See RECORD.

RECORD LOCKING Think about an airline reservation. You call up. You want to change your reservation. While the airline has your record open, your travel agent calls up to change it. You change your reservation. Your travel agent changes it. Which one ends up in the "permanent" record? Confusion reigns. Clearly it makes sense to only allow one person to access one record at once and lock everyone else out. Record locking is the most common and most sophisticated means for multi-user LAN applications to maintain data integrity. In a record locking system, users are prevented from working on the same data record at the same time. That way, users don't overwrite other users' changes and data integrity is maintained. But though it doesn't allow users into the same record at the same time, record locking does allows multiple users to work on the same file simultaneously. So multi-user access is maximized. Contrast with file locking, which only allows a single user to work on a file at a time.

RECORDED ANNOUNCEMENT INTERCEPT Provides a recorded message to an intercepted call indicating why the call cannot be completed, as an alternative to attendant intercept or intercept one for DID and CCSA calls to restricted or unassigned numbers.

RECORDED ANNOUNCEMENT SERVICE A special type of central office trunk which when dialed, will connect the caller to a prerecorded message.

RECORDED TELEPHONE DICTATION Phone users can dial into centralized telephone dictation equipment. The dictation equipment is usually handled as a trunk connection or it can be wired on an extension level.

RECORDER A device many large phone users use to record conversations with their callers. Recording truck dispatches can help a company gain the upper hand in customer service. Purchasing departments may use the recorder to remind vendors of their promises. The financial department can document money transfer orders and investments. Recorders come in several sizes. There are cassette recorders with standard speed and slow extended play speed. Open or reel-to-reel recorders have features similar to cassette recorders. Cassette recorders may be voice-operated (VOX) or started by a recorder coupler. Channel capacities available today include 7, 10, 14, 20, 28, 30, 40, 56 and 60 channels, depending on the manufacturer. Some recorders can search for and recall conversations recorded with an option called "autosearch."

RECOVERY The way a computer or telephone system resumes operation after overcoming a problem with the hardware (say a power failure) or a program error. Some phone systems recover quickly by themselves. Some recover slowly by themselves. Some need human intervention. These are the slowest. Check yours out. If your recovery is slow, and if you local power company is unreliable, you might consider backing your computer up with an uninterruptible power supply.

RECTIFIER A device for converting Alternating Current (AC) into Direct Current (DC). AC current comes out of the commercial power supply — 120 volts, 60 Hz. DC power is what drives telephone systems and the circuits that move the transmission around. Typically that DC power ranges from 5 to 48 volts.

RED ALARM In T-1, a red alarm is generated for a locally detected failure such as when a condition like OOF exists for 2.5 seconds, causing a CGA, (Carrier Group Alarm).

RED BOX A device that produces tones similar to those produced by dropping coins into a pay phone to inform the operator or automatic machinery that money has been deposited. The red box is used to defraud telephone companies. It is so named because they are usually built small enough to be placed in the "crush proof box" of a packet of Marlboro cigarettes. Red boxes are illegal.

REDUNDANCY 1. That part of any message which can be eliminated without losing the important information. 2. Having one or more "backup" systems available in case of failure of the main system.

REDUNDANCY CHECK A technique of error detection involving the transmission of additional data related to the basic data in such a way that the receiving terminal, by comparing the two sets of data, can determine to a high degree of probability whether there has been an error in transmission.

REDUNDANT BITS The extra bits included in a transmission for purposes of detecting and/or correcting errors. See REDUNDANCY CHECK.

REED RELAY Two tiny pieces of metal encapsulated in a tiny nitrogen-filled glass tube. When a current is passed through a magnet around the nitrogen-filled glass capsule, one arm of the metal reed relay moves and makes contact with the other. In this way it acts as a "switch." Reed relay switches are reliable. Because they are metal, they can carry great amounts of data. They are rapidly becoming obsolete.

REFERENCE CLOCK A clock of high stability and accuracy that is used to govern the frequency of a network and mutually synchronize clocks of lower stability.

REFERENCE LEVEL The measure of a value used as a starting point for further measurements. In communications applications this term usually refers to a power level of a signal or a noise. A common reference level is 0 dBm, that is, 1 milliwatt.

REFERENCE NOISE RN. A reference level of noise power.

REFRACTIVE INDEX A ratio of the velocity of light in a vacuum to the velocity of light in another medium, like glass.

REFRESH RATE With conventional CRT displays, the rate per unit of time at which a displayed image is renewed in order to appear stable. Typically, 50 times per second, or 50 Hz (in Europe), or 60 times per second, or 60 Hz (in the United States).

REGENERATE To restore a signal to its original shape. Signals need to be restored because they become distorted and acquire noise during transmission. Analog signals cannot be regenerated because it is very hard for telecommunications equipment to distinguish between unwanted noise and wanted noise (i.e. your voice) in an analog signal. Digital signals can be more easily regenerated since they consist of "ones" and "zeros." If digital signals are flattened or distorted, a simple logic circuit — "Is it a zero or a one?" — can restore the signal to its original clean squared shape.

REGENERATIVE REPEATER A device which regenerates incoming signals and retransmits these signals on an outgoing circuit. See REGENERATE.

REGIONAL CENTER A control center (Class 1 office) connecting sectional centers of the telephone system together.

REGISTER A device capable of storing a specified amount of data, such as one word. The register holds the information for manipulation by the telephone system or a computer. In an automatic telephone system, a register receives dialed pulses or pushbutton tones and then uses that information to control the switch.

REGISTERED TERMINAL EQUIPMENT Terminal equipment which is registered for connection to the telecommunications network in accordance with Subpart C of Part 68 of the FCC's Rules. If a terminal device has been properly registered it will have an identification number permanently affixed to it.

REGISTRATION NUMBER (FCC PART 68) Approval number given to telephone equipment to certify that a particular device passes the tests defined in Part 68 of the FCC Rules. These tests certify the phone won't cause any harm to the public network. They do not attest to the commercial value of the product, nor whether it will (or won't) sell. See REGISTRATION PROGRAM.

REGISTRATION PROGRAM FCC program governing the direct connection of terminal equipment, whether customer-provided or telephone company-provided, to the telecommunications network without the need for a protective connecting arrangement (PCA). An applicant for equipment registration is required to show the equipment meets technical standards developed by the FCC. See REGISTRATION NUMBER and PART 68.

REGRESSION ANALYSIS A method of forecasting the future by plotting events in the past and assuming there'll be some similarity in the future. About as accurate as any other pseudoscientific method.

REGULATED Controlled for uniformity. Many aspects of telecom are regulated — from the input voltage powering a telecom system to the output signal of a microwave system. 2. Adhering to the rules, and sundry whims of a government agency. Most aspects of the telephone business are under the control of a government agency to some degree. Their rules cover everything from certifying of expenses which may be capitalized to specifying how many seconds the subscriber can be forced to wait for dial tone (three seconds). Stripped to bare essentials, a regulatory agency can only do two things. First, it can allow the regulated entity to raise its prices to a point where nobody wants to buy anymore. Second, it can stop competitors coming into the business. The first (high price) is the reason no one (or few people, anyway) send telegrams. The second (keep out the competition) reason gets stymied because new technology — e.g. cheap local microwave — comes along to force the regulatory agency's hand. In the long run, no regulated entity survives because it has a regulated monopoly. It survives because it provides good service at a fair price.

REGULATORY GROUPS Refers to local, State or Federal entities that issue orders, findings, etc. that are binding upon providers and users of telecommunications and services.

REJ Abbreviation for REJect.

REL Release Message. The fifth of the ISUP call set-up messages. A message sent in either direction indicating that the circuit identified in the message is being released due to the reason (cause) supplied and is ready to be put into the idle state on receipt of the Release Complete Message. See ISUP and COMMON CHANNEL SIGNALING.

RELATIONAL DATABASE The most popular method of creating a database system. In its simplest definition (and this is not a data processing dictionary) a relational database is actually a collection of data files that "relate" to each other through at least one common field. For example, one's employee number can be the common thread through several data files — payroll, telephone directory, etc. One's employee number might thus be a good way of relating all the files together in one gigantic data base management system (DBMS).

RELATIVE TRANSMISSION LEVEL The ratio of the test-tone power at one point to the test-tone power at some other point in the system chosen as a reference point.

RELAX A release tool for an Ericsson AXE.

RELAY An electrically activated switch used to operate a circuit. It connects one set of wires to another. Typically the relay opens and closes because a surrounding magnetic field is turned on or off. Older telephone switches used many relays to switch (i.e. complete) their calls. Relays come in many forms. There are hermetically-sealed relays, in which thin metal contacts are sealed in an airtight glass or metal enclosure. There are also mercury relays in which a small tube of mercury tilts and completes or breaks a circuit. See also REED RELAY.

RELAY RACK Open ironwork designed to mount and support electronic equipment. A relay rack is to electronic equipment what a distribution frame is to wire. See DISTRIBUTION FRAME.

RELEASE 1. A call comes into a switchboard. The operator calls you to tell you it's for you. Then he/she "releases" the call to you. On most switchboards there's a button labelled "RLS." That's the release button. 2. The ending of an inbound ACD call by hanging up. 3. The feature key on most ACD instruments labelled Release.

RELEASE LINK CAPABILITY The ability for an originating switching system, on receipt of a new destination address from the current terminating switching system, to release the transmission link to that terminating switching system and continue call processing using the new destination address. Definition from Bellcore in reference to its concept of the Advanced Intelligent Network.

RELEASE LINK TRUNK RLT. Telecommunications channel used with Centralized Attendant Service to connect attendant-seeking calls from a branch location to a main location.

RELEASE WITH HOWLER If a phone stays off-hook without originating a call (or the receiver is accidentally knocked off), the system transmits a loud tone over the line and then disconnects the line and the phone. The central office effectively then ignores them (the line and the phone) until someone puts the receiver back on-hook again.

RELIABILITY A measure of how dependable a system is once you actually use it. Very different from MTBF (Mean Time Between Failures). And very different from availability. See MTBF.

RELOCATABLE CODE Machine language programs that can reside in any portion of memory.

REMOTE ACCESS Sending and receiving data to and from a computer or controlling a computer with terminals or PCs connected through communications (i.e. phone) links.

REMOTE ACCESS TO PBX SERVICES Allows a user outside the PBX to access the PBX by dialing it over a normal phone line. You dial the number. It answers. It may or may not say anything. It may just give you dial tone. You now punch in an authorization code. If your code is acceptable, the PBX gives you another dial tone. That dial tone is effectively the one all users within the PBX get. Once you have this dial tone, you can dial another extension, jump on the company's WATS network, get into the dictation unit, access its voice mail, or whatever. Suffice, you are inside the PBX. You can do whatever anyone else inside the PBX can do.

REMOTE BATCH PROCESSING Processing in a computer system in which batch programs and batch data are entered from a remote terminal or a remote PC (personal computer) over phone lines.

REMOTE CALL FORWARDING RCF. This is a neat service. It allows a customer to have a local telephone number in a distant city. Every time someone calls that number, that call is forwarded to you in your city. Remote call forwarding is very much like call forwarding on a local residential line, except that you have no phone, no office and no physical presence in that distant city. Remote Call Forwarding exists purely in the central office. You can also think of it as measured Foreign Exchange. Companies buy Remote Call Forwarding for three reasons: 1. To encourage distant customers to call them by giving them a local number in their own city to call. (This the most obvious reason for an IN-WATS line, a FX or a RCF line). 2. They buy RCF over IN-WATS or FX lines because they don't have the volume to justify these potentially more expensive lines. 3. Companies buy RCF lines as overflow lines from IN-WATS and FX lines. They use their RCF lines when the other lines (FX and IN-WATS) get busy during peak busy periods. Remote Call Forwarding calls are typically charged at the same price as normal DDD calls (i.e. the most expensive to call). And you can't, as yet, reprogram RCF calls easily. You have to place an order with your friendly telco and wait...

REMOTE CONCENTRATOR A remote multiplexer. A device which places more than one distant user on two cable pairs. The idea of a remote concentrator is to substitute electronics for cable. It's simply cheaper to put electronics on either end of two cable pairs and drive many conversations through those wires, than running extra cables (digging streets, erecting poles, etc.)

REMOTE DIAGNOSTICS You own a phone system. You have a service company. There's some problem with it. Instead of sending a technician out, your service company dials your PBX from a data terminal or PC and "asks" your PBX in computerese what's wrong with it. If it isn't too broken, it will come back and give you some indication. This is called remote diagnostics. Some service companies call all their customers' phone systems every morning and run routine remote diagnostics on their switch. It's like going to the doctor for a daily physical. Sometimes this test may find a problem before the user is even aware. Sometimes the problem can be repaired on-line. If not, the service company will have to dispatch a technician. Remote diagnostics is a good idea. More phone systems should have it. To do remote diagnostics on a telephone system, you will typically need a phone line dedicated to the PBX and a modem on either end.

REMOTE JOB ENTRY RJE. Remote Job Entry occurs in computer operations where work or input is sent in remotely over phone lines. That "work" might include the day's sales of a distant store.

REMOTE LINE CONCENTRATOR A multiplexer. A device that "concentrates" several users' lines on a fewer number of trunks. Typically, a remote line concentrator is used because it's cheaper, easier or more flexible to substitute electronics for cable. See REMOTE CONCENTRATOR.

REMOTE LINE SWITCH A line unit mounted near a cluster of users and equipped with intracalling capability.

REMOTE LINE UNIT A remote line concentrator without intracalling capability. See REMOTE CONCENTRATOR and REMOTE LINE SWITCH.

REMOTE MAINTENANCE FACILITY See REMOTE DIAGNOSTICS.

REMOTE OFFICE TEST LINE ROTL. A testing device that acts in conjunction with a central controller and a responder to make two-way transmission and supervision measurements.

REMOTE OPERATIONS SERVICE ELEMENT ROSE. An application layer protocol that provides the capability to perform remote operations at a remote process. Definition from Bellcore in reference to its concept of the Advanced Intelligent Network.

REMOTE ORDER WIRE An order wire is a line on which maintenance and monitoring is done. A remote order wire is an order wire that has been extended to a distant point that may be more convenient.

REMOTE PROGRAMMING Dial your phone system with your friendly personal computer, modem and a communications software package and you can change the telephone system's programming remotely. This feature is great for companies with telephone systems in many locations. They can all be run from one central point. This feature is also great if you want some changes made on your system. It's obviously a lot cheaper for your vendor to make those changes from his office rather than have to visit yours. It's also a lot faster. See REMOTE DIAGNOSTICS.

REMOTE SITE (LOCATION) A location for a DCE device which is not at the central or control site. A typical application would have a terminal at the remote site and the host computer at the central or control site.

REMOTE STATION Any piece of equipment attached to a LAN by a telephone company supplied link. Technically, that includes all devices that aren't servers. Usually it refers to a workstation at a distant location, linked to the main LAN by a modem and connected through a serial port "gateway." See MODEM.

REMOTE STATION LAMP FIELD For use at multi-line phones, usually manned by secretaries who answer many phone lines.

REMOTE SWITCHING SYSTEM A technique of handling the switching functions of a remote location by relaying the calls through a more sophisticated switching system in a central location. See also REMOTE CONCENTRATOR.

REMOTE TERMINAL A terminal connected to a computer over a phone line.

REMOTE TRAFFIC MEASUREMENT Traffic and feature usage data can be transmitted by the system to a distant service technician.

REMOVABLE CARTRIDGE SYSTEM A high-capacity storage system that can be removed from the PC. A removable cartridge systems consists of a drive mechanism and the cartridges used to store data. The most well-known removable cartridge system is the Bernoulli Box by Iomega Corp.

REN Ringer Equivalency Number. Part of the FCC certification number approving a telephone terminal product for direct sale to the end user as not doing harm to the network. The REN consists of a number and a letter which indicates the frequency response of that telephone's ringer. "A" = 20 Hz or 30 Hz "B" = a range from 15.3 Hz to 68 Hz. The remaining letters represent ringers that will work on very narrow ranges such as "C" = 15.3 Hz to 17.4

Hz, etc. The number indicates the quantity of ringers which may be connected to a single telephone line and still all ring. The total of all RENs of the telephones connected to the one line must not exceed the value 5 or some or all of the ringers may not operate.

REORDER TONE The Reorder tone sounds like a busy signal but is twice as fast. It means that all switching paths are busy. A busy signal means that the line called is in use. A reorder (or fast busy) tone means all the circuits are busy. But you have a much better chance of getting one out of many than one out of one. So if you hear a reorder signal, dial back immediately.

REPAIR SERVICE ANSWERING RSA. Functions that support the initial handling and entry of subscriber reported troubles. They enable subscribers to request trouble verification tests, to to initiate a trouble report and to obtain information on the status of an open trouble report. Definition from Bellcore in reference to its concept of the Advanced Intelligent Network.

REPEATER A device inserted at intervals along a circuit to boost, and amplify an analog signal being transmitted. A repeater is needed because the quality and strength of a signal decays over distance. You will find repeaters in cables and in microwave systems. Repeaters may also regenerate a digital signal — "squaring it" and "cleaning" it up — but not changing it. Regenerating the signal removes noise and thus reduces the likelihood of errors. You can only regenerate digital signals. You cannot regenerate analog signals. You can regenerate digital signals because a machine can tell what's a signal and what's noise in a digital signal. But no machine exists to do that with an analog signal.

REPEATING COIL A transformer which connects one telephone circuit with another without any DC connection between the circuits.

REPERFORATOR/TRANSMITTER RT. A teletypewriter unit consisting of a reperforator and a tape transmitter, each independent of the other.

REPLY A transmitted message which serves as a response to an original message. (What else?)

REPORT PROGRAM GENERATOR A computer language for processing large data files.

REPORT-ONLY EVENT An event that the ASC (AIN Switch Capabilities) reports to a SLEE (Service Logic Execution Environment) but the ASC does not suspend processing events for the connection segment. Definition from Bellcore in reference to its concept of the Advanced Intelligent Network.

REQUEST TO SEND RTS. One of the control signals on a standard RS-232-C connector. It places the modem in the originate mode so it can begin to send.

RESALE CARRIER A long distance company that does not own its own transmission lines. It buys lines from other carriers and then resells them to its subscribers. Some resale carriers have their own switches. Some don't. Some have a mix of their own lines and leased lines. Most long distance carriers — including MCI and US Sprint — have a mix of their own lines and leased lines.

RESERVE POWER A telephone system may be equipped with storage batteries to provide primary power during a commercial power failure. No loss of service will occur during transition to battery power. All this is a long way of saying your phone system is backed by batteries, typically lead acid (the same ones used in your car).

RESIDENT PROGRAM See RAM-RESIDENT PROGRAM.

RESIDENTIAL AND LIGHT COMMERCIAL WIRING Refers to the wiring system and all of its appurtenances required to provide convenient and useful telephone services to residences and light commercial buildings.

RESIDUAL ERROR RATE The ratio of the number of bits, unit elements, characters or blocks incorrectly received but undetected or uncorrected by the error-control equipment to the total number of bits, unit elements, characters or blocks sent.

RESISTANCE Any electrical conductor will resist the flow of electrical current. As it resists the flow of current, so the current becomes weaker. Resistance generates heat and occasionally light. It is technically defined as a property or a characteristic of a conductor, i.e. the metal through which the electricity flows. It is measured in Ohms.

RESISTOR A device whose function is to put resistance into an electrical circuit.

RESOLUTION A measure of the quality of a transmitted image. Beginning with the scan processing in the transmitter and ending with the display and/or printing process in the receiver, resolution is a basic parameter of any image transmission system. It affects the design of all its subsystems. In the scanner, the resolution is a function of the spot size which the scanner optics and associated electronics "look" at the scene and through which the system can uniquely identify the smallest distance along the scan line. Resolution is measured in picture elements (pixels). The number of picture elements per inch determines the sharpness of what it is you're transmitting.

RESONANCE The condition that exists when inductive reactance equals capacitive reactance. In a series circuit it results in maximum current at the resonant frequency. In a parallel circuit it results in maximum voltage at the resonant frequency.

RESONANT CAVITY Closed metal container which has the characteristics of a parallel resonant circuit.

RESPONDER A test line that can make transmission and supervision measurements through its host switch under control of a remote computer.

RESPONSE An answer to an inquiry. In IBM's SNA, the control information sent from a secondary station to the primary station under SDLC.

RESPONSE TIME The time it takes a system to react to a given input. When operating a terminal connected to a computer, response time would be the time between the operator pressing the last key of a series of keys and the appearance of a response on the operator's display. In a data communications system, response time includes the transmission time, the processing time, the searching for records time and the transmission time back to the originator. Response time is very critical in applications like airline reservation systems. Here the customer is on the phone awaiting a reply. That time is critical in whether the customer perceives he's getting good or bad service. Response times of more than three seconds are not acceptable in situations where the customer is waiting on the phone to buy something. Response time is a function, inter alia, of the number of phone lines you lease or use. You can save a lot of phone line costs by cutting back on lines. But you'll extend response time. Life, as always, is a trade-off.

RESTART A central office word for the rebooting a personal computer. In telephony, a system initiated action designed to restore overall service capacity.

RESTORE Typically, to put a telephone system back into full operation.

RESTRICTION Phone systems can disallow people or extensions from making certain calls. If they're not allowed to make long distance calls, this is called toll restriction. See TOLL RESTRICTION. There are other forms of restriction, like being able to only use the company's internal network.

RESTRICTION FROM OUTGOING CALLS Phone users may be restricted from placing outgoing calls. See CLASS OF SERVICE.

RESTRICTION SERVICES These features allow the attendant to control the restriction of phones or groups of phones. It can be very useful in hotels and motels to turn off service to room phones during the time between check out and check in of quests. Here are some examples of restriction services:

- CONTROLLED OUTWARD RESTRICTION: Phones can be restricted from making dialed outgoing calls while inward calls are completed normally.
- CONTROLLED STATION-TO-STATION RESTRICTION: Originating phone calls to other extensions in the system are blocked, however, normal incoming and outgoing calls can be completed.
- CONTROLLED TERMINATION RESTRICTION: Phones can complete outgoing calls normally, but incoming calls are directed to either the attendant or an intercept tone or recording.
- CONTROLLED TOTAL RESTRICTION: Restricted phone lines cannot make or receive any calls.

RETRACTILE CORD A coiled cord that springs back to its original length when you let it go. Telephone handset cords are the most common retractile cords. There are wide quality variations among retractile cords. Western Electric (oops AT&T Technologies) has set a very good standard for retractile cords. But not everyone conforms to it. If you want to quickly see the quality difference among various coil cords, take six from different manufacturers and hang them over your office door and come back in a week. You'll see a bunch touching the floor. Others will still be taut. Another way is simply to connect them to your phone, one by one, and listen to the differences. Some simply sound weaker. Cheaper ones tend to sound worse. (So what's new?)

RETRANSMISSIVE STAR In optical fiber transmission, a passive component that permits the light signal on an input fiber to be retransmitted on multiple output fibers. The signal comes in on one fiber, hits a star-type connector which splays the transmission out. A retransmissive star is formed by heating together a bundle of fibers to near their melting point. Such a device is used mainly in fiber-based local networks. It's also called star coupler. When you see one you'll be surprised how crude this device looks, despite its fancy name.

RETRIAL After failing to complete a call, a person tries again. This is called a "retrial." The term is used in traffic engineering. It's critical in figuring needed trunking capacity. See QUEUING THEORY, POISSON and TRAFFIC ENGINEERING.

RETROFIT KIT A conversion kit which makes a standard pay phone into one which will accept credit cards.

RETRY In the bisync protocol, the process of resending the current block of data a prescribed number of times until it is accepted.

RETURN A carriage return. This key on some keyboards is also called "Enter." Touching the CR (Carriage Return) gives you two functions: a "line terminating function" and a "new line function", abbreviated "NL". Simply put, a Return at the end of a line, terminates that line and begins a new one.

RETURN LOSS A measure of the similarity of the impedance of a transmission line and the impedance at its termination. It is a ratio, expressed in decibels, of the power of outgoing signal to the power of the signal reflected back from an impedance discontinuity.

RETURN TO ZERO RZ. Method of transmitting binary information such that, after each encoded bit, voltage returns to the zero level.

REVENUE ACCOUNTING OFFICE RAO. A telephone company center using mainframe computers for billing other data processing. Functions performed include receipt and processing of AMA (Automatic Message Accounting) data and preparation of the subscriber's bill. Definition from Bellcore in reference to its concept of the Advanced Intelligent Network.

REVERSE BATTERY SUPERVISION A way of telling the originating central office that the called telephone has been answered (i.e. it has gone off-hook). The voltage of the line at the originating end is reversed. Reverse battery supervision, which puts a signal at the user's premises, is very useful for devices like call accounting systems (knowing precisely when to begin the billing cycle) and telemarketing systems (knowing precisely when to transfer the machined-dialed call over to the operator). See also ANSWER SUPERVISION.

REVERSE CHANNEL 1. A (typically) small-bandwidth channel used for supervisory or error-control signaling. Signals are transmitted in the opposite direction to the data that is sent. 2. The channel in a dial-up telephone circuit from the called party to the calling party.

REVERSE INTERRUPT In Bisync, a control character sequence (DLE) sequence sent by a receiving station instead of ACK1 or ACK0 to request premature termination of the transmission in progress.

REVERSE MATCHING Attaching the name and address to a phone number. A It's a job usually done by a specialized service bureau. Called "reverse" matching because the service bureaus started in business by attaching phone numbers to lists containing names and their addresses. With ANI (Automatic Number Identification), we get the phone numbers of people calling us. But we don't get their names and addresses. We need to get this information for many reasons. The obvious being that getting this information on-line and fast saves asking the caller for it and typing all the stuff in. That saves time on the phone — as much as 20 seconds. And fewer questions about boring stuff like phone number, address, city, state, zip means less typing time (also called data entry time, less clerking time) and more time to explain the specials we're selling today. In short, the fewer questions we ask, the less we type and the more stuff we can sell. Reverse matching can be done instantly on-line via a direct data hookup to a distant specialized service bureau or it can be done at the end of the month when we receive our 800 phone bill containing the phone numbers of the people who called us that month.

REVERSE TRANSFER An Inter-Tel term for a phone feature in which a call on common hold at any phone may be retrieved from any phone anywhere in the phone system.

REVERSE VIDEO A video display with all the characters reversed. Characters which are normally white on the screen appear black. And blacks appear white. Reverse video is used to emphasize or enhance things — like those characters to be printed in italics or bold.

REVISABLE-FORM DOCUMENT An electronic document with its formatting information intact, readable and modifiable.

REWRITABLE OPTICAL DISKS They look like CD-ROMS but they're not. On one side you can store 284 megabytes or 335 megabytes depending on how large you make the sectors — either 512-byte sectors or 1,024-byte, respectively. All the optical disks conform to standards set up by ISO. They fit between Winchester hard drives and tape drives. Compared with hard drives, they are very very slow. And the optical drives are not cheap — at least $4,000 at this writing. However, the optical disks are cheap and make reasonably good secondary storage devices.

RF Radio Frequency. Electromagnetic waves operating between 10 kHz and 3 MHz propagated without guide (wire or cable) in free space. If you have a home computer that lets you use your home TV set as a video display device, then the computer has an RF Generator. This means that this device is generating an RF carrier to carry the video signal information.

RFI Request For Information. General notification of an intended purchase of equipment or equipment and lines sent to potential suppliers to determine interest and solicit general descriptive product materials, but not prices or a formal request. See RFQ for a detailed explanation.

RFP A Request For Proposal. A detailed document prepared by a buyer defining his requirements for service and equipment sent to one or several vendors. A vendor's response to an RFP will typically be binding on the vendor, i.e. he will be obliged to deliver what he says in his RFP at the prices and following the conditions explained in that RFP. See RFQ for a detailed explanation.

RFQ Request For Quotation. A document prepared by a buyer defining his needs for service and equipment in fairly broad terms and sent to one or several vendors. The RFQ is much less detailed than the RFP. Let's start at the beginning of the buying process. We have a buyer who wants a phone system. His first step may be to issue a formal or informal RFI — Request For Information. In effect, the RFI says "Please tell me what you have. I have a vague idea of what I want but I don't know exactly what is available to suit my needs. Please send me some information."

After a buyer gets his responses to his RFI's, he may issue an RFQ — Request For Quotation. An RFQ may include a tentative configuration of the type of phone system the user wants, plus some listing of features the buyer is interested in. In the RFQ, the buyer asks for some rough ballpark of the possible price for such a system. Usually the "price" is within plus or minus 10% of where it will eventually be in the final configuration. In short, an RFQ's purpose is not to buy, but to find out what's out there and what it might cost. The purpose may be to allocate a budget or to put aside some money for the forthcoming purchase.

An RFP — Request For Proposal — is much more formal and definitive. Its purpose is simple. The buyer wants to buy something. The RFP contains a list of what the buyer wants, when he wants it, how it should be installed, how it should delivered, what financing may be necessary. It is now up to the vendor/s to respond with their configuration, their precise prices and their terms and conditions of sale. Whatever the vendor responds with — called a Response to an RFP — constitutes a definite offer. At this point, the buyer can negotiate the terms of the vendor's Response to his RFP. This will lead to the writing, and eventual signing of a contract. Or the buyer may simply decide to accept the Vendor's Response. Often that Response may have a line at the back of it — "I accept the terms and conditions of this response." If the buyer signs this, then the Response to the RFP becomes a valid contract.

RH Request Header or Response Header.

RHEOSTAT A variable resistor.

RIBBON CABLE Multi-wire cable that is flat instead of round. In ribbon cable, the conductors are laid side by side. Ribbon cable can be more easily laid under carpeting because it is flat and thus, can extend phone and computer services to places otherwise hard to reach. There are disadvantages to ribbon cable. Because ribbon cable is flat, it's hard to twist its individual wire conductors around each other (thus humming can be a problem). It is hard to put a metal shielding around the twisted wire pairs. It is hard to put coax cable into ribbon cable. It is hard to make ribbon cable sufficiently strong to withstand thousands of high heels trampling it. It is hard to make ribbon cable which turns a corner... But there has been enormous progress in ribbon cable. And ribbon cable is finding greater use in buildings. These days it even carries commercial A.C. power.

RING 1. As in Tip and Ring. One of the two wires (the two are Tip and Ring) needed to set up a telephone connection. 2. Also a reference to the ringing of the telephone set. 3. The design of a Local Area Network (LAN) in which the wiring loops from one workstation to another, forming a circle (thus, the term "ring"). In a ring LAN, data is sent from workstation to workstation around the loop in the same direction. Each workstation (which is usually a PC) acts as a repeater by re-sending messages to the next PC in the ring. The more PCs, the slower the LAN. Network control is distributed in a ring network. Since the message passes through each PC, loss of one PC may disable the entire network. However, most ring LANs recover very quickly should one PC die or be turned off. If it dies, you can remove it physically from the network. If it's off, the network senses that and the token ignores that machine. In some token LANs, the LAN will close around a dead workstation and join the two workstations on either side together. If you lose the PC doing the control functions, another PC will jump in and take over. This is how the IBM Token-Passing Ring works. See TOPOLOGY, BYPASS CABLE and TOKEN RING.

RING AGAIN The PBX remembers the last number called by a phone and will redial it when the feature is activated.

RING BACK TONE The sound you hear when you're calling someone else's phone. The tone you hear is generated by a device at your central office and may bear no relationship to the sound the phone at the other end is emitting — or not emitting. If your call didn't go through the first time, always call back at least once. See RINGING TONE.

RING BANDING A method of color coding insulated conductors by means of a small band of colored ink applied circumferentially at regular intervals along the axis of the insulated conductor.

RING BATTERY Commonly unfiltered -24 VDC source that supplies operating power to all local KSU components. Also called the B Battery.

RING CONDUCTOR One conductor of a phone line.

RING CYCLE A ring cycle in North America is typically six seconds long, two of ringing, four of silence, then repeated.

RING INDICATOR Modem interface signal defined in RS-232-C which indicates to the data terminal equipment that a call is coming in.

RING ISOLATOR A device placed on a telephone line to disconnect the ringer when it is an idle state. It is used for noise prevention.

RING LATENCY The time required to repeat the frame at a phone on a ring.

RING NETWORK A network that links PBXs, computers, terminals, printers and other devices in a circular communications link. See RING.

RING SIGNAL The pulse ringing voltage output of the local Interrupter KSU. Typically, this signal is 105 VAC with a duty cycle of 2 seconds on and 4 seconds off.

RING TRIP The process of stopping the AC ringing signal at the central office when the telephone being rung is answered.

RINGDOWN CIRCUIT A tie line connecting phones in which picking up one phone automatically rings the other phone. In a ringdown circuit, a ringing current (AC) is sent down the line. That current may light a lamp, set off a bell, buzz a buzzer. The idea is to alert the person at the other end to the incoming call.

RINGDOWN INTERFACE A private line two-wire interface also called Loop Start Trunk.

RINGER A bell in a telephone which indicates if a phone call is coming in. These days "ringers" are electromechanical and clunky (old-style) or small and electronic (new style). The new electronic ones are cheaper, but less interesting to listen to. Most sound like bleating sheep in heat.

RINGER EQUIVALENCE NUMBER REN. A number required in the U.S. for registering your telephone equipment with the phone company. Add together the REN's of all the telephones on a single line. The sum of those numbers should never exceed five otherwise none of your bells will work and you won't hear an incoming call. (Your central office simply doesn't send sufficient current down the line.) The alphabetic character after the number refers to the ringing frequency of the alternating current sent down the line to ring the bell. If the letter is "A", the ringer frequency is about 20 Hertz. Most single line phones have a Ringer Equivalence of 1.0A. If the letter is "B", the ringer will respond to any current coming down the line. Any other letter, and you are probably on a party line where the ringer frequency is used for party selection. In Canada, they use the term "Load Number" instead of Ringer Equivalence. The numbers are different, but the concept is the same. See LOAD NUMBER.

RINGER ISOLATOR A device in the phone which disconnects the ringer when ringing voltage is not present.

RINGING Alternating Current (AC) sent out from the central office along the local loop to the subscriber. It's typically 70 to 90 volts at 17 Hz to 20 Hz. You can get a mild shock if you have your hands on a telephone circuit when ringing current comes along. The rest of the time, the lines are harmless.

RINGING GENERATOR An optional KTU facility that generates the AC ringer voltage from the 24 VDC local Key System Power Supply source. Typically, this voltage is 90 to 115 (nominally 105) VAC at 30 Hertz.

RINGING KEY A key that sends a ringing current.

RINGING SIGNAL Any AC or DC signal transmitted over a line or trunk for the purpose of alerting someone or some thing at the distant end of an incoming call.

RINGING TONE A low tone which is one second ON and three seconds OFF. It indicates that ringing current is being sent by the central office to the person receiving the call. Ringing tone is not produced by the calling party's central office — but by the called party's central office. Thus, it is possible for you to hear ringing tone but for the person you are calling not to hear anything. As a general rule, if the person doesn't answer, call them a second time. Often, they'll say "The phone never rang." This will not be a lie, but simply a temporary glitch in their central office.

RINGING TRANSFER A PBX feature which allows you to choose which bells in a group of phones will ring when a call is coming in for that group.

RINGING VOLTAGE In addition to talk battery, a Central Office provides ringing signaling. Ring Voltage is generally 70 to 90 volts at 17 Hz to 20 Hz. See also RINGING.

RINGMATE A New York Telephone service which allows you to add one or two additional numbers to your existing phone number. You can tell which phone is ringing by the sound of the ringing. You can, of course, only speak on one line at once. The purpose of the service is to help you identify who's calling you and decide whether or not to answer.

RIP-CORD A cord placed directly under the jacket of a cable in order to facilitate stripping (removal) of the jacket.

RISC Reduced Instruction Set Computer. Computers based on an unusual high speed processing technology that uses a far simpler set of operating commands. These commands greatly speed a computer's performance, especially for calculation-intensive operations such as those performed by scientists and computer-aided design (CAD) and computer-aided manufacture (CAM) engineers. RISC is a design that achieves high performance by doing the most common computer operations very quickly. In contrast, the microprocessors used in most PCs are based on a design called CISC (Complex Instruction Set Computing). CISC does not execute instructions as quickly as RISC but it has more commands and accomplishes more with each command. Programs written for RISC are typically not compatible with those written for CISC processors.

RISER The conduit or path between floors of a building into which telephone and other utility cables are placed to bring service from one floor to another. Your risers should be twice the size you ever think you'll need in the next 30 years. It's expensive to build risers after the building is built. Very expensive.

RIT Rate of Information Transfer. The amount of information that can be communicated from a sender to a receiver in a given length of time.

RJ Registered Jack.

RJE Remote Job Entry. A Remote Job Entry terminal is used for the transmission of "batch" data to a remote computer system. Processed information is then returned to the printer in the terminal. This type of processing from a remote site is a standard method of data transmission. See IBM.

RJXXX Registered Jack

RLC Release Complete Message. The sixth ISUP call set-up message. A message sent in either direction in response to the receipt of a Release Message, or if appropriate to, a Reset Circuit Message when the circuit concerned has been brought into the idle condition. See ISUP and COMMON CHANNEL SIGNALING.

RLCM Remote Line Concentrating Module

RLL Run Length Limited. A type of data coding used for disk drives.

RLT Release-Link Trunks.

RMATS Remote Maintenance and Test System. That equipment and programming used to run, maintain and test a telephone system remotely — usually by dialing in on a special phone line.

RMS Root Mean Square. Method of measuring amplifier power.

RNR Abbreviation for not ready to receive.

RO Receive Only.

ROAMING A mobile telephone user who uses service in more than one basic service area, i.e. he roams from area to area.

ROBBED-BIT SIGNALING In T-1, refers to the use of the least significant bit of every word of frames 6 and 12 (D4), or 6, 12, 18 and 24 (ESF) for signaling purposes.

ROH Receiver Off Hook.

ROI Return On Investment.

ROLL-CALL POLLING A technique in which every station is interrogated sequentially by a central computer system.

ROLMNET II ANALYSIS AND SUPPORT A service provided by the Rolm Analysis Center (RAC) that analyzes current call patterns and trunking facilities, chooses alternative facilities, and recommends the most cost effective long distance network based on the customer's needs. It also compares the present facilities to the proposed network and calculates cost savings.

ROLMPHONE DATA (RPD) INTERFACE A group of printed circuit cards forming the interface between Rolm digital desktop products and the CBX (Rolm's name for its PBX) for transmission of digital data. It accommodates ROLMphone telephones equipped with DataCom Modules, as well as Cedar, Cypress and Juniper desktop products. Compare with ROLMPHONE INTERFACE.

ROLMPHONE INTERFACE RPI. A group of printed circuit cards forming the interface between Rolm digital desktop products and the CBX for transmission of digitized voice signals. In addition to the ROLMphones, the RPI also accommodates connections to Cypress, Cedar and Juniper. Compare with ROLMPHONE DATA INTERFACE.

ROLMPHONES A family of electronic telephones which only work on the Rolm line of PBXs (which Rolm calls CBXs). As of writing, these phones include the ROLMphone 400, ROLMphone 240 and ROLMphone 120. In addition, Rolm has telephone/workstation devices called Cypress, Cedar and Juniper and will probably have more by the time you read this.

ROM Read Only Memory. Computer memory which can only be read from. New data cannot be entered and the existing data is non-volatile. This means it stays there even when power is turned off. A ROM is a memory device which is programmed at the factory and whose contents thereafter cannot be altered. In contrast is the device called RAM, whose contents can be altered. See READ ONLY MEMORY.

ROOM CUT-OFF Hotel/motel guest telephones restricted from outgoing calls when the guest room is unoccupied.

ROOM STATUS AND SELECTION Provides the capability to store and display the occupancy and cleaning status and the type number of each guest room. This helps housekeeping management, maid locating and room selection. Also, communications between the front desk and the housekeeper are speeded up via real-time maid activity and checkout audit printouts to indicate which rooms need cleaning next. The occupancy status is normally changed by the maid or inspector dialing from the room telephone.

ROSE 1. Remote Operations Service Element. An application layer protocol that provides the capability to perform remote operations at a remote process. Definition from Bellcore in reference to its concept of the Advanced Intelligent Network. 2. As in Bodin. The very thoughtful lady who helps us, our friends and customers. We couldn't survive without Rose. Call her and tell her this. 1-212-691-8215.

ROTARY DIAL The circular telephone dial. As it returns to its normal position (after being turned) it opens and closes the electrical loop sent by the central office. Thus it generates pulses for each digit dialed. You can hear the "clicks". The number "seven," for example consists of seven "opens and closes," or seven clicks. You can dial on a rotary phone without using the rotary dial. Simply depress the switch hook quickly, allowing pauses in between to signify that you're about to send a new digit. It's a good party trick.

ROTARY DIAL CALLING The telephone system will accept dialing from conventional rotary dial sets, although pushbutton dial sets offer faster calling and greater reliability.

ROTARY HUNT You buy several phone lines. Let's say 212-691-8215, 212-691-8216, 212-691-8217, 212-691-8218. Someone dials you on your main number — 212-691-8215. It's busy. (That's our number.) The central office slides the call over to 212-691-8216. If that number is busy, it slides it over to 212-691-8217, and so on. This is called rotary hunt. It hunts to the next line in the rotary group. In the old days, the phone lines you could rotary hunt to had to be in numerical sequence. But now with modern stored program control central offices, your lines in rotary hunt can be very different as long as they're all on the same exchange.

ROTARY OUTPUT TO CENTRAL OFFICE Most central offices are equipped to provide tone dial service. In cases where the telephone company central office trunks are not designed to accept tone signaling, your on-premise phone system (PBX, key system or single line phone) will translate the number entered by a phone in tones into rotary dial pulses which can be processed by the central office.

ROTARY REGISTER A Rolm CBX printed circuit card that converts offhook bits corresponding to dial pulses into digital words suitable for computer processing.

ROTARY SENDER A Rolm CBX printed circuit card that receives digital code words from the computer and converts them into digital pulses. These are routed to an interface card which performs the proper outpulsing conversion.

ROTATIONAL MAILBOXES Information only mailboxes whose information is automatically changed on a time-sensitive or usage-sensitive basis.

ROTS Rotary Out-Trunk Switches.

ROUNDTRIP PROPAGATION DELAY Roundtrip propagation delay from a burst modem to a burst modem will be about 470 milliseconds to 570 milliseconds (About half a second). See SATELLITE TRANSMISSION DELAY.

ROUTE ADVANCE This feature routes outgoing calls over alternate long distance lines when the first choice trunk group is busy. The phone user selects the first choice route by dialing the corresponding access code. The phone equipment automatically advances to alternate trunks and trunk groups, based on the user's class of service. Route advance is a more primitive form of least cost routing. See LEAST COST ROUTING.

ROUTE LIST A sequence of trunk groups that can be searched for a particular route. This list is comprised of trunk groups and configuration attributes (e.g. Class of Service) governing the use of a particular trunk group.

ROUTE INDICATOR An address or group of characters in the heading of a message defining the final circuit or terminal to which the message is to be delivered.

ROUTE OPTIMIZATION The Rolm way of saying Least Cost Routing. See LEAST COST ROUTING and ROUTE OPTIMIZATION II.

ROUTE OPTIMIZATION II A Rolm product which offers automatic long distance cost control through Least Cost Routing, Queuing, Toll Restriction and the use of alternate long distance carriers. See also LEAST COST ROUTING, QUEUING and TOLL RESTRICTION.

ROUTER Roughly like a bridge, but more protocol-dependent. A router can usually link only LANs with the identical protocol — two Starlan LANs, two

NetWare LANs, etc. Bridges are more protocol-independent, and can link more dissimilar LANs, though they can't link entirely dissimilar networks. That requires a gateway. Like bridges, routers restrict a LAN local traffic to itself, only passing data on to the bridged, or routed LAN when that data is specifically intended for it. Contrast to a repeater, which indiscriminately passes all data along, regardless of its destination. See also INTERNETWORKING and BRIDGES.

ROUTING The process of selecting the correct circuit path for a message.

ROUTING CODE The combination of characters or digits required by the switching system to route a transmission to its desired destination.

ROUTING DATA BASE Distance table in DNA.

ROUTING LABEL The part of a signaling message identifying its destination.

ROUTING TABLE 1.Incoming Calls: A routing table is a user definable list of steps which are treatment instructions for an incoming call. Ideally these steps should be addressed and the call treatment begun before the call is answered. A routing table should consist of a minimum of steps that include agent groups, voice response devices, announcements (delay and informational) music on hold, intraflow and interflow steps, route dialing (machine based call forwarding). A significant issue in the structure of routing tables is "look-back" capability, where no one previously interrogated resource is abandoned by the system (i.e. an agent group is now ignored, even though an agent is now available, because the ACD does not consider previous steps in the routing table).

2. Outgoing Calls: For a specific calling site, this table lists the long distance routing choices for each location to be dialed. There may be only one choice (route) listed for some or all destinations or there may be several choices for some destinations. (It depends how many outgoing lines and how many outgoing trunk groups you have.) If there are several choices then they will be ranked by some criteria (least cost, best quality, etc.).

RPD See ROLMPHONE DATA INTERFACE.

RPI See ROLMPHONE INTERFACE.

RPG REPORT PROGRAM GENERATOR.

RPL Rolm Processing Language. A high-level programming language that gives the programmer access to the underlying CBX II 9000 processor architecture so that real-time communications capabilities of the processor microcode can be used.

RPOA Recognized Private Operating Agency. A term used by the CCITT to describe those companies designated as operating telephone companies — if the country's phone networks are not run by government-owned administrations, such as the PTT's in Europe.

RPQ Request for Price Quotation. Solicitation for pricing for a specific component, software product, service or system. See also RFQ.

RR Abbreviation for Ready to Receive.

RS Record Separator.

RS-232-C Also known as RS-232. A set of standards specifying various electrical and mechanical characteristics for interfaces between computers, terminals and modems. The RS-232-C standard, which was developed by the EIA (Electrical Industries Association), defines the mechanical and electrical characteristics for connecting DTE and DCE data communications devices. It defines what the interface does, circuit functions and their corresponding connector pin assignments. The standard applies to both synchronous and asynchronous binary data transmission. Most personal computers use the RS-232-C interface to attach modems. Some printers also use RS-232-C. You should be aware that despite the fact that RS-232-C is an EIA "standard," you cannot necessarily connect one RS-232-C equipped device to another one (like a printer to a computer) and expect them to work intelligently together. That's because different RS-232-C devices are often wired or pinned differently and may also use different wires for different functions. The "traditional" RS-232-C plug has 25 pins. The new IBM PC AT, most AT compatibles and the Toshiba T1100 Plus have a "new" RS-232-C plug with only nine pins. This smaller plug does essentially the same thing as its bigger cousin, but you need an adapter cable to connect one to another. They're freely available. See also interface and the RS-232-C diagram. See the APPENDIX for description of the pins and what they do.

RS-422-A Electrical characteristics of balanced-voltage digital interface circuits.

RS-423-A Electrical characteristics of unbalanced-voltage digital interface circuits.

RS-449 Another "standard" data communications connector. This one uses 37-pins and is designed for higher speed transmission. Each signal pin has its own return line, instead of a common ground return and the signal pairs (signal, return) are balanced lines rather than a signal referenced to ground. This cable typically uses twisted pairs, while a RS-232-C cable usually doesn't. See the APPENDIX.

RS-499-1 Addendum 1 to RS-449. (What else?)

RSC Remote Switching Center

RT Reorder Tone.

RT Remote Terminal

RTAN Real Time ANI.

RTS Request To Send. One of the control signals on a standard RS-232-C connector. It places the modem in the originate mode so it can begin to send. See the APPENDIX.

RTV Real-Time Video. DVI software that implements quick-and-dirty, realtime video compression. Once called "edit-level video," it stores video as only 10 frames per second. Meant for use while developing DVI applications.

RU Request Unit or Response Unit. A basic unit of data in SNA.

RUN To start a software program.

RUN LENGTH ENCODING A facsimile encoding process that converts an expanse of white or black to a code corresponding to the length of the run.

RUN TIME The time it takes to execute a software program.

RZ Return to Zero. A method of transmitting binary information where voltage returns to a zero (reference) level after each encoded bit.

SAA Systems Application Architecture. A set of specifications written by IBM describing how users should interface with applications and communications programs. The idea is to give all software "a common feel" so that training will be less burdensome. According to IBM advertising, "SAA will make it possible for everyone in an organization to access information regardless of its location. What's more, all software written to SAA specifications will provide similar screen layouts, menus and terminology."

SAG The downward curvature of a wire or cable due to its weight.

SALES AUTOMATION See SALES FORCE AUTOMATION.

SALES FORCE AUTOMATION The use of computers and computer software by salespeople to boost their sales. There are two types of sales force automation — those totally self-contained on the computers of salespeople (mostly laptops) or those which communicate with headquarters computer over phone lines. There are many purposes of the phone communication — sending orders in, finding out about backorders, getting updates on "specials," dropping letters and memos in, getting new prices, new products, new technical specs, etc. Salespeople routinely show 10% to 20% sales gains armed with a laptop PC and sales automation software (also called "personal contact") software. The publisher of this dictionary runs a regular trade show on Sales Force Automation. It's called "SaleTech." Call 1-800-LIBRARY for more information.

SAMPLING Converting continuous signals, like voice or video, into discrete values, e.g. digital signals. See also PCM and DIGITAL SIGNAL PROCESSING.

SANITY CHECK A check to confirm the service capability of a switching system. This test has not been applied to the author of this dictionary.

SAPI Northern Telecom term for Service Access Point Identifier.

SASS Shared Access for Switched Services. An AT&T offering combining MEGACOM WATS and MEGACOM 800 to enable both outgoing and incoming MEGACOM service on the same T-1 circuit.

SATELLITE 1. A microwave receiver, repeater, regenerator in a geosynchronous orbit 22,300 miles above the earth. 2. Something distant to the main something. See MAIN DISTRIBUTION FRAME and SATELLITE TRANSMISSION.

SATELLITE BUSINESS SYSTEMS SBS. A satellite long distance carrier originally owned jointly by IBM, Aetna Insurance and Comsat, but now owned by MCI, which, in turn, is now partly owned by IBM. SBS started out to serve the data communications transmission marketplace but found that marketplace too small to be profitable. It then started to serve the voice transmission marketplace and did somewhat better. Satellite Business Systems no longer exists as a separate entity. It has been merged into MCI, which may, one day, be merged into IBM. See SBS.

SATELLITE CLOSET A walk-in or shallow closet that supplements a backbone closet. See BACKBONE CLOSET.

SATELLITE COMMUNICATIONS The use of geostationary orbiting satellites to relay information.

SATELLITE COMMUNICATIONS CONTROL SCC. The earth station equipment that controls such communications functions as access, echo suppression, forward error correction and signaling.

SATELLITE DELAY COMPENSATOR A device that compensates for the absolute delay in a satellite circuit communicating with data terminal equipment (DTE) with the DTE's own protocol.

SATELLITE DISTRIBUTION FRAME An intermediate point for connecting wires running between a group of phones and the Main Distribution Frame located elsewhere in the building. A fat multi-conductor cable comes from the main distribution frame to the satellite distribution frame, where it splits into individual cables to individual phones or workstations. The satellite distribution frame is usually located in a satellite wiring closet or cabinet. These wires are ultimately connected to the telephone system. See DISTRIBUTION FRAME.

SATELLITE FACILITY A transmission system using a satellite in a geostationary orbit above the earth and a number of earth stations.

SATELLITE LINK Microwave link using a satellite to receive, amplify and retransmit signals. Typically that satellite is in a geosynchronous orbit.

SATELLITE OPERATION A configuration of multiple PBXs or one big PBX and several smaller PBXs. The configuration gives a company with several nearby locations a unified system of centralized trunks, centralized attendants, overall call detail recording and many of the advantages of a private network. The key advantage of satellite operation is that one big centralized telephone system can contain most of the intelligence and computer smarts for the total system. This advantage is heavily economic. A variation on satellite operation is called CENTRALIZED ATTENDANT SERVICE (CAS).

SATELLITE PREMISES CHANNEL This is the cable connecting arrangement between a dedicated earth station and the Customer Provided Equipment.

SATELLITE PROCESSOR A computer with little computing power used for operations that do not require the full processing power of the main machine.

SATELLITE TRANSMISSION A form of transmission which sends signals to an orbiting satellite which receives them, amplifies them and returns those signals back to earth. Satellite transmission provides great clarity but suffers from delay. See SATELLITE TRANSMISSION DELAY.

SATELLITE TRANSMISSION DELAY Referring to the time it takes a signal to travel from one satellite earth station to the satellite in the sky then to the satellite earth station at the other end. Since most communications satellites orbit the earth at a distance of approximately 22,300 miles, the total distance the signal travels is 44,600 miles. Since radio waves travel at the speed of light (186,000 miles per second), simple arithmetic will show a delay of approximately one-quarter of one second thus, 44,600 divided by 186,000 = 0.239 second. If you are waiting for a reply, double this time. (You double the distance.)

SATURN A family of excellent digital PBXs made by Siemens and sold by Siemens Information Systems of Boca Raton, FL.

SAVE AND REPEAT Another way of saying "Autodial." Electronic phones may be able to save a number so you can dial it later by simply hitting one button on the phone. This feature is similar to a "Last Number Redial" button, except that button just dials the last number called. "Save and Repeat" puts a number into temporary storage for dialing at another time. Phones should have both auto-redial and save-and-repeat buttons.

SBS Satellite Business Systems. A long distance satellite company that started out as a joint venture between Lockheed and MCI, was sold to IBM Aetna and Comsat and then eventually was given to MCI in exchange for shares issued to IBM. SBS never made any money. But that was irrelevant. Its job was to help IBM sell computer networks. See SATELLITE BUSINESS SYSTEMS.

SCA Supplemental Communications Authority. The authority granted by the Federal Communications Commission to transmit on a subcarrier.

SCAI Switch to Computer Applications Interface. A Northern Telecom protocol that defines how switches talk to outboard computers, i.e. computers which are external to the switch and contain such a database of customer buying information. Using SCAI, calls and data screens about a calling customer can be presented to the agent simultaneously.

SCAN Switched Circuit Automatic Network.

SCANNER A device used to input graphic images into the computer. Scanners look at or "scan" a piece of paper and put the image's information into digital form. The information can then be recognized by the computer. A scanner is also in a fax machine that "looks" at the original document and determines the brightness level of each pixel to be transmitted. See also Optical Character Recognition.

SCANNS Multiplexers which perform the vital functions of monitoring and control within System 75s and 85s Automated Building Management feature. The SCANNS continuously scan sensors and send the resulting data to local control units.

SCAN TIME The time between two successive polls to a workstation on a data communications network.

SCATTERING A cause of lightwave signal loss in optical fiber transmission. The diffusion of a light beam caused by microscopic variations in the material density of the transmission medium.

SCC Specialized Common Carrier. Another term for a long distance carrier in competition with AT&T. The word "Specialized" came about because these long distance carriers purported to provide "specialized" circuits for business customers. At one stage they were also known as OCCs, or Other

Common Carriers (i.e. other than AT&T). These days, both terms have fallen into disrepute. All long distance carriers — including AT&T — are called InterExchange Carriers (IXCs).

SCCP Part of the SS7 protocol. It provides additional routing and management functions for transfer of messages other than call set-up between signaling points. See also SIGNALING SYSTEM 7 and COMMON CHANNEL SIGNALING.

SCEPTRE A consumer videotex interactive terminal which, when used with a TV set and a phone line, allows the consumer to interact with a videotex data base service.

SCHEMATIC Diagram which details the electrical elements of a circuit or system.

SCO An AT&T specialized network maintenance organization providing a single point of contact for resolving customer network faults.

SCOPE A slang term for cathode ray oscilloscope.

SCP 1. Service Control Point. A remote database within the System Signaling 7 network. The SCP supplies the translation and routing data needed to deliver advanced network services. The SCP translates an 800-IN-WATS number to the required routing number. See also TCAP. 2. Northern Telecom term for a Satellite Communications Processor.

SCRAMBLER A device which deliberately distorts a voice or data conversation so that only another like device can figure out the content of the message. Analog scramblers invert the frequencies of speech. Digital scramblers first convert speech to digital form and then encrypt. Both types also perform the reverse process. The sophistication (i.e. complexity) of a scrambler determines its price.

SCRATCH PAD A part of the random access memory of a computer or telephone system which can be used to temporarily store data. See REGISTER.

SCREENED TRANSFER You are transferring a call from your phone to your boss. You dial a code for transfer, then dial your boss. The caller you're transferring is automatically put on hold. You speak to your boss, tell her who you're putting through. She okays the transfer, then you hit another digit and the call goes right through. This is called screened transfer. An unscreened transfer occurs when you simply dial your boss's office and send the call through without announcing it. Most PBXs have the ability to do both screened and unscreened calls.

SCROLLING Browsing through information at a video terminal. Scrolling is the continuous movement of information either vertically or horizontally on a video screen as if the information were on a paper being rolled under it.

SCSI (Pron. scuzzy.) A new disk drive control technology called Small Computer System Interface. A single S.C.S.I. adapter card plugged into an internal IBM PS/2 micro channel PC slot can control as many as seven different hard disks, optical disks, tape drives and scanners — without siphoning power away from the computer's main processor. S.C.S.I. disk drives also work incredibly fast — often as fast as 10 to 15 millisecond average seek time.

SDEC Northern Telecom term for Satellite Data Exchange Controller.

SDI Northern Telecom term for Serial Data Interface.

SDF Sub Distribution Frame. Intermediate cross connect points, usually located in wiring or utility closets. A trunk cable or LAN backbone is run from each SDF to the MDF (Main Distribution Frame).

SDLC Synchronous Data Link Control. A bit-oriented synchronous communications protocol developed by IBM where the message may contain any collection or sequence of bits without being mistaken for a control character. SDLC is used in IBM's SNA — System Network Architecture. See HDLC and IBM.

SDMA Station Detail Message Accounting. See CALL ACCOUNTING.

SDRM Sub-rate Data Multiplexing. Refers to a service where a DSO (64 Kbps) channel may contain one 56 Kbps signal, five 9.6 Kbps signals, ten 4.8 Kbps signals or twenty 2.4 Kbps signals. Although speeds may be mixed, the highest speed determines the number of signals supported.

SDN Software Defined Network. See SOFTWARE DEFINED NETWORK, SDN SERVING OFFICE, VIRTUAL NETWORK and the APPENDIX

SDN SERVING OFFICE One of many AT&T-supplied switching nodes in an SDN network. See also SOFTWARE DEFINED NETWORK and the APPENDIX.

SEALING CURRENT A designation for a powering situation that consists of a wet loop without span power.

SEAMLESS In a LAN environment, it means that what takes place between the user and the application accessed is transparent. The user doesn't perceive he's on a network because his programs run as though they were on his personal computer.

SECAM Sequential and memory color TV system adopted by France and most Eastern European and Middle Eastern countries.

SECONDARY EQUIPMENT Used telecommunications equipment.

SECONDARY MARKET The market for used business telecommunications and computer equipment. The magazine serving this market is called TELECOM GEAR. It's a monthly. You can get your free subscription by calling 1-800-322-5156.

SECONDARY PROTECTION Primary protection is a device that sits at your building entrance between your phone line coming in from outside and your line going into and up your building. The phone company is responsible for installing primary protection. Secondary protection sits on your floor just next to your phone system. Secondary protection is designed to protect your phone equipment from spikes, surges and high electricity that might affect your phone lines between the primary protection downstairs and the secondary protection upstairs. Secondary protection typically costs $20 to

$30 a line. It's worth every penny.

SECRETARIAL HUNTING The secretary's station number is programmed as the last number in one or more hunt groups. If all phones within a hunt group are busy the call will hunt to the secretary.

SECRETARIAL INTERCEPT A PBX feature. Causes calls for an executive to ring his/her secretary — even if the executive's direct extension number was dialed. The executive's phone will ring only if the secretary's phone is placed on "Do Not Disturb" or the secretary transfers the call in.

SECTIONAL CENTER A control center connecting primary telco switching centers. A Class 2 office.

SECTORING The process of dividing a mobile cellular radio cell into 180-, 120- or 60-degree assigned to the cell.

SECURE VOICE Voice signals that are encoded or encrypted to prevent unauthorized listening.

SECURENET A service from Southwestern Bell in which customers' dedicated circuits are routed through a serving central office to a "primary" hub. In addition, a secondary path is routed via a SWBT-designated alternate serving central office and an alternate hub. The service is designed to give Southwestern Bell customers better reliability.

SECURITY A way of insuring data on a LAN is protected from unauthorized use. Network security measures can be software-based, where passwords restrict users' access to certain data files or directories. This kind of security is usually implemented by the network operating system. Audit trails are another software-based security measure, where an ongoing journal of what users did what with what files is maintained. Security can also be hardware-based, using the more traditional lock and key.

SECURITY ACCESS MANAGER SAM. An AT&T computer-based building access security system.

SECURITY BLANKING The ability of a switch to blank out the called digits for certain extensions so no called number detail is printed. Senior executives in serious takeover negotiations find this feature useful. There have been instances of people figuring out which company another company is about to buy based on telephone calling records. If you have this information, you can buy the company's stock before the bid is announced and make a lot of money. This feature — security blanking — is designed to avoid such occurrences.

SECURITY CODE A user identification code required by computer systems to protect information or information resources from unauthorized use.

SECURITY STUD A cylindrically shaped metal finger that holds open the door to a Cash Box until the box is removed for collection.

SEEK TIME The time it takes to find some information on a disk (hard or soft) in a computer. Average seek time is a critical measure of the speed of a computer disk drive.

SEGMENT 64 characters. Use as a method of data communications billing by some overseas phone companies

SEIZE To access a circuit and use it, or make it busy so that others cannot use it.

SELECTIVE CALLING The ability of the transmitting phone to specify which of several phones on the a line is to receive a message.

SELECTIVE PAGING TO STATION A phone can page to individual phone instruments.

SELECTIVE RINGING A method of ringing only the desired party on a party line.

SELECTIVE SIGNALING A method of in-band signaling used on private networks to tell switches to switch the call.

SELECTIVITY Ability of a tuner or receiver to get only a desired station while rejecting other adjacent stations. The higher the figure expressed in decibels (dB), the better the selectivity.

SELF DIAGNOSTICS Your phone system tells you when something is wrong with it by sending you a "message" via the operator console or through one of the data ports on the phone system.

SELF EXTINGUISHING The characteristic of a material whose flame is extinguished after the igniting flame is removed.

SELF INDULGENCE The author's writing of occasional irrelevant "definitions" in this dictionary.

SELF TEST The capability of a PBX to run programs at regular intervals to test its own operation and signal when failures have occurred or are about to occur without human intervention.

SEMAPHORE A message sent when a file is opened to prevent other users from opening the same file at that time. Its purpose is to preserve the integrity of data (i.e. stop it from being messed with) while you're using it.

SEMI-AUTOMATIC MESSAGE SWITCHING A network control technique whereby an operator manually switches a message to a destination according to the address information contained in the message header.

SEMI-RIGID A cable containing a flexible inner core and a relatively inflexible sheathing material, such as a metallic tube but, which can be bent for coiling or spooling and placing in duct or cable run.

SEMICONDUCTOR Material which has a resistance to electricity somewhere between a conductor (e.g. a copper wire) and an insulator (e.g. plastic). Hence the word "semi" conductor. Silicon and germanium are the two most commonly-used semiconductor materials. The flow of current in a semiconductor can be changed by light or the presence or absence of an electric or magnetic field.

SENDER Equipment in the originating telephone system which outpulses (sends out) the routing digits and the called person's number. Senders are necessary in computerized (stored program control) switches because the switch needs to know all the digits of the numbers you are calling before it chooses and seizes a trunk.

SENSITIVITY The input signal level required for a tuner, amplifier, etc., to produce a stated output. The lower the required input, the higher the sensitivity. Measured in mV (microvolts).

SENSITIVITY ANALYSIS The process of rerunning a financial study to figure the degress to which changing the assumptions changes the result of the analysis.

SENT PAID A utility industry term that describes all calls charged to the originating number or collected as coins in a pay telephone.

SEPARATION Extent to which two stereo channels are kept apart. Expressed in decibels, the larger the number, the better the separation and stereo effect.

SEPARATOR Pertaining to wire and cable, a layer of insulating material such as textile, paper, etc. placed between a conductor and its insulation, between a cable jacket and the components it covers or between various components of a multi-conductor cable. It can be utilized to improve stripping qualities and/or flexibility, or can offer additional mechanical or electrical protection to the components it separates.

SEPARATIONS AND SETTLEMENTS A complex set of accounting procedures developed by the traditional telephone industry. The procedures classify telephone plant as intrastate or interstate, and return revenues from long distance phone calls to local telephone companies. As part of Deregulation and Divestiture, this procedure is being replaced by per minute access charges.

SEQUENCING The process of dividing a data message into smaller pieces for transmission, where each piece has its own sequence number for reassembly of the complete message at the destination end. Similar to packetizing. See PACKET.

SEQUENTIAL Pertaining to events occurring in a specific time or code order.

SEQUENTIAL ACCESS The need to read data — one record after another in sequence — before getting to the information you want. Magnetic tape, for example, requires you to read the entire tape up to where your information is. This is because the computer cannot tell where on the tape your information is because records on tape files are often of variable length. Most Random Access files, usually kept on a disk drive, require records to be of a fixed length, such as 80 characters per record. Then when you seek record 23, the computer seeks character 1840 in the file (23 x 80), and takes the next 80 characters as the record you want. Using the analogy of music recorded on records and magnetic tape, a phonograph record needle has the capability of random access because the needle can be set down in the spaces between cuts on the record. With mag tape, you must fast forward past all the music you don't want before you get to the music you want to hear. Also, if the computer tape drive is fast forwarding, it cannot count characters to find the record, and must read in the data you don't want (and throw it away), before it gets to the data you need. Random access is much faster than sequential access.

SERIAL CALL Telephone system feature set up by the attendant when an incoming calling party wishes to speak with more than one person internally. When the first party hangs up, the call automatically moves to the second person the outside party wants to speak with. When that person hangs up, then the call automatically goes to the third person, etc.

SERIAL INTERFACE The "lowest common denominator" of data communications. A mechanism for changing the parallel arrangement of data within computers to the serial (one bit after the other) form used on data transmission lines and vice versa. At least one serial interface is usually provided on all computers for the connection of a terminal, a modem or a printer. Sometimes also called a serial port. See RS-232-C and SERIAL INTERFACE CARD.

SERIAL INTERFACE CARD A printed circuit card which drops into one of the expansion slots of your computer and changes the parallel internal communications of your computer into the one-bit-at-time serial transmission for sending information to your modem or to a serial printer.

SERIAL MEMORY Memory medium to which access is in a set sequence and not at random.

SERIAL PORT An input/output port (plug) that transmits data out one bit at a time, as opposed to the parallel port which transmits data out eight bits, or one byte at a time. Most personal computers (PCs) have at least one serial and one parallel port. In a typical configuration, the serial port is used for a modem while the parallel port is used for a printer. For a diagram of a typical 25-pin RS-232-C serial port, see the APPENDIX at the back of this book.

SERIAL PROCESSING Method of data processing in which only one bit is handled at a time.

SERIAL TRANSMISSION Sending pulses one after another rather than several at the same time (parallel). When transmitting data over a telephone line there is only one set of wires. Therefore, the only logical way to transmit it is to send the data in serial mode. It is possible to use eight different frequencies to transmit a character all at once (parallel), but these modems are ridiculously expensive. See SERIAL PORT and PARALLEL.

SERIALIZE To change from parallel-by-byte to serial-by-bit.

SERIES RF TAP A bugging device. It is a radio transmitter which is installed in series with one wire of the telephone circuit. Normally a parasite (i.e. takes power from the phone line). Transmits both sides of the conversation. It transmits only when the phone is off-hook.

SERVER A computer providing a service, such as shared access to a file system, a printer or an electronic mail system to LAN users. Usually a combination of hardware and software. There are variations on the same theme. They are called file servers and print servers.

SERVICE AREA The geographic area served by a supplier. The area in which the supplier, theoretically, stands ready to provide his service. The service area of New York Telephone is most (not all) of New York State.

SERVICE BUREAU A data processing center that does work for others. There are many ways of bringing work to a service bureau, including mailing it and transmitting it over phone lines. If it comes over phone lines, the service is likely to be called "time sharing."

SERVICE CHARGE DETAIL A listing of all the telephone equipment installed as part of a specific telephone system. Usually provided by the vendor or maintenance organization.

SERVICE CONTROL POINT SCP. A network system in the Advanced Intelligent Network Release 1 architecture that contains SLEE (Service Logic Execution Environment) functionality and communicates with AIN Release 1 Switching Systems in processing AIN Release 1 calls. Definition from Bellcore in reference to its concept of the Advanced Intelligent Network.

SERVICE CREATION The set of activities that must be performed to create a new service to be offered to subscribers and the associated service-specific operations capabilites to support the new service. Definition from Bellcore in reference to its concept of the Advanced Intelligent Network.

SERVICE DISPLAY Displays a specific service being presently in effect.

SERVICE FUNCTION A primary or secondary service function.

SERVICE INDEPENDENT BAF The finite set of BAF structures and modules needed to record usage of Advanced Intelligent Network Release 1 services. The set is said to be robust because it will be designed to record future AIN Release 1 services that have not yet been identified. Definition from Bellcore in reference to its concept of the Advanced Intelligent Network.

SERVICE LINE An exchange line associated with multiple data station installations to provide monitoring and testing of both customer and Telco data equipment.

SERVICE LOGIC EXECUTION ENVIRONMENT SLEE. A functional group residing in an SCP (Service Control Point) or Adjunct that contains the Service Logic and Control, Information Management, AMA (Automatic Message Accounting) and Operations FEs (Functional Entity). This composite set of capabilities, which includes FC routines, provides a functionally consistent interface to SLPs (Service Logic Program) independent of the underlying operating system. Definition from Bellcore in r eference to its concept of the Advanced Intelligent Network.

SERVICE NEGOTIATION The functionality needed to gather subscriber Advanced Intelligent Network Release 1 business needs; provide answers, AIN Release 1 service/feature descriptions, prerequisite non-AIN services, availability and costs; reserve AIN Release 1 resources (e.g. 800 number and 900 number); identify required network resources; and identify available AIN Release 1 services/features by wire center. Definition from Bellcore in reference to its concept of the Advanced Intelligent Network.

SERVICE OBJECTIVE Goal statement referring to the quality of service you provide a customer. You, the vendor, are not guaranteeing that service — just stating it as your objective.

SERVICE OBSERVATION 1. A generic word used by telephone companies to check the quality of the service they're providing. Some of it is done automatically with machinery. Some of it is done by senior operators who listen in on the conversations of other operators dealing with their subscribers. In short, the senior operators "observe" the service the junior operators are providing. 2. As a feature of some telephone systems, the Service Observation (SOB) command provides the capability to automatically record data about completed calls, incomplete calls and abnormal calls for the purpose of qualitative supervision of call traffic conditions.

SERVICE ORDER A request for service or equipment from a telecommunications vendor or carrier.

SERVICE PERIOD The time during which the telephone company furnishes a circuit.

SERVICE POINTS The points on the customer's premises where such channels or facilities are terminated in switching equipment used for communications with phones or customer-provided equipment located on the premises.

SERVICE TERMINAL The equipment needed to terminate the channel and connect to the phone apparatus or customer terminal.

SERVICE TRAFFIC MANAGEMENT STM. The SLEE (Service Logic Execution Environment) functionality for detecting overloads associated with a specific service and for sending Automatic Code Gap messages to the appropriate entities. The SN&M (Service Negotiation and Management) OA (Operations Application) also provides STM(Service Traffic Management)-related capabilities.

SERVING OFFICE An office of AT&T or its Connecting or Concurring Carriers, from which interstate communications services are furnished.

SERVING WIRE CENTER The wire center from which service is provided to the customer.

SES Severly Errored Seconds. Errored seconds during which the error rate exceeded 10.

SESSION A connection between two things (PC to PC, terminals to mainframe, etc.) and measured from beginning to end. Also a data conversation between two devices, say, a dumb terminal and a mainframe. It is possible to have more than one session going between two devices simultaneously.

SESSION LAYER The fifth layer — the network processing layer — in the

OSI Reference Model, responsible for binding and unbinding logical links between users. It manages, maintains and controls the dialogue between the users of the service.

SF Single Frequency. A method of in-band signaling. Single frequency signaling typically uses the presence or absence of a single specified frequency (usually 2,600 Hz). See SIGNALING.

SHADOW MASK The most common type of color picture tube in which the electron beam is directed through a perforated metal mask to the desired phosphor color element.

SHANNON A measurement of the quality of information in a message represented by one or the other of two equally probable, exclusive and exhaustive states.

SHARED LOGIC Simultaneous use of a single computer by multiple users.

SHARED SERVICES Providing PBX-based communications and processing services to the unaffiliated tenants and/or the building manager/owner of a commercial building in a standalone or campus environment.

SHARED TENANT SERVICES Providing centralized telecommunications services to tenants in a building or complex.

SHARON A beautiful lady. She deserves better than this small mention.

SHEATH The outer jacket (usually metal or plastic) surrounding copper and fiber cables that prevents water damage to the cables inside.

SHELF LIFE The useful life of components when not in use — such as being stored on a shelf as spare parts or in a warehouse awaiting shipment. Batteries tend to have the shortest shelf life of most telecommunications components. Today, the shelf life is less a problem of shelf decay and more a problem of technological obsolescence.

SHIELD A metallic layer consisting of type, braid, wire or sheath provided to reduce stray electrical fields and provide for safety of personnel.

SHIELDED PAIR Two insulated wires in a cable wrapped with metallic braid or foil to prevent the wires acting as antennas and picking up external interference (e.g. a local TV station).

SHIELDING The process by which electrical conductors are wrapped with metallic foil or braid to insulate them from interference and thus provide high quality transmission. Many devices can cause interference to cables (i.e. multiple conductors) carrying telecommunications conversations. Such things include high voltage AC power lines, machinery with motors, machines which make rays of some type (X-Ray systems, TV sets etc.). By wrapping conductors around the cable cores, these cables are less likely to be affected by these outside forces and the noise they create on telephone lines. Shielding will also lessen the chance that the information movement along the cable will interfere with signals on other, adjacent cables. The need for shielding stems from this phenomenon: If you send an electrical signal along one pair of cables, those cables will give off a small amount of electrical energy — called magnetic radiation. That radiation will cause electromagnetic interference with a cable close by. If you "shield" the pair carrying the electrical signal, you will cut down the susceptibility of those cables to interference from other cables. LANs should always be installed with the best quality shielded cable. They will run better with shielded cable. Never skimp on the quality of the cable you're installing for LANs. Most telephones don't require shielded cable unless the cable serving them is passing through some area of high electro-mechanical interference.

SHIFT 1. The movement of data to either the right or the left of an existing position in a data field. 2. The code control function of converting the characters from upper to lower case, or vice versa.

SHIFT CHARACTER The control character which defines the shift function.

SHIFT REGISTER A register in which a clock pulse causes the stored data to move to the right or left one bit position. See ZERO STUFFING.

SHOCK A sudden stimulation of the nerve and convulsive contraction of the muscles caused by a discharge of electricity through the body. The severity depends on the amount and duration of the current and whether the path of the current is through a vital organ.

SHORT A circuit impairment that exists when two conductors of the same pair, which normally make up an operating electrical circuit, touch or are connected.

SHORT BUS A high-speed common channel in the AT&T ISN packet controller over which all messages between sending and receiving devices pass.

SHORT CIRCUIT A near zero resistance connection between any two wires that disrupts transmission where two pairs are involved usually called a "cross." It disrupts transmission and may cause an excessive current flow.

SHORT HAUL Between a few hundred yards and 20 miles. Many people would argue with this definition.

SHORT HAUL MODEM A data set designed for use in communicating data up to distances of 25 miles over a dedicated unloaded copper pair. Many people would argue with this definition.

SHT Short Hold Time.

SI Shift In.

SIA Securities Industries Association.

SIDE CIRCUIT A metallic, single pair circuit arranged to derive a phantom circuit. The phantom circuit is derived by center tapping a repeating coil in each of two side circuits.

SIDE HOUR Any hour that is not the Busy Hour.

SIDEBAND The frequencies on either side of the main frequency in a telecommunications signal. In the early days these sideband frequencies were not used because they were too "noisy," unreliable and were not needed. Now, technology has improved and frequencies are in short supply, more and more transmission vendors are making use of their sidebands, and thus substantially broadening the throughput of their existing transmission paths. Sideband technology has made great strides especially in through-the-air microwave transmission.

SIDETONE A part of the design of a telephone handset which allows you to hear your own voice while speaking. The idea is to let you know that the telephone you're speaking on is working. Too much sidetone becomes an echo and is bad. Too little sidetone makes the channel unerring.

SIGN ON/SIGN OFF The process of identifying oneself to a machine so as to gain access. In the case of an ACD system this process allows statistics to be kept for this person individually. It also allows for the movement of the person around the system while statistics are accumulated in one logical file.

SIGN-ON To go through the process of beginning a working session between you, your data terminal or PC and a computer system.

SIGNAL 1. An electrical wave used to convey information. 2. An alert. 3. An acoustic device (e.g. a bell) or a visual device (e.g. a lamp) which calls attention. To transmit an information signal or alerting signal.

SIGNAL CONDITIONING The amplification and/or modification of electrical signals to make them more appropriate for transmission over a certain medium — cable, microwave, etc.

SIGNAL CONVERTER The equipment which changes the data signal into a form suitable for the transmission medium, or the reverse. The converter can also work with DC/AC current. The signal converter comprises a modulator and/or demodulator.

SIGNAL GROUND SGD. In RS-232-C signaling, Signal Ground establishes a common reference level for the voltages of all other signals (such as RXD/TXD), except Frame Ground.

SIGNAL LEVEL The strength of a signal, generally expressed in either absolute units of voltage or power, or in units relative to the strength of the signal at its source.

SIGNAL TO NOISE RATIO The ratio of the usable signal being transmitted to the noise or undesired signal. Usually expressed in decibels. This ratio is a measure of the quality of a transmission.

SIGNAL TRANSFER POINT The packet switch in the Common Channel Interoffice Signaling (CCIS) system. The CCIS is a packet switched network operating at 4800 bits per second. CCIS replaces both SF (Single Frequency) and MF (Multi-frequency) by converting dialed digits to data messages. See SIGNALING SYSTEM 7.

SIGNALING Pertains to the transmission of electrical signals to and from the user's premises and the telephone company central office. Examples of central office signals to the user's premises are ringing (audible alerting) signals, dial tone, speech signals, etc. Signals from the user's telephone include off-hook (request for service), dialing (network control signaling), speech to the distant party, on-hook (disconnect signal), etc. See SIGNALING SYSTEM 7.

SIGNALING CONNECTION CONTROL PART SCCP. Part of the SS7 protocol that provides communication between signaling nodes by adding circuit and routing information to the signaling message. The ISDN-UP (Integrated Services Digital Network User Part) and TCAP (Transaction Capabilities Application Part) use the SCCP (Signaling Connection Control Part) and the MTP (Message Transfer Part) to transport information. Definition from Bellcore in reference to its concept of the Advanced Intelligent Network.

SIGNALING SYSTEM 7 SS7. All phone systems need signaling. According to James Henry Green, author of the Dow Jones-Irwin Handbook of Telecommunications, signals have three basic functions:

1. SUPERVISING. Monitoring the status of a line or circuit to see if it is busy, idle or requesting service. Supervision is a term derived from the job telephone operators perform in manually monitoring circuits on a switchboard. On switchboards, supervisory signals are shown by a lit lamp indicating a request for service on an incoming line or an on-hook condition of a switchboard cord circuit. In the network (i.e. the automated part of the network), supervisory signals are indicated by the voltage level on signaling

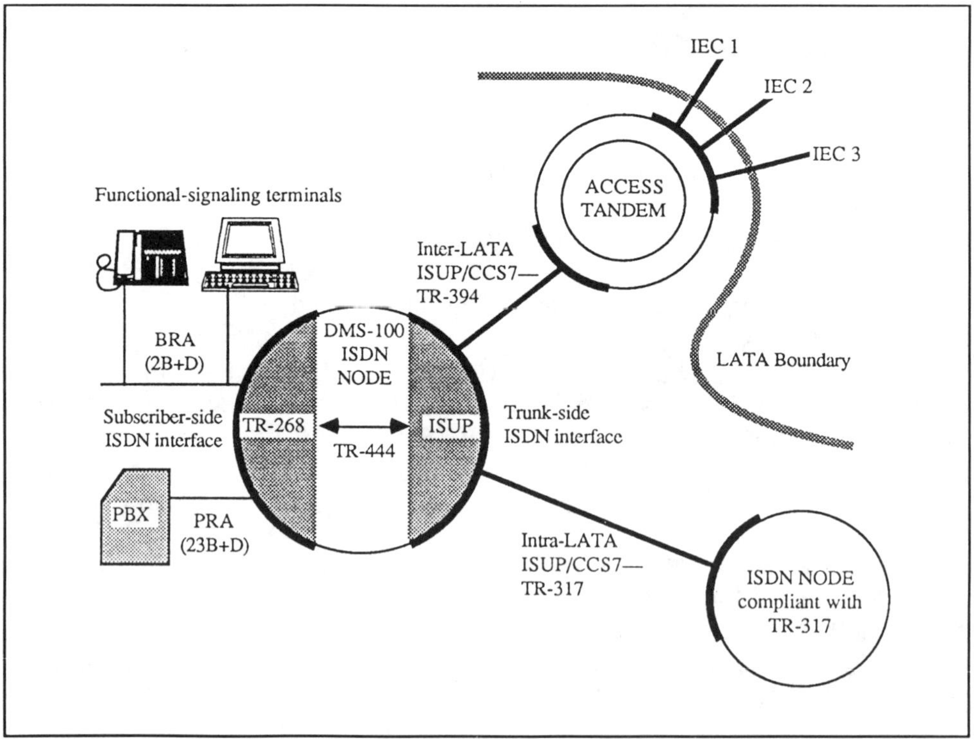

courtesy Northern Telecom

leads, or the on-hook/off-hook status of signaling tones or bits.

2. ALERTING. Indicates the arrival of an incoming call. Alerting signals are bells, buzzers, whoofers, tones, strobes and lights.

3. ADDRESSING. Transmitting routing and destination signals over the network. Addressing signals are in the form of dial pulses, tone pulses or data pulses over loops, trunks and signaling networks.

Most signaling today is MF (multi-frequency) and SF (single frequency) and is in-band. This means that it goes along and occupies the same circuits as those which carry voice conversations. There are two problems with this. First, about 35% of all toll calls are not completed because the phone doesn't answer or is busy, or there are equipment problems along the way. The circuit time used in signaling is substantial, expensive and wasteful. Second, in-band signaling is vulnerable to fraud. So the idea of out-of-band signaling came about. It got the name of Common Channel Interoffice Signaling (CCIS) because it used a communications network totally separate from the switched voice network. In North America, CCIS started out as an AT&T packet switched network operating at 4800 bits per second. Each of the packet switches in this network (they are no longer exclusively AT&T's) are called Signal Transfer Points — STPs. CCIS has the following advantages over SF/MF signaling:

Fraud is reduced. "Talk-off" is reduced. (Talk-off occurs when your voice contains enough 2600 Hz energy to activate the tone-detecting circuits in the central office.) Signaling is faster allowing circuits and conversations to be set up and torn down (i.e. disconnected) faster. Signals can be sent in both directions simultaneously and during voice conversation if necessary. Network management information is routed over the CCIS network. For example, when trunks fail, switching systems can be told with CCIS data messages to reroute traffic around problem areas.

The older CCIS signaling is being replaced with a newer out-of-band signaling system called CCITT Signaling System 7. According to an AT&T technical paper delivered at the International Switching Symposium in Spring, 1987, CCITT Signaling System 7 is being required by telecommunications administrations worldwide (i.e. all the local country-owned telephone companies) for their networks. AT&T continued with the introduction of digital switches and transmission equipment with 56 kbps and 64 kbps transmission rates, the International Telegraph and Telephone Consultative Committee (CCITT in French) in 1980 approved the CCITT 7 recommendations optimized for digital networks. This new protocol uses destination routing, octet oriented fields, variable length messages and a maximum message length allowing for 256 bytes of data. Addition of flow control, connectionless services and Integrated Services Digital Network (ISDN) capabilities were approved by CCITT in 1984. A major characteristic of CCITT #7 is its layered functional structure. Its transport functions are divided into four levels, three of which constitute the Message Transfer Part (MTP). The fourth consists of a common Signaling Connection Control Part (SCCP).

The SS7 protocol consists of four basic sub-protocols:

- Message Transfer Part (MTP), which provides functions for basic routing of signaling messages between signaling points.
- Signaling Connection Control Part (SCCP), which provides additional routing and management functions for transfer of messages other than call set-up between signaling points.
- Integrated Services Digital Network User Part (ISUP), which provides for transfer of call set-up signaling information between signaling points.
- Transaction Capabilities Application Part (TCAP), which provides for transfer of non-circuit related information between signaling points.

Signaling System 7 provides two major capabilities:

1. Fast call set-up, via high-speed circuit-switched connections.
2. Transaction capabilities which deal with remote data base interactions. What this means in its simplest terms and in one simple application is that Signaling System 7 information can tell the called party who's calling and, more important, tell the called party's computer. A scenario: when you call a direct mail order business, Signaling System 7 will send a signal as to which phone is calling. The agent's CRT screen will pop the caller's name and perhaps the caller's most recent buying information. The agent may answer the phone "Good morning, Mr. Newton. Did you enjoy the three khaki pants we sent you last week?..." Signaling System 7 will be an integral part of ISDN. It will enable us to extend full PBX and Centrex-based services like call forwarding, call waiting, call screening, call transfer, etc. outside the switch to the full international network. In effect, with Signaling System 7, the entire network will acquire the "smarts" of today's smartest electronic digital PBX. See also MTP, SCCP, ISUP and TCAP.

SIGNIFICANT HOUR Any hour that influences the sizing of a trunk group.

SILICON A neutral element found primarily in raw form in sand from which transistor chips are made. See SEMICONDUCTOR.

SILICON AVALANCHE DIODE A fast-acting surge protector which features a narrow voltage clamping range.

SILICON VALLEY A heavily industrialized area in and around San Jose, CA, which accounts for much of the semiconductor, integrated circuit and microprocessor production in the United States.

SIMPLEX Operating a channel in one direction only with no ability to operate in the other direction. For example one side of a telephone conversation is all that could be carried by a Simplex line.

SIMPLEX LOOP POWERING In T-1, refers to the powering of the digital signal pairs that are simplex in nature (Tip or Ring) and that may have voltage applied to maintain the required 60 mA dc current to control repeater signal regeneration, loopbacks, keep alive signals and alarms.

SIMULTANEOUS PERIPHERAL OPERATIONS ON LINE SPOOL. Temporarily storing programs, data or output on magnetic tape or in RAM for later output or execution. Many PCs use a small software spooling program which accepts material to be printed very quickly, stores it in a portion of RAM, then feeds that material to the printer at a speed the printer can handle. See SPOOLING.

SINGING An undesirable whistle or howl on a transmission circuit. It is caused by unstable operation of the circuit created by excessive gain or unbalanced hybrid coils. This is the same effect observed when you increase the volume on a public address system until the system squeals or "sings."

SINGING RETURN LOSS The loss at which a circuit oscillates or sings at the extreme low and high ends of the voice band.

SINGLE ADDRESS MESSAGE A message which is to be transmitted to only one specific terminal, as opposed to a broadcast or group message.

SINGLE DIGIT DIALING Provides for single-digit dialing to reach a preselected phone or group of phones.

SINGLE ENDED TERMINAL DEVICE A device which terminates only one line at a given time.

SINGLE FREQUENCY SIGNALING The use of one tone — typically 2600 Hz — to indicate if the phone line is busy or idle (supervision) and to convey dial pulse signals from one end of a trunk or line to the other, using the presence or absence of a single specified frequency.

SINGLE LINE INSTRUMENT A telephone set normally used to access only one line. However when used with advanced telephone systems, additional lines can be accessed by dialing specific codes rather than by depressing keys.

SINGLE MODE FIBER An optical waveguide which is constructed to propagate (i.e. carry) only the single wavelength selected for transmission.

SINGLE NUMBER SERVICE An optional feature for 800 IN-WATS Services which allows a subscriber who has or wants to have both intrastate and interstate 800 service to use the same 1-800 number for both services. If you'd like to buy another copy of this dictionary, call 1-800-LIBRARY. That phone number will be answered at our office in New York City. It will work for calls from inside and from outside New York State.

SINGLE SIDEBAND TRANSMISSION A type of carrier transmission where one sideband is transmitted and the other is suppressed. The carrier wave can be either transmitted or suppressed.

SINGLE SLOT Current standard for coin phone construction that utilizes one slot for the deposit of all acceptable coins.

SINGLE WIRE LINE A transmission path which uses a single conductor and a ground return to complete a circuit. Used a lot in rural areas.

SINK That part of a communications system which receives information.

SIR Speaker Independent Recognition. See SPEAKER INDEPENDENT RECOGNITION.

SITA Society of International Aeronautical Telecommunications. The international data communications network used by many airlines.

SIX DIGIT TRANSLATION We have a long distance number 212-691-8215. The ability of a switching system to do six digit translation means that it can "look at" 212-691 and figure how to route the phone call. The criterion of choosing which way to send the call is, most often, the least expensive way. Six digit translation is often an integral part of Least Cost Routing programs within the phone system which tell the calls to go over the lines perceived by the user to be the least cost way of getting the call from point A to point B. There are typically two types of "least cost routing" translation — that which examines the first three digits of the phone number (i.e. just the area code) and the first six digits of the phone number (i.e. the area code and the three digits of the local central office). Six digit translation is preferred because it allows you more flexibility in routing, particularly to big area codes, like 213 in LA, where there are long distance calls within the area code. See also LEAST COST ROUTING and ALTERNATE ROUTING.

SKEW The deviation from synchronization of two or more signals.

SLAVE A device which operates under the control of a master — another device or system. Slave switching systems are common in rural areas. The master central office might be in town A. Twenty miles away there's a smaller town. It makes no economic sense to serve those subscribers each on single local dedicated loops from Town A. Best solution: place a "slave" central office in that distant town and drive its software, diagnostics and changes from the main central office in Town A. See also REMOTE CONCENTRATOR.

SLC-96 Pronounced "SLICK 96." A product of AT&T Technologies. It's a short haul multiplexing device which enables up to 96 telephone customers to be served on three pairs of wires. SLC stands for Subscriber Loop Carrier.

SLIC An AT&T term for Subscriber's Line Interface Circuit, a device that interfaces the SLC series of AT&T products of local subscriber pair gain or multiplexing devices. See SLC-96.

SLIP/SLIP RATE The loss (or rate of loss) of a data bit on a T-1 link due to a frame misalignment between the timing at a transmit node and timing at a receive node.

SLOTTED ALOHA A random access technique extending pure ALOHA to the case in which messages may only be transmitted in slotted intervals of time.

SLOTTED RING A LAN architecture in which a constant number of fixed-length slots (packets) circulate continuously around the ring. A full/empty indicator within the slot header indicates when a workstation or PC attached to the LAN may place information into the slot. Think of a slotted ring LAN as an empty train that constantly travels in a circle, being filled and emptied at different terminals (workstations).

SMA 905/906 (Subminature type A) A former microwave connector modified by Amphenol to become the "standard" fiber optic connector. The 905 version is a straight ferrule design, where as the 906 is a stepped ferrule design and uses a plastic sleeve for alignment.

SMART PHONE A microcomputer-controlled electronic telephone with lots of features. Typically single line with a simple tip and ring interface (i.e. not proprietary to any special key system or PBX).

SMARTCALL Smartcall is a name registered by GTE for services more advanced than conventional Custom Calling call enhancement services, such as speed calling or call waiting. Calling Number Identification is a GTE Smartcall service. Other services include Automatic Call Return, Automatic Busy Redial, Call Tracing Service, Protected Number Service, VIP Alert, Call Block, etc.

SMARTHOUSE The National Society of Home Builders has registered SmartHouse. BellSouth has trademarked SuperHouse. And GTE has registered SmartPark. One day, fiber optic will snake to everyone's house, bringing the potential of immense information services. Until that day comes they'll be lots of interesting demonstrations at distant trade shows.

SMARTPARK GTE's registered trademark for a fiber-optic wired industrial park offering a wide variety of voice, data and video transmission and switching services. "The GTE SmartPark services help protect tenants from communications obsolescence and eliminates the need for relocation when their telecommunications requirements expand," says Harrison Coleman, national SmartPark product manager.

SMDA Station Message Detail Accounting. Another name for telephone call accounting. See CALL ACCOUNTING SYSTEM.

SMDI Station Message Desk Interface or Simplified Message Desk Interface. The SMIS is the data link from the central office if you have ESSX, Centrex or Centron (etc.) that gives you your stutter dial tone or message waiting light. In essence, SMDI is a data line from the central office containing information and instructions to your on-premises voice mail box. With SMDI, the calling person is not required to re-enter the called phone number (or in any other way identify the called party) once the call terminates to the messaging system.

SMDR Station Message Detail Reporting. Another name for telephone call accounting. See SMDR PORT and CALL ACCOUNTING SYSTEM.

SMDR PORT Modern PBXs and some larger key systems have an Station Message Detail Recording (SMDR) electrical plug, usually an RS-232-C receptacle, into which one plugs a printer or a call accounting system. The telephone system sends information on each call made from the system to the outside world through the SMDR port. That information — who made the call, where it went, what time of day, etc. — will be printed by the printer or will be "captured" by the call accounting system on a floppy or a hard magnetic disk and later processed into meaningful management reports.

See CALL ACCOUNTING SYSTEM.

SMI Structure of Management Information. The set of rules and formats for defining, accessing and adding objects to the Internet MIB. SMI was elevated to full standard status in May 1990.

SMRT, SINGLE MESSAGE-UNIT RATE TIMING USA telephone company tariff under which local calls are timed in 5-minute increments — with a single message unit charge applied to each complete or partial increment.

SMSA Standard Metropolitan Statistical Area. A metropolitan area consisting of one or more cities as defined by the Office of Management and Budget and used by the FCC to allocate the cellular radio market.

SMTP, SIMPLE MAIL TRANSFER PROTOCOL In local area networking technology, protocol that operates at layers 5 through 7 of the Open Systems Interconnection (OSI) model.

SNA Systems Network Architecture. An IBM product. The most successful computer network architecture in the world. See IBM and SYSTEMS NETWORK ARCHITECTURE.

SNEAK CURRENT An unwanted but steady current which seeps into a communication circuit. It is usually too weak to cause immediate damage, but if unchecked could potentially create harmful heating effects.

SNIGLET Any word that does not appear in the dictionary, but should. A term invented by Rich Hall of the HBO Television program "Not Necessarily The News". An example of a sniglet is the definition of "Hozone." It's obviously where socks go when they don't come back from the laundry.

SNMP Simple Network Management Protocol. In 1988, the Department of Defense and commercial TCP/IP implementors designed a network management architecture for the needs of the average internet (a collection of disparate networks joined together with bridges or routers). Although SNMP was designed as the TCP's stack network management protocol, it can now manage virtually any network type and has been extended to include non-TCP devices such as 802.1 Ethernet bridges. SNMP is widely deployed in TCP/IP (Transmission Control Protocol/Internet Protocol) networks, but actual transport independence means it is not limited to TCP/IP. SNMP has been implemented over Ethernet as well as OSI transports. SNMP became a TCP/IP standard protocol in May 1990.

SO Serving Office. Central office where IXC (InterExchange Carrier) has POP (Point Of Presence).

SOH Start Of Header. A transmission control character used as the first character of the heading of an information message.

SOFT COPY A copy of a file or program which resides on magnetic medium, such as a floppy disk, or any form that is not a hard copy — which is paper.

SOFT KEY There are three types of keys on a telephone: hard, programmable and soft. HARD keys are those which do one thing and one thing only, e.g. the touchtone buttons 1, 2, 3, * and # etc. PROGRAMMABLE keys are those which you can program to do produce a bunch of tones. Those tones might be "dial mother." They might be "transfer this call to my home for the evening." They might be "go into data mode, dial my distant computer, log in and put in my password." SOFT keys are the most interesting. They are unmarked buttons which sit below or above on the side of a screen. They derive their meaning from what's presently on the screen. And what's on the screen will change based on where the call is at that moment — in a conference call, about to set up a conference call, about to go into voice mail, into voice mail, programming a speed dial number, etc.

SOFT SECTORED A floppy disk whose sector boundaries are marked with records instead of holes. Soft-sectored disks have typically one hole. Hard sectored disks have many holes. A soft-sectored disk won't work on disk drives which use hard-sectored drives and vice versa — even though the disks might be the same size. Soft-sectored disks are now much more common.

SOFT SELECTABE/SOFT STRAPPABLE Refers to an option that is controllable throught software rather than hardware.

SOFTWARE The detailed instructions to operate a computer. The term was created to differentiate instructions (i.e. the program) from the hardware. See PROGRAM, HARDWARE and FIRMWARE.

SOFTWARE DEFINED NETWORK SDN. An AT&T network offering for large companies with many locations. The AT&T Software Defined Network Service Description of July 1986 describes SDN as a service developed for multi-location businesses which allows network managers to tailor their network to their own specific communications needs. Call processing information is stored in a database that is accessed during a call. Calls are transferred over AT&T facilities to either a location that is a dedicated part of the network (for "on-net calling") or to non-dedicated facilities that are part of the network ("on-net" calling). Any company location can become part of a network through SDN dedicated access lines to an AT&T SDN serving office. Here is further explanation of SDN by Siemens Information Systems, whose Saturn PBX has the capability to interface to and mesh neatly with an AT&T SDN network. Here is Siemens' explanation (it's good): When a company establishes an SDN, each phone on the network has a unique seven digit number. This number may or may not be the same as the Listed Directory Number (LDN). When a call is placed at one PBX, it is sent over a dedicated access line to the long distance network. The call is received by the SDN Serving Office and digits are sent via a CCIS (Common Channel Interoffice Signaling) link to the Network Control Point (NCP) for analysis and routing. There is one NCP per SDN network. The NCP contains the unique database for the company using the SDN. The NCP analyzes the digits received against the database, determines whether it is an on-net or off-net call, and sets up the path over which the call will be rerouted on the long distance network. If it is an on-net call, the NCP translates the unique seven digit locator code to one that will be recognized by the AT&T network, sends the call over the network to another SDN Serving Office, and completes the call over dedicated lines to the PBX being called. There is a discount for any call which remains on-net throughout. If the call is off-net, the digits dialed are sent over the long distance network to a Central Office that is not part of the SDN. The call is then completed to the corporate PBX over DID (Direct Inward Dial) lines. Since the introduction of route selection features in PBXs, the caller now has the ability to dial the 10-digit LDN (Long Distance Number) and have the PBX make the decisions on the route and make the decisions on any digit translation or deletion that is necessary to route the call. The CCIS network which carries SDN call signaling is a packet switching network operating at 4,800 bits per second. It will eventually be replaced by CCITT 7 Signaling, a more powerful internationally accepted signaling system. See SIGNALING SYSTEM 7.

SOFTWARE INTERFACES Language between programs which allows one program to call upon another for assistance in processing.

SOFTWARE SUPERVISION "Answer Supervision" is knowing when the person at the other end answers the phone. The main reason for wanting to know this is so that a phone company can start billing the call. There are two ways of doing answer supervision. You can get it from the nation's phone system, i.e. the distant office signals back across the country when the called person picks up the phone. Or you can fake it with "software supervision." Essentially this means there's electronics which "listens" to the call. If it "hears" voice or something like voice, it assumes the conversation has started and it's time to start billing the call. Software supervision is not accurate. But when you haven't got access to real answer supervision (for whatever reason) it's better than the previous alternative, which was "timeout." In timeout answer supervision, the carrier simply assumed the call had begun after a certain number of seconds — like 30 — had elapsed with the calling person hanging up. This meant, for example, if you called Grandma and she wasn't there, but you left it ringing, 'cause you knew she took time to answer the phone, then you'd be charged for the call — even though she didn't answer phone!

SOHO Small Office Home Office. An acronym for a new market opening up. In New York City, there's an area called SOHO. It stands for South of Houston Street.

SOLDER A metal or metallic alloy used when melted to join metallic surfaces. To unite or join by solder.

SOLID STATE Any semiconductor device that controls electrons, electric fields and magnetic fields in a solid material — and typically has no moving parts.

SONET Synchronous Optical NETwork. A family of fiber-optic transmission rates from 51.84 Mbps to 13.22 Gbps, created to provide the flexibility needed to transport many digital signals with different capacities, and to provide a standard for manufacturers to design from. Sonet is an optical interface standard that allows interworking of transmission products from multiple vendors (i.e. mid-span meets). It defines a physical interface, optical line rates known as Optical Carrier (OC) signals, frame format and an OAM&P protocol (Operations, Administration, Maintenance, And Provisioning). The OC signals have electrical called Synchronous Transport Signals (STSs). The base rate is 51.84 Mb/s (OC-1/STS-1) and higher rates are direct multiples of the base rate.

SONET was created by the Exchange Carriers Standards Association for the American National Standards Institute (ANSI). The standard is being defined in phases — Phase 1, adopted in March of 1988 by ANSI, and Phase 2, planned or completion by February of 1990. SONET has also been adopted by the Consultive Committee for International Telephone and Telegraph (CCITT).

SONET was initiated by Bellcore on behalf of the Regional Bell Operating Companies to attain these goals: Multi-vendor interworking, to be cost effective for existing services on an end-to-end basis, to create an infrastructure to support new broadband services and for enhanced operations, administration, maintenance and provisioning (OAM&P).

SONET, according to Northern Telecom, offers many advantages over asynchronous transport including: Opportunity for back-to-back multiplexing, digital cross-connect panels; Easy evolution to broadband transport; Compatibility with evolving operations standards; Enhanced performance monitoring and Extension of OAM&P capabilities to end users.

SONET transmission equipment interleaves STSs in simple integer multiples to form a synchronous high speed signal. This permits easy access to low speed signals (e.g. DS-O, DS-1, etc.) without multi-stage multiplexing and demultiplexing. The low speed signals are mapped into sub-STS-1 signals called Virtual Tributaries (VTs).

SONET uses a 51.84 Mb/s STS-1 signal as the basic building block. Higher rate signals are multiples of STS-1 (e.g. the STS-12/OC-12 signal has a rate of 12 x 51.84 Mb/s or 622.080 Mb/s). The frame format consists of 90 x 9 bytes. The SONET frame format is divided into two main areas: Synchronous Payload Envelope (SPE) and Transport Overhead (TOH). The SPE contains the information being transported by the frame. The TOH supports the OAM&P functions of SONET, and includes a data communication channel that provides an OAM&P communication path between multiple interconnected SONET network elements.

The SPE can handle payloads in any of three ways:

1. As a continuous 50.11 Mb/s envelope for carrying asynchronous DS-3, and other payloads requiring up to 50.11 Mb/s capacity in asynchronous (byte invisible) or byte visible format.
2. In a VT structured envelope to accommodate DS-1, DS-1C, DS-2, European CEPT1, or future VT based services (see chart below). These signals can have either an asynchronous or byte visible format.
3. As concatenated payloads to accommodate services requiring more than 50.11 Mb/s capacity. For example, three STS-1 SPEs may

be concatenated (combined) to transport a broadband ISDN signal of 135 Mb/s.

SOP Standard Operating Procedure.

SOURCE That part of a communications system which transmits information.

SOURCE ADDRESS The part of a message which indicates who sent the message. Just like the top left-hand address on the envelope.

SOURCE CODE A computer program which can be translated by another program into a program that will run on a particular computer. The program which finally runs on that computer is known as the object code.

SORT To order a collection of records — for example, a telephone directory — in some specified way, say, in alphabetical order. Computers can sort in virtually any way you ask them to. Most companies don't produce sufficient "sorts" on their telephone directories.

SOUTHWESTERN BELL CORPORATION One of the seven Regional Holding Companies formed at Divestiture. It includes Southwestern Bell and other companies.

SP Support Processor. Sending Program. Signal Present. Signal Processor. Signaling Point.

SPACE In digital transmission, the space is equated to the zero (0) and the mark is equated to the one (1). In telecommunications, space is the absence of a signal. Equivalent to a binary "O".

SPACE DIVERSITY Protection of a radio signal by providing a separate antenna located a few feet below the regular antenna on the same tower to assume the load when the regular transmission path on the same tower fades because of rain, a bird flying through it, etc.

SPACE DIVISION MULTIPLEXING Each distinct signal or message travels over a separate physical path such as its own wire or wire pair within a cable.

SPACE DIVISION SWITCHING Method for switching circuits in which each connection through the switch takes a physically separate path.

SPACE HOLD A no traffic line condition where a steady space is transmitted.

SPACE SEGMENT This is the imprecise term used to describe the band of frequency purchased by the satellite customer. The customer can purchase a portion of the bandwidth of a single transponder or the customer can purchase one or more entire transponder bandwidths.

SPACECRAFT SWITCHED TIME DIVISION MULTIPLE ACCESS SSTDMA. A method of sharing the capacity of a communications satellite by on-board switching of signals aimed at earth stations.

SPAG Europe's Standards Promotion and Application Group.

SPAN Refers to that portion of a high speed digital system than connects a C.O. (Central Office) to C.O. or terminal office to terminal office.

SPAN LINE A T-1 link.

SPAN POWERED In T-1, refers to the application of a varying voltage (+130V to -130V) to the digital cable pairs to maintain a 60mA DC current at each repeater and at the customer premises (this power is generally used for regeneration, loop backs, keep alive signals and alarms).

SPARK TEST A test designed to locate pin-holes in a wire's insulation by application of an electrical potential across the material for a very short period of time while the wire is drawn through an electrode field with one end of the wire grounded.

SPE Synchronous Payload Envelope. In Sonet, three different payload structures are defined to address different input requirements: 1. Direct-to-STS-1 line rate multiplexing takes 28 DS-Is, 14 DS-ICs or 7 DS-2s directly into the 51.84 Mbps rate. Each is uniquely transported within the SPE. 2. Asynchronous DS-3 Multiplexing takes a complete asynchronous DS-3 bundle (the output of an M13 for example) into the SPE. 3. Synchronous DS-3 Multiplexing maps a Syntran DS-3 signal to the SPE.

SPEAKER INDEPENDENT (VOICE) RECOGNITION SIR. Technologies for the automated conversion of speech to accurate and meaningful textual information (typically ASCII). SIR is used to accept input from callers to voice processors where the callers are using rotary dial phones instead of touchtone — Dual Tone Multi-Frequency (DTMF) — phones. SIR can substitute for the numbers on the DTMF keypad and can add the benefit of a few basic voice commands, e.g., Yes, No, Help, etc.

Because computer processing demands are formidable with speaker independent recognition, accurate speaker independent products are created with limited vocabularies. In contrast, trainable or speaker dependent recognizers can feature larger vocabularies at lower prices. SIR has been slowly gaining acceptance in telephone applications. SIR is increasingly used in automated operator assistance applications. SIR will see increased use as system builders respond to pressures to provide voice processing functions to the enormous rotary phone installed base domestically and abroad.

SPECIFIC GRAVITY The ratio of the weight of any volume of substance to a weight of an equal volume of some substance taken as a standard, usually water for liquids and hydrogen for gases.

SPEECH CONCATENATION A term used in voice processing for economical digitized speech playback that uses independently recorded files of phrases or file segments linked together under application program control to produce a customized response in natural sounding language. For example, order status, bank balances, bus schedules or lottery results, etc. Concatenation is done for speed and economy. It lends itself to limited and structured vocabularies that are best stored in RAM (Random Access Memory) or speedily accessible from disk. Concatenation does not replace Text-To-Speech (TTS) as a method of getting the voice processer to deliver its responsese. Concatenation, however, can be an excellent complement to

TTS when a voice application demands broad, real time vocabulary production. See TEXT-TO-SPEECH.

SPECTRUM ANALYZER Tuneable RF instrument which displays a portion of the RF spectrum with amplitude of signals on the vertical axis and frequency on the horizontal axis on a screen. Used in TSCM to analyze transmissions for the characteristics of an illegitimate transmitter (radio bug).

SPAGHETTI CODE A program written without thought, logic or structure. And whose "logic" is therefore very difficult to follow. Some would say this definition covers most software written today. That's unfair.

SPARE PAIRS In existing distribution systems, twisted pairs that are not being used and can be used to serve new communications devices. Spare pairs are exactly what they sound like — spare pairs of cables. Best to install as many spares as you can when you initially wire up a building or office. Remember Newton's Rule: You'll always need twice as much cabling as you ever dreamed in your wildest dreams you'd need.

SPATA SPeech And daTA. Watch for this expression to pick up steam once true integration of voice and data occurs. The expression does not come from the sentence: "Spata to integrate today than tomorrow."

SPATIAL DATA MANAGEMENT A technique which allows users access to information by pointing at picture symbols on the screen.

SPC Stored Program Control. All phone systems these days are SPC. There's stored software, which is the program, which controls the computer or microprocessor which in turn controls the operation of the switch. Thus switches are stored program control.

SPE Switch Processing Element.

SPEAKERPHONE A telephone which has a speaker and microphone for hands free, two-way conversation.

SPECIAL ACCESS A dedicated line from a customer to a long distance company provided by a local phone company.

SPECIAL BILLING NUMBER A phone number assigned to certain customers for billing purposes. It cannot be called. It may be given to an operator as the calling number on an outgoing paid call, or it may be used as a "third number billed" number. It's designed as a measure of security and accounting convenience.

SPECIAL NIGHT ANSWERING POSITION Provides either a console or a pre-assigned single extension phone to answer all incoming night calls.

SPECIAL SERVICES A variety of services that are separate from the public switched network.

SPECIALIZED COMMON CARRIER A company providing domestic long distance telecommunications services other than AT&T. See OTHER COMMON CARRIERS.

SPECTRAL EFFICIENCY The efficiency of a microwave system in its use of the radio spectrum, usually expressed in bits per Hz for digital radios and KHz per voice channel in analog radios.

SPECTRUM A continuous range of frequencies, usually wide in extent within which waves have some specific common characteristics.

SPECTRUM ANALYZER Tuneable RF (radio frequency) instrument which displays a portion of the RF spectrum with amplitude of signals on the vertical axis and frequency on the horizontal axis on a screen.

SPEED DIAL A feature that enables a PBX or PBX phone to store certain telephone numbers and dial them automatically when a code is entered. See SPEED DIALING.

SPEED DIALING Permits fast dialing of frequently used numbers. A repertory of numbers may be stored in the instrument and/or in the telephone switch. Usually a button or one, two or three digits are dialed to activate speed dialing.

SPIKE MIKE Contact microphone for listening through walls.

SPIKES Electrical anomalies represented as short duration, instantaneous, very high voltage fluctuations on an electrical service.

SPIN STABILIZATION A method of preventing a satellite from tumbling by spinning it about its axis.

SPIRAL WRAP A term given to describe the helical wrap of a tape or thread over a core.

SPIRIT COMMUNICATIONS SYSTEM A small electronic key system from AT&T. A SPIRIT telephone system supports as few as three outside lines and eight telephones (or, with an expansion unit, up to 24 outside lines with 48 phones).

SPLICE Verb. The joining of two or more cables together by splicing the conductors pair-to-pair.

SPLASHING A "splash" happens when an Alternate Operator Service (AOS) company, located in a city different to the one you're calling from, connects your call to the long distance carrier of your choice in the city the AOS operator is in. Splashing does not imply backhauling, but if often happens. For example, let's say you're calling from a Hotel Magnificent in Chicago. You ask AT&T handle your call. The AOS, located in Atlanta, "splashes" your call over to AT&T in Atlanta. But you're calling Los Angeles. Bingo. Your AT&T call to LA is now more expensive than it would be if you had been connected to AT&T in Chicago.

SPLINT A perjorative word for US Sprint, a long distance company now owned largely by United Telecom, Kansas City.

SPLIT Same as Group. See ACD or AUTOMATIC CALL DISTRIBUTOR.

SPLIT ACCESS TO OUTGOING TRUNKS Two separate trunk groups provided for direct outward dialing which can be accessed by dialing the same trunk access code. Controlled on class of service basis.

SPLIT CHANNEL MODEM A modem which divides a communications channel into separate send and receive channels. Most modems which use the dial-up phone network are split channel — meaning they can transmit and receive simultaneously over a two wire circuit. See also SPLIT

STREAM MODEM, which is another term for the same thing.

SPLIT LINK When one multiplexer uses two links to communicate to two separate multiplexers.

SPLIT PAIR Something that happens in cable splicing when one wire of a pair gets spliced to the wire of an adjacent pair. You could call it a split pair. It's more accurate to call it a mistake.

SPLIT STREAM MODEM A modem which can handle multiple, independent channels over a single transmission path.

SPLITTING Permits operator to consult privately with one party on a call without the other party's hearing. Or permits a three-party telephone conference user to consult privately with one side of the conference while the other is effectively put on hold. Jumping from one party to the other is called "Swapping."

SPOOL Abbreviation for Simultaneous Peripheral Operation On Line. A program or piece of hardware that controls data going to an output device. See SPOOLING.

SPOOLING Simultaneous Peripheral Operations On Line. Spooling means temporarily storing programs or program outputs on magnetic tape, RAM or disks for output or processing. The word "Spooling" is mostly associated with printers. Here's an example: Pretend that a lot of people on your Local Area Network all want to send their reports to the printer today. Instead of each person having control of the printer and relinquishing it only when they're through, each user tells the print Spooler what file they want printed. The program, called the spooler, places the print request in the print queue. When your request reaches the top of the queue, your report is printed out. Using a PC as print spooler slows it down. Best not to use it for much else.

SPOT BEAM ANTENNA A satellite antenna capable of illuminating or focussing on a narrow portion of the earth's surface.

SPREAD SPECTRUM A modulation technique in which the information content is spread over a wider bandwidth than the frequency content of the original information.

SPRINT A trademark of US Sprint, a long distance telephone company now owned largely by United Telecom, Kansas City.

SPUD A special long-handled shovel used to loosen soil in a hole into which you're going to put a telephone pole.

SPURS 1. The sharp metal devices on the climbers used by telephone linepersons (people who climb telephone poles). Such climbing spurs make a mess of telephone poles. 2. The cowboy devices awarded by US WEST to privileged persons who have done US WEST some nice favor or are otherwise deserving of honor.

SQL Structured Query Language. Invented by IBM, SQL is a powerful database language used for creating, maintaining and viewing database data. It is becoming somewhat of a standard in the mainframe and minicomputer world, and it is on its way to becoming a PC standard. When it is a standard, different computer systems running different DBMSs will easily be able to communicate and exchange data with each other by simply trading SQL commands. SQL is commonly used with database servers. Unfortunately, there doesn't see to be a "standard" SQL. Like there isn't a standard UNIX, etc.

SQUARE OPERATION If there are fewer than eight lines in a Merlin system, all users can access all lines. See SQUARED KEY SYSTEM.

SQUARED KEY SYSTEM What is a squared key system? No one knows where the word "squared" came from. So if our explanation bears no relation to the word "squared," sorry. But it goes like this (we think): In the old days there were 1A2 phone systems. These 1A2 phones had buttons on them. These buttons could correspond to trunks — any trunk. These were called non-squared systems. Then came electronic key systems. Each trunk had to "appear" (i.e. be) the same button on each phone. These electronic key systems were called squared systems. There are advantages and disadvantages. Squared systems are portrayed as having one advantage: You can go to any phone anywhere in the system and punch any button for any trunk and know it to be the same button for the same trunk. Thus less confusion. But this means you can only have as many trunks on your key system as you have trunk buttons on your key telephones. In a non-squared system — a 1A2, the newer hybrids or some of the newer programmable key systems — you can have more trunks than you have buttons on each phone. Some phones will have trunks that others don't have and vice versa. Thus you can have more trunks on your phone system than you have buttons on your phones. This means, for example, that four executives can have each have private lines and access to four trunks on a six button phone. (The other button is for Hold.)

SS7 Signaling System 7. See SIGNALING SYSTEM 7.

SSB Single SideBand. See SINGLE SIDEBAND.

SSCP System Services Control Point. A host based network entity in SNA that manages the network configuration, coordinates network operator and problem determination requests, maintains network address and mapping tables and provides directory support and session services.

SSP Service Switching Point

ST 1. Start signal to indicate end of outpulsing. 2. Straight Tip. A fiber-optic connector designed by AT&T which uses the bayonet style coupling rather than screw-on as the SMA uses. The ST is generally considered the eventual replacement for the SMA type connector.

STACK A set of data storage locations that are accessed in a fixed sequence.

STAKO An Ericsson committee for component standardization.

STAND ALONE Any device that can perform independently of something else.

STANDBY PROCESSOR A spare computer exists which can direct PBX operations if the primary one fails. Some standbys are just sitting there, installed but not turned on. They require someone to turn them on. Some standbys are actually running all the time, as the main one is. If the main one crashes, the standby processor is ready to take over.

STANDARDS Agreed principles of protocol. Standards are set by committees working under various trade and international organizations. RS standards, such as RS-232-C are set by the EIA, the Electronics Industries Association. ANSI standards for data communications are from the X committee. Standards from ANSI would look like X3.4-1967 which is the standard for the ASCII code. The CCITT does not put out standards, but rather, publishes "recommendations", owing to the international egos involved. "V" series recommendations refer to data transmission over the telephone network, while "X" series recommendations, such as X.25 (properly pronounced "Eks dot twenty five"), refer to data transmission over public data networks. Notice that the ANSI standards have the year they were approved as part of the name of the standard, while CCITT recommendations do not. The placement of the "dot" is another clue as to whose confusing standard belongs to whom.

When you're buying a phone system, at minimum it should conform to four standards:

- Emissions compliance according to the FCC Part 15;
- Telephone compliance according to the FCC Part 68;
- Safety standards set by the National Electric Code, OSHA and the Underwriters Laboratories 1459;
- Bellcore compliance (from the Network Equipment Building System publication and their Generic Physical Design Requirements for Telecommunications Products and Equipment publication.

STANDARD JACK The means of connecting customer premises equipment to a circuit as specified in the FCC Registration Program.

STANDARD METROPOLITAN STATISTICAL AREA SMSA. A metropolitan area consisting of one or more cities as defined by the Office of Management and Budget and used by the FCC to allocate the cellular radio market.

STANDARDIZED TEST TONE A single frequency signal at a standardized power level.

STANDING WAVE When you look at it on an oscilloscope the pattern of the wave is perfectly flat, i.e. horizontal. It's caused by two sine waves of the same frequency moving in opposite directions. In effect, they cancel each other out.

STAR A topology in which all phones or workstations are wired directly to a central service unit or workstation that establishes, maintains and breaks connections between the workstations. Virtually all phone systems are stars configurations. ISDN BRI bus will be the first phone system to operate on a bus. In datacom language, the center of a star is called the hub. The advantage of a star is that it is easy to isolate a problem node. However, if the central node fails, the entire network fails. The star network we're all most familiar with is our local telephone exchange. At the center (the hub) rests the central office. Spanning out in a star are the lines going to the individual workstations (telephones) in peoples' houses and offices.

STAR COUPLER A device that couples multiple fibers at a central point and distributes the signal from one fiber into all others simultaneously.

STAR NETWORK A computer network with peripheral nodes all connected to one or more computers at a centrally located facility.

STARLAN A local area network developed by AT&T which uses twisted pair telephone wires in a star configuration. It transmits data at 1M bits per second, using the CSMA/CD access method, over unshielded twisted pair. It is compatible with AT&T's Premises Distribution System, a large cabling system. Starlan connects to the Information Systems Network, a larger data communications switching system for high-speed terminal-to-host and host-to-host connectivity. Starlan software provides transparency and ease of use to the end-user through the AT&T menu program. AT&T is based in Bridgewater, NJ.

START BIT In asynchronous data communications, characters are sent at arbitrary intervals, i.e. when the operator hits a key. In order for the computer to make heads or tails of what's coming in, each character starts its transmission with a Start Bit. This way, if the first bit of the character to be transmitted is a 0, the fact of receiving a Start Bit (always a 1) tips off the computer that the next bit is part of a transmitted character and not just part of the inter-character gap. See STOP BIT.

START ELEMENT 1. The start pulse of a transmission character. It is used for synchronization of the following bits in a serial transmission process. 2. One of the input or output points in a communications system. This would include a telephone set, a data terminal, a computer communications port.

START OF HEADING SOH. A control character used in data communications that designates the beginning of the message header.

START OF MESSAGE SOM. A control character used in data communications that designates the beginning of the message.

START OF TEXT STX. A control character used in data communications that designates the beginning of the information being transmitted.

START STOP TRANSMISSION The technique of asynchronous data transmission wherein each character is comprised of a start element at its beginning and a stop element at its end. Start-stop elements allow the receiving device to determine where the transmitted bits for one character ends and the next begins.

STAT MUX Informal for statistical multiplexer.

STAT V Trademark for MICOM's series of combined statistical multiplexer and APV products.

STATE PUBLIC SERVICE COMMISSION PSC. The State legislative body responsible for among other things, regulating the operation of telephone companies and other persons involved in the furnishing of telephone service. Some states' PSCs are called Public Utilities Commissions. See the next definition.

STATE UTILITY COMMISSIONS Each state has a utility commission responsible for the regulation of telephone service provided wholly within that state. Regulation extends to introduction of new services, their prices, who will provide them, as well as discontinuance of existing services.

STATIC Interference caused by natural electric disturbances in the atmosphere, in your office, in your home. Static electricity can play havoc with telephone systems. Properly grounding your phone system to a true cold water pipe (not one that connects to a PVC plastic piper) is the most minimal protection.

STATION A dumb word for a telephone. Also called an instrument, or a telephone instrument. An extension station is one connected "behind" a PBX or key system. In other words, the PBX or key system is between the station and the telephone central office. We tried to remove the word "station" from this dictionary, but failed. We suspect the word comes from the very old days when the telephone industry was regulated by the Interstate Commerce Commission, (the ICC) which also regulated the railroad industry.

STATION APPARATUS The equipment which is installed on the customer's premises, including phones, ancillary electronics and small hardware.

STATION BATTERY A separate power source which provides the necessary DC power to drive a telephone system. Normally, telephones are powered by a central source, i.e. their PBX or central office. See BATTERY.

STATION BUSY INDICATION Provides a visual indication at a telephone of the busy or idle status of another telephone.

STATION BUSY LAMPS Lamps located on a station instrument, providing visual indication of each busy phone in the system. Busy Lamp Fields (BLFs) often come on key systems and sometimes on smaller PBXs. They're very handy.

STATION BUSY OVERRIDE Preselected phones have the privilege and ability to preempt busy circuits and override a private conversation.

STATION CALL TRANSFER A phone user can transfer incoming and outgoing calls to another phone without attendant assistance.

STATION CAMP-ON Phones can camp-on to a busy extension. The camped-on phone will be notified of the camp-on by a special beep signal. The person at the other end may or may not hear the signal.

STATION CODE The final four digits of a standard seven or 10 digit telephone number.

STATION DIRECT STATION SELECTION The phone user places a call to an extension within the PBX by pushing a single pushbutton on his phone.

STATION EQUIPMENT Telephone instruments and associated equipment furnished to subscribers. We suspect that the word "station" came from early telephone industry which was regulated by the same government agency which regulated the railroad business.

STATION HUNTING This feature allows a calling phone which places a call to a busy phone to proceed to the next idle phone in the hunt group. This jump is done automatically. See also ROTARY HUNT, which is the same thing for trunks.

STATION KEEPING The process on board a satellite for keeping it at its assigned longitude and inclination.

STATION MESSAGE DETAIL RECORDING Now refers to the RS-232-C "port" or plug found on the back of most modern PBXs and some larger key systems. See CALL ACCOUNTING SYSTEM and CALL DETAIL RECORDING.

STATION MESSAGE REGISTERS Message unit information centrally recorded on a per-station basis for each completed outgoing call.

STATION MESSAGE WAITING Special light on a phone to alert hotel/motel guests of messages waiting at the front desk.

STATION MONITORING Selected phones can monitor (i.e. listen in on) any other phones in the system.

STATION OVERRIDE SECURITY Designated phones can be shielded against executive busy override (presumably other executives).

STATION PROTECTOR A gas discharge, carbon block or other device that short circuits harmful voltages to ground in the event of lightning strikes on the phone line.

STATION REARRANGEMENT AND CHANGE Allows a user to move phones, change the features and/or restrictions assigned to phones and administer features associated with telephones.

STATION REVIEW A study of how people in an organization use the telephones and what communications needs are not being satisfied.

STATION RINGER CUTOFF Allows the ringer on the telephone to be turned off. Not always a good idea, since calls may still come in for that phone, but no one may pick them up because they don't hear it ring.

STATION TONE RINGING Electronic tone ringer that replaces the bell.

STATION TO STATION CALL A directly dialed call. No operator is used. Most calls are now directly dialed. Some long distance companies don't even have operators to help complete calls. AT&T still does.

STATION TRANSFER SECURITY If trunk call is transferred from one phone to another, and the second phone does not answer within a predetermined time, the trunk call will automatically go to the attendant.

STATION VISUAL SIGNALING Lamp on a phone which indicates flashing incoming, steady busy, and "wink" hold visual conditions associated with that phone.

STATISTICAL MULTIPLEXING A way of multiplexing a channel so that many data communications conversations may fit on the channel simultaneously. In statistical multiplexing a channel is only assigned to communicating devices when they actually have data to send or receive. See also FAST PACKET MULTIPLEXING.

STATISTICS PORT In network management systems, interface for reporting events and status.

STATMUX A statical multiplexer. See STATISTICAL MULTIPLEXING.

STATUS INFORMATION Information about the logical state of a piece of equipment.

STATUS SIGNAL UNIT Signal unit of CCS used to initiate transmission on a link or to recover from loss of transmission.

STC Society of Telecommunications Consultants. They're based in New York City and set standards of behavior for the consulting community.

STD Subscriber Trunk Dialing. An non-North American term for direct distance dialing, i.e. dialing long distance calls directly without an operator's assistance.

STDM Statistical Time Division Multiplexer. STDMs are TDMs with an added microprocessor that provides more intelligent data flow control and enhanced functionality, such as error control and more sophisticated user diagnostics. The major difference between TDMs and STDMs is that stat muxes dynamically allocate time slots on the link to inputting devices on an as-needed basis (rather than in round-robin fashion where all devices are polled in preordained order). Therefore, there is no idle time on the link because a device does not have information to send. Unlike TDMs, STDMs have buffers for holding data from attached devices. They can handle a combined input speed (aggregate speed) that exceeds the speed of the communications link.

S10 REGISTER Hayes, the modem people, invented their "Command Set." This command set lets you control your Hayes compatible modem. In the Command Set there are "S" registers which set how the modem responds to events like anwsering. Should it answer on the first, second, third, etc. ring. There are 27 registers. The most important S register is S10. This register sets the time between loss of carrier and internal modem disconnect. The factory setting is 1.3 seconds. Drop carrier for 1.3 seconds and your modem will turn itself off. This is long enough for all conditions, except the awful "call waiting" signal you get at hotels and at home. There is a solution: Get your communications software to "go local." Then type *ATS10=20.* That will increase your S10 register to two seconds. If you have a 300 or 1200 baud you'll have to do this every time you turn on your modem. If you have a 2400 baud modem (the only one to get), you type *ATS10=20&W* only once. The "&W" writes it into your 2400 baud's non-volatile memory. If you want to check to see if you did it right, type *ATS10?* That will reply by saying 020. That means 20 tenths of a second, or two seconds. If that still doesn't work for you, increase S10 to three seconds.

Other S registers control how long your modem waits for the other end to answer, how long its dialing "pause" is, how quickly it outpulses tones for dialing, etc.

STEP One movement of an electromechanical switch which typically corresponds to one impulse from a rotary dial or one impulse from a touch tone phone which has been converted to a rotary dial.

STEP BY STEP An electromechanical type of central office. Usually referred to by the initials SXS.

STEP CALL The phone user can, upon finding that the called phone is busy, call an idle nearby phone by merely dialing an additional digit.

STEP DOWN 1. Reduce the voltage. 2. A feature of fax machines that makes them drop their transmission speed when the quality of the phone lines they are transmitting over begins to deteriorate. Dropping the transmission speed is the major way of getting the faxes through on "dirty" lines. All Group III fax machines have "step-down" as a built in feature, or should have.

STEP INDEX FIBER A type of optical fiber with a uniform index of refraction throughout the core.

STEPPED INDEX Referring to a type of optical fiber which exhibits a uniform refractive index at the core and a sharp decrease in the refractive index at the core-cladding interface.

STOP BIT The Stop Bit is an interval at the end of each Asynchronous Character that allows the receiving computer to pause before the start of the next character. The Stop Bit is always a 0. See START BIT.

STOP ELEMENT The last element of a character in asynchronous serial transmission, used to ensure recognition of the next start element.

STOP/START TRANSMISSION A method of transmission in which a group of bits are preceded by a start bit and followed by a stop bit. Also called asynchronous transmission. See ASYNCHRONOUS.

STORAGE UNIT A device in which information can be recorded and retained for later retrieval and use.

STORE AND FORWARD In communications systems, when a message is transmitted to some intermediate relay point and stored temporarily. Later the message is sent the rest of the way. Not very convenient for voice conversations, but useful for telex type, and other one-way transmission of messages. Telephone answering machines, as well as voice mailboxes are considered forms of Store and Forward message switching.

STORED PROGRAM CONTROL SPC. The routing of a phone call through a switching matrix is handled by a program stored in a computer-like device, which may well be a special-purpose computer. Before SPC switches came along, the rotary dialing of the phone caused the elements of the switch to directly "step" through their dialing path. This was slow and cumbersome, since dialing can be slow. Also subscribers can abort half way (they made a mistake) and this can mess up the switch's efficiency. Thus the move to stored program control switches was very significant. These days virtually all switches as stored program control. Nothing happens in the switching matrix until the stored program control receives all the dialing digits and decides what to do with them.

STP Signal Transfer Point. The packet switch in the nation's emerging Common Channel Interoffice Signaling (CCIS) system. The CCIS is a packet switched network operating at 4800 bits per second. CCIS replaces both SF (Single Frequency) and MF (Multi-frequency) by converting dialed digits to data messages. It will run faster with the introduction of Signaling System 7. See SIGNALING SYSTEM 7.

STRAIGHTFORWARD OUTWARD COMPLETION Operator can place an outgoing call for phone user. Also called "Through Supervision."

STRAND A single uninsulated wire.

STRAND LAY The distance of advance of one strand of a spirally stranded conductor, in one turn, measured axially.

STRANDED CONDUCTOR A conductor composed of groups of wires twisted together.

STRANDED COPPER A type of electrical wire conductor comprised of multiple copper wires twisted together forming a single conductor and then covered with an insulating jacket.

STREAMING TAPE BACKUP A device to back up files and programs. A streaming tape backup looks very much like a large audio cassette. It records data sequentially.

STRING A sequence of characters that is handled as a unit by the computer.

STROWGER, ARMOND The world's first Phone Phreak. The man who invented the telephone dial as a method of allowing the user to complete calls without the Operator getting in the way. In Kansas City in the late 1800s, 'Ol Armond was an undertaker who wasn't getting much business. That's because the girlfriend of a rival undertaker was a telephone operator, and when she got a call asking for the local undertaker, she forwarded the calls to her boyfriend. This story may or may not be apocryphal. But it's a great story.

STRUCTURED QUERY LANGUAGE SQL. A relational database language (ANSI Standard) that consists of a set of facililties for defining, manipulating and controlling data.

STS Synchronous Transport Signal

STS-1 Synchronous Transport Signal Level - 1. The basic rate (51.840 Mbps) and associated byte interleaved multiplex structure that all Sonet products/offerings are based (i.e.,n times the STS-1 rate).

STUNT BOX A device to 1. control the nonprinting functions of a teletypewriter terminal, such as a carriage return and line feed and 2. a device to recognize line control characters.

SUB (SUBSTITUTE CHARACTER) A control character used in the place of a character that has been found to be invalid or in error.

SUB-ADDRESSING A name for an ISDN service which enables many different types of terminals — phones, fax machines, PCs, etc. — to be connected to the ISDN user interface and uniquely identified during a call request. See ISDN.

SUBCARRIER A carrier which modulates a main carrier so that two different modulating signals can be transmitted simultaneously, one on the main carrier and one on the subcarrier.

SUBROUTINE A piece of software that performs a useful function that will be needed often. The code for the subroutine is stored on disk (like a letter, etc.) and dropped into a larger program as needed. A nicely written subroutine saves you "re-inventing the wheel."

SUBSCRIBER A person or company who has telephone service provided by a phone company. In other industries, subscribers are called customers. Some telephone companies are beginning to call their subscribers customers. Thank goodness.

SUBSCRIBER LINE The telephone line connecting the local telco central office to the subscriber's telephone instrument or telephone system.

SUBSCRIBER LINE CHARGE A monthly charge on subscribers created by the Federal Communications Commission and paid to the local telephone company. The logic for this charge has something to do with reimbursing the local phone companies for some costs which it is not recovering elsewhere. In reality, it's just another rate increase.

SUBSCRIBER LOOP The circuit that connects the telephone company's central office to the demarcation point on the customer's premises. The circuit is most likely a pair of wires. But it could be three wires if some external signaling is being used. It could also be four wires if the circuit was a four-wire full duplex leased line.

SUBSCRIBER LOOP CARRIER See SLC-96.

SUBSCRIBER PLANT FACTOR A planning factor used by common carriers to allocate investment in phone equipment, subscriber lines and the nontraffic sensitive portion of the central office equipment.

SUBSCRIBER'S DROP Wire which runs from a cable terminal or distribution point to the subscriber's premises.

SUBSET A contraction for Subscriber Set, or telephone set.

SUBSTATION An additional phone which has been established as an extension to the main phone or primary line.

SUBVOICE-GRADE CHANNEL A communications channel of such narrow dimensions (bandwidth) that it cannot handle voice conversations. Usually used for slow data transmission such as Teletype or telemetry.

SUMMARY BILLING New York Telephone will give you one monthly consolidated phone bill — no matter how many New York Telephone number accounts you have in your billing area.

SUPERPATH New York Telephone's Superpath services offer end-to-end digital transmissions at 1.544 Mbps (T-1) or 44.736 Mbps (T-3).

SUN TRANSIT OUTRAGE Satellite circuit outrage caused by direct radiation of the sun's rays on an earth station receiving antenna.

SUPER TRUNK A trunk between the master and the hub headends in a hub CATV system.

SUPERGROUP Sixty voice channels. In more technical terms: the assembly of five 12-channel groups occupying adjacent bands in the spectrum for the purpose of simultaneous modulation or demodulation.

SUPERHOUSE The National Society of Home Builders has registered SmartHouse. BellSouth has trademarked SuperHouse. And GTE has registered SmartPark. One day, fiber optic will snake to everyone's house, bringing the potential of immense information services. Until that day comes they'll be lots of interesting demonstrations at distant trade shows.

SUPERIMPOSED RINGING A way of stopping party line phone users from hearing each other's ring by superimposing a DC (direct current) voltage over the ringing signal and using it to alert a vacuum tube or semiconductor device in only the phone instrument that we want to ring. See also SUPERPOSED RINGING.

SUPERPOSED CIRCUIT An additional channel obtained from one or more circuits, normally provided for other channels, in such a manner that all the channels can be used simultaneously without mutual interference.

SUPERPOSED RINGING Party-line telephone ringing in which a combination of alternating and direct currents is used, the objective being to only ring the bell in the phone of the one whose call is coming in. See also SUPERIMPOSED RINGING for a better explanation.

SUPERVISION Supervision of a phone call is detecting when a called party has picked up his phone and when that party has hung up. Supervision is used primarily for billing purposes. Not all long distance carriers have supervision capability. It depends on how "equal accessed" they have chosen to be. See ANSWER SUPERVISION, SOFTWARE SUPERVISION and SIGNALING SYSTEM 7.

SUPERVISORY CALL This service feature allows the attendant, after connecting an incoming CO line or tie line call to the wanted phone, to continuously supervise the call in progress.

SUPERVISORY CONTROL Characters or signals which automatically actuate equipment or indicators at a remote terminal.

SUPERVISORY LAMP A lamp which shows the operator whether the person is speaking (off-hook) or is not speaking (on-hook). These days such lamps are called BUSY LAMP FIELDS. In some smaller key systems, all phones have them. Busy lamp fields are an operator's best friend.

SUPERVISORY PROGRAMS Computer programs designed to coordinate service and augment the machine components of the system, and coordinate and service application programs.

SUPERVISORY RELAY A relay which, during a call, is controlled by the transmitter current supplied to a subscriber line to receive from the associated phone signals that control the actions of operators or switching mechanisms.

SUPERVISORY SIGNAL 1. A signal which indicates whether a circuit is in use, or not in use, and which indicates change in use, and/or 2. A signal used to indicate the various operating states of circuit combinations.

SUPPRESSED CARRIER TRANSMISSION A transmission technique in which only the sidebands (one or both) are transmitted and the main carrier is not transmitted and thus not used.

SUPPRESSORS, ECHO Echo is controlled in long distance circuits with devices called echo suppressors. These devices automatically insert loss in the return path of a four-wire circuit. All long distance circuits are four-wire — two wires for each of the two paths (receiving and transmitting). The echo suppressor jumps back and forth between the two transmission paths. Properly adjusted, an echo suppressor puts only sufficient loss in a circuit so a listener can interrupt the talker. With very long circuits — 22,300 miles — in satellites, a better way is needed. They're called echo cancellers.

SURCHARGE A charge imposed in accordance with the Commission's Access Reconsideration decision in CC Docket 78-72, Phase 1, FCC 83-356. released August 22, 1983 and updated too many times since. The monthly charge is about $2.00 and is going up to $3.50. This charge is said to compensate the local phone company for long distance commissions (called settlements and separations) lost and now replaced with per minute access charges.

SURFACE OUTLET A Communications Outlet (modular jack) that is installed on the surface of the mounting location. The premises wire serving such an outlet may or may not be concealed behind the mounting surface.

SURGE PROTECTOR A device which plugs between the phone system and the commercial AC power outlet. It is designed to protcct the phone system from high voltage spikes (also called surges) which might damage the phone system. When a surge occurs on the power line, the surge protector sends the overload to ground. How fast it sends it to ground is a subject that could fill a book. The type of surge protector that you buy will be determined mostly by the speed you need to protect your equipment.

SURGES The increased flow of current through an electrical device brought about by an instantaneous change in its resistance or impedance.

SUSAN A nice name for a wife. Everyone should have such a good one.

SWISS ARMY KNIFE The one tool to have when you can't have more than one. Be sure it has a normal screwdriver, a phillips head screwdriver and a pair of scissors. A corkscrew also is useful.

SWITCH A mechanical, electrical or electronic device which opens or closes circuits, completes or breaks an electrical path, or selects paths or circuits.

SWITCH HOOK Also called Hook Switch. The little plunger at the top of most telephones which is depressed (pushed down) when the handset is resting in its cradle (on-hook). When the handset is raised, the plunger pops up (the phone goes off-hook). This Switch Hook can be used to signal for various services such as calling the attendant or transferring calls.

SWITCH HOOK FLASH A signaling technique whereby the signal is originated by momentarily depressing the switch hook. See SWITCH HOOK.

SWITCH OVER When a failure occurs in the equipment, a switch may occur to an alternative piece of equipment.

SWITCH ROOM The room in which you put phone equipment. Also called the Phone Room. (What else?) The Phone Room should be large, clean and should stay at roughly seventy degrees and 50% humidity. You, the customer, are responsible for the quality and condition of your phone room. The messier it is, the hotter it is, the dirtier it is, the poorer your phone system (and its technicians) will function.

SWITCH TRAIN In a telecom circuit (typically a step-by-step central office), the series of switching devices which a call moves through in sequence.

SWITCHBOARD The attendant position of a PBX. Most of them don't actually have "boards" (they were big), they have consoles (they're much smaller and they fit on desks). Switchboards are desks.

SWITCHBOARD CABLE A cable used within and between the central office main frames and the switchboard.

SWITCHED ACCESS A method of obtaining test access to telecommunications circuits by using electromechanical circuitry to switch test apparatus to the circuit.

SWITCHED CARRIER In data terms, physical line specification selection indicating a half duplex line in a bisync network.

SWITCHED CIRCUIT AUTOMATIC NETWORK SCAN. A service arrangement at certain Telco premises to interconnect private line telephone service channels of a switched service network provided to certain agencies of the federal Government.

SWITCHED LINE A circuit which is routed through a circuit switched network, such as the telephone or telex network.

SWITCHED LOOP OPERATION Each call requiring attendant assistance is automatically switched to one of several switched loops on an attendant position.

SWITCHED NETWORK See PSTN.

SWITCHED PRIVATE LINE NETWORK A network which results from combining point-to-point circuits with switches.

SWITCHED SERVICE NETWORK A private line network that uses scan and/or CCSA type common control switching.

SWITCHED VIRTUAL CIRCUIT A call which is only established for the duration of a session and is then disconnected.

SWITCHING Connecting the calling party to the called party. This may involve one or many physical switches.

SWITCHING ARRANGEMENT A circuit component which enables a Customer to establish a communications path between two phones on a network.

SWITCHING CENTERS There are four levels in the North American switching hierarchy run at AT&T. They are: Class 1 — Regional Center, Class 2 — Sectional Center, Class 3 — Primary Center, Class 4c — Toll Center and Class 4P — Toll Point. In addition, the local Bell operating companies run a fifth level in the hierarchy, called the Class 5 — End Office.

SWITCHING EQUIPMENT Premises equipment which performs the functions of establishing and releasing connections on a per call basis between two or more circuits, services or communications systems.

SWITCHWAY New York Telephone's Switchway is switched 56 Kbps service. Switchway lets you dial up and transmit data at up to 56,000 bits per second. It is a totally digital service — from one end to the other. Think of it as a dial-up service for computers. It's billed like a voice line — a monthly charge plus so much per minute. Switchway lines are assigned normal telephone numbers. SWITCHWAY lines require either a 2-wire or 4-wire non-loaded metallic connection. You can dial in and around New York City using Switchway. You can call further across the country by using Switchway to connect to long distance companies, like AT&T, MCI and Sprint.

SX A family of excellent PBXs made by Mitel of Boca Raton, Florida. There's the analog SX-10, SX-20, SX-50, SX-100 and SX-200, and the digital SX-2000.

SXS Step By Step. The earliest central office. An electromechanical system. Unbelievably reliable when kept clean.

SYMBOL An abbreviated, predetermined representation of any relationship, association or convention.

SYN, SYN CHARACTER, SYNCHRONOUS IDLE In synchronous transmission. Control character in character-oriented protocols used to maintain synchronization and as a time-fill in the absence of data. The sequence of two SYN characters in succession is used to maintain synchronization following each line turnaround. Contrast with flag.

SYN(C) Synchronization character.

SYNC BITS Synchronizing bits (more properly bytes or characters) used in synchronous transmission to maintain synchronization between transmitter and receiver.

SYNCHRONOUS 1. The condition that occurs when two events happen in a specific time relationship with each other and both are under control of a master clock. 2. Synchronous transmission means there is a constant time between successive bits, characters or events. The timing is achieved by the sharing of a single clock. Each end of the transmission synchronizes itself with the use of clocks and information sent along with the transmitted data. Synchronous is the most popular communications method to and from mainframes. In synchronous transmission, characters are spaced by time, not by start and stop bits. Because you don't have to add these bits, synchronous transmission of a message will take fewer bits (and therefore less time) than an asynchronous transmission. But because precise clocks and careful timing are needed in synchronous transmission, it's usually more expensive to set up synchronous transmission. See ASYNCHRONOUS

SYNCHRONOUS DATA LINK CONTROL SDLC. A data communications line protocol associated with the IBM Systems Network Architecture. See SYSTEMS NETWORK ARCHITECTURE.

SYNCHRONOUS NETWORK A network in which all the communication links are synchronized to a common clock.

SYNCHRONOUS TRANSMISSION Transmission in which the data characters and bits are transmitted at a fixed rate with the transmitter and receiver synchronized. Synchronous transmission eliminates the need for start and stop bits. See SYNCHRONOUS and ASYNCHRONOUS.

SYNCHRONOUS TRANSPORT SIGNAL LEVEL. STS-1. The basic logical building block signal in its electronic form with a rate of 49.92 Mbps.

SYNCHRONIZATION BIT A binary bit used to synchronize the transmission and receipt of characters in data communications.

SYNCHRONIZE To cause two systems to work at the same speed.

SYNDROME Basic element of decoding procedure. Identifies the bits in error.

SYNTAX The set of rules for using a programming language. It is the grammar used in programming statements.

SYNTAX ERROR An error caused by incorrect programming statements according to the rules of the language being used. Sometimes the computer will throw up "SN" to indicate a syntax error.

SYNTHESIZED VOICE Human speech approximated by a computer device that concatenates basic speech parts (or phonemes) together. Usually has a metallic, germanic sound.

SYNTRAN SYNCHRONOUS TRANSMISSION A restructured DS-3 signal format for synchronous transmission at the 4.736 Mbps DS-3 level of the North American Hierarchy.

SYSGEN Acronym for SYStem GENeration.

SYSOP The SYStem OPerator of a PC-based electronic bulletin board/mail service. SYSOPs (pron. sis-ops) typically put computers and modems on phone lines, then published the phone number, then invited people with computers to call them and leave them messages and interesting software programs which they had written. These programs then became "public domain," or freeware. And other callers were invited to download these programs for their own use. See also BBS.

SYSTEM An organized assembly of equipment, personnel, procedures and other facilities designed to perform a specific function or set of functions.

SYSTEM 25 The System 25 PBX from AT&T is a digital phone system for businesses with 20 to 150 telephones.

SYSTEM BUILD This is the original manufacturer system building that occurs when the order is placed by the buyer with the vendor. The basic configuration is set up to reflect the users needs at that point in time. Thereafter, if any changes occur to reflect changes in the operating environment, the manufacturer must reconfigure the system to reflect this change. There is usually a reprogramming charge and a delay associated with the change.

SYSTEM CLOCK The clock designated as the reference for all clocking in a network of eleconic devices such as a multiplexer or transmission facilities management system.

SYSTEM CONNECT The method by which connection is physically made to the cost computer or local area network.

SYSTEM GAIN The amount of free space path loss that a radio can overcome by a combination of enhancing transmitted power and improving receiver sensitivity.

SYSTEM RELOAD A process allowing stored data to be written from a tape into the system memory. Picture: your telephone system goes dead. For whatever reason it loses all memory of its generic programming and your specific programming (whose extension gets what, etc.). You have to quickly grab the backup (hopefully you have it on tape or magnetic disk) and load it back into your telephone system's memory. This is called system reload. Sometimes it's done automatically. Sometimes you have to do it manually.

SYSTEM SEGMENT A conceptual subset of a system, usually referring to one which can be functionally replaced without damaging the capability of the system.

SYSTEM SIDE Defines all cabling and connectors from the host computer or local area network to the cross connect field at the distribution frame.

SYSTEMS ANALYSIS Analysing an organization's activities to figure the best way of applying computer systems to its organization.

SYSTEMS ANALYST A person who performs systems analysis and who follows through with methods, techniques and programs to meet the need.

SYSTEMS APPLICATION ARCHITECTURE SAA. A set of specifications written by IBM to describe how users should interface with applications and communications programs. The idea is to give all software "a common feel" so that training will be less burdensome. According to IBM advertising, "SAA will make it possible for everyone in an organization to access information regardless of its location. What's more, all software written to SAA specifications will provide similar screen layouts, menus and terminology."

SYSTEMS NETWORK ARCHITECTURE SNA. IBM's very successful computer network architecture. Easily the most successful computer network architecture in the world. It is as successful in the computer networking world as AT&T's telephone network design is in that industry. The best explanation we've ever read of SNA is in James Henry Green's Dow Jones-Irwin Handbook of Telecommunications. (You can get a copy of this great book by calling the Telecom Library at 1-800-LIBRARY.) Here is an excerpt:

"SNA is a tree-structured architecture, with a mainframe host computer acting as the network control center. The boundaries described by the host computer, front-end processors, cluster controllers and terminals are referred to as the network's domain. Unlike the switched telephone network that establishes physical paths between terminals for the duration of a session, SNA establishes a logical path between network nodes, and it routes each message with addressing information contained in the protocol. The network is therefore incompatible with any but approved protocols. SNA uses the SDLC data link protocol exclusively. Devices using asynchronous or binary synchronous can access SNA only through protocol converters...SNA works in seven layers roughly analogous to ISO's seven level OSI model. Unlike OSI, however, SNA is fully defined at each level. SNA was first announced in 1974 and is the basis for much of the OSI model, but it differs from OSI in several significant respects." For more on these differences, see page 96 in Green's Handbook.

The following is a description we received from IBM's PR department: "What is SNA?" In general, SNA is the description of the rules that enable IBM's customers to transmit and receive information through their computer networks. SNA may also be viewed as three distinct but related entities: a specification, a plan for structuring a network and a set of products. First, SNA is a specification governing the design of IBM products that are to communicate with one another in a network. It is called an architecture because it specifies the operating relationships of those products as part of system. Second, SNA provides a coherent structure that enables users to establish and manage their networks and, in response to new requirements and technologies, to change or expand them. Third, SNA may be viewed as a set of products: combinations of hardware and programming designed in accordance with the specification of SNA. In addition to a large number of computer terminals for both specific industries and general applications, IBM's SNA product line includes host processors, communication controllers, and adapters, modems and data encryption units. The SNA product line also includes a variety of programs and programming subsystems. Telecommunications access methods, network management programs, distributed applications programming and the network control program are examples.

SYSTEMS SOFTWARE A type of program used to enhance the operating systems and the computer systems they support.

T Tip.

T CARRIER A time-division multiplexed, phone company-supplied, digital transmission facility operating at an aggregate data rate of 1.544 Mbit/s. See T-1.

T CONNECTION T-shaped three-way conductor for distributing an incoming signal in two outgoing ways. Same shape as a T-connection in the road.

T INTERFACE 4-wire ISDN circuit. The more common ISDN circuit is called the "U" interface. See U INTERFACE and ISDN.

T TAP A passive line interface used for extracting data from a circuit. Also, for extracting optical signals from a fiber cable or electrical signals from a coaxial cable.

T-1 Also spelled T1. A digital transmission link with a capacity of 1.544 Mbps (1,544,000 bits per second). T-1 uses two pairs of normal twisted wires, the same as you'd find in your house. T-1 normally can handle 24 voice conversations, each one digitized at 64 Kbps. But, with more advanced digital voice encoding techniques, it can handle more voice channels. T-1 is a standard for digital transmission in North America. T-1 links can often be connected directly to new PBXs and many new forms of short-haul transmission, such as short-haul microwave systems. It is not compatible with T-1 in Europe. For a full explanation of T-1 see Bill Flanagan's book The Guide to T-1 Networking. (Call 1-800-LIBRARY for your copy.) See also the following five definitions.

T-1 FRAMING Digitization and coding of analog voice signals requires 8,000 samples per second (two times the highest voice frequency of 4,000 Hz) and its coding in 8-bit words yields the fundamental T-1 building block of 64 Kbps for voice. This is termed a Level 0 Signal and is represented by DS-0 (Digital Signal at Level 0). Combining 24 such voice channels into a serial bit stream using Time Division Multiplexing (TDM) is performed on a frame-by-frame basis. A frame is a sample of all 24 channels (24 x 8 = 192) plus a synchronization bit called a framing bit, which yields a block of 193 bits. Frames are transmitted at a rate of 8,000 per second (corresponding to the required sampling rate), thus creating a 1.544 Mbps (8,000 x 193 = 1,544 Mpbs) transmission rate, the standard North American T-1 rate. This rate is termed DS-1. See also D-4 FRAMING and EXTENDED SUPER-FRAME FORMAT. See also T-2, T-3 and T-4.

T-1 SPAN LINE See Span

T-I CHANNEL Either of the two external ports of a TDI or RDI which provides for transmitting or receiving eight TDM channels.

T-SPAN A telephone circuit or cable through which a T-carrier runs. See T-1.

T1 See T-1 (as in T-ONE).

T-1C 3.152 million bits per second. Capable of handling 48 voice conversations. T-1C is further up the North American digital carrier hierarchy. See T-1.

T-2 6.312 million bits per second. Capable of handling at least 96 voice conversations depending on the encoding scheme chosen. T-2 is four times the capacity of T-1. T-2 is further up the North American digital carrier hierarchy. See T-1.

T-3 28 T-1 lines or 44.736 million bits per second. Commonly referred to as 45 megabits per second. Capable of handling 672 voice conversations. T-3 runs on fiber optic and is typically called FT-3. T-3 is further up the North American digital carrier hierarchy. See T-1.

T-4 274.176 million bits per second. Capable of handling 4,032 voice conversations. T-4 has 168 times the capacity of T-1. T-4 can run on coaxial cable, waveguide, millimeter radio or fiber optic. T-4 is further up the North American digital carrier hierarchy. See also T-1.

TA A Terminal Adapter allows existing non-ISDN terminals to operate on ISDN lines. It provides conversion between a non-ISDN terminal device and the ISDN user/network interface.

TABLE DRIVEN Describing a logical computer process, widespread in the operation of commun- nications devices and networks, in which a user-entered variable is matched against an array of predefined values. Frequently used in network routing, access security and modem operation. It involves a table lookup that is a reference to a collection of predefined values.

TABLE HOOK-UP METHOD An information retrieval system in which the input information and the related output information are stored as a pair. When a particular input is given, the table is accessed and the output data which coincides with the input is taken out.

TABLES A collection of data in which each item is arranged in relation to the other items. Many telephony functions use "lookup tables" to determine the routing of calls. These tables solve the problem, "If the call is going to this exchange in this area code, then use this trunk and this routing pattern." See TABLE DRIVEN.

TABS AT&T's Telemetry Asynchronous Block Serial Protocol.

TAFAS Trunk Answer From Any Station. The ability to answer an incoming phone call from any telephone attached to the system.

TAIL CIRCUIT A feeder circuit or an access line to a network.

TAIL-END-HOP-OFF TEHO. In a private network with several nodes (locations), TEHO occurs when a call placed from one location on the network to a location not on the network leaves the network at the node closest to its destination.

TALK-OFF Talk-off is one hazard of in-band signaling. Talk-off occurs when your voice has enough 2600 Hz energy to activate the 2600 Hz tone-detecting circuits in the central office. The 2600 Hz tone is used for in-band signaling. See SIGNALING SYSTEM #7.

TALKING BATTERY The DC voltage supplied by the central office to the subscriber's loop to operate the carbon transmitter in the handset.

TALKING PATH The tip and ring conductors of a telephone circuit.

TANDEM The connection of networks or circuits in series. That is, the connection of the output of one circuit to the input of another. See TANDEM SWITCH.

TANDEM CALL A call processed by two or more switches. Also used to designate this type of call at a switch where a connection is established from one trunk to another (tandem trunking). See TANDEM SWITCH.

TANDEM DATA CIRCUIT A data channel passing through more than two data circuit-terminating equipment (DCE) devices in series.

TANDEM OFFICE A major phone company switching center for the switched telephone network. It serves to connect central offices when direct interoffice trunks are not available.

TANDEM SWITCH Tandem is a telephony term meaning to "connect in series." Thus a tandem switch connects one trunk to another. A tandem switch is an intermediate switch or connection between an originating telephone call location and the final destination of the call. The tandem point passes the call along. A PBX can often handle tandem calls from other/to other locations as well as process calls to, from and within its own location.

TANDEM TIE TRUNK SWITCHING The PBX permits tie lines to "tandem" through the switch. This means an incoming tie line call from a distant PBX receives a dial tone instead of automatically connecting with the operator. The caller can then dial a connection with either a phone on the PBX or an outgoing line. The outgoing line can be a local trunk in which case the distant PBX has access to a form of foreign exchange service, or another tie line which links a third system. This system of tie lines is widely used to form a corporate communications system, allowing economical connections between distant offices. To provide tie line tandeming ability, the PBX must be able to detect when either tie line goes on-hook at the distant end so that it can break its tandem connection and allow the tie lines to be used for other calls.

TANDEM TRUNKS Trunks between an end office and a tandem switching machine or between tandem switching machines. Tandem trunks can provide direct routing or alternate routing capability when direct trunks are occupied.

TANK TEST A voltage dielectric test in which the wire or cable test sample is submerged in water and voltage is applied between the conductor and water as ground.

TAP An electrical connection permitting signals to be transmitted onto or off a bus. The link between the bus and the drop cable that connects the workstation to the bus. Also a device used on CATV cables for matching impedance or connecting subscriber drops.

TAP BUTTON A button found on single line phones behind a PBX or Centrex. The tap button gives a precisely measured Hookswitch flash. The purpose of this button is to signal the PBX that it is about to receive a command — typically a transfer. To transfer a call on a single line phone, you typically depress the hookswitch, then punch out the extension you want to transfer the call to, announce the call when someone answers, then hang up and the PBX or Centrex transfers the call. The problem with using a hookswitch to make this transfer is that if you depress the hookswitch for too long you will cut the call off. As a result, some manufacturers put a tap button on their single line phones. This button gives the precise hookswitch signal for the precise length of time necessary — no more, no less. The Tap Button is also called a Flash button or a Tap Key.

TAP KEY Also called Tap Button or Flash Key. A button on a phone that accomplishes the same function as a switch-hook but is not a switch-hook. See TAP BUTTON.

TAPE DRIVE The physical unit that holds, reads and writes magnetic tape.

TAPE READER A device which reads information recorded on punched paper tape or magnetic tape.

TAPERED RATE A proposal by New York Telephone to give discounts to large customers who might be considering bypass.

TARGA Truevision Advanced Raster Graphics Adapter.

TARIFF Documents filed by a regulated telephone company with a state public utility commission or the Federal Communications Commission. The tariff, a public document, details services, equipment and pricing offered by the telephone company (a common carrier) to all potential customers. Being a "common carrier" means it (the phone company) must offer its services to everybody at the prices and at the conditions outlined in its public tariffs. Tariffs do not carry the weight of law behind them. If you or the telephone company violate them, no one will go to jail. The worst that can happen to you, as a subscriber, is that your service will be cut off, or threatened to be cut off. Regulatory authorities do not normally approve tariffs. They accept them — until they are successfully challenged before a hearing of the regulatory body or in court (usually Federal Court). Many tariffs were accepted by regulatory commissions only to be struck down in court as unlawful, discriminatory, not cost-justified, etc. Monies collected under the tariff have been refunded and unnecessary equipment removed. In these new, competitive days, many telephone companies are violating their own tariffs by charging less money than their tariffs say they should, or bundling services together at a discount. They are also providing service and equipment on terms less onerous than outlined in their tariffs. Many users now regard tariffs as starting bargaining points, rather than ending bargaining points.

TARIFF 12 A user-specific long distance tariff of AT&T. Tariff 12 gives AT&T the ability to price its long distance services for one company practically any which way it feels — giving them a mix of services at stable prices over the long term with significant volume discounts. As this dictionary was going to the printer, a federal appeals court overturned the Federal Communications Commission's April 1989 decision allowing AT&T to offer custom networks and ordered the FCC to reopen its investigation into the legality of the Tariff 12 deals.

TARIFF 15 A user-specific long distance tariff of AT&T. Tariff 15 gives AT&T the ability to price its long distance services for one company practically any way it feels. Tariff 15 is single-customer discounting. Some of AT&T competitors claim the tariff is "illegal."

TAS Telephone Answering Service.

TASI Time Assignment Speech Interpolation. A money-saving analog multiplexing procedure which keeps the connection to the circuit as long as someone is speaking and lets other conversations use the circuit during the intervals (measured in microseconds) when there's no speaking. Since a long distance circuit is usually only half used — one person speaking, one person listening — at least 50% of the circuit can be used by someone else. TASI is typically used by long distance companies on submarine cable across the Atlantic and the Pacific. Unfortunately, the flip-flopping around of circuit allocation by TASI means that the first tiny bit of a conversation is often lost. This can be disastrous for data. The key in data is to keep transmitting. The key in voice is to say something like "Ah" to seize the channel and then say what you want. TASI is very much like a very fast version of mobile dispatch radio. A modern version of TASI is called DIGITAL SPEECH INTERPOLATION.

TASI is somewhat comparable to statistical multiplexing of data.

TASK MANAGEMENT Allocating resources and overseeing the sequence of tasks completed by the computer.

TAT TransAtlantic Telephone cable.

TC Transmission Control.

TCA TeleCommunications Association. A major association of West-of-the-Rockies telecommunications management professionals. Every September, TCA runs the TCA Show in San Diego. It's one of the biggest telecom shows of the year.

TCAM Telecommunications Access Method. A popular telecommunications software package to run on IBM 370 computers. See IBM.

TCAP An ISDN application protocol. In addition to PRA and ISUP, the third major ISDN protocol in the delivery of advanced network services is TCAP, a CCS7 application protocol that provides the platform to support non-circuit related, transaction-based information exchange between network entities. This capability is required by transaction-based services that must exchange information between a pair of signaling nodes in a CCS7 network. Examples of these services include enhanced dial-800 service, automated credit card calling and virtual private networking. The TCAP protocol enables these services to access remote databases called service control points (SCPs) to process part of the call. The SCP supplies the translation and routing data needed to deliver advanced network services — like translating a dial calls into the required routing number. TCAP is useful also in coordinating some enhanced call-related services. For example, network ring again requires the connection of two users when both stations become idle. In this case, TCAP is used to coordinate between the users' switches while waiting for each line to become idle. And it can do this without tying up network trunks.

One of the major advantages of TCAP is that it provides a set of protocol building blocks for use in a variety of service definitions. The TCAP building blocks are subdivided into the transaction sublayer and the component sublayer. For more on TCAP, see the 1988-3 issue of Northern Telecom's Telesis publication.

TCM 1. Traveling Class Mark. 2. Trellis Coding Modulation

TCP Transmission Control Protocol. ARPAnet-developed transport layer protocol. Corresponds to OSI layers 4 and 5, transport and session. See also IP.

TCP/IP Transmission Control Protocol/Internet Program. A set of protocols developed by the Department of Defense to link dissimilar computers across networks. TCP/IP is an important and established internetworking protocol that works at the third and fourth layers of the OSI model. Developed by the Department of Defense, TCP/IP is designed to be rugged and robust, and to guarantee delivery of data in the most demanding circumstances. TCP/IP is more and more popular with networking and computer vendors who want to connect their equipment to a variety of other systems and protocols. TCP/IP has been implemented on everything from PC LANs to minis and mainframes.

TCR Transaction Confirmation Report. A report from a fax machine listing the faxes received and transmitted. It provides details about each fax, including date, time, the remote fax's number, results, total pages.

TDC Time Division Controller.

TDF Trunk Distributing Frame.

TDI Transmit Division Intertie.

TDM See TIME DIVISION MULTIPLEXING.

TDM NETWORK A Rolm term: The assembly of interface cards and buses for connecting phones to each other, to outside trunks, etc., and to certain shared electronics within the CBX (Rolm term for PBX).

TDMA See TIME DIVISION MULTIPLE ACCESS.

TE ISDN Terminal Equipment.

TECHNICAL CONTROL CENTER A testing center for telecommunications circuits. The center provides test access and computer-assisted support functions to aid in circuit maintenance.

TEDDY BEAR A stuffed animal named after President "Teddy" Roosevelt, a keen hunter who once took pity on a baby bear.

TEEN SERVICE A feature of some central offices which allows two telephone numbers to be assigned to a single party phone line. Each number has a distinctive ringing patter so that the called parties can recognize which line is ringing. The inventor of this service named it after the fact that his teenage children were always receiving phone calls. And he wanted a way for them to recognize when the calls were for them and when they were for the parents. Sadly, this phenomenon now begins earlier in life, with children as young as six receiving their own calls. We speak from experience.

TEHO See TAIL END HOP-OFF (traffic engineering).

TEI Northern Telecom term for Terminal Endpoint Identifier.

TELBANKING Banking transactions conducted through telecommunications.

TELCO The local telephone company. Often a term of endearment. Americanism for telephone company.

TELECOMMUNICATIONS 1. The art and science of "communicating" over a distance by telephone, telegraph and radio. Any transmitting or receiving of information as signals or sounds or images by electrical means. 2. A fancy word for "telephony," which it replaced and which many thought meant only analog voice, but didn't.

TELECOMMUNICATIONS BROKER A person or an organization which buys telecommunications services at bulk rates and resells these services at below "normal" i.e. retail prices.

TELECOMMUNICATIONS LINES Telephone and other communications lines used to transmit messages from one location to another.

TELECOMMUNICATIONS NETWORK The public switched telephone exchange network.

TELECOMMUTING The process of commuting to the office through a communications link rather than transferring one's physical presence. In short, working at home on a computer, a modem and maybe a facsimile machine, rather than going into the office.

TELECONFERENCING A conference of more than two people linked by telecommunications. Can be audio only; can be video one-way and audio the other; can be video both ways. For years, teleconferencing has been heralded as a great coming event, and a significant replacement for travel. The death of travel has not happened because teleconferencing remains expensive, cumbersome, lacking in the human touch and difficult to initiate. Few companies have teleconferencing facilities in their offices. So, to hold a teleconference you often have to travel somewhere — a local hotel ballroom, the local AT&T office, etc. Teleconferencing will not displace travel. But it is growing and growing rapidly. It is developing its own special niche in the telecommunications travel-continuum. That niche is increasingly for events like new product announcements, price changes, new Vision statements — happenings which need to be broadcast quickly to many people, and which often generate questions from the dispersed audience.

TELECOPIER A fancy word for a facsimile machine.

TELEFAX A high-speed, 64 kilobit per second facsimile service that uses Group 4 fax machines and one Bearer channel of an ISDN circuit, or any other 64 kbps circuit. Group 4 fax machines take about six seconds to transmit a page. They're fast and impressive.

TELEGRAM Hard-copy information, in written, printed or pictorial form, routed to the general telegraph service for transmission and delivery to the addressee. Telegrams are dying due to the high cost of delivery.

TELEGRAPHY Aging data transmission technique characterized by maximum data rates of 75 bits per second and signaling where the direction, or polarity, of DC current flow is reversed to indicate bit states.

TELEMARKETING Marketing and sales conducted via the telephone. There are two sides to telemarketing — incoming and outgoing. Incoming telemarketing is largely run through 800 toll-free IN-WATS numbers and local FX (foreign exchange) lines. Outgoing telemarketing is organized over OUT-WATS lines. An expanding range of telecom gadgetry is being developed to automate telemarketing — including automated outbound dialers, voice processing technology and automatic call distributors. The tone recognition, voice detection and transaction audiotex and transaction processing capabilitities of voice processing gear can be used to enhance all telemarketing applications.

TELEMETRY A communications system for the transmission of digital or analog data which represents status information on a remote process, function or device.

TELEPHONE 1. An invention of the devil. 2. The most intrusive device ever invented. 3. The biggest time waster of all time, as in: "What did you do all day?" "Nothing. Just spent the day on the phone." 4. Also a truly remarkable invention. Here's a list of the eight things a telephone does, according to Understanding Telephone Electronics:

1. When you lift the handset, it signals you wish to use the worldwide phone system.
2. It indicates the phone system is ready for your wish by receiving a tone, called a dial tone.
3. It sends the number of the telephone to be called.
4. It indicates the progress of your call by receiving tones — ringing, busy, etc.
5. It alerts you to an incoming call.
6. It changes your speech into electrical signals for transmission to someone distant. It also changes the electrical signals it receives from the distant person to speech so you can understand them.
7. It automatically adjusts for changes in the power supplied to it.
8. When you hang up, it signals the phone system your call is finished.

And, most remarkably, most simple telephones cost under $50. Wait until you see what ISDN phones will cost.

TELEPHONE AMPLIFIER A device to amplify the sound of the receiver. Something no phone should be without. Some devices work strictly on line power. They can only increase volume by 10 dB, which is often not enough (especially if you're over 40). The best telephone amplifiers are powered by

AC/DC adapters. Newer ones are powered by nicad batteries. They will amplify to 20 dB.

TELEPHONE CHANNEL A transmission path suitable for carrying voice signals. Defined by its ability to transmit signals in a frequency range of about 300 to 3000 Hz.

TELEPHONE CIRCUIT Electrical connection permitting the establishment of telephone communication in both directions between two telephone exchanges.

TELEPHONE EXCHANGE A switching center for connecting and switching phone lines. A European term for what North Americans call central office.

TELEPHONE FREQUENCY Any frequency within that part of the audio frequency range essential for the transmitting speech, i.e. 300 to 3000 Hz.

TELEPHONE MANAGEMENT SYSTEM The term originally meant a system for controlling telephone costs by:

1. Automatically selecting lower-cost long distance routes for placed calls. 2. Automatically restricting certain people's abilities to make some or all long distance calls. 3. Automatically keeping track of telephone usage by extension, time of day, number called, trunk used and sometimes by person calling and client or account to be billed for call.

These days the terms means those three functions plus a whole lot more, typically those associated with professionally managing the corporate or government telecommunications expenses, including (but not limited to):

Computerized inventory monitoring,

Computerized traffic engineering and network design,

Departmental telephone bill allocation and invoicing,

Automated telephone directory, etc.

Project tracking,

Automated equipment and service ordering.

In short, all the functions of professional telecommunications management that can be automated or organized in some way on a computer. The telecommunications management system thus refers to the computer hardware and the software. For more on this subject see the latest June issue of TELECONNECT Magazine. See also CALL ACCOUNTING SYSTEM.

TELEPHONE MESSAGE MANAGEMENT SYSTEM TMMS. This IBM software product permits detailed personalized call answering in the CBX II 9000 environment. Which sounds like voice mail to us. We stole this definition from a glossary Rolm supplied us.

TELEPHONE RECEIVER Telephone earpiece. Device that converts electrical energy into sound energy, designed to be held to the ear.

TELEPHONE SERVICE REPRESENTATIVE TSR. Another word for agent — the person who answers the phone on an automatic call distributor. See AGENT.

TELEPHONE SIGNALING DEVICE A gadget which indicates that the phone is ringing. May also be hooked up to lamps or overhead lighting to cause those lights to flash when the phone is ringing.

TELEPHONY Converting voices and other sounds into electrical impulses for transmission by wire or other means over distances greater than what you can hear by shouting.

TELEPORTS The definition written by Gary Stix in the August 12, 1986 issue of Computer Decisions reads, "High bandwidth telecommunications distribution systems that allow major local users to obtain local, private services and long distance services. The most notable example is the New York Teleport," which is located on Staten Island. Teleports traditionally consist of two things — a fiber optic/coaxial cable network around a city and a collection of nearby satellite antennas. The cable network collects transmissions from larger customers and takes them to the antennas for shipping to and from distant offices. Teleport companies are now more successful as local communications companies than they are as long distance gateways. Which is understandable, since the cost of local calls has gone up, while the cost of long distance calls has gone down.

TELEPRINTER A teletypewriter. Also called a telex machine.

TELEPROCESSING An IBM term for data communications.

TELETEX A new CCITT standard for text and message transmission which is replacing Telex. Teletex operates at 2400 baud, about 50 times faster than telex. Teletex uses ASCII to encode its characters for transmission.

TELETEXT A data communications information service used to transmit information from remote data banks to viewers. Teletext originated in Europe and was originally designed for public consumption. It didn't prove successful. Now teletext is proving somewhat more successful among corporations for the internal dissemination of information.

TELETRAFFIC OPTIMIZER PROGRAM Derives data by processing actual calls instead of using an analytical model based on estimates or summaries.

TELETRAINING Education and training through telecommunications.

TELETYPE A specific type of teletypewriter.

TELETYPEWRITER TTY. A telegraph device capable of transmitting and receiving alphanumeric information over communications channels. It may also contain a keyboard similar to that of a typewriter or computer but usually with fewer keys. See TELETYPE.

TELEVISION A standard TV channel today fits into a frequency bandwidth of six megahertz.

TELEWATCH New York Telephone's Telewatch is a maintenance service which periodically tests NYTel analog DID trunks for transmission loss, noise and trouble.

TELEX A worldwide switched message service. Telex service is offered in the United States by the Western Union Telegraph Company, MCI, ITT,

RCA, FTCC and TRT. Telex has one gigantic advantage: Overseas it's very popular and widely used. Contacting overseas businesses by telex is often far more reliable and faster than contacting them by telephone. Telex is good for overseas time zone differences because you can send a message to an unattended telex machine. It also delivers a printed record. Telex is relatively inexpensive usually costing a little less than a phone call. Telex has one disadvantage: It's very slow and not very accurate with virtually no data communications error checking procedures. Telex is being rapidly displaced by faster, more accurate forms of data communications, including the public packet switched networks and the various electronic mail services, and most recently by massive competition from low-cost facsimile machines. See TELETEX.

TELNET Terminal-remote host protocol developed for ARPAnet.

TELPAK A discontinued AT&T service that gave large customers discounts on purchases of multiple analog private lines. Telpak was to discourage users from building their own private microwave systems. Users who bought Telpak, however, were not allowed to resell any of the circuits, though they were allowed to share them. The FCC ruled Telpak as being discriminatory against competition. (It was too cheap.) It may still exist on an intrastate basis in some states. Telpak typically came in bundles of 12, 24, 60 and 240 voice lines. The bigger the bundle, the cheaper the per circuit cost.

TEMPERATURE RATING The maximum temperature at which the insulating material may be used in continuous operation without loss of its basic properties.

TEMPORARY STATION DISCONNECTION Allows the attendant to completely remove selected phones from service at any time on a temporary basis.

TENANT SERVICE Some businesses acquire a telephone system too large for their needs so they sell parts of the service to smaller offices in their own building or in the surrounding community. There are two ways to make money on tenant service — renting phone equipment or re-selling long distance lines. There's more money on re-selling long distance lines.

TENSILE STRENGTH A term denoting the greatest longitudinal tensile stress a substance can bear withour tearing apart or rupturing.

TERMINAL 1. The point at which a telephone line ends, or is connected to other circuits of a network. 2. An input/output device for communicating with computers. Typically has a keyboard and a CRT (TV screen) display. See TERMINALS.

TERMINAL CONFIGURATION The functional interconnection of the components of a terminal. For example, a keyboard-printer may be configured to transmit keystrokes without printing them. Printing is only performed on data retrieved from the communication line. Terminals with multiple components can be configured in a variety of ways.

TERMINAL EMULATION A microcomputer or personal computer pretends to be (i.e. emulates) a data terminal. It does this with special printed circuit boards inserted into its motherboard and/or special software. For example, TELECONNECT uses the communications software program called Crosstalk to emulate a DEC VT-100, a Digital Equipment Corporation VT-100 terminal. We do this because emulating a DEC VT-100 works better with certain software programs we call up remotely.

TERMINAL EQUIPMENT Terminal Equipment usually refers to the telephones and other equipment at the end of telephone lines.

TERMINAL NODE In IBM's SNA, a peripheral node that is not user-programmable, having less intelligence and processing capability than a cluster node.

TERMINAL REPEATER A repeater for use at the end of a trunk line.

TERMINAL SERVER A device that allows the input/output of a variety of terminals to be multiplexed onto a LAN cable. A terminal server has a single network interface and several ports for terminal connections. The advantage of a terminal server is it allows many terminals to be connected to a host via a single existing LAN cable, rather than a variety of point-to-point cables. Digital Equipment's DECnet makes heavy use of terminal servers.

TERMINAL TABLE An ordered collection of information that identifies each line, phone, component or application program from which a message can be sent.

TERMINALS The screws or soldering lugs to which an external circuit can be connected.

TERMINALS TO LONG DISTANCE OPERATOR Commonly known as "toll terminals", they provide special trunks directly to the long distance telephone company operators. Upon completion of long distance calls, the toll operator will ring the attendant (or hotel operator) and give them "time and charges" for the phone call just ended.

TERMINATE 1. To connect a wire conductor to something, typically a piece of equipment. 2. To end one's telecommunications service or equipment rental.

TERMINATED 1. The condition of a wire or cable pair which is connected to (terminated on) binding posts or a terminal block. 2. The condition of a circuit connected to a network which has the same impedance the circuit would have if it were infinitely long.

TERMINATED LINE A telephone circuit with a resistance at the far end equal to the characteristic impedance of the line, so no reflections or standing waves are present when a signal is entered at the near end. Compare with bridge tap.

TERMINATING CHANNEL The name for the circuit in a private line channel that connects a local central office with the CBX/PBX or telephone instrument at the customer's premises.

TERMINATING OFFICE The switching center (i.e. the central office) of the person you're calling (the "called party").

TERMINATION RESTRICTION Prevents a user from receiving any calls on the phone line. A DID call to the restricted termination routes to an attendant, an announcement or intercept tone at customer option. All other calls route to intercept tone.

TERMINATION OF SERVICE The end of service of a line or equipment. All pursuant to the regulations set forth in the tariff.

TERRESTRIAL Long distance facilities which are entirely on land and do not use satellites. This includes microwave, coaxial cable, optical fiber, normal cable, etc. There are reasons to prefer terrestrial facilities over satellite facilities, though satellites also have many advantages:

1. No echo or delay in voice conversation. Some people find satellite conversations disturbing because of the delay. 2. No significant reduction in data throughput. Most data communications protocols send their data in "chunks" and require an acknowledgement from the other end when one chunk has been received before the next chunk can be sent. When it takes a long time for an acknowledgement to be received (as in a satellite circuit), the effective throughput of data becomes very slow.

When you're trying to send one one-way signal to many locations, satellites do a better and cheaper job.

TEST, FRIENDLY BUSY A test to see if a line is busy. The subscriber does not know the line is being tested. Such a test is usually performed if someone calling that number requests it.

TEST BOARD A switchboard equipped with testing apparatus.

TEST CENTER Equipment for detecting and diagnosing faults and problems with communications lines and the equipment attached to them. If centralized, a facility where a network manager or technician can gain access to (almost) any circuit in a network for the purpose of running diagnostic testing. Also called a network control center.

TEST DESK A desk equipped with equipment to test and repair subscriber lines. See also TEST CENTER.

TEST SET A telephone handset with extra electronics designed to test telephone circuits. Also called a butt set, since it typically hangs on the technician's tool belt near the wearer's butt... Well, that's one explanation. Another is that it's called a "butt" set because it allows the use to "butt in" to a conversation and listen to its quality, etc.

TEST SHOE A device that is applied to a circuit at a distributing frame to gain test access to circuit conductors.

TEST TONE A tone used to find trouble on phone lines.

TEXT Transmitted characters which make up the body of a message.

TEXT-TO-SPEECH SYNTHESIS TTS. Technologies for converting textual (ASCII) information into synthetic speech output. Used in voice processing applications requiring production of broad, unrelated and unpredictable vocabularies, e.g., products in a catalog, names and addresses, etc. This technology is appropriate when system design constraints prevent the more efficient use of speech concatenation alone. See SPEECH CONCATENATION.

TGB Trunk Group Busy.

TGC Transmission Group Control in IBM's SNA.

TGW Trunk Group Warning.

TH Transmission header, an SNA term.

THE PHONE COMPANY Also known by the initials TPC. In the 1966 James Coburn movie "The President's Analyst", the evil worldwide conspiracy was run by TPC, which turned out to be The Phone Company. Some people believe the movie was not fiction.

THERMAL NOISE Noise created in an electronic circuit by movement and collision of electrons.

THERMOPLASTIC Material that will resoften and distort from its formed shape when heated above a critical temperature peculiar to the material.

THERMOSET A plastic material which is crosslinked by a heating process known as curing. Once cured, thermosets cannot be reshaped.

THERMOSTAT Device responding to temperature changes, used to control heating and cooling equipment.

THIN ETHERNET An Ethernet technology that uses a smaller diameter coaxial cable than standard Ethernet. Also called "Cheapernet" due to the smaller cabling cost. Thin Ethernet systems tend to have transceivers located on the network interface card, rather than in external boxes. PCs connect to the Thin Ethernet bus via a coaxial "T" connector. Thin Ethernet is now the most common ethernet cable.

THIRD PARTY CALL Any call charged to a number other than that of the origination or destination party. It's not a good idea to let your employees make third party calls to one or more of your phone numbers. Best to ask them to place the calls on their personal phone credit cards. This way, they will spend a modicum of time justifying their exorbitant phone calls.

THIRD WIRE TAP The activating of a telephone handset microphone by using a third wire, thus bypassing the hook switch.

THREE SLOT An obsolete pay phone that is identified by three separate coin slots.

THREE-WAY CALLING A local phone company feature that allows a phone user to add another user to an existing conversation and have a three party conference call.

THREE-WAY CONFERENCE TRANSFER A PBX feature. By depressing the switchhook, a user can dial another extension and either hang up and transfer the call, get information from the called party and then resume the first call or bridge all parties together for a three-way conference call.

THRESHOLD OF PAIN 1. The present price of local telephone service. 2. Unbearable noise.

THROUGH DIALING Allows the attendant on a phone system to select a trunk and pass dial tone to a restricted phone user so that user may directly dial an outside call.

THROUGHPUT The actual amount of useful and non-redundant information which is transmitted or processed. Throughput is the end result of a data call. It may only be a small part of what was pumped in at the other end. The relationship of what went in one end and what came out the other is a measure of the efficiency of that communications link — a function of cleanliness, speed, etc.

TIA Telecommunications Industry Association. A new Washington lobbying and trade association, the result of the merger of the USTA (United States Telephone Association) and the EIA (Electronic Industries Association.

TIC An AT&T term for a digital carrier facility used to transmit a DS-1 formatted digital signal at 3.152 Mbps.

TICK TONE Clicking noise heard on some PBX lines indicating that the digits dialed will shortly be repeated to the central office.

TICKER A one-way telex machine used to typically report stock or commodity prices. The machine prints on ticker tape, which is about one inch wide and perfect for throwing out windows at passing celebrities. Thus the term "Ticker Tape Parade."

TICKET A telephone industry term for a filled-out form, usually a form for billing someone for a call. There are all sorts of tickets, including ones on paper, ones on computer and ones automatically generated without human intervention.

TIE A telephone industry term for joining cables and/or wires together.

TIE DOWN Verb meaning to terminate a wire on a main, intermediate or satellite distribution frame.

TIE LINE A dedicated circuit linking two points without having to dial the normal phone number. A tie line may be accessed by lifting a telephone handset or by pushing one, two or three buttons.

TIE TRUNK A dedicated circuit linking two PBXs.

TIE TRUNK ACCESS Allows a phone system to handle tie lines which can be accessed either by dialing a trunk group access code or through the attendant.

TIE/communications The largest key system seller in the US. It's based in Shelton, CT.

TIGHT JACKET BUFFER A buffer construction which uses a direct extrusion of plastic over the basic fiber coating. This construction serves to protect the fiber from crushing and impact loads and to some extent from the microbending induced during cabling operations. See also LOOSE TUBE BUFFER.

TIGHTLY COUPLED Describing the interrelationship of processing units that share real storage, that are controlled by the same control program and that communicate directly with each other. Compare with loosely coupled.

TIME ASSIGNMENT SPEECH INTERPOLATION See TASI.

TIME CONGESTION The time resources (outgoing trunks) are busy.

TIMED DETECTION As a substitute for answer supervision, some long distance phone companies use call timing and estimate that a call is completed if the caller remains off-hook for 30 seconds or more. This is not necessarily accurate, of course. The caller might be holding, thinking the person is in the shower, out in the garden, etc. Little does the caller know he is now being charged to listen to ringing signals. A long distance phone company that is "equal accessed" doesn't have this problem. A long distance company that isn't equal accessed — one that you have to dial directly with a local call — might well have this problem. Rule: When in doubt, don't wait too long on the phone listening to endless ringing. Hang up. Count to ten. Then redial.

TIME DIVERT TO ATTENDANT A system feature which automatically transfers a phone to the attendant if the phone has been left off-hook too long.

TIME DIVISION CONTROLLER TDC. A device which commands functions, monitors status and connects channels of TDM cards.

TIME DIVISION MULTIPLE ACCESS TDMA. A technique used in satellite communications to interweave multiple conversations into one transponder so as to appear to get simultaneous conversations. A variation on TASI.

TIME DIVISION MULTIPLEX TDM. A technique for transmitting a number of separate data, voice and/or video signals simultaneously over one communications medium by quickly interleaving a piece of each signal one after another. Here's our problem. We have to transport the freight of five manufacturers from Chicago to New York. Each manufacturer's freight will fit into 20 rail boxcars. We have three basic solutions. First, build five separate railway lines from Chicago to New York. Second, rent five engines and schlepp five complete trains to New York on one railway track. Or, third, join all the boxcars together into one train of 100 boxcars and run them on one track. The train might look like this: Engine, Boxcar from Producer A, Box Car from Producer B, Producer C, Producer D, Producer E, and then the order begins again...Boxcar from Producer A, Producer B...Moving one large train of 100 boxcars is likely to be cheaper and more efficient than moving five smaller trains each of 20 boxcars on five separate railway tracks. Time Division Multiplexing, thus, represents substantial savings over have five separate networks (five separate tracks) and sending five separate transmissions (five separate trains).

This is what Time Division Multiplexing is all about. And the analogy is perfect. Take one large train (fast communications channel) and interleave pieces (boxcars) from each conversation one after another. If you do this fast enough, you'll never notice you've broken the conversations apart, moved them separately, and then put them back together at the distant end. In TDM, you "sample" each voice conversation, interleave the samples, send them on their way, then reconstruct the several conversations at the other end. There are several ways to do the sampling. You can sample eight bits (one byte) of each conversation, or you can sample one bit. The former is called word interleaving; the latter bit interleaving. The basic goal of multiplexing — whether it be time division multiplexing, or any other form — is to save money, to cram more conversations (voice, data, video or facsimile) onto fewer phone lines. To substitute electronics for copper. See MULTIPLEXING.

TIME DIVISION MULTIPLEXER TDM. A device which derives multiple channels on a single transmission facility by connecting bit streams one at a time at regular intervals. It interleaves bits or characters from each terminal or device using the time. See TIME DIVISION MULTIPLEX.

TIME DIVISION SIGNALING Signaling over a time-division multiplex system in which all voice channels share a common signaling channel, with time division providing the separation between signaling channels. See SIGNALING SYSTEM 7.

TIME DIVISION SWITCHING The connection of two circuits in a network by assigning them to the same time slot on a common time division switched bus.

TIME DOMAIN REFLECTOMETER TDR. A testing device that acts on radar-like principles to determine the location of metallic circuit faults.

TIME MULTIPLEXED SWITCH The space switch of which the cross point settings are changed in each time slot.

TIME OF DAY DISPLAY The time and date displays on phones. Actually, it's very useful information. Sometimes it's not displayed on the operator's console. As a result, the operator may never know that every phone in the office is showing the wrong time and date.

TIME OF DAY ROUTING This feature automatically changes access to certain types of lines at times when the lines change from being expensive to cheap, or vice versa. For example, it's cheaper to use WATS lines before 8:00 AM in the morning. A company has offices in New York and Los Angeles. It might be cheaper to route calls to Chicago in the morning over the tie lines to LA and then out the LA WATS lines to Chicago, than to go directly out the New York WATS lines.

TIME OUT In telecommunications and computer networks, an event which occurs at the end of a predetermined interval of time is called Time Out. For example if you lift the phone off the cradle and do not proceed to dial, after a certain number of seconds you will hear either a voice telling you to get on with it or a howling sound of some sort. Data networks have the same thing. Don't do anything for x minutes and the system will knock you off the air, i.e. hang up on you. In more technical terms, time out is the amount of time that hardware or software waits for an expected event before taking corrective action. In its most common form, time out is the amount of time an OCC or telephone system waits after your call goes through before it begins billing or timing the call. Also see ANSWER SUPERVISION.

TIME SLOT In time division multiplexing or switching, the slot belonging to a voice, data or video conversation. It can be occupied with conversation or left blank. But the slot is always present. You can tell the capacity of the switch or the transmission channel by figuring how many slots are present.

TIME SPACE TIME SYSTEM TST. The most common form of switching matrix for small digital telephone exchanges in which a space switch is sandwiched between two time switches.

TIME SWITCH A device incorporating a clock which arranges to switch equipment on or off at predetermined times.

TIMED RECALL Your PBX can be instructed to place a call at a designated time. When the time comes, your PBX rings your phone. When you answer your phone, the PBX places the call.

TIMED REMINDERS At 20-second intervals, timed reminders will alert an attendant that a call is still waiting, a called line has not yet been answered or a call is still on hold. Timed reminders can be made longer or shorter. They can alert attendants to all sorts of events and non-events.

TIMESHARING The use of one computer by many users at one time. Each user is typically sitting in front of a data terminal and connected to the master computer through communications lines — local or long distance. The user asks the computer to work on his task, whether it be a simple as looking up some stock prices, checking an airline reservation or doing some accounting calculations. It appears to each user as if he/she has a computer dedicated to his own task, but the computer is large and powerful, and is moving rapidly from one user's task to the next. Timesharing's advantages are twofold: 1. The user may find it cheaper to time share a computer than to buy his own. 2. The computer may have valuable and extensive information in it, which would be virtually impossible to duplicate or handle in many stand-alone computers. Timesharing was more popular when computers were more expensive.

TIMING JITTER In digital carrier systems, an accumulative relative timing discrepancy between digital signal elements.

TINNED WIRE Copper wire coated with tin to make soldering easier.

TINSEL A component of some phone line cord conductors. Tinsel is made by rolling copper into very thin, narrow rolls and then winding several strands of tinsel around a non-metallic core (a string) and then placing an insulating cover over the resulting conductor. A cord is then built up of two or more conductors encased in a plastic jacket. The essential reason for this type of construction is to obtain good cord flexibility and long life.

TIP 1. The first wire in a pair of wires. The second wire is called the "ring" wire. 2. A conductor in a telephone cable pair which is usually connected to positive side of a battery at the telephone company's central office. It is the phone industry's equivalent of Ground in a normal electrical circuit. See TIP & RING.

TIP & RING An old fashioned way of saying "plus" and "minus," or ground and positive in electrical circuits. Tip and Ring are telephony terms. They derive their names from the operator's cordboard plug. The tip wire was connected to the tip of the plug, and the ring wire was connected to the slip ring around the jack. A third conductor on some jacks was called the sleeve. That's it. Nothing more sinister. Nothing more interesting.

TIP CABLE A small cable connecting terminals on a distributing frame to cable pairs in the cable vault.

TIP CONDUCTOR The first conductor of a customer line.

TIP SIDE That conductor of a circuit which is associated with the tip of a plug, or of a telephone circuit.

TL Tie Line.

TLF Trunk Link Frame.

TLP Transmission Level Point.

TNL Terminal Net Loss.

TOGGLE 1. A flip-flop switch that changes for every input pulse. 2. Any simple two-position switch.

TOKEN 1. A unique combination of bits. When a LAN workstation receives a token, it has now been given permission to transmit. See token passing. 2. Here is a Rolm definition: The floating master message which coordinates use of the CBX control packet network among the nodes connected to it. See TOKEN PASSING, TOKEN BUS and TOKEN RING.

TOKEN BUS A local network access mechanism and topology in which all phones or workstations attached to the bus listen for a broadcast token or supervisory frame. That token confers on them the right to communicate over the share channel, the token bus. See TOKEN PASSING.

TOKEN PASSING A method whereby each device on a local area network receives and passes the right to use the single channel on the LAN. The key to remember is that a token passing, or token ring LAN has only one channel. It's a high-speed channel. It can move a lot of data. But it can only move one "conversation" at a time. The Token acts like a traffic cop. It confers the privilege to send a transmission. Tokens are special bit patterns or packets, usually several bits in length, which circulate from node to node when there is no message traffic. Possession of the token gives exclusive access to the network for transmission of a message. The token is generated by one device on the network. If that device is turned off or fails, another device will assume the token creation task. See TOKEN RING and IBM TOKEN RING.

TOKEN RING A ring type of local area network (LAN) in which a supervisory frame, or Token, must be received by an attached terminal or workstation before that terminal or workstation can start transmitting. The workstation with the token then transmits and uses the entire bandwidth of whatever communications media the token ring network is using. A token ring is a baseband network. Token ring is the technique used by IBM, Arcnet, and others. A token ring LAN can be wired as a circle or a star, with all workstations wired to a central wiring center, or to multiple wiring centers. Despite the wiring, a token ring LAN always works logically as a circle, with the token passing around the circle from one workstation to another. The advantage of token ring LANs is that media faults (broken cable) can be fixed easily. It's easy to isolate them. Token rings are typically installed in centralized closets, with loops snaking to served workstations. Some other LANs require your going up in the ceiling and finding coax taps. All the work on a token ring can be done on one or several panels. These panels allow you to isolate workstations, and thus isolate faults. Help on this definition courtesy Tim Becker, Lanquest Group, Santa Clara, CA. See also TOKEN PASSING and IBM TOKEN RING.

TOLL CALL A call to any location outside the local service area. A long distance call.

TOLL CENTER A Class Four central office.

TOLL CONNECTING TRUNK A trunk used to connect a Class 5 office (local central office) to the direct distance dialing network.

TOLL DENIAL Permits phone user to make local calls but denies completion of toll calls or calls to the toll operator without the assistance of the attendant. See TOLL RESTRICTION.

TOLL RESTRICTION To curb a telephone user's ability to make long distance calls. Toll restriction capability on modern PBXs and key telephone systems has been increasing in sophistication. Some PBXs now allow selective restriction based on specific extensions, users or geography. In other words, Joe Smith, the president, could call everywhere. John Doe in accounting might only be allowed to call Chicago and Houston, where our two factories are located. Mary Johnson, the seller for the western U.S., might only be allowed to call Denver and points west. There's considerable debate as to how useful toll restriction really is.

TOLL STATION A Telco phone from which established long distance message rates are charged for all messages sent over company lines.

TOLL TESTBOARD Manual test position at which toll circuits are tested and repaired.

TOLL TERMINAL A phone only furnished with long distance service.

TOLL TERMINAL ACCESS Allows hotel/motel guest phones to access toll calling trunks.

TOLL TICKET Ticket is the telephone company term for a bill. A toll ticket is a bill containing the calling number, called number, time of day, date and call duration. Some phone systems generate their own bills automatically. Some still need an operator. It depends on the equipment and the type of call.

TOLL TRUNK A communications channel between a toll office and a local central office.

TONE DIAL A pushbutton telephone dial that makes a different sound (in fact, a combination of two tones) for each number pushed. The correct name for tone dial is "Dual Tone MultiFrequency" (DTMF). This is because each button generates two tones, one from a "high" group of frequencies — 1209, 1136, 1477 and 1633 Hz — and one from a "low" group of frequencies — 697, 770, 852 and 841 Hz. The frequencies and the keyboard, or tone dial, layout have been internationally standardized, but the tolerances on individual frequencies vary between countries. This makes it more difficult to take a touchtone phone overseas than a rotary phone.

You can "dial" a number faster on a tone dial than on a rotary dial, but you make more mistakes on a tone dial and have to redial more often. Some people actually find rotary dials to be, on average, faster for them. The design of all tone dials is stupid. Deliberately so. They were deliberately designed to be the exact opposite (i.e. upside down) of the standard calculator pad, now incorporated into virtually all computer keyboards. The reason for the dumb phone design was to slow the user's dialing down to the speed Bell central offices of early touch tone vintage could take. Today, central offices can accept tone dialing at high speed. But sadly, no one in North America makes a phone with a sensible, calculator pad or computer keyboard dial. On some telephone/computer workstations you can dial using the calculator pad on the keyboard. This is a breakthrough. It a lot faster to use this pad. The keys are larger, more sensibly laid out and can actually be touch-typed (like touch-typing on a keyboard.) Nobody, but nobody can "touch-type" a conventional telephone tone pad. A tone dial on a telephone can provide access to various special services and features — from ordering your groceries over the phone to inquiring into the prices of your (hopefully) rising stocks.

TONE DISABLING A method of controlling the operation of communications equipment by transmitting a certain tone over the phone line.

TONE RINGING Either a steady or oscillating electronic tone at the phone to tell you someone is calling.

TONE SENDER 1. A printed circuit card in Rolm CBX which supplies the data bus with the digital representations of the following tones: dial, ring, busy, error, howler (off-hook timeout) and pulse (after flashing). 2. A printed circuit card which generates the following tones: dial, ring, busy, error, howler (off-hook timeout) and pulse (after flashing).

TONE SIGNALING The transmission of supervisory, address and alerting signals over a telephone circuit by means of tones. Typically in-band. See also SIGNALING SYSTEM #7.

TONE TO DIAL PULSE CONVERSION Converts DTMF (Dual Tone Multiple Frequency) signals to dial pulse signals when trunks going to carry outgoing calls are not equipped to receive tone signals. A lot of electronic phones with touchtone dials have a sliding switch that allows you to choose whether the phone will outpulse in rotary, or whether it will touchtone out. You choose whichever your trunk line will accept.

TOP Technical and Office Protocol.

TOPOLOGY The geometric form describing a network. The arrangement of links and nodes in a network, typically conceived as one of several abstract types of layout, such as distributed bus, ring or star.

TOPS Traffic Operator Position System. A system to help a telephone company operator complete toll calls.

TOPS MPX Northern Telecom's Traffic Operator Position System designed on a token ring for interface between operator positions and the IBM Directory Assistance system database.

TORN TAPE RELAY SYSTEM A store and forward message switching system which uses punched paper as the storage medium.

TOUCHTONE A trademark owned by AT&T for Tone Dialing. The author apologizes to AT&T for using this word throughout this dictionary. It's simply a nicer word than the alternative, pushbutton.

TP Abbreviation for Transport Protocol or Twisted Pair.

TPAD Terminal Packet Assembler/Disassembler linked to a cluster controller or terminal device, taking native protocol input and converting it to X.25 for transmission over a packet network.

TPDU Abbreviation for Transport Protocol Data Unit.

TPI Tracks Per Inch. A measurement of how much data can be stored on a disk.

TRAC Northern Telecom term for Technical Recommendations Approval Committee.

TRACE AGENT This is a command used in the Infoswitch product line to report all the events and transactions an agent has been involved in over a defined period of time.

TRACE PACKET A special kind of packet in a packet-switching network which functions as a normal packet but causes a report of each stage of its progress to be sent to the network control center.

TRACER STRIPE When more than one color coding stripe is required, the first or widest stripe is the base stripe. The other, usually narrower stripes are the tracer stripes.

TRACK A storage channel on a disk or tape which can be magnetically encoded.

TRACK ACCESS TIME The time it takes to move the pickup head on a disk drive from one track to another.

TRACKING 1. Figuring where a satellite is and keeping track of it. This is not an easy job, given the vastness of space. 2. The effect created in compressed video when the speed of the transmission is not great enough to keep up with the speed of the action. Tracking creates a tearing effect on the video picture.

TRACTOR FEEDER A device which attaches to a computer printer and allows the printer to use continuous, sprocket-fed, paper. Such paper has a row of evenly spaced holes on both sides. Those holes coincide with the pins on the tractor feeder. In all tractor-fed printers, the tractor moves the paper, not the printers's platen.

TRADER TURRET A very large key telephone used by traders of commodities, securities, etc. Turrets typically have many line buttons. Each one corresponds to a trunk, an autodial or tie-line circuit to another trader or a financial institution. The objective of turrets is to allow the trader to be in instant communication with others who might want to buy or sell that which he is trying to sell or buy. See the June issue of TELECONNECT for an annual roundup of turrets.

TRAFFIC The amount of activity during a given period of time over a circuit, line or group of lines, or the number of messages handled by a data communications switch. There are many measures of "traffic." Typically it's so many minutes of voice conversation, or so many bits of data conversation. See also TRAFFIC ENGINEERING and QUEUING THEORY.

TRAFFIC CAPACITY The number of CCS (hundred call seconds) of conversation a switching system is designed to handle in one hour. This is the simple definition. See TRAFFIC ENGINEERING.

TRAFFIC CARRIED See TRAFFIC OFFERED AND CARRIED.

TRAFFIC CONCENTRATION The average ratio of the traffic during the busy hour to the total traffic during the day.

TRAFFIC DATA TO CUSTOMER The owner of a call accounting system can poll his PBXs daily or hourly and get traffic measurements, including peg counts, usage and overflow data. Summary reports, exception reports and complete traffic register outputs can be obtained.

TRAFFIC ENGINEERING The science of figuring how many trunks, how much switching equipment, how many phones, how much communications equipment you'll need to handle the telephone, voice, data and video traffic you're estimating. Traffic engineering suffers from several problems:

1. You are basing your future needs on past traffic. (Clearly, you can modify these numbers based on what you think might happen.)
2. Most traffic engineering is based on one or more mathematical formulas, all of which approach but never quite match the real world situation of an actual operating phone system. Computer simulation is the best method of predicting one's needs, but it's expensive in both computer and people time.
3. Most people in the telecommunications industry do not understand traffic engineering, have not worked with it sufficiently and so make horrendous (i.e. dumb and costly) mistakes.
4. Since there are now over 600 long distance companies in the United States and several thousand different-priced ways of dialing between major cities (most at different prices), traffic engineering has become very complex.

TRAFFIC LOAD Total traffic carried by a trunk during a certain time interval.

TRAFFIC MONITOR PBX feature that provides basic statistics on the amount of traffic handled by the system.

TRAFFIC OFFERED AND CARRIED People pick up the phone and try to place their calls. This is "Traffic Offered" to the switch. The calls that get through the switch and onto lines is called "Traffic Carried." The difference between traffic offered and carried is the traffic that was lost or delayed because of congestion. There are two basic ways of measuring traffic — erlangs and CCS (or hundred call seconds).

TRAFFIC MEASUREMENT Memory and other software in a telephone system which collect telephone traffic data such as number of attempted calls, number of completed calls and number of calls encountering a busy. The objective of traffic measurement is to enter the results into traffic engineering and so arrange one's incoming and outgoing trunks to get the best possible service. See TRAFFIC ENGINEERING.

TRAFFIC OVERFLOW Occurs when traffic flow exceeds the capacity of a particular trunk group and flows over to another trunk group.

TRAFFIC PATH A path over which individual communications pass in sequence.

TRAFFIC RECORDER A device which measures traffic activity on a transmission channel. It's a recorder, not a processor. It's dumb.

TRAFFIC TABLE A computer database into which a PBX enters a count of feature activity. Certain detected operating errors are also entered in the traffic table.

TRANSACTION It is a completed event that can be assembled in chronological sequence for an audit trail.

TRANSACTION CAPABILITIES APPLICATION PART TCAP. The application layer protocol of SS7. Transaction capabilities in the SS7 protocol are functions that control non-circuit related information transferred between two or more signaling nodes. Definition from Bellcore in reference to its concept of the Advanced Intelligent Network.

TRANSACTION DETAIL The detail of a transaction record.

TRANSACTION FILE A collection of transaction records. A transaction data entry program allows for the creation of new transaction files used to update the data base.

TRANSCEIVER A device capable of both sending and receiving information.

TRANSCODER A device that combines two 1.544 megabit per second bit streams into a single 1.544 megabit per second bit stream to enable transmission of 44 or 48 voice conversations over a DS-1 medium.

TRANSDUCER A device which converts one form of energy into another. The diaphragm in the telephone receiver and the carbon microphone in the transmitter are transducers. They change variations in sound pressure (your voice) to variations in electricity, and vice versa.

TRANSFER A telephone system feature which provides the ability to move a call from one extension to another. It is probably the most commonly used and misused feature on a PBX. Before you buy a PBX, check out how easy it is to transfer a call. If you have a single line phone, you should simply hit the touch-hook, hear a dial tone and then dial the chosen extension number and hang up. This sounds easy in principle, but many people find it difficult since they associate the touch-hook with hanging up the phone. Some companies have gotten around this by putting a "hookflash" button on the phone itself. Such a button is like having an autodial button which just makes the exact short tone you make when you quickly hit the hookflash button. An even better solution is an electronic phone with a button specially marked "transfer," or a button next to a screen which lights up "transfer." Failing to efficiently transfer a call is the easiest way to give your customers the wrong impression of your firm. Think of how many times have you called a company only to be told it wasn't the fellow's job and he will transfer the call, but "If we get cut off, please call Joe back on extension 2358."

TRANSFER DELAY A characteristic of system performance that expresses the time delay in processing information through a data transmission system.

TRANSFER RATE The speed of data transfer — in bits, bytes or characters per second — between devices.

TRANSFORMER An electrical device used to reduce the voltage in a circuit. One reason for using a transformer is that commercial power is typically 120 or 240 volts while many phone systems (and other computer-type "things") work best on 48, 24 or lower voltage.

TRANSHYBRID LOSS The transmission loss between opposite ports of a hybrid network, that is between the two ports of the four-wire connection.

TRANSIENTS Intermittent, short duration signal impairments or mess ups. See HIT.

TRANSIENT MOBILE UNIT A mobile unit communicating through a foreign base station.

TRANSITION PROBABILITIES Probabilities of moving from one state to another.

TRANSISTOR The transistor was invented in 1947 by John Bardeen, Walter H. Brattain and William Shockley of Bell Laboratories. Here is an explanation of how a transistor works, taken from "Signals, The Science of Telecommunications" by John Pierce and Michael Noll:

> "To understand how a transistor works, we must look at the laws of quantum mechanics. We commonly picture an atom as a positive nucleus surrounded by orbiting electrons ... Vacuum tubes rely on the ability of electrons to travel freely with any energy through a vacuum. Transistors rely on the free travel of electrons through crystalline solids called semiconductors ... Semiconductors (such as silicon or gallium arsenide) differ from pure conductors, such as metals, in how full of electrons are the energy bands that allow free travel."

And depending on their design, transistors can act as amplifiers or switches.

TRANSLATE To change the digits dialed on your phone into digits necessary for routing the call across the country. See TRANSLATIONS.

TRANSLATIONS Translations are changes made by the network to dialed telephone numbers to allow the call to progress through the network. Sometimes the translations are made automatically. Take one series of dialed numbers; convert them to another. Sometimes, translations are done with the help of "lookup" tables, also called databases. Here's an example of translations done with the help of a database. TELECONNECT Magazine has a WATS line, 1-800-LIBRARY. If you dial it on the phone, you'll see it is really 1-800-542-7279. But this is not its real number. When someone in California dials 1-800-LIBRARY, AT&T's long distance network recognizes the "1-800" portion of the call and sends it to a special AT&T central office in Utah. When the call arrives, a computer looks up the number 542-7279 in its database and translates that to 1-212-206-6871 and puts the call back into the network. Within seconds, that number in New York, 212-206-6871, which we think is our IN-WATS line, rings.

TRANSLITERATE To convert the characters of one alphabet to the corresponding characters of another alphabet.

TRANSMISSION Sending electrical signals carrying information over a line to a destination.

TRANSMISSION BUS The circuits mounted on the backplane of the AT&T ISN packet controller that carry data packets from sending device interface modules into the switch and back to the receiving device interface modules. See also BACKPLANE.

TRANSMISSION CODE A code by which information is sent and received on a transmission system.

TRANSMISSION CONTROL Category of control characters intended to control or help transmission of information over telecommunication networks.

TRANSMISSION FACILITY A piece of a telecommunications system through which information is transmitted.

TRANSMISSION LEVEL The power of a transmission signal at a specific point on a transmission facility. See DECIBEL.

TRANSMISSION LEVEL POINT TLP. A designated point on a circuit where the transmission level has been specified by the designer. Referencing this point in relation to others in the network can determine the performance of the network.

TRANSMISSION LIMIT The wavelengths above and below which the fiber ceases to be transparent and therefore, can no longer transmit information.

TRANSMISSION MEDIA Anything, such as wire, coaxial cable, fiber optics, air or vacuum, that is used to carry an electrical signal which has information.

TRANSMISSION OBJECTIVES A stated set of desired performance characteristics for a transmission system.

TRANSMIT BUS In AT&T's Information Systems Network (ISN), the circuit on the backplane of the packet controller that transports message packets from sending device interface modules to the switch module.

TRANSMIT DIGITAL INTERTIE TDI. A 16-channel serial converter which converts the TDM Data Bus from parallel format to serial format for transmission between nodes.

TRANSMITTER The device in the telephone handset which converts speech into electrical impulses for transmission.

TRANSMITTER DISTRIBUTOR A device in a teletypewriter system which converts the information from the parallel form in which it is used in the keyboard-printer to and from the serial form which it is transmitted on the transmission line.

TRANSMITTER START CODE A coded control character or code sequence transmitted to a remote terminal instructing that terminal to begin sending information.

TRANSMULTIPLEXER A device that takes a bunch of voice analog phone conversations and converts them directly into a T-1 1.544 megabit per second bit stream — without the need for de-multiplexing the bunches down to individual conversations, then digitizing them, then bundling them up into a T-1 digital bit stream. A transmultiplexer does it all in one go.

TRANSPARENCY A data communications mode that allows equipment to send and receive bit patterns of virtually any form. The user is unaware that he is transmitting to a machine that receives faster or slower, or transmits to him faster or slower, or in a different bit pattern. All the translations are done somewhere in the network. He is unaware of the changes occuring — they are transparent. ISDN is planned to be transparent.

TRANSPARENT When applied to telephone communications, the provision of a feature or service such as Automatic Route Selection in a such a way that the user is unaware of it and it has no affect on the way he uses the telephone. It's "transparent" to him. Translations are transparent to the telephone user. See TRANSLATIONS and TRANSPARENCY.

TRANSPARENT MODE 1.The operation of a digital transmission facility during which the user has complete and free use of the available bandwidth and is unaware of any inter- mediate processing. Generally implies out-of-brand signaling (also called Clear Channel). 2.In BSC data transmission, the suppression of recognition of control charac- ters, to allow transmission of raw binary data without fear of misinterpretation.

TRANSPONDER A transponder is a fancy name for radio relay equipment on board a communications satellite. Just like its domestic microwave counterpart (which you see along highways), a transponder will receive a signal, amplify it, change its frequency and then send it back to earth. Transponders typically have 36 MHz bandwidth. Full motion, full color TV video requires a 6 MHz analog channel.

TRANSPORT LAYER Layer 4 in the OSI data communications model that, along with the underlying network, data link and physical layers, is responsible for the end-to-end control of transmitted information and the optimized use of network resources. Also serves the session layer.

TRANSPORT MEDIUM The actual medium over which transmission takes place including copper wire, fiber optics, microwave and satellites, to name a few.

TRANSPOSITION Interchanging the relative position of conductors at regular intervals to reduce crosstalk.

TRANSVERSE PARITY CHECK Type of parity error checking performed on a group of bits in a transverse direction for each frame. See PARITY CHECK.

TRAP A mechanism permitting a device to automatically send an alarm for certain network events to a management station. Typically, network management information is gained by polling network nodes on a regular basis. This strategy can be modified when a trap is set from a network node. With traps, a node alerts the management station of a catastrophic problem. The management station can then immediately initiate a polling sequence to the node to determine the cause of the problem. This strategy is often called trap-directed polling.

TRAP AND TRACE An old telephone company term. Equipment and procedures for determining the source of an incoming call.

TRAVELING CLASS MARK TCM. A code that accompanies a long distance call. When Automatic Route Selection (ARS) or Uniform Numbering/Automatic Alternate Routing (UN/AAR) selects a tie trunk to a distant tandem PBX, the traveling class mark (TCM) is sent over the tie trunk. It is then used by the distant system to determine the best available long distance line consistent with the user's calling privileges. The TCM indicates the restriction level to be used based on the phone, trunk or attendant originating the call or the authorization code, if dialed.

TREE A network topology shaped like a branching tree. (What else?) It is characterized by the existence of only one route between any two network nodes. Most CATV distribution networks are tree networks.

TREE MAILBOX A special function mailbox that provides the caller with a menu and allows selections from the menu using single digit commands.

TRELLIS CODING A method of forward error correction used in certain high-speed modems where each signal element is assigned a coded binary value representing that element's phase and amplitude. It allows the receiving modem to determine, based on the value of the preceding signal, whether or not a given signal element is received in error.

TRELLIS CODING MODULATION TCM. A modem modulation technique in which sophisticated mathematics are used to predict the best fit between the incoming signal and a large set of possible combinations of amplitude and phase changes. TCM provides for transmission speeds of 14,400 bps and above on single voice grade phone lines.

TRFR TRansFeR.

TRIBUTARY CIRCUIT A circuit connecting an individual phone to a switching center.

TRIBUTARY PBX An exchange within the main PBX configuration but with its own listed number.

TRIGGER The combination of the occurrence of an event and the satisfaction of trigger criteria. Definition from Bellcore in reference to its concept of the Advanced Intelligent Network.

TRL Transistor Resistor Logic.

TROPOSPHERE A layer of the earth's atmosphere. You can bounce certain frequency radio signals off it and use it as an elementary transmission reflector.

TROUBLE NUMBER DISPLAY The operator will know what the trouble is with the phone system by seeing a number pop up on her/his console. That number may pop up automatically or the operator may have to hit the ALM (for ALARM) or similar button.

TROUBLES PER HUNDRED Troubles per hundred is a criterion for acceptable customer service which telephone companies and public utility commissions have agreed upon. It's measured in terms of the number of complaints received per hundred telephones in one month. Six complaints per hundred is considered the maximum for acceptable service. See QUALITY OF SERVICE.

TROUBLE TICKET Form used to report problems. Often incorrectly filled-in. Check.

TROUBLE UNIT A weighting figure applied to telephone circuit or circuits to indicate expected performance in a given period.

TRUNK A telephone communication path or channel between two points, one of them usually being a telephone company central office or switching center.

TRUNK ACCESS NUMBER The number of the trunk over which a call is to be routed.

TRUNK ANSWER FROM ANY PHONE When a call comes in, something rings. You can now answer the incoming call from any phone. To do so, you must dial a special code or hit a special feature button on your phone. When TELECONNECT'S PBX bells ring, all we have to do is to touch "6" on any phone and we can answer the incoming call.

TRUNK DATA MODULE TDM. Provides the interface between the DCP signal and a modem or Digital Service Unit (DSU).

TRUNK DIRECT TERMINATION An option on switchboards which terminates a trunk group on one key (or button) on the console.

TRUNK EXCHANGE A telephone exchange dedicated primarily to interconnecting trunks.

TRUNK GROUP A group of essentially like trunks that go between the same two geographical points. They have similar electrical characteristics. A trunk group performs the same function as a single trunk, except that on a trunk group you can carry multiple conversations. You use a trunk group when your traffic demands it. Typically, the trunks in a trunk group are accessed the same way. You dial your Band 5 WATS trunk group by dialing 62, for example. If the first trunk of that group is busy, you choose the second, then the third, etc. See TRUNK HUNTING.

TRUNK GROUP WARNING Alerts the attendant when a preset number of trunks in a group are busy. See TRUNK GROUP.

TRUNK HUNTING Switching incoming calls to the next consecutive number if the first called number is busy.

TRUNK MAKE BUSY A fancy name for saying that, by punching a few buttons on the console, you can make any trunks in your PBX or key system busy, effectively putting the trunk out of service. You may want to do this if your trunk is acting up. By busying it out at the console, you are effectively denying its use to anyone in the company. Thus you are protecting yourself from further complaints. Hopefully, it will be repaired promptly.

TRUNK MONITORING Feature which allows individual trunk testing to verify supervision and transmission. You dial an access code and then the specific trunk number from the attendant console. You want the ability to test a specific trunk because normally you might be only accessing a trunk group when you dial an access code. Thus, each time you dial into the trunk group, you might end up on another individual trunk. Some PBXs have a variation of trunk monitoring, whereby if a user encounters a bad trunk, he can dial a specific code, then hang up. The PBX recognizes these digits and makes a trouble report on that specific trunk, possibly reporting it to the operator, keeping it in memory for later analysis or dialing a remote diagnostic center and reporting its agony.

TRUNK NUMBER DISPLAY The specific trunk number of an incoming call can be displayed on the attendant console, enabling your attendant to instantly identify the origin of certain calls. For example, if you have several tie lines to branch offices, your attendant knows immediately which office is calling. Many newer PBXs have displays on individual telephones, which show the actual trunk being used for outgoing and incoming calls. This provides an additional measure of control. You might, for example, speak faster if you knew the call was coming in on your INWATS line. You might also answer the call differently if you know what trunk it's coming in on. For example, you might be running several, totally-separate businesses from the same console. Each business has a different number. The only way you know what to answer — Joe's Bakery or Mary's Real Estate — is by the trunk.

TRUNK ORDER A document (or data system equivalent) used in an operating telephone company to request a change to a trunk group.

TRUNK QUEUING A feature whereby your phone system automatically stacks requests for outgoing circuits and processes those requests on, typically, a first-in/first-out basis. See QUEUING THEORY.

TRUNK RESERVATION The attendant can hold a single trunk in a group and then extend it to a specific phone. This means, for example, that a WATS line can be held for someone special — a heavy caller, the president of the firm, etc.

TRUNK RESTRICTION Some people may not be allowed to use certain trunks at certain times. The sophistication of trunk restriction depends on the switch and the way it's programmed.

TRUNK TO TIE TRUNK CONNECTIONS The ability of the switching system to provide the attendant with the capability of extending an incoming trunk call to a tie trunk terminating some place else.

TRUNK TO TRUNK BY STATION A PBX feature which permits the user who established a three-way conference involving himself and two trunks to drop from the call without disconnecting the trunk-to-trunk connection.

TRUNK TO TRUNK CONNECTIONS The attendant can establish connections between two outside parties on separate trunks. Call your office on your IN-WATS. Ask the operator to extend that call to the VP who happens to be at his home. The operator must place an outside call to the VP on an outside trunk and join that call to the incoming call. Sometimes it works.

TRUNK TO TRUNK CONSULTATIONS Allows a phone connected to an outside trunk circuit to gain access to a second outside trunk for "outside" consultation. No conference capability is available with this feature.

TRUNK TRANSFER BY STATION Permits the user who established a three-way conference involving two lines to drop from the call without disconnecting the trunk-to-trunk connection.

TRUNK VERIFICATION BY CUSTOMER Provides the attendant or phone user access to individual lines in a trunk group to check their condition. See also TRUNK MONITORING.

TRUNK VERIFICATION BY STATION Provides a warning tone if a phone user enters a busy trunk.

TSAP Abbreviation for "Transport Service Access Point" in the OSI transport protocol layer.

TSCM Technical Surveillance CounterMeasures. Commonly called debugging, sweeps or electronic sweeping.

TSI Time Slot Interchange. A way of temporarily storing data bytes so they can be sent in a different order than they were received. Time Slot Interchange is a way to switch calls.

TSO Time Share Operation.

TSPS Traffic Service Position System permits operator positions serving public phones and HOBIC operations to be located remotely from the CO which services the pay phone or the hotel, or the hospital, etc.

TSR 1. Telephone Service Representative. Also, agent. See AGENT. 2. Terminate and Stay Resident. A term for loading a software program in an MS-DOS computer in which the program loads into memory and is always ready for running at the touch of a combination of keys, e.g. Alt M, or Ctrl ESC. Here's some information from Jackie Fox writing in PC Today: You can't load TSRs willy-nilly and expect them to work with each other. Some will get along with each other. Others won't. When you install a TSR, it goes to a location in RAM (Random Access Memory) called the Interrupt Vector Table. The interruprt vector table is like a hotel lobby, and TSRs are like guests waiting for messages. The TSR watches every incoming keystroke to see if it's the special hot key combination (message), the TSR is waiting for. If it isn't, the TSR passes it back to the regular program. What if you have four or five TSRs loaded? The one you loaded last has seniority. It checks the incoming keystrokes first. If the TSR recognizes the keystroke combination as its own hot-key combination, it takes over. If not, it passes it along to the next TSR. This process is called interrupt handler chaining. If none of the TSRs recognize that particular combination, they pass it along to DOS so it can process it as a regular keystroke combination. Not all TSRs pass instructions along the way they should. Some TSRs intercept keystrokes and never pass them on. Some TSRs never restore their original addresses. Sometimes two TSRs fight over the same hot key combination. Then you end up with a frozen keyboard. The basic problem is there are no rules for loading and running TSRs.

TST Time-Space-Time system.

TTD Temporary Text Delay. The TTD control sequence (STX ENQ) is sent by a sending station in message transfer state when it wants to retain the line but is not ready to transmit.

TTL Transistor Transistor Logic.

TTS Text To Speech. A term used in voice processing. See TEXT-TO-SPEECH.

TTTN Tandem Tie Trunk Network.

TTY A teletypewriter.

TUNABLE OPERATING SYSTEM PARAMETERS Tuning an operating system is the same as optimizing it, in that you rewrite commands and programs so they operate faster and more efficiently. Any new operating system needs to be tuned to the specific machine on which it is running.

TUR Traffic Usage Recorder.

TURNAROUND TIME The actual time required to reverse the direction of transmission from sender to receiver or vice versa when using a half-duplex circuit. The turnaround time is needed for line propagation effects, modem timing and computer reaction.

TURNKEY SYSTEM An entire telephone system with hardware and software assembled and installed by a vendor and sold as a total package. The term "turnkey" means the buyer is presented with the key to the thing he has just bought. He turns the key and the system will do everything it is supposed to do, including work. Most telephone systems are purchased Turnkey. An integral part of a contract to buy a turnkey phone system is the terms and conditions for the acceptance of the system. Someone has to define what it means for the thing to work, what you expect from it — so you, the buyer, can formally accept the system and thus incur an obligation to pay for it. Defining Acceptance Conditions is no small task on bigger phone systems.

TURRET A very large key system for financial traders, emergency teams at nuclear power stations and others who need single phone button access to hundreds of people. By simply pushing one button, the user can dial one of hundreds of people. These buttons may be connected to tie lines, foreign exchange lines. They may even be DDD lines with autodial capability. Like all good key systems, the buttons have a lamping display which shows if the particular line is idle, busy, ringing, on hold, etc.

TVC Trunk Verification by Customer. See TRUNK VERIFICATION BY CUSTOMER.

TVS Trunk Verification by Station. See TRUNK VERIFICATION BY STATION.

TWINAX Twinaxial Cable made up of two central conducting leads of coaxial cable.

TWIST Signals at different frequencies are transmitted with differing response by the transmission system. Usually refers to distortion of DTMF signals.

TWISTED PAIR Two wires twisted around each other to reduce induction (thus interference) from one wire to the other. Several sets of twisted pair wires may be enclosed in a single cable. Twisted pair is the normal cabling from a central office to your home or office, or from your PBX to your office phone. Twisted pair wiring comes in various thicknesses. As a general rule, the thicker the cable is, the better the quality of the conversation and the longer cable can be and still get acceptable conversation quality. However, the thicker it is, the more it costs.

TWO-OUT-OF-FIVE CODE A decimal code system in which each decimal digit is represented by five binary bits, two of which are ones and three are zeroes.

TWO-PARTY HOLD ON CONSOLE Allows an attendant to hold a call with both a calling and a called phone (or trunk) connected. Such a feature is required for activation of Attendant Lockout, Serial Call and Trunk-to-Trunk connections features.

TWO-PARTY STATION SERVICE PBX system with two internal phones, each with selective ringing. Resembles rural two party service of old.

TWO-TIER PRICING A complex and now largely obsolete AT&T pricing plan which imposed two monthly "rate elements" on every hardware piece of an AT&T telephone system. Tier A was a fixed rate, not subject to rate increases. It was fixed for a certain number of months, say 60. It was, allegedly, to pay for the system. At the end of the 60 months, Tier A disappeared, as though it were a full-payout lease and you now owned the equipment (which you didn't.) Tier B is the second element in this pricing scheme. It covers maintenance, and it is subject to rate increases. AT&T doesn't offer two-tier pricing any longer. Many two-tier contracts are now finding their Tier A payments ceasing. Remember, the equipment still belongs to AT&T.

TWO-TONE KEY Same as frequency shift keying.

TWO-WAY SPLITTING PBX feature. Allows a telephone user to jump back and forth between two calls. Try this: Someone calls you. You both decide you want to speak to a third person. You call that person and conference the three of you together. Then you decide you want to consult with one of the people confidentially. So you "split" one from the other and you speak to one. Then you swap back and forth between the two, speaking to one and then the other in complete privacy. It's easier to do this sort of complicated phone transaction on a phone with a LCD screen. Fortunately, these are becoming more common these days.

TWO-WAY TRUNK A trunk which can be seized from either end. Can be used to carry conversations into or out of a telephone system, i.e. most trunks. Some trunks are set up as one-way only. A classic one-way trunk is a IN-WATS line. It is designed to only receive calls.

TWO-WIRE CIRCUIT A transmission circuit composed of two wires — signal and ground — used to both send and receive information. In contrast, a four wire circuit consists of two pairs. One pair is used to send. One pair is used to receive. All trunk circuits — long distance circuits — are four wire. A four wire circuit costs more but delivers better reception. All local loop circuits — those coming from a Class 5 central office to the subscriber's phone system — are two wire, unless you ask for a four-wire circuit and pay a little more.

TWT Traveling Wave Tube.

TWX (Pronounced TWIX.) Teletype Writer eXchange. An automatic teletypewriter (i.e. telex-like) switching service where subscribers may dial any other subscriber and send and receive a message. Formerly owned by AT&T and sold to Western Union in 1972. It differed from Telex in that TWX used AT&T's normal long distance phone network, was thus more ubiquitous, was faster than Telex and was incompatible with Telex, which Western Union owned. However, Western Union, in a major accomplishment, got them to talk to each other.

TYPE APPROVAL A concept in which a design is approved by an agency and all devices subsequently manufactured according to that design are automatically approved.

TYPE 66 PUNCHDOWN BLOCK A standard, solderless terminal wiring block used today. Invented by Western Electronic.

TYPEBAR Linear type element in a printer containing the printable symbols.

TYPING REPERFORATOR Same as receive only typing reperforator.

U INTERFACE Two wire ISDN circuit — essentially today's standard one pair telephone company local loop made of twisted-wire. The "U" interface is the most common ISDN interface. It carries 160,000 bits per second from the central office to your home or office. Of those 160,000 bits, two are used for 64,000 bps Bearer (B) channels and one is used by the subscriber for 16,000 bps of data (the D channel). The other 16,000 bps is used by the network for signaling between the black box on the subscriber premises and the central office. The idea is to get the ISDN "U" interface working to 18,000 feet — the average length of a North American subscriber local loop. You screw the two "U" wires (local loop pair) coming in from your local ISDN CO into a black box about the size of desk printing calculator, called an NT-1. Out the side of the black box comes four wires, which are called the "S Bus." Onto these four wires you can attach, in a loop configuration (also called single bus), as many as eight ISDN terminals — telephones, fax machines, etc. See ISDN.

UART Universal Asynchronous Receiver/Transmitter. A device, usually an integrated circuit chip that performs the parallel-to-serial conversion of digital data to be transmitted and the serial-to-parallel conversion of digital data that has been transmitted. For example, UART converts the incoming serial data from a phone line into the parallel form best manipulated inside a computer. UART also does the opposite. It converts the computer's parallel data into serial data suitable for asynchronous transmission on phone lines.

UCD Uniform Call Distributor. A device for allocating incoming calls to a bunch of people. Less full-featured than an Automatic Call Distributor. For a bigger explanation see UNIFORM CALL DISTRIBUTOR.

UDP User Datagram Protocol. UDP provides basic transport.

UG UnderGround.

UHF The Ultra High Frequency part of the radio frequency spectrum ranging between 300 MegaHertz and 3 GigaHertz.

UIS Universal Information Services. AT&T's vision of a single fully-integrated, user-defined digital network with a universal port of entry. Very similar to ISDN, now aggressively adopted by AT&T.

UL APPROVED Tested and approved by the Underwriters Laboratories. The Underwriters Laboratories, Inc. was established by the National Board of Fire Underwriters to test equipment affecting insurance risks of fire and safety. Most phone systems are tested and approved. Most of the testing focuses on the power supply feeding the phone system. The power supply is that little black box that plugs into the AC wall outlet at one end, takes 120 volt AC and converts it to low voltage DC power that the phone system typically runs on. If the power supply tests OK, then that's usually sufficient UL testing. For it is the power supply — and what happens to the commercial AC power that feeds into the power supply — that determines the potential fire hazard of your phone system. After many fire deaths in recent years, most local communities are a lot more concerned about UL Approval of installed telephone equipment. Fire departments have been known to zealously enforce these rules.

In addition to the UL approval, the other major fire concern is the use of proper wire in new building construction, with especial emphasis on teflon-covered cable in plenum ceilings.

ULP Abbreviation for "Upper Layer Protocol." Layer above TCP.

ULSI Ultra Large Scale Integration, the technique of putting millions of transistors on a single integrated circuit. Compare with LSI (Large Scale Integration) and VLSI (Very Large Scale Integration).

ULTRAVIOLET Portion of the electromagnetic spectrum between the short wavelength extreme of the visible spectrum (about 0.4 microns) and 0.04 microns. Light in the ultraviolet spectrum is used for erasing EPROMS.

ULTRAVIOLET FIBER Special fiber which extends the usable range into the UV region of the spectrum.

UNATTENDED Equipment working without a human attendant or operator. There are pros and cons to operators. On the pro side, they offer a personalized service that's absolutely critical to customer goodwill. On the con side, they can be slow and cumbersome. They can be very irksome when you know you could do that task yourself, but have to wait for the operator. Some companies have only one main number. Some companies use a main number and DID — on their Centrex and their PBX. Some companies use an automated attendant and an operator. There's more flexibility with DID and a main number, or Centrex DID and a main number. Customers without knowledge dial the main number. Customers with knowledge can dial direct DID numbers. See also AUTOMATED ATTENDANTS.

UNATTENDED CALL Calls placed by a computerized dialing system in anticipation of an agent being available to answer the call. A called party is detected answering the phone and no agent is available to serve the call. The system hangs up on the party so as not to create any greater nuisance than has already occurred. The telemarketing industry does not believe that an unattended call can be queued for the next available agent.

UNBALANCED LINE A telephone circuit in which the voltages on the two conductors are not equal with respect to ground. Unbalanced lines give poor phone service. Lines can become unbalanced when they come from the central office or when they are in the PBX or the on-site phone system. Problems can and should be repaired for decent quality results.

UNBUNDLED Services, programs, software and training sold separately from the hardware.

UNDERLYING CARRIER A common carrier providing facilities to another common carrier which then provides services to end users.

UNDERWRITERS LABORATORIES, INC A non-profit laboratory which examines and tests devices, materials and systems for safety, not for satisfactory operation. See also UL APPROVED.

UNEQUAL ACCESS Refers to long distance phone companies who do not take advantage of Judge Harold Greene's Equal Access divestiture provisions. Rather than a carrier selection code, unequal access carriers require you to dial a local seven digit number and punch in an authorization code. If the carrier elected to pay for Equal Access, you would just dial directly the same 10 digits you do today, and your local telephone company would give your billing number to your long distance company.

UNERASE A command for getting back files you've accidentally erased. See MS-DOS.

UNGROUNDED Not connected to ground. PBXs, key systems and other phone systems will not work well when not connected to a solid ground because they have no place to send high voltage spikes (static electricity, lightning strikes, etc.) Improper grounding is probably the most common cause of phone system faults. Our feeling: the better the ground, the better the phone system performance. One way of grounding is the third wire of an electrical outlet. This may be OK if you check where that wire is ultimately connected to. You can ground to the metal cold water pipe. But that may connect to a plastic PVC pipe one floor below. Best to check. A ground ultimately ending firmly routed a dozen feet below the ground is best. Books have been written on the subject of grounding for telephony. See Lees abc Teletraining books, available from the Telecom Library at 1-800-LIBRARY or 212-691-8215.

UNIBOL A UNIX version of COBOL.

UNIDIRECTIONAL The transmission of information in one direction only.

UNIFORM CALL DISTRIBUTION See UNIFORM CALL DISTRIBUTOR.

UNIFORM CALL DISTRIBUTOR A device for distributing many incoming calls uniformly among a group of people (typically called "agents" because of the early use of these machines by the airline, hotel and car reservation industry). These days the term Uniform Call Distributor is falling into disrepute as the newer term, Automatic Call Distributor comes in. According to incoming call experts, a Uniform Call Distributor is generally less "intelligent," and therefore less costly than an ACD. A UCD will distribute calls following a predetermined logic, for example "top down" or "round robin." It will not typically pay any heed to real-time traffic load, or which agent has been busiest or idle the longest. Also, a UCD's management reports tend to be rudimentary, consisting of simple pegs counts, as opposed to an ACD, which can produce reports on the productivity of agents.

UNIFORM NUMBERING PLAN A uniform seven-digit number assignment made to each phone in a private corporate network. Such a plan allows routing of calls to distant phones from any on-net telephone without any differences in the dialed number. Without a uniform numbering plan, you would dial your boss in New York differently if you were in the company's Chicago office and differently again if you were in your company's San Francisco office. With a uniform numbering plan, it would be the same from all locations. The nation's long distance network has, obviously, a uniform numbering plan.

UNIFORM SERVICE ORDER CODE See USOC.

UNIFORM SPECTRUM RANDOM NOISE Noise distributed over the spectrum in such a way that the power per unit bandwidth is constant. Also known as "white" noise.

UNINTERRUPTIBLE POWER SUPPLY UPS. (Pronounced "UPs.") An auxiliary power unit for a telephone system that provides continuous power in case you lose commercial power. An UPS is typically a bank of wet cell batteries (similar to automobile batteries) engineered to power a phone system up to eight hours without any re-charging. A UPS system can also include a gasoline-powered generator. And if the generator works (make sure it has gas), you can power your phone system for much longer. According to Bell Labs, however, over 90% of all power outages last less than five minutes.

UNIQUE ADDRESSING The addressing of a node by using the software-programmable address assigned to each one upon system initialization. For example, TELECONNECT's LAN has a "unique" addressing scheme. Each workstation is known by the operator's first name.

UNITED STATES TELEPHONE ASSOCIATION USTA. The largest trade association of telephone companies. Based in Washington, its primary role is to ensure no regulation or legislation is passed that is unfavorable to the telephone industry. Its secondary aim is to hold trade shows/conventions each year. Its third aim is education. It has a sister organization, the United States Telephone Suppliers Association, which is now merged with the EIA, forming the TIA. See the next definition.

UNITED STATES TELEPHONE SUPPLIERS ASSOCIATION USTSA. This is the association of suppliers — manufacturers and wholesalers — affiliated with the United States Telephone Association (USTA). It is based in Chicago. Its aims are to promote sales of its members' products to international and domestic telephone companies through conventions. It has merged with the Electronic Industries Association to become the TIA — Telecommunications Industry Association.

UNIVERSAL ACCESS NUMBER A single number dialed from anywhere in the country which will route a customer to one or several locations for service, advice, etc. The definition varies depending on whose networking scheme you're dealing with.

UNIVERSAL ADDRESSING The addressing of a node by the use of the universal addresses which all nodes recognize.

UNIVERSAL ASYNCHRONOUS RECEIVER-TRANSMITTER UART. A device that converts outgoing parallel data from your computer to serial transmission and converts incoming serial data to parallel for reception.

UNIVERSAL INFORMATION SERVICES UIS. AT&T's vision for the future of the telecommunications industry, where network providers everywhere can give any customer any kind of voice, data or image service in any place, at any time, in any combination and with maximum convenience and economy. UIS is very much like ISDN. The word UIS seems to be disappearing as AT&T embraces ISDN.

UNIVERSAL INTEGRATED SERVICES See UNIVERSAL INFORMATION SERVICES.

UNIVERSAL MAILBOX Allows a user of unified messaging services to have single access to all messages from internal and external electronic mail systems. A nice idea given today's lack of standardization among electronic mail services. Not yet a reality.

UNIVERSAL NIGHT ANSWER A feature of telephone systems that permits any phone to pick up any incoming trunk call when the Attendant's console is unmanned (unpersonned?) and the phone system is set up (typically at the console) for "Night Answer."

UNIVERSAL PAY PHONE Description for a coin-and-credit-card phone.

UNIVERSAL SENDER Allows the dialed number to be sent out by the user.

UNIVERSAL SERVICE Originally conceived by the first chairman of the Bell System, Theodore Vail, universal service has been the goal of the entire telephone industry, including its Federal and state regulators, since the 1920s. The idea of universal service is to have residential telephone service priced sufficiently low so anyone in the United States can afford it. Keeping residential service low has been the reason why local business service is usually priced much higher -- though the two services are usually identical. Universal Service is now effectively accomplished. It has become a political rallying cry, used to justify the strange and wonderful pricing schemes the phone industry and its regulators create with little regard for the actual costs of providing those services.

UNIVERSAL TURRET A very large key system for financial traders, emergency teams at nuclear power stations and others who need single phone button access to hundreds of people. By simply pushing one of the button in front of them, the user can dial one of hundreds of people. These buttons may be connected to tie lines, foreign exchange lines. They may even be DDD lines with autodial capability. Like all good key systems, the buttons have a lamping display which shows if the particular line is idle, busy, ringing, on hold, etc.

UNIVERSAL WALL JACK There's really no such animal. Every manufacturer of installation gadgetry is trying to propagate the idea that their jack is universal, when it really isn't. The "universal" wall jack we installed in our new offices is actually four jacks — 1. Four pairs for two PBX voice lines (one electronic two-pair phone and one tip and ring phone) and one spare. 2. One RS-232-C 12-conductor shielded cable for connecting to centralized printers, for connecting to a dataPBX and for permanent null-modem connection of computers. 3. One for connecting to our high-speed, one megabit per second LAN, and 4. One spare twisted, shielded, stranded pair for a second LAN, or whatever comes along.

UNIX An immensely powerful and complex operating system for computers. UNIX is developed, marketed, championed and trademarked by AT&T. It needs a computer with a large amount of RAM memory to support its power. It has been used extensively in universities, and is only now emerging onto the business scene. UNIX allows a computer to handle multiple users and multiple programs simultaneously. It works on many different computers. This means you can often take applications software which runs on UNIX and often move it — with little changing — to a bigger, different computer, or to a smaller, different computer. This process of moving programs to other computers is known as "porting." UNIX was developed in 1969 by Ken Thompson of AT&T Bell Laboratories.

UNLOADED LINE A telephone line with its loading coils removed to increase the distance and speed with which data may be transmitted over the line. A fee is usually charged for removing the coils.

UNMA AT&T's Unified Network Management Architecture.

UPLINK In satellites, it's the link from the earth station up to the satellite. The link from the satellite down to the earth station is called the downlink. The two are differentiated because customers often buy uplinks and downlinks from different suppliers — especially in international telecommunications.

UPLOAD To transmit a data file from your computer to another computer. The opposite of download, which is receiving a file on your computer from another computer. Upload means the same as TRANSMIT, while DOWNLOAD means the same as receive. Before you upload or download, check at least three times you're going the direction you want. It's very easy to erase files (weeks of work) if you make a mistake and confuse uploading and downloading. (Don't laugh. We've done it several times. Dumb!)

UPS See UNINTERRUPTIBLE POWER SUPPLY. Also stands for United Parcel Service, a package deliverer that regularly lives up to its self-imposed, relatively speedy delivery schedule.

UPSTREAM In a broadband network, the signal from the transmitting stations to the headend. See UPSTREAM CHANNEL.

UPSTREAM CHANNEL A collection of frequencies on a CATV channel reserved for transmission from the terminal next to the user TV set to (upstream to) the CATV company's computer. Such signals might be requests for pay movies.

UPSTREAM OPERATIONS Functions that provide a BCC (Bellcore Client Company) control of features and service configurations and subject to BCC control, some service management capabilities for subscribers. These functions include Service Negotiation and Management, Service Provisioning and Repair Service Answering/Work Force Administration. Definition from Bellcore in reference to its concept of the Advanced Intelligent Network.

UPTIME Colloquial expression for the uninterrupted amount of time that network or computer resources are working and available to a user. In short, time between failures or periods of nonavailability (as for maintenance).

UPWARD COMPATIBLE Any device that can be easily organized, fixed or configured to work in either a different, expanded operating environment or some enhanced mode. Software is said to be upward compatible if a computer larger than the one for which it was written can run the program.

URBAN SERVICE Any of the grades of service regularly furnished inside base or locality rate areas, or outside base or locality rate areas at base or locality rates plus zone connection charges or incremental rates. Another way of saying expanded metropolitan phone service.

US WEST One of the seven Regional Holding Companies formed at divestiture. It includes Mountain Telephone, Northwestern Bell and Pacific Northwest Bell among other service entities and entrepreneurial adventures.

USA DIRECT An AT&T service designed for those calling the U.S. from overseas. Callers in foreign countries dial a toll-free number in that country. That call gets them to an AT&T operator in the U.S. who lets them make calls to the U.S. with their AT&T calling card or by making a collect call. AT&T calls the service USADirect — one word. It would look like a mistake if I spelled it that way in this dictionary. MCI has a similar service called "Call USA."

USAGE BASED Usage-Based refers to a rate or price for telephone service based on usage rather than a flat, fixed monthly fee. Until a few years ago, most local phone service in the United States was charged on a flat rate basis. Increasingly, phone companies are switching their local charging over to usage-based. Flat-rate calling will probably disappear within a few years. Allegedly, usage based phone service pricing is fairer on those phone subscribers who don't use their phone much. Usage based pricing is not consistent throughout the U.S. Typically, you get charged for each call. And the charging is very much like that for long distance — by length of call, by time of day and by distance called. See also FLAT RATE.

USAGE SENSITIVE A form of Measured Rate Service. See USAGE BASED.

USART Universal Synchronous/Asynchronous Receiver/Transmitter. An integrated circuit chip that handles the I/O (input/output) functions of a computer port. It converts data coming in parallel form from the CPU into serial form suitable for transmission, and vice versa.

USER ACCESSIBLE TABLES There are many tables (databases) inside a phone system. They include the extensions with privileges and long-distance dialing selections (see LEAST COST ROUTING). In the old days, most PBX and phone system tables were not accessible to the user, on the assumptions that 1. The user would screw the tables up, and/or 2. Really didn't care about getting access. Things have changed. Users now want faster and greater control over their own destiny. So, many manufacturers are making their tables user accessible.

USER AGENT Generally refers to the windows and menus used to make interfacing to UNIX easier.

USER ID Persistent information in an ASC (AIN Switch Capabilities) that the ASC communicates to the SLEE (Service Logic Execution Environment) as a parameter in a message to the SLEE. The SLEE uses this parameter to identify the set of information related to the user (e.g., customer record) that service logic needs to perform its task. If a user does not subscribe to any Advanced Intelligent Network Release 1 feature but invokes an AIN Release 1 feature, the user ID in the ASC may correlate in the SLEE to a set of default information to be used by service logic.

USER LOOP A 2- or 4-wire circuit connecting a user to a PBX or other phone system.

USER MESSAGE Part of a CPN message directing a destination node to accomplish some task.

USER TO USER MESSAGING An ISDN service enabling voice and computer data to be transmitted simultaneously — for example, enabling one person to transmit a spreadsheet file to another so both can examine it on their individual screens, and for each to have the ability to change the spreadsheet and have the changes appear instantly on the other person's screen, and then discuss the changes.

USER'S SET Apparatus located on the premises of a communications user. Designed to work with other parts of his system.

USITA United States Independent Telephone Association, the old name for the United States Telephone Association. See USTA.

USOC Universal Service Order Code. (Pronounced "U-Sock.") An old Bell System term identifying a particular service or equipment offered under tariff. There was nothing "Universal" or consistent about USOC codes. Many services and equipment were called different things by different Bell operating companies. Since Divestiture, there is absolutely no consistency and little relevance left in USOC codes. Each Bell operating company is busily creating its own billing codes and terms.

USP Usage Sensitive Pricing. A tariff for local service under which the subscriber only pays for the telephone service he uses. This is done for gas and electric service.

USRT Universal Synchronous Receiver/Transmitter. Integrated circuit that performs conversion of parallel data to serial for transmission over a synchronous data channel.

USTA See UNITED STATES TELEPHONE ASSOCIATION.

USTSA See UNITED STATES TELEPHONE SUPPLIERS ASSOCIATION.

UTILITY PROGRAM A program which performs generalized functions.

UTILITY ROUTINE A routine in general support of the operation of a computer, including input/output, diagnostic, tracing or monitoring.

UTP Unshielded Twisted Pair. Twisted pair cable without individual or overall shielding.

UV A microvolt.

V & H Vertical and Horizontal grid coordinates. AT&T Bell Labs assigned pair of numbers that locates each telephone company's central office or rate center on a grid of the North American Continent. The V & H numbers are used to determine the "airline distance" between any two rate centers. Long

V & H COORDINATES OF MAJOR CONTINENTAL US CITIES

	V	H
ALABAMA	**V**	**H**
Birmingham	7518	2304
Huntsville	7267	2535
Mobile	8167	2367
Montgomery	7692	2247
ARIZONA		
Flagstaff	8746	6760
Phoenix	9135	6748
Tucson	9345	6485
Yuma	9385	7171
ARKANSAS		
Fayetteville	7600	3872
Hot Springs	7827	3554
Pine Bluff	7803	3358
CALIFORNIA		
Anaheim	9250	7810
Bakersfield	8947	8060
Fresno	8669	8239
Long Beach	9217	7856
Los Angeles	9213	7878
Oakland	8486	8695
Redwood City	8556	8682
Sacramento	8304	8580
San Bernadino	9172	7710
San Diego	9468	7629
San Francisco	8492	8719
San Jose	8583	8619
Santa Monica	9227	7920
Santa Rosa	8354	8787
Sunnyvale	8576	8643
Van Nuys	9197	7919
COLORADO		
Denver	7501	5899
Fort Collins	7331	5965
Grand Junction	7804	6438
Greeley	7345	5895
Pueblo	7787	5742
CONNECTICUT		
Bridgeport	4841	1360
Hartford	4687	1373
New Haven	4792	1342
New London	4700	1242
Stamford	4897	1388
DELAWARE		
Wilmington	5326	1485
DC		
Washington	5622	1583
FLORIDA		
Clearwater	8203	1206
Daytona Bch	7791	1052
Ft Lauderdale	8282	0557
Jacksonville	7649	1276
Miami	8351	0527
Orlando	7954	1031
Tallahassee	7877	1716
Tampa	8173	1147
GEORGIA		
Atlanta	7260	2083
Augusta	7089	1674
Macon	7364	1865
Savannah	7266	1379
IDAHO		
Boise	7096	7869
Pocatello	7146	7250
ILLINOIS		
Chicago	5986	3426
Joliet	6088	3454
Peoria	6362	3592
Rock Island	6276	3816
Springfield	6539	3518
INDIANA		
Bloomington	6417	2984
Fort Wayne	5942	2982
Indianapolis	6272	2992
Muncie	6130	2925
South Bend	5918	3206
Terre Haute	6428	3145
IOWA		
Burlington	6449	3829
Cedar Rapids	6261	4021
Des Moines	6471	4275
Dubuque	6088	3925
Iowa City	6313	3972
Sioux City	6468	4768
KANSAS		
Dodge City	7640	4958
Topeka	7110	4369
Wichita	7489	4520
KENTUCKY		
Danville	6558	2561
Frankfort	6462	2634
Madisonville	6845	2942
Paducah	6982	3088
Winchester	6441	2509
LOUISIANA		
Baton Rouge	8476	2874
New Orleans	8483	2638
Shreveport	8272	3495
MAINE		
Augusta	3961	1870
Lewiston	4042	1391
Portland	4121	1384
MARYLAND		
Baltimore	5510	1575
MASSACHUSETTS		
Boston	4422	1249
Framingham	4472	1284
Springfield	4620	1408
Worchester	4513	1330
MICHIGAN		
Detroit	5536	2828
Flint	5461	2993
Grand Rapids	5628	3261
Kalamazoo	5749	3177
Lansing	5584	3081
MINNESOTA		
Duluth	5352	4530
Minneapolis	5777	4513
St. Paul	5776	4498
MISSISSIPPI		
Biloxi	8296	2481
Jackson	8035	2880
Meridian	7899	2639
MISSOURI		
Joplin	7421	4015
Kansas City	7027	4203
St. Joseph	6913	4301
Springfield	7310	3836
MONTANA		
Billings	6391	6790
Helena	6336	7348
Missoula	6336	7650
NEBRASKA		
Grand Island	6901	4936
Omaha	6687	4595
NEVADA		
Carson City	8139	8306
Las Vegas	8665	7411
Reno	8064	8323
NEW HAMPSHIRE		
Concord	4326	1426
Manchester	4354	1388
Nashua	4394	1356
NEW JERSEY		
Atlantic City	5284	1284
Camden	5249	1453
Hackensack	4976	1432
Morristown	5035	1478
Newark	5015	1430
New Brunswick	5085	1434
Trenton	5164	1440
NEW MEXICO		
Albuquerque	8549	5887
Las Cruces	9132	5742
Santa Fe	8389	5804
NEW YORK		
Albany	4639	1629
Binghamton	4943	1837
Buffalo	5076	2326
Nassau	4961	1355
New York City	4977	1406
Poughkeepsie	4821	1526
Rochester	4913	2195
Syracuse	4798	1990

Troy	4616	1633
Westchester	4912	1330
NORTH CAROLINA		
Asheville	6749	2001
Charlotte	6657	1698
Fayetteville	6501	1385
Raleigh	6344	1436
Winston-Salem	6440	1710
NORTH DAKOTA		
Bismarck	5840	5736
Fargo	5615	5182
Grand Forks	5420	5300
OHIO		
Akron	5637	2472
Canton	5676	2419
Cincinnati	6263	2679
Cleveland	5574	2543
Columbus	5872	2555
Dayton	6113	2705
Toledo	5704	2820
OKLAHOMA		
Lawton	8178	4451
Oklahoma City	7947	4373
Tulsa	7707	4173
OREGON		
Medford	7503	8892
Pendleton	6707	8326
Portland	6799	8914
PENNSYLVANIA		
Allentown	5166	1585
Altoona	5460	1972
Harrisburg	5363	1733
Philadelphia	5257	1501
Pittsburgh	5621	2185
Reading	5258	1612
Scranton	5042	1715
RHODE ISLAND		
Providence	4550	1219
SOUTH CAROLINA		
Charleston	7021	1281
Columbia	6901	1589
Spartanburg	6811	1833
SOUTH DAKOTA		
Aberdeen	5992	5308
Huron	6201	5183
Sioux Falls	6279	4900
TENNESSEE		
Chattanooga	7098	2366
Johnson City	6595	2050
Knoxville	6801	2251
Memphis	7471	3125
Nashville	7010	2710
TEXAS		
Amarillo	8266	5076
Austin	9005	3996
Corpus Christi	9475	3739
Dallas	8436	4034
El Paso	9231	5655
Fort Worth	8479	4122
Houston	8938	3563
Laredo	9681	4099
Lubbock	8596	4962
San Antonio	9225	4062
UTAH		
Logan	7367	7102
Ogden	7480	7100
Provo	7680	7006
Salt Lake City	7576	7065
VERMONT		
Burlington	4270	1808
VIRGINIA		
Blacksburg	6247	1867
Leesburg	5634	1685
Lynchburg	6093	1703
Norfolk	5918	1223
Richmond	5906	1472
Roanoke	6196	1801
WASHINGTON		
Bellingham	6087	8933
Kennewick	6595	8391
North Bend	6354	8815
Seattle	6336	8896
Spokane	6247	8180
Yakima	6533	8607
WEST VIRGINIA		
Clarksburg	5865	2095
Morgantown	5764	2083
Wheeling	5755	2241
WISCONSIN		
Appleton	5589	3776
Eau Claire	5698	4261
Green Bay	5512	3747
La Crosse	5874	4133
Madison	5887	3796
Milwaukee	5788	3589
Racine	5837	3535
WYOMING		
Casper	6918	6297
Cheyenne	7203	5958

distance phone calls are priced on the basis of airline distance between two rate centers or telephone central offices. You calculate airline distance based on Pythagoras' theorem. The formula is thus: the airline distance is the square root of the sum of V1 (vertical number of the first town) minus V2 (vertical number of the second town) squared and h1 (horizontal number of the first town) minus h2 (horizontal number of the second town) squared. This square root is then divided by 10.

V PATH CUSTOM NETWORK SERVICE V PATH is a network service from New York Telephone for voice and data transmissions specifically designed for large, multi-location business customers within a regional calling area. V PATH is designed to provide the features of a private network using public switched lines.

V SERIES RECOMMENDATIONS CCITT standards dealing with data communications operation over the telephone network. The idea of standards is simple. If you have them and if every manufacturer conforms, then every modem can talk to every other one. That's the idea. But it's not always that simple. Sometimes you have to conform to several standards. For example, in the higher speed modems, for example those at 9,600 bps, you have to conform to speed (that's one standard). You have to conform to error control. That's another standard. And you also have to conform to data compression — if you are using data compression. ISDN terminal adapters are V series recommendations, too. CCITT uses the term "bis" to designate the second in a family of related standards and "ter" designates the third in a family.

V.13 CCITT standard for simulated carrier control. Allows a full-duplex modem to be used to emulate a half-duplex modem with interchange circuits changing at appropriate times.

V.14 CCITT standard for asynchronous-to-synchronous conversion without error control. Allows a modem that is actually synchronous to be used to carry start/stop (async) characters. If a V.42 modem connects with another modem that doesn't have error-control, it falls back

to V.14 operation to work without error-control.

V.17 New CCITT standard for simplex (one-way transmission) modulation technique for use in extended Group 3 Facsimile applications only. Provides 7200, 9600, 12000, and 14400 bps trellis-coded modulation (the modulation scheme is similar to V.33).

V.21 CCITT standard for 300 bit per second duplex modems for use on the switched telephone network. V.21 modulation is used in a half-duplex mode for Group 3 fax negotiation and control procedures (CCITT T.30).

V.22 CCITT standard for 1,200 bit per second duplex modems for use on the switched telephone network and on leased circuits.

V.22 bis CCITT standard for 2,400 bit per second duplex modems for use on the switched telephone network. V.22 bis also provides for 1200bps operation for V.22 compatibility. Bis is used by the CCITT to designate the second in a family of related standards. "ter" designates the third in a family. See V SERIES.

V.23 V.23 is the standard for a modem with a 600 bps or 1200 bps "forward channel" and a 75 bps "reverse" channel for use on the switched telephone network.

V.24 CCITT definitions for interchange circuits between data terminal equipment (DTE) and data communications equipment (DCE) equipment.

V.25 Automatic calling and/or answering equipment on the general switched telephone network, including disabling of echo suppressors on manually established calls.

V.25 bis. V.25 bis is an automatic calling and answering command set including ability to work with async, bisync, and HDLC devices. Provides a small subset of the functions of the Hayes Standard AT Command Set.

V.26 V.26 is the CCITT standard for 2400 bps modem for use on 4-wire leased lines.

V.26 bis CCITT standard for 1.2/2.4 kbps modem. It is important to note that V.26 bis is a half-duplex modem (1200 or 2400 bps in only one direction at a time); it provides an optional 75 bps reverse channel as well.

V.26 ter V.26 ter is a FULL DUPLEX 2400bps modem, like V.22 bis. The difference is that V.26 ter uses echo cancellation (like V.32) instead of frequency division (like V.22 bis), making it more expensive than V.22 bis. It was intended to serve as a fallback mode from V.32, but most manufacturers ignored it and provide V.22 bis as a fallback instead (V.26 ter is used only in a few installations in France, as far as we know).

V.27 CCITT standard for 4,800 bits per second modem with manual equalizer for use on leased telephone-type circuits. May be full-duplex on four-wire leased lines, or half-duplex on two-wire lines.

V.27 bis CCITT standard for 2.4/4.8-kbit/s modem with automatic equalizer for use on leased telephone-type circuits. 2.4 Kbps modem for 4-wire leased circuits. Either speed (2400 is a fallback) can be used on either 4-wire leased lines (full duplex) or 2-wire leased lines (half-duplex). It also provides an optional 75 bps reverse channel.

V.27 ter CCITT standard for 2.4/4.8-kbit/s modem for use on the switched telephone network. Half-Duplex only. V.27 ter is the modulation scheme used in Group 3 Facsimile for image transfer at 2400 and 4800 bps.

V.28 V.28, entitled "Electrical Characteristics for Unbalanced Double-Current Interchange Circuits" provides the CCITT equivalent of the electrical characteristics defined in EIA-232.

V.29 CCITT standard for 9,600 bits per second modem for use on point-to-point leased circuits. V.29 also provides fallback rates of 4800 and 7200 bps. V.29 can be full-duplex on 4-wire leased circuits, or half-duplex on two-wire and dial-up circuits. V.29 is the modulation technique used in Group 3 fax for image transfer at 7200 and 9600bps.

V.32 CCITT standard for 9,600 bit per second two-wire full duplex modem operating on dial-up lines. If you're buying a 9,600 bps modem for use on the normal switched phone lines, make sure it conforms to V.32. Very important. V.32 also provides fallback operation at 4800bps, and can operate on leased lines as well as dial-up. See also V.42 ERROR CORRECTION and V.42 bis DATA COMPRESSION.

V.32 bis New CCITT standard for full-duplex transmission on two-wire leased and dial-up lines at 4800, 7200, 9600, 12000, and 14400 bps. Provides backward compatibility with V.32. Includes "rapid rate renegotiation" feature to allow quick and smooth rate changes when line conditions change.

V.33 CCITT standard for 14,400 and 12,000 bps modem for use on four-wire leased lines.

V.35 CCITT standard for trunk interface between a network access device and a packet network that defines signaling for data rates greater than 19.2 kbps. V.35 was a definition of a GROUP band modem (meaning, one that used the bandwidth of several telephone circuits). V.36 and V.37 are other group band modems. V.35 just happened to describe, in an appendix, electrical characteristics for a high speed interface. IBM decided to use this for other things, but it was never stan

dardized for those purposes. The CCITT, in the 1988 Blue Book, says "It is the opinion of the CCITT that the information contained in Recommendation

V.35 is out of date. Therefore it is not recommended to use the techniques described in this Recommendation for new designs. Alternative techniques are described in Recommendations V.36 and V.37. It should be noted that other Recommendations make reference to the electrical characteristics described in Appendix II to this Recommendation [V.35]. As these characteristics are expected to allow interworking with V.11 characteristics, use of V.11 circuits is recommended in those cases." V.35 is no longer published by the CCITT.

V.42 ERROR CORRECTION CCITT error-correction standard specifying both MNP4 and LAP-M. The CCITT title says "Error-correcting procedures for DCEs using Asynchronous-to-Synchronous Conversion". It also notes in the text that it applies only to full-duplex devices. The CCITT modulation schemes with which V.42 may be used are V.22, V.22 bis, V.26 ter, and V.32, and V.32 bis. LAPM, based on HDLC, is the "primary" protocol, on which all future extensions will be based. The Alternative Protocol specified in Annex A of the Recommendation is for backward compatibility with the "installed base" of error-correcting modems.

V.42 bis DATA COMPRESSION Recently-approved CCITT data compression standard. It compresses files at average ratio of 3.5:1 and can yield file transfer speeds of up to 9,600 bps on a 2,400 bps modem, or 38,400 bits per second with a 9,600 bps modem when combined with V.42 depending upon the type of data being transferred. If you're buying a 9,600 modem for use over dial-up phone lines, make sure it has V.42 bis data compression, V.42 error correction and conforms to V.32. V.42 bis was approved by the CCITT because of its technical merits. Existing data compression methods (MNP 5 for example) only provided up to two-to-one compression. Also, V.42 bis provides for built-in "feedback" mechanisms, so that the modem can monitor it's own compression performance. If the DTE starts send pre-compressed or otherwise uncompressible data, V.42 bis can automatically suspend it's operation to avoid expansion of the data. It continues to monitor performance even when sending data "in the clear", and when a performance improvement can be gained by reactivating compression, it will do so automatically. V.42 bis was selected because it would work with a wide variety of different implementations — different amounts of memory, different processor speeds, etc. Because of this, there WILL be differences between various manufacturer's products in terms of THROUGHPUT performance (although they will all properly compress and decompress, some will do it faster than others). If maximum throughput is important, users should check benchmark tests to find the modem that provides the best performance.

V.54 CCITT standard for loop test devices in modems. Defines local and remote loopbacks.

VAC Voice Activity Compression.

VACANT CODE An unassigned area code, central office or station code.

VACANT CODE INTERCEPT Routes all calls made to an unassigned "level" (first digit dialed) to the attendant, a busy signal, a "reorder" signal or to a recorded announcement.

VACANT NUMBER INTERCEPT Routes all calls of unassigned numbers to the attendant, a busy signal or a prerecorded announcement.

VAD Value Added Dealer. Another term for Value Added Reseller (VAR). Essentially, VARs or VADs are companies who buy equipment from computer or telephone manufacturers, add some of their own software and possibly some peripheral hardware to it, then resell the whole computer or telephone system to end users, typically corporations.

VAIL, Theodore N. Theodore N. Vail began his career with the Bell System as general manager of the Bell Telephone Company in 1878. He later became the first president of the American Telephone & Telegraph Company in 1885. He left AT&T two years later. After pursuing other interests for 20 years, he returned as president of AT&T in 1907, retiring in 1919 as chairman of the board. Vail believed in "One policy, one system, universal service." He regarded telephony as a natural monopoly. He saw the necessity for regulation and welcomed it.

VALIDATION Generally, all long distance carriers, operator service providers and private payphone companies will not put a call through unless they can "validate," the caller's telephone company calling card, home/business phone number or credit card. Until the advent of US West's Billing Validation Service and other similar databases in 1987, the companies who needed to validate their callers' billing requests had to turn back the caller or accept the call on faith. Validating a user's calling card is, simply, a Yes-No. If the card number is validated, it is Yes. Getting the validation involves a data call from the provider to the owner of the database. There are many ways of doing this, including a dedicated trunk and an port through an X.25 network.

VALIDITY CHECK Any check designed to insure the quality of transmission.

VALUE ADDED Refers to a voice or data network service that uses available transmission facilities and then adds some other service or services to increase the value of the transmission.

VALUE ADDED CARRIER A voice or data common carrier that adds special service features, usually computer related, to services purchased from other carriers and then sells the package of service and features.

VALUE ADDED NETWORK A data communications network in which some form of processing of a signal takes place, or information is added to the signal by the network. No one knows exactly what a VAN is. The general idea is that a VAN buys "basic" transmission and sometimes switching services from local and long distance phone companies and adds something else — typically an interactive computer with a database or a storage. In this way, the VAN adds value to basic communications services. Dial-up stockmarket quoting services are VANs. Electronic mail providers are VANs. The classic VAN is a packet-switched operation like Tymnet, GTE Telenet, MCI Mail or AT&T Mail. But there are also VANs, which use Telenet, to add more value and make even more services. VANs could be important ISDN customers, with their customers using the D channel. In the US, some Information Providers also call themselves VANs.

VALUE ADDED SERVICE A communications facility using common carrier networks for transmission and providing extra data features with separate equipment. Store and forward message switching, terminal interfacing and host interfacing features are common extras.

VALUFLEX A New York Telephone service which lets you make and receive regular phone calls and 800-number calls from local areas on your normal business phone lines. There are big advantages here. You don't have to rent additional phone lines. You don't have to expand your existing phone system — or buy a new one (if getting extra lines means you'd grow out). And you can combine your incoming 800 lines with features you can get on business lines — like call forwarding, conferencing, etc. Have your 800 calls come into your office during the day. Have them call forwarded at night to your home. 800 Valuflex is aimed at smaller business.

VALVE The original British word for an electron tube.

VAMPIRE TAP In local area networking technology, a cable tap that penetrates through the outer shield to make connection to the inner conductor of a coax cable.

VAN Value Added Network.

VAPORWARE A semi-affectionate slang term for software which has been announced and perhaps even demonstrated, but not delivered to commercial customers. Hyperware is hardware which has been announced but has not yet been delivered.

VARIABLE CALL FORWARDING An optional feature of AT&T's 800 IN-WATS service. It allows the subscriber to route calls to certain locations based on time of day or day of week.

VARIABLE FORMAT MESSAGE A message in which the page format of the output is controlled by format characters embedded in the message itself. The alternative is to have the format determined by prior agreement between the origin and the destination.

VARIABLE LENGTH RECORD A file in a database containing records not of uniform length and in which the distinctions between fields are made with commas, tabs or spaces. Records become uniform in length either because they are uniform to start with or they are "padded" with special characters.

VARIABLE QUANTIZING LEVEL VQL. A speech-encoding technique that quantizes and encodes an analog voice conversation for transmission at 32,000 bits per second.

VARIABLE TERM PRICING PLAN VTPP. A rate plan developed by AT&T to replace two-tier pricing. VTPP generally provides for two, four, five or six year contracts, over which period the customer is promised stable prices for some — not all — of the equipment and/or tariffed services he uses. Generally, under VTPP, the customer does not end up owning any of the equipment. VTPP has now been replaced by more normal ways of doing commercial business — outright sale, leasing, etc.

VARIABLE TIMING PARAMETER Timing durations for features such as hold recall, camp-on recall, off-hook duration, and many other programmable telephone system services.

VARIOLOSSER A device with a variable level of attenuation which is controlled by an external signal. Often this signal is the level of the signal being attenuated, that is the higher the level of the signal the more it is attenuated.

VAX line of minicomputers made by Digital Equipment Corporation (DEC).

VC Virtual circuit; In packet switching, network facilities that give the appearance to the user of ä an actual end-to-end circuit. A dynamically variable network connection where sequential user data packets may be routed differently during hte course of a "virtual connection." Virtual circuits allow many users to share transmission facilities simultaneously.

VCA See VOICE CONNECTING ARRANGEMENT.

VCR VideoCassette Recorder (or Player).

VDT Video Display Terminal. A data terminal with a TV screen.

VECTOR A quantity in the visual (video) telecommunications industry that describes the magnitude and direction of an object's movement — for example, a head moving to the right.

VELOCITY OF LIGHT The speed of light in a vacuum is 186,280 miles per second, or 299,792 kilometers per second.

VELOCITY OF PROPAGATION The speed at which a signal travels from a sender, through a transmission line and finally arrives at the receiver.

VELOCITY OF SOUND The velocity of sound varies with the medium carrying it. In air at 0 degrees centigrade, it's 331 meters per second. In glass at 20 degrees centigrade, its 5485 meters per second.

VENDOR CODE Software written by the same company that manufactured the computer system on which it is running (or not running...).

VENDOR INDEPENDENCE The ability to allow devices manufactured by different vendors, often using different protocols, to talk to (communicate) with each other.

VERIFICATION A service of a phone company operator who dials into a busy or otherwise impossible-to-reach line and checks that line and reports on that check to the caller. Phone companies are beginning to charge for this service. As of writing, AT&T, for example, was charging 40 cents to verify the line was busy and 70 cents additional for the operator to interrupt the conversation and say another call was coming in.

VERIFICATION TRUNK A trunk to which an operator has access and which will switch through to a called line even if the line is busy.

VERTICAL That part of a wiring grid which connects the host computer of Main Distribution Frame (MDF) to equipment located on other fields.

VERTICAL BLANKING INTERVAL The interval between television frames in which the picture is blanked to enable the trace (which "paints" the screen) to return to the upper left hand corner of the screen, from where the trace starts, once again, to paint a new screen. Several companies are eyeing the vertical blanking interval as a place to send digital data, including news and weather information. The vertical blanking interval was the basis of teletext, a 1970s technology that, with the help of a decoder, displays printed information on the TV screen. Teletext has never caught on in the U.S. in part because the amount of data that could be transmitted comfortably was small.

VERTICAL REDUNDANCY CHECK VRC. A check or parity bit added to each character in a message such that the number of bits in each character, including the parity bit, is odd (odd parity), or even (even parity). See PARITY.

VERTICAL SERVICE Options that the customer can add to his basic service such as touchtone, conference calling, speed dialing, etc. No one can explain why it's called "vertical" service.

VERY LARGE SCALE INTEGRATION Semiconductor chip with several thousand active elements or logic gates — the equivalent of several thousand transistors on a single chip. VLSI is the technique for making the micro chip, the so-called "computer on a chip."

VF Voice Frequency.

VG Voice Grade.

VGA Variable Graphics Array. A graphics standard developed by IBM for the IBM PC. VGA allows the PC's screen to generate any of four levels of resolution — with one of the sharpest being 640 horizontal picture elements, known as pels or pixels, by 480 pels vertically. VGA is superior to earlier graphics standards, such as CGA and EGA. VGA is barely adequate for CAD-CAE. See MONITOR for all the numbers on pixels in various screens.

VHF Very High Frequency; portion of the electromagnetic spectrum with frequencies between 30 and 300 MHz.

VHI Virtual Host Interface.

VIA NET LOSS VNL. A planning factor used in allocating the attenuation losses of trunks in a transmission network. A specified value for this loss is selected to obtain a satisfactory balance between loss and talker echo performance.

VIDEO COMPRESSION A method of transmitting analog television signals over a narrow digital channel by processing the signal digitally. You can compress an analog TV signal into one T-1 signal of 1.544 megabits per second. More advanced compression techniques will enable video signals to be compressed into fewer bits per second. One increasingly common method allows a full-color reasonably full-motion video to be compressed into two 56 kbps channels.

VIDEO SIGNAL Transmission of moving frames or pictures of information requiring frequencies of 1 to 6 MegaHertz. A commercial quality full-color, full-motion TV signal requires 6 MHz.

VIDEO TELECONFERENCING The real-time, and usually two-way, transmission of digitized video images between two or more locations. Teleconferencing requires a wideband transmission facility. Transmitted images may be freeze-frame (where television screen is repainted every few seconds to every 20 seconds) or full motion. Bandwidth requirements for two-way videoconferencing range from 6 MHz for analog, full-motion, full-color, commercial grade TV to two 56 kbps lines for digitally encoded reasonably full motion, full color, to 1,544 Mbit/s for very good quality, full-color, full motion TV.

VIDEOTEX Two-way interactive electronic data transmission or home information retrieval system using the telephone network and (sometimes) through-the-air piggybacked TV signals as the transmission media. Videotex has not been successful because of its (erstwhile) need for expensive, proprietary (i.e. dedicated) equipment and lack of variety in information offered. There are various forms of videotex. The "classic" European version of interactive videotext typically works at 75 baud going out from the terminal and 1200 baud coming in from the central office. Some American versions ape the European system. Some have 1200 baud both ways. In interactive videotext, you can do everything from sending serious electronic mail to your business suppliers to holding raunchy conversations with perverts in distant cities. As long as you pay your bills, no European PTT seems to care about what you transmit or receive. In France, videotex is called Minitel.

VIEWDATA Another name for Videotex.

VINES Virtual networking software which is the core of the LAN from Banyan, Westboro, MA.

VIRTUAL In the telephone industry, "Virtual" is something that pretends to be something it isn't, but can be made to appear to be that thing. A virtual private line is effectively a dial-up phone line with an auto-dialer on it. To the user, it appears to be a private line. (But the phone company can re-sell that capacity when it's not in use.) The concept of "virtual" is to give the telephone company an excuse to lower the price to the end user. See VIRTUAL NETWORK.

VIRTUAL BANDING In WATS services, virtual banding is the ability of trunks to carry traffic to all WATS bands, with billing based on the end points of the call instead of the band over which the traffic went.

VIRTUAL CALL CAPABILITY Provides set-up and clearing on a per call basis. Each call placed appears to have a dedicated connection for the duration of the call.

VIRTUAL CIRCUIT A communications link that appears to be a dedicated point-to-point circuit. Also, a system that delivers data packets in guaranteed sequential order, just as they would arrive over a real point-to-point circuit. There is no guarantee that the packets were sent in order or over the same route, yet they are reassembled together correctly at the receiving end. By this reassembling, it appears there is an actual point-to-point connection.

VIRTUAL MACHINE FACILITY VM/370. An IBM system control program, essentially an operating system that controls the concurrent execution of multiple virtual machines on a single System/370 mainframe.

VIRTUAL NETWORK A network that is programmed, not hard-wired, to meet a customer's specifications. Created on as-needed basis. Also called Software Defined Network by AT&T. See SOFTWARE DEFINED NETWORK and VIRTUAL PRIVATE NETWORK.

VIRTUAL PRIVATE NETWORK A carrier-provided service in which the public switched network provides capabilities similar to those of private lines, such as conditioning, error testing, and higher speed, full-duplex, four-wire transmission with a line quality adequate for data. A virtual private network eliminates or partly eliminates the need for fixed point-to-point private line because it provides on-demand dial-up circuits or bandwidths that can be dynamically allocated.

VIRTUAL ROUTE Virtual circuit in IBM's SNA. See SYSTEMS NETWORK ARCHITECTURE.

VIRTUAL ROUTE PACING CONTROL SNA congestion control at the path control level. See SYSTEMS NETWORK ARCHITECTURE.

VIRTUAL STORAGE The concept of storage space that may be viewed as addressable main storage to a computer user, but is actually auxiliary storage (usually peripheral mass storage) mapped into real addresses. The amount of virtual storage is limited by the addressing scheme of the computer.

VIRTUAL TELECOMMUNICATION ACCESS METHOD VTAM: (Pronounced "Vee-Tam.") A program component in an IBM computer which handles some of the communications processing tasks for an application program. VTAM also provides resource sharing, a technique for efficiently using a network to reduce transmission costs.

VIRTUAL TERMINAL VT. A universal terminal. The ISO virtual terminal (VT) protocol is designed to describe the operation of a so-called universal terminal so any terminal can talk with any host computer.

VISTA A videotext service offered in Canada.

VISUALLY IMPAIRED ATTENDANT SERVICE Visually impaired attendant service capability is achieved by augmenting the normal visual signals provided on a standard attendant position with special tactile devices and/or audible signals which enable a visually impaired person to operate the position.

VLF Very Low Frequency. That portion of the electromagnetic spectrum having continuous frequencies ranging from about 3 Hz to 30 kHz.

VLSI Very Large-Scale Integration. The art of putting hundreds of thousands of transistors onto a single quarter-inch square integrated circuit. Compare with LSI and ULSI.

VM Virtual memory. See VIRTUAL STORAGE.

VOICE ACTIVITY COMPRESSION VAC. A method of conserving

transmission capacity by not transmitting pauses in speech.

VOICE APPLICATIONS PROGRAM System software providing the necessary logic to carry out the functions requested by telephone system users. It is responsible for actual call processing, making the various voice connections and providing user features, such as Call Forwarding, Speed Dialing, Conference, etc.

VOICE CALLING One manufacturer describes this as allowing a phone user to have calls automatically answered and connected to his phone's loudspeaker. Not a common definition.

VOICE CIRCUIT The typical analog telephone channel coming into your house or office. It has a bandwidth between 300 Hz and 3000 Hz. This is not sufficient for high fidelity voice transmission. You'd probably need at least 10,000 Hz. But it's sufficient to recognize and understand the person on the other end.

VOICE COIL The element in a dynamic microphone which vibrates when sound waves strike it. The coil of wire in a loudspeaker through which audio frequency current is sent to produce vibrations of the cone and reproduction of sound.

VOICE COMPRESSION Refers to the process of electronically modifying a 64 Kbps PCM voice channel to obtain a channel of 32 Kbps or less for the purpose of increased efficiency in transmission.

VOICE CONNECTING ARRANGEMENT VCA. A device that, once upon a time, was necessary for connecting your own phone system to the nation's switched telephone network. Most phones now have the protective circuitry of VCAs built into them.

VOICE COUPLER An interface arrangement once provided by the telephone company to permit direct electrical connection of customer-provided voice terminal equipment to the national telephone network. No longer needed because of the FCC's Registration Program.

VOICE DIALING The ability to tell your phone to dial by talking to it. Say, "Call Police" and it will automatically dial the police. This feature has enormous benefits for handicapped people. It will have greater benefits for normal people when the technology of voice recognition improves.

VOICE DIGITIZATION The conversion of an analog voice signal into binary (digital) bits for storage or transmission.

VOICE FREQUENCY VF. An audio frequency in the range essential for transmission of speech. Typically from about 300 Hz to 3000 Hz.

VOICE FREQUENCY TELEGRAPH SYSTEM A telegraph system permitting use of up to 20 channels on a single voice circuit by frequency division multiplexing.

VOICE GRADE A communications channel which can transmit and receive voice conversation in the range of 300 Hertz to 3000 Hertz.

VOICE HOGGING See VOICE SWITCHED.

VOICE MAIL SYSTEM A device to record, store and retrieve voice messages. There are two types of voice mail devices — those which are "stand alone" and those which profess some integration with the user's phone system. A stand alone voice mail is not dissimilar to a collection of single person answering machines, with several added features. You can instruct the machines (voice mail boxes) to forward messages among themselves. You can organize to allocate your friends and business acquaintances their own mail boxes so they can dial, leave messages, pick up messages from you, pass messages to you, etc. You can also edit messages, add comments and deliver messages to a mailbox at a pre-arranged time. Messages can be tagged "urgent" or "non-urgent" or stored for future listening. The range of voice mail options varies among manufacturers.

An integrated voice mail system includes two additional features. First, it will tell you if you have any messages. It does this by lighting a light on your phone and/or putting a message on your phone's alphanumeric display. Second, if your phone rings for a certain number of rings (you set the number), the phone will transfer your caller automatically to your voice mail box, which will answer the phone, deliver a little "I am away" message and then receive and record the caller's message.

There are other levels of integration. You might have a phone which has "soft" buttons and an alphanumeric display. That display might label your phone's soft buttons like those on a cassette recorder — forward, reverse, slow, fast, stop, etc. so you can go through your messages any way you like. Telenova has such a phone. It's very impressive.

There are pros and cons to voice mail systems. Some employees will hide behind them, forwarding calls from their customers into voice mail boxes and never returning them. Some employees will make good use of them. They dial in for their messages, research what the customer wants and return the voice mail calls quickly. Many voice mail systems are being combined with automated attendants. Some people hate voice mail systems. Others love them. It all depends on how the system is used, managed and sold.

See also AUDIOTEX, AUTOMATED ATTENDANTS, INFORMATION CENTER MAILBOXES, ENHANCED CALL PROCESSING and VOICE PROCESSING.

VOICE MESSAGE SERVICE A leased service typically over dial up phone lines which provides the ability for a phone user to access a voice mail system and leave a message for a particular phone user. See VOICE MAIL SYSTEM.

VOICE MESSAGING Recording, storing, playing back and distributing phone messages. New York Telephone has an interesting way of looking at voice messaging. NYTel sees it as four distinct areas: 1. Voice Mail, where messages can be retrieved and played back at any time from a user's "voice mailbox"; 2. Call Answering, which routes calls made to a busy/no answer extension into a voice mailbox; 3. Call Processing, which lets callers route themselves among destinations via their touch-tone phones; and (4.)

Information Mailbox, which stores general recorded information for callers to hear.

VOICE OVER TIE/communications name for a totally wonderful feature on a phone system — namely that while you are speaking to someone on the phone, your operator can talk to you "over" the conversation you're having. What happens is that you hear your operator in your telephone's handset receiver, but the person you're speaking with can't. You can reply to the operator (telling him/her you'll be one minute, please call back, etc.) by hitting a Privacy or DoNotDisturb button on your phone. Voice Over has major benefits. It saves on long distance calls you don't have to return. It closes deals that can't wait. And it gives customers immediate answers. In short, it improves corporate efficiency and customer satisfaction.

VOICE PAGING ACCESS Gives attendants and phone users the ability to dial loudspeaker paging equipment throughout the building. An unbelievably useful feature, if your people are prone to wander.

VOICE RECOGNITION Computer recognition of a human voice.

VOICE RESPONSE UNIT VRU. Think of a Voice Response Unit (also called Interactive Voice Response Unit) as a voice computer. Where a computer has a keyboard for entering information, an IVR uses remote touchtone telephones. Where a computer has a screen for showing the results, an IVR uses a digitized synthesized voice to "read" the screen to the distant caller. An IVR can do whatever a computer can, from looking up train timetables to moving calls around an automatic call distributor (ACD). The only limitation on an IVR is that you can't present as many alternatives on a phone as you can on a screen. The caller's brain simply won't remember more than a few. With IVR, you have to present the menus in smaller chunks.

VOICE RING Multiple Digital Intertie Buses connected in series to all nodes. Provides extra channels for voice data transmission when direct link (DI) channels are busy.

VOICE STORE AND FORWARD Voice mail. A PBX service that allows voice messages to be stored digitally in secondary storage and retrieved remotely by dialing access and identification codes. See VOICE MAIL SYSTEM.

VOICE SWITCHED A device which responds to voice. When the device hears a voice, it turns on and transmits it, muting the receive side. The most common voice-switched device is the desk speakerphone. With voice switching, it's easy to hog a circuit. Just keep making a noise. Watch out for voice hogging. If you're calling someone and waiting for them by listening in on your speakerphone, mute your speakerphone. This way you'll hear them when they answer.

VOICEMUX 100 Trademark for MICOM's combined TDM and APV products.

VOLATILE STORAGE Computer storage that is erased when power is turned off. RAM is volatile storage.

VOLT The standard unit of electromotive force or electrical pressure. One volt is the amount of pressure that will cause one ampere of current to flow through one ohm of resistance.

VOLT METER An instrument for measuring voltages, resistance and current.

VOLTAGE Potential difference between two points. The measurement of electrical potential in a conductor.

VOLTAGE RATING The highest voltage that may be continuously applied to a wire in conformance with standards or specifications.

VOLUME UNIT VU. The unit of measurement for electrical speech power in communications work. VUs are measured in decibels above 1 milliwatt. The measuring device is called a VU meter.

VOTING RECEIVERS A group of mobile base phone receivers operating on the same frequency as a control unit to pick the best signal from among them.

VOX Voice Operated transmission.

VOYCALL An early key system manufacturer, which made a combination 1A2 handsfree intercom telephone system. It was wood grained, inlaid into black plastic. An impressive phone system. Sadly, no more.

VPOTS Very Plain Old Telephone Service. No automated switching.

VPU Virtual Physical Unit.

VQL VARIABLE QUANTIZING LEVEL Speech-encoding technique that quantizes and encodes an analog voice conversation for transmission, nominally at 32 Kbps.

VRC Vertical Redundancy Check. **VRPRS** Virtual Route Pacing ResponSe in SNA.

VRU See VOICE RESPONSE UNIT.

VS See VIRTUAL STORAGE.

VS&F Voice Store and Forward. Voice is digitally encoded, sent to large storage devices and later forwarded to the recipient. See VOICE MAIL.

VSAT Very Small Aperture Terminal. A relatively small satellite antenna, typically 1.5 to 3.0 meters in diameter, used for transmitting and receiving one channel of data communications. You see VSATs on top of retail stores which use them for transmitting the day's receipts and receiving instructions for sales, etc.

VSCBX A Rolm PBX called a Very Small Computerized Branch EXchange.

VTAM Virtual Telecommunications Access Session. In an IBM 370 or compatible, VTAM is a method to give users at remote terminals access to applications in the main computer. VTAM provides resource sharing, a technique for efficiently using a network to reduce transmission costs. See SYSTEMS NETWORK ARCHITECTURE.

VUI First came the CLI (Command-Line Interface). Then came the GUI (Graphical User Interface). Get ready for the VUI: the Video User Interface. Actually, you don't need to get ready for it any time soon, but you might start wondering how to use it.

VW-1 A test used by Underwriters Laboratories to classify wires and cables by their resistance to burning. (Formerly designated as FR-1.)

WACK Wait before transmitting positive ACKnowledgement. In Bisynch, this DLE sequence is sent by a receiving station to indicate it is temporarily not ready to receive.

WAFER A thin disk of a purified crystalline semiconductor, typically silicon, cut into chips after processing. Typically, a wafer is about one-fiftieth of an inch thick and four or five inches in diameter.

WAIT ON BUSY An English term for the American term "Camp On" or "Call Waiting." A service allowing the subscriber to make a call to a busy phone line, wait until the call is over, then be connected automatically.

WALK TIME The time required to transfer permission to poll from one station to another.

WALKIE-TALKIE Hand-held radio transmitter and receiver. Like the police carry. Probably the best named device in telecom. You walkie, you talkie.

WALL OUTLET A phone outlet positioned at shoulder height to accept a wall telephone set. The typical installation includes a special modular jack containing two mounting bosses that insert into key-hole slots in the base of the telephone set. Electrical connection is made by a short cord or a lug element that is integral to the telephone set base.

WALL PHONE A phone that is mounted on the wall. Where else would a wall phone be mounted? Some new phones — especially some key systems — come so you can use them on the desk or mount them on a wall, without extra hardware. Some desk phones cannot be mounted on a wall. This is a disadvantage when you run out of space on your desk, as you will with all the computers and workstations you'll be putting there.

WALL THICKNESS A term expressing the thickness of a layer of applied insulation or jacket.

WAN Wide Area Network. Uses common carrier-provided lines that cover an extended geographical area. Contrast with LAN. See WIDE AREA NETWORK.

WANGNET Wang Laboratories' proprietary broadband LANs. Used as the brand name for Wang's LAN products.

WARBLE-TONE A tone changing in frequency at a slow enough rate to give the effect of warbling, like a duck.

WARC World Administrative Radio Conference. Sets international frequencies. Just before Telecom '87, WARC allocated important new frequencies for satellite-based land mobile (satellite to truck, etc.) and radiodetermination navigation services (electronic maps for your car). WARC is part of the 154-member International Telecommunication Union. CCITT is part of the ITU. See CCITT.

WATS Wide Area Telecommunications Service: basically discounted toll service provided by all long distance and local phone companies. AT&T started WATS but forgot to trademark the name, so now every supplier uses it as a generic name. There are two types of WATS services — in and out WATS, i.e. those WATS lines that allow you to dial out and those on which you receive incoming calls (the typical 800 line service). You subscribe to in- and out-WATS services separately. In the old days you needed separate in and out lines to handle the in and out WATS services. But these days you can choose to have in- and out-WATS on the same line. This is not particularly brilliant traffic engineering, since you can't receive an incoming 800 call if you're making an outgoing call. But I do know someone who has an 800 line on his cellular phone!

Many users inside companies think their company's WATS lines (and thus their WATS calls) are free, so they speak longer. This can kill the idea of buying WATS lines to save money. In the old days, interstate WATS was charged at effectively a flat rate and thus, there was some reason to believe that marginal WATS calls were 'free.' These days EVERY WATS call costs money. EVERY one! Without exception. See 800 SERVICE and PLANT TEST NUMBER.

WATT A unit of electrical power. That amount of power required to maintain a current of one amp under the pressure of one volt. See OHM's LAW.

WAVEFORM The characteristic shape of a period signal usually shown as a plot of amplitude over a period of time.

WAVEGUIDE A hollow, finely engineered metallic tube used to transmit microwave radio signals from the microwave antenna to the radio and vice versa. Waveguides comes in various shapes — rectangular, elliptical or circular. They are very sensitive and should be handled very gently.

WAVELENGTH The length of a wave measured from any point on one wave, to the corresponding point on the next wave, such as from crest to crest. There is a direct proportion between the wavelength of a radio signal and its frequency.

WAVELENGTH DIVISION MULTIPLEXING A way of increasing the capacity of an optical fiber by simultaneously operating at more than one wavelength. Similar to frequency division multiplexing.

WAY OPERATED CIRCUIT A circuit shared by three or more phones on a party line basis. One of the phones usually operates as the control point.

WAY STATION One of thc phones, other than the central controller, on a way operated circuit. See WAY OPERATED CIRCUIT.

WCV See Weighted Call Value.

WDM Wavelength Division Multiplexing. A technique in fiber-optic transmission for using different light wavelengths to send data parallel-by-bit (one discrete wavelength per bit), serial-by-character. One multimode fiber can act as an 8-bit parallel bus.

WEATHER TRUNK GROUP A trunk group used to provide customers with weather information.

WECO Western Electric COmpany.

WEIGHTED CALL VALUE WCV. The average handling time of a call transaction. ACD vendors count this differently. Typically, a combination of the talk time and the after-call work or wrap-up time.

WESTAR Family of communications satellites owned and operated by Western Union.

WET CIRCUIT A circuit carrying direct current.

WET LOOP POWERING Defined as local power (non-Span provided) with use of copper pairs (power is looped at the last repeater).

WET T-1 A T-1 line with a Bell Operating Company powered interface.

WETTING AGENT A chemical which reduces surface tension in a liquid, motivating the liquid to spread more evenly on a surface.

WHITE NOISE Noise (as compared to information) whose frequency is broad and uniform. The garbage you hear behind a phone conversation. The noise you hear when you're trying to sleep somewhere — anywhere — in New York City. White noise is fairly equally distributed across all frequencies.

WHO-ARE-YOU CODE WRU. A control character which operates the answerback unit in a terminal (typically a telex terminal) for identification of sending and receiving stations in a network.

WIDE AREA NETWORK WAN. An data network typically extending a LAN (local area network) outside the building, over telephone common carrier lines to link to other LANs in remote buildings in possibly remote cities. A WAN typically uses common-carrier lines. A LAN doesn't. WANs typically run over leased phone lines — from one analog phone line to T-1 (1.544 Mbps). The jump between a local area network and a WAN is made through a device called a bridge or a router. Bridges operate independently of the protocol employed. They will work, according to Jeff Weiss, of Cryptall Communications, with all present and expected future communications packages. Routers are specific to the protocol being employed. New routing software is needed for each new protocol or protocol deviation. See BRIDGE, ROUTER and DIGITAL HIERARCHY.

WIDE AREA TELEPHONE SERVICE See WATS and 800 SERVICE.

WIDE FREQUENCY TOLERANT POWER PLANT PBX power facilities are provided that will operate from AC energy sources which are not as closely regulated as commercial AC power. The wide tolerant plant will tolerate average frequency deviations of up to plus or minus 3 Hz or voltage variations of -15% to +10% as long as both of the conditions do not occur simultaneously. This feature permits operation with customer provided emergency power generating equipment.

WIDEBAND Refers to a channel wider in bandwidth than a voice-grade channel.

WIDEBAND PACKET TRANSPORT Transmission of addressed, digitized message fragments (packets) interleaved among the addressed fragments of other messages at a rate high enough to support general purpose telecommunications services.

WIDEBAND SWITCH Switch capable of handling channels wider in bandwidth than voice-grade lines. Radio and TV switches are examples of wideband switches.

WILLFUL INTERCEPT The act of intercepting messages intended for a station experiencing a line or equipment malfunction.

WINCHESTER DISK A sealed hard disk. The Winchester magnetic storage device was pioneered by IBM for use in its 3030 disk system. It was called Winchester because "Winchester" was IBM's code name for the secret research project that led to its invention. A Winchester hard disk drive consists of several "platters" of metal stacked on top of each other. Each of the platter surfaces is coated with magnetic material and is "read" and "written" to by "heads" which float across (but don't touch) the surface. The whole system works roughly like the old-style Wurlitzer jukebox. There are several advantages to a Winchester disk system: 1. It can store, read and write enormous quantities of information. Some Winchesters have a capacity of over 100 megabits. 2. You can access information on a Winchester faster than with any other permanent computer storage medium. 3. Winchesters are reliable and relatively inexpensive. There are also disadvantages: 1. They are very sensitive to rough handling (they hate being moved). 2. They are very sensitive to the organization of their directory track (lose that and you're in big trouble). 3. When Winchesters "crash" (i.e. the heads touch the surface of the rotating platters), you can lose an enormous amount of precious data — possibly millions of bytes of data.

WINDING Coils of wire usually found in transformers and used to boost inductance.

WINDOW 1. A flow-control mechanism in data communications, the size of which is equal to the number of frames, packets or messages that can be sent from a transmitter to a receiver before any reverse acknowledgment is required. It's called a pacing group in IBM's SNA. 2. A box on the CRT (cathode ray tube) of your personal computer or terminal. A software program is running inside the box. It's possible with new "windows" software to run several programs simultaneously, each accessible and visible through the "window" on your CRT. 3. A technique of displaying information on a screen in which the viewer sees what appears to be several sheets of paper much as they would appear on a desktop. The viewer can shift and shuffle the sheets on the screen. Windowing can show two files simultaneously. For example, in one window you might have a letter you're writing to someone and in another window, you might have a boilerplate letter from which you can take a paragraph or two and drop it in your present letter. Being able to see the two letters on the screen makes writing the new letter easier.

WINDOW CONTROL A credit or token scheme in which a limited number of messages or calls are allowed into the system.

WINDOW SIZE The minimum number of data packets that can be transmitted without additional authorization from the receiver.

WINDOWING A technique of running several programs simultaneously — each in running a separate window. For example, in one window you might run a word processing program. In another, you might be calculating a spreadsheet. In a third, you might be picking up your electronic mail.

WINK A momentary interruption in SF (single frequency) tone indicating the distant central office is ready to receive the digits you just dialed.

WINK OPERATION A type of control for phone systems using address signaling.

WINK SIGNAL A short interruption of current to a busy lamp causing it to flicker. Indicates there is a line on hold.

WIRE CENTER The location where the telco terminates subscriber outside cable plant (i.e. their local lines) with the necessary testing facilities to maintain them. Usually the same location as a class 5 central office. However, testing facilities can be centralized within a single CO to remotely monitor and trouble-shoot the lines terminated in other COs. Theoretically, each of these class 5 COs could represent a wire center. Depending on the size of the serving area, it is likely that test facilities would be centralized in one or two of the central offices and these would represent the wire centers.

WIRE CENTER SERVING AREA That area of an exchange served by a single wire center.

WIRE PRINTER A matrix printer which uses a set of wire hammers to strike the page through a carbon ribbon, generating the matrix characters.

WIRED LOGIC A required logic function implemented in hardware, not software.

WIRED-FOR CAPACITY The wired-for capacity represents the upper limit of capacity for a particular configuration. To bring to a phone system to its "wired for capacity," all that's necessary is to fill the empty slots in the system's metal shelving (its cage) with the appropriate printed circuit boards. "Wired-for Capacity" is a marginally useful term, giving little indication of the type of printed circuit boards — trunk, line, special electronic line, special circuit, etc. — that can be installed. And many PBXs allow only their printed circuit boards to go into assigned slots. Your PBX cabinet might, for example, have plenty of empty space for extra printed circuit boards, but it may not have any more space for boards which service electronic phones. Thus, it is effectively maxed out.

WIRE PAIR Two separate conductors traveling the same route, serving as a communications channel.

WIRE STRIPPER A tool which takes the insulation off a wire without hurting the metal conductor.

WIRELESS Without wires. An English and Australian word for radio.

WIRELINE FCC regulations restrict providers of cellular telephone service in any given market to one wireline carrier (the local telephone company) and one non-wireline carrier (any company other than the local telephone company).

WIRETAPPING To listen in clandestinely to someone else's conversation. Other than scrambling, there is no known method to protect your telephone call against wiretapping, no matter what equipment you buy from companies advertising their wares nationally. Wiretapping can be accomplished without physical connection to a phone line, though technically this would be called "bugging." For all intents and purposes you should consider your telephone conversations as public and treat your conversations as such.

WIRING CLOSET Termination point for customer premises wiring, offering access to service personnel. Generally serves a specific area, with cross-connected multiple wiring closets.

WIRING GRID The overall architecture of building wiring.

WOO WOO TONE A tone on a phone line indicating the number is unavailable. Also the words to a neat Jeffrey Osborne song, as in "Will you woo woo with me?"

WORD A collection of bits the computer recognizes as a basic information unit and uses in its operation. Usually defined by the number of bits contained in it, e.g. 8, 16 or 32 bits. Here's another explanation: A group of characters capable of being processed simultaneously in the processor and treated by computer circuits as an entity.

WORD LENGTH The number of bits in a word.

WORDS PER MINUTE WPM. The speed of printing, typing or communications. 100 WPM is 600 characters per minute (six characters per average word) or 10 characters per second. In ASCII, asynchronous transmission at this rate is also 100 or 110 bits per second, depending on the number of stop bits.

WORKSTATION Input/output equipment at which someone works. A station at which a user can send data to or receive data from a computer for the purpose of performing a job. These days, there are things called integrated voice/data workstations which also include a telephone.

WORLD NUMBERING ZONE One of eight geographic areas used to assign a unique telephone address to each telephone subscriber.

WORM Write Once, Read Many times. Refers to the new type of optical disks (similar to compact discs) which can be written to only once, but read many times. In other words, once the data is written, it cannot be erased. WORM disks typically hold around 600 megabytes. See also ERASABLE OPTICAL DRIVE.

WPM See WORDS PER MINUTE.

WRAP 1. In data communications, to place your diagnostic and test equipment around parts of a network so you can monitor their use (i.e. do network diagnostics on them). You are, in essence, wrapping your products around theirs. 2. To make a connection between a flexible wire and a hard tag by tightly wrapping the cable around the tag. There are automatic wire wrapping tools available for this job.

WRAP-UP Between-call work state that an ACD agent enters after releasing a caller. It's the time necessary to complete the transaction that just occurred on the phone.

WRAP-UP DATA Ad hoc data gathered by an agent in the ACD system following a call.

WRITE To record information on a storage device, usually disk or tape.

WRITE PROTECT Using various hardware and software techniques to prohibit the computer from recording (writing) on storage medium. You can write protect a 5 1/4 diskette by simply covering the little notch with a small metal tag.

WTNG WaiTiNG.

WYSIWYG (pron. Whiz-i-wig) What You See Is What You Get. A word processing term meaning what you see on your computer screen is what you will see printed on paper. The exact typeface, the correct size, the right layout, etc. Some word processors do WYSIWYG. Others don't. You usually need a screen with graphics to get the full effect.

X

X An abbreviation for the word "cross," as in crossbar. 5XB would be the abbreviation for a No. 5 Crossbar.

X-AXIS Horizontal axis on a graph or chart.

X-OFF/X-ON A flow control protocol for asynchronous serial transmission. Flow control is a method of adjusting information flow. For example, in transmitting between a computer and a printer, the computer sends the information to be printed at 9600 baud. That's several times faster than the printer can print. The printer, however, has a small memory. The computer dumps to the memory, called a buffer, at 9600 baud. When it fills up, the printer signals the computer that it is full and please stop sending. When the buffer is ready to receive again, the printer (which also has a small computer in it) sends a signal to the desktop computer (the one doing the printing) to please start sending again. X-OFF means turn the transmitter off (xmit in Ham radio terms). It is the ASCII character Control-S. X-ON means turn the transmitter on. It is the ASCII character Control-Q. You can use these characters with many microcomputer functions. For example, if you do DIR in MS-DOS and you want to stop the fast rush of files, then type Control-S.

X-Y A specific variety of electromechanical switch. Does the same things as a Strowger step-by-step switch but in a horizontal plane. It's so called because it's a two motion switch with horizontal and vertical movements. The first pulse sends the switch horizontally to the right place, then the next pulse sends it vertically up to the right place and so on, until it has switched the call through. One of the most reliable switches ever produced. Unfortunately, it's slow, space-consuming and unable to be programmed with many new customer-pleasing features.

X.1 International user classes of service in public data networks and ISDNs.

X.2 International user services and facilities in public data networks.

X.3 Packet Assembly/Disassembly (PAD) facility in a public data network. X.3 defines a set of 18 parameters that regulate basic functions performed by a PAD to control an asynchronous terminal. The setting of these parameters governs such characteristics as terminal speed, terminal display, flow control, break handling and data forwarding conditions, and so on.

X.20 Interface between data terminal equipment (DTE) and data circuit-terminating equipment (DCE) for start-stop transmission services on public data networks.

X.20 bis Used on public data networks of data terminal equipment (DTE) that is designed for interfacing to asynchronous duplex V-series modems.

X.21 Interface between data terminal equipment (DTE) and data circuit-equipment (DCE) for synchronous operation on public data networks.

X.21 bis Used on public data networks of data terminal equipment (DTE) that is designed for interfacing to synchronous V-series modems.

X.24 List of definitions for interchange circuits between data terminal equipment (DTE) and data circuit-terminating equipment (DCE) on public data networks.

X.25 From its beginning as an international standards recommendation from CCITT, the term X.25 has come to represent a common reference point by which mainframe computers, word processors, mini-computers, VDUs, microcomputers and a wide variety of specialized terminal equipment from many manufacturers can be made to work together over a type of data communications network called a packet switched network. On a packet switched data network (private or public), the data to be transmitted is cut up into blocks. Each block has a header with the network address of the sender and that of the destination. As the block enters the network, the number of bits in the block are put through some mathematical functions (an algorithm) to produce a check sum. The check sum is attached as a "trailer" to the packet as it enters the network. Packets may travel different routes through the network. But, ultimately, the packets are routed by the network to the node where the destination computer or terminal is located. At the destination, the packet is disassembled. The bits are put through the same algorithm, and if the digits computed are the same as the ones attached as the trailer, there are no detected errors. An ACK, or acknowledgement, is then sent to the transmitting end. If the check sum does not match, a NAK, or Negative Acknowledgement is sent back, and the packet is retransmitted. In this manner, high speed, low error rate information can be transmitted around the country using shared telecommunications circuits on public or private data networks.

X.25 is the protocol providing devices with direct connection to a packet switched network. These devices are typically larger computers, mainframes, minicomputers, etc. Word processors, personal computers, workstations, dumb terminals, etc. do not support the X.25 packet switching protocols unless they are connected to the network via PADs — Packet Assembler/Disassemblers. A PAD converts between the protocol used by the smaller device and the X.25 protocol. This conversion is performed on both outgoing (from the network) and incoming data (to the network), so the transmission looks transparent to the terminal. (See TRANSPARENT.) There's a very good book on X.25 called X.25 Explained, Protocols for packet switching networks by R. J. Deasington of IBM. It is available from Telecom Library on 1-800-LIBRARY, or 1-212-691-8215.

X.28 DTE/DCE interface for start-stop-mode data terminal equipment accessing the packet assembly/disassembly facility (PAD) in a public data network situated in the same country.

X.29 Procedures for the exchange of control information and user data between a packet assembly/disassembly facility (PAD) and a packet mode DTE or another PAD.

X.32 Interface between Data Terminal Equipment (DTE) and Data Circuit Terminating Equipment (DCE) operating in a packet mode and accessing a packet switched public data network via a public switched telephone network or a circuit switched public data network. X.32 describes the functional and procedural aspects of the DTE/DCE interface for DTEs accessing a packet switched public data network via a public switched network.

X.75 An international standard for linking X.25 packet switched networks. See X.25.

X.121 International Numbering Plan for public data networks. X.121 defines the numbering system used by data devices operating in the packet mode.

X.150 DTE and DCE test loops in public data networks.

X3.15 Bit sequencing of ASCII in serial-by-bit data transmission.

X3.16 Character structure and character parity sense for serial-by-data communications in ASCII.

X3.36 Synchronous high speed data signaling rates between data terminal equipment and data circuit-terminating equipment.

X3.41 Code extension techniques for use with 7-bit coded character set of ASCII.

X3.44 Determination of the performance of data communications systems.

X3.79 Determination of performance of data communications systems that use bit-oriented control procedures.

X3.92 Data encryption algorithm.

X.400 A newer series of OSI standards for the transmission of electronic text and graphic mail between unlike computers and terminals. There are many X.400 standards. In short, X.400 sets up how the mail messages are encoded and X.25 sets up how they are transmitted. The X. standards are a sub-set of and conform to X.25.

XBAR Crossbar.

XC Cross connect.

XENIX Microsoft trade name for a 16-bit microcomputer operating system derived from AT&T Bell Labs' UNIX.

XFR TransFeR.

XMIT Transmit.

XMODEM Also called "Christiansen Protocol". An error-correcting data transmission protocol created by Ward Christiansen of Chicago for transmitting files between microcomputers. Many communications packages for microcomputer systems now have three ways of transmitting a file between computers. (A file might be anything — a letter, an article, a sales call report, a Lotus 1-2-3 spreadsheet.) The first method of transmitting a file is if the other computer is using the same software package you are using, e.g. Crosstalk's own proprietary protocol. The second method is simply the "fast typist" command. This tells the software to find the file and type it fast, as if a typist were actually at the keyboard. The third is the XMODEM protocol, which is included in Crosstalk, Relay Gold and other modern PC software packages. The XMODEM protocol sends information in 128 bytes blocks of data. Some sums (check sums) are done on each block and the result is sent along with the block. If it does not check out at the other end, the computer at the other end sends a request (a NAK — Negative AcKnowledgement) to re-transmit that block once again. If the block checks out, the computer sends an ACK — an Acknowledgement. In this way, relatively error-free transmission can be accomplished.

XMODEM protocol used to be common among computer hobbyists but is now popular among business users of microcomputers. If you're buying a telecommunications software program for your microcomputer — IBM, Radio Shack, Compaq, Apple, etc. — it's a good idea to buy a program with XMODEM present. AT&T Mail supports XMODEM protocol. So does TELECONNECT Magazine's own E-mail InfoBoard system (212-989-4675). MCI Mail does not support XMODEM protocol. We don't know why. We wish they did. See also BINARY TRANSFER. There are many variations of XMODEM including MODEM7, YMODEM, Y-MODEM-G and ZMODEM. Most common communications software packages only support (i.e. will handle) the original version of XMODEM (checksum) and the newer CRC variation. A recent study in Byte Magazine (March, 1989) showed ZMODEM to be a far more efficient file transfer protocol than XMODEM, YMODEM, or W/XMODEM. See also YMODEM and ZMODEM.

XNMS Trademark for MICOM's IBM PC-based packet data network (PDN) network management system software products.

XNS Xerox Network Services, their communications protocol. Used by some companies on Ethernet LANs. In local area networking technology, special communications protocol used between networks. XNS/ITP functions at the 3rd and 4th layer of the Open Systems Interconnection (OSI) model. Similar to transmission control protocol/internet protocol (TCP/IP).

XPAD An eXternal Packet Assembler/Disassembler.

XRB Transmit Reference Burst.

YAGI ANTENNA A type of directional antenna.

YELLOW ALARM An alarm signal sent back toward the source of a failed transmit circuit in a DS-1 2-way transmission path.

YELLOW PAGES A directory of telephone numbers classified by type of business. It was printed on yellow paper throughout most of the twentieth century until it was obsoleted in the early 21st century by electronic directories delivered on disposable laser disks. As a concession to history, the laser disks are now painted bright yellow.

YMODEM A faster transfer variation of XMODEM. In YMODEM, XMODEM's 128-byte block grew to YMODEM's 1024 bytes (1 kilobyte). YMODEM combines the 1K block and the 128-byte block modems into the same protocols. YMODEM, or 1K as it is known, became the thrifty way to send files (i.e. it saved on phone time). Enhancements were added, such as auto-fallback to 128-byte blocks if too many errors were encountered (because of bad phone lines, etc.) See XMODEM for a much larger explanation of file transfer using X, Y and ZMODEM protocols.

ZAP To erase all or part of a program or data. ZBTSI Zero Byte Time Slot Interchange. A technique used with the T carrier extended superframe format (ESF) in which an area in the ESF frame carries information about the location of all-zero bytes (eight consecutive "O"s) within the data stream.

ZEDIT The best front-end word processor ever written. For your copy call Telecom Library, 1-800-999-0345.

ZENER DIODE A particular type of semiconductor which acts as a normal rectifier until the voltage applied to it reaches a certain point. At this point — at the zener voltage or the avalanche voltage — the zener diode becomes conducting.

ZERO BIT The high-order bit in a byte or a word.

ZERO CODE SUPPRESSION The insertion of a "one" bit to prevent the transmission of eight or more consecutive "zero" bits. Used primarily with digital T-1 and related telephone-company facilities which require a minimum "ones density" keep the individual subchannels of a multiplexed, high-speed facility active. Several different schemes are currently employed to accomplish this. Proposals for a standard are being evaluated by the CCITT.

ZERO FREQUENCY The frequency (wavelength) at which the attenuation of the lightguide is at a minimum.

ZERO SLOT LAN A Local Area Network (LAN) that uses a PC's serial port to transmit and receive data. It doesn't require a network interface card to be installed in a slot in the PC, thus the name "zero-slot" LAN. RS-232 LANs usually use standard RS-232 or phone cable to link PCs. Software does the rest of the work. Due to the slow speed of serial communications on a PC, RS-232 LANs are usually restricted to speeds of around 19.2K bits per second. What they lose in speed, however, they make up in low price.

ZERO STUFFING Get a cup of coffee right now. Synchronous data transmission is done by sending what IBM and AT&T call Frames, and what everyone else calls Packets. A frame starts off by sending a bit pattern of 01111110 (notice the six 1s in a row). Synchronous transmission is for sending a bit stream, which means that the bits may (but probably do not) have any relation to the transmission of characters. This is especially true when sending digitized voice. As the bits pass to the receiver, they go through a shift register. When the flag signifying the end of a frame goes by, the last 16 bits in the shift register are the check digits. The receiver computes the check digits based on the data bits that have gone by. As the sender sent the data, it computed the check digit, sent it after the end of the frame, and then sent the flag. If the receiver computes the same check digit that the sender sent, then one can be reasonably assured the data came through without error. But that's not what I came to talk to you about. I came to talk about Zero Stuffing. The problem is that somewhere in the bit stream, there is the possibility of there being six 1 bits in a row. To the receiving computer, six 1s means a flag. Therefore the sending computer, if it "sees" six 1 bits, will send five 1 bits, and stuff a zero in the bit stream. In fact, if it sees even five 1 bits, it will stuff a zero anyway, so there will be no ambiguity. The rule is, "If there are five ones in a row and it is NOT the end of a frame, stuff a zero into the bit stream." This way the receiver will know that this is in no way the end of the frame yet. Now if the receiver sees six 1's in a row, it knows without a doubt that it IS at the end of a frame, and should proceed with the error checking.

ZERO TEST LEVEL POINT A level point used as a reference in determining loss in circuits. Analogous to using sea level when defining altitude. Written as 0 TLP.

ZERO TRANSMISSION LEVEL POINT ZTLP In telephony, a reference point for measuring the signal power gain and losses of telecommunications circuit, at which a zero dBm signal level is applied. Usually referenced to the output signal level at the transmitting switch in a telephone circuit.

ZERO TRANSMISSION LEVEL REFERENCE POINT A point in a circuit to which all relative transmission levels are referenced. The transmission level at the transmitting switchboard is frequently taken as the zero transmission level reference point.

ZIP CODE The specific five-digit code assigned to each post office to facilitate mail delivery. The Postal Service is beginning to use nine-digit zip codes. The additional four digits will determine the precise letter carrier routing from the post office into the street. Some post offices now optically read zip codes. Allegedly this speeds up delivery.

ZIP TONE Short burst of dial tone to an ACD agent headset indicating a call is being connected to the agent console.

ZMODEM Both XMODEM and YMODEM transmit, then receive, then transmit. The handshake (ACK or NAK) happens when the sender isn't sending. ZMODEM adds full duplex-transmission to the transfer protocol. ZMODEM does not depend on any ACK signals from the host computer. It keeps sending unless it receives a NAK, at which time it falls back to the failed block and starts to retransmit at that point. ZMODEM was written by Chuck Forsberg. With XMODEM or YMODEM you must start over if you're disconnected before completion. With ZMODEM you can transfer 90% of the file on one phone call, get knocked off the line and come back and transmit the last 10%. For a big explanation of protocol transmission, see XMODEM. See also YMODEM.

ZONE One of a series of specified areas, beyond the base rate area of an exchange. Service is furnished in zones at rates in addition to base rates.

ZONE BITS 1. One or two leftmost bits in a commonly used system of six bits for each character. 2. Any bit in a group of bit positions that are used to indicate a specific class of items, i.e., numbers, letters, commands.

ZONE PAGING Ability to page a specific department or area in or out of a building. "Page John in the Accounting Department." Zone paging is useful for finding people who wander, like most of us.

ZULU TIME Greenwich Mean Time.

(and finally...)

ZZZYANDOTTIE, ARCHIMEDES The last name in the Manhattan Telephone directory. Mr. Zzzyandottie beat out Adam Zyzzmjac for the honor.

Common Channel Signaling

IAM Parameters

Parameter	Type	Length (octets)
Message type	F	1
Nature of connection indicators	F	1
Forward call indicators	F	2
Calling party's category	F	1
User service information	V	3-5
Called party number	V	3-11
Calling party number	O	6-9
* Charge number	O	4-9
* Originating line information	O	3
* Transit network selection [1]	O	5
* Carrier selection	O	3
* Service code	O	3

* Additional internetwork parameters
[1] Sent on international calls only

F = Mandatory fixed length parameter
V = Mandatory variable length parameter
O = Optional parameter of fixed or variable length

CABLE PIN CONFIGURATIONS

RS-232 Interface

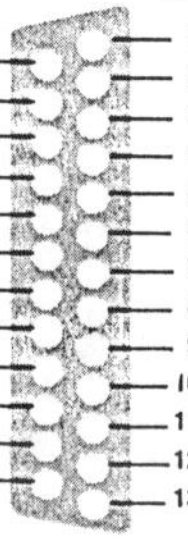

SIGNAL DESIGNATION	PIN NUMBER	PIN NUMBER	SIGNAL DESIGNATION
		1	PROTECTIVE GROUND
SECONDARY TRANSMITTED DATA	14	2	TRANSMITTED DATA
DCE TRANSMITTER SIGNAL ELEMENT TIMING	15	3	RECEIVED DATA
SECONDARY RECEIVED DATA	16	4	REQUEST TO SEND
RECEIVER SIGNAL ELEMENT TIMING	17	5	CLEAR TO SEND
DIVIDED CLOCK RECEIVER	18	6	DATA SET READY
SECONDARY REQUEST TO SEND	19	7	SIGNAL GROUND/COMMON RETURN
DATA TERMINAL READY	20	8	RECEIVED LINE SIGNAL DETECTOR
SIGNAL QUALITY DETECTOR	21	9	POSITIVE DC TEST VOLTAGE
RING INDICATOR	22	10	NEGATIVE DC TEST VOLTAGE
DATA SIGNAL RATE SELECTOR	23	11	EQUALIZER MODE
DTE TRANSMITTER SIGNAL ELEMENT TIMING	24	12	SECONDARY DATA CARRIER DETECT
BUSY	25	13	SECONDARY CLEAR TO SEND

RS-449 Interface

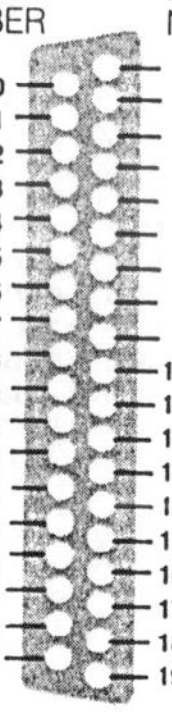

SIGNAL DESIGNATION	PIN NUMBER	PIN NUMBER	SIGNAL DESIGNATION
		1	SHIELD
RECEIVE COMMON	20	2	SIGNALING RATE INDICATOR
	21	3	
SEND DATA	22	4	SEND DATA
SEND TIMING	23	5	SEND TIMING
RECEIVE DATA	24	6	RECEIVE DATA
REQUEST TO SEND	25	7	REQUEST TO SEND
RECEIVE TIMING	26	8	RECEIVE TIMING
CLEAR TO SEND	27	9	CLEAR TO SEND
TERMINAL IN SERVICE	28	10	LOCAL LOOPBACK
DATA MODE	29	11	DATA MODE
TERMINAL READY	30	12	TERMINAL READY
RECEIVER READY	31	13	RECEIVER READY
SELECT STANDBY	32	14	REMOTE LOOPBACK
SIGNAL QUALITY	33	15	INCOMING CALL
NEW SIGNAL	34	16	SELECT FREQUENCY
TERMINAL TIMING	35	17	TERMINAL TIMING
STANDBY/INDICATOR	36	18	TEST MODE
SEND COMMON	37	19	SIGNAL GROUND

V.35 Interface

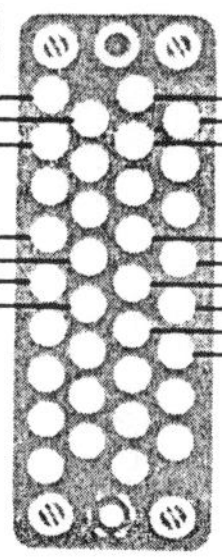

SIGNAL DESIGNATION	PIN NUMBER	PIN NUMBER	SIGNAL DESIGNATION
SIGNAL GROUND	B	A	CHASSIS GROUND
CLEAR TO SEND	D	C	REQUEST TO SEND
RECEIVE LINE SIGNAL DETECT	F	E	DATA SET READY
RECEIVED DATA	R	P	TRANSMITTED DATA
RECEIVED DATA	T	S	TRANSMITTED DATA
RECEIVE TIMING	V	U	TERMINAL TIMING
RECEIVE TIMING	X	W	TERMINAL TIMING
		Y	TRANSMIT TIMING
		AA	TRANSMIT TIMING

IEEE-488 Interface

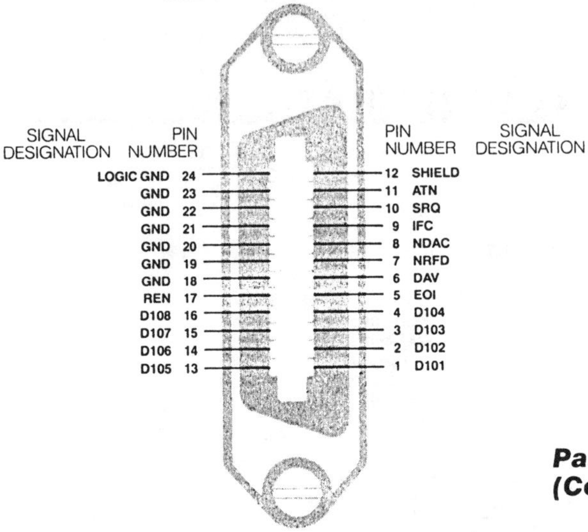

Parallel Interface (Centronics type)

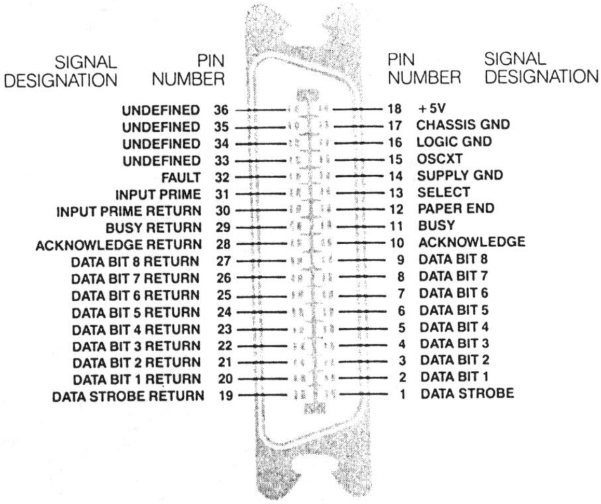

IBM PC Parallel Interface

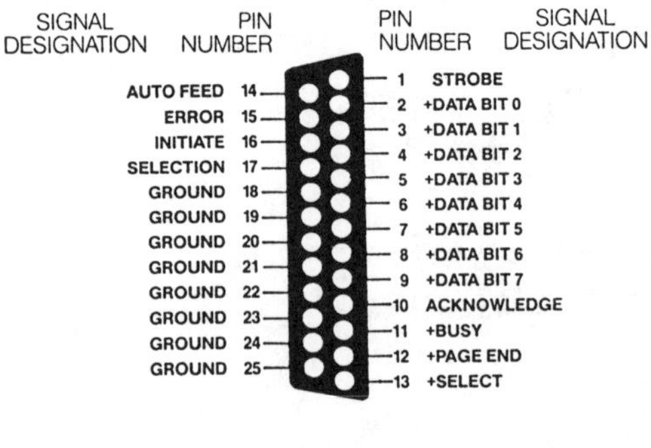

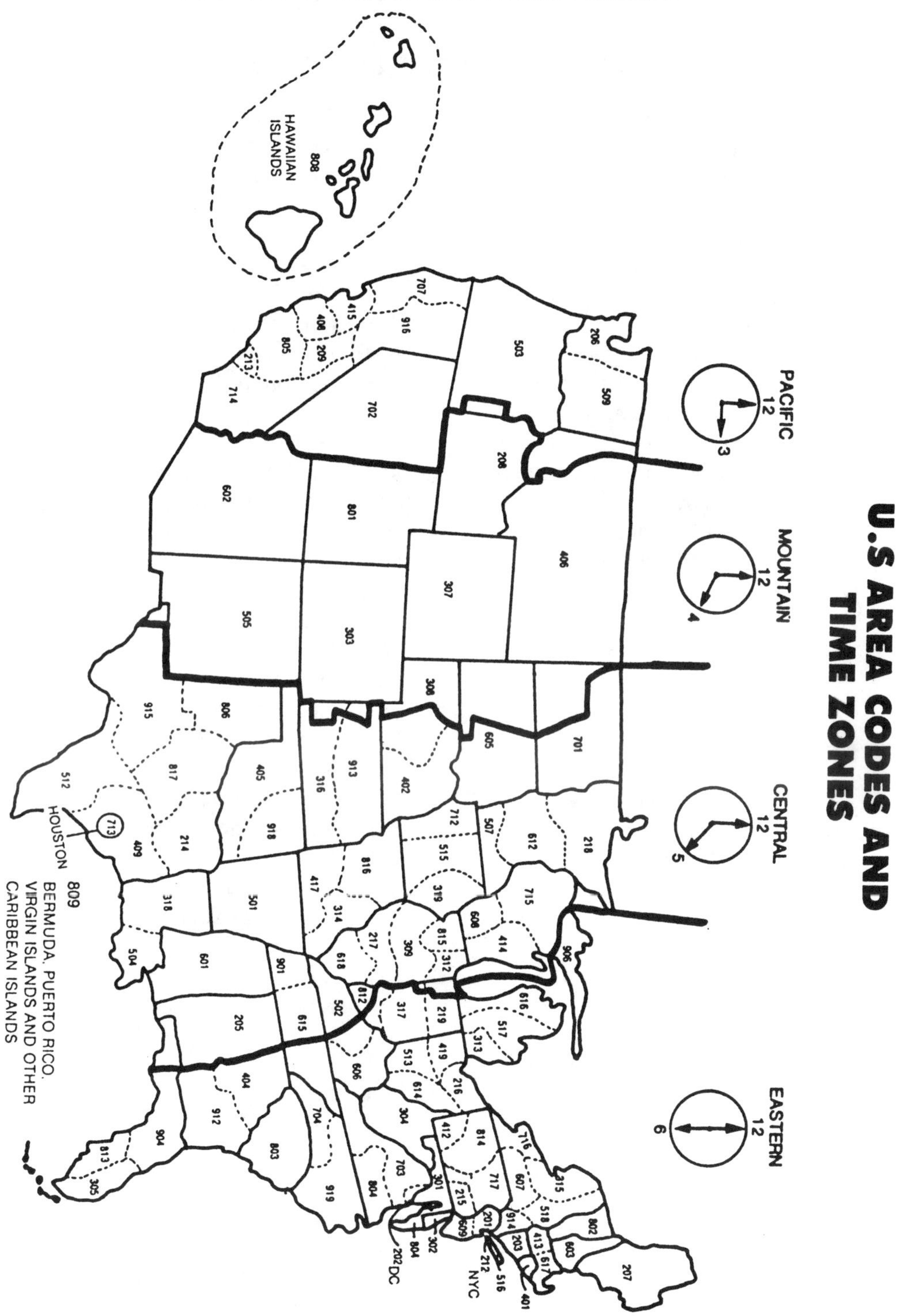
U.S AREA CODES AND
TIME ZONES
PACIFIC
MOUNTAIN
CENTRAL
EASTERN
808
HAWAIIAN
ISLANDS
HOUSTON
NYC
DC
809
BERMUDA, PUERTO RICO,
VIRGIN ISLANDS AND OTHER
CARIBBEAN ISLANDS

NORTH AMERICAN AREA CODES

201 Northern New Jersey
202 Washington DC
203 Connecticut
204 Manitoba, Canada
205 Alabama
206 Washington (Seattle)
207 Maine
208 Idaho
209 California
212 New York (Manhattan, Bronx)
213 California (Los Angeles)
214 Texas (Dallas)
215 Pennsylvania (Philadelphia)
216 Ohio (Cleveland)
217 Illinois (Springfield)
218 Minnesota (Duluth)
219 Indiana (South Bend)

301 Maryland
302 Delaware
303 Colorado
304 West Virginia
305 Florida (Miami)
306 Saskatchewan, Canada
307 Wyoming
308 Nebraska (North Platte)
309 Illinois (Peoria)
312 Illinois (Chicago)
313 Michigan (Detroit)
314 Missouri (St Louis)
315 New York (Syracuse)
316 Kansas (Wichita)
317 Indiana (Indianapolis)
318 Louisiana (Shreveport)
319 Iowa (Dubuque)

401 Rhode Island
402 Nebraska
403 Alberta, Yukon, Northwest Territories, Canada
404 Georgia (Atlanta)
405 Oklahoma (Oklahoma City)
406 Montana
407 Florida (Boca Raton)
408 California (Silicon Valley, Cupertino)
409 Texas (Beaumont)
412 Pennsylvania (Pittsburgh)
413 Massachusetts (Springfield)
414 Wisconsin (Milwaukee)
415 California (San Francisco)
416 Ontario (Toronto) Canada
417 Missouri (Springfield)
418 Quebec (Quebec City) Canada
419 Ohio (Toledo)

501 Arkansas
502 Kentucky (Louisville)
503 Oregon
504 Louisiana (New Orleans)
505 New Mexico
506 New Brunswick
507 Minnesota (Rochester)
508 Massachusetts (Worcester)
509 Washington (Spokane)
512 Texas (San Antonio)
513 Ohio (Cincinnati)
514 Quebec (Montreal) Canada
515 Iowa (Des Moines)
516 New York (Long Island)
517 Michigan (Lansing)
518 New York (Semi-Upstate)
519 Ontario, Canada

601 Mississippi
602 Arizona
603 New Hampshire
604 British Columbia, Canada
605 South Dakota
606 Kentucky (Covington)
607 New York (Binghamton)
608 Wisconsin (Madison)

609 New Jersey (Trenton)
612 Minnesota (Minneapolis)
613 Ontario (Ottawa) Canada
614 Ohio (Columbus)
615 Tennessee (Nashville)
616 Michigan (Grand Rapids)
617 Massachusetts (Boston)
618 Illinois (Centralia)
619 California (San Diego)

700 Information Services
701 North Dakota
702 Nevada
703 Virginia (Arlington)
704 North Carolina (Charlotte)
705 Ontario (North Bay) Canada
706 Northwest Mexico
707 California (Santa Rosa)
709 Newfoundland, Canada
710 Government Special Services
712 Iowa (Council Bluffs)
713 Texas (Houston)
714 California (Anaheim)
715 Wisconsin (Eau Claire)
716 New York (Buffalo)
717 Pennsylvania (Harrisburg)
718 New York (Brooklyn, Queens, Staten Island)
719 Colorado

800 IN-WATS Service
801 Utah
802 Vermont
803 South Carolina
804 Virginia (Richmond)
805 California (Bakersfield)
806 Texas (Amarillo)
807 Ontario (Thunder Bay) Canada
808 Hawaii
809 Bermuda, Puerto Rico, Virgin Islands & Caribbean Islands
812 Indiana (Evansville)
813 Florida (Fort Meyers)
814 Pennsylvania (Altoona)
815 Illinois (Rockford)
816 Missouri (Kansas City)
817 Texas (Fort Worth)
818 California (Burbank)
819 Quebec (Sherbrooke) Canada

900 DIAL-IT Services
901 Tennessee (Memphis)
902 Nova Scotia,Prince Edward Island, Canada
903 Texas (Dallas suburbs)
904 Florida (Jacksonville)
905 Mexico City, Mexico
906 Michigan (Escanaba)
907 Alaska
908 New Jersey (New Brunswick)
912 Georgia (Savannah)
913 Kansas (Topeka)
914 New York (Westchester County)
915 Texas (Sweetwater)
916 California (Sacramento)
918 Oklahoma (Tulsa)
919 North Carolina (Raleigh)

(Note: There are only two numbers -- 909 and 917 -- still up for grabs. Stay tuned.

CANADA AND ALASKA AREA CODES AND TIME ZONES

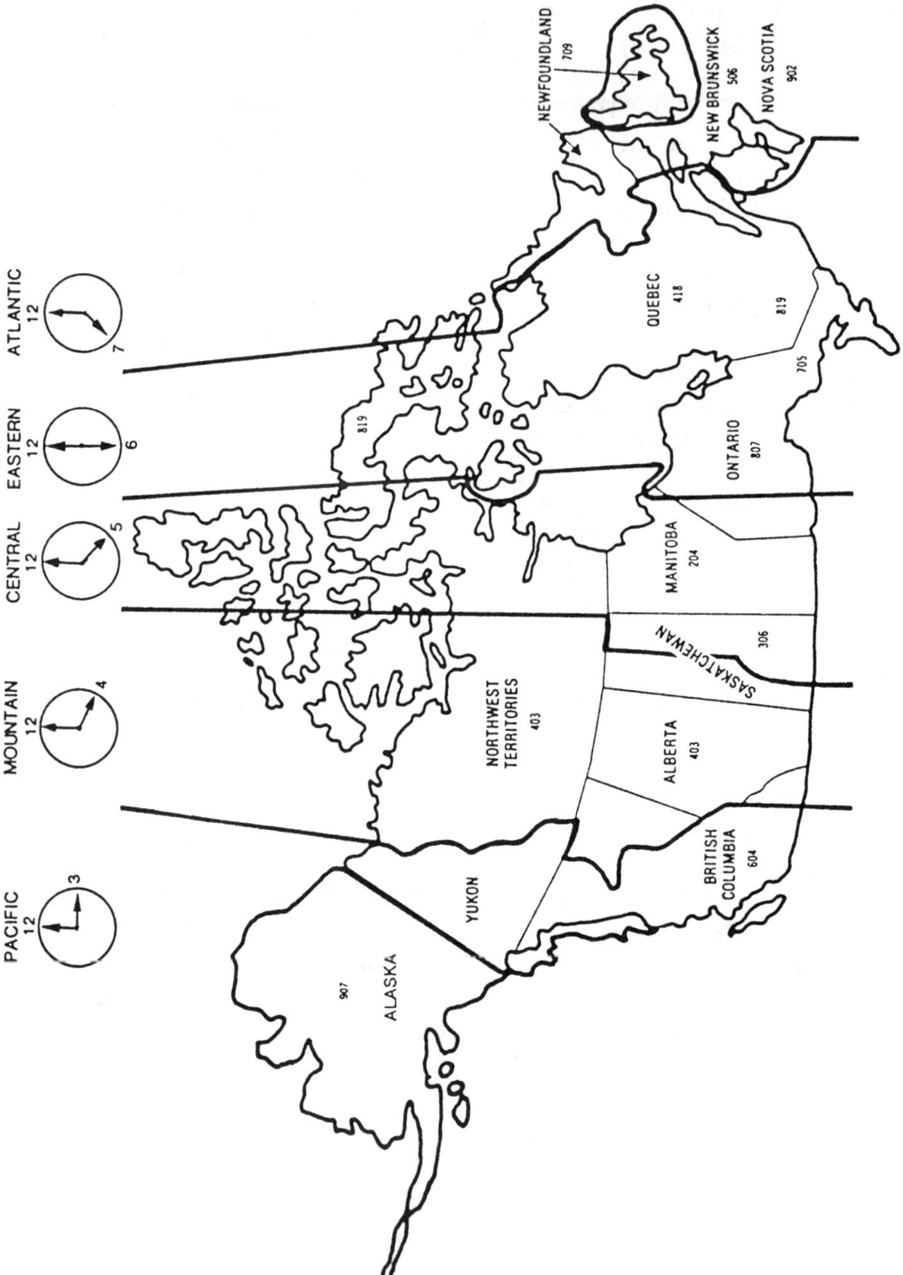

How to Use your Calling Cards Abroad

	AT&T	MCI
Argentina	001-800-200-1111	800-333-1111
Australia	0014-881-011	0014-881-100
Austria	022-903-011	—
Belgium	11-0010	11-00-12
Bermuda	1-800-872-2881	1-800-623-0484
Brazil	000-8010	000-8012
Chile	000 + -312	000 + -316
Columbia	980-11-0010	980-16-0001
Denmark	0430-0010	0430-0022
Finland	9800-100-10	9800-102-80
France	19 + -00-11	19 + -00-19
Germany	0130-0010	—
Greece	00800-1311	00800-1211
Hong Kong	008-1111	008-1121
Italy	172-1011	172-1022
Japan	0039-111	0039-121
Netherlands	06 + -022-91-11	06 + -022-91-22
Norway	050-12-011	—
Spain	—	900-99-0014
Sweden	020-795-611	020-795-922
Switzerland	046-05-0011	0460-50-222
Taiwan	—	0
UK	0800-89-0011	0800-89-0222
USA Info	1-800-874-4000	1-800-444-4444

+ means wait for second dial tone

Venture-Speak Terms Defined

Here's a short glossary of the terms you find in financial reports, and what they *really* mean.

Acquisition strategy: The current products have no market.

Basically on plan: We're expecting a revenue shortfall of 25%.

Bio-tech business model: Potential bigger fools have been identified.

Considerably ahead of plan: Hit plan in one of the last three months.

Core business: Our product line is obsolete.

Currently revising the budget: The financial plan is in total chaos.

Cyclical business: We posted a huge loss last year.

Entreprenurial CEO: He is totally uncontrollable, bordering on maniacal.

Highly leveraged network: No longer works, but has friends who still do.

Ingredients are there: Given two years, we might find a workable strategy.

Investing heavily in R&D: We're trying desperately to catch the competition.

Limited downside: It can't get much worse.

Long selling cycle: Yet to find a customer who likes the product.

Major opportunity: It's our last chance.

Niche strategy: A small-time player.

Passive investor: He calls once a year to see if the company is still in business.

Repositioning the business: We've recently written off a multi-million dollar investment.

Selective investment strategy: The board is spending more time on yachts than airplanes.

Somewhat below plan: We expect a revenue shortfall of 75%.

Strategic investor: One who will pay a preposterous price.

Too early to tell: Results so far have been grim.

Turnaround opportunity: It's a lost cause.

Unique: We have no more than six competitiors.

Window of opportunity: Without more money, the company is dead.

NOTES
(AND WORDS TO ADD TO THE NEXT EDITION)

NOTES
(AND WORDS TO ADD TO THE NEXT EDITION)

This page intentionally
not left blank.